For Hans Dieter Betz,
in friendship.
LLW

L. L. Welborn
An End to Enmity

Beihefte zur Zeitschrift für die neutestamentliche Wissenschaft

und die Kunde der älteren Kirche

Herausgegeben von
James D. G. Dunn · Carl R. Holladay
Hermann Lichtenberger · Jens Schröter
Gregory E. Sterling · Michael Wolter

Band 185

De Gruyter

L. L. Welborn

An End to Enmity

Paul and the "Wrongdoer" of Second Corinthians

De Gruyter

ISBN 978-3-11-026327-5
e-ISBN 978-3-11-026330-5
ISSN 0171-6441

Library of Congress Cataloging-in-Publication Data

Welborn, L. L., 1953–
   An end to enmity : Paul and the "wrongdoer" of Second Corinthians / Larry L. Welborn.
   p. cm. – (Beihefte zur Zeitschrift für die neutestamentliche Wissenschaft und die Kunde der älteren Kirche, ISSN 0171-6441 ; Bd. 185)
   Includes bibliographical references and index.
   ISBN 978-3-11-026327-5 (hardcover : alk. paper)
   1. Bible. N.T. Corinthians, 2nd – Socio-rhetorical criticism.   2. Paul, the Apostle, Saint – Adversaries.   I. Title.
   BS2675.52.W44   2011
   227'.3067–dc23

2011018150

Bibliographic information published by the Deutsche Nationalbibliothek

The Deutsche Nationalbibliothek lists this publication in the Deutsche Nationalbibliografie; detailed bibliographic data are available in the Internet at http://dnb.d-nb.de.

© 2011 Walter de Gruyter GmbH & Co. KG, Berlin/Boston

Printing: Hubert & Co. GmbH & Co. KG, Göttingen
∞ Printed on acid-free paper

Printed in Germany

www.degruyter.com

An End to Enmity:
Paul and the 'Wrongdoer' of Second Corinthians
L. L. Welborn

In
Honorem
Edwin A. Judge

Contents

Acknowledgements IX

Abbreviations XIII

Preface XIX

Chapter One: Introduction 1

Chapter Two: History of Scholarship 3

Chapter Three: Inferences from Exegesis 23

Chapter Four: Social and Rhetorical Conventions 212

Chapter Five: Prosopography 289

Chapter Six: History of a Friendship 382

Bibliography 485

Index of Ancient Sources 529

Index of Modern Authors 559

Acknowledgements

It is a joy to be able to thank all those whose insight, criticism, and generous support have contributed to this book. At the top of the list is the person to whom the book is dedicated: Edwin Judge. In the spring of 2006, I was invited to present lectures as the Visiting Fellow at the annual conference of the Society for the Study of Early Christianity at Macquarie University. The knowledge that Edwin Judge would be my respondent on this occasion lent a special intensity to the preparation of lectures in which I sought to build upon the insights of Edwin Judge and his student Peter Marshall into the social and rhetorical conventions that governed friendship, enmity, and reconciliation in the Greco-Roman world. My anxiety at facing Edwin Judge as respondent proved to be as fruitful as it was unfounded. On the long flight back from Sydney, Australia, to Dayton, Ohio, I found myself perusing a manuscript of 120 pages and assumed (wrongly, as it turned out) that I would soon be able to transform the manuscript into a little book on the episode of Paul's conflict with the "wrongdoer" of 2 Corinthians. Over the past four years, Edwin Judge has become the most significant influence upon my development as a historian of early Christianity, generously devoting hours to discussion of the questions that animate my research. I now owe Edwin Judge as much gratitude as I feel towards my old mentor Arnaldo Momigliano, who first taught me how knowledge of Greco-Roman history can be made useful for the study of the New Testament.

Readers of this book will surely discern that its origin, and hence my indebtedness, lies farther back than the spring of 2006. I first encountered the enigma of the ἀδικήσας when serving as a research assistant for Hans Dieter Betz in the preparation of his Hermeneia commentary on 2 Corinthians 8 and 9. In composing the footnotes for the present book, I was pleased to be reminded that Hans Dieter Betz had already proposed the most plausible solution to the problem of the nature of the offense of the ἀδικήσας against Paul. While a student at the University of Chicago, I also profited from several conversations with David Epstein, then assistant to President Hannah Gray, about personal enmity in Roman politics.

Like other students of 2 Corinthians, my research took direction from insights in the epilogue to the English edition of Dieter Georgi's *The Opponents of Paul in Second Corinthians*. I found special inspiration in Georgi's suggestion that "the problem of the ἀδικήσας in 2 Cor. 2 and 7 may yield more information...Paul's preceding negative experience, a painful visit (2 Cor. 2:1–4), is commonly understood as being an insult. But the style and form of communication are remarkable. Paul's 'evasive' approach by way of circumlocution needs to be more carefully analyzed. The results of that analysis may further clarify the conflict itself." Conversations with Dieter Georgi in the fall of 2001 encouraged me to pursue a better understanding of the social conventions that guided Paul's employment of the rhetorical figure of *periphrasis* in approaching the subject of the one who did wrong and caused pain in 2 Cor. 2 and 7.

My friend and teacher John Fitzgerald illuminated aspects of Paul's pursuit of reconciliation with the Corinthians through his essay on "Paul and Paradigm Shifts." In my attempt at a partial prosopography of mid first-century Roman Corinth, I received extraordinary assistance from Glen Bowersock, who tirelessly corrected my efforts until the results appeared "somewhat more plausible." I am grateful to my friend Donald Dale Walker for stimulating correspondence on 2 Cor. 10:10, and especially for his insight into the term ἐξουθενημένος.

Several scholars made their own work available to me before publication: Jon Hall sent an advance copy of his *Politeness and Politics in Cicero's Letters*; David Konstan shared his essay on "Remorse, Repentance and Forgiveness in the Classical World": Steven Friesen sent his study of "The Wrong Erastus" at the most timely moment.

Several colleagues and friends read portions of the manuscript, or responded to papers based upon the manuscript delivered at meetings of the Society of Biblical Literature in Aukland, Boston, and New Orleans. I am especially grateful to Helmut Koester, who read and commented on the entire manuscript, to Dale Martin, who read drafts of several sections, and to Robert Jewett, who offered constructive criticism and encouragement. I also wish to thank John Barclay, Paul Barnett, Jeremy Barrier, Bernard Barsky, Ward Blanton, Alexandra Brown, Cavan Concannon, Susan Eastman, Neil Elliott, Christopher Forbes, Paul Holloway, Israel Kamudzandu, Yung Suk Kim, Gerd Lüdemann, Peter Marshall, Brent Nongbri, Daniel Patte, Thomas Schmeller, and Ekkehard and Wolfgang Stegemann.

At Fordham University I have found the supportive and stimulating academic community I have sought throughout the years. I have drawn special inspiration from conversations with my colleagues Ben Dunning, George Demacopoulos, Brad Hinze, Karina Hogan, Patrick Hornbeck, Elizabeth Johnson, Matthew McGowan, Robert Penella, Michael Peppard, John Seitz, and Maureen Tilley, among others. I am grateful for the work of graduate assistants who have contributed to the completion of this project: Michael Azar, Allan Georgia, and Brett Kendall. All of my projects in recent years have blossomed under the leadership of my department chair, Terrence Tilley.

I return to the invitation to deliver the lectures at Macquarie University that provided the occasion for the composition of this book. Four friends associated with Macquarie University and the Society for the Study of Early Christianity showed unwarranted confidence in my abilities: Alanna Nobbs (Head of the Department of Ancient History), Don Barker (Secretary of SSEC), Mark Harding (Dean of the Australian Colleges of Theology), and Jim Harrison (Professor of New Testament at the Wesley Institute); their advocacy and friendship created the conditions for an extraordinarily productive period in my research. I am grateful to Rachel Yuen-Collingridge of Macquarie University for gracious assistance with searches through the *Thesaurus Linguae Graecae*. I recall with pleasure stimulating conversations with Brad Bitner and Julien Ogereau, PhD students in New Testament at Macquarie.

Some of the material in Chapter 3 was previously published in the *Journal for the Study of the New Testament* 32 (2009) 39–56 and in *Novum Testamentum* 52 (2010) 207–220. I thank the editors for permission to republish this material here.

My commitment to this project has been sustained through four years of research and writing by the lively interest of my mother Ann Welborn, the affection of my wife Diane, and the advice of my sons Locke (who crafted the wording of the title) and Mark (who improved my literary style), for all of whom I feel an inexpressible gratitude.

Nerantza, Greece, June 29, 2010   L. L. Welborn

Abbreviations

AB	Anchor Bible
ABD	*Anchor Bible Dictionary.* Edited by D. N. Freedman. 6 vols. New York, 1992
AGJU	Arbeiten zur Geschichte des antiken Judentums und des Urchristentums
AJA	*American Journal of Archaeology*
AnBib	Analecta biblica
ANF	Ante-Nicene Fathers
ANRW	*Aufstieg und Niedergang der römischen Welt: Geschichte und Kultur Roms im Spiegel der neueren Forschung.* Edited by H. Temporini and W. Haase. Berlin, 1972-
AusBR	*Australian Biblical Review*
BA	*Biblical Archaeologist*
BDAG	Bauer, W., F. W. Danker, W. F. Arndt, and F. W. Gingrich, *A Greek-English Lexicon of the New Testament and Other Early Christian Literature.* 3d ed. Chicago, 1999.
BBB	Bonner biblische Beiträge
BDF	Blass, F., A. Debrunner and R. W. Funk, *A Greek Grammar of the New Testament and Other Early Christian Literature.* Chicago, 1961
BETL	Bibliotheca ephemeridum theologicarum lovaniensium
BGU	Aegyptische Urkunden aus den Museen zu Berlin: Griechische Urkunden I-VIII 1895-1933.
BHTh	Beiträge zur historischen Theologie
Bib	*Biblica*
BibInt	*Biblical Interpretation*
BJRL	*Bulletin of the John Rylands University Library of Manchester*
BR	*Biblical Research*
BSac	*Bibliotheca Sacra*
BWANT	Beiträge zur Wissenschaft vom Alten und Neuen Testament
BZ	*Biblische Zeitschrift*
BZNW	Beihefte zur Zeitschrift für die neutestamentliche Wissenschaft
CAH	Cambridge Ancient History
CBQ	*Catholic Biblical Quarterly*

CIG	*Corpus inscriptionum graecarum.* Edited by A. Boeckh. 4 vols. Berlin, 1828–1877
CIJ	*Corpus inscriptionum Judaicarum*
CIL	*Corpus inscriptionum latinarum*
CJ	*Classical Journal*
CP	*Classical Philology*
CPSP	*Cambridge Philological Society Proceedings*
CQ	*Classical Quarterly*
CNT	Commentaire du Nouveau Testament
CW	*Classical World*
EA	*Epigraphica Anatolica*
ETL	*Ephemerides theologicae lovanienses*
EBib	Etudes bibliques
EDNT	*Exegetical Dictionary of the New Testament.* Edited by H. Balz, G. Schneider. ET. Grand Rapids, 1990–1993
EKKNT	Evangelisch-katholischer Kommentar zum Neuen Testament
EvQ	*Evangelical Quarterly*
FGH	*Die Fragmente der griechischen Historiker.* Edited by F. Jacoby. Leiden, 1954–1964
FRLANT	Forschungen zur Religion und Literatur des Alten und Neuen Testament
GCS	Die griechische christliche Schriftsteller der ersten [drei] Jahrhunderte
GRBS	*Greek, Roman, and Byzantine Studies*
HDR	Harvard Dissertations in Religion
HNT	Handbuch zum Neuen Testament
HNTC	Harper's New Testament Commentaries
HR	*History of Religions*
HSCP	*Harvard Studies in Classical Philology*
HTR	*Harvard Theological Review*
ICC	International Critical Commentary
IG	*Inscriptiones graecae.* Editio minor. Berlin, 1924-
IGR	*Inscriptiones Graecae ad res Romanas pertinentes*
ILLRP	*Inscriptiones Latinae Liberae Res Republicae.* Edited by A. Degrassi. Rome, Vol. 1^2 (1965), Vol. 2 (1963)
ILS	*Inscriptiones Latinae Selecta.* Edited by H. Dessau. Leipzig, 1892–1916
Int	*Interpretation*
JAARSup	*Journal of the American Academy of Religion Supplement*
JAC	*Jahrbuch für Antike und Christentum*

JBL	*Journal of Biblical Literature*
JGRChJ	*Journal of Greco-Roman Christianity and Judaism*
JHS	*Journal of Hellenic Studies*
JR	*Journal of Religion*
JRH	*Journal of Religious History*
JRS	*Journal of Roman Studies*
JSHRZ	*Jüdische Schriften aus hellenistisch-römischer Zeit*
JSNT	*Journal for the Study of the New Testament*
JTS	*Journal of Theological Studies*
KEK	Kritisch-exegetischer Kommentar über das Neue Testament (Meyer)
KJV	King James Version
LCL	Loeb Classical Library
LSJ	Liddell, H. G., R. Scott, and H. S. Jones, *A Greek-English Lexicon*. 9th ed. with revised supplement. Oxford, 1996
LXX	Septuagina
MAMA	*Monumenta Asiae Minoris Antiqua*. Manchester and London, 1928–1993
MRF	*Mimorum Romanorum Fragmenta*. Edited by M. Bonaria. Geneva, 1955
NEB	New English Bible
NewDocs	*New Documents Illustrating Early Christianity*. Edited by G. H. R. Horsley and S. Llewelyn. North Ryde, N.S.W., 1981-
NHC	Nag Hammadi Codices
NHL	*Nag Hammadi Library in English*. Edited by J. M. Robinson. 4th rev. ed. Leiden, 1996
NHS	Nag Hammadi Studies
NZK	*Neue kirchliche Zeitschrift*
NovT	*Novum Testamentum*
NovTSup	Novum Testamentum Supplements
NRSV	New Revised Standard Version
NTAbh	Neutestamentliche Abhandlungen
NTD	Das Neue Testament Deutsch
NTOA	Novum Testamentum et Orbis Antiquus
NTS	*New Testament Studies*
OCD	*Oxford Classical Dictionary*. Edited by S. Hornblower and A. Spawforth. 3 ed. Oxford, 1996
OGIS	*Orientis graeci inscriptiones selectee*. Edited by W. Dittenberger. 2 vols. Leipzig, 1903–1905

PG	Patrologiae cursus completes...Series graeca. Edited by J.-P. Migne. 166 vols. Paris, 1857–1883
PGM	*Papyri graecae magicae: Die griechischen Zauberpapyri.* Edited by K. Preisendanz. Berlin, 1928
PL	Patrologia cursus completes...Series prima [latina]. Edited by J.-P. Migne. 221 vols. Paris, 1844–1865
PW	Pauly, A. F. *Paulys Realencyclopädie der classischen Altertumswissenschaft.* New edition G. Wissowa. 49 vols. Munich, 1980
RE	*Real-Encyclopädie der classischen Altertumswissenschaft.* Edited by August Friedrich von Pauly and Georg Wissowa. Stuttgart, 1894-
RESuppl	Supplement to Pauly-Wissowa
RAC	*Reallexicon für Antike und Christentum.* Edited by T. Klauser, et al. Stuttgart, 1950-
RB	*Revue bibique*
REA	*Revue des etudes anciennes*
RGG	*Religion in Geschichte und Gegenwart.* Edited by K. Galling. 7 vols. 3d ed. Tübingen, 1957–1965
RhM	*Rheinisches Museum für Philologie*
SBB	Stuttgarter biblische Beiträge
SBL	Society of Biblical Literature
SBLDS	Society of Biblical Literature Dissertation Series
SBLSS	Society of Biblical Literature Semeia Studies
SBS	Stuttgarter Bibelstudien
SC	Sources chrétiennes. Paris: Cerf, 1943-
SCHNT	Studia ad corpus hellenisticum Novi Testamenti
SEÅ	*Svensk exegetisk årsbok*
SEG	*Supplementum epigraphicum Graecum*
SHAW	Sitzungsberichte der Heidelberger Akademie der Wissenschaften
SIG	*Sylloge inscriptionum graecarum.* Edited by W. Dittenberger. 4 vols. 3d ed. Leipzig,1915–1924
SNTSMS	Society for New Testament Studies Monograph Series
SNTU	Studien zum Neuen Testament und seiner Umwelt
SO	Symbolae osloenses
SP	Sacra Pagina
Str-B	Strack, H. L., and P. Billerbeck. *Kommentar zum Neuen Testament aus Talmud und Midrasch.* 6 vols. Munich, 1922–1961
SUNT	Studien zur Umwelt des Neuen Testaments

SVF	*Stoicorum veterum fragmenta.* Edited by H. von Arnim. 4 vols. Leipzig, 1903–1924
TAM	*Tituli Asiae Minoris.* Edited by E. Kalinka and R. Herberdey. Vienna: Hoelderi, 1901.
TAPA	*Transactions of the American Philological Association*
TDNT	*Theological Dictionary of the New Testament.* Edited by G. Kittel and G. Friedrich. Translated by G. W. Bromiley. 10 vols. Grand Rapids, 1964–1976
TLZ	*Theologische Literaturzeitung*
TRE	*Theologische Realenzyklopädie.* Edited by G. Krause and G. Müller. Berlin, 1977–2007.
TU	Texte und Untersuchungen
TynBul	*Tyndale Bulletin*
TZ	*Theologische Zeitschrift*
WBC	Word Biblical Commentary
WUNT	Wissenschaftliche Untersuchungen zum Neuen Testament
YCS	Yale Classical Studies
ZAC	*Zeitschrift für antikes Christentum*
ZNW	*Zeitschrift für die neutestamentliche Wissenschaft und die Kunde der älteren Kirche*
ZPE	*Zeitschrift für Papyrologie und Epigraphik*
ZThK	*Zeitschrift für Theologie und Kirche*
ZwTh	*Zeitschrift für wissenschaftliche Theologie*

Preface

Any attempt to reconstruct the history of Paul's relationship with the Corinthians necessitates a hypothesis regarding the composition of the two canonical letters to Corinth, a desideratum reflected in the subtitle of a recent essay on Paul's letters to Corinth: "The Interpretive Intertwining of Literary and Historical Reconstruction."[1] The necessity of literary-critical hypotheses resides not only in the historical quest of contemporary scholars,[2] but also in the problematic nature of the canonical epistles themselves, which exhibit abrupt transitions, changes in tone and content, repetitions, inconsistencies in reports of events, and differences in outlook and judgment. Especially problematic is the impression that different portions of canonical 2 Corinthians reflect different situations in the relationship between Paul and the Corinthians. Indeed, the composition of 2 Corinthians is so problematic that the unity of 2 Corinthians must be regarded as a hypothesis in need of demonstration.[3]

A majority of scholars regard 2 Corinthians as a composite text, differing only with respect to the number and sequence of the letters.[4] A preface is not the place to examine the evidence for various partition theories in detail.[5] Rather, we must content ourselves with a summary of the

---

1   Margaret M. Mitchell, "Paul's Letters to Corinth: The Interpretive Intertwining of Literary and Historical Reconstruction" in *Urban Religion in Roman Corinth*, ed. by Daniel N. Schowalter and Steven J. Friesen (Cambridge, MA: Harvard University Press, 2005) 307–338.
2   Johannes Weiss in his review of Halmel in *TLZ* 19 (1894) 513.
3   So already Philipp Vielhauer, *Geschichte der urchristlichen Literatur* (Berlin: Walter de Gruyter, 1975) 151.
4   See the extensive *Forschungsberichte* in Hans Dieter Betz, *2 Corinthians 8 and 9: A Commentary on Two Administrative Letters of the Apostle Paul* (Philadelphia: Fortress Press, 1985) 3–36; Reimund Bieringer and Jan Lambrecht, *Studies on 2 Corinthians* (Leuven: Leuven University Press, 1994) 67–130; Margaret E. Thrall, *A Critical and Exegetical Commentary on the Second Epistle to the Corinthians*, 2 vols. (Edinburgh: T & T Clark, 1994) 1.3–49.
5   See the scrupulous examination of the evidence by Max Krenkel, *Beiträge zur Aufhellung der Geschichte und der Briefe des Apostels Paulus* (Braunschweig: Schwetschke, 1895) 154–377.

textual features which lead scholars to conclude that 2 Corinthians is a collection of letters.

First, the discrepancy between chs. 10–13 and other portions of the canonical epistle is conspicuous. It is not so much the reversal in tone between 9:15 and 10:1 as the contrast in content that leads scholars to doubt that chs. 10–13 originally formed the continuation of chs. 1–9. One need only compare Paul's reference to "the obedience of you all" in 7:15 with his readiness "to punish every disobedience" in 10:6 to see that these statements presuppose different situations. One might also contrast Paul's account of the "godly grief" that has produced "repentance" in 7:10–11 with his fear that he will have "to mourn over many who previously sinned and have not repented" in 12:20–21. The various attempts at harmonization of these discrepancies have not proven convincing—from Lietzmann's famous "sleepless night,"[6] to recent appeals to the rhetorical structure of 2 Corinthians,[7] or to Paul's psychagogical purposes.[8] That statements so contrary originally stood in the same epistle seems to me impossible, and necessitates the partition of 2 Corinthians.

Second, chs. 8 and 9 are discrete appeals for partnership in the collection.[9] After a lengthy discussion of the collection in ch. 8, Paul introduces the subject anew in ch. 9, and treats it thoroughly, as if it had not been previously mentioned.[10] Although both chapters treat the collection, they do not relate to one another, differing in tone, purpose, strategy and style. Ch. 8 holds up the churches of Macedonia as models of generosity for the Corinthians, while ch. 9 boasts of the readiness of the Achaians in an appeal to the people of Macedonia. Thus, chs. 8 and 9 must have been originally independent pieces of correspondence.

---

6 Hans Lietzmann, *An die Korinther I/II* (Tübingen: Mohr Siebeck, 1949) 139: "Mir genügt z.B. die Annahme einer schlaflos durchwachten Nacht zwischen c. 9 und c. 10 zur Erklärung."
7 E.g., Frederick J. Long, *Ancient Rhetoric and Paul's Apology: The Compositional Unity of 2 Corinthians* (Cambridge: Cambridge University Press, 2004).
8 Ivar Vegge, *2 Corinthians—a Letter about Reconciliation: A Psychagogical, Epistolographical and Rhetorical Analysis* (Tübingen: Mohr Siebeck, 2008).
9 As demonstrated by Betz, *2 Corinthians 8 and 9*, pursuing an insight that goes back to Johann Salomo Semler.
10 The general point remains valid, despite the observations on the connecting particles in 9:1 by Stanley K. Stowers, "Περὶ μὲν γάρ and the Integrity of 2 Cor. 8 and 9," *NovT* 32 (1990) 340–348.

Third, the passage 2:14–7:4 interrupts the account of Paul's search for Titus in 2:12–13 continued seamlessly in 7:5–6. As Johannes Weiss observed, "This separation of what belongs together is unheard-of and intolerable from a literary point of view, since 2:13 and 7:5 f. fit onto each other as neatly as the broken pieces of a ring."[11] The attempt to construe Paul's apology for his apostolic office in 2:14–7:4 as a "digression" within the narrative[12] fails to convince, since the apology has no point of departure in what precedes, and makes no connection with what follows.[13] An excursus of such length (6 pages in Nestle-Aland!) has no parallel in the letters of Paul.[14] The judgment of Dieter Georgi remains valid: "The seams in 2:13/14 and 7:4/5 are the best examples in the entire New Testament of one large fragment secondarily inserted into another text. The splits in 2:13/14 and 7:4/5 are so basic, and the connections between 2:13 and 7:5 so obvious, that the burden of proof now lies with those who defend the integrity of the canonical text, and they have not brought any good new arguments to support their claims."[15]

Finally, the paragraph 6:14–7:1 tears apart the context of what is demonstrably the strongest peroration in the Pauline corpus in 6:11–13; 7:2–4.[16] The passage contains *hapax legomena* and stylistic peculiarities.[17] The thought has more in common with the Qumran literature than with

---

11   Johannes Weiss, *The History of Primitive Christianity*, 2 vols., trans. by F. C. Grant (New York: Wilson-Fredrickson, 1937) 1.349.
12   An explanation which goes back to J. A. Bengel, *Gnomon Novi Testamenti* (1742); Eng. trans. *Gnomon of the New Testament*, 3 vols., trans. by A. Fausset (Edinburgh: T & T Clark, 1877) 2.361; followed by a number of subsequent interpreters, e.g., C. F. G. Heinrici, *Der zweite Brief an die Korinther* (Göttingen: Vandenhoeck & Ruprecht, 1900) 36, 251–52; Nils Hyldahl, "Die Frage nach der literarischen Einheit des Zweiten Korintherbriefes," *ZNW* 64 (1973) 289–306.
13   L. L. Welborn, "Paul's Letter of Reconciliation in 2 Corinthians 1:1–2:13; 7:5–16 and Ancient Theories of Literary Unity" in *Politics and Rhetoric in the Corinthian Epistles* (Macon: Mercer University Press, 1997) 95–131, esp. 114–18.
14   Vielhauer, *Geschichte der urchristlichen Literatur*, 152.
15   Dieter Georgi, *The Opponents of Paul in Second Corinthians* (Philadelphia: Fortress Press, 1986) 335; similarly, Vielhauer, *Geschichte der urchristlichen Literatur*, 152.
16   See the discussion of this passage, with extensive bibliography, in Thrall, *Second Epistle*, 1.22–36.
17   Nils A Dahl, "A Fragment and Its Content: 2 Corinthians 6:14–7:1" in *Studies in Paul* (Minneapolis: Augsburg, 1977) 62–91.

the letters of Paul.[18] Hence, 6:14–7:1 has long been recognized as an interpolation,[19] probably non-Pauline in authorship.[20] A redactor has inserted an exhortation to separation from unbelievers into a Pauline appeal for openness between followers of Christ.[21]

Thus, five authentic letters of Paul and one non-Pauline interpolation emerge from literary criticism of 2 Corinthians. The compelling rationale for the partition of canonical 2 Corinthians was clearly articulated by Philipp Vielhauer a generation ago: "The characteristic of 2 Corinthians which more than any other makes a literary-critical analysis necessary is that the incoherence lies in the composition of the whole, while the individual large sections, e. g., 2:14–7:4 and 10–13, are within themselves exceptionally well disposed."[22]

The single criterion for determining the original sequence of the letters collected in 2 Corinthians is the phenomenon of the "cross-references": that is, passages in later letters which refer back to earlier ones. On the basis of the most conspicuous of these cross-references, Adolf von Hausrath identified 2 Cor. 10–13 as the "letter of tears" mentioned in 2:3–4.[23] With subtle insight, James Kennedy disclosed the numerous cross-references that connect chs. 1–2 and 7 with chs. 10–13.[24] Consider, for example, 1:23 ("it was to spare you that I did not come again to Corinth") and 13:2 ("if I come again, I will not spare"). Or, compare 2:3 ("I wrote as I did, so that when I came, I might not suffer pain…") with 13:10 ("So I write these things while I am away from you, so that when I come, I may not have to be severe…"). Or, compare 2:9 ("I wrote for this

---

18 Joseph A. Fitzmyer, "Qumran and the Interpolated Paragraph in 2 Corinthians 6:14–7:1," *CBQ* 23 (1961) 273–280.
19 Christian Emmerling, *Epistola Pauli ad Corinthios posterior* (Lipsiae: Barth, 1823) 77; Krenkel, *Beiträge*, 332–33.
20 Hans Dieter Betz, "2 Cor. 6:14–7:1: An Anti-Pauline Fragment?" *JBL* 92 (1972) 88–108.
21 Stephen J. Hultgren, "2 Cor. 6:14–7:1 and Rev. 21:3–8: Evidence for the Ephesian Redaction of 2 Corinthians," *NTS* 49 (2003) 39–56; Richard I. Pervo, *The Making of Paul; Constructions of the Apostle in Early Christianity* (Minneapolis: Fortress Press, 2010) 40.
22 Vielhauer, *Geschichte der urchristlichen Literatur*, 151.
23 Adolf Hausrath, *Der Vier-Capitel-Brief des Paulus an die Korinther* (Heidelberg: Bassermann, 1870).
24 James H. Kennedy, "Are There Two Epistles in 2 Corinthians?" *The Expositor* 6 (1897) 231–238, 285–304; idem, *The Second and Third Epistles of St. Paul to the Corinthians* (London: Methuen, 1900); idem, "The Problem of Second Corinthians," *Hermathena* 12 (1903) 340–376.

reason: to test you and to know whether you are obedient in everything") with 10:6 ("We are ready to punish every disobedience when your obedience is complete"). As Kennedy observed, "in each of these pairs—the act, or purpose, or feeling, which in 2 Cor. 10–13 is present or future, in 2 Cor. 1–9 is spoken of as belonging to the past."[25] In a number of instances, Paul can be seen to soften the harsh language of chs. 10–13 by a conciliatory use of the same terms in chs. 1–2 and 7: for example, in 10:1–2 Paul boasts "I have confidence against you," but in 7:16 asserts "I have complete confidence in you."

Utilizing the criterion of the cross-references, Margaret Mitchell has recently argued that Paul's defense of the conduct of Titus and an unnamed brother in 12:18 refers back to the mission of Titus and the brother in 8:6, 22,[26] reviving an insight of Johannes Weiss.[27] Thus, Mitchell has concluded, rightly, in my view, that 2 Cor. 8 is the earliest of the letters which make up our 2 Corinthians.[28]

A consequent application of the criterion of the cross-references would lead us to place 2:14–7:4 (minus the interpolated passage) after 10–13.[29] An older generation of scholars including Adolf von Hausrath, Paul Schmiedel, James Kennedy, Kirsopp Lake and Alfred Plummer, among others recognized several instances in 2:14–6:13; 7:2–4 where Paul refers back to statements in 10–13.[30] Thus, in 3:1 and 5:12, where Paul asks "Are we beginning again to recommend ourselves" (ἀρχόμεθα πάλιν ἑαυτοὺς συνιστάνειν), and asserts "We are not commending ourselves to you again" (οὐ πάλιν ἑαυτοὺς συνιστάνομεν ὑμῖν), Paul is clearly referring back to passages in chs. 11 and 12 where he felt obliged to engage in "self-commendation" (cf. 12:11).[31] As Kennedy

---

25 Kennedy, "Are There Two Epistles in 2 Corinthians?" 234.
26 Mitchell, "Paul's Letters to Corinth," 326–333.
27 Weiss, *Primitive Christianity*, 1.353, 357.
28 Mitchell, "Paul's Letters to Corinth," 324, 328.
29 See already N. H. Taylor, "The Composition and Chronology of Second Corinthians," *JSNT* 44 (1991) 67–87, esp. 71–75.
30 Hausrath, *Der Vier-Capitel-Brief des Paulus*, 22, 23, 26; Paul Wilhelm Schmiedel, *Die Briefe an die Korinther* (Freiburg: Mohr, 1891) 61; Kennedy, *The Second and Third Epistles*, 81–89; idem, "The Problem of Second Corinthians," 350–351; Kirsopp Lake, *The Earlier Epistles of St. Paul. Their Motive and Origin*, 2nd ed. (London: Rivingtons, 1914) 154; Alfred Plummer, *A Critical and Exegetical Commentary on the Second Epistle of St. Paul to the Corinthians* (Edinburgh: T & T Clark, 1915) xxxi-xxxiii.
31 Hausrath, *Der Vier-Capitel-Brief des Paulus*, 22; Schmiedel, *Die Briefe an die Korinther*, 61.

observed, "The word πάλιν implies that Paul has done on a recent occasion that very thing which he now assures them that he will do no more."³² In 5:13, where Paul alludes apologetically to a previous moment when he appeared to be "beside himself," he is probably referring to the experience described in 12:1–6.³³ In 4:2, where Paul underlines his refusal to "practice cunning" (μὴ περιπατοῦντες ἐν πανουργίᾳ) or to "falsify (δολοῦντες) the word of God," he is likely recalling his earlier rebuttal of the charge of being "crafty" (πανοῦργος) and taking the Corinthians in "by deceit" (δόλῳ) in 12:16.³⁴ Paul's retrospective assertion that "we defrauded no one" (οὐδένα ἐπλεονεκτήσαμεν) in 7:2 recalls his earlier denial that he had "defrauded" (ἐπλεονέκτησα) the Corinthians through Titus and the brother in 12:17–18.³⁵ All of these cross-references were apparent to interpreters of previous generations, along with numerous, less conspicuous instances of "softening" of words and phrases, such as καύχησις and πεποίθησις, used in a harsh and uncomplimentary fashion in chs. 10–13, but upon which Paul confers a new, conciliatory sense in 2:14–7:4.³⁶

That the cross-references between 2:14–7:4 and 10–13 are no longer recognized by scholars, and are largely ignored, is owing, in my view, to a wrong direction taken by scholarship, when Günther Bornkamm supported the suggestion of his student Walter Schmithals that 2:14–7:4 preceded 10–13.³⁷ Schmithals' suggestion regarding the posi-

---

32 Kennedy, "The Problem of Second Corinthians," 350–351.
33 Hausrath, *Der Vier-Capitel-Brief,* 23; Schmiedel, *Die Briefe an die Korinther,* 61; Kennedy, "The Problem of Second Corinthians," 361, calling attention to the past tense of ἐξέστημεν in 5:13.
34 Plummer, *Second Epistle,* xxxi.
35 Plummer, *Second Epistle,* xxxiii.
36 Kennedy, "The Problem of Second Corinthians," 340–346; Lake, *The Earlier Epistles of St. Paul,* 161; Plummer, *Second Epistle,* xxxi. Cf. Taylor, "The Composition and Chronology of Second Corinthians," 74–75.
37 Günther Bornkamm, *Die Vorgeschichte des sogenannten Zweiten Korintherbriefes.* SHAW.PH 1961, 2. Abhandlung (Heidelberg: Winter, 1961) 7–36, esp. 23: "So sprechen gute Gründe für die jüngst vertretene Annahme, dass zwischen der ersten Apologie und dem Schmerzenbrief abermals unterschieden werden muss. Die erstere wäre dann noch früher geschrieben, in einem Augenblick, wo Paulus erstmals Kunde von den neuen Aposteln und der Bedrohung der Gemeinde bekommen hatte, aber von einem Sieg der Gegner über sie noch nicht die Rede sein könnte." Bornkamm's only argument for placing 2:14–7:4 before 10–13 is the reference in 10:10 to "weighty and strong letters" of Paul, which he takes to be a reference to 2:14–7:4. But Bornkamm must concede: "Gewiss kann sich das auf unsern I. Korintherbrief beziehen."

tion of 2:14–7:4 within the Corinthian correspondence was based upon the highly questionable assumption that Paul "misunderstood" the situation in Corinth, and that the "cautious polemic" of 2:14–7:4 reflects Paul's misunderstanding.[38] A preface is not the place for an analysis of a misstep in the history of scholarship, even when that misstep has had major consequences.[39] But it would repay the efforts of scholars who, as Johannes Weiss eloquently confessed, "have come to love the highly personal, truly human, psychologically interesting and religiously profound writing known as 2 Corinthians, and who know that they will have no rest until they have understood its composition to some extent,"[40] to re-read the relevant pages of Bornkamm's influential essay on the pre-history of 2 Corinthians, and to observe with what tortured arguments Bornkamm endeavored to dispel the appearance of the cross-references between 2:14–7:4 and 10–13, once he had decided to support the assumption of his student Schmithals regarding the placement of 2:14–7:4 within the Corinthian correspondence.[41]

---

38 Walter Schmithals, *Gnosticism in Corinth: An Investigation of the Letters to the Corinthians* (Nashville: Abingdon, 1971) 99. In comparison with the explicit Auseinanderstezung of chs. 10–13, Schmithals finds the polemic of 2:14–6:13; 7:2–4 "cautious": "The cautious polemic cannot be without reason. It fits into a time in which Paul was compromised by recent prejudiced utterances in Corinth and had received information about this exposure." Thus, Schmithals bases his argument for the placement of 2:14–6:13; 7:2–4 on the supposition that 1 Corinthians "contained inaccurate or misinformed statements of the apostle on the situation in Corinth." Paul received a report of this from the returning Timothy, in consequence of which he became more cautious in his next letter.

39 Bornkamm was followed by Dieter Georgi, *Die Gegner des Paulus im 2. Korintherbrief: Studien zur religiösen Propaganda in der Spätantike* (Neukirchen-Vluyn: Neukirchener Verlag, 1964); Hans Dieter Betz, *Der Apostel Paulus und die sokratische Tradition: Eine exegetische Untersuchung zu seiner 'Apologie' in 2 Kor 10–13* (Tübingen: Mohr-siebeck, 1972); idem, *2 Corinthians 8 and 9*; Mitchell, "Paul's Letters to Corinth," 333–335; among others.

40 Weiss, review of Halmel in *TLZ* 19 (1894) 513.

41 Bornkamm, *Vorgeschichte*, 23 n.88: "Keinesfalls darf man aus πάλιν (3:1; 5:12) schliessen, dass II Kor 10–13 vorangegangen sein müssen, da dort das Motiv der Selbstempfehlung eine so bedeutende Rolle spielt." [But why not?] Bornkamm goes on to explain: "Was II Kor 10–13 als Selbstempfehlung begegnet, ist in Wahrheit ja eine Parodie und also in den Augen der Gegner keine Empfehlung für Paulus." [One might counter that parody is indicative of Paul's *attitude* toward the requirement of "self-commendation," but Paul still felt obliged to engage in self-commendation, as he acknowledges in 12:11.] Consequently, Bornkamm is left without a referent in 2 Corinthians for 3:1 and 5:12, and must seek it in 1 Corinthians: "Der Vorwurf und Verdacht der Selbstempfehlung, den Pau-

Consistent application of the criterion of the cross-references establishes the following sequence of letters and letter-fragments within 2 Corinthians (I append generic titles for purposes of identification):

2 Cor. 8, Appeal for Partnership in the Collection
2 Cor. 10–13, Polemical Apology
2 Cor. 2:14–6:13; 7:2–4, Conciliatory Apology
2 Cor. 1:1–2:13; 7:5–16, Therapeutic Epistle
2 Cor. 9, Appeal for Partnership in the Collection

I readily concede that the order of the fragments could be different than that given here: passages such as 10:6 ("being ready to punish every disobedience") might refer back to 7:15 ("remembering the obedience of you all"). Terms such as καύχησις and πεποίθησις might first have been used in commendation and affection in 2:14–6:13; 7:2–4, and later in a bitter and ironic sense in 10–13. But there are consequences of reversing the direction of the cross-references: Paul would then seem to mock at his own terms of endearment. Employing an apt metaphor, James Kennedy observed: "They are like the valves of the heart which revealed to Harvey the secret of the circulation of the blood by opening in one direction only."[42]

With a minority of critics,[43] I am unable to persuade myself that 1 Corinthians is a unified composition. In 1 Corinthians, as in 2 Corinthi-

---

lus 3:1; 5:12 abwehrt, weist allerdings auf frühere seiner Äusserungen zurück, mit denen er seiner Gemeinde lastig fallen konnte." Then, Bornkamm asserts that the whole search is useless: "Doch ist es müssig, sie näher zu bestimmen," and proceeds to generalize the act of self-commendation throughout 1 Corinthians: "Tatsächlich hat Paulus ja niemals auf solche 'Selbstempfehlungen' verzichten können und schon der I. Kor ist von ihnen durchzogen (I, 3:10; 4:1 ff.; 4:15 f.; 8:13; bes. 9:1 ff.; 9:26 f.; 11:1; 14:18 f.; 15:10)." [But if 1 Cor. is "durchzogen von Selbstempfehlungen," why is the same not true of 2 Cor. 10–13?] Thus, Bornkamm's argument that 2 Cor. 3:1 and 5:12 cannot refer to 2 Cor. 10–13 collapses under its own weight.

42 Kennedy, "Are There Two Epistles in 2 Corinthians?" 299.
43 Johannes Weiss, *Der erste Korintherbrief* (Göttingen: Vandenhoeck & Ruprecht, 1910) xxxix-xliii; Wolfgang Schenk, "Der 1. Korintherbrief als Briefsammlung," *ZNW* 60 (1969) 219–243; Vielhauer, *Geschichte der urchristlichenLiteratur*, 140–141; Christophe Senft, *La première épître de Saint Paul aux Corinthiens* (Neuchatel: Neuchatel-Delachaux, 1979) 17–25; Michael Bünker, *Briefformular und rhetorische Disposition im 1. Korintherbrief* (Göttingen: Vandenhoeck & Ruprecht, 1983) 51–59; Robert Jewett, "The Redaction of 1 Corinthians and the Trajectory of the Pauline School," *JAARSup* 46 (1978) 389–444; Hans Josef Klauck, *1. Korintherbrief* (Würzburg: Echter, 1984).

ans, one encounters abrupt transitions, frequent changes of theme, and generally loose construction.⁴⁴ Assigning portions of 1 Corinthians to separate letters would be justified only if the passages in question presupposed different situations. This appears to be the case in three instances: Paul's attitude toward the factions (contrast 11:18–19 with 1:10–12), Paul's advice on food sacrificed to idols (contrast 10:1–11 with 8:1–13), and Paul's announcement of his travel plans (contrast 16:5–9 with 4:17–21).⁴⁵ Hence, I divide 1 Corinthians into three letters, composed in the following order:

1 Cor. 10:1–22; 6:12–20; 10:23–11:34, On Association with the Immoral and Idolaters
1 Cor. 7–9, 12–16, Response to the Corinthians' Questions
1 Cor. 1:1–6:11, Counsel of Concord

The strongest argument for the unity of canonical 1 Corinthians derives from rhetorical analysis, which identifies 1 Corinthians as a deliberative appeal for concord (1:1–4:21), with advice on divisive issues organized under subheadings (5:1–16:24).⁴⁶ Yet a single letter is not consistent with the several occasions and sources of information evident in the text of 1 Corinthians: an anonymous report (11:18), the Corinthians' letter (7:1), a visit by Stephanas and his colleagues (16:17), and a report from Chloe's people (1:11).

I freely acknowledge the hypothetical character of my literary analysis of Paul's Corinthian correspondence. Other theories can be made plausible, including those which defend the unity of canonical 1 Corinthians. But there are a finite number of interpretive possibilities, and not every theory provides a satisfactory explanation of the textual evidence. I emphasize once again the necessity of some theory of literary composition for any attempt to reconstruct the history of Paul's relationship with Corinth. Given the reciprocal nature of literary analysis and historical reconstruction in the case of Paul's letters to Corinth, I would like to think that my investigation of Paul's relationship with the wrongdoer may contrib-

---

44 Vielhauer, *Geschichte der urchristlichen Literatur*, 140–141.
45 Similarly, Vielhauer, *Geschichte der urchristlichen Literatur*, 141.
46 Margaret M. Mitchell, *Paul and the Rhetoric of Reconciliation: An Exegetical Investigation of the Language and Composition of 1 Corinthians* (Tübingen: Mohr-Siebeck, 1991). For critique of the hypothesis that all of 1 Corinthians qualifies as deliberative rhetoric, see R. Dean Anderson, *Ancient Rhetorical Theory and Paul* (Kampen: Kok Pharos, 1996).

ute something to a better understanding of the compositional history of Paul's Corinthian correspondence.

Chapter One
Introduction

> *Cum ad Corinthios ejusdem apostoli litterae iterantur, venia fit plane, sed incertum cui, quia nec persona nec causa proscribitur.*
>
> Tertullian *De pudicitia* 14

In 2 Corinthians chapters 2 and 7, Paul refers to an individual who has done him "wrong" and has caused him "pain."[1] The gravity of the incident is indicated by the consequences, to which allusion is made in the context: Paul postponed his planned visit to Corinth (1:15–16, 23; 2:1), and instead wrote a tearful letter (2:3–4), which he feared would cause the Corinthians pain (7:8).[2] Given the importance of the episode,[3] one might assume that scholars would devote much effort to the discovery of the nature of the offence and the identity of its perpetrator. But in the past generation, only three articles treated the subject thematically.[4] The reason for the neglect of the subject is not hard to find, and was already suggested by Tertullian: in the interest of forgiveness and reconciliation, Paul draws a curtain of anonymity over the wrongdoer and discreetly avoids description of his wrong. Thus, prudent historians of the

---

1   2 Cor. 2:5; 7:12. That Paul is dealing with the same situation and the same individual in 2 Cor. 2:5–11 and 7:5–12, see ch. 3 below, pp. 23–25.
2   Hans Conzelmann, *Geschichte des Urchristentums* (Göttingen: Vandenhoeck & Ruprecht, 1969) 87; Günther Bornkamm, *Paul* (New York: Harper & Row, 1971) 77.
3   Frances Young and David F. Ford, *Meaning and Truth in 2 Corinthians* (Grand Rapids: Eerdmans, 1987) 22: "One suspects that the person concerned lies at the root of the crisis of confidence between Paul and the church."
4   C. K. Barrett, "Ο ΑΔΙΚΗΣΑΣ (2 Cor. 7.12)" in *Verborum Veritas*, eds. O. Böcher and K. Haacker (Wuppertal: Theologischer Verlag-Brockhaus, 1970) 149–57; repr. in idem, *Essays on Paul* (Philadelphia: Westminster, 1982) 108–17; Margaret E. Thrall, "The Offender and the Offence: A Problem of Detection in 2 Corinthians" in *Scripture: Meaning and Method*, ed. B. P. Thompson (Pickering: Hull University Press, 1987) 65–78; Colin G. Kruse, "The Offender and the Offence in 2 Corinthians 2:5 and 7:12," *EvQ* 88.2 (1988) 129–39.

twentieth century were prepared to admit that this was a case where they were unable to reach safe conclusions because the evidence was insufficient. Kirsopp Lake asked, "Who was the offender, and what was his offence?" and answered, "The one thing that is certain here is that no confident answer can ever be given."[5] And T. W. Manson conceded, "What exactly happened on this occasion we do not know and have no means of discovering."[6]

We shall see that close reading of the text of 2 Corinthians, and study of the words that Paul chooses to describe the wrong, will lift the veil of Pauline discretion to a considerable degree, disclosing, in broad outline, the type of offence that was committed, and the relationship of the wrongdoer both to Paul and to the Corinthians. But no amount of exegetical artistry will reveal the identity of the one who did Paul wrong. If progress is to be made in detection, it can only result from taking Paul's silence seriously and asking about its cause.

This book will argue that Paul does not mention the name of his enemy because he is following a rhetorical convention well established in the Greco-Roman world. Later, when reconciliation is achieved, Paul is at liberty to mention his erstwhile opponent. We shall argue that Paul does so in another context, and again in accordance with social convention. Thus the conventions that conceal the identity of the wrongdoer reveal him in the end.

The prosopographic data supplied by Paul's epistles permit us to assign the individual who has done Paul wrong to the upper class—indeed, he is the Christian of highest social standing at Corinth. The archaeological record of Roman Corinth enables us to form some estimate of the career and influence of a man such as the one who became the leader of the opposition to Paul in Corinth.

Thus, a close reading of the text of Paul's epistles in the context of the social conventions that governed friendship, enmity, and reconciliation in the Greco-Roman world makes it possible to reconstruct the history of Paul's conflict and reconciliation with a powerful convert to Christianity at Corinth.

---

5   Lake, *The Earlier Epistles of St. Paul*, 169.
6   T. W. Manson, *Studies in the Gospels and Epistles*, ed. M. Black (Manchester: Manchester University Press, 1962) 213.

Chapter Two
History of Scholarship

For eighteen-hundred years, there was no doubt as to the identity of the wrongdoer of 2 Cor. 2 and 7: he was equated with the incestuous man of 1 Cor. 5.[1] Tertullian was the exception in the history of interpretation. Tertullian argued that the two cases could not be identical, because Paul's accounts of the situations, and especially his verdicts in the two cases, were entirely different: in 1 Cor. 5 Paul speaks explicitly of one who has committed fornication and defiled his father's marriage bed, but in 2 Cor. 2 Paul speaks discreetly, indeed almost obscurely, of one who has caused pain and should now be forgiven;[2] the former case is placed under a sentence of "condemnation" (*condemnatio*), while the latter is subject only to "censure" (*increpatio*).[3] Having dissociated the wrongdoer from the incestuous man, Tertullian sought for another whom Paul could have intended when he spoke in 2 Cor. 2 of one who had pained the Corinthian church, and found him among the factious of 1 Cor. 1–4 who were inflated with pride against the apostle.[4] As

---

1 John Chrysostom, *Hom. 1 Cor.* 15:1 (*MPG* 61.121); *Hom. 2 Cor.* 4:3 (*MPG* 61.421), with other ancient commentators, including Ambrosiaster, Theodoret, and Theophylact. See the judgment of G. Estius, *In Omnes Divi Pauli Apostoli epistolas commentariorum Tomus Prior* (Douai, 1614), cited in C. F. Georg Heinrici, *Das zweite Sendschreiben des Apostel Paulus an die Korinther* (Berlin: Hertz, 1887) 14: "transit ad mentionem hominis qui praecipuam tristitiae causam dederat... Eundem hunc esse cum illo quem prius ob incestum jusserat tradi Satanae, nullus est commentatorum qui dubitet." Representatives of the traditional view in the 20th century include: Heinrici, *Der zweite Brief,* 12; Philip E. Hughes, *Paul's Second Epistle to the Corinthians* (Grand Rapids: Eerdmans, 1962) 59–65; Kruse,"The Offender and the Offence," 129–39.

2 Tertullian, *Pud.* 13–14, ed. Franciscus Oehler, *Quinti Septimi Florentis Tertulliani Quae Supersunt Omnia* (Leipzig: Weigel, 1853) 1.817–21. On Tertullian as the exception in the history of interpretation, see Heinrici, *Das zweite Sendschreiben,* 14–15; Thrall, "The Offender and the Offence," 66.

3 Tertullian, *Pud.* 14; cf. Heinrici, *Der zweite Brief,* 11–12.

4 Tertullian, *Pud.* 14; cf. Heinrici, *Der zweite Brief,* 12.

remarkable as Tertullian's insights seem to us today,[5] his interpretation remained without effect upon the tradition, because his views were held to be tainted by Montanism, in the service of whose rigorous discipline Tertullian sought to remove any scriptural foundation for the authority of the Catholic bishops to absolve penitent fornicators and adulterers.[6] Thus the history of interpretation followed the path marked out by Chrysostom rather than Tertullian, seeing in 2 Cor. 2 and 7 Paul's expression of gratitude for the punishment which the church had inflicted upon the incestuous man.[7]

A new chapter in the history of interpretation of 2 Corinthians opened in 1830, with the publication by Friedrich Bleek of two hypotheses which had implications for the identity of the wrongdoer.[8] Bleek sought to demonstrate that the letter to which Paul refers in 2 Cor. 2:3–4 as a "painful epistle" is not, as customarily assumed, 1 Corinthians, but a letter written between 1 and 2 Corinthians, a letter which is now lost.[9] Moreover, on the basis of 2 Cor. 12:14 and 13:1, Bleek contended that Paul must have been in Corinth a second time before the composition of 2 Corinthians, and that it is to such an occasion that Paul refers in 2 Cor. 2:1 as a "painful visit."[10] Thus Bleek ventured a suggestion in the direction of Tertullian's interpretation: Paul's painful epistle was written in response to a grave insult which a member of the Corinthian community gave to Paul on his second visit.[11] Bleek grasped the implications of this reconstruction for the traditional identification of the

---

5   See the judgment of Plummer, *Second Epistle*, 54: "Tertullian's vigorous argument almost suffices without any others."
6   On the role of Tertullian's Montanism, see Heinrici, *Das zweite Sendschreiben*, 14–15; E.-B. Allo, *Saint Paul: Seconde Épître aux Corinthiens* (Paris: Gabalda, 1956) 57–58; Hughes, *Paul's Second Epistle*, 62–63; Thrall, "The Offender and the Offence," 66.
7   Heinrici, *Der zweite Brief*, 12; Hughes, *Paul's Second Epistle*, 62–64.
8   Friedrich Bleek, "Erörterungen in Beziehung auf die Briefe Pauli an die Korinther," *ThStKr* 3 (1830) 614–32. For Bleek as the first in the modern era to question the traditional identification of the wrongdoer with the incestuous man, see Krenkel, *Beiträge*, 293; Heinrici, *Der zweite Brief*, 12, 14–15.
9   Bleek, "Erörterungen," 625–32.
10 Bleek, "Erörterungen," 614–24.
11 Bleek, "Erörterungen," 629, concluding "dass irgend ein Einzelner sich auf besonders auffallende Weise gegen die Anordnungen des Paulus—im Allgemeinen oder in einer besonderen Hinsicht—widersetzt hätte, der aber nach dem durch Titus überbrachten Schreiben durch die Gemeinde bestraft und in die gehörigen Schranken zurückgeführt ware."

wrongdoer with the incestuous man: in Paul's discussion of the letter that he wrote and the wrongdoer who occasioned it, everything turns upon a *personal relationship* between Paul and an unnamed individual, something that would not have been true with a case of incest.[12] Yet, Bleek was not prepared to give up the traditional identification, and evidently saw no alternative. Bleek imagined a scenario in which, after the incestuous man had received Paul's judgment in 1 Cor. 5, he hardened his heart and persisted in the practice, and the community did nothing to hinder him. Paul learned of this development from Timothy, and wrote another letter in which he gave the church grief and moved them to take action against the sinner.[13]

With the rise of historical consciousness in the nineteenth century, it became more and more difficult to reconcile the differences between the incestuous man of 1 Cor. 5 and the wrongdoer of 2 Cor. 2 and 7. Reconstructions of developments between 1 Corinthians and 2 Corinthians in the service of the traditional identification became more speculative and complex. The account that finally provoked a reaction and led to a decisive break with tradition was, ironically, that of the great historian of the early church, F. C. Baur.[14] Baur explained that Paul's demand for the expulsion of the incestuous man from the community in 1 Cor. 5 went unheeded in Corinth and only served to expose Paul to criticism by opponents who disparaged his authority. Later, Titus arrived in Corinth and carried out a less drastic punishment. Realizing that his measures had been too hasty and daring, Paul wrote in 2 Cor. 2 to retract his demands in principle, seeking to efface the negative impression he had produced by indulgence and appeasement.[15] In sharp debate with Baur, Heinrich Ewald argued that Paul could not have granted personal forgiveness such as he expresses in 2 Cor. 2:10 to one who was guilty of the sin of

---

12 Bleek, "Erörterungen," 630. Bleek was followed by Heinrich Ewald, *Die Sendschreiben des Apostels Paulus* (Göttingen: Dieterich, 1857) 226–27; August Neander, *Auslegung der beiden Briefe an die Korinther* (Berlin: Reimer, 1859); Adolf Hilgenfeld, *Historisch-kritische Einleitung in das Neue Testament* (Leipzig: Fues, 1875) 286, among others.
13 Bleek, "Erörterungen," 630.
14 Ferdinand Christian Baur, *Paulus, der Apostel Jesu Christi: Sein Leben und Wirken, seine Briefe und seine Lehre, ein Beitrag zu einer kritischen Geschichte des Urchristentums* (Stuttgart: Becher & Müller, 1845, ²1866) 1.334–35.
15 Baur, *Paulus*, 335; followed by Albert Klöpper, *Kommentar über das zweite Sendschreiben des Apostel Paulus an die Gemeinde zu Korinth* (Berlin: Reimer, 1874) 59, 163–64; Heinrich Julius Holtzmann, "Das gegenseitige Verhältnis der beiden Korintherbriefe," *ZwTh* 22 (1879) 467–68.

incest and whose expulsion from the community he had clearly demanded.[16] Ewald proposed that, on the occasion of Paul's second visit to Corinth, one of the Corinthians, probably a leader of the church, openly accused Paul of misconduct so serious that, had it been proven, would have sufficed to deprive Paul of his apostolic legitimacy.[17]

Ewald's arguments for the distinction of the wrongdoer from the incestuous man were accepted by a number of scholars and became the basis for further research.[18] As attention shifted from 1 Corinthians to 2 Corinthians, scholars discovered clues to the status of the wrongdoer, the nature of his offence, and his role in the opposition to Paul. Analysis

---

16 Heinrich Ewald, "Bemerkungen über die Paulusbriefe," *Jahrbücher der biblischen Wissenschaft* 2 (1850) 229–30: "Er [Baur] meint z.b., der Apostel habe bei dem 2 Cor, 2,5 ff. bezeichneten manne jenen blütschänder 1 Cor. 5,1–5 im sinne: indem er nach 1 Cor. 5 dessen ausstossung aus der Gemeinde gefordert, habe er, wie er 2 Cor. 2 selbst einsehe, einen zu gewagten und übereilten schritt gethan, durch welchen er, weil er die beabsichtigte folge nicht hatte, sich nur eine blösse gegeben habe und den er nun 2 Cor. 2 im grunde selbst zurücknehme; jene forderung habe in Corinth einem sehr übeln eindruck gemacht, den der Apostel jetzt durch nachgiebigkeit und begütigung zu verwischen suche. Jawohl, wenn der Apostel ein mann etwa wie Dr. Baur erster prof. der ev. theologie in Tübingen gewesen wäre, so liesse sich solcherlei zeug erdichten und mitanhören! Zumglück war er ein ganz anderer mann, und zumglück haben seine worte nicht im geringsten einen solchen sinn. Einen Christen der ihn persönlich beleidigt hatte konnte der Apostel gern verzeihen: von einem blütschänder konnte, nachdem er einmal dessen ausstossung gefordert, bei ihm garnichtmehr die rede seyn. Ist den unsern Kirchengeschichtern der geist der apostolischen Kirche so gänzlich unfassbar? Aber dann sollten sie wenigstens den sinn der worte der quellen nicht verdrehen."
17 Ewald,"Bemerkungen," 230; idem, *Sendschreiben*, 226–27.
18 Adolf Hilgenfeld, "Die Christusleute in Korinth," *ZwTh* 3 (1865) 241–43; idem, "Paulus und die korinthischen Wirren," *ZwTh* 9 (1871) 103–104; idem, "Paulus und Korinth," *ZwTh* 26 (1888) 193–94; Willibald Beyschlag, "Über die Christuspartei in Korinth," *ThStKr* 38 (1865) 253–54; idem, "Zur Streitfrage über die Paulusgegner des zweiten Korintherbriefes," *ThStKr* 44 (1871) 670; Karl Heinrich von Weizsäcker, "Paulus und die Gemeinde in Korinth," *Jahrbücher für deutsche Theologie* 19 (1873) 643–45; idem, *Das apostolische Zeitalter der christlichen Kirche* (Freiburg: Mohr, 1886, ²1892) 306–309; Paul Wilhelm Schmiedel, *Hand-Commentar zum Neuen Testament*, vol. 2 (Freiburg: Mohr, Siebeck, 1891, ²1892) 46, 79–80, 220–21; Otto Pfleiderer, *Das Urchristentum, seine Schriften und Lehren in geschichtlichem Zusammenhang beschrieben* (Berlin: Reimer, 1887, ²1902) 103–104; Krenkel, *Beiträge*, 257, 283–96; Johannes Weiss, *Das Urchristentum*, ed. R. Knopf (Göttingen: Vandenhoeck & Ruprecht, 1917); English trans. *The History of Primitive Christianity*, 2 vols., trans. by F. C. Grant (New York: Wilson-Erickson, 1937) 1.342–44.

of Paul's argument and rhetoric in 2 Cor. 1:1–2:13 and 7:5–16 led to the conclusion that the occasion both of Paul's absence from Corinth and of his painful epistle was an incident in Corinth in which two individuals were involved: Paul was wronged by a prominent member of the Corinthian church, and had something of which to forgive.[19] Yet the community could not be entirely excused of complicity: indeed, the wrong of 2:5 and 7:12 was an insult in which the tensions between Paul and the community culminated.[20] Although Paul never says precisely in what the invective against him consisted, chapters 10–13 contain much polemical material. The speaker for the opposition against Paul was discovered behind the indefinite pronouns and the third-person verbs in 10:7, 10:10, and 10:11.[21] Calumnies against Paul reverberate throughout the apologetic of these chapters: accordingly, Paul was represented as weak, a contemptible speaker, a boastful fool, crafty and deceitful, one in whom the power of Christ was not present.[22] It was clear that the wrongdoer could not be one of the Jewish apostles who had entered the Corinthian community from outside, since such a person would not have stood under the jurisdiction of the Corinthian church, and would not have been brought to grief and repentance by Paul.[23] Yet the whole of 2 Corinthians makes it likely that the wrongdoer was a Corinthian Christian who had been influenced by the Judaizers: in this sense, the affair of the wrongdoer could be said to belong to the history of the Jewish-Christian opposition to Paul.[24] Such was the new understanding of the

---

19 Ewald, *Sendschreiben*, 227; Neander, *Auslegung*, 293: "dass etwa einer aufgetreten sei, der dem apostolischen Ansehen Pauli übermütig trotzte und dadurch eine Spaltung in der Gemeinde hervorzurufen drohte"; Krenkel, *Beiträge*, 257; Wilhelm Bousset, *Der zweite Brief an die Korinther* (Göttingen: Vandenhoeck & Ruprecht, ²1908) 175; Weiss, *Primitive Christianity*, 1.342–43.

20 Ewald, *Sendschreiben*, 227; Neander, *Auslegung*, 293; Schmiedel, *Die Briefe an die Korinther*, 46, 220–21; Richard Drescher, "Der zweite Korintherbrief und die Vorgänge in Korinth seit Abfassung des ersten Korintherbriefs," *ThStKr* 70 (1897) 49; Weiss, *Primitive Christianity*, 1.342–43.

21 Karl König,"Der Verkehr des Paulus mit der Gemeinde zu Korinth," *ZwTh* 40 (1897) 514; Weiss, *Primitive Christianity* 1.343.

22 Hilgenfeld, *Historisch-kritische Einleitung*, 286: "In der korinthischen Gemeinde wird jemand öffentlich erklärt haben, Paulus, der vorgebliche Apostel rühme sich masslos und sei vor lauter Einbildung ganz von Sinnen gekommen, ein reiner Narr geworden." See also König, "Verkehr," 516, 520–21; Weiss, *Primitive Christianity*, 1.343–44.

23 König, "Verkehr," 516; Weiss, *Primitive Christianity*, 1.343–44.

24 Weizsäcker, "Paulus und die Gemeinde in Korinth," 643, who concludes, "dass der ganze Vorfall in die Geschichte der jüdaistischen Agitation gehört, wenn auch

offender and his offence which emerged by the end of the nineteenth century in the succession of Bleek and Ewald.[25]

Nevertheless, a minority of eminent scholars maintained the identity of the wrongdoer with the incestuous man, even in the face of a new, critical consensus.[26] It is important to grasp their reasons for doing so, because their resistance ultimately sharpened understanding of the nature of the offence against Paul. First, some weight must be granted to tradition: especially in cases where the evidence seems insufficient, preference is naturally given to the form in which knowledge has been transmitted.[27] Second, the new hypothesis regarding the offender and the offence had become intertwined in the history of scholarship with a critique of the integrity of 2 Corinthians, so that some scholars felt obliged to reaffirm the traditional identification of the wrongdoer, in order to defend the unity of the canonical text.[28] It will be recalled that Ewald's proposal to distinguish the wrongdoer from the incestuous man rested upon Bleek's critique of the assumption that 1 Corinthians is the "letter of tears" mentioned in 2 Cor. 2:3–4.[29] Once the equation of the "painful epistle" with 1 Corinthians was given up, it was inevitable that scholars would search for the letter elsewhere in the Pauline corpus. Within a generation, Adolf Hausrath found the "lost" letter in 2 Cor. 10–13,[30] a proposal which has garnered much support in the history of scholarship,[31] and which remains

---

der Mann nicht einer von den auswärts Gekommenen, sondern ein Mitglied der Gemeinde gewesen zu sein scheint." See also Hilgenfeld, *Historisch-kritische Einleitung*, 283–86; König, "Verkehr," 516.

25 Weiss, *Primitive Christianity*, 1.342–44, summarizing the development in scholarship of the preceding century.
26 Hausrath, *Der Vier-Capitel-Brief des Paulus*, 7, 28; Heinrich Julius Holtzmann, "Das gegenseitige Verhältnis der beiden Korintherbriefe," ZwTh 22(1879) 466–68; Julius Ferdinand Räbiger, *Kritische Untersuchungen über den Inhalt der beiden Briefe des Apostels Paulus an die korinthische Gemeinde mit Rücksicht auf die in ihr herrschenden Streitigkeiten* (Breslau: Morgenstern, 1886) 230; Heinrici, *Das zweite Sendschreiben*, 13–22; idem, *Der zweite Brief*, 11–16; Carl Holsten, "Einleitung in die Korintherbriefe," ZwTh 44 (1901) 355–56.
27 Heinrici, *Der zweite Brief*, 11, 16; cf. Hughes, *Paul's Second Epistle*, 62.
28 E.g., Klöpper, *Kommentar*, 9, 27; Holtzmann, "Das gegenseitige Verhältnis," 455–92, esp. 464–68; Heinrici, *Der zweite Brief*, 5–32, esp. 11–16.
29 Bleek, "Erörterungen," 625–32; Ewald, *Sendschreiben*, 226–27.
30 Hausrath, *Der Vier-Capitel-Brief des Paulus*; see also idem, *Neutestamentliche Zeitgeschichte*, 4 vols. (Heidelberg: Bassermann, 1875) 3.302–14.
31 Schmiedel, *Die Briefe an die Korinther*, 2.74–80; Carl Clemen, *Die Einheitlichkeit der paulinischen Briefe, an Hand der bisher mit bezug auf sie angestellten Interpolations- und Compilationshypothesen geprüft* (Göttingen: Vandenhoeck & Ru-

for many the most convincing explanation of the internal references in Paul's Corinthian correspondence.[32] Third, defenders of the traditional identification of the wrongdoer with the incestuous man called attention to a certain "resonance" between the language of 1 Cor. 5:1–5 and 2 Cor. 2:5–11: in both passages, the person in question is denoted circumspectly by means of indefinite (τις) and correlative (τοιοῦτος) pronouns; in both passages, there is mention of Satan and of Christ.[33] Moreover, Paul's declaration that the Corinthians had proven themselves

---

precht, 1894) 19–68; Weiss, *Primitive Christianity*, 1.347–49; J. Héring, *La seconde Épître de Saint Paul aux Corinthiens* (Neuchâtel and Paris: Delachaux et Niestle, 1958); Rudolf Bultmann, *Der zweite Brief an die Korinther*, ed. E. Dinkler (Göttingen: Vandenhoeck & Ruprecht, 1976) 20–23; Walter Schmithals, *Die Gnosis in Korinth: Eine Untersuchung zu den Korintherbriefen* (Göttingen: Vandenhoeck & Ruprecht, 1969) 84–94; Dieter Georgi, *Die Gegner des Paulus im 2. Korintherbrief: Studien zur religiösen Propaganda in der Spätantike* (Neukirchen-Vluyn: Neukirchener Verlag, 1964), English trans. *The Opponents of Paul in Second Corinthians* (Philadelphia: Fortress Press, 1986) 9–13; Bornkamm, *Vorgeschichte*, esp. 172–78, revised and reprinted, with an addendum, in idem, *Geschichte und Glaube*, vol. 2 (Munich: Kaiser, 1971) 162–94; Vielhauer, *Geschichte der urchristlichen Literatur*, 142–56; Betz, *2 Corinthians 8 and 9*, 3–25; L. L. Welborn, "The Identification of 2 Corinthians 10–13 with the 'Letter of Tears'," *NovT* 37 (1995) 138–53; Mitchell, "Paul's Letters to Corinth," 307–38; Calvin Roetzel, *2 Corinthians* (Nashville: Abingdon, 2007) 32–33 and *passim*.

32 Kennedy, "Are There Two Epistles in 2 Corinthians?" 231–38, 285–304; idem, *The Second and Third Epistles*; James Moffatt, *The Historical New Testament* (New York: Schribner's, 1901) 174–91; Gerald H. Rendall, *The Epistles of Paul to the Corinthians* (London: Macmillan, 1909) 4–6; Lake, *The Earlier Epistles of St. Paul*, 151–64; Plummer, *Second Epistle*, xxii-xxvi, xxxi-xxxiii; R. H. Strachan, *The Second Epistle of St. Paul to the Corinthians* (New York: Harper, 1935) xiv-xx; Francis Watson, "2 Cor. x-xiii and Paul's Painful Letter to the Corinthians," *JTS* 35/2 (1984) 324–46; Welborn, "The Identification of 2 Corinthians 10–13," 138–53.

33 Baur, *Paulus*, 1.333; A. Sabatier, *L'Apôtre Paul. Esquisse d'une histoire de sa pensée* (Strasbourg: Treuttel et Wurtz, 1870) 142; Klöpper, *Kommentar*, 157; Hausrath, *Neutestamentliche Zeitgeschichte*, 2.700–701; Johann Christian Karl von Hofmann, *Die heilige Schrift neuen Testaments zusammenhängend untersucht*, 2. Theil, 3. Abteilung: *Der zweite Brief Pauli an die Korinther* (Nördlingen: Beck, ²1877) 105–106; Heinrici, *Der zweite Brief*, 16; Theodor Zahn, *Introduction to the New Testament*, 3 vols. (Edinburgh: T & T Clark, 1909) 1.348; Hughes, *Paul's Second Epistle*, 64 n.6; G. W. H. Lampe, "Church Discipline and the Interpretation of the Epistles to the Corinthians" in *Christian History and Interpretation*, eds. W. R. Farmer, C. F. D. Moule, R. R. Niebuhr (Cambridge: Cambridge University Press, 1967) 353–54.

"guiltless in the matter" (ἁγνοὶ τῷ πράγματι) of the wrongdoer in 2 Cor. 7:11 was construed as a reference to the "immorality" (πορνεία) of the incestuous man in 1 Cor. 5:1.[34] We shall see that the verbal similarities between these passages are too general to support an identification of the individuals involved, and that when the common vocabulary is examined in context, it highlights the differences, and even contradictions, between the two cases. Yet, for scholars who were inclined to defend the traditional identification of the wrongdoer with the incestuous man, the occurrence of similar expressions in 1 Cor. 5 and 2 Cor. 2 furnished a thread of continuity between the two cases.

More consequential than the arguments advanced in support of the traditional identification was a criticism of the new understanding of the offence against Paul as an "insult."[35] Several scholars questioned whether the punishment imposed upon the one who had caused pain in 2 Cor. 2:6 was not a disproportionate use of force, if Paul were merely dealing with a personal insult,[36] and wondered aloud whether it would not be "petty" of the apostle to respond to an insult in such a severe manner.[37] Eventually, Theodor Zahn focused attention on the verb Paul uses in 2 Cor. 7:12 to describe the nature of the offence.[38] Zahn demonstrated that the verb ἀδικεῖν ("to wrong") is nowhere used in the Septuagint or the New Testament with the unambiguous meaning "to insult" or "to slander." Rather, "to wrong someone" (ἀδικεῖν τινά) is defined as "voluntarily causing injury contrary to the law."[39] While an injury to reputation might fall into this category, Zahn questioned why Paul would not have written "the insulter" (ὁ ὑβρίσας) and "the insulted" (ὁ ὑβρισθείς), or "the

---

34 Klöpper, *Kommentar*, 54, 361; Holtzmann, "Das gegenseitige Verhältnis," 466; James Denney, *The Second Epistle to the Corinthians* (London: Armstrong, 1894) 2–3; Hughes, *Paul's Second Epistle*, 64 n.6.
35 Klöpper, *Kommentar*, 156–57; Holtzmann, "Das gegenseitige Verhältnis," 466; Heinrici, *Das zweite Sendschreiben*, 15; Zahn, *Introduction*, 1.349; Hans Windisch, *Der zweite Korintherbrief* (Göttingen: Vandenhoeck & Ruprecht, 1924, repr. 1970) 238.
36 Klöpper, *Kommentar*, 156–57; Holtzmann, "Das gegenseitige Verhältnis," 466; Windisch, *Der zweite Korintherbrief*, 238.
37 Heinrici, *Der zweite Brief*, 15; C. Holsten, "Einleitung in die Korintherbriefe," *ZwTh* 44 (1901) 355; Zahn, *Introduction*, 1.349; Allo, *Saint Paul*, 61–62.
38 Zahn, *Introduction*, 1.349; cf. Heinrici, *Der zweite Brief*, 16.
39 Zahn, *Introduction*, 1.349, citing Aristotle *Rhet.* 1.10.3.

Chapter Two. History of Scholarship

reviler" (ὁ λοιδορήσας) and "the reviled" (ὁ λοιδορηθείς), had he intended to speak of a personal insult.[40]

Thus, the attempt to maintain the traditional identification of the wrongdoer with the incestuous man produced one truly valuable insight into the nature of the offence against Paul: the wrong was more than a personal insult, however grave, public, and calumnious; the kind of action denoted by ἀδικεῖν was an injury with a legal aspect.[41] Beyond this, the defense of the traditional identification served to illustrate the hypothetical character of the new proposal that emerged in consequence of Bleek and Ewald, and the greater intellectual satisfaction of being able to identify the wrongdoer with another figure in the Corinthian correspondence.[42] Moreover, the debate between the critics and the traditionalists revealed that every attempt to reconstruct the events and persons to which allusion is made in the text involves a theory of the literary unity of the writings known to us as 1 and 2 Corinthians. Finally, the similarity of vocabulary between 1 Cor. 5:1–5 and 2 Cor. 2:5–11 proved intriguing to a number of scholars and seemed to leave open the possibility that the persons in question might be the same, even if the offences described were different.

The attempt to maintain the traditional identification of the wrongdoer with the incestuous man was abandoned at the beginning of the twentieth century,[43] and has been revived only as a subsidiary argument within defenses of the unity of 2 Corinthians.[44] It is important to comprehend the reasons why the traditional view was finally abandoned, despite its attractions, because the debate and its resolution delineate the pa-

---

40 Zahn, *Introduction*, 1.349; followed by Werner Georg Kümmel, *Introduction to the New Testament* (Nashville: Abingdon, 1975) 198.
41 Already emphasized by Krenkel, *Beiträge*, 305; followed by Windisch, *Der zweite Korintherbrief*, 238.
42 Heinrici, *Der zweite Brief*, 16; cf. Thrall, *Second Epistle*, 1.65.
43 James Moffatt, *An Introduction to the Literature of the New Testament* (New York: Scribner's, 1910) 122: "It should no longer require to be proved that this offender is not the incestuous person of 1 Cor. V.1, but someone who had wronged Paul himself."; Plummer, *Second Epistle*, xv, 54, who mentions only Zahn, among major scholars, as a defender of the traditional identification of the wrongdoer with the incestuous man.
44 Alan M. G. Stepheson, "A Defence of the Integrity of 2 Corinthians" in *The Authorship and Integrity of the New Testament* (London: SPCK, 1965) 86; Hyldahl, "Die Frage nach der literarischen Einheit," 305–306; David R. Hall, *The Unity of the Corinthian Correspondence* (London: T & T Clark, 2003) 227–35.

rameters within which the identity of the wrongdoer may be fruitfully investigated.

First, it is clear that Paul regards *the wrong* that has been committed in the two cases very differently. In 1 Cor. 5, Paul deals with a report of "sexual immorality" (πορνεία), indeed "a kind of immorality that is not found even among the pagans" (5:1). But in 2 Cor. 2 and 7, there is no evidence that the wrongdoer has engaged in an immoral act; neither the verb λυπεῖν ("to cause pain") nor ἀδικεῖν ("to inflict injury") possesses the specificity or intensity necessary to designate such a shameful act as incest.[45] The incestuous man of 1 Cor. 5 has sinned against God and has transgressed God's law; not so the wrongdoer of 2 Cor. 2 and 7, who has caused pain to Paul and the Corinthians, and whose forgiveness comes from his fellow Christians, rather than God.[46]

Second, Paul's account of *the response* of the Corinthians to the two incidents is strikingly different, indeed antithetical. In 1 Cor. 5, Paul is indignant with the Corinthians because they have tolerated the presence of the sinner in the community; they are arrogant, when they should have been sorrowful.[47] But in 2 Cor. 2 and 7, it is the Corinthians who are sorrowful and indignant and eager to clear themselves of complicity;[48] Paul approves the punishment which the Corinthians have imposed upon the wrongdoer, and finds that the church has proven its obedience in everything.[49]

Third, *the attitude* that Paul adopts in the case of the wrongdoer in 2 Cor. 2 is incommensurate with the judgment passed upon the incestuous man in 1 Cor. 5. Would Paul not have fallen into self-contradiction, had he advised the Corinthians to forgive and restore the one whom he had earlier commanded to be expelled from the church and handed over to Satan? The absolution of the incestuous man would have amounted to a repudiation of his earlier instructions regarding fornicators and adulter-

---

45   Krenkel, *Beiträge*, 285–86; Plummer, *Second Epistle*, 54; Allo, *Saint Paul*, 55, 57–58.
46   Krenkel, *Beiträge*, 285–86.
47   Krenkel, *Beiträge*, 290; Plummer, *Second Epistle*, 54; Allo, *Saint Paul*, 58; Victor Paul Furnish, *II Corinthians* (Garden City: Doubleday, 1984) 164–65.
48   Krenkel, *Beiträge*, 290; Plummer, *Second Epistle*, 55; Allo, *Saint Paul*, 55; Furnish, *II Corinthians*, 164–65.
49   Krenkel, *Beiträge*, 290; Plummer, *Second Epistle*, 55.

ers in 1 Cor. 5, and would have given new life to the immoral practices among the Corinthians.[50]

Fourth, *the penalty* that is imposed in the two instances is fundamentally different. In 1 Cor. 5, Paul decrees that the incestuous man is to be expelled from the community: in solemn assembly, the Corinthians are "to hand the man over to Satan for the destruction of the flesh" (5:5). While it is not clear precisely what was involved in the execution of this sentence, Paul's language suggests a punishment that is drastic and permanent, such as excommunication.[51] In 2 Cor. 2:6, by contrast, Paul declares himself satisfied with a much less severe penalty, a "rebuke" or "censure," judging from the term that Paul uses (ἐπιτιμία).[52] Paul's subsequent appeal to the Corinthians to forgive and console the wrongdoer in 2 Cor. 2:7–8 is simply inconceivable, if the same case is in view as in 1 Cor. 5.[53]

Fifth, *the outcome* that is envisioned in consequence of the penalties is mutually exclusive. In 1 Cor. 5, any hope for the salvation of the incestuous man awaits the coming of the day of the Lord (5:5). No provision is made for the repentance of the incestuous man, and indeed, the possibility seems to be excluded by the permanence of his expulsion from the community.[54] But in 2 Cor. 2, Paul appeals to the Corinthians to forgive and console the wrongdoer, "lest he be overwhelmed by excessive sorrow" (2:7). It is clear that Paul aims at the restoration of the wrongdoer to the fellowship of the community, and that no special absolution is needed beyond a reaffirmation of love (2:8). As Tertullian observed long ago, Paul would doubtless have expressed his pardon very differently, had the one whom he condemned with special indignation in 1 Cor. 5 repented, contrary to expectation.[55]

---

50 Krenkel, *Beiträge*, 287–89; Lietzmann, *An die Korinther I-II*,105; Allo, *Saint Paul*, 59–60; Furnish, *II Corinthians*, 165; R. P. Martin, *2 Corinthians* (Waco: Word, 1986) 38; Thrall, *Second Epistle*, 1.64.
51 Krenkel, *Beiträge*, 290–91; Allo, *Saint Paul*, 57; F. F. Bruce, *1 and 2 Corinthians* (London: Oliphants, 1971) 185; Furnish, *II Corinthians*, 165.
52 Krenkel, *Beiträge*, 302; C. K. Barrett, *A Commentary on the Second Epistle to the Corinthians* (New York: Harper & Row, 1973) 90–91. Further on ἐπιτιμία, see below, ch. 3, pp. 42–43.
53 Ewald, "Bemerkungen," 229; Krenkel, *Beiträge*, 289; Allo, *Saint Paul*, 57–58; Bruce, *1 and 2 Corinthians*, 185; Furnish, *II Corinthians*, 165.
54 Krenkel, *Beiträge*, 290; Philipp Bachmann, *Der zweite Brief des Paulus an die Korinther* (Leipzig: Deichert, 1922) 113; Windisch, *Der zweite Korintherbrief*, 92; Furnish, *II Corinthians*, 166; Thrall, *Second Epistle*, 1.64.
55 Tertullian, *Pud.* 13; cf. Plummer, *Second Epistle*, 54.

As suggested earlier, the verbal similarities between 1 Cor. 5:1–5 and 2 Cor. 2:5–11, which held such attraction for defenders of the traditional identification of the wrongdoer, are discovered, upon closer inspection, to be superficial, and actually indicative of fundamental differences between the two cases, when the vocabulary is examined in context. Note the different role assigned to Satan in the two passages: in 1 Cor. 5:5, Satan is the agent of destruction of the flesh; the realm of Satan's activity is circumscribed; he claims as his prey only the gross sinners. But in 2 Cor. 2:11, Satan threatens to outwit and plunder the entire community, if the wrongdoer is not forgiven and comforted.[56] The authority of Christ is invoked in the two passages, but to very different effects: in 1 Cor. 5:4, the Lord Jesus provides the sanction and warrant for the judgment that is executed upon the incestuous man, whereas in 2 Cor. 2:10, Christ bears witness to the altruistic motive for Paul's forgiveness.[57] In both passages, Paul uses the pronouns τις and τοιοῦτος to refer to an unnamed individual (1 Cor. 5:1, 5; 2 Cor. 2:5, 6, 7), but the reasons are distinct in each instance: in 1 Cor. 5, Paul aims to ostracize the sinner, while in 2 Cor. 2, anonymity serves the goal of reconciliation.[58] Finally, the attempt to construe the term πρᾶγμα in 2 Cor. 7:11 as an allusion to the πορνεία of 1 Cor. 5:1 overlooks the fact that in his only other use of the word πρᾶγμα in the Corinthian correspondence, in 1 Cor. 6:1, Paul refers to a lawsuit, or to the occasion for litigation.[59]

The greater part of these arguments against the identification of the wrongdoer with the incestuous man were forcefully articulated by the scrupulous exegete Max Krenkel at the end of the nineteenth century.[60] Subsequently, no major commentator on 2 Corinthians has attempted to defend the traditional identification.[61] In the final edition of his Meyer commentary, Georg Heinrici retreated from the robust, psycholo-

---

56 Schmiedel, *Die Briefe an die Korinther*, 221; Krenkel, *Beiträge*, 290–91; Bachmann, *Der zweite Brief*, 113; Windisch, *Der zweite Korintherbrief*, 92; Allo, *Saint Paul*, 57; Furnish, *II Corinthians*, 165; Thrall, *Second Epistle*, 1.62.
57 R. V. G. Tasker, *The Second Epistle of Paul to the Corinthians* (London: Tyndale Press, 1958) 55; Furnish, *II Corinthians*, 165; Thrall, *Second Epistle*, 1.62–63.
58 Bachmann, *Der zweite Brief*, 133; Furnish, *II Corinthians*, 164; Thrall, "The Offender and the Offence," 67.
59 Krenkel, *Beiträge*, 292; Furnish, *II Corinthians*, 165; Thrall, *Second Epistle*, 1.63.
60 Krenkel, *Beiträge*, 284–92. The impact of Krenkel's careful exegesis can still be traced in Thrall's commentary.
61 Numbered in this group: Allo, Bachmann, Barrett, Betz, Bousset, Bruce, Bultmann, Furnish, Grässer, Héring, Lietzmann, Martin, Plummer, Roetzel, Strachan, Thrall, Wendland, Windisch, and Wolff.

gizing explanations by which he had earlier sought to fill in the gaps between 1 Cor. 5 and 2 Cor. 2,[62] and took refuge in a prudent agnosticism in the face of textual ambiguities.[63] Thus one hears no more about the anxiety of the Corinthian Christians lest their own hidden sins be brought to light as a motive for their procrastination in carrying out the punishment of the incestuous man.[64] Gone is the colorful, dramatic portrait of the transformation of an impenitent sinner, who had scorned divine law and human taboo, into "a bruised reed in danger of completely breaking."[65] Instead, Heinrici contented himself with exposing the weaknesses of all hypotheses, and finally expressed his preference for the traditional identification of the wrongdoer as the simplest solution.[66]

Attempts to revive the traditional identification of the wrongdoer with the incestuous man during the past century have mostly taken the form of subsidiary arguments within defenses of the literary unity of 2 Corinthians, as already noted.[67] These attempts have not produced any

---

62 Heinrici, *Das zweite Sendschreiben*, 19–21.
63 Heinrici, *Der zweite Brief*, 26, 28–30, resolving "dass Sichere zu ermitteln, und wenn die Briefe, wie sie überliefert sind, in den Grundzügen ein klares Bild der Kämpfe des Paulus um das Seelenheil seiner Gemeinde, um die Autorität seines Apostolats und die Lauterkeit seines Characters ergeben, sich in bezug auf die Undeutlichkeiten und Möglichkeiten von secundärer Bedeutung zu bescheiden."
64 Heinrici, *Das zweite Sendschreiben*, 20: "Dazu kommt, dass die Forderung, ein Gemeindeglied, dessen Frevel man doch wohl um seiner sonstigen Verdienste oder Vorzüge willen übersehen hatte, auszuschliessen, nicht nur beschämte, sondern auch mannichfache Interessen kreuzte und verletzte. Wer weiss es nicht, wie jedes auch noch so berechtigte Eingreifen gegen eine irgendwie geschätzte oder angesehene Person Gegenströmungen hervorlockt, zumal wenn die That des in Anspruch Genommenen die verwandten Schossünden anderer nach ihrer Verwerflichkeit empfindlich beleuchtet? Auch macht der schliessliche Erfolg der Strafe es wahrscheinlich, dass der Schuldige sofort das Seine dazu gethan habe, die That als weniger straffällig hinzustellen, um seinen Einfluss in der Gemeinde nicht einzubüssen. Hieraus erklärt sich dann das Zögern, wo nicht die Abneigung, dem Willen des Apostels sich zu fügen. Wie viel Beschönigungen findet das böse Gewissen! Und die starke Neigung zu geschlechtlichen Sünden war night mit einem Schlage zu tilgen."
65 Heinrici, *Das zweite Sendschreiben*, 19: "Nicht mehr sprach ein verstockter Sünder, den die Gemeinde in ihrer Mitte duldete, göttlichem und menschlichem Rechte Hohn, sondern das geknickte Rohr drohte ganz zu zerbrechen." Cf. idem, *Der zweite Brief*, 93.
66 Heinrici, *Der zweite Brief*, 16.
67 Hughes, *Paul's Second Epistle*, 59–65; Stepheson, "Defence of the Integrity of 2 Corinthians," 82–97, esp. 86; Hyldahl, "Die Frage nach der literarischen Ein-

new arguments in favor of the traditional identification, nor have they engaged the difficulties which the traditional identification encountered in historical criticism.[68] Instead, it is now asserted that the focus of scholarship on the offender and the offence fundamentally mistakes Paul's purposes, both in 1 Cor. 5 and in 2 Cor. 2 and 7: Paul's principal concern throughout his correspondence was to test the obedience of the Corinthians, who were puffed up with pride in their own wisdom and knowledge; Paul's insistence upon the punishment of the incestuous man was a test of the Corinthians' submission to his apostolic authority, a test which they passed, when they punished the offender and brought him to repentance.[69] But this attempt to dispose of the problem by redefining the issue fails to take account of differences between 1 Cor. 5 and 2 Cor. 2 and 7, precisely in regard to Paul's concern for the spiritual well-being of the congregation as a whole: in 1 Cor. 5, Paul is concerned about the moral purity of the community, and the Corinthians are commanded to remove the incestuous man from their midst; in 2 Cor. 2 and 7, by contrast, Paul's concern is for the healing of a broken community, and this can be achieved by restoring the penitent wrongdoer to fellowship.[70] Precisely when one focuses upon Paul's concern for the Corinthians in the relevant passages, two very different situations come into view.

Two major, new hypotheses regarding the identity of the wrongdoer in 2 Corinthians were put forward in the twentieth century.[71] Both hypotheses have their roots in the critique of the traditional interpretation during the nineteenth century, and thus seek clues to the identity of the wrongdoer in the pages of 2 Corinthians, without recourse to the case of the incestuous man. Both hypotheses are informed by analyses of pertinent features of the argument and language of 2 Corinthians, and draw legitimate exegetical inferences. Yet each proposal is in its own way highly speculative, positing events for which there is no evidence

---

heit," 298–306, esp. 305–306; Hall, *Unity of the Corinthian Correspondence*, 100–101, 202–203, 223–35.

68 These are the principal defects of the studies by Kruse, "The Offender and the Offence," 129–39 and Hall, *Unity of the Corinthian Correspondence*, 227–35. See the comments of Furnish, *II Corinthians*, 164.

69 D. R. Hall, "Pauline Church Discipline," *TynBul* 20 (1969) 3–26, esp. 15–17; idem, *Unity of the Corinthian Correspondence*, 227–35.

70 Rightly, Windisch, *Der zweite Korintherbrief*, 92; Furnish, *II Corinthians*, 166.

71 Barrett, "Ο ΑΔΙΚΗΣΑΣ," 149–57; repr. in idem, *Essays on Paul*, 108–17; Thrall, "The Offender and the Offence," 65–78; summarized in idem, *Second Epistle*, 1.61–69.

in the text. And neither hypothesis provides the satisfaction of identifying the wrongdoer with any precision, the principal attraction of the traditional interpretation. Nevertheless, it is essential to engage these hypotheses in detail, because each embodies insights that contribute to a positive identification of the wrongdoer and a plausible reconstruction of events.

C. K. Barrett's essay of 1970, entitled "Ο ΑΔΙΚΗΣΑΣ," seeks to resolve an apparent tension in Paul's account of the complicity of the Corinthians in the affair of the wrongdoer, by positing that the offender was a visitor to Corinth, whose challenge to Paul's apostolic authority and insult to his person at first went unanswered by the Corinthian Christians, who failed to show the proper zeal in defending their apostle, but who later, under the good influence of Titus, repented of having listened to the intruder, punished the offender, and vindicated themselves in the matter.[72] Barrett's hypothesis arises out of close exegesis of two verses in particular, 7:9 and 7:11. In the former passage, Paul rejoices in the fact that his painful epistle has moved the Corinthians to repentance. If the Corinthians had something of which to repent, then they must have shared in the guilt of the wrongdoer in some fashion. The complicity of the Corinthians is confirmed by consideration of the words Paul uses to describe the Corinthians' attitude toward the situation in which they found themselves: ἀπολογία ("eagerness to clear oneself"), ἀγανάκτησις ("indignation"), and ἐκδίκησις ("punishment"). As Barrett recognized, these are "defensive words" which imply an underlying charge.[73] On the other hand, Paul pronounces the Corinthians' innocence emphatically and unequivocally at the end of vs. 11: "In every way you have proved yourselves guiltless in the matter."[74] The desire of the Corinthians to vindicate themselves is likewise indicated by other terms that Paul uses to describe their response, especially ζῆλος ("zeal") and σπουδή ("earnestness"). How is one to resolve the apparent contradiction in Paul's statements about the Corinthians? Barrett sought to restore balance to our understanding of the role of the Corinthians by locating the wrongdoer outside the Corinthian church, as a kind of fulcrum upon which the response of the Corinthians turned. Barrett speculated that the wrongdoer was the leader of an ad-

---

72 Barrett, "Ο ΑΔΙΚΗΣΑΣ," 108–17, esp. 113–15; followed by Jerome Murphy-O'Connor, *Paul: A Critical Life* (Oxford: Oxford University Press, 1996) 293–94.
73 Barrett, "Ο ΑΔΙΚΗΣΑΣ," 112–13.
74 Barrett, "Ο ΑΔΙΚΗΣΑΣ," 112–13.

vance contingent of Judaizing opponents who make their full appearance in the last four chapters of 2 Corinthians.[75]

It is easy to expose the weakness of Barrett's hypothesis. Barrett constructs his proposal out of materials from chapter 7. But Paul's instructions concerning the punishment and forgiveness of the wrongdoer in 2:5–11 make clear that the person in question is a member of the Corinthian church.[76] The wrongdoer is subject to the discipline of the Corinthians and submits to the penalty which they impose, conditions which would hardly have been accepted by a visitor to Corinth, an interloping apostle.[77] It is impossible to imagine that the leader of the group of apostles opposed to Paul would have experienced such remorse over the insult he had given to Paul that he would be in danger of drowning in excessive sorrow, as Paul fears in 2:7. The polemics of 2 Cor. 10–13 make clear that Paul's apostolic rivals had considered theological and ecclesiastical reasons for challenging the legitimacy of Paul's apostleship.[78] Moreover, the concern that Paul displays for the welfare of the wrongdoer, whom the Corinthians are to forgive, console, and love (2:7–8), is appropriate to one of his own converts, a member of the Corinthian church, but difficult to understand in relation to an intruder who had claimed superior rights for himself as an apostle and had belittled the authority of Paul.[79]

Because Barrett's hypothesis is encumbered by defects, there is a danger that one may overlook two genuine insights embodied in his interpretation. First, Barrett perceives a connection between the wrongdoer's challenge to Paul's authority and the Jewish-Christian opposition to Paul. Thus Barrett revives an understanding of the situation which goes back to the Tübingen School of the nineteenth century: the affair of the wrongdoer belongs to the history of Jewish Christian agitation against Paul. For Adolf Hilgenfeld and Carl Weizsäcker, this much was clear,

---

75 Barrett, "Ο ΑΔΙΚΗΣΑΣ," 113–15; similarly, Murphy-O'Connor, *Paul*, 293–94.
76 So, already, König, "Verkehr," 516; Kümmel, *Introduction*, 208. In criticism of Barrett on this point, Furnish, *II Corinthians*, 396; C. Wolff, *Der zweite Brief des Paulus an die Korinther* (Berlin: Evangelische Verlaganstalt, 1989) 43; Thrall, "The Offender and the Offence," 71; Murray J. Harris, *The Second Epistle to the Corinthians* (Grand Rapids: Eerdmans, 2005) 225.
77 Gerd Lüdemann, *Paulus, der Heidenapostel Band II: Antipaulinismus im frühen Christentum* (Göttingen: Vandenhoeck & Ruprecht, 1989) 126 n.78.
78 Ernst Käsemann, "Die Legitimität des Apostels. Eine Untersuchung zu II Korinther 10–13," *ZNW* 41 (1942) 33–71; Betz, *Der Apostel Paulus*; Georgi, *Opponents of Paul*, 83–238.
79 Thrall, "The Offender and the Offence," 71.

even if the wrongdoer was not a Jewish-Christian apostle who had entered the community from without, but rather a member of the Corinthian church.[80] Such an assumption alone does justice to the polemic against Paul that reverberates throughout 2 Corinthians, especially in chs. 10–13, and whose final echoes are audible in the cautious apologetic of chs. 1–2 and 7. Only such an assumption suffices to explain how an insult done to Paul, even one which challenged his apostolic authority, could have acquired such importance that it became the occasion for Paul's prolonged absence from Corinth and a letter written "with many tears."[81]

Second, and perhaps more importantly, Barrett uncovers a certain tension between the wrongdoer and the rest of the Corinthian Christians. There is an unmistakable ambiguity in their relationship: on the one hand, the Corinthians have proven their innocence by punishing the wrongdoer; in this respect, the wrongdoer stands over against the Corinthian church. But on the other hand, the Corinthians have something of which to repent, even if their complicity consisted merely in acquiescence; in this respect, the wrongdoer stands within the Corinthian congregation, or is closely associated with it. Barrett sought to reflect this ambiguity by placing the wrongdoer at the boundary of the Corinthian community, as a visitor, an intruder, but not himself a Corinthian. We have identified the flaws in Barrett's proposal, but ambiguity remains and demands an explanation. If the wrongdoer is not to be sought outside the Corinthian church, then perhaps he stands above the congregation, as a person of higher social status, the patron of the Christian groups at Corinth.[82]

The second new hypothesis of the twentieth century regarding the identity of the wrongdoer was that of Margaret Thrall.[83] Thrall postulated that the wrongdoer was a member of the Corinthian church who, on the occasion of Paul's second visit to Corinth, robbed Paul of money that

---

80 Hilgenfeld, "Die Christusleute in Korinth," 243; idem, "Paulus und die korinthischen Wirren," 103–104; Weizsäcker, "Paulus und die Gemeinde in Korinth," 643–44.
81 So, already, Drescher,"Vorgänge in Korinth," 49; König, "Verkehr," 512–14; Weiss, *Primitive Christianity*, 1.342–43.
82 Presciently, Ewald, *Sendschreiben*, 227: "ja einer der angesehensten, vielleicht ein mitglied des vorstandes, vergass sich so weit das ser ihm offen in der gemeinde unwürdiges vorwarf"; similarly, Weiss, *Primitive Christianity*, 1.342–43.
83 Thrall, "The Offender and the Offence," 65–78; summarized in idem, *Second Epistle*, 1.61–69.

had been entrusted to him by another Corinthian Christian as a contribution to the collection for the poor saints in Jerusalem. When Paul confronted the wrongdoer with his crime, he denied the charge, and questioned the apostle's motives. The congregation as a whole was uncertain whom to believe, and hence did not immediately accept Paul's version of events. Unable to persuade the Corinthians to take action against the wrongdoer, and fearing that some in the congregation might have been accomplices in the theft, Paul departed from Corinth in grief. Upon returning to Ephesus, Paul wrote a severe epistle which caused such revulsion of feeling among the Corinthians that they were moved to investigate the crime more thoroughly and to impose a punishment upon the wrongdoer.[84]

Thrall acknowledged that her reconstruction was "pure hypothesis."[85] And, indeed, her proposal is so speculative that one could be excused for omitting it from a history of critical scholarship on the subject. But then, one might fail to recognize the importance of two pieces of textual evidence to which Thrall's hypothesis is an ingenious response. The idea that the wrongdoing involved a robbery was suggested to Thrall by the verb ἀδικεῖν, whose meaning was clarified by exegetical research following Zahn.[86] It will be recalled that Zahn established, appealing to Aristotle, that ἀδικεῖν is to be defined as "voluntarily causing injury contrary to the law."[87] Subsequently, research by Max Krenkel and Hans Windisch made the sense of ἀδικεῖν more precise: in a number of relevant instances, ἀδικεῖν is used in reference to an illegal injury in which money was involved: thus in Philemon 18, Matt. 20:13, and Lev. 6:2–5 (LXX).[88] This is probably also the sense of the term in 1 Cor. 6:7–8, where the lawsuits in question seem to be civil in nature, concerned with money or property.[89] Thrall's hypothesis was strongly influenced by a passage

---

84 Thrall, "The Offender and the Offence," 71–76. Thrall asserts that she is building upon the suggestions of Krenkel and Windisch.
85 Thrall, "The Offender and the Offence," 75.
86 Zahn, *Introduction*, 1.349; followed by Windisch, *Der zweite Korintherbrief*, 238.
87 Aristotle *Rhet.* 1.10.3: ἔστω δὴ τὸ ἀδικεῖν τὸ βλάπτειν ἑκόντα παρὰ τὸν νόμον.
88 Krenkel, *Beiträge*, 305–307, who speaks of a "Schädigung an Hab und Gut"; Windisch, *Der zweite Korintherbrief*, 238.
89 So, already, Krenkel, *Beiträge*, 305; followed by Windisch, *Der zweite Korintherbrief*, 238–39. On the civil nature of the lawsuits, see now Bruce W. Winter, "Civil Litigation: 1 Corinthians 6:1–11" in idem, *Seek the Welfare of the City: Christians as Benefactors and Citizens* (Grand Rapids: Eerdmans, 1996) 105–22, esp. 107.

Chapter Two. History of Scholarship

in Philo's *Special Laws* where the term ἀδικεῖν seems to refer to the pilfering of a deposit entrusted to a friend by a third party.[90] We may leave on one side Thrall's robbery scenario which, because it is "pure hypothesis," can neither be proved nor disproved. But we should hold fast to Thrall's inference that, in the wrong done to Paul by an unnamed individual, money was somehow involved.

Less speculative, but more original, was Thrall's intuition regarding the collection for the poor saints in Jerusalem as the context for the action of the wrongdoer.[91] Unfortunately, Thrall did not elaborate this insight or seek to ground it in exegesis of passages in 2 Corinthians where Paul responds to allegations of misconduct in the administration of the collection. 2 Cor. 8 and 9 reveal how much importance the collection had assumed in Paul's thinking about the legacy of his apostleship to the Gentiles, how crucial the contribution of the wealthy Corinthians had become to the success of the collection, and how much difficulty Paul encountered in allaying suspicions and persuading the Corinthians to complete their gift.[92] In 2 Cor. 12:16–18 Paul denies the accusation that he sought to "defraud" the Corinthians through his emissary Titus.[93] As we shall see, this statement is best understood as a reference to the mission of Titus to Corinth in connection with the collection, discussed in 2 Cor. 8.[94] Thus, Thrall's suggestion that the collection was the occasion for the offence against Paul has far-reaching implications.

The history of research into the identity of the wrongdoer in 2 Corinthians has produced mainly negative results. By "negative," what is meant is that the labor of almost two centuries has been expended on the demolition of the traditional identification, the separation of the wrongdoer from the incestuous man. Only when this critical task was

---

90 Philo *Spec.* 4.34; Thrall, "The Offender and the Offence,": 73–74. The text was already discussed in connection with 2 Cor. 7:12 by Windisch, *Der zweite Korintherbrief,* 238.
91 Thrall, "The Offender and the Offence," 74–76. A connection between the action of the wrongdoer and Paul's collection for the poor in Jerusalem was already posited by Betz, *2 Corinthians 8 and 9,* 97.
92 Dieter Georgi, *Die Geschichte der Kollekte des Paulus für Jerusalem* (Hamburg: Reich, 1965; English trans. *Remembering the Poor: The History of Paul's Collection for Jerusalem* (Nashville: Abingdon, 1992); Betz, *2 Corinthians 8 and 9,* esp. 37–86.
93 See the discussion of the charge of πλεονεξία in 2 Cor. 12:16–18 below in ch. 3.
94 So, already, Barrett, *Second Epistle,* 325; followed by Mitchell, "Paul's Letters to Corinth," 326–27. See the discussion of 2 Cor. 12:18 as a retrospective reference to 2 Cor. 8:6, 18 in ch. 3 below, pp. 173–177.

complete, could scholars turn to a constructive search for evidence in 2 Corinthians, and establish the following facts: the wrongdoer was a member of the Corinthian church; he was influenced by Jewish-Christian opponents of Paul; his offence took place on the occasion of Paul's second visit to Corinth; the wrong was an injury in which money was somehow involved; the context of the injurious action was the collection for the poor saints in Jerusalem; the Corinthians were somehow complicit in the wrong done to Paul.[95] These facts are not insignificant, and yet, they do not lead to a positive identification of the wrongdoer. And attempts to go beyond these basic facts have resulted in speculative hypotheses that are not capable of confirmation. In retrospect, it is clear that what was lost when the traditional identification was abandoned was a control outside the text of 2 Corinthians, an instance with which the evidence of 2 Corinthians could be correlated, and by which the results could be verified. Our study will seek to establish a control outside the text by invoking the social and rhetorical conventions in which Paul and the Corinthians participated, and by which their relationships were governed. Only when such a framework has been articulated will it be possible to verify a hypothesis regarding the identity of the wrongdoer. But first, we must turn back to the text of 2 Corinthians, to make sure that we have extracted all the relevant information, that we have isolated every trait that might contribute to a positive identification of the wrongdoer.

---

95 Compare the list of "traits précis" in Allo, *Saint Paul*, 55.

Chapter Three
Inferences from Exegesis
2 Cor. 1:1–2:13; 7:5–16

We begin with a point that has been assumed throughout the history of scholarship, but which is so fundamental, and has such far-reaching implications, that it must be stated explicitly: Paul is dealing with the same situation in 2 Cor. 2:5–11 and 7:5–12.[1] In both passages, Paul speaks of "pain" (λύπη) that has been caused to the Corinthians. In 2:1–11, Paul defends himself against the charge that he wrote as he did in a previous epistle in order to cause pain to his readers; his intention was rather to prove his love and to test their obedience (2:4, 8). Paul sets opposite the community as a whole an individual member who has pained not only Paul but all the Corinthians, and has been punished by a verdict of the majority (2:5–6). In 7:5–12, Paul concedes that he has pained his readers by means of a letter; but the letter has also had the good effect that the Corinthians have been moved to repentance and have carried out the punishment of the wrongdoer, and thus have given proof of their obedience. When two paragraphs in the same writing present so many conspicuous points of contact, there can be no doubt that in both places we are confronted with the same situation, and that we are justified in combining the evidence of the two passages, supplementing the statements of the one passage with the other.[2] Naturally, the connections would be closer and more significant if, as Johannes Weiss proposed, 2 Cor. 1:1–2:13; 7:5–16 was originally an independent letter.[3] But even without this hy-

---

1 The identity of the situations in 2 Cor. 2:5–11 and 7:12 is recognized by all interpreters, including those who equate the wrongdoer with the incestuous man of 1 Cor. 5. Cf. Holtzmann, "Das gegenseitige Verhältnis," 465; Bultmann, *Der zweite Brief*, 52.
2 Krenkel, *Beiträge*, 252–53.
3 Weiss, *Primitive Christianity*, 1.345–53; followed by A. Loisy, "Les épîtres de S. Paul," *Revue d'histoire et de literature religieuses* 7 (1921) 213–50; Bultmann, *Der zweite Brief*, 20–23; Bornkamm, *Vorgeschichte*, 21–23, 29–31; Georgi, *Opponents of Paul*, 9–13, 335; Betz, *2 Corinthians 8 and 9*, 141–44; L. L. Welborn, "Like Broken Pieces of a Ring: 2 Cor. 1:1–2:13; 7:5–16 and Ancient Theories

pothesis, it is clear that the two texts treat the same painful incident under slightly different aspects: ch. 2 seeks to conciliate the sorrowful wrongdoer; ch. 7 conciliates the penitent Corinthians.

The first and most obvious implication of the fact that chs. 2 and 7 deal with the same situation is that the one who caused pain (ὁ λελυπηκώς) and the one who did wrong (ὁ ἀδικήσας) are the same individual.[4] This point has seldom been disputed in the history of interpretation, but, as we shall see, its consequences have not been fully appreciated.[5] It should also go without saying that the offence was committed by a single individual. So much is clearly indicated by the singular pronouns in ch. 2 and the singular participle in ch. 7: thus, 2:5, "if someone (τις) has caused pain"; 2:6, "sufficient for such a one" (τῷ τοιούτῳ)"; 2:7, "lest such a one (ὁ τοιοῦτος) be overwhelmed"; 2:8, "reaffirm your love for him (εἰς αὐτόν)"; 2:10, "to whom (ᾧ) you forgive anything"; and 7:12, "the one who did the wrong (τοῦ ἀδικήσαντος)."[6] A few scholars have sought to construe the singular pronouns in these verses as references to a class of individuals, and the singular participle, ὁ ἀδικήσας, as a general or collective singular covering a group of sinners.[7] Even if a few of the singulars—that is, the indefinite and correlative pronouns—might be taken as designations of a category of persons—thus, "anyone" and "such a person"—the personal and relative pronouns—"to him" and "to whom"—cannot easily be understood in this way.[8] If Paul had intended to speak of a group of wrongdoers and their unjust acts in 7:12, there is no reason why Paul should not have used the plural participle; indeed, a collective singular would seem to be out of place.[9] Thus we may regard it as estab-

---

of Literary Unity," *NTS* 42 (1996) 559–83; Mitchell, "Paul's Letters to Corinth," 318–35; Roetzel, *2 Corinthians*, 26–32.

4 Krenkel, *Beiträge*, 283; Windisch, *Der zweite Korintherbrief*, 237.
5 The failure to keep this identity in mind leads Barrett ("Ο ΑΔΙΚΗΣΑΣ," 112–15) to search for the wrongdoer outside the Corinthian community; conversely, Allo (*Saint Paul*, 55) fails to place sufficient emphasis upon the λύπη caused by the wrongdoer in his list of "traits précis."
6 Windisch, *Der zweite Korintherbrief*, 237; Allo, *Saint Paul*, 56–57; Barrett, "Ο ΑΔΙΚΗΣΑΣ," 109; Betz, *Der Apostel Paulus*, 11 n.40; Thrall, "The Offender and the Offence," 72.
7 Joseph Sickenberger, *Die beiden Briefe des heiligen Paulus an die Korinther* (Bonn: Hanstein, 1921) 35–37; Eduard Golla, *Zwischenreise und Zwischenbrief* (Freiburg: Herder, 1922) 41–42.
8 Drescher, "Vorgänge in Korinth," 49; Barrett, "Ο ΑΔΙΚΗΣΑΣ," 116 n.7; Furnish, *II Corinthians*, 164.
9 Windisch, *Der zweite Korintherbrief*, 237 n.2.

lished that a single individual was responsible for the painful and injurious act, even if others were somehow involved. Before letting go of this point, we should not fail to notice the source of whatever ambiguity attaches to the question of whether the one who caused pain and the one who did wrong are one and the same individual: the source is Paul's rhetoric, that is, his evasive manner of speaking, his determined use of circumlocutions.

A second, less obvious, but no less certain implication of the identity of the situations in chs. 2 and 7 is that "the one who was wronged" (ὁ ἀδικηθείς) in 7:12 is none other than Paul himself.[10] To be sure, this point was obscured for most of the history of interpretation by the force of the traditional identification of the wrongdoer with the incestuous man. According to the traditional view, the wronged party was the father of the perpetrator of incest, whose marital bed was defiled and whose rights were injured by the shameful act of his son.[11] The difficulties with this interpretation were noted long ago and were among the reasons why the traditional identification was abandoned: the father is mentioned in 1 Cor. 5:1 only in passing, and without any indication of concern for his "rights"; instead, Paul devotes all of his attention to the punishment of the son.[12] Moreover, if the one who was wronged were the father of the incestuous man, one would expect some mention of him in 2 Cor. 2:5–11, where the forgiveness of the penitent is discussed; surely the father would have had more to forgive in this situation than Paul, whose forgiveness is explicitly granted in 2:10.[13]

---

10 So, the majority of interpreters: e.g., Bleek, "Erörterungen," 630; Ewald, *Sendschreiben*, 227; Schmiedel, *Die Briefe an die Korinther*, 46; Drescher, "Vorgänge in Korinth," 49; König, "Verkehr," 514–16; Weiss, *Primitive Christianity*, 1.342–43; Plummer, *Second Epistle*, xvi, 54–55, 225; Lietzmann, *An die Korinther I-II*, 105; Bachmann, *Der zweite Brief*, 112; Allo, *Saint Paul*, 56; Bruce, *1 and 2 Corinthians*, 164, 185; Barrett, "Ο ΑΔΙΚΗΣΑΣ," 111; idem, *Second Epistle*, 89; Bultmann, *Der zweite Brief*, 51; Georgi, *Opponents of Paul*, 339–40; Furnish, *II Corinthians*, 166; Reimund Bieringer, *The Corinthian Correspondence* (Leuven: Leuven University Press, 1996) 11–12.
11 Baur, *Paulus*, 1.335; Klöpper, *Kommentar*, 59, 163–64; Holtzmann, "Verhältnis," 467–68; Heinrici, *Der zweite Brief*, 16, 93; Zahn, *Introduction*, 1.349; Hughes, *Paul's Second Epistle*, 64; Kruse, "The Offender and the Offence," 131–36; Hall, *Unity*, 228–29.
12 Windisch, *Der zweite Korintherbrief*, 237.
13 Krenkel, *Beiträge*, 286–87; Bachmann, *Der zweite Brief*, 307; Thrall, *Second Epistle*, 1.65.

Although the majority of interpreters since the beginning of the twentieth century have rightly taken Paul to be "the one who was wronged," a minority look for another person in the congregation, or among Paul's associates.[14] It is important to grasp the cause of this ambiguity, since it points the way toward an understanding of Paul's rhetoric and the social conventions by which his rhetoric was governed. A group of scholars, giving full weight to the legal connotations of the verb ἀδικεῖν, posit that the offence was an injury done to one member of the Corinthian church by another, perhaps in respect to property or possessions, through a civil lawsuit like those against which Paul warned in 1 Cor. 6:1–11; the injured party turned to Paul for redress, when the Corinthian church failed to take up his cause against the avaricious wrongdoer.[15] The problems with this suggestion come readily to mind: if the one who was wronged were a member of the Corinthian church, why does Paul not urge him to forgive the offender, when he appeals to the rest of the congregation to do so in 2:7–8? And if the wronged party had already pardoned the offender, why does Paul not say as much in 2:10? Why is the only mention of personal forgiveness Paul's own?[16] We should not fail to notice that what debilitates this hypothesis is the failure to take full account of the identity of the situations in chs. 2 and 7.

A second group of scholars propose that the ἀδικηθείς was one of Paul's close associates, such as Timothy or Titus, the only named individuals who are known to have been sent to Corinth by Paul as envoys.[17] On the occasion of one such mission, whether to instruct the Corinthians (1 Cor. 4:17) or to organize the collection (2 Cor. 8:6, 16, 23), Paul's representative was gravely maligned.[18] To be sure, the attack was really

---

14 Beyschlag, "Christuspartei," 254; Pfleiderer, *Urchristentum*, 106–107; Krenkel, *Beiträge*, 305–307; Windisch, *Der zweite Korintherbrief*, 238–39; Allo, *Saint Paul*, 55–56, 62; K. Prümm, *Diakonia Pneumatos I: Theologische Auslegung des zweiten Korintherbriefs* (Freiburg: Herder, 1967) 403–404.
15 Krenkel, *Beiträge*, 305–307; Windisch, *Der zweite Korintherbrief*, 238–39; Allo, *Saint Paul*, 55–56, 62.
16 Thrall,"The Offender and the Offence," 69; idem, *Second Epistle*, 1.68.
17 Identifying Timothy as the ἀδικηθείς, Beyschlag, "Christuspartei," 254; Pfleiderer, *Urchristentum*, 106–107; perhaps Timothy, Furnish, *II Corinthians*, 396; Frank J. Matera, *II Corinthians* (Louisville: Westminster, 2003) 18; a close coworker of Paul, so Allo, *Saint Paul*, 55–56, 62; Prümm, *Diakonia Pneumatos*, 403–404.
18 Beyschlag, "Christuspartei," 254.

aimed at Paul, but Timothy or Titus was the immediate object of insult.[19] This theory would have the seeming advantage of reconciling Paul's unusual manner of speaking about the injured party in 7:12, as if he were some third person, with the clear implications of other statements in the context, that a challenge to Paul's apostolic authority was involved.[20] But this hypothesis is vulnerable to objections like those which ruled out of consideration the identification of the ἀδικηθείς with a member of the Corinthian church. Timothy cannot be the one who was wronged, because he is the nominal co-author of 2 Corinthians, or better of 2 Cor. 1:1–2:13; 7:5–16. In any case, Timothy should have been mentioned in 2:5–11, and especially in 2:10, where Paul declares his personal forgiveness, for otherwise it appears that Timothy was not yet ready to be reconciled.[21] Nor can Titus have been the injured party, since he is mentioned repeatedly in the epistle (2:13; 7:6, 13, 14), and his readiness to forgive the offender would surely have been made clear in 2:5–11.[22]

Reflecting upon the various hypotheses regarding the identity of the one who was wronged, several factors seem to be involved in the reluctance of scholars to acknowledge what the texts of chs. 2 and 7 make obvious and unavoidable: namely, that Paul himself is the only one who could have been wronged (7:12), such that he would be individually pained (2:5) and have cause for the expression of personal forgiveness (2:10). First, there is an unwillingness by certain scholars to countenance the diminution of Paul's authority and the humiliation of his person entailed in the notion that Paul was the one wronged; for such scholars, the apostle must always have been in control and could never have suffered such a humiliating defeat.[23] Second, the term ἀδικηθείς is felt to be too objective as a self-designation for a writing as intensely personal as 2 Corinthians.[24] Heinrici asserts that it is not Paul's manner to speak of himself

---

19 Pfleiderer, *Urchristentum*, 107.
20 Windisch, *Der zweite Korintherbrief*, 238.
21 Windisch, *Der zweite Korintherbrief*, 238; Allo, *Saint Paul*, 62; Barrett, "Ο ΑΔΙ-ΚΗΣΑΣ," 116 n.19; Thrall, "The Offender and the Offence," 69.
22 Windisch, *Der zweite Korintherbrief*, 238; Allo, *Saint Paul*, 62; Thrall, *Second Epistle*, 1.66.
23 R. Mackintosh, "The Brief Visit to Corinth," *Expositor* 6 (1908) 226–34, esp. 226; Allo, *Saint Paul*, 55, 61, 62; Hughes, *Paul's Second Epistle*, 59; Harris, *Second Epistle*, 226–27.
24 Krenkel, *Beiträge*, 303; Windisch, *Der zweite Korintherbrief*, 238; Thrall, *Second Epistle*, 1.68.

in the third person.²⁵ The latter observation directs our attention to the third and most significant source of ambiguity regarding the identity of the one who was wronged: the rhetorical figure of *periphrasis* (περίφρασις) which Paul employs throughout 2 Cor. 1–2 and 7, but especially whenever he approaches the subject of the one who caused pain and did wrong.²⁶ At this point, we need not explore the social convention that guided Paul's choice of this figure, but may simply note the presence of the figure and seek to define its role in Paul's unusual manner of speaking of himself as the ἀδικηθείς. We shall see that Paul's objective reference to himself in the third person is only the most extreme instance of a pattern of circumspection that characterizes every reference to the wrong that he has suffered.

The paragraph in which the subject of "the one who caused pain" is cautiously broached (2:5–11) begins with a conditional sentence so general that it almost suggests a hypothetical assumption, "But if (εἰ) someone has caused pain,...", except that the apodosis goes on to reveal that pain has certainly been caused and that it has touched "all" of the Corinthians (2:5).²⁷ Yet, Paul's reserve in speaking about the matter is so complete that one questions, for a moment, whether anything has occurred—the style is so suspended, the expression so inexact. Out of reluctance to give the incident its proper name, the action is denoted only by its effect, "pain" (λύπη), and this is immediately mitigated by two qualifying phrases—"to some degree" (ἀπὸ μέρους), and "not to exaggerate it" (ἵνα μὴ ἐπιβαρῶ).²⁸ Above all, Paul's caution in approaching the guilty party is so great that he refers to him only where the sentence structure makes it necessary, and then only by means of the most indefinite expressions—"someone" (τις), "such a one" (τοιοῦτος), "him" (αὐτόν), "whom" (ᾧ)—so that, not only do we remain ignorant of his name, but we are scarcely able to discover his status in the community, or his

---

25 Heinrici, *Das zweite Sendschreiben*, 21; idem, *Der zweite Brief*, 93.
26 Georgi, *Opponents of Paul*, 340; Peter Marshall, *Enmity in Corinth: Social Conventions in Paul's Relations with the Corinthians* (Tübingen: Mohr Siebeck, 1987) 342. See the discussion of this figure in ch. 4 below.
27 H. A. W. Meyer, *Der zweite Brief an die Korinther* (Göttingen: Vandenhoeck & Ruprecht, 1870) 169; Heinrici, *Der zweite Brief*, 92–93; Plummer, *Second Epistle*, 55–56; Windisch, *Der zweite Korintherbrief*, 84.
28 See the discussion of various constructions of these phrases in Heinrici, *Der zweite Brief*, 94–95, with references to older scholarship; Windisch, *Der zweite Korintherbrief*, 85; Allo, *Saint Paul*, 36; Thrall, *Second Epistle*, 1.172–73.

relationship to Paul.²⁹ Even in granting forgiveness to the wrongdoer, Paul is entirely indirect: the penitent must receive Paul's κεχάρισμαι out of the mouth of the Corinthians—"to whom you forgive anything, I too" (ᾧ δέ τι χαρίζεσθε, κἀγώ). But this is immediately qualified by another conditional—"if I have forgiven anything" (εἴ τι κεχάρισμαι). And finally, Paul's forgiveness is deflected and dispersed by reference to the welfare of the community as its motive and goal—"[it was] for your sake in the presence of Christ" (2:10).³⁰

The remarkable evasiveness of Paul's rhetoric in this paragraph must be borne in mind, when seeking to assess Paul's apparent denial that he has been caused pain in 2:5. For clearly, the statement, οὐκ ἐμὲ λελύπηκεν, is not meant to be taken literally; otherwise Paul could not acknowledge, as he does very gingerly in 2:10, that he has something of which to forgive.³¹ Moreover, the preceding verses, 2:1–4, speak very poignantly of the renewed pain that Paul sought to avoid by not coming to Corinth, and of the "anguish of heart" and "many tears" with which he wrote to the Corinthians.³² Clearly Paul has been caused pain, and has apparently suffered a great deal. How, then, should we understand Paul's statement "he has not pained me"? Max Krenkel already grasped the mechanism of Paul's rhetoric in 2:5, as well as in 7:12: Krenkel observed that when a negative statement is followed by a positive assertion introduced by the strong adversative ἀλλά, then the first statement is in no sense intended to be an unqualified negation, rather the combination gives expression to the thought, "not the one thing is the principal point upon which everything depends, but the other."³³ A good example of this usage outside the Pauline corpus is found in John 6:32, "Truly, truly I say to you, it was not Moses who gave you the bread from heaven, but it is my Father who

---

29 Meyer, *Der zweite Brief*, 169; Windisch, *Der zweite Korintherbrief*, 83–84.
30 Plummer, *Second Epistle*, 62; Windisch, *Der zweite Korintherbrief*, 84, 90–91.
31 Bachmann, *Der zweite Brief*, 112; Windisch, *Der zweite Korintherbrief*, 85; Lietzmann, *An die Korinther I-II*, 105; Allo, *Saint Paul*, 38, 56; Bruce, *1 and 2 Corinthians*, 185; Thrall, *Second Epistle*, 1.171; Harris, *Second Epistle*, 223.
32 Weiss, *Primitive Christianity*, 1.345; Plummer, *Second Epistle*, 50–51; Windisch, *Der zweite Korintherbrief*, 82; Thrall, *Second Epistle*, 1.170.
33 Krenkel, *Beiträge*, 298–99; see already Heinrici, *Sendschreiben*, 134. Cf. M. Zerwick, *Analysis Philologica Novi Testamenti Graeci* (Rome: Pontifical Biblical Institute , 1966) §445: "In disjunctive propositions, it is a Semitic peculiarity to express one member negatively so as to lay more stress on the other, saying 'not A but B' where the sense is 'not so much A as B'," citing as examples Matt. 10:20; Mark 9:37; Luke 10:20; John 7:16; 12:44; 1 Cor. 1:17; similarly, BDF §448 (1).

gives you the true bread from heaven." It is not the intention of the evangelist here to deny the reality of the manna miracle; indeed, it is recognized only a few verses later in John 6:49.[34] Thus, in 2 Cor. 2:5, Paul is to be understood as saying, "It is not the pain which has been caused me that is the principal focus of attention and the occasion for discipline, but the pain caused you."[35] And in 7:12, Paul would say, "It was not consideration of the one who did wrong nor the one who suffered wrong which primarily motivated me to write, but in order to make manifest the zeal which you have for us before God."[36] Beyond Paul's circumspect rhetoric, we catch a glimpse of the real situation: an ordinary view of the incident would have suggested that it was, in fact, Paul who had been personally pained.[37] About the social relationship that evoked this extraordinary rhetoric, and Paul's objective in employing this figure, there will be much discussion later.[38]

Thus, Paul's unusual, third-person reference to himself as "the one who was wronged" (ὁ ἀδικηθείς) may now be recognized as the most extreme instance of a rhetoric of circumspection that pervades the relevant paragraphs of chs. 2 and 7. Indeed, we can now see that Paul's language is more evasive the closer the proximity to the epicenter of wrong, and correspondingly more self-revealing at a greater distance from the injurious act. Paul's forgiveness is expressed explicitly in 2:10, though with care not to be too direct. The personally painful consequence of the wrong is covered by a rhetorical disclaimer in 2:5, but not in such a way as to negate the fact. When the offence is finally mentioned in 7:12, Paul adopts an objective form of self-reference, which almost effaces his person from the incident. Yet, when full account is taken of the similarity of the situations in chs. 2 and 7, and when the relevant paragraphs are read

---

34 Krenkel, *Beiträge*, 298–99.
35 Krenkel, *Beiträge*, 299; Moffatt, *Introduction*, 122; Windisch, *Der zweite Korintherbrief*, 84–85; Bruce, *1 and 2 Corinthians*, 185; Furnish, *II Corinthians*, 389; Wolff, *Der zweite Brief*, 42; Thrall, *Second Epistle*, 1.171; Harris, *Second Epistle*, 223.
36 Krenkel, *Beiträge*, 299.
37 Ewald, *Sendschreiben*, 227; Schmiedel, *Die Briefe an die Korinther*, 221; Hilgenfeld, *Historisch-kritische Einleitung*, 286; Lietzmann, *An die Korinther I-II*, 105; Windisch, *Der zweite Korintherbrief*, 84–85, 236–39; Bachmann, *Der zweite Brief*, 112; Allo, *Saint Paul*, 56; Barrett, *Second Epistle*, 89; Furnish, *II Corinthians*, 160, 166, 389–90; Thrall, *Second Epistle*, 1.171.
38 See ch. 4 below.

with sensitivity to Paul's rhetoric, there is no mystery about the identity of "the one who was wronged"—it was Paul himself.

A third implication of a close, comparative reading of chs. 2 and 7 is that the Corinthian church was somehow involved in the wrong done to Paul.[39] It must be acknowledged, from the outset, that the part played by the Corinthian church in the affair of the wrongdoer was a complicated one. This can be grasped immediately by considering the two very different roles that are assigned to the Corinthians: according to 2:5–11, the Corinthians have been pained; they have imposed punishment upon an individual, and are now urged to forgive; but in 7:5–12, the Corinthians have repented; they have experienced mourning, eagerness to clear themselves, longing and zeal. In the one instance, the Corinthians serve as judge and jury; in the other, they are somehow complicit in the offence. Yet, the two depictions of the Corinthians are not unrelated: the motif of vindication that dominates ch. 7 is already sounded in 2:9; and, conversely, the hurtful individual, whose punishment is ordered in ch. 2, reappears at the close of the latter paragraph in 7:12.[40] Thus, it is clearly a single, complex incident to which reference is made in chs. 2 and 7, an incident in which the Corinthians are variously involved. Several aspects of the Corinthians' involvement emerge from analysis of the relevant texts.

First, the vocabulary that Paul chooses to describe the Corinthians' response to his painful epistle in 7:7 and 7:11 leaves no room for doubt about their complicity in the affair of the wrongdoer.[41] Paul's severe letter had awakened in the Corinthians "longing" (ἐπιπόθησις), "mourning" (ὀδυρμός), "zeal" (ζῆλος), "earnestness" (σπουδή), "eagerness to clear oneself" (ἀπολογία), "indignation" (ἀγανάκτησις), "alarm" (φόβος), "longing" (ἐπιπόθησις), "zeal" (ζῆλος), and "vengeance" (ἐκδίκησις). Paul's account of the Corinthians' response focuses on their emotions, rather than their actions, because he seeks to provide therapy for the pain that his previous epistle has caused.[42] But for our purposes, Paul's report is useful, because it opens a window into the Corinthians' conscience, and reveals that, at the time of Titus' visit, and after receiving

---

39 Drescher, "Vorgänge in Korinth," 49; König, "Verkehr," 512–14; Windisch, *Der zweite Korintherbrief*, 84; Bornkamm, *Vorgeschichte*, 9.
40 Windisch, *Der zweite Korintherbrief*, 84.
41 Windisch, *Der zweite Korintherbrief*, 234–35; Hughes, *Paul's Second Epistle*, 267, 274–75; Furnish, *II Corinthians*, 386–89, 395.
42 L. L. Welborn, "Paul's Appeal to the Emotions in 2 Corinthians 1.1–2.13; 7.5–16," *JSNT* 82 (2001) 31–60.

Paul's severe epistle, the Corinthians had suffered a shock and were in considerable distress.[43] Taken in isolation, some of the words used to describe the Corinthians' attitude might be regarded as "neutral," as far as their innocence or complicity is concerned: thus, ἐπιπόθησις might be construed as longing for Paul's presence, or σπουδή as sincere commitment to Paul's cause.[44] But as expressions of "godly grief," and as fruits of "repentance" (7:9–10), these terms must all be understood as descriptive of the Corinthians' concern to amend a wrong in which they have been involved.[45] ὀδυρμός, "mourning," is a particularly strong expression for the sorrow of a community that has gained remorseful insight into the consequences of its actions, and that now regards its previous conduct toward the apostle as an offence.[46] ἀπολογία, "eagerness to clear oneself," presupposes that the Corinthians have been charged with something, that they feel compelled to defend themselves, and that they now seek vindication.[47] ἀγανάκτησις, "indignation," is not only anger at the wrongdoer who has caused so much pain, but, as an aspect of the Corinthians' "repentance," must be understood as anger against themselves, as discontent over their involvement in the matter.[48] The term φόβος furnishes the clearest indication that the Corinthians suffer from a guilty conscience, for it is best understood as "fear" at the prospect that the apostle might come to Corinth and make severe use of his authority to punish, as he

---

43 Windisch, *Der zweite Korintherbrief*, 234.
44 Barrett, "Ο ΑΔΙΚΗΣΑΣ," 113; Windisch, *Der zweite Korintherbrief*, 228. BDAG 377 s.v. ἐπιπόθησις, 939–40 s.v. σπουδή.
45 Windisch, *Der zweite Korintherbrief*, 228, 235; Hughes, *Paul's Second Epistle*, 267; Bruce, *1 and 2 Corinthians*, 218; Thrall, *Second Epistle*, 1.498.
46 LSJ 1199 s.v. ὀδυρμός, "lamentation": γήξας ὀδυρμῶν πενθίμων τε δακρύων Euripides *Phoen.* 1071; θρήνων ὀδυρμοί Euripides *Tro.* 609; ὀδυρμοὺς καὶ οἴκτους Plato *Resp.* 387D. See also BDAG 692 s.v. ὀδυρμός: TestSol 4:2; Matt. 2:18; Josephus *B.J.* 5.31; *A.J.* 2.238; 2 Macc. 11:6. Cf. Windisch, *Der zweite Korintherbrief*, 228; Hughes, *Paul's Second Epistle*, 267; Bruce, *1 and 2 Corinthians*, 218; Thrall, *Second Epistle*, 1.489.
47 LSJ 208 s.v. ἀπολογία: Lysias 14.29; see also BDAG 117 s.v. ἀπολογία. *Diccionario Griego-Español III* (Madrid: Instituto de Filología, 1991) 434 s.v. ἀπολογία. Cf. Windisch, *Der zweite Korintherbrief*, 235; Hughes, *Paul's Second Epistle*, 274; Harris, *Second Epistle*, 542.
48 LSJ 6 s.v. ἀγανάκτησις II; BDAG 5 s.v. ἀγανάκτησις: Appian *Bell. civ.* 1, 10 §39; 4, 124 §521; *PGrenf* II. 82.17–18; Josephus *B.J.* 4.342; *Diccionario Griego-Español I* (Madrid: Instituto de Filología, 2008) 17 s.v. ἀγανάκτησις: Thucydides 2.41; Dio Cassius 36.43.1. Cf. Windisch, *Der zweite Korintherbrief*, 235; Plummer, *Second Epistle*, 223; Hughes, *Paul's Second Epistle*, 274; Harris, *Second Epistle*, 542.

had threatened to do in 2 Cor. 13:1–10.⁴⁹ The series of terms in 7:11 is not casually constructed, but is an intentional creation, as indicated by the fact that exactly seven terms are chosen,⁵⁰ and that each term is emphasized by the anaphoric use of ἀλλά, thus, *"what* eagerness to clear yourselves, *what* indignation, *what* alarm, etc."⁵¹ Paul describes the stages of an emotional progress by which the Corinthians have lived through their repentance from complicity in the wrong, culminating in their willingness to punish (ἐκδίκησις) the wrongdoer. Only upon the completion of this sequence, does Paul declare that the Corinthians have cleared themselves of guilt in the matter (7:11b).⁵²

A second aspect of the Corinthians' complicity is so obvious from the context that it hardly needs to be pointed out, except that Paul calls attention to it repeatedly: Paul himself was the victim of the wrong in which the Corinthians were involved. In 7:7, where Paul summarizes what Titus reported from Corinth, the three attitudes of the Corinthians—"longing, mourning, and zeal"—are explicitly qualified by the phrase *"on behalf of me"* (ὑπὲρ ἐμοῦ).⁵³ And again, at the climax of the longer list of emotions that comprised the Corinthians' repentance, Paul explains in 7:12 that his purpose in writing a painful epistle had been "to disclose to you the zeal that you have *for us* (ὑπὲρ ἡμῶν) before God."⁵⁴ In both cases, the qualifying phrases emphasize that it was Paul himself who was the victim of the Corinthians' involvement in wrongdoing. Two fine, rhetorical points darken and enrich the self-portrait of Paul as the victim of the Corinthians' neglect, or something worse, and as suffering the despairing consequences. The anaphoric use of the second person pronoun in 7:7, drawn forward to a position of emphasis, and repeat-

---

49 Windisch, *Der zweite Korintherbrief*, 235; Hughes, *Paul's Second Epistle*, 274; Furnish, *II Corinthians*, 388–89.
50 Windisch, *Der zweite Korintherbrief*, 234. Cf. Rom. 8:35, where seven terms are also chosen.
51 BDF §448 (6); Meyer, *Der zweite Brief*, 333; Windisch, *Der zweite Korintherbrief*, 234; Bachmann, *Der zweite Brief*, 303; Lietzmann, *An die Korinther I-II*, 132; Hughes, *Paul's Second Epistle*, 274; Thrall, *Second Epistle*, 1.493.
52 Windisch, *Der zweite Korintherbrief*, 236; Plummer, *Second Epistle*, 223; Hughes, *Paul's Second Epistle*, 275; Barrett, "Ο ΑΔΙΚΗΣΑΣ," 113; Furnish, *II Corinthians*, 395.
53 Windisch, *Der zweite Korintherbrief*, 228.
54 Windisch, *Der zweite Korintherbrief*, 236; Bultmann, *Der zweite Brief*, 62; Thrall, *Second Epistle*, 1.496. Note the variant in the ms. tradition: τὴν σπουδὴν ὑμῶν τὴν ὑπὲρ ὑμῶν D* F 0243. 629 *pc*. But the majority reading (τὴν σπουδὴν ὑμῶν τὴν ὑπὲρ ἡμῶν) is to be preferred.

ed before each of the Corinthians' attitudes as reported by Titus—thus, "*your* longing, *your* mourning, *your* zeal"—strongly suggests that all of these emotions had previously been felt by Paul, and had gone unrequited.⁵⁵ Similarly, the result clause at the end of 7:7, in which Paul describes the consoling effect of Titus' report from Corinth, retains the thought of an ominous consequence that might have resulted instead of joy: the adverb μᾶλλον, "rather," is to be taken in the sense of "instead,"⁵⁶ and marks an alternative to the anxious and crestfallen mood of vss. 5–6, in which Paul awaited news from Corinth; thus, even as Paul speaks of his joy, he recalls, by means of contrast, the hurtful attitude of the congregation toward him—their indifference, their insouciance, their neglect—which produced, for a time, the very opposite of joy.⁵⁷

A third aspect of the Corinthians' involvement in the wrong done to Paul emerges from careful analysis of Paul's statements about the grievous effect of the crime in 2:5–7: in some respect, the Corinthians' complicity was limited, their participation qualified.⁵⁸ In 2:5, where Paul broaches the subject of the one who caused pain, not only to Paul himself, but also, and more importantly, to all of the Corinthians, he interjects two qualifying phrases, ἀπὸ μέρους and ἵνα μὴ ἐπιβαρῶ, whose purpose is to limit and mitigate some aspect of the situation.⁵⁹ The exact meaning of these phrases in the present instance is unclear, because each may be construed with different elements of the sentence.⁶⁰ The prepositional phrase ἀπὸ μέρους, "in part," can be taken to modify πάντας ὑμᾶς, in which case, Paul would be saying that not all of the Corinthians have been caused pain, but only "some of you," "a portion of you."⁶¹ But ἀπὸ μέρους may also qualify the verb λελύπηκεν, in which case, the phrase

---

55 Plummer, *Second Epistle*, 219; Denney, *Second Epistle*, 252; Hughes, *Paul's Second Epistle*, 267; Furnish, *II Corinthians*, 386.
56 Windisch, *Der zweite Korintherbrief*, 228–29; Allo, *Saint Paul*, 195; cf. BDAG 614 s.v. μᾶλλον 3. For other interpretations of μᾶλλον χαρῆναι, see Plummer, *Second Epistle*, 219.
57 Windisch, *Der zweite Korintherbrief*, 229.
58 Krenkel, *Beiträge*, 257; Windisch, *Der zweite Korintherbrief*, 83–84; Allo, *Saint Paul*, 55.
59 Heinrici, *Der zweite Brief*, 94; Windisch, *Der zweite Korintherbrief*, 85; Barrett, "Ο ΑΔΙΚΗΣΑΣ," 110; Bultmann, *Der zweite Brief*, 52.
60 For various possible constructions of the sentence, see Heinrici, *Der zweite Brief*, 94–95, with reference to older scholarship, i.e., Bengel, Mosheim, B. Weiss, Hofmann; more recently, Thrall, *Second Epistle*, 1.172–73.
61 Schmiedel, *Die Briefe an die Korinther*, 219–21; Lietzmann, *An die Korinther I-II*, 106; Plummer, *Second Epistle*, 52, 56; Bultmann, *Der zweite Brief*, 52.

limits the degree of pain; Paul would be saying that not all of the Corinthians have been equally grieved, but only "in some measure," or "to some degree."[62] A similar ambiguity characterizes the phrase ἵνα μὴ ἐπιβαρῶ. If the verb ἐπιβαρεῖν is used transitively, the phrase means "so as not to lay a burden upon" someone; the context allows either the offender or the Corinthians as the object; Paul would then be seeking to soften the harsh effect of his statement upon those who are judged worthy of blame.[63] But the majority of interpreters take the verb as an intransitive, expressing Paul's desire "not to exaggerate" the extent of the pain that has been caused.[64] Because Paul uses both of the expressions ἀπὸ μέρους and ἐπιβαρεῖν elsewhere, and with a range of meanings,[65] it is difficult to avoid the conclusion that the ambiguity in this instance is intentional, and supplements the evasive style that characterizes the entire paragraph. In any case, these phrases suggest a limit to the Corinthians' complicity in the wrong done to Paul: either they were not all involved, or they were not involved to the same degree.

In 2:6, Paul introduces a further distinction that has implications for our assessment of the Corinthians' involvement in the affair of the wrongdoer: Paul declares, "Sufficient for such a one is this punishment by the majority." It now emerges that the punishment imposed upon the offender was the verdict of a majority of the Corinthian Christians. The expression οἱ πλείονες, "the majority,"[66] implies here, as it does else-

---

62 Bachmann, *Der zweite Brief,* 112; Windisch, *Der zweite Korintherbrief,* 85; Allo, *Saint Paul,* 36; Barrett, *Second Epistle,* 89; Thrall, *Second Epistle,* 1.172; Harris, *Second Epistle,* 224.
63 The verb ἐπιβαρεῖν is used transitively in 1 Thess. 2:9. For older interpreters who took ἐπιβαρεῖν as transitive (in 2 Cor. 2:5), see Heinrici, *Der zweite Brief,* 94–95; Hughes, *Paul's Second Epistle,* 65 n.8. For examples of the transitive use, see Dionysius of Halicarnassus *Ant. rom.* 4.9; 8.73; Appian *Bell. civ.* 4, 31 §133; *SIG* 807,16 [c. 54 AD].
64 Plummer, *Second Epistle,* 56; Windisch, *Der zweite Korintherbrief,* 85; Lietzmann, *An die Korinther I–II,* 106; Bultmann, *Der zweite Brief,* 52; Furnish, *II Corinthians,* 155; Thrall, *Second Epistle,* 1.172; Harris, *Second Epistle,* 224.
65 ἀπὸ μέρους—2 Cor. 1:14; Rom. 11:25; 15:15, 24; ἐπιβαρεῖν—1 Thess. 2:9; 2 Thess. 3:8 (deutero-Pauline).
66 BDAG 848 s.v. πολύς 1.β, "the majority." Some commentators interpret οἱ πλείονες as "the many," on the analogy of Hebrew *ha-rabbim,* as a term for the whole community, rather than the majority: i.e., Barrett, *Second Epistle,* 91; Martin, *2 Corinthians,* 37, appealing to the usage of *ha-rabbim* in the literature of the Qumran community (e.g., 1 QS VI.8ff; CD XIII.7), and positing a Hebraism in Josephus' discussion of the self-government of the Essenes (*B.J.* 2.146). Against this interpretation, see Herbert Braun, *Qumran und das Neue Testament,* 2 vols.

where in Paul,⁶⁷ the existence of a "minority" who were of a different opinion about the treatment of the wrongdoer.⁶⁸ Indeed, closer inspection of the exact wording of 2:6 discloses not merely an implicit contrast between two groups, but actually suggests a contrast between two verdicts, emphasized by the demonstrative pronoun αὕτη, and the repetition of the article: thus the phrase ἡ ἐπιτιμία αὕτη ἡ ὑπὸ τῶν πλειόνων (this punishment, namely the one [decided upon] by the majority") has as its counterpart ἡ ἐπιτιμία ἐκείνη ἡ ὑπὸ τῶν ἐλασσόνων ("that punishment, namely the one [recommended] by the minority").⁶⁹ Traditionally, interpreters have seen in the minority a dissident group opposed to Paul, who argued for a more lenient penalty, or perhaps, no penalty at all.⁷⁰ But consideration of the context leads to the opposite conclusion: the minority was the party of Paul, who wished for a more severe treatment of the offender than the majority had voted.⁷¹ Only this interpretation is consistent with Paul's statements in 2:9 and 7:15, which speak of "obedience in everything" and "the obedience of you all." If there were still a discontent and rebellious minority, how could *all* be praised for their obedience?⁷² Moreover, the expression ἱκανόν, placed at the head of 2:6 for emphasis, suggests that some were not "satisfied" with the punishment imposed by

---

(Tübingen: Mohr Siebeck, 1966) 1.152, 198: the Greek equivalent of *rabbim* is πολλοί (not πλείονες), as in Dan. 9:27; 11:33, 39; 12:3 (LXX). Moreover, a careful reading of Josephus' account of the way in which the Essenes governed themselves suggests that here, too, οἱ πλείονες must be taken in the ordinary Greek sense of "the majority." See the discussion of the issue in Furnish, *II Corinthians*, 155–56; Thrall, *Second Epistle*, 1.175.

67 1 Cor. 9:19; 10:5; 15:6; 2 Cor. 9:2; Phil. 1:14.
68 Krenkel, *Beiträge*, 302; Plummer, *Second Epistle*, 58; Windisch, *Der zweite Korintherbrief*, 86–87; Furnish, *II Corinthians*, 155–56; Thrall, *Second Epistle*, 1.174–76.
69 Krenkel, *Beiträge*, 302.
70 Heinrici, *Der zweite Brief*, 97; Hughes, *Paul's Second Epistle*, 68–69; Bultmann, *Der zweite Brief*, 52; Lietzmann, *An die Korinther I-II*, 198; Bornkamm, *Vorgeschichte*, 9; Allo, *Saint Paul*, 54–55; Kümmel, *Introduction*, 208, 213; among others.
71 Krenkel, *Beiträge*, 302; Zahn, *Introduction*, 1.333–35; Kennedy, *Second and Third Corinthians*, 100–109; Lake, *Earlier Epistles*, 170–72; Plummer, *Second Epistle*, 58; Bachmann, *Der zweite Brief*, 118; Windisch, *Der zweite Korintherbrief*, 87; Harris, *Second Epistle*, 229.
72 Krenkel, *Beiträge*, 302; Kennedy, *Second and Third Epistles*, 106–107; Barrett, *Second Epistle*, 215; Furnish, *II Corinthians*, 391.

the majority and wished for something more "adequate."⁷³ Finally, this interpretation is confirmed by the way in which Paul continues in 2:7: "so that, on the other hand, you should instead forgive..."; the adverbial expression τοὐναντίον μᾶλλον, literally "on the contrary rather," following ἱκανόν, indicates that there were still some who felt that the punishment was insufficient, and who had hitherto refused to forgive.⁷⁴

The picture of the Corinthians' involvement in the affair of the wrongdoer which has emerged from a close reading of 2 Cor. 2 and 7 is complex and interesting. We may summarize what we have learned thus far, and, at the same time, indicate the limits of our knowledge. The Corinthians were complicit in a wrong done to Paul by a particular individual. The seriousness of their complicity is demonstrated, both by Paul's perception that the Corinthians have something of which to repent, and by the Corinthians' manifestation of the emotional symptoms of remorse. All of the Corinthians were pained by the action of the wrongdoer, but not all were sensible of it to the same degree, a distinction which suggests varying levels of complicity within the congregation. A majority decided upon a punishment which Paul deemed "sufficient," but a minority wished for a harsher penalty, and were not eager to forgive; from this difference, one may legitimately infer that the majority were more closely associated with the wrongdoer, the minority with Paul.

Nevertheless, much remains unclear about the involvement of the Corinthians in the affair of the wrongdoer. It is difficult to ascertain in what, specifically, the complicity of the Corinthians consisted. Was it

---

73   Krenkel, *Beiträge*, 302; Windisch, *Der zweite Korintherbrief*, 86. It is uncertain whether ἱκανόν refers to the severity or the duration of the punishment, though the former fits the context better: so, BDAG 472 s.v. ἱκανός 3.b–ἱκανὸν ἡ ἐπιτιμία *"the punishment is severe enough"*; see the discussion in Furnish, *II Corinthians*, 156. On the lack of agreement in gender between the neuter adjective ἱκανόν and the feminine subject ἐπιτιμία, interpreters offer various explanations: a reflection of classical usage (BDF §131); a substantival use of the neuter adjective, as in the case of the synonym ἀρκετόν in Matt. 6:34, likewise used with a feminine subject (Heinrici, *Der zweite Brief*, 95; Harris, *Second Epistle*, 228). Hughes (*Paul's Second Epistle*, 66 n.11) suggests that ἱκανόν is a Latinism (= *satis*), referring to Luke 22:38, ἱκανόν ἐστι, and Mark 15:15, τὸ ἱκανὸν ποιῆσαι = *satisfacere*.
74   Plummer, *Second Epistle*, 58; Windisch, *Der zweite Korintherbrief*, 88; Lietzmann, *An die Korinther I-II*, 106; Bultmann, *Der zweite Brief*, 53; Furnish, *II Corinthians*, 156; Harris, *Second Epistle*, 229. See BDAG 614, s.v. μᾶλλον 3: "marker of an alternative to something, *rather* in the sense *instead* (of something)." Contra Vegge, *2 Corinthians*, 74–75, who argues for a temporal understanding of ἱκανόν in 2:6.

merely insensitivity to the harm done to Paul by some in the congregation who regarded the incident as a purely personal matter between the offender and Paul?[75] Did the complicity of the Corinthians consist in nothing more than their reluctance to punish the offender?[76] To be sure, a deeper complicity is indicated by the tenor of the Corinthians' emotional response to Paul's severe epistle, as we have demonstrated. The wrongdoer must have drawn the majority of the community more deeply into his crime, for only thus is it really comprehensible that Paul would postpone his planned visit and endure such a prolonged absence from Corinth (1:15–16, 23; 2:1–2), and feel constrained to compose a letter written "with many tears" (2:3–4), and deem it necessary to send Titus on a special mission from Asia (2:12–13; 7:5 ff.).[77] But it is not yet clear in what way the majority of the Corinthians would have shown their support for the wrongdoer, nor how they might have participated in his injurious act. We must hope that further light will be thrown upon these matters by examination of the vocabulary that Paul uses to describe the incident and its aftermath, and, eventually, by a widening of the textual basis to include other portions of 2 Corinthians, especially chs. 10–13.

We have now extracted from the text of 2 Cor. 2 and 7 all relevant information that exegesis can yield regarding the principal actors in the incident under discussion—the wrongdoer, Paul, and the Corinthians. Before passing on to an examination of the nature of the offence, we may briefly consider *the relationships* between the actors in this drama. About the relationship between Paul and the wrongdoer, very little can be said at this point, because of Paul's highly evasive style and his consistent use of circumlocutions. Entirely lacking are any of the terms from the Pauline thesaurus by which the functions of members of the Christian community are customarily designated: ἀδελφός, συνεργός, κοινωνός, σύζυγος, συστρατιώτης, etc.[78] Paul does not betray whether the offender is an early or a recent convert, whether he is a householder, whether he has devoted himself to the service of the saints—the kind of information

---

75 Krenkel, *Beiträge*, 257.
76 Thrall, *Second Epistle*, 1.495.
77 Drescher, "Vorgänge in Korinth," 49; Weiss, *Primitive Christianity*, 1.342–43.
78 E. Earle Ellis, "Paul and his Co-Workers," *NTS* 17 (1971) 437–38; Wayne A. Meeks, *The First Urban Christians: The Social World of the Apostle Paul* (New Haven: Yale University Press, 1983) 9–10; see in general, Wolf-Henning Ollrog, *Paulus und seine Mitarbeiter. Untersuchungen zu Theorie und Praxis der Paulinischen Mission* (Neukirchen-Vluyn: Neukirchener Verlag, 1979).

otherwise included when converts are mentioned.[79] Although Paul refers throughout to a particular individual and a specific, problematic act, a personal apostrophe, such as one finds in Phil. 4:2–3, is wanting.[80] In 2 Cor. 1–2 and 7, Paul never deals with the wrongdoer directly, but only through the medium of the congregation. In sum, Paul's rhetoric is so circumspect that only one inference about his relationship to the wrongdoer is permitted: Paul regards the wrongdoer as a person of significant influence; only thus can one explain the extreme caution exhibited whenever Paul approaches the subject of the wrongdoer. Although Paul has been wronged and pained, he finds it expedient, perhaps even necessary, to counsel the forgiveness of the one whom the majority have judged leniently.[81]

Fortunately, rather more can be said about the relationship of the wrongdoer to the Christian community: the offender was himself a member of the Corinthian congregation.[82] It is difficult to imagine that anyone other than a member of the Corinthian church would have submitted to a penalty imposed by the Corinthians, as 2:6 indicates has happened.[83] The strongest evidence is furnished by 2:7, where Paul expresses his concern lest the wrongdoer be "overwhelmed by excessive sorrow." The verb that Paul uses here to depict the potential fate of the wrongdoer is frightful in its force: καταπίνειν in the passive voice means "to be swallowed up by waters," "to be drowned."[84] The image is that of a man being drowned by his own tears.[85] Paul intensifies the portrait of grief by adding

---

79 E.g., 1 Cor. 16:12–15; 16:19; 1:14; 1:16; Phil. 4:2–3; Phlm. 1–2.
80 Windisch, *Der zweite Korintherbrief*, 84.
81 Bachmann, *Der zweite Brief*, 133; Windisch, *Der zweite Korintherbrief*, 84; Thrall, *Second Epistle*, 1.177.
82 Ewald, *Sendschreiben*, 227; Weiss, *Primitive Christianity*, 1.342; Kümmel, *Introduction*, 208; Thrall, *Second Epistle*, 1.177.
83 Klöpper, *Kommentar*, 158–59; Kümmel, *Introduction*, 208; Thrall, *Second Epistle*, 1.67, 177; Harris, *Second Epistle*, 227.
84 BDAG 524 s.v. καταπίνω 1.b, "of waters, waves, *swallow up*"; passive, "be drowned," Ex. 15:4 v.l. See esp. the transferred sense, in reference to mental and emotional states, in Philo *Gig.* 13; *Deus* 181. Cf. Hughes, *Paul's Second Epistle*, 67 n.12: "The intensive force of the compound καταπίνειν should be brought out: 'to swallow up completely' or 'engulf'," citing as examples of this forcefulness Matt. 23:24; 1 Cor. 15:54; 2 Cor. 5:4; Heb. 11:9; 1 Peter 5:8; Rev. 12:6.
85 Furnish, *II Corinthians*, 156. Cf. Thrall, *Second Epistle*, 1.177; Harris, *Second Epistle*, 229–30.

the comparative adjective περισσότερος, "excessive."⁸⁶ Making allowances for hyperbole, one must still ask: who but a member of the Corinthian congregation would have felt so deeply about a penalty imposed by the Corinthians as to experience such remorse?⁸⁷

Nevertheless, there are indications that the wrongdoer was no ordinary Corinthian. We recall that Barrett already sensed a tension in the relationship between the wrongdoer and the Corinthian church.⁸⁸ The exceptional status of the wrongdoer is underlined by the language Paul uses in counseling his forgiveness in 2:7–8: the Corinthians are "to try to conciliate" (παρακαλέσαι) and "to ratify" (κυρῶσαι) love for the wrongdoer; this is highly respectful treatment, with a surprising degree of formality.⁸⁹ In this instance, the verb παρακαλεῖν has the sense "to appease," or "to speak kindly"; it is the means of dealing with someone who is angry, the proper form of address for elders.⁹⁰ Here, as elsewhere, κυροῦν is used in the technical, legal sense of "the confirmation of an act or decision."⁹¹ Paul's juxtaposition of the terms κυροῦν and ἀγάπη gives rise to

---

86 BDAG 806 s.v. περισσότερος a: *"excessive."* Cf. Harris, *Second Epistle*, 229: "The comparative περισσότερος functions as an elative superlative, so that τῇ περισσοτέρᾳ λύπῃ means 'by excessive sorrow' or 'by excess of grief'."
87 König, "Verkehr," 516; Kümmel, *Introduction*, 208; Thrall, *Second Epistle*, 1.67, 177; Harris, *Second Epistle*, 225.
88 Barrett, "Ο ΑΔΙΚΗΣΑΣ," 113–15.
89 Bachmann, *Der zweite Brief*, 119.
90 BDAG 765 s.v. παρακαλέω 5: 2 Macc. 13:23, τοὺς Ιουδαίους παρεκάλεσσεν, "he [Antiochus] conciliated the Jews"; Luke 15:28, παρεκάλει αὐτόν, "he [the father of the prodigal son] tried to appease him [the elder brother]"; Acts 16:39, παρεκάλεσαν αὐτούς, "conciliated them"; 1 Cor. 4:13, δυσφημούμενοι παρακαλοῦμεν, "when slandered, we speak kindly"; 1 Tim. 5:1, Πρεσβυτέρῳ μὴ ἐπιπλήξῃς ἀλλὰ παρακάλει ὡς πατέρα, "Do not rebuke an elder, but speak kindly as to a father." Cf. Furnish, *II Corinthians*, 156.
91 LSJ 1014 s.v. κυρόω 1; BDAG 579 s.v. κυρόω 1: Dio Chrysostom 59 [76], 1; *SIG* 368, 25; 695, 68–69; *OGIS* 383, 122; *I.Eph.* VI.2054, cited in *New Documents Illustrating Early Christianity*, Vol. 4, ed. G. H. R. Horsley (North Ryde: Macquarie University, 1987) 171 §82; *PAmh* 97, 14; *PTebt* 294, 16. For other examples from the papyri of the use of κυρόω in a legal sense, see J. H. Moulton and G. Milligan, *The Vocabulary of the Greek Testament illustrated from the Papyri and other non-literary Sources* (London: Hodder & Stoughton, 1930; repr. Grand Rapids: Eerdmans, 1976) 366; J. Behm, "κυρόω," *TDNT* 3 (1965)1098–99. Paul uses the verb in a legal sense in Gal. 3:15, κεκυρωμένην διαθήκην, "a will that has been ratified." A number of interpreters find the technical, legal sense present in 2 Cor. 2:8: Bachmann, *Der zweite Brief*, 119; Windisch, *Der zweite Korintherbrief*, 89; Allo, *Saint Paul*, 40; Hughes, *Paul's Second Epistle*, 67 n.14; C. Spicq, *Agape in the New Testament* (St. Louis: Herder,

an uneasy oxymoron: a formal resolution of love.⁹² Why must the wrongdoer be treated with such tact and caution in extending the gift of forgiveness? Ewald suggested long ago that the wrongdoer may have been a member of the upper class, a person of status and substance.⁹³ This suggestion finds support in Paul's final comment about the wrongdoer in ch. 2: apprehending the possibility that the man might be lost to the Christian community, Paul uses a term, πλεονεκτεῖν, which has a financial connotation: "we might be defrauded."⁹⁴

Turning now to an examination of the language Paul uses to speak of the incident, we begin at a distance from the wrongdoing, that is, with the forgiveness that Paul urges, and work our way back towards the injurious act, in keeping with our earlier insight into the logic of Paul's rhetoric. First, it can be established that the wrong was an act of the type for which the forgiveness of the Corinthian church was appropriate. This is a significant limitation in two directions: on the one hand, in respect to divine law, and on the other hand, in respect to human law. It is striking that nowhere in 2:5–11 does Paul make reference to divine forgiveness.⁹⁵ This omission is all the more remarkable, when one considers that the verb by which Paul designates the response that the Corinthians are to make to the wrongdoer in 2:7 and 2:10, χαρίζεσθαι, is the verb Paul ordinarily uses to refer to the gracious benefits conferred by God.⁹⁶ Thus the absence of any mention of divine forgiveness in this instance can only be intentional. The wrong is of a kind for which human forgiveness is sufficient; it is covered by the graciousness of fellow-Christians. Paul's usage effectively excludes the sin of incest, and many other sins

---

    1963) 185–87; Prümm, *Diakonia Pneumatos I*, 66; Furnish, *II Corinthians*, 157; Thrall, *Second Epistle*, 1.177–78; Harris, *Second Epistle*, 230.

92 Behm, "κυρόω," *TDNT* 3 (1965)1098–99; Furnish, *II Corinthians*, 157; Thrall, *Second Epistle*, 1.178.

93 Ewald, *Sendschreiben*, 227: "…ja einer der angesehensten, vielleicht ein mitglied des vorstandes."

94 LSJ 1416 s.v. πλεονεκτέω II.2: Menander *Mon.* 259; Dio Chrysostom 67 [17], 8; Dio Cassius 52.37; passive: Xenophon *Mem.* 3.5.2; Demosthenes 41.25. BDAG 824 s.v. πλεονεκτέω 1: Dionysius of Halicarnassus *Ant. rom.* 9, 7; Plutarch *Marc.* 315; Ps.-Lucian *Amor.* 27; *OGI* 484, 27. Cf. G. Delling, "πλεονεκτέω," *TDNT* 6 (1968) 266–74. Paul uses the term in reference to a charge of fraud brought against him by someone in Corinth in 2 Cor. 12:17–18; 7:2. The financial nuance of πλεονεκτεῖν in 2 Cor. 2:11 is noted by Hughes, *Paul's Second Epistle*, 72 n.22 and Furnish, *II Corinthians*, 158.

95 Windisch, *Der zweite Korintherbrief*, 88.

96 E.g., 1 Cor. 2:12; Gal. 3:18; Phil. 1:29. Cf. Furnish, *II Corinthians*, 156.

(cf. 1 Cor. 6:9–11) for which divine forbearance would be necessary.[97] On the other hand, the wrong cannot have fallen within the scope of criminal law, for over such matters the Corinthian church had no jurisdiction; thus violent crimes, adultery, forgery, and the like, are excluded.[98] Nor can one believe that any but the most trivial of civil offences could have been pardoned by the Christian assembly, which was, after all, a completely private religious organization without any public standing.[99] Thus the "ordinary cases" (βιωτικὰ κριτήρια) for which Paul deems it proper to appoint judges within the church, according to 1 Cor. 6:5, may have been included;[100] but it seems doubtful that a case of outright robbery, such as Thrall imagines having taken place,[101] could have been dismissed by the "forgiveness" of the Christian assembly.

Second, on the principle that the punishment should suit the crime, there is good reason to investigate more thoroughly the meaning of the term ἐπιτιμία in 2:6. In most translations and commentaries, ἐπιτιμία is rendered "punishment,"[102] and this may well be the general sense of the term.[103] But the cognate ἐπιτίμιον was the established term for "penalty," and was commonly in use.[104] The only occurrence of ἐπιτιμία in the New Testament is in this verse of 2 Corinthians! Elsewhere, ἐπιτιμία denotes "punishment" in general only in Wisdom 3:10 and in an Egyptian

---

97 Bultmann, *Der zweite Brief*, 52; Kümmel, *Introduction*, 283; Bruce, *1 and 2 Corinthians*, 185; Prümm, *Diakonia Pneumatos I*, 68; Furnish, *II Corinthians*, 165–66.
98 O. F. Robinson, *The Criminal Law of Ancient Rome* (London: Duckworth, 1995).
99 W. Cotter, "The *Collegia* and Roman Law: state restrictions on voluntary associations" in *Voluntary Associations in the Greco-Roman World*, ed. John S. Kloppenborg and S. G. Wilson (London: Routledge, 1996) 74–89; Richard S. Ascough, *Paul's Macedonian Associations* (Tübingen: Mohr Siebeck, 2003) 43–46; Bruce W. Winter, "Gallio's Ruling on the Legal Status of Early Christianity (Acts 18:14–15)," *TynBul* 50 (1999) 213–24.
100 Bruce W. Winter, "Civil Litigation in Corinth: The Forensic Background to 1 Cor. 6:1–8," *NTS* 37 (1991) 559–71.
101 Thrall, "The Offender and the Offence," 71–76; idem, *Second Epistle*, 1.67–69.
102 Heinrici, *Der zweite Brief*, 95; Plummer, *Second Epistle*, 52, 57; Lietzmann, *An die Korinther I/II*, 106; Furnish, *II Corinthians*, 153, 155; Wolff, *Der zweite Brief*, 44; Thrall, *Second Epistle*, 1.163, 173–74, 176; Harris, *Second Epistle*, 227.
103 Moulton-Milligan, *Vocabulary*, 248 s.v. ἐπιτιμία d; LSJ 667 s.v. ἐπιτιμία II; BDAG 384 s.v. ἐπιτιμία.
104 LSJ 667 s.v. ἐπιτίμιον 2: in singular, Aristophanes *Thesm.* 1026; Aristotle *Oec.* 1349b30; *IG* 2.1104; *PHal.* 1.208. Cf. Windisch, *Der zweite Korintherbrief*, 86; Thrall, *Second Epistle*, 1.173.

papyrus of the first century A.D.[105] Thus it seems best to derive the specific content of ἐπιτιμία from the verb ἐπιτιμᾶν, which is common in the New Testament and in ancient literature generally, with the meaning "to rebuke, reprove, censure," also "speak seriously or warn," in order to prevent an action or bring one to an end.[106] This understanding of ἐπιτιμία is supported by the Latin church fathers, whose renderings vary, but who consistently express the idea of censure or reproof.[107] Of course, a wide range of actions are subject to censure. But if there were any correspondence between the punishment and the crime, then ἐπιτιμία may suggest something about the area in which the offence occurred. We naturally find ourselves asking whether the wrong may have involved an accusation, an allegation, or a charge against Paul.[108]

Third, further insight may be gained into the relationship of the offender both to Paul and to the Corinthians by examination of the word that Paul uses to describe the *consequence* of the wrong, namely, λύπη (2:5). Because the meaning of λύπη is broad and, from a modern point of view, rather ambiguous,[109] it might seem an unpromising source of inferences about a specific act and its circumstances: physically, λύπη can denote any pain, including that caused by sickness or injury, hunger or thirst, heat or cold;[110] in the psychological sense in which the term is

---

105 Wis. 3:10: οἱ δὲ ἀσεβεῖς καθὰ ἐλογίσατο ἕξουσιν ἐπιτιμίαν ("But the impious will have punishment as their reasoning demands"); *OGIS* 669.43.
106 BDAG 384 s.v. ἐπιτιμάω 1: Thucydides 4.28.1; Demosthenes *Or.* 1.16; *SIG* 344, 55; Sir. 11:7; Josephus *A.J.* 5.105. See the arguments of Bachmann, *Der zweite Brief*, 117 n.3, 119; Barrett, *Second Epistle*, 90; Martin, *2 Corinthians*, 30, 37; David E. Fredrickson, "Paul's Bold Speech in the Argument of 2 Corinthians 2:12–7:16," PhD diss., Yale University (1991) 23–36; idem, "Paul, Hardships, and Suffering" in *Paul in the Greco-Roman World*, ed. J. Paul Sampley (Harrisburg: Trinity Press International, 2003) 180–81.
107 Tertullian: *increpatio*; Augustine: *correptio*; Ambrosiaster, Vulgate: *objurgatio*; cited by Plummer, *Second Epistle*, 57.
108 Ewald, *Sendschreiben*, 227; Betz, *2 Corinthians 8 and 9*, 97. On defamation as a form of *iniuria* in Roman law, see Max Kaser, *Das römische Privatrecht* (Munich: C. H. Beck, 1955) 3.520–22.
109 See the comments on λύπη-words in Greek by William V. Harris, *Restraining Rage: The Ideology of Anger Control in Classical Antiquity* (Cambridge, MA: Harvard University Press, 2001) 343; David Konstan, *The Emotions of the Ancient Greeks: Studies in Aristotle and Classical Literature* (Toronto: University of Toronto Press, 2006) 245.
110 Herodotus 7.16; Sophocles *Aj.* 338; *El.* 654; Euripides *Orest.* 1105; Aeschines *Ag.* 791–92; Plato *Phileb.* 31B-F, 36 A; *Phaed.* 85 A. LSJ 1065, s.v. λυπέω,

used in 2 Cor. 2 and 7, λύπη can refer to distress, anxiety, sorrow or grief, bordering upon the modern concept of depression,[111] but also frustration and annoyance, especially at insults.[112] A factor complicating whatever conclusions might be drawn from Paul's use of the term is that throughout the relevant portions of 2 Corinthians, λύπη has both an active and a passive dimension: thus, the wrongdoer has caused pain both to Paul and to the Corinthians (2:5), but now he is in danger of drowning in excessive sorrow (2:7); Paul has grieved the Corinthians by means of an epistle (2:4; 7:8), but Paul had suffered pain on the occasion of a previous visit from those who should have made him rejoice (2:1–3); the Corinthians have caused Paul pain, distress and anguish of heart (2:3–4), but have themselves been grieved to the point of remorse by Paul's painful epistle (7:8–9).[113] In all of these instances, Paul uses forms of λύπη and λυπεῖν. Whether because of the inherent breadth and ambiguity of the term, or the variety of situations in which it is used by Paul, virtually no exposition of λύπη is to be found in the commentaries, nor does λύπη appear among the list of *"traits précis"* which are taken to clarify the problem of the offender and the offence in essays devoted to the subject.[114] Nevertheless, we shall see that attention to the usage of λύπη in texts contemporary with 2 Corinthians will illuminate the relationship of the wrongdoer to Paul and the Corinthians, in three respects.

First, Paul's use of the verb λυπεῖν to describe the consequence of the wrongdoer's action suggests that the wrongdoer was a person of higher social status than Paul, or the Corinthians in general. In the vast majority of instances, λύπη is pain produced within an asymmetrical relationship of power. This is obviously true in all those cases where λύπη is the result of destructive, impersonal forces, such as death and misfortunes.[115] But inequality also characterizes social relationships in which λύπη is suffered:

λύπη; Moulton-Milligan, *Vocabulary*, 382 s.v. λυπέω, λύπη. See esp. Rudolf Bultmann, "λύπη," *TDNT* 4 (1967) 313–24.

111 Aeschylus *Ag.* 791; Sophocles *Oed. Col.* 1217; Thucydides 6.59; Euripides *Orest.* 396–98; Antiphon fr. 107; Andocides 2.8; Plato *Phileb.* 31B-F, 36 A. LSJ 1065 s.v. λύπη 2; BDAG 604–605 s.v. λύπη. See esp. Bultmann, "λύπη," *TDNT* 4 (1967) 313–14. On λύπη as depression, see the observations of Harris, *Restraining Rage*, 17.

112 E.g., *PRyl.* 1.28.211; *PPetr.* 2.13; Herodas 5; Josephus *A.J.* 8.356; Dio Chrysostom 45.3; cf. Bultmann, "λύπη," *TDNT* 4 (1967) 313.

113 König, "Verkehr," 509.

114 Allo, *Saint Paul*, 55.

115 E.g., *PGrenf.* 2.36; *POxy.* 1.115; *POxy.* 12.1481; Moulton-Milligan, *Vocabulary*, 382 s.v. λυπέω; Bultmann, "λύπη," *TDNT* 4 (1967) 313.

in most situations, the one who inflicts pain is the one who has the power to do so; thus, kings and tyrants grieve their subjects; masters hurt their slaves; husbands distress their wives, and fathers their children.[116] Paul's younger contemporary, Plutarch, acknowledges that slaves are most often the victims of λῦπαι, "because of the absolute power we possess, there being no one to oppose or prevent us."[117] Plutarch pictures the household of an irascible man who is driven by "a craving to pain someone else" (τοῦ λυπεῖν ἕτερον ὄρεξις): the tokens of pain are visible "on the faces of the servants and in the marks branded upon them and their fetters; the only music heard within the house is wailing cries, as the stewards are being lashed within and the serving-maids being tortured, so that those who witness the pains (αἱ λῦπαι) caused by anger in gratifying its desires and pleasures must feel pity."[118] Analyzing the motives of those who cause pain, Plutarch observes that those who succumb most readily to "the inclination to inflict a hurt" (ἡ πρὸς τὸ λυπῆσαι ἔνδοσις) are those whose power is the most petty, and whose grasp upon it is the most tenuous, for instance, "the miser with his steward, the glutton with his cook, the jealous man with his wife, the conceited man hearing himself maligned."[119] Plutarch urges the gentlemen of his own social class, for whom his essay on the cure of anger is written, to join him in a "fast from evil," and to pass "a few sober and wineless days, without anger," assuring them that the placid and gentle spirit they will attain will be "without sorrow" (ἄλυπος) to those who come in contact with it.[120]

An impressive, and rather pitiable, example of the "pain" endured by social inferiors in a dependent relationship is provided by an Egyptian papyrus letter of the mid-first century A.D.[121] Sarapion and Heracleides are evidently clients and business agents whose affairs have recently taken a turn for the worse. Near the beginning of the letter, Sarapion reports to

---

116 E.g., Plutarch *Mor.* 463 A-B, with examples of those who inflict λῦπαι upon others, in *Mor.* 457 A-B, 460F. See also LSJ 1066 s.v. λυπηρός II; BDAG 604 s.v. λυπέω 1; 605 s.v. λυπηρός 1.
117 Plutarch *Mor.* 459B. See the commentary by Hans Dieter Betz and John Dillon, "De cohibenda ira (*Moralia* 452E-464D" in *Plutarch's Ethical Writings and Early Christian Literature*, ed. Hans Dieter Betz (Leiden: Brill, 1978) 189–90.
118 Plutarch *Mor.* 463 A; see also *Mor.* 457 A-B: ἡ πρὸς τό λυπῆσαι ἔνδοσις ("the inclination to inflict pain"); cf. Betz, "De cohibenda ira," 193.
119 Plutarch *Mor.* 457B-C.
120 Plutarch *Mor.* 464C-D; cf. Betz, "De cohibenda ira," 195–96.
121 *BGU* IV.1079 [41 AD]. Cf. Stanley K. Stowers, *Letter-Writing in Greco-Roman Antiquity* (Philadelphia: Westminster, 1986) 110.

Heracleides: "I received your letter…and I read it and was distressed (ἐλυπήθην)."[122] Sarapion advises his partner to act in accordance with the wishes of a more powerful man: "Comply with Ptollarion at all times; perhaps he can help you. Say to him, 'I am different, different from all the rest. I am a child. I have sold you my merchandise for a talent too little. I do not know what my patron will do to me. We have many creditors. Do not ruin us.' Beg him every day. Perhaps he will pity you. By complying with him, you stand a better chance of gaining his friendship."[123]

To be sure, there are instances where a slave or a client is said to have caused pain to his master or patron. Thus, the jealous mistress in Herodas' fifth mime-poem warns her slave girl: "Do not vex me at all!" (μή με λύπει τι).[124] But an honest assessment of the power differential in such cases would prevent us from regarding the λύπη caused by the slave as genuine pain. In Herodas' mime, the jealous mistress had just ordered a slave to be flogged and tattooed, when a sympathetic servant interceded on the fellow's behalf to persuade the mistress to remit the punishment, and was silenced with the warning "Don't vex me at all!" Hence, when a man of Plutarch's class speaks of the λῦπαι which he daily suffers on account of slaves and clients, we are right to translate "annoyances" and "frustrations."[125] Such cases do not weaken our inference regarding the social status of the wrongdoer in 2 Corinthians, whose power sufficed, according to Paul, to cause pain to an entire community (2:5). There are those rare instances when a group of inferiors join forces to inflict real pain upon someone powerful. The rhetor Polyaenus uses λυπεῖν to describe the humiliation and outrage experienced by a king who was deposed by his subjects.[126] A similar, though less serious, case of collective punishment of someone powerful lies before us in 2 Cor. 2:5–11, and, if Paul is not exaggerating, the result was an experience of profound and genuine sorrow (2:7). Nevertheless, Paul's use of λυπεῖν to describe the consequence of the wrongdoer's action strongly suggests that the one who caused pain was a person of status and power (at least within the Christian community).

---

122 *BGU* IV.1079, 9.
123 *BGU* IV.1079, 10–24, 26–27.
124 Herodas *Mime* 5, 73.
125 Plutarch *Mor.* 460C; cf. Aulus Gellius *Noct. att.* 1.26.
126 Polyaenus 8, 47; BDAG 604 s.v. λυπέω 1.

Second, Paul's use of λυπεῖν and λύπη implies that the hurt suffered by himself and the wrongdoer occurred in the context of a friendship. This may seem a surprising inference, given Paul's explicit references to injury, alienation and anguish in the relationship (2:1–4; 7:12). Yet, friendship was understood to create a special vulnerability to pain; consequently, much of the discourse about pain in ancient authors explores a potential inherent in friendship. Aristotle already offered an explanation for this in his discussion of the causes of anger: people are angry when they are pained (ὅταν λυπῶνται), and are more angry when they are pained by friends than by those who are not, because they think that they have a right to be treated well by friends rather than ill.[127] Probing more deeply the psychogenesis of anger, Plutarch observes that, whereas the occasions of anger are different for different persons, "yet in the case of practically all of them, there is present a belief that they are being despised and neglected;"[128] the resulting pain is worse when we think ourselves despised by friends, Plutarch explains,[129] or "when one whom we have supposed a true friend quarrels and finds fault with us."[130] Turning confessional, Plutarch reveals that his own strong inclination to trust his friends leaves him vulnerable to much pain: "Consequently, like men who attempt to walk on empty air, the more I give myself up to loving a person, the more I go astray, and when I stumble and fall, the greater my distress."[131] In the epistolary handbook attributed to Libanius, the example of the "grieving style" of letter (λυπητική) includes the following explanation: "For the griefs (λῦπαι) men cause their friends are exceedingly difficult to heal, and hold greater insults than those they receive from their enemies."[132]

An illuminating example of the special potential for pain inherent in friendship is provided by yet another papyrus letter of the first century

---

127 Aristotle *Rhet.* 2.2.8–9, 15, 1379a; cf. *Pol.* 1327b40–1328a16. See the commentary on this passage by William M. A. Grimaldi, *Aristotle: "Rhetoric", Pt. 2 – A Commentary* (New York: Fordham University Press, 1988) 35–36, 41–42.
128 Plutarch *Mor.* 460D; cf. Aristotle *Rhet.* 2.3, 1380a8 ff. See the comments of Betz, "De cohibenda ira," 191.
129 Plutarch *Mor.* 461E, 462B.
130 Plutarch *Mor.* 463B.
131 Plutarch *Mor.* 463C. Cf. Betz, "De cohibenda ira," 193.
132 Ps.-Libanius *Ep. Char.* 90 in Abraham J. Malherbe, *Ancient Epistolary Theorists* (Atlanta: Scholars Press, 1988) 80–81; my translation modifies Malberbe..

A.D.[133] Chairemon, the gymnasiarch in Arsinoe, writes to his friend, Apollonius, who is evidently also his brother in the cultic association (κοινόν) of the Dioscuri.[134] The greater part of the letter is concerned with the administration of the estates which Chairemon possesses. Yet the letter is marked by a more personal and intimate tone than one customarily encounters in papyrus letters.[135] In the prescript, Chairemon greets Apollonius as his "best and dearest" (φίλτατος). Within a few lines, the subject of friendship is explicitly mentioned, but in a qualified manner which hints at some tension: "Now concerning the matter in question, as it suits you, I will give thanks for your forethought, if you do not forget your friendship (φιλοφροσύνη) towards me."[136] The fragmentary state of the papyrus makes it impossible to tell what has troubled the relationship between the friends, but letters have somehow been involved. Twice Chairemon apologizes; he wishes for Apollonius to have his full apology (ἀπέχεις οὖν τὴν ἀπολογίαν).[137] Toward the end of the letter, Chairemon expresses his confidence "that you will not grieve me, for I have understood how you love me" (δὲ ὅτι [ο]ὐ [μή] με λοιπήσῃς [= λυπήσῃς], α[ἰ]σθόμενος πῶς με φιλεῖς).[138] Then he warns, "But if you fail, you will give me an eternal grief (ἐὰν δὲ ἀστοχήσῃς [αἰω]νίαν μοι λοίπην [= λύπην] [π]αρέχιν μέλλις).[139] Chairemon closes with the reassurance, "For you can trust in my judgment, as I am neither unjust (ἄδικος) nor desirous of what belongs to others."[140]

A further and, in my view, decisive indication that the pain suffered by Paul and the wrongdoer implies the rupture of a previous friendship is provided by consideration of the genre of the letter in which Paul's treatment of the wrongdoer is found.[141] In this regard, we follow the sugges-

---

133 *BGU* II.531 [ca. 70–80 AD]. This letter belongs to a correspondence which includes *BGU* I.248, 249; II.531, 594, 595; III.850. See also Bror Hjalmar Olsson, *Papyrusbriefe aus der frühesten Römerzeit* (Uppsala: Almquist and Wiksells, 1925) nos. 41–45, 47.
134 *BGU* I.248; Olsson, *Papyrusbriefe*, 122–23: Ὄμνυμι δὲ σοι κατὰ τ[ῶ]ν Δ[ιο]σκ[ο]ύρων ὧν κοινῇ σεβόμεθα...ἐπιθυμεῖν τῶν ἠθῶν σου ἀπολαῦσαι ὅμως τ[έ]λειον ε[ὑ]ρήσεται τῆς τύχης ἐπιτρεπούσας περὶ τοῦ κοινοῦ.
135 Olsson, *Papyrusbriefe*, 120.
136 *BGU* II.531, 6–8; Olsson, *Papyrusbriefe*, n. 43, p. 120.
137 *BGU* II.531, 13, 20–22; Olsson, *Papyrusbriefe*, n. 43, pp. 128–29.
138 *BGU* II.531, 18–19.
139 *BGU* II.531, 19–20.
140 *BGU* II.531, 20–22.
141 On the importance of genre in ancient composition generally, see Malcolm Heath, *Unity in Greek Poetics* (Oxford: Clarendon Press, 1989) 17–18, 20–

tion of Hans Windisch,[142] that the sections 1:1–2:13 and 7:5–16 of the writing known to us as 2 Corinthians correspond to the "therapeutic" or "conciliatory" type of letter described in the handbook on epistolary style attributed to Libanius.[143] Naturally, this suggestion would have greater force, if, as Johannes Weiss argued, 2 Cor. 1:1–2:13; 7:5–16 were originally an independent letter.[144] But even if these chapters are only portions of a larger epistle, defined according to the criterion of style,[145] inferences drawn from the function of this type of writing would still be significant. Libanius defines the "therapeutic" (θεραπευτική) letter as "that in which we conciliate someone who has been caused grief (τινα λυπηθέντα) by us for some reason."[146] Libanius adds that "some also call this the apologetic type (ἀπολογητική)." The definition makes clear that the function of this type of letter is the healing of λύπη.[147] The sample letter that Libanius provides permits us to identify the elements of the social relationship which are constitutive of this type of writing. One who wishes to compose a conciliatory letter is instructed to write in this way: "In addition to making the statements that I did, I went on (to put them) into action, for I most certainly did not think that they would ever cause you sorrow (τὸ γὰρ σύνολον οὐκ ἐνόμιζον σέ ποτε λυπηθήσεσθαι). But if you were upset by what was said or done, be assured, most excellent sir, that I shall most certainly no longer mention what was said. For it is my aim always to heal my friends rather than to cause them sorrow (σκοπὸς

22, 38, 150–54; Francis Cairns, *Generic Composition in Greek and Roman Poetry* (Edinburgh: Edinburgh University Press, 1972). On the importance of genre for understanding ancient letters, see Olsson, *Papyrusbriefe*, 8–9; K. Berger, "Hellenistische Gattungen im Neuen Testament," *ANRW* II.25.2, 1289–90; Stowers, *Letter-Writing*, 49–57 and passim.

142 Windisch, *Der zweite Korintherbrief*, 8.
143 V. Weichert, *Demetrii et Libanii qui feruntur* ΤΥΠΟΙ ΕΠΙΣΤΟΛΙΚΟΙ *et* ΕΠΙΣΤΟΛΙΜΑΙΟΙ ΧΑΡΑΚΤΗΡΕΣ (Leipzig: Teubner, 1910); text and translation of Ps-Libanius in Malherbe, *Ancient Epistolary Theorists*. On the authorship and date of this handbook, see J. Sykutris, "Proclus, Περὶ ἐπιστολιμαίου χαρακτῆρος," *Byzantinisch-Neugriechische Jahrbücher* 7 (1928–29) 108–18.
144 Weiss, *Primitive Christianity*, 1.349.
145 Loisy, "Les épîtres de Paul," 213; Windisch, *Der zweite Korintherbrief*, 8.
146 Ps.-Libanius *Ep. Char.* 19 in Malherbe, *Ancient Epistolary Theorists*, 68–69.
147 On the role of social function in determining the genre of ancient letters, see Stanley K. Stowers, "Social Typification and the Classification of Ancient Letters" in *The Social World of Formative Christianity and Judaism*, ed. P. Borgen and J. Neusner (Philadelphia: Fortress Press, 1988) 78–90; idem, *Letter-Writing*, 51–57.

γάρ μοι θεραπεύειν ἀεὶ τοὺς φίλους ἐστὶν ἤπερ λυπεῖν)."[148] The essential elements of this type of letter are as follows: 1) the writer and the recipient are friends; 2) the recipient has been grieved by the writer; 3) the writer is attempting to conciliate the recipient, so as to restore the relationship.[149]

Without entering here into the detailed exegesis that will be supplied later,[150] it is already clear how closely 2 Cor. 1:1–2:13; 7:5–16 corresponds to the therapeutic type of letter. Paul writes in order to conciliate the Corinthians in respect to "grief" (λύπη) which he has caused by his words and actions. Paul had promised to come to Corinth (1:15–16), but instead of paying the promised visit (1:23; 2:1), he had written a letter that caused the Corinthians considerable distress (2:3–4; 7:8). Among those who had been pained by Paul's epistle, there was one who suffered more than all the rest; indeed, there is now a danger that this one will be "overwhelmed by excessive sorrow" (2:7). Paul writes to conciliate all of the Corinthians; but he offers special instructions, and evidently feels a deeper concern, for one individual (2:7–8). That there should be so much pain in the relationship between Paul and the wrongdoer, pain given and pain received, and that Paul should work so hard to heal the breach, appealing for forgiveness, reconciliation and love, argues for a special friendship.

The discussions of pain that we have briefly consulted permit a final, concise inference regarding Paul's use of λύπη to describe the effect of the wrong: the offence would seem to fall into the category of the most serious kind of "slight," namely "insult." Aristotle specifies "injury" and "pain" as the effects of "insult."[151] It is worth quoting Aristotle's definition in full, because the modern understanding of "slight" and "insult" differs markedly from the ancient concepts. Aristotle explains: "He who insults (ὁ ὑβρίζων) another slights (ὀλιγωρεῖ) him; for insult (ὕβρις) consists in causing injury (βλάπτειν) or pain (λυπεῖν) whereby the sufferer is dis-

---

148 Ps. Libanius *Ep. Char.* 66 in Malherbe, *Ancient Epistolary Theorists*, 76–77. See also no. 107 (θεραπευτική) of the exempla found in certain codices of Ps.-Libanius in V. Weichert, *Demetrii et Libanii*, 62–63.
149 The analysis offered here follows the approach of Stowers, "Social Typification," 78–90. The essential elements of this social relationship are present in other conciliatory letters, e.g., Cicero *Fam.* 5.8; Apollonius of Tyana *Ep.* 45; Marcus Aurelius apud Philostratus *Vit. soph.* 2.1.562–63.
150 See ch. 6 below, pp. 464–72.
151 Aristotle *Rhet.* 2.2.5, 1378b; cf. 1373b38–1374a17. See the discussion of ὕβρις in Aristotle by Grimaldi, *Aristotle, Rhetoric II*, 28–29.

graced (αἰσχύνη ἐστὶ τῷ πασχόντι)."¹⁵² For our purposes, "slight," ὀλιγωρία, is better translated "contempt," whether through act or expression.¹⁵³ But the crucial term here is ὕβρις, which is a more serious offence in Paul's world than is suggested by "insult." ὕβρις is "insolence" that typically arises from the possession of wealth;¹⁵⁴ it is "degrading treatment," by which the powerful act out their sense of superiority over others.¹⁵⁵ Similarly, Plutarch realizes that it is "the suspicion of contempt or arrogance" that makes the wrongs and pains we suffer from others intolerable.¹⁵⁶ We may infer that the pain Paul experienced was the result of an "insult." The content of the insult and the context in which it took place remain to be determined. But the fact that Paul suffered λύπη as a result of the offence suggests that he was treated with contempt and was put to shame.

We may add a coda to our examination of Paul's use of λυπεῖν to describe the effect of the wrong: Paul's use of the perfect tense, λελύπηκεν, shows that the pain caused by the wrongdoer's action was still being felt at the time of composition of this epistle.¹⁵⁷ This is a necessary inference, because elsewhere in the epistle Paul uses the verbal tenses with such

---

152 Aristotle *Rhet.* 2.2.5, 1378b14–17, with the commentary of Grimaldi, *Aristotle, Rhetoric II*, 28–29. My translation modifies the LCL.
153 Aristotle *Rhet.* 2.2.3–4, 1378b10–1379a8; *Pol.* 1315a18. See the discussion of ὀλιγωρία in Grimaldi, *Aristotle, Rhetoric II*, 22, 26–27. Cf. LSJ 1216 s.v. ὀλιγωρία.
154 LSJ 1841 s.v. ὑβρίζω II, ὕβρις 1. G. Bertram, "ὕβρις," *TDNT* 8 (1972) 295–307, esp. 298, on violence of the rich against the poor. On wealth producing ὕβρις, see esp. Theognis 751; Euripides *fr.* 438; Aristophanes *Plut.* 563–64; Aristotle *Rhet.* 2.2.6, 1378b; 2.5, 1383a1–3; 2.16.1–4, 1390b32–34, 1391a18–19; *Eth. nic.* 4.3.1; Dio Chrysostom 76.7. See the discussion of ὕβρις in Kenneth James Dover, *Greek Popular Morality in the Time of Plato and Aristotle* (Oxford: Oxford University Press, 1974) 110–11; D. M. MacDowell, "Hybris in Athens," *Greece and Rome* 23 (1976) 16; Peter Marshall, *Enmity in Corinth: Social Conventions in Paul's Relations with the Corinthians* (Tübingen: Mohr Siebeck, 1987) 182–87; Ryan K. Balot, *Greed and Injustice in Classical Athens* (Princeton: Princeton University Press, 2001).
155 Aristotle *Rhet.* 2.2.5–6, 1378b, with the comments of Grimaldi, *Aristotle, Rhetoric II*, 32; see also *Rhet.* 1.13.10; *Eth. nic.* 4.3.21; 7.6.4. See the discussion in N. R. E. Fisher, "Hybris and Dishonor," *Greece and Rome* 23 (1976) 177–93, esp. 180, 182; idem, *Hybris. A Study in the Values of Honour and Shame in Ancient Greece* (Warminster: Aris and Phillips, 1992); Douglas Cairns, *"Hybris,* Dishonour, and Thinking Big," *JHS* 116 (1996) 1–32.
156 Plutarch *Mor.* 460D.
157 Windisch, *Der zweite Korintherbrief,* 84; Allo, *Saint Paul,* 59–60.

care to distinguish moments and stages in his ongoing relationship with the Corinthians, e. g. in 7:8.[158]

Moving closer to the epicenter of wrong, we come to the term by which Paul designates the respect in which the Corinthians have cleared themselves of guilt associated with the wrongdoer, namely, πρᾶγμα (7:11). In translations and commentaries, πρᾶγμα is rendered "matter" or "affair," and the word certainly has this very general meaning: thus, "the matter under discussion."[159] But πρᾶγμα has a special meaning in a legal context as "the matter of contention," "the subject of dispute."[160] In the papyri, πρᾶγμα ἔχειν πρός τινα is "to have a lawsuit with someone."[161] In Aristotle's analysis of the motives of injustice, τὸ πρᾶγμα designates the action of a wrongdoer which, unless it escapes detection, becomes the subject of a legal proceeding.[162] Especially significant is Paul's own use of πρᾶγμα in 1 Cor. 6:1 to speak of the "grievance" that leads one to seek redress in the public court.[163] All of this suggests that the wrong done to Paul was a serious matter of the sort that might have been the subject of a legal dispute.

We come, finally, to the term by which Paul refers to the offence: ἀδικεῖν/ἀδικεῖσθαι. It is entirely understandable that this term should have received the attention of scholars from Zahn to Thrall,[164] for it is Paul's only explicit mention of the injurious act. The history of research has disclosed that the verb has legal and financial connotations that are not immediately apparent to a modern reader.[165] Before we engage these findings and seek to sort out the implications, it is important to recognize that ἀδικεῖν, like λυπεῖν, has a broad meaning, and a generic usage

---

158 On the careful differentiation of tenses in 2 Cor.7:8 (ἐλύπησα...μεταμέλομαι...μετεμελόμην...), see Windisch, *Der zweite Korintherbrief*, 231; Harris, *Second Epistle*, 535–36. On the consequent difficulties of syntax, see Barrett, *Second Epistle*, 208–10; Furnish, *II Corinthians*, 387.
159 E.g., Plummer, *Second Epistle*, 223; Hughes, *Paul's Second Epistle*, 275. See also BDAG 858 s.v. πρᾶγμα 1.
160 BDAG 859 s.v. πρᾶγμα 4; Xenophon *Mem.* 2.9.1; Polyaenus 6.36; Josephus *C. Ap.* 2.177. Cf. Windisch, *Der zweite Korintherbrief*, 235–36.
161 E.g., *POxy.* 743, 19 [1 BC]; 706, 4; *BGU* I.22, 9; *PRyl.* II.113, 13; cf. Moulton and Milligan, *Vocabulary*, 532 s.v. πρᾶγμα 2; BDAG 859 s.v. πρᾶγμα 4.
162 Aristotle *Rhet.* 1.11.29–12.2, 1372a.
163 Krenkel, *Beiträge*, 305; Weiss, *Der erste Korintherbrief*, 146 n.1; Windisch, *Der zweite Korintherbrief*, 236.
164 Zahn, *Introduction*, 1.349; Krenkel, *Beiträge*, 305–306; Windisch, *Der zweite Korintherbrief*, 11, 238–39; Thrall, "The Offender and the Offence," 71–76.
165 Thrall, "The Offender and the Offence," 71–73.

in conciliatory epistles. The transitive ἀδικεῖν τινα is generally "to wrong someone," "to treat someone unjustly."[166] It is the counterpart in human affairs of "impiety" (ἀσεβεῖν) towards God, as shown by the broad, structural contrast drawn by Apollonius of Tyana in his 58th epistle.[167] Even Aristotle's definition of τὸ ἀδικεῖν, to which appeal is made by Zahn and Thrall, participates in this general sense, as becomes clear when the definition is read in context. At the beginning of his analysis of propositions used in accusation and defense, Aristotle defines what is meant by acting unjustly: "Let injustice, then, be defined as voluntarily causing injury contrary to the law" (῎Εστω δὴ τὸ ἀδικεῖν τὸ βλάπτειν ἑκόντα παρὰ τὸν νόμον).[168] That Aristotle does not intend to restrict the scope of ἀδικεῖν to legal violations is indicated by a clarification, which he introduces in the next sentence: by "law," νόμος, Aristotle means not only the particular, written laws by which cities are governed, but also the general, unwritten principles, whatever they may be, which are recognized by all (κοινὸν δὲ ὅσα ἄγραφα παρὰ πᾶσιν ὁμολογεῖσθαι).[169] When Aristotle later repeats the definition of "being wronged" (τὸ ἀδικεῖσθαι), the reference to law is omitted: "Being wronged is to suffer injustice at the hands of one who voluntarily inflicts it."[170] It is this general sense of ἀδικεῖν as "to hurt unjustly" which is found in philosophical discussions of the causes of grief and anger from Chrysippus to Plutarch.[171]

Evidently unnoticed by scholars of 2 Corinthians is the fact that ἀδικεῖν has an established usage in letters of the conciliatory style employed by Paul in 2 Cor. 1:1–2:13; 7:5–16. A textbook example of the conventional use of ἀδικεῖν in a conciliatory epistle is presented by the letter of

---

166 BDAG 20 s.v. ἀδικέω 1c. See, e.g., Aristotle *Rhet.* 1.10; Demosthenes *Or.* 21.129; Epictetus 3.24.81; Sir. 4:9; 13:3; 1 Cor. 6:7–8; 2 Cor. 7:2; Gal. 4:12; Phlm. 18; Matt. 20:13 Acts 25:10. Cf. Windisch, *Der zweite Korintherbrief*, 238.
167 Apollonius of Tyana *Ep.* 58 apud Philostratus *Vit. soph.* 1.361, 25: ἀσεβεῖς μὲν τὸν θεόν, ἀδικεῖς δὲ τὸν υἱόν.
168 Aristotle *Rhet.* 1.10.3, 1368b6; cf. Grimaldi, *Aristotle, Rhetoric I*, 229–30.
169 Aristotle *Rhet.* 1.10.3, 1368b7–9.
170 Aristotle *Rhet.* 1.13.5, 1373b27–28; cf. *Eth. nic.* 5.8, 1135b25–29.
171 Chrysippus in *SVF* III.395 = Stobaeus *Ecl.* 2.91.10; cf. Diogenes Laertius 7.113; Poseidonius fr. 155 apud Lactantius *Ir.* 17.33; Cicero *Tusc.* 4.21; Seneca *Ira* 1.12.2–5; cf. Lactantius *Ir.* 17.13; Plutarch *Mor.* 457C. See the discussion in Harris, *Restraining Rage*, 61–62; Konstan, *The Emotions of the Ancient Greeks*, 65–66.

Marcus Aurelius to his friend and former teacher Herodes Atticus.[172] In the portion of the letter preserved by Philostratus, the emperor assures his aggrieved friend of his good will, while deflecting his anger upon certain unnamed members of Herodes' household. Marcus counsels: "Do not regard yourself as unjustly treated (μηδὲ ἡγεῖσθαι ἀδικεῖσθαι), if after I detected the crimes of some of your household, I chastised them with a punishment as mild as possible."[173] Seeking to move his old friend toward reconciliation, Marcus urges: "But if I grieved you in anything, or am still grieving you (εἰ δέ τι λελύπηκα σε ἢ λυπῶ), demand reparations (ἀπαίτησον δίκας) from me in the temple of Athena in your city at the time of the Mysteries."[174]

The fifth pseudonymous epistle of Euripides is a conciliatory apology to his friend Cephisophon regarding Euripides' decision to leave Athens and accept the hospitality of king Archelaus of Macedon.[175] The decision has had an impact upon the circle of Euripides' comrades, and rumors have circulated regarding Euripides' motives.[176] Euripides writes to explain his departure from Athens, to justify his acceptance of gifts from Archelaus, and to heal the breach in his relations with his friends. Early in the letter, Euripides refers to "those who are wronging us" (τούτοις ἀδικήσαις ἡμᾶς) by allegations of covetousness.[177] Euripides assures his friends that his departure to Macedon has not altered his affection for them, nor diminished the benefits they may hope to receive from his friendship.[178] In closing, Euripides commends Cephisophon for writing to him on matters of importance, but then gently remonstrates with his friend: "but just as you did well in writing, you did wrong (ἀδικεῖν

---

172 Philostratus *Vit. soph.* 2.1.562–63; text and translation in *Philostratus and Eunapius: Lives of the Sophists*, ed. W. C. Wright (Cambridge, MA: Harvard University Press, 1968) 174–75. Philostratus states that he extracts from the letter only that which bears upon his narrative. All of Philostratus *Vit. soph.* 2.1.559–63 should be read as background.
173 Philostratus *Vit. soph.* 2.1.562.
174 Philostratus *Vit. soph.* 2.1.563.
175 Text and translation in Rudolf Hercher, *Epistolographi Graeci* (Paris: Didot, 1873) 277–79; H. U. Gösswein, *Die Briefe des Euripides* (Meisenheim am Glan: Hain, 1975). Cf. J. Sykutris, "Epistolographie," *RE* Suppl. 5 (1931) 211; Hans Josef Klauck, *Ancient Letters and the New Testament* (Waco: Baylor University Press, 2006) 116.
176 Ps.-Euripides *Ep.* 5.1–2, 4, Hercher, *Epistolographi Graeci*, 277–78.
177 Ps.-Euripides *Ep.* 5.2, Hercher, *Epistolographi Graeci*, 278.
178 Ps.-Euripides *Ep.* 5.6, Hercher, *Epistolographi Graeci*, 278–79.

σε), if you gave any support to the things spoken against us by those who are not worthy."[179]

An entirely characteristic usage of ἀδικεῖν in a conciliatory letter is found in the fifth pseudepigraphic epistle of Aristotle, addressed to his friend and successor as head of the Lyceum, Theophrastus.[180] The epistle begins as one might expect of an exchange between philosophers, that is, with a definition: "a present wrong" (ἡ πρόχειρος ἀδικία) is more easily treated than one that has rankled for a long time. The former may be calmed by a thoughtful word or gesture, but the treatment of an ancient enmity is compared to a doubtful passage through a roiling sea of "distress."[181] Thus, Aristotle declares, "it is necessary not to wrong (μὴ ἀδικεῖν) friends especially, not even on a reasonable pretext." The philosopher concludes with the concession that it is beyond the capacity of a human being to avoid doing wrong (τὸ μὴ ἀδικεῖν) altogether, but that it is a very good thing to bring someone who has erred to a place of safety and a calm mind.[182]

Other examples might be adduced,[183] but these suffice to demonstrate that a reference to "wrongdoing" was an established feature of the conciliatory epistle, and that the meaning of ἀδικεῖν in such letters tended to be rather general. Only in rare instances, where the historical circumstances happen to be known, or may be reconstructed from allusions in the text, is it possible to ascertain specifically of what the wrongdoing consisted. In the case of Marcus' letter to Herodes, the background is supplied by Philostratus' *Lives of the Sophists* and by a lengthy inscription recording a letter of Marcus Aurelius to the Athenians.[184] But we should not fail to notice that it is contrary to the purposes of a conciliatory epistle to dwell upon the details of the wrong whose hurt the writer seeks to assuage. We recall that in the model of a conciliatory letter sup-

---

179 Ps.-Euripides *Ep.* 5.6, Hercher, *Epistolographi Graeci*, 279.
180 Ps.-Aristotle *Ep.* 5; text and translation in Hercher, *Epistolographi Graeci*, 174; M. Plezia, *Aristotelis epistolarum fragmenta cum testament* (Warsaw: Academia Scientiarum Polona, 1968). Cf. Sykutris, "Epistolographie," 202; Klauck, *Ancient Letters*, 112–13.
181 Ps.-Aristotle *Ep.* 5, 3–8; Hercher, *Epistolographi Graeci*, 174.
182 Ps.-Aristotle *Ep.* 5, 10–13, Hercher, *Epistolographie Graeci*, 174.
183 E.g., Demosthenes *Ep.* 2.16; Apollonius of Tyana *Ep.* 46.
184 C. P. Jones, "A New Letter of Marcus Aurelius to the Athenians," *ZPE* 8 (1971) 161–83; G. H. R. Horsley, "Marcus Aurelius to the Athenians, Appeal for Reconciliation" in *NewDocs*, Vol. 4 (North Ryde: Macquarie University, 1987) 83–87. Cf. James H. Oliver, *Marcus Aurelius. Aspects of Civic and Cultural Policy in the East* (Princeton: Princeton University Press, 1970) 1–84.

plied by Libanius, the writer assures his friend, "if you were upset by what was said or done, I shall most certainly no longer mention what was said."[185] These observations are offered, not in order to deny that inferences may be drawn from Paul's use of ἀδικεῖν, but only as a reminder of the constraints upon knowledge imposed by the genre.

Now, to the implications of Paul's use of ἀδικεῖν and ἀδικεῖσθαι to refer to what an unnamed individual did and what he himself suffered. First, there is an undeniably legal aspect to the term, as Zahn pointed out long ago.[186] But it is important to determine, insofar as possible, in what this legal aspect consists, whether, that is, the action denoted by ἀδικεῖν is in itself a violation of law, or generally involves a legal context. Fortunately, a number of relevant texts, for the most part, those already cited by Zahn and Windisch, permit us to make a determination. In Sirach 4:9, the teacher instructs a student who is preparing for a legal vocation: "Rescue the one who is being wronged (ἀδικούμενον) from the hand of the one doing wrong (ἀδικοῦντος); and do not be faint-hearted in giving your verdict (ἐν τῷ κρίνειν σε)." In Acts 25:10, Paul seeks to have his trial transferred to a different venue, and thus explains to the Roman governor Festus: "I am appealing to Caesar's tribunal; this is where I should be tried. I have done no wrong (ἠδίκησα) to the Jews, as you very well know." The most relevant text is probably 1 Cor. 6:7–8, where Paul offers a final, evaluative comment on the tendency of some Christians in Corinth to have recourse to the civil courts to settle disputes: "In fact, to have lawsuits at all with one another is already a defeat for you"; then Paul asks, "Why not rather be wronged (ἀδικεῖσθε)? Why not rather be defrauded?" and observes, "But you yourselves wrong (ἀδικεῖτε) and defraud—and brothers at that!" These texts, and others that might have been cited,[187] already make clear that the action denoted by ἀδικεῖν and ἀδικεῖσθαι is not in itself a violation of law, an "illegal action," as Thrall would have it,[188] but an action which generally involves the parties in a legal context. In most cases, the one who was wronged turns to the court for redress; but in some cases, the wrongdoer seeks to exploit the court for his own advantage. It is because wrongdoing in a civil society generally involves the parties in a legal dispute that ὁ ἀδικήσας comes to mean "the accused" or "the culprit," and ὁ ἀδικηθείς "the

---

185 Ps.-Libanius *Ep. Char.* 66; Malherbe, *Ancient Epistolary Theorists*, 76–77.
186 Zahn, *Introduction*, 1.349; see further Windisch, *Der zweite Korintherbrief*, 238.
187 E.g., Gal. 4:12; 2 Cor. 7:2; BDAG 20 s.v. ἀδικέω 1c.
188 Thrall, "The Offender and the Offence," 73–74.

accuser" or "the victim" in legal terminology.[189] Returning to Aristotle's definitions of ἀδικεῖν and ἀδικεῖσθαι in the *Rhetoric*, we are reminded that his penetrating analysis of the motives of those who do wrong and the character of those who suffer from it is offered as instruction for forensic speakers who are preparing rhetorical arguments for the courts.[190]

Next, the verb ἀδικεῖν has a specialized meaning in a number of relevant instances: "to injure someone in a financial matter," "to cause a loss," "to defraud."[191] In Lev. 6:2–5 (LXX = 5:21–24), the verb is used of defrauding a neighbor. In *The Special Laws* (4.34), Philo deals with the case of a deposit entrusted to a friend, which is then stolen by thieves: if the thieves are not caught, the depository should not have to make good the theft, for this would have the absurd result that an innocent party who had committed no fraud (τὸν μηδὲν ἠδικηκότα) would be injured by a friend who had, in fact, been defrauded (ἀδικηθέντα) by others.[192] In Matt. 20:13, the vineyard owner replies to a laborer who expects more pay: "Friend, I am doing you no wrong (ἑταῖρε, οὐκ ἀδικῶ σε); did you not agree with me for the usual daily wage?" In Philemon 18–19, Paul assures Philemon that he will stand surety for the slave Onesimus: "If he has wronged you in any way or owes you anything (εἰ δέ τι ἠδίκησέν σε ἢ ὀφείλει), charge that to my account…I will repay it." In 1 Cor. 6:7–8, we recall, Paul connects "being wronged" (ἀδικεῖσθαι) with "being defrauded" (ἀποστερεῖσθαι) in expressing his disapproval of Christians engaged in civil litigation.

In a number of conciliatory letters, where the circumstances of the wrong happen to be known, or may be inferred, money is predictably at the root of things. In the case of Herodes Atticus, the "wrong" which Marcus did to his old friend was the judgment that he should make financial concessions to his fellow-Athenians in a dispute that had come before the emperor's court;[193] Herodes had evidently refused to honor his father's *fideicommissa* to the people of Athens.[194] In the

---

189 Rightly, Windisch, *Der zweite Korintherbrief*, 238; Aristotle *Eth. nic.* 5,2, 1129a33 on the ἄδικος as the "violator of law"; cf. Gottlob Schrenk, "ἄδικος," *TDNT* 1 (1964) 149–50.
190 This is the assumption throughout the discussion of ἀδικία in *Rhet.*1.10–14, see esp. 1.10.6.
191 BDAG 20 s.v. ἀδικέω 1c, 2; Windisch, *Der zweite Korintherbrief*, 238.
192 Philo *Spec.* 4.34; see the discussion of this text in Thrall, "The Offender and the Offence," 73.
193 Philostratus *Vit. soph.* 2.1.550–61.
194 Oliver, *Marcus Aurelius*, 27.

fifth pseudonymous epistle of Euripides, the "wrong" consisted of an allegation that Euripides had failed to distribute to his friends and comrades any of the money given to him by king Archelaus, on account of his covetousness.[195] In the conciliatory epistle of Apollonius of Tyana to Hestiaeus, the misunderstanding between the philosopher and his brother is said to be "on the point of money."[196] In the letter to his "best and dearest" Apollonius, Chairemon alludes to the possibility that his friend and business partner has withheld some of the profits from his estates;[197] Chairemon had evidently given voice to this suspicion in a previous letter;[198] now he writes to apologize, and at the same time, assures his friend that he is "neither unjust (ἄδικος) nor desirous of what belongs to others."[199] In light of the regularity with which ἀδικεῖν implies an injury in a financial matter, we are entitled to ask whether money was not somehow involved in the wrong done to Paul.[200]

A summary of what we have learned from an examination of ἀδικεῖν and ἀδικεῖσθαι would fairly state that the evidence does not support the hypothesis of Thrall, that the wrong took the form of a theft of money entrusted to Paul by a third party.[201] The meaning of ἀδικεῖν is too broad, and the usage of the term too generic, to warrant such a specific conclusion. Nevertheless, the general and special meanings of ἀδικεῖν, taken together, permit two inferences: the wrong involved Paul and a Corinthian Christian in a legal dispute, and a fraudulent use of money was somehow a factor. It remains to be determined in what legal context Paul and the wrongdoer participated, whether before a civic court or in a quasi-judicial proceeding within the church. Nor is it yet clear in what sense money was involved in the injurious act, that is, whether someone was actually defrauded, or an allegation was made of financial misconduct. We must hope that a widening of the textual basis beyond 2 Cor. 2 and 7 will eventually allow us to answer these questions.

---

195 Ps.-Euripides *Ep.* 5.3–4; Hercher, *Epistolographi Graeci*, 278.
196 Apollonius of Tyana *Ep.* 35 and 45; cf. Philostratus *Vit. soph.* 1.18; 3.33; 8.2. See the commentary on *Ep.* 35 and 45 by Robert Penella, *The Letters of Apollonius of Tyana. A Critical Text with Prolegomena, Translation and Commentary* (Leiden: Brill, 1979) 48–51, 62–65.
197 *BGU* II.531; Olsson, *Papyrusbriefe*, no. 43, p. 128.
198 *BGU* I.248; Olsson, *Papyrusbriefe*, no. 41, p. 122.
199 *BGU* II.531, Col. I. 11, 13, 21; Col. II. 21–22; Olsson, *Papyrusbriefe*, 128–29.
200 So, already, Windisch, *Der zweite Korintherbrief*, 238–39.
201 Thrall, "The Offender and the Offence," 74–76; idem, *Second Epistle*, 1.68–69, 171, 495.

Looking back over all of the terms that Paul uses to refer to the affair of the wrongdoer—that is, χαρίζεσθαι, ἐπιτιμία, λυπεῖν, πρᾶγμα, and ἀδικεῖν, we may draw all our inferences together in the form of a working hypothesis: Paul was wronged by a member of the Corinthian church; the majority of the Corinthians were complicit in the injurious act; the wrongdoer was a person of high social status, and had enjoyed a friendship with the apostle; Paul experienced the wrong as a contemptuous insult; the offence involved Paul and the wrongdoer in a legal dispute, in which a fraudulent use of funds was somehow a factor.

We should acknowledge that our additive approach contrasts with the method employed by a number of scholars who insist upon making distinctions, assuming that if the act were an "unjust injury," it could not, at the same time, have been an "insult."[202] But this assumption is exploded by attentive reading of Aristotle's analysis of injustice, for Aristotle perceives that "insult" (ὕβρις) is often the concomitant of "injustice" (ἀδικία) and "injury" (βλάβη); whether it is or not is a question of the offender's purpose.[203] Ben Sira makes the realistic and poignant observation: "A rich man does wrong (ἠδίκησεν), and even adds insults; a poor man suffers wrong (ἠδίκηται), and must add apologies" (Sirach 13:3). An advantage of our additive approach is that it permits inferences derived from one term to complement, or qualify, as the case may be, inferences derived from another. We offer a final example from Aristotle: analyzing the frame of mind of those who commit wrong, Aristotle observes, "Men who commit wrong think that they are most likely to be able to do so with impunity, if they are eloquent, business-like, experienced in judicial trials, if they have many friends, and if they are wealthy."[204] It will be recalled that our conclusion regarding the social status of the wrongdoer was based upon analysis of λυπεῖν; that inference is reinforced and confirmed by the study of ἀδικεῖν.

---

202 Zahn, *Introduction*, 1.349; Kümmel, *Introduction*, 198; Thrall, "The Offender and the Offence," 72; idem, *Second Epistle*, 1.67.
203 Aristotle *Rhet.* 1.13.10, 1374a; 2.2.5, 1378b; 2.2.12, 1379a; Grimaldi, *Aristotle, Rhetoric II*, 28–29.
204 Aristotle *Rhet.* 1.12.2, 1372a; Grimaldi, *Aristotle, Rhetoric I*, 269–70.

2 Cor. 10–13

We may now seek to widen the textual basis beyond 2 Cor. 2 and 7, in our search for clues to the identity of the offender and the nature of his offence. In this undertaking, 2 Cor. 10–13 has a special importance. In agreement with a hypothesis that goes back to Adolf Hausrath,[205] we identify 2 Cor. 10–13 with the "letter of tears" mentioned by Paul in 2 Cor. 2:3–4. Certainly no other portion of the Corinthian correspondence seems to reflect so exactly that state of mind which Paul discloses in 2:4; for the tone of 2 Cor. 10–13 alternates between belligerence and weakness, confidence and woundedness, anger and grief. There are moments of bitter resentment, as when Paul "boasts" that he had received no financial support from the Corinthians (in 11:7–11), and moments of profound self-abnegation, as when Paul concedes that he was too "weak" to discipline the Corinthians (in 11:16–21). One can well imagine that the letter preserved in these four chapters was written "out of much affliction and anguish of heart, through many tears" (2:4).

Moreover, the state of the relationship between Paul and the Corinthians reflected in chs. 10–13 corresponds remarkably well with that which we have reconstructed through exegesis of chs. 2 and 7. We recall that the Corinthians had "repented" of their involvement in the wrong done to Paul (7:9–10). Among the signs of the Corinthians' "godly grief" were "eagerness to clear" themselves, "indignation," and "fear" (7:11). Titus had reported the "longing, mourning, and zeal" of the Corinthians on Paul's behalf (7:7). Paul takes care not to mention the precise nature of the Corinthians' guilt in his conciliatory epistle, so as not to cause further grief.[206] But the matter in which the Corinthians were complicit must have been very serious, because it led Paul to endure a prolonged absence from Corinth and to write an anguished "letter of tears" (1:23–2:4). It was the purpose of Paul's severe epistle not only to bring about the Corinthians' repentance (7:9), but also to provoke the Corinthians' "zeal" on behalf of Paul's apostleship (7:12), a zeal

---

205 Hausrath, *Der Vier-Capitel-Brief des Paulus*; see, more recently, Watson, "Paul's Painful Letter," 324–46; Welborn, "The Identification of 2 Corinthians 10–13 with the 'Letter of Tears'," 138–53.
206 In keeping with the aims of a conciliatory epistle, according to Ps.-Libanius *Ep. Char.* 66; Malherbe, *Ancient Epistolary Theorists*, 76–77; cf. Welborn, "The Identification of 2 Corinthians 10–13 with the 'Letter of Tears'," 146–47.

that had evidently not been manifested on the occasion of Paul's last visit to Corinth.[207]

Turning now to chs. 10–13, we find that the relationship between Paul and the Corinthians is just as painful as chs. 1–2 and 7 have led us to expect, except that the conflict seems to be in an earlier, more contentious stage, without any signs of remorse. To echo the warlike imagery that Paul uses in the first paragraph of ch. 10,[208] the Corinthians are in open revolt against their apostle: they have thrown up a "stronghold" of arguments (10:4); behind a "towering fortress" of mutinous thoughts (10:5), they harbor questions about the legitimacy of Paul's apostleship—whether Paul "belongs to Christ" (10:7), whether "Christ is speaking" in him (13:3).[209] The Corinthians have compared Paul with certain other apostles (10:12–13), and have found him wanting in a number of respects: Paul is untrained in speech and deficient in knowledge (11:4–6);[210] his manner of supporting himself betrays a lack of confidence in his rights as an apostle (11:7–11);[211] he lacks the authority which other apostles possess to impose discipline upon the unruly (11:16–21a).[212] Because Paul does not manifest the signs of an apostle, the Corinthians have challenged Paul to "commend himself" (12:11–

---

207 Windisch, *Der zweite Korintherbrief*, 228; Bruce, *1 and 2 Corinthians*, 218.
208 Abraham J. Malherbe, "Antisthenes and Odysseus, and Paul at War," *HTR* 76 (1983) 143–73; Laurie Brink, "A General's Exhortation to his Troops: Paul's Military Rhetoric in 2 Cor. 10:1–11," *BZ* 49 (2005) 191–201; 50 (2006) 74–89; Raymond F. Collins, *The Power of Images in Paul* (Minneapolis: Liturgical Press, 2008) 170–71.
209 On the issue of Paul's legitimacy (δοκιμή) in 2 Cor. 10–13, see, in general, Ernst Käsemann, "Die Legitimität des Apostels," *ZNW* 41 (1942) 33–71; Betz, *Der Apostel Paulus*, 56–57, 67–68, 99–100, 132–37; more specifically, D. W. Oostendorp, *Another Jesus. A Gospel of Jewish-Christian Superiority in II Corinthians* (Kampen: Kok, 1967) 19; Margaret E. Thrall, "Super-Apostles, Servants of Christ, and Servants of Satan," *JSNT* 6 (1980) 42–57, esp. 54.
210 For a summary of views on this text, see Martin, *2 Corinthians*, 342–43; see further Bruce W. Winter, *Philo and Paul among the Sophists: Alexandrian and Corinthian Responses to a Julio-Claudian Movement*, 2nd ed. (Grand Rapids: Eerdmans, 2002) 184, 223–28.
211 Betz, *Der Apostel Paulus*, 100–102; Ronald F. Hock, *The Social Context of Paul's Ministry: Tentmaking and Apostleship* (Philadelphia: Fortress Press, 1980) 56–60, 64; Furnish, *II Corinthians*, 506–508.
212 Plummer, *Second Epistle*, 317; Windisch, *Der zweite Korintherbrief*, 348–49; Bachmann, *Der zweite Brief*, 381; Hughes, *Paul's Second Epistle*, 401; Watson, "Paul's Painful Letter," 343–44; Thrall, *Second Epistle*, 2.720–21.

12), a requirement which Paul regards as unprincipled boasting (11:21b, 30; 12:1, 5–6), and treats ironically (11:21b-12:10).²¹³

Behind the searing polemic of these chapters lies an incident, which is never described, but whose outline one is nevertheless able to trace. As one would expect of the exigence of a discourse,²¹⁴ the incident is alluded to in the exordium (10:1–6) and in the peroration (13:5–10): in the final verse of the former (10:6), Paul speaks of a "disobedience" (παρακοή) which he is "ready to punish";²¹⁵ in the latter (13:7), recapitulating, but at the same time, looking hopefully forward, Paul prays that the Corinthians "may not do anything wrong" (μὴ ποιῆσαι κακὸν μηδέν).²¹⁶ It is this "disobedience," this "wrong," which has evoked the discussion of Paul's authority to punish that dominates the opening and closing paragraphs of the letter.²¹⁷ In 10:1–11, Paul warns the Corinthians that, despite his appearance of weakness and gentleness (10:1), he is prepared to inflict punishment upon them when he next comes to Corinth (10:6, 11). Paul wishes that he would not have to show such hostility (10:2), and would prefer to wait until the Corinthians have turned fully to obedience (10:6); but he is armed with weapons of the spirit (10:3–5), and is prepared to use them, if necessary, against those who remain obdurate (10:6). Those who doubt Paul's authority to punish (10:8) are given to understand that what Paul threatens by letter when absent (10:9), he will do when present (10:11). In 13:1–4, looking toward his impending visit to Corinth, Paul warns the congregation that he will punish those who have not repented when he returns. Paul reminds the Corinthians that he had issued this warning previously, on the occasion of his second visit: "If I come again, I will not be lenient" (13:2). In closing the letter, Paul explains that he has written these things to the Corinthians while ab-

---

213 Windisch, *Der zweite Korintherbrief*, 316; Betz, *Der Apostel Paulus*, 67, 72–73, 82–85, 89–95; Josef Zmijewski, *Der Stil der paulinischen 'Narrenrede': Analyse der Sprachgestaltung in 2 Kor 11,1–12,10 als Beitrag zur Methodik von Stiluntersuchungen neutestamentlicher Texte* (Bonn: Hanstein, 1972) 234–35.
214 On rhetorical exigence, see Lloyd F. Bitzer, "The Rhetorical Situation," *Philosophy and Rhetoric* 1 (1968) 1–14. On the *stasis* of 2 Cor. 10–13, see Brian K. Peterson, *Eloquence and the Proclamation of the Gospel in Corinth* (Atlanta: Scholars Press, 1998).
215 On the parallels between 2 Cor. 10:1–10 (the *exordium*) and 13:1–10 (the *peroration*), see H.-G. Sundermann, *Der schwache Apostel und die Kraft der Rede: Eine rhetorische Analyse von 2 Kor 10–13* (Frankfurt: Lang, 1996) 47.
216 Plummer, *Second Epistle*, 274; Furnish, *II Corinthians*, 461, 578.
217 Watson, "Paul's Painful Letter," 343–44.

sent, so that when he next comes to Corinth, he will not have to be "severe" in using the "authority" that the Lord has given him (13:10).

Without entering here into the detailed exegesis that will be supplied later, it is already possible to discern something about the incident that underlies 2 Cor. 10–13 and its consequences for Paul and the Corinthians: on the occasion of Paul's second visit to Corinth, there was an affront to Paul so serious that it sufficed to call into question his apostolic legitimacy.[218] About the precise nature of the offence, much remains to be determined. But it is clear that Paul regarded the insult as an act of "disobedience" (παρακοή) and a "wrong" (κακόν) that merited punishment. Indeed, Paul issued a threat on that occasion that he would inflict punishment when he returned to Corinth: "If I come again, I will not spare" (13:7). Yet, it is also clear that Paul failed to punish anyone when he was present and had the opportunity to do so. Paul presents his failure to inflict punishment as an act of leniency (10:1; 13:7),[219] a reprieve to allow the Corinthians to turn to obedience (10:6). But from the Corinthians' point of view, Paul's reluctance to inflict punishment must have seemed evidence of "weakness," the final and decisive proof that Paul lacked the authority that should characterize an apostle.[220] It is for this reason that Paul is repeatedly obliged to take up the charge of "weakness" in chs. 10–13 (10:1, 10; 11:21; 13:3–4, 9) and to argue, paradoxically, that "weakness" is the form in which the power of Christ is revealed, and the mode of existence of Christ's true apostle (11:21b-12:10, esp. 11:29, 30; 12:5, 9–10).[221] Enough has been said so that it

---

218 Ewald, *Sendschreiben*, 226–27; Schmiedel, *Hand-Commentar*, 221; Plummer, *Second Epistle*, xvi, xviii, 55, 225; Weiss, *Primitive Christianity*, 1.342–43; Bultmann, *Der zweite Brief*, 51; Bruce, *1 and 2 Corinthians*, 164; Watson, "Paul's Painful Letter," 340, 343.
219 Donald Dale Walker, *Paul's Offer of Leniency (2 Cor. 10:1): Populist Ideology and Rhetoric in a Pauline Letter Fragment* (Tübingen: Mohr Siebeck, 2002) 318–19 and passim.
220 Weiss, *Primitive Christianity*, 1.343; Watson, "Paul's Painful Letter," 343–45. On the judgment that Paul is "weak" in 2 Cor. 10:10, see Betz, *Der Apostel Paulus*, 53, 96. On the possibility that the expression ὡς ὅτι ἡμεῖς ἠσθενήκαμεν in 2 Cor. 11:21 reflects what the Corinthians have been saying about Paul (interpreting ὅτι as recitative), see Windisch, *Der zweite Korintherbrief*, 348; Barrett, *Second Epistle*, 533 n.23; Thrall, *Second Epistle*, 2.719–20.
221 Betz, *Der Apostel Paulus*, 96, 140; Watson, "Paul's Painful Letter," 345; Scott B. Andrews, "Too Weak Not to Lead: The Form and Function of 2 Cor. 11:23b-33," *NTS* 41 (1995) 263–76; Jan Lambrecht, "Strength in Weakness," *NTS* 43 (1997) 285–90.

is clear that the situation underlying chs. 10–13 is very much the same as that presupposed in chs. 1–2 and 7, except that, in the latter chapters, we see the event at a later stage, after the Corinthians have repented.[222]

In widening the textual basis of our inquiry beyond 2 Cor. 2 and 7, we will be seeking places in chs. 10–13 where the offender and the offence are prefigured, or, more accurately, where they are already present, but in a manner corresponding to the earlier, conflicted stage in the relationship between Paul and the Corinthians. An analogy may be helpful: just as we may come across a glove or a hat in our house, and from these items surmise something about the person who inadvertently left them, and may eventually return to reclaim what he has forgotten, so we may discover in chs. 10–13 words and phrases that point forward to the wrongdoer of chs. 2 and 7, and may infer from these that he has been present. The phenomenon that we will be analyzing is, thus, the counterpart of the "cross-references" that J. H. Kennedy discovered in the text of 2 Corinthians at the turn of the twentieth century.[223] Kennedy demonstrated that in a number of passages in chs. 1–2 and 7 Paul is clearly referring back to what he had earlier written in chs. 10–13, in some cases echoing the same words, and in others employing euphemisms. To cite only one example, in 13:2 Paul had threatened, "if I come again, I will not spare (οὐ φείσομαι)," then in 1:23 Paul explains, "it was to spare (φειδόμενος) you that I did not come again to Corinth." Kennedy noticed that, in every instance, the action or feeling which in chs. 10–13 is described as present or future, in chs. 1–2 and 7 is regarded as belonging to the past.[224] Kennedy further observed that these backward references have the effect of conferring upon the harsh words and feelings of chs. 10–13 a new, therapeutic significance.[225] In our investigation, we will be reversing the polarity of this textual phenomenon, searching for words and phrases in chs. 10–13 that harshly anticipate Paul's conciliatory style in chs. 1–2 and 7. As we have already acknowledged, this procedure assumes the hypothesis that the "letter of tears" should be identified with 2 Cor. 10–13. Regarding chs. 10–13 as the severe epistle, whose painful effect Paul seeks to conciliate in chs. 1–2 and 7, we dis-

---

222 Weiss, *Primitive Christianity*, 1.345–46; Watson, "Paul's Painful Letter," 346.
223 Kennedy, "Are There Two Epistles in 2 Corinthians?" 233–36, 294–300; idem, *Second and Third Epistles*.
224 Kennedy, *Second and Third Epistles*, 63–68, 79–94; followed by Lake, *Earlier Epistles*, 57–58.
225 Kennedy, *Second and Third Epistles*, 99–100.

cover additional information about the offender and the offence in several areas.

In a number of passages in 2 Cor. 10–13, Paul seems to refer to an individual by means of singular pronouns, in most instances the same indefinite and correlative pronouns, namely, τις and τοιοῦτος, used in reference to the wrongdoer in 2:5–11. If 2 Cor. 10–13 is rightly identified with the "painful epistle," it would seem likely that some of the pronouns in these chapters should refer to the wrongdoer. In a perceptive essay published at the end of the nineteenth century, Karl König already detected the wrongdoer behind ὁ τοιοῦτος in 10:11, who is given to understand that Paul will carry out his threat to punish.[226] Johannes Weiss pursued this insight in his reconstruction of the events underlying 2 Cor. 10–13.[227] More recently, Francis Watson posited that the offender is referred to as τις in 10:7, who is confident that he belongs to Christ, and as ὁ τοιοῦτος in 10:11; Watson also called attention to the third person singular verb φησίν in 10:10, which quotes an opinion derogatory of Paul.[228] These are not the only instances of singular pronouns and singular verb-forms in chs. 10–13.[229] But each case must be evaluated inde-

---

226 König, "Verkehr," 481–554, esp. 514–16.
227 Weiss, *Primitive Christianity*, 1.342–44. Barrett ("ΑΔΙΚΗΣΑΣ," 115; idem, *Second Epistle*, 256, 260) also argues in favor of understanding 2 Cor. 10:7, 10, 11 as references to a particular individual.
228 Watson, "Paul's Painful Letter," 345–46: "In x.7–11, τινας (x.2) has been replaced by τις (x.7) or ὁ τοιοῦτος (x.11), which correspond exactly to ii.5 ff., where the offender is referred to as τις (ii.5) or τῷ τοιούτῳ (ii.6). Evidently this individual is the leader of a group of rebels (τινας, x.2) within the congregation (cf. also the third person singular in φησίν, x.10)." Similarly, Hans-Josef Klauck, *2. Korintherbrief* (Würzburg: Echter, 1986) 79; Lars Aejmelaeus, *Streit und Versöhnung. Das Problem der Zusammensetzung des 2. Korintherbriefes* (Helsinki: Finnish Exegetical Society, 1987) 197; David G. Horrell, *The Social Ethos of the Corinthian Correspondence. Interests and Ideology from 1 Corinthians to 1 Clement* (Edinburgh: T & T Clark, 1996) 308–309; Peterson, *Eloquence and the Proclamation of the Gospel*, 48–51, 72. Most recently, Margaret M. Mitchell, "The Corinthian Correspondence and the Birth of Pauline Hermeneutics" in *Paul and the Corinthians: Studies on a Community in Conflict. Essays in Honour of Margaret Thrall*, ed. T. J. Burke and J. K. Elliott (Leiden: Brill, 2003) 34: "The picture we can reconstruct from these terms [φόβος and ἐδίκησις in 7:11] is that some single person, probably the voice behind φησίν in 10:10 (and τις in 10:7 and τοιοῦτος in 10:11) who had done Paul an injustice (ὁ ἀδικήσας versus ὁ ἀδικηθείς in 7:12), had been punished."; Roetzel, *2 Corinthians*, 99–100.
229 2 Cor. 10:18; 11:4, 16, 20; 12:6.

pendently, because it may be nothing more than a way of expressing a generalization.[230] A complicating factor is the Corinthians' demand that Paul demonstrate the legitimacy of his apostleship by comparing himself with other apostles. In some cases, a singular pronoun or a singular participle may refer to one of these rival missionaries. But where the context makes it clear that a specific individual is intended, and that this individual is a Corinthian, it is appropriate to ask whether Paul might be referring to the wrongdoer. Analysis of such passages promises to disclose new insights into the values of the wrongdoer and his attitude toward Paul.

An observation on the structure of Paul's discourse in chs. 10–13 permits us to make some distinctions among Paul's uses of the pronouns. One might expect that references to the Corinthians would be concentrated at the beginning and the end of the letter, in the exordium (10:1–6) and proposition (10:7–11) of the former, and in the exhortation (12:14–13:4) and peroration (13:5–10) of the latter; for in these sections Paul is concerned with his relationship to his readers and the occasion of the epistle.[231] By contrast, one would expect to find fewer pronouns referring to the Corinthians in the argumentative sections of the epistle (10:12–12:13), where Paul defends the legitimacy of his apostleship through ironic comparison with other apostles. When singular pronouns and singular verb-forms are encountered in the "proofs" section of Paul's argument, we may reasonably ask whether such cases refer to a rival missionary whose credentials as an apostle the Corinthians regard as fully established.[232]

Paul's assault upon the rebellious congregation in the opening paragraphs of ch. 10 unfolds in three stages, like concentric circumvallations, corresponding to the loci of opposition. At the outset, Paul addresses all of the Corinthians, designated by the second person plural pronoun (ὑμεῖς), and alludes to a lowly estimate they have formed of his behavior and person (10:1). But before a verse has passed, Paul counters a group of "some" (τινες) who bring a more serious charge against his apostleship, questioning the spiritual basis of his existence (10:2). Breaking through the "fortification" of the faction opposed to his apostleship (10:3–6),

---

230 Note the caution expressed by Furnish, *II Corinthians*, 466, 468, referring to the generalized meaning of εἰ τις in Rom. 8:9b; 1 Cor. 3:12; Phil. 3:4, and the general sense of φησίν ("one says") in Hellenistic Greek.
231 Furnish, *II Corinthians*, 459, calling attention to the emphatic ὑμῶν in 2 Cor. 10:6; Sundermann, *Der schwache Apostel*, 45, 47.
232 Barrett, "ΑΔΙΚΗΣΑΣ," 115; Betz, *Der Apostel Paulus*, 13.

Paul confronts the ringleader of the resistance, a single individual, designated by the pronouns τις (10:7) and τοιοῦτος (10:11); indeed, we hear the voice of the rebel leader, through a direct quotation of his negative estimate of Paul's presence and discourse in 10:10, and we hear Paul's menacing response to "such a person" in 10:11. The organization of Paul's polemical apology places a single individual at the center of a community which, as a whole, is portrayed as opposed to Paul. We must assume that this individual shares the derogatory opinions about Paul attributed to the Corinthians generally in 10:1, and to "some" of the Corinthians in 10:2. Thus an attempt to reconstruct the attitudes of the wrongdoer must take account not only of the judgment implicit in 10:7 and the direct quotation in 10:10, but must also assess the invective of 10:1–6.[233]

2 Cor. 10:1–11

Paul opens his polemical apology[234] by countering a judgment which he evidently attributes to all of the Corinthians: "I who am humble when face to face with you, but bold toward you when I am away" (10:1). The conventional translation of the key terms in this sentence—"humble" and "bold"—cannot fail to confuse the modern reader and obscure the point at issue.[235] Two thousand years after the revolution of values that accompanied the rise of Christianity, "humility" is generally seen as a virtue, indeed, the quintessential feature of Christian ethics.[236] But

---

233 Watson, "Paul's Painful Letter," 345–46; Walker, *Paul's Offer of Leniency*, 258–59, 318–22.
234 Hans Dieter Betz, *II Corinthians 10–13 and the Socratic Tradition* (Claremont: Center for Hermeneutical Studies, 1970); idem, *Der Apostel Paulus*, esp. 13–42; Georgi, *Opponents of Paul*, 336–37; John T. Fitzgerald, "Paul, the Ancient Epistolary Theorists, and 2 Corinthians 10–13" in *Greeks, Romans, and Christians*, ed. D. L. Balch (Minneapolis: Fortress Press, 1990) 190–200; David E. Aune, "Corinthians, Second Letter to the" in *The Westminster Dictionary of New Testament and Early Christian Literature* (Louisville: Westminster John Knox, 2003) 115–117.
235 Windisch, *Der zweite Korintherbrief*, 292.
236 Adolf von Harnack, "Sanftmut, Huld und Demut in der alten Kirche" in *Festgabe für Julius Kaftan zu seinen 70. Geburtstag*, ed. A. Titius (Tübingen: Mohr Siebeck, 1920) 113–29; R. Leivestad, "ΤΑΠΕΙΝΟΣ – ΤΑΠΕΙΝΟΦΡΩΝ," *NovT* 8 (1966) 36–47; W. Grundmann, "ταπεινός," *TDNT* 8 (1972) 18–19; Francesco D'Agostino, *Epieikeia. Il tema dell' equita nell' antichità greca* (Milan: Giuffrè, 1973) 159.

the word translated "humble," ταπεινός, is used here strictly in its pre-Christian sense of "lowly," "servile," "submissive."[237] That this is the case is evident from the attitude with which it is immediately contrasted, θαρρεῖν, which is "to be confident," "to be courageous,"[238] and from the fact that ταπεινός is glossed by ἀσθενής, "weak," and ἐξουθενημένος, "contemptible," when the judgment upon Paul is formulated more explicitly and at greater length in 10:10.[239] Moreover, the structure of the sentence in 10:1–2 makes clear that, in describing himself as ταπεινός, Paul is taking up the language of others, rather than speaking for himself: the relative clause in which the judgment ταπεινός is embedded (ὅς κατὰ πρόσωπον μὲν ταπεινὸς ἐν ὑμῖν, κτλ.) interrupts the appeal begun in 10:1, "I beseech you" (παρακαλῶ ὑμᾶς), and resumed in 10:2, "I ask you" (δέομαι), in order to give, parenthetically, the reason why an entreaty is necessary.[240] How serious and problematic the charge of being ταπεινός appeared to Paul is indicated by the fact that he twice recurs to the point in the discourse that follows—in 11:7, recalling the conditions of his subsistence in Corinth, and in 12:21, fearing what might happen when he returns.[241]

Because the quality denoted by ταπεινός is so remote from the modern sense of "humble," it is necessary to examine some of the usages, if we would understand the estimation of Paul embodied in this term. As an attitude and behavior, ταπεινός describes the quality of being "pliant," "submissive," "cringing," "abject."[242] It is the attitude required of Andromache, wife of Hector, when she has become a slave after the fall of Troy, and is warned by her new mistress Hermione, "Instead of your former haughty spirit, you must now crouch low abased (ταπεινή) and grovel

---

237 BDAG 989 s.v. ταπεινός 1, 2; Grundmann, "ταπεινός," 1–2; Barrett, *Second Epistle*, 247; Furnish, *II Corinthians*, 456.
238 Windisch, *Der zweite Korintherbrief*, 292; Furnish, *II Corinthians*, 456.
239 Heinrici, *Der zweite Brief*, 312, 317; Plummer, *Second Epistle*, 273; Bachmann, *Der zweite Brief*, 342; Windisch, *Der zweite Korintherbrief*, 293; Lietzmann, *An die Korinther I/II*, 140; see the discussion in Thrall, *Second Epistle*, 2.602–604.
240 Windisch, *Der zweite Korintherbrief*, 293–94; Hughes, *Paul's Second Epistle*, 348; Furnish, *II Corinthians*, 456.
241 Barrett, *Second Epistle*, 247; Furnish, *II Corinthians*, 456; cf. Windisch, *Der zweite Korintherbrief*, 334.
242 BDAG 989 s.v. ταπεινός 1, 2; Grundmann, "ταπεινός," *TDNT* 8 (1972) 2; see esp. Xenophon *Mem.* 3.10.5: "self-abasement and servility" (καὶ τὸ ταπεινόν τε καὶ ἀνελεύθερον); Plato *Leg.* 728E: τὰ δὲ ταπεινάς τε καὶ ἀνελευθέρους ("lowly and servile").

at my knee."²⁴³ In Xenophon's dialogue *Hiero*, the despot explains that "the needier the people are, the more submissive (ταπεινότεροι) he finds them to be."²⁴⁴ Aristotle characterizes those who are capable of living at the will of another as "servile" (θητικοί) and "submissive" (ταπεινοί), and categorizes their behavior as "slavish" (δουλικόν).²⁴⁵ In the face of danger or adverse circumstances, one who is ταπεινός exhibits an abject spirit.²⁴⁶

In applying the term ταπεινός to Paul, the Corinthians express the judgment that Paul behaves submissively, in a cringing and abject manner, when he is face to face with them, but shows a boldness born of confidence, when he is at a distance.²⁴⁷ The occasion for the formulation of this judgment was, most immediately, Paul's behavior on his second visit to Corinth, when he suffered an affront to his apostolic dignity, and was unable, or unwilling, to respond to the offence.²⁴⁸ It is this humiliating experience that Paul recalls in 12:20–21, as he anticipates, with considerable apprehension, his impending third visit to Corinth.²⁴⁹ Paul expresses his fear, "lest, when I come, my God should humiliate me again (πάλιν...ταπεινώσῃ με) in your presence" (12:20).²⁵⁰ It is important to notice that vss. 20 and 21 are constructed in parallel.²⁵¹ Thus, although vs. 20 is presented as an anxious anticipation of what may happen in the future, it is likely that Paul is already recollecting the painful experience of his previous visit, as he clearly is in vs. 21, where he countenances the possibility of being "again humiliated." In vs. 20 Paul voices the fear that, when he comes, neither he nor the Corinthians will find each other to be what they wish. Paul fears that among the Corinthians he will find "strife, jealousy, angry outbursts, intrigues, slanders, whisperings, arrogant opinions, disorders."²⁵² This is no mere "vice catalogue," as

---

243 Euripides *Andr.* 164–65; Grundmann, "ταπεινός," 8.2.
244 Xenophon *Hier.* 5.4; LSJ 1757 s.v. ταπεινός 2. See also Herodotus 7.14; Euripides *fr.* 716; Aristophanes *Pr.* 322; Xenophon *Anab.* 2.5.13.
245 Aristotle *Eth. nic.* 4.3, 1125a2–3.
246 Josephus *B.J.* 1.312–13.
247 Cf. Arthur J. Dewey, "A Matter of Honor: A Socio-Historical Analysis of 2 Corinthians 10," *HTR* 78 (1985) 209–17.
248 Weiss, *Primitive Christianity*, 1.343.
249 Weiss, *Primitive Christianity*, 1.342, 343.
250 Construing πάλιν with ταπεινώσῃ, rather than ἐλθόντος: thus, Plummer, *Second Epistle*, 369; Hughes, *Paul's Second Epistle*, 472 n.166; Barrett, *Second Epistle*, 330; Furnish, *II Corinthians*, 562; Thrall, *Second Epistle*, 2.865.
251 Windisch, *Der zweite Korintherbrief*, 407–408; Bultmann, *Der zweite Brief*, 241.
252 Compare the translation of Barrett, *Second Epistle*, 329.

demonstrated by the restriction of the terms to conditions which are symptomatic of the rupture of a relationship and the breakdown of a community of mutual support and trust.[253] How much this list contributes to a reconstruction of the poisonous social atmosphere in which Paul was wronged, we shall later discover.[254] More pertinent to the immediate point is Paul's next statement: "and [I fear] lest I be found by you not the sort of man you desire" (vs. 20c). What is hinted at here is explicated in the corresponding colon of vs. 21: Paul fears that the Corinthians will again find him ταπεινός.[255]

Johannes Weiss tried to imagine the character of Paul's response to the wrongdoer on the occasion of his second visit to Corinth, with specific reference to the term ταπεινός: "When Paul arrived... one of the Corinthians flung insolent insults in his face without anyone uttering a word of protest. And what of Paul? He appears to have been as though paralyzed. So dreadfully had he been affected, not so much by the insult of the individual as by the defection of the church (2 Cor. 7:9, 11–12) that he gave up all idea of reply and demand for satisfaction and punishment (2 Cor. 13:2). With feeble words and the loss of personal dignity (Greek ταπεινός), he abandoned the field. He had suffered a grievous humiliation (2 Cor. 12:21), a heavy defeat."[256] Weiss' reconstruction is the fullest acknowledgement by a New Testament scholar that Paul suffered "humiliation" on the occasion of his second visit to Corinth.[257] Yet, even Weiss' clear-eyed account does not capture the shameful sense of degradation expressed by the Greek ταπεινός.[258]

Assuming that the judgment embodied in the term ταπεινός is not mere hyperbole, it is surely understandable that the Corinthians would have been disconcerted by Paul's behavior on the occasion of his second visit, for the Paul whom the Corinthians had come to know through his

---

253 Eduard Schweizer, *Church Order in the New Testament* (London: SCM Press, 1979) 197; Furnish, *II Corinthians*, 567.
254 See below, on 2 Cor. 12:20–21.
255 Windisch, *Der zweite Korintherbrief*, 407–408; Furnish, *II Corinthians*, 568.
256 Weiss, *Primitive Christianity*, 1.343.
257 Thrall, "The Offender and the Offence,' 69–70, on the contrasting reconstructions of Weiss and Allo.
258 Xenophon *Mem.* 3.10.5, where the ταπεινός is explicated as "one who is the embodiment of what is ugly, depraved and hateful" (τὰ αἰσχρά τε καὶ πονηρὰ καὶ μισητά); Dionysius of Halicarnassus *Ant. rom.* 8.32.3, where ταπεινός climaxes a list of deprivations, including "resourceless, homeless, etc." Cf. BDAG 989 s.v. ταπεινός 2.

epistles and envoys during the years of absence while he resided in Ephesus[259] was the epitome of "confidence." In reading the writing known to us as 1 Corinthians, one is immediately struck by the tone of assurance that pervades every part of the epistle, whether Paul is correcting the Corinthians' understanding of the body and sexuality (6:12–20), or warning against the dangers of idolatry (10:1–11:1), or criticizing abuses at the Lord's Supper (11:17–34), or giving directions concerning marriage and divorce (7:1–40), or offering advice on the matter of food sacrificed to idols (8:1–13), or explaining his decision not to make use of certain rights that are his as an apostle (9:1–27), or instructing on the proper use of spiritual gifts (12:1–14:40), or presenting a reasoned proof of the resurrection of the body (15:1–58), or ordering the collection for the saints (16:1–4).[260] In all of this, there are moments of extraordinary trust in his own judgment, as in 7:12, where Paul offers counsel on his own authority, without appealing to the teaching of Christ ("I say—I and not the Lord"). Even in 1 Cor. 1:1–6:11, where Paul warns against factions in the Corinthian church,[261] and counters the description of his gospel as "foolishness,"[262] the dominant tone is one of irony, not pleading; Paul writes in a state of controlled excitement, but there is no sign of weakness, no evidence of inability to cope.[263] On the contrary, Paul portrays himself as the spiritual father of the Corinthians (4:14–17),[264] and threatens disciplinary action: "Some of you, thinking that I am not coming to you, have become arrogant. But I will come to you soon, if the Lord wills, and I will find out not the talk of these arrogant people but their power. For the kingdom of God is not in talk but in power. What

---

259 Following the early chronology of Gerd Lüdemann, *Paul, Apostle to the Gentiles: Studies in Chronology* (Philadelphia: Fortress Press, 1984), esp. 164–70, who dates Paul's arrival in Corinth to the early 40s, on the basis of Acts 18:2; Suetonius *Claud.* 25; Dio Cassius; followed by John Knox, "Chapters in a Life of Paul" in *Colloquy on New Testament Studies*, ed. Bruce Corley (Macon: Mercer University Press, 1983) 359–61; Horrell, *Social Ethos*, 74.
260 Weiss, *Der erste Korintherbrief*, XV, XLIII.
261 Weiss, *Der erste Korintherbrief*, XXIX–XXXIX; L. L. Welborn, "On the Discord in Corinth: 1 Corinthians 1–4 and Ancient Politics" in idem, *Politics and Rhetoric in the Corinthian Epistles* (Macon: Mercer University Press, 1997) 1–42.
262 L. L. Welborn, *Paul, the Fool of Christ: A Study of 1 Corinthians 1–4 in the Comic-Philosophic Tradition* (London: T & T Clark, 2005).
263 Weiss, *Der erste Korintherbrief*, 25, 27, 29–30, 106; Karl Plank, *Paul and the Irony of Affliction* (Atlanta: Scholars Press, 1987) 33–70.
264 N. H. Young, "*Paidagogos*: The Social Setting of a Pauline Metaphor," *NovT* 29 (1987) 150–76; Welborn, *Paul, the Fool of Christ*, 86–90.

would you prefer? Am I to come to you with a stick, or with love in a spirit of leniency?" (4:18–21). In dealing with the case of the incestuous man, Paul assumes the authority to pronounce judgment *in absentia* (5:3), and indicates that his spirit is present "with the power of our Lord Jesus," when the Corinthians are assembled (5:4).[265]

What can account for the contrast in Paul's attitude and behavior when he is absent from Corinth, on the one hand, and when he is "face to face" with the Corinthians, on the other? Re-examining the usages of ταπεινός, one notices that a person is never described as ταπεινός in general, as is the case with a modern condition such as "depression" that is characterized by obscure etiology, but one is always ταπεινός in relation to another who is more powerful, more noble, more free: thus, the slave is ταπεινός before the master, the poor in the presence of the rich, the lowly and undistinguished opposite the nobles, the abject in comparison with the "great-souled."[266] It is suggestive that, in the clause under consideration (10:1), the counterpart of "being absent" (ἀπών) is not "being present" in general,[267] but the more lively expression κατὰ πρόσωπον, used elsewhere by Paul of a challenging, "face to face" encounter.[268] These considerations reinforce the conclusions that emerged from our exegesis of ch. 2, specifically from Paul's use of the verbs παρακαλεῖν and κυροῦν in counseling the Corinthians "to try to conciliate" the wrongdoer through a "reaffirmation of love": at the center of the group opposed to Paul is a figure who must be treated with extreme tact and caution because he is a person of high status and influence, a person before whom Paul seems to have lost face.

In focusing, as we have thus far, on ταπεινός as descriptive of attitude and behavior, we have not yet plumbed the depths of the value judgment embodied in this term. As further exegesis of 2 Cor. 10:1 and 11:7 will demonstrate, an understanding of the deeper, social foundation of the word ταπεινός is crucial for reconstruction of the wrongdoer's attitude toward Paul. In the usages of ταπεινός surveyed above, one cannot have failed to notice that the demeanor so described is assumed to be charac-

---

265 Weiss, *Der erste Korintherbrief*, 126–28; Wolfgang Schrage, *Der erste Brief an die Korinther* (Neukirchen-Vluyn: Neukirchener Verlag, 1991) 1.373.
266 Euripides *Andr.* 164–65; Xenophon *Mem.* 3.10.5; *Hier.* 5.4; Plato *Phaedr.* 257C; Aristotle *Pol.* 4.11, 1295b18–21; James 1:9–10; Luke 1:52; cf. BDAG 989 s.v. ταπεινός 1.
267 Windisch, *Der zweite Korintherbrief*, 293.
268 Gal. 2:11—Paul's confrontation with Cephas in Antioch. Cf. Furnish, *II Corinthians*, 456.

teristic of and inherent to certain social conditions—namely, those of slavery and poverty. In Xenophon's account of how behavior gives expression to the character of the soul, "self-abasement" (τὸ ταπεινόν) is the concomitant of "servility" (ἀνελεύθερον), just as "dignity" (τὸ μεγαλοπρεπές) is the natural comportment of a freeman (ἐλευθέριον).[269] According to Aristotle, those who have grown up in extreme poverty (οἱ δὲ καθ' ὑπερβολὴν ἐν ἐνδείᾳ) are "wholly of an ignoble disposition" (ταπεινοὶ λίαν), and hence unfit to govern.[270] In Josephus' account of the revolutionary putsch in Jerusalem during the Jewish war, the Zealots put to death all persons of social consequence, all, that is, except the ταπεινοί: "and none escaped save someone who was utterly lowly (σφόδρα τις ἦν ταπεινός), whether on account of ignoble birth (ἀγένεια) or (mis)fortune (τύχη)."[271] Even manual laborers are regarded as ταπεινοί, since labor dulls the mind: Aristotle explains, "we call vulgar the industries that earn wages; for they make the mind preoccupied (ἄσχολος) and degraded (ταπεινή)."[272] Thus, Lucian is counseled to abandon his work as a sculptor and to pursue an intellectual career as an orator or a philosopher, for if he continues to cut stones, he "must put on a filthy tunic, assume a servile appearance (καὶ σχῆμα δουλοπρεπὲς ἀναλήψῃ), and hold bars and gravers and sledges and chisels in your hands, with your back bent over your work; you will be a groundling, with groundling ambitions, altogether humble (καὶ πάντα τρόπον ταπεινός); you will never lift your head, or conceive a single manly (ἀνδρῶδες) or liberal (ἐλεύθερον) thought."[273]

The firm connection of the term ταπεινός with the demeanor expected of the lower classes suggests that the judgment pronounced by the Corinthians upon Paul was not merely the reflection of his behavior on one occasion or another, but a more deeply rooted assumption about the comportment inherent in Paul's social class as someone who supported himself by the work of his hands.[274] Features of Paul's argument in 2 Cor. 10–13 support this inference, and lead us back to passages in 1 Corinthians where Paul acknowledges that his way of life and self-presentation give the impression of "foolishness," "weakness," and "disrepute." In the remaining usage of the verb ταπεινόω in 2 Cor. 11:7, Paul refers to

---

269 Xenophon *Mem.* 3.10.5; cf. Barrett, *Second Epistle*, 247.
270 Aristotle *Pol.* 4.11, 1295b18–21.
271 Josephus *B.J.* 4.365.
272 Aristotle *Pol.* 8.2, 1337b12–15.
273 Lucian *Somn.* 13; cf. Hock, *The Social Context of Paul's Ministry*, 35–36.
274 Windisch, *Der zweite Korintherbrief*, 334; Hock, *Social Context*, 60, 63–64.

the humiliation involved in his decision to support himself by working with his own hands, rather than accepting benefactions from the wealthy in Corinth.²⁷⁵ Paul asks ironically,²⁷⁶ "Did I commit a sin by demeaning myself (ἐμαυτὸν ταπεινῶν) so that you might be exalted, because I proclaimed the gospel of God to you free of charge (δωρεάν)?" The structure of the Greek sentence makes clear the implicit connection between social inferiority and the means of Paul's subsistence.²⁷⁷ The infinitival expression ἁμαρτίαν ποιεῖν ("to commit a sin") can take as its object either a participle or a ὅτι clause.²⁷⁸ Paul exploits both possibilities in order to contrast the absurdity of the Corinthians' judgment with the purity of his own motives. Thus the two phrases which ironically elucidate Paul's "wrongful act" (ἁμαρτία) are constructed as parallels,²⁷⁹ with the result that ἐμαυτὸν ταπεινῶν ("demeaning myself"), corresponds to the adverbial expression δωρεάν ("free of charge"),²⁸⁰ drawn forward to the beginning of the clause in order to reinforce the parallel construction.²⁸¹ The apostle's "self-abasement" consisted in the fact that he lived while in Corinth "without taking money" from the Corinthians. How Paul managed to subsist, while devoting his best energies to preaching, without taking gifts from the Corinthians, we know from other texts: Paul worked with his own hands (1 Cor. 4:12) as a σκηνοποιός (Acts 18:3).²⁸² Nevertheless, Paul's efforts at self-support proved insufficient to supply his needs, as he acknowledges in the following verses: while Paul was in Corinth, he "fell into want" (ὑστερηθείς), lacking even the basic necessities of

---

275 Plummer, *Second Epistle*, 302; Hughes, *Paul's Second Epistle*, 384; E. A. Judge, "St. Paul and Socrates," *Interchange* 14 (1973) 115; idem, "The Social Identity of the First Christians: A Question of Method in Religious History," *JRH* 11 (1980) 214; Furnish, *II Corinthians*, 508.
276 Betz, *Der Apostel Paulus*, 101; Wolff, *Der zweite Brief*, 220; Paul Barnett, *The Second Epistle to the Corinthians* (Grand Rapids: Eerdmans, 1997) 513.
277 Windisch, *Der zweite Korintherbrief*, 334.
278 Windisch, *Der zweite Korintherbrief*, 334.
279 Windisch, *Der zweite Korintherbrief*, 334; Lietzmann, *An die Korinther I/II*, 146; Bultmann, *Der zweite Brief*, 207.
280 Windisch, *Der zweite Korintherbrief*, 334.
281 Plummer, *Second Epistle*, 303; Windisch, *Der zweite Korintherbrief*, 335.
282 On the meaning of σκηνοποιός and the relationship of Paul's trade to his social status, see Ron Hock, "Paul's Tentmaking and the Problem of His Social Class," *JBL* 97 (1978) 555–64; idem, *Social Context*, 20–21, 36, 60, 63–64. For the suggestion that σκηνοποιός refers to a "maker of stage properties," see s.v. σκηνοποιός. in BDAG 928–29.

food, clothing and shelter,[283] and was obliged to accept assistance from poor Christians in Macedonia, taking money which they could ill afford to spare (2 Cor. 11:8–9).[284]

As strange as it may seem to modern sensibilities, the evidence is nonetheless clear that men of the social class of Cicero and Seneca regarded artisanal labor of the sort by which Paul sought to sustain himself as "degrading."[285] Cicero says flatly: "All artisans are engaged in vulgar trades; for no workshop can have anything noble about it."[286] Seneca demurs: "I am not led to include painters within the liberal arts, no more than sculptors or workers in marble."[287] Those who followed intellectual professions as teachers of rhetoric or philosophy were expected to accept gifts in return for their services.[288] The exceptional philosopher who refused to take money, and who chose instead to support himself by working, caused consternation and eventually raised questions about the value of his wisdom.[289] This attitude is reflected in Antiphon's criticism of Socrates, as recounted by Xenophon: "Socrates, I for my part believe you to be a just, but by no means a wise man. And I think you realize it yourself. Anyhow, you decline to take money for your society. Yet if you believed your cloak or house or anything you possess to be worth money, you would not part with it for nothing or even less than its value. Clearly,

---

283 Zmijewski, 'Narrenrede,' 133 argues that the aorist participle ὑστερηθείς should be regarded as an ingressive aorist; followed by Thrall, *Second Epistle* 2.686. Cf. Phil. 4:12.

284 Cf. Phil. 4:15. On the "abysmal poverty" of the Macedonian Christians, see 2 Cor. 8:2, with the commentary of Betz, *2 Corinthians 8 and 9*, 43–44, 50–51.

285 E.g., Cicero *Off.* 1.42.150–51; Seneca *Ep.* 88.18, 21, 23. See the discussion in Ramsay MacMullen, *Roman Social Relations 50 B.C. to A.D. 284* (New Haven: Yale University Press, 1974) 114–20; Hock, *Social Context*, 36; S. R. Joshel, *Work, Identity, and Legal Status at Rome: A Study of the Occupational Inscriptions* (Norman: University of Oklahoma Press, 1992) 68–69.

286 Cicero *Off.* 1.42.150; cf. MacMullen, *Roman Social Relations*, 115; Hock, *Social Context*, 36.

287 Seneca *Ep.* 88.18; see also Valerius Maximus 8.14.6; cf. MacMullen, *Roman Social Relations*, 115.

288 E.g., Lucian *Merc. cond.* See the references to gifts and benefits conferred upon philosophers, rhetors, and poets in Glen W. Bowersock, *Augustus in the Greek World* (Oxford: Clarendon, 1965) 30–41; Peter White, *Promised Verse: Poets in the Society of Augustan Rome* (Cambridge, MA: Harvard University Press, 1993) 14–27, 276 n. 21. Cf. Hock, *Social Context*, 53–55; Marshall, *Enmity in Corinth*, 1–18.

289 Hock, "Paul's Tentmaking and the Problem of His Social Class," 555–64, esp. 561; idem, *Social Context*, 56–59, 64.

then, if you set any value on your society, you would insist on getting the proper price for that too. It may well be that you are a just man because you do not cheat people through avarice; but wise you cannot be, since your knowledge is not worth anything."²⁹⁰ Similarly, the Stoic Musonius, who worked on a farm, was aware that his means of supporting himself would prompt objections: "What, perhaps someone might say, is it not preposterous for an educated man who is able to influence the young to the study of philosophy to work the land and to do manual labor just like a peasant?"²⁹¹

In 1 Cor. 9 we find Paul already defending his decision not to accept financial support from the Corinthians.²⁹² We shall later discuss the patronal relationship which Paul was expected to embrace, when we explore the evidence for the wrongdoer's support of one of Paul's apostolic rivals.²⁹³ At this point, it is only important to note that Paul's determination to preach the gospel "free of charge" (ἀδάπανος) to the Corinthians (1 Cor. 9:18) raised questions about his apostolic legitimacy: "Am I not an apostle?" Paul asks in mock amazement (1 Cor. 9:1).²⁹⁴ In 1 Cor. 1–4, with partisanship of Paul's rivals openly expressed, the critique of Paul's means of subsistence is more focused and pejorative: it is no longer Paul's refusal of support, but the vulgarity of his occupation which, among other aspects of his person, contributes decisively to the impression that he is "foolish," "weak," and "dishonored" (1 Cor. 4:10).²⁹⁵ Notice that in 1 Cor. 4:12 the acknowledgement, "we labor, working with our own hands" (κοπιῶμεν ἐργαζόμενοι ταῖς ἰδίαις χερσίν) climaxes the series of adversities ("we are hungry and thirsty, we are poorly clothed and beaten and homeless") by which Paul warrants and illustrates the humiliating predicates μωροί, ἀσθενεῖς, ἄτιμοι.²⁹⁶ It is abundantly clear that

---

290 Xenophon *Mem.* 1.6.12; cf. Barrett, *Second Epistle*, 281–82.
291 Musonius *frag.* 11, Cora Lutz, *Musonius Rufus: The Roman Socrates* (New Haven: Yale University Press, 1942) 82,22–24. Cf. Hock, *Social Context*, 58.
292 See the discussion in Gerd Theissen, "Legitimation and Subsistence: An Essay on the Sociology of Early Christian Missionaries" in *The Social Setting of Pauline Christianity: Essays on Corinth* (Philadelphia: Fortress Press, 1982) 44–54; Hock, *Social Context*, 60–62; Gordon Fee, *The First Epistle to the Corinthians* (Grand Rapids: Eerdmans, 1987) 392; Winter, *Paul Among the Sophists*, 164–72; Thrall, *Second Epistle*, 2.701–704.
293 See below on 2 Cor. 11:4, 20, pp. 128–29, 139–50.
294 Weiss, *Der erste Korintherbrief*, 232.
295 Theissen, *Social Setting*, 44–46; Hock, *Social Context*, 36, 60.
296 Weiss, *Der erste Korintherbrief*, 112; Hock, "Paul's Tentmaking and the Problem of His Social Class," 555–64.

Paul's banausic occupation was a source of embarrassment for some in Corinth. The description of Paul as ταπεινός embodies a judgment about the demeanor expected of one who supported himself by the work of his hands.

It is obvious whose values are reflected in the term ταπεινός: it embodies the negative judgment of the upper class upon all who are of low social status—slaves, the poor, the undistinguished—all those who lack the resources to cope.[297] For this reason, ταπεινός is often linked with other terms that express the disdain of the upper class for the commoners, e. g., φαῦλος ("base")[298] and αἰσχρός ("ugly").[299] ταπεινός belongs to MacMullen's "lexicon of snobbery," the linguistic mechanism by which the upper class enhanced the feeling of social distance from the poor, the uneducated, the lowborn.[300] Along these lines, we are led to a conclusion that coincides with the results of our exegesis of 2 Cor. 2 and 7, specifically with the implications of Paul's use of the verbs λυπεῖν and ἀδικεῖν to describe the actions of the wrongdoer: the individual who was at the center of the opposition to Paul, and whose values are deposited in the judgment ταπεινός, was a person of high social status. It may seem surprising that the wrongdoer's estimate of Paul's behavior and person should be attributed to the Corinthians in general (ἐν ὑμῖν, 10:1). But historians are increasingly aware of the phenomenon of the diffusion of tastes and values within a vertically organized society like Roman Corinth.[301] That Paul is conscious of appearing ταπεινός before the Corinthians furnishes additional evidence of the influence of the wrongdoer upon the congregation as a whole.

The fact that the term ταπεινός belongs to the lexicon of the upper class and gives expression to its consciousness of social superiority raises the problem of the balance of ideology and reality in such language.

---

297 W. Grundmann, "ταπεινός," *TDNT* 8 (1972) 1–4; Barrett, *Second Epistle*, 247; BDAG 989 s.v. ταπεινός 1.
298 E.g., Isocrates *Or.* 10.12.
299 Xenophon *Mem.* 3.10.5; Demosthenes *Or.* 18.178; Plutarch *Cat. Min.* 32.
300 MacMullen, *Roman Social Relations*, 138–41, where ταπεινός would fit well alongside βάναυσος, *vulgus*, etc; cf. Zwi Yavetz, *Plebs and Princeps* (London: Oxford University Press, 1969) Appendix 1, for a list of adjectives for the lower class.
301 Andrew Wallace-Hadrill, "Patronage in Roman society: from republic to empire" in *Patronage in Ancient Society*, ed. A. Wallace-Hadrill (London: Routledge, 1990) 71–78; Timothy L. Carter, "'Big Men' in Corinth," *JSNT* 19 (1997) 45–70; Judith Perkins, *Roman Imperial Identities in the Early Christian Era* (London: Routledge, 2009) 62–72.

Does Paul concur, in any sense other than an ironic sense, with this negative value judgment?[302] We must allow, I think, that the term ταπεινός possessed reality as a characterization of Paul's behavior and person to the degree that Paul, the wrongdoer, and the Corinthians participated in the social structure which gave meaning to the term. Of course, as a Jew shaped by the Jewish Scriptures, Paul would have had access to a very different usage of ταπεινός—as a description of the humble spirit appropriate to a human being before God.[303] But there is no trace of this sense in 2 Cor. 10–13, where ταπεινός and ταπεινόω are used exclusively with the pejorative meaning shaped by aristocratic Greek culture.[304] Yet, there is evidence in the sentence structure of 2 Cor. 10:1 that ταπεινός is a substitute for and a corrective of a nearly synonymous term by which Paul had previously described himself, namely, πραΰς, "gentle."[305] Paul opens his polemical apology with an appeal (παρακαλῶ ὑμᾶς), strengthened by the words διὰ τῆς πραΰτητος καὶ ἐπιεικείας τοῦ Χριστοῦ ("through the meekness and gentleness of Christ"). At first, the phrase appears to be only the typical formula of invocation, such as Paul often employs, virtually interchangeable with διὰ τοῦ ὀνόματος τοῦ κυρίου ἡμῶν Ἰησοῦ Χριστοῦ ("through the name of our Lord Jesus Christ") in 1 Cor. 1:10, or διὰ τῶν οἰκτιρμῶν τοῦ θεοῦ ("through the mercies of God") in Rom. 12:1.[306] But students of the Corinthian correspondence will recall that Paul had used the term πραΰτης in a minatory fashion in his previous letter (1 Cor. 4:21), confronting the Corinthians with the alternative: "What would you prefer? Am I to come to you with a stick, or with

---

302 On the sense in which Paul might have appropriated the term ταπεινός used by his critics, see the discussion in Furnish, *II Corinthians*, 460; Thrall, *Second Epistle*, 2.603–604; Walker, *Paul's Offer of Leniency*, 29–30.
303 Grundmann, "ταπεινός," *TDNT* 8 (1972) 6–17 on the use of ταπεινός in the Septuagint and in Hellenistic Judaism. See esp. Matt. 11:29; 1 Cor. 7:6; Rom. 12:16. Cf. Leivestad, "ΤΑΠΕΙΝΟΣ – ΤΑΠΕΙΝΟΦΡΩΝ," 46–47.
304 Windisch, *Der zweite Korintherbrief*, 293; Barrett, *Second Epistle*, 247; Furnish, *II Corinthians*, 456; Walker, *Paul's Offer of Leniency*, 21, 29–30.
305 On the sentence structure of 2 Cor. 10:1, and the consequent relation of ταπεινός to πραΰτης, see Windisch, *Der zweite Korintherbrief*, 291–92; R. Leivestad, "The Meekness and Gentleness of Christ. II Cor. x.1," *NTS* 12 (1966) 156–64; Betz, *Der Apostel Paulus*, 46; Furnish, *II Corinthians*, 460.
306 See also 1 Cor. 1:10; Phlm. 9; Rom. 15:30; cf. Windisch, *Der zweite Korintherbrief*, 291; Carl J. Bjerkelund, *Parakalo: Form, Funktion und Sinn der parakalo-Sätze in den paulinischen Briefen* (Oslo: Universitetsforlaget, 1967) 164–67; Furnish, *II Corinthians*, 455; Thrall, *Second Epistle* 2.599–600.

love in a spirit of gentleness (πνεύματι πραΰτητος)?"[307] Why should Paul have felt obliged, at the beginning of his polemical apology, written in the aftermath of the incident in Corinth which had caused him so much pain, to revive a term, πραΰτης, the recollection of which must have caused him considerable embarrassment, given his failure to carry out the threatened punishment? And why should Paul now nuance πραΰτης by the addition of ἐπιείκεια, so that the sense of "leniency" displaces "gentleness" in the resulting combination, best translated "leniency and clemency"?[308] And why, finally, should Paul now attribute to Christ a quality which in his previous epistle he had claimed as his own, evoking a characteristic trait of the messianic king well known from the Psalms (Ps. 44[45]:5) and the Prophets (Zech. 9:9)?[309] Although certainty is unattainable in such cases, the following scenario suggests itself: on the occasion of his second visit to Corinth, Paul represented his reluctance to inflict punishment as a manifestation of his "spirit of gentleness" (πνεῦμα πραΰτητος); the local leader of the opposition to Paul retorted, "What you call 'gentleness' (πραΰτης) is really just ταπεινότης—the cringing, abject weakness that always characterizes someone of your class!"

If this reconstruction is plausible, then there are two consequences for the emergent image of the wrongdoer. First, the wrongdoer was a person of considerable verbal skill, sensitive to the nuances of words, able and willing to engage with Paul in a kind of linguistic fencing. The wrongdoer skillfully exploited the connotations of "meekness" and "humility" inherent in the word πραΰς, when he substituted the pejorative synonym ταπεινός.[310] We shall see that this inference is supported by exegesis of 2 Cor. 10:1–11 in general, and by the vocabulary of 10:10 in particular. Second, the wrongdoer reveals an acerbity in partisan conflict which is not typical of men of the upper class in speaking with social inferiors. As our investigation has shown, ταπεινός was a potent, derogatory label

---

307 Weiss, *Der erste Korintherbrief*, 123. On the threat of punishment, see Elizabeth Castelli, *Imitating Paul: A Discourse of Power* (Louisville: Westminster John Knox, 1991) 98–111; E. M. Lassen, "The Use of the Father Image in Imperial Propaganda in 1 Cor. 4:14–21," *TynBul* 42 (1991) 127–36.
308 Walker, *Paul's Offer of Leniency*, 62–67, 258–59, 326–29.
309 Furnish, *II Corinthians*, 455.
310 Appreciating the irony of ταπεινός following πραΰτης, and attributing the use of ταπεινός to Paul's critics: Plummer, *Second Epistle*, 273; Barrett, *Second Epistle*, 246–47; Bultmann, *Der zweite Brief*, 185; Furnish, *II Corinthians*, 460. On the possibility that ταπεινός in 2 Cor. 10:1 embodies an ironic twist upon πραΰτης, see Walker, *Paul's Offer of Leniency*, 258–59.

in the Greco-Roman world. When one considers how careful patrons were to avoid words that might imply the social inferiority of their protégés,[311] the wrongdoer's application of the term ταπεινός to Paul seems to be an act of calculated humiliation.

Next (2 Cor. 10:2), we come to a more serious charge, a moralistic judgment, which Paul attributes to "some" (τινες), but not to all, of the Corinthians: that Paul and his colleagues (ἡμεῖς) have been guilty of conducting their affairs "according to human standards" (κατὰ σάρκα).[312] On the theory that 2 Cor. 10–13 should be identified with the "letter of tears" mentioned in 2 Cor. 2:4, we may plausibly infer that the group of "some" who render this negative judgment are identical with the group later described as "the majority" (οἱ πλείονες) in 2:6, who are satisfied with the more lenient punishment imposed upon the wrongdoer.[313] Thus the group which dares to question the spiritual basis of Paul's existence is the party of the wrongdoer, the association of those who, in ways that have yet to be determined, stand more directly under the wrongdoer's influence.

How seriously Paul took the allegation of this group is indicated by the escalation of the rhetoric of "confidence" in 10:2. The verb θαρρεῖν is resumed from the preceding verse, and undergoes a double expansion: first, by the addition of πεποίθησις, "self-confidence," and then by the absolute use of the infinitive τολμῆσαι, which intensifies the sense of "courage" into "daring."[314] It is difficult to capture the heightened bravado in translation: "I ask that, when I am present, I will not have to be bold with that self-confidence by which I count on daring to oppose some peo-

---

311 Richard Saller, *Personal Patronage under the Early Empire* (Cambridge: Cambridge University Press, 1982) 7–15; idem, "Patronage and Friendship in Early Imperial Rome: Drawing the Distinction" in *Patronage in Ancient Society*, ed. A. Wallace-Hadrill (London: Routledge, 1989) 49–61.

312 Windisch, *Der zweite Korintherbrief*, 295: "Während das erste Zitat wohl auch in der Gemeinde verbreitet war, beschränkte sich die zweite Parole, der 'fleischliche Wandel' nur auf den Kreis der persönlichen Gegner (τινές)." On κατὰ σάρκα as a heightened, moralistic critique, see Plummer, *Second Epistle*, 275; Tasker, *Second Epistle*, 133; Furnish, *II Corinthians*, 461.

313 So, already, Krenkel, *Beiträge*, 302; Kennedy, *Second and Third Epistles*, 99–109; Lake, *Earlier Epistles*, 170–72; Plummer, *Second Epistle*, 58; Bachmann, *Der zweite Brief*, 118; Tasker, *Second Epistle*, 53; Harris, *Second Epistle*, 229. See above on 2 Cor. 2:6, pp. 35–37.

314 Windisch, *Der zweite Korintherbrief*, 294. On the context and connotations of the terms θαρρεῖν, πεποίθησις, and τολμᾶν, see Betz, *Der Apostel Paulus*, 67–68.

ple...."³¹⁵ That the courage which Paul seeks to summon is activated by the hostility of others is signaled by the prepositional phrase ἐπί τινας, best translated *"against* certain persons," rather than "toward some."³¹⁶ It is suggestive, moreover, that Paul makes a preemptive raid on his opponents' thought-process by using the verb λογίζεσθαι in his own sense ("count on," "reckon on," 10:2a), before alluding to the use of λογίζεσθαι made by certain persons in their "evaluation" of his conduct (10:2b).³¹⁷

The reproach of certain persons against Paul is embodied in the phrase κατὰ σάρκα περιπατοῦντες, "comporting oneself according to human standards." At first sight, the scope of the judgment seems unbounded, encompassing all aspects of Paul's behavior; for κατὰ σάρκα (literally "according to the flesh") is ordinarily used in Paul's letters to describe a way of life that is unredeemed by the Spirit, life governed by human norms and oriented toward worldly advantages.³¹⁸ Thus the charge of living κατὰ σάρκα would seem to be so general as to provide little insight into specific attitudes of the wrongdoer and his supporters toward Paul. Because the condemnation of human standards implied in the phrase κατὰ σάρκα περιπατοῦντες seems so comprehensive, a number of interpreters have taken these words to be the slogan of a hypothetical group of Gnostics in the church at Corinth, who thereby seek to deny to Paul the status of a "spiritual person" (πνευματικός).³¹⁹ We shall discover not only that this hypothesis is unnecessary but also that more detailed information regarding the basis of the wrongdoer's critique of Paul may be derived from the language of 10:2–3, when attention is paid to the role of the phrase κατὰ σάρκα περιπατοῦντες in the debate between

---

315 Compare the translation of Barrett, *Second Epistle*, 248.
316 Rightly, Hughes, *Paul's Second Epistle*, 348; Barrett, *Second Epistle*, 248; Furnish, *II Corinthians*, 457.
317 Windisch, *Der zweite Korintherbrief*, 295; Georgi, *Opponents of Paul*, 235; Furnish, *II Corinthians*, 456 suggest that λογίζεσθαι is a term being used by Paul's critics which he now wishes to redirect against them.
318 Eduard Schweizer, "σάρξ," *TDNT* 7 (1971) 131–35; BDAG 914–16 s.v. σάρξ; Barrett, *Second Epistle*, 249–50. In general, see Alexander Sand, *Der Begriff "Fleisch" in den paulinischen Hauptbriefen* (Regensburg: Pustet, 1967); Robert Jewett, *Paul's Anthropological Terms. A Study of Their Use in Conflict Settings* (Leiden: Brill, 1971) 23–40, 49–166.
319 Wilhelm Lütgert, *Freiheitspredigt und Schwarmgeister in Korinth* (Gütersloh: Bertelsmann, 1908); Windisch, *Der zweite Korintherbrief*, 295; Bultmann, *Der zweite Brief*, 132–41; Walter Schmithals, *Gnosticism in Corinth: An Investigation of the Letters to the Corinthians* (Nashville: Abingdon, 1971).

Paul and the Corinthians, and when the provenance of the verb λογίζεσθαι is investigated.

We should begin by observing that the prepositional phrase κατὰ σάρκα is characteristically Pauline: κατὰ σάρκα is found a total of eighteen times in the authentic Pauline epistles.[320] The same is true of the verb περιπατεῖν in the non-literal sense "to conduct one's life," "comport oneself," "behave": "In the New Testament this use of the word is decidedly Pauline."[321] Moreover, the phrase κατὰ σάρκα is used here with the same negative connotation that it has elsewhere in Paul, where life "according to the flesh" is set over against life "according to the Spirit."[322] The evidence strongly suggests that the phrase κατὰ σάρκα περιπατοῦντες has been lifted directly from Paul, and is now turned ironically, one might almost say maliciously, against him. The use that is made of the phrase κατὰ σάρκα περιπατοῦντες exhibits the same eristic tendency that appeared in the substitution of ταπεινός for πραΰς in 10:1, the same capacity for verbal combat.

The phrase κατὰ σάρκα is used for the first time in Paul's Corinthian correspondence with a negative nuance in 1 Cor. 1:26, where Paul qualifies the wisdom of the privileged few who, for the most part, have not been "called" by the gospel of Christ.[323] A number of recent studies have contributed to an emerging consensus that Paul's critique of "eloquent wisdom" (σοφία λόγου) in 1 Cor. 1–4 was occasioned by the enthusiasm of the wealthy few at Corinth for the rhetorical sophistication exhibited by certain rival evangelists, especially Apollos.[324] I would argue that it was a decisive moment in the history of Paul's relationship with the Corinthians, when he chose to characterize those who enjoyed

---

320 BDAG 916 s.v. σάρξ 2cα; Schweizer, "σάρξ," *TDNT* 7 (1971) 132–33.
321 BDAG 803 s.v. περιπατέω 2.
322 Windisch, *Der zweite Korintherbrief*, 295; Schweizer, "σάρξ," *TDNT* 7 (1971) 131–32; Tasker, *Second Epistle*, 133; Barrett, *Second Epistle*, 250.
323 Weiss, *Der erste Korintherbrief*, 35; Anthony C. Thiselton, *The First Epistle to the Corinthians* (Grand Rapids: Eerdmans, 2000) 180–81.
324 A. D. Litfin, *St. Paul's Theology of Proclamation: 1 Corinthians 1–4 and Greco-Roman Rhetoric* (Cambridge: Cambridge University Press, 1994) 162; Winter, *Paul Among the Sophists*, 141–42, 164–65, 172–79, 195–200; D. P. Ker, "Paul and Apollos—Colleagues or Rivals?" *JSNT* 77 (2000) 75–97, esp. 91–92; J. F. M. Smit, "What is Apollos? What is Paul? In Search for the Coherence of First Corinthians 1.10–4.21," *NovT* 44 (2002) 231–51, esp. 246–47; Welborn, *Paul, the Fool of Christ*, 103–109, 117–18.

the benefits of learned culture, the σοφοί,[325] as κατὰ σάρκα. Paul then proceeded to generalize this judgment, describing all of the Corinthians as "fleshly people" (σάρκινοι), as "infants in Christ," who must be fed with milk rather than solid food (1 Cor. 3:1–3).[326] In this way, the phrase κατὰ σάρκα entered the polemic between Paul and the Corinthians, and reproach engendered reproach.

So much for the background of the phrase κατὰ σάρκα. But to what aspect of Paul's behavior have "certain persons" applied this negative judgment? It is possible, and indeed necessary, to seek greater specificity in this case, because the verb περιπατεῖν, as Paul uses it, always connotes "behavior," and, for the most part, behavior regarded from an ethical perspective.[327] Here the verb λογίζεσθαι, which describes the critical process by which Paul has been "evaluated" (10:2b), provides a crucial datum. It is striking that the verb λογίζεσθαι appears so frequently in 2 Cor. 10–13: 10:2 (twice); 10:7, 11; 11:5; 12:6. Especially important are the uses of this verb in 10:7 and 10:11 to denote the thoughts of a certain anonymous individual, who is indicated by the pronouns τις and ὁ τοιοῦτος—in our view, the wrongdoer. The repetition of λογίζεσθαι and its persistent connection with persons hostile to Paul suggest that this term was chosen by Paul's critics with care, because it was germane to the realm of Paul's perceived misbehavior.[328] The verb λογίζεσθαι is primarily an accounting term: thus, "to reckon," "to calculate," "to place on someone's account," "to credit."[329] Thus, in *OGIS* 595,15: τὰ ἕτερα ἀναλώματα ἑαυτοῖς ἐλογισάμεθα, ἵνα μὴ τὴν πόλιν βαρῶμεν ("We charged the other expenses to our account, in order not to burden the city").[330] This is

---

325 Weiss, *Der erste Korintherbrief*, 35; Winter, *Paul Among the Sophists*, 189, 192–94, 199; Welborn, *Paul, the Fool of Christ*, 126–29.
326 On the characterization of the Corinthians as σάρκινοι, σαρκικοί, and νηπιοί, see Weiss, *Der erste Korintherbrief*, 71–73; W. Grundmann, "Die ΝΗΠΙΟΙ in der urchristlichen Paränese," *NTS* 5 (1958/59) 188–205; Hans Conzelmann, *1 Corinthians*. Hermeneia (Philadelphia: Fortress Press, 1975) 71; Raymond F. Collins, *First Corinthians* (Collegeville: Michael Glazier, 1999) 139–41; Winter, *Paul Among the Sophists*, 174–75; Thistelton, *First Epistle*, 288–89.
327 BDAG 803 s.v. περιπατέω 2; Heinrich Seesemann, "πατέω and Compounds in the NT 3. περιπατέω," *TDNT* 5 (1967) 944–45.
328 Georgi, *Gegner des Paulus*, 222–23, 227–28; Furnish, *II Corinthians*, 456; Barnett, *Second Epistle*, 460 n.24.
329 Moulton and Milligan, *Vocabulary of the Greek Testament*, 377–78; BDAG 597 s.v. λογίζομαι 1.a; H. W. Heidland, "λογίζομαι," *TDNT* 4 (1967) 284.
330 Moulton and Milligan, *Vocabulary of the Greek Testament*, 377–78; BDAG 597 s.v. λογίζομαι 1.a. See also *PFay.* 21, 9.

the sense of λογίζεσθαι in a number of Paul's own usages.³³¹ Especially significant is 2 Cor. 12:6, where Paul refrains from boasting, "lest someone (τις) may credit (λογίσηται) me beyond what he sees in me or hears from me."³³² Even when the term is used in a transferred sense of cognitive processes, the commercial provenance is sometimes relevant, and is assumed in the logic of Paul's metaphors.³³³ While it would be unwise to press the linguistic evidence further,³³⁴ we naturally find ourselves asking whether the behavior in which Paul has engaged, and which is reckoned by his critics to be κατὰ σάρκα, might not lie in the area of his financial accounting, his bookkeeping.

In the passages of 2 Cor. 10–13 we have examined thus far, the negative estimations of Paul have been attributed to some or to all of the Corinthians. We have inferred, on the basis of the structure of Paul's argument in 10:1–11, that the derogatory opinions expressed in 10:1 and 10:2 were held *a fortiori* by the wrongdoer, indeed, that he is their promulgator. This inference anticipates the situation in 2 Cor. 7, where Paul acknowledges the complicity of the community in the wrong done by an individual. Now, in 10:7, we encounter a viewpoint that is explicitly attributed to "a certain person" or "someone" (τις): "If someone is confident in himself that he belongs to Christ, let him consider this again by himself, that just as he is of Christ, so also are we" (εἴ τις πέποιθεν ἑαυτῷ Χριστοῦ εἶναι, τοῦτο λογιζέσθω πάλιν ἐφ' ἑαυτοῦ, ὅτι καθὼς αὐτὸς Χριστοῦ, οὕτως καὶ ἡμεῖς).

It is important to give our reasons for referring the indefinite pronoun τις to a specific individual in this instance and, moreover, to a Corinthian, rather than an outsider, since the history of interpretation tends to construe the pronoun in a general sense ("anyone," "whoever"),³³⁵ or to identify the individual intended as the leader of a group of missionaries

---

331 E.g., Gal. 3:6; Rom. 4:3, 4, 5, 9, 10, 22, 23–24; 2 Cor. 12:6; BDAG 597 s.v. λογίζομαι 1.a.
332 Windisch, *Der zweite Korintherbrief*, 381; Lietzmann, *An die Korinther I/II*, 172; Héring, *Saint Paul*, 95; Barrett, *Second Epistle*, 312; Bultmann, *Der zweite Brief*, 225; Zmijewski, *"Narrenrede,"* 359; Furnish, *II Corinthians*, 527.
333 E.g., 1 Cor. 4:1, ἡμᾶς λογιζέσθω ἄνθρωπος ὡς ὑπηρέτας Χριστοῦ, where the stewards, or household managers, have responsibility for financial accounts; cf. Collins, *First Corinthians*, 168, 172; Welborn, *Paul, the Fool of Christ*, 242–44.
334 Note the caution of Windisch, *Der zweite Korintherbrief*, 295.
335 E.g., Plummer, *Second Epistle*, 280; L. J. Koch, *Fortolkning til Paulus' andet Brev til Korinthierne* (Copenhagen: J. Frimodts Forlag, 1958) 358; Furnish, *II Corinthians*, 466; Martin, *2 Corinthians*, 307; Barnett, *Second Epistle*, 470; Thrall, *Second Epistle*, 2.623; Vegge, *2 Corinthians*, 304.

opposed to Paul.³³⁶ In favor of taking the pronoun as a reference to a particular person, rather than as a generalization, are several nuances of Paul's language. First, the verb πέποιθεν ("is confident") introduces a subjective element that is unnecessary for a generalization, but appropriate to an account of the thought process of a specific individual.³³⁷ If Paul had intended a comparison between himself and any reader in Corinth, he might simply have written, "If anyone reckons that he belongs to Christ, then so do I!" But Paul inserts the verb πέποιθεν at the beginning of the premise, in a position of emphasis. πέποιθεν entails the sense of an unjustified conceit, or an unfounded certainty,³³⁸ a connotation which comes more fully to expression in the variant reading of Codex Vaticanus: δοκεῖ πεποιθέναι.³³⁹ A subjective moment is also present in the reflexive pronoun ἑαυτῷ, whether the dative is translated "in himself" or "with regard to himself."³⁴⁰ Especially expressive of subjective reflection is the prepositional phrase ἐφ' ἑαυτοῦ, "by himself," that is, "by his own lights," or "on his own merits,"³⁴¹ suggesting a judgment that one makes "for oneself" in a moment of reflection.³⁴² Indeed, the effect of the addition of the phrase ἐφ' ἑαυτοῦ to the directive τοῦτο λογιζέσθω πάλιν is subtly humiliating.³⁴³ A final, personalizing feature is the brief repetition of the premise, καθὼς αὐτὸς Χριστοῦ ("just as he is of Christ"), inserted rather awkwardly within the desired conclusion. All of these elements (πέποιθεν, ἑαυτῷ, ἐφ' ἑαυτοῦ, καθὼς αὐτὸς Χριστοῦ) lend a subjective and individual cast to the sentence, but are strictly speaking unnecessary to a straightforward comparison designed to establish the equality of Paul's claim to belong to Christ; they retard the flow of the sentence, while at the same

---

336 Barrett, *Second Epistle*, 256, 260; Wolff, *Der zweite Brief*, 200.
337 Windisch, *Der zweite Korintherbrief*, 300.
338 LSJ 1345 s.v. πείθω B.III; Rom. 2:19; Phil. 3:3–4; Luke 18:9; 2 Chron. 32:15 (LXX); *BGU* IV.1147, 17. Cf. Plummer, *Second Epistle*, 280; Windisch, *Der zweite Korintherbrief*, 302.
339 See the discussion of this variant in Windisch, *Der zweite Korintherbrief*, 301, 302 n.1; Thrall, *Second Epistle*, 2.619 n.172.
340 Cf. Luke 18:9. Plummer, *Second Epistle*, 280; Windisch, *Der zweite Korintherbrief*, 302; Barrett, *Second Epistle*, 256; Wolff, *Der zweite Brief*, 200–201.
341 BDAG 365 s.v. ἐπί 8; Windisch, *Der zweite Korintherbrief*, 301; Furnish, *II Corinthians*, 466; Thrall, *Second Epistle*, 2.623 n.205.
342 Windisch, *Der zweite Korintherbrief*, 301, 302; Barrett, *Second Epistle*, 256; Furnish, *II Corinthians*, 466.
343 Windisch, *Der zweite Korintherbrief*, 300, 302; Furnish, *II Corinthians*, 466.

time heightening its rhetorical effect.[344] To a reader sensitive to such nuances, these features suggest that the pronoun τις in 10:7 refers to a specific individual.

In favor of regarding the person denoted by the pronoun in 10:7 as a local Corinthian, rather than an interloping apostle, are certain aspects of the structure and form of Paul's argument. First, the location of the claim by "someone" to be "of Christ" in one of the opening paragraphs of the discourse suggests that the person who makes this claim is among the primary addressees of the letter. Paul's (forced) comparison of himself with other apostles does not begin until 10:12. But in 10:7–11 Paul is still speaking directly to the Corinthians (note the second person pronouns, ὑμῶν and ὑμᾶς, in 10:8 and 10:9), to those who have read his letters and have experienced his presence and have heard him speak (10:10). Second, Paul's evocation of the claim of "someone" to be "of Christ" takes the form of an apostrophe.[345] To apostrophize someone who belongs to the community of addressees is rhetorically appropriate, but to apostrophize a person outside the community, an itinerant apostle, who would have no opportunity to read the letter, might be thought strange.[346]

Before seeking to comprehend the content of the claim to "belong to Christ," we should clarify, insofar as possible, the character and purpose of this assertion, and its critical implications for Paul. That the phrase Χριστοῦ εἶναι captures a slogan or catchword of some sort,[347] expressing the speaker's identity and sense of community, is indicated by the concision with which the expression is introduced in the premise of Paul's apostrophe: in this way, someone has formulated the depth of his sense of relationship to Christ. Moreover, the conjunction ὅτι, which prefaces the brief reformulation of the claim in the latter part of the verse, not only specifies what is to be taken into consideration (τοῦτο λογιζέσθω..., ὅτι),[348] but also signals a quotation,[349] reminding the reader of what

---

344 Windisch, *Der zweite Korintherbrief*, 300: "Der Satz bekommt so etwas Schwerfälliges; aber seine Wirkung wird gesteigert: er muss langsam und mit Betonung jedes Wortes gesprochen Werden."
345 Windisch, *Der zweite Korintherbrief*, 300, 302.
346 Windisch, *Der zweite Korintherbrief*, 302.
347 Windisch, *Der zweite Korintherbrief*, 301; Bultmann, *Der zweite Brief*, 190; Schmithals, *Gnosticism in Corinth*, 197; Georgi, *Gegner des Paulus*, 227–28; Theissen, *Social Setting*, 46–47.
348 Furnish, *II Corinthians*, 466. Cf. Rom. 2:3 (λογίζῃ δὲ τοῦτο,...ὅτι).
349 BDAG 731 s.v. ὅτι 1d; cf. Barrett, *Second Epistle*, 256, 260.

"someone" has said, namely, that he is "of Christ" (αὐτὸς Χριστοῦ). At the same time that someone expresses his sense of belonging to Christ in this way, the emphatic nature of that claim also implies some doubt as to whether Paul shares the sense of relationship embodied in the phrase Χριστοῦ εἶναι.[350]

What is the meaning of the claim by someone in Corinth to "belong to Christ"? The history of interpretation demonstrates that the meaning of the phrase Χριστοῦ εἶναι is anything but clear.[351] We may begin by eliminating untenable hypotheses, and in the process delimit the context in which a viable meaning may be found. First, it is unlikely that the claim to "belong to Christ" is associated with the party slogan ἐγὼ εἰμι Χριστοῦ ("I am of Christ") in 1 Cor. 1:12.[352] Analysis of 1 Cor. 1:12 suggests that the latter phrase is not a quotation of a slogan actually used by one of the factions at Corinth, but a Pauline parody of the tendency to partisanship that had manifested itself in the church, the absurdly hyperbolic climax of a series of parodic cries—"I am [a partisan] of Christ!"[353] But even if the "Christ party" actually existed and employed such a slogan, there is little possibility of a connection with the claim of "someone" to "belong to Christ" in 2 Cor. 10:7, for Paul proceeds to claim for himself what "someone" is confident of possessing—"we, too, are Christ's!"— a conclusion entirely inconsistent with Paul's determined opposition to partisanship in 1 Cor. 1–4.[354]

Second, it is improbable that the claim to "belong to Christ" expresses the consciousness of a distinctive, spiritual relationship with Christ on the part of a group of Corinthian Gnostics.[355] Although this theory has

---

350 Windisch, *Der zweite Korintherbrief,* 301; Barrett, *Second Epistle,* 256–57.
351 Georgi, *Gegner des Paulus,* 2–9; Furnish, *II Corinthians,* 476; Jerry L. Sumney, *Identifying Paul's Opponents: The Question of Method in 2 Corinthians* (Sheffield: Sheffield Academic Press, 1990) 92; Thrall, *Second Epistle,* 2.620–22.
352 Against, e.g., Hughes, *Paul's Second Epistle,* 356; Allo, *Saint Paul,* 246–47, 272–74; Schmithals, *Gnosticism in Corinth,* 192, 197–206. See the critique of this view by Windisch, *Der zweite Korintherbrief,* 301; Bruce, *1 and 2 Corinthians,* 231; Barrett, *Second Epistle,* 257; Furnish, *II Corinthians,* 476; Thrall, *Second Epistle,* 2.620–21.
353 Weiss, *Der erste Korintherbrief,* XXXVI-XXXIX,16–18; Mitchell, *Paul and the Rhetoric of Reconciliation,* 83, 86; Welborn, *Politics and Rhetoric,* 60–61.
354 Plummer, *Second Epistle,* 280; Barrett, *Second Epistle,* 257; Bultmann, *Der zweite Brief,* 190; Furnish, *II Corinthians,* 476; Wolff, *Der zweite Brief,* 200; Thrall, *Second Epistle,* 2.621.
355 Rightly rejected as improbable by Furnish, *II Corinthians,* 476; Sumney, *Identifying Paul's Opponents,* 92; Thrall, *Second Epistle,* 2.621.

been vigorously propounded by distinguished scholars,[356] it founders on Paul's claim to equality of relationship in 10:7b: Paul's bold assertion, "so also are we!" (οὕτως καὶ ἡμεῖς) would give the trump card to his theological opponents![357]

The majority of interpreters refer the pronoun τις in 10:7 to an outsider, a rival apostle, whose claim to "belong to Christ" is construed as the assertion of a special relationship to Jesus as the Christ, either through personal acquaintance with Jesus of Nazareth as one of his original disciples,[358] or through authorization to ministry by Jesus as an "apostle" or "servant" of Christ.[359] If either of these interpretations is correct, then Paul's claim to equality of relationship is manifestly unfounded, for Paul did not have any acquaintance with Jesus and was not one of his original disciples;[360] moreover, Paul elsewhere shows himself painfully aware that his status as an apostle rests on a different basis than those who derived their authorization from Jesus, or who were commissioned by the Jerusalem church.[361] In evaluating the hypothesis that the claim to "belong to Christ" in 10:7 refers to the status of an apostle, we should not fail to notice that those who explain the phrase Χριστοῦ εἶναι in this way consistently appeal to passages outside the context of 10:7—to 11:13, where Paul's missionary rivals are called "apostles of Christ" (ἀπόστολοι Χριστοῦ), and to 11:23, where the same persons are characterized as "servants of Christ" (διάκονοι Χριστοῦ).[362] Indeed, Heinrici even pronounces the addition of δοῦλος ("servant") to Χριστοῦ in the Western text of 10:7 "a correct gloss" ("eine richtige Glosse").[363] Whatev-

---

356 Lütgert, *Schwarmgeister in Korinth*, 89–92; Bultmann, *Der zweite Brief*, 189; Héring, *Saint Paul*, 72; 72; Schmithals, *Gnosticism in Corinth*, 63–65, 197–98.
357 Wolff, *Der zweite Brief*, 200; Thrall, *Second Epistle*, 2.621; Harris, *Second Epistle*, 688–89.
358 Klöpper, *Kommentar*, 433; Hughes, *Paul's Second Epistle*, 356; Martin, *2 Corinthians*, 307–308.
359 Windisch, *Der zweite Korintherbrief*, 301–303; Georgi, *Gegner des Paulus*, 227–28; Barrett, *Second Epistle*, 257–58; Furnish, *II Corinthians*, 476; Sumney, *Identifying Paul's Opponents*, 158; Thrall, *Second Epistle*, 2.622; Harris, *Second Epistle*, 691.
360 Windisch, *Der zweite Korintherbrief*, 301, 302; Barrett, *Second Epistle*, 257; Bultmann, *Der zweite Brief*, 189; Furnish, *II Corinthians*, 476; Thrall, *Second Epistle*, 2.621.
361 Theissen, *Social Setting*, 46–47, 66–67.
362 E.g., Hughes, *Paul's Second Epistle*, 356; Barrett, *Second Epistle*, 257; Furnish, *II Corinthians*, 476; Thrall, *Second Epistle*, 2.622.
363 Heinrici, *Der zweite Brief*, 326; cf. Bachmann, *Der zweite Brief*, 349.

er the enigmatic phrase "belonging to Christ" (Χριστοῦ εἶναι) may mean, it is surely wrong, methodologically, to begin the search by importing the sense of "servant" or "apostle" from another context. We must be content to seek the meaning of Χριστοῦ or Χριστοῦ εἶναι without supplement, and we must restrict our search to the immediate context of 10:7, where "someone" emphatically expresses his confidence in his relationship to Christ by employing this phrase.

What, then, is the meaning of "belonging to Christ" in this context? And why should the individual who expresses his sense of identity in this way seem to deny the depth of that relationship to Paul? The simplest and most obvious answer, and the one that remains most firmly within the bounds of what is implied by the genitive, is that Χριστοῦ εἶναι means "being a Christian."[364] This is also the meaning which is clearly indicated by the usage of Χριστοῦ elsewhere in Paul's epistles (e.g., 1 Cor. 3:23; 15:23; Gal. 3:29).[365] So the point at issue in 10:7 is not apostleship, but Christian existence: "If someone is confident that he is a follower of Christ, let him bear in mind that I am one too!"[366] The problem with this obvious explanation is that it seems to imply too much or too little: negatively, it entails the absurd suggestion that Paul is not a Christian; positively, it is so inclusive that it leaves no room for the insinuation that something is lacking in Paul's relationship to Christ.[367] The commentators are right to insist that something is missing in the obvious meaning of Χριστοῦ εἶναι in 10:7.[368]

In this case, the aporia lies not in the text, but *in ourselves.* Ironically, the internal barrier against which modern interpreters struggle is one that was erected within the tradition by Paul; our difficulty in understanding measures the triumph of Paulinism. How is one to understand what it would have meant to "belong to Christ," *prior to* the rupture in the community of "Abraham's offspring" (Gal. 3:29) which Paul's mission to the

---

364 Meyer, *Der zweite Brief*, 400; Plummer, *Second Epistle*, 280; Käsemann, "Die Legitimität des Apostels," 34–36; Oostendorp, *Another Jesus*, 18–19; Walker, *Paul's Offer of Leniency*, 321–22 n.159.
365 Weiss, *Der erste Korintherbrief*, 91; cf. Windisch, *Der zweite Korintherbrief*, 301: "Durch den Sprachgebrauch bei Paulus wird [für die Erklärung des Χριστοῦ εἶναι an uns. Stelle die einfache Zugehörigkeit zu Christus, das Christsein] entschieden am meisten empfohlen…"; Furnish, *II Corinthians*, 466.
366 Walker, *Paul's Offer of Leniency*, 321–22 n.159.
367 Windisch, *Der zweite Korintherbrief*, 301–302; Barrett, *Second Epistle*, 257–58.
368 Windisch, *Der zweite Korintherbrief*, 300; Barrett, *Second Epistle*, 256; Thrall, *Second Epistle*, 2.619; Harris, *Second Epistle*, 688.

Gentiles brought about? How is one to understand what it would have meant to "be a Christian" *prior to* the new form which Paul gave to Christian existence through his concept of participation in the cross of Christ? The challenge to the interpreter is to recover an understanding of "belonging to Christ" that antedates the crucial developments in Paul's thinking which produced what became the normative definition of "being a Christian."[369]

We are helped in this problematic undertaking by the fact that the transition from one sense of "belonging to Christ" to another runs directly through the letters of Paul. Thus one may glimpse the outlines of an older concept in several passages in Paul's earlier epistles. In 1 Cor. 15:23 Paul expounds the eschatological consequences of the coming (παρουσία) of Christ: for "those who belong to Christ" (οἱ τοῦ Χριστοῦ), his coming will mean life from the dead (ζῳοποιηθεῖν), participation in the resurrection.[370] In Gal. 3:29 Paul climaxes his account of the new identity in Christ by assuring the Galatians: "If you belong to Christ (εἰ δὲ ὑμεῖς Χριστοῦ), then you are Abraham's seed, heirs (κληρονόμοι) according to the promise."[371] In 1 Cor. 3:21–23 Paul seeks to elevate the consciousness of the Corinthians beyond their petty preoccupation with human leaders by reminding them of the spiritual riches and eschatological sovereignty which is theirs as the people who "belong to Christ": "For all things are yours, whether Paul or Apollos or Cephas, whether the world or life or death, whether things present or things to come; all things are yours!"[372] The final line of vs. 23 supplies, in the form of a coda, the reason for the subordination of all things to the Corinthians, at the same time that it reminds them of the one to whom they are subordinate: "and you belong to Christ (ὑμεῖς δὲ Χριστοῦ), and Christ be-

---

369 Udo Schnelle, *Wandlungen im paulinischen Denken* (Stuttgart: Katholisches Bibelwerk, 1989) esp. 49–54; Hans Dieter Betz, *Galatians: A Commentary on Paul's Letter to the Galatians*. Hermeneia (Philadelphia: Fortress Press, 1979) 181–201; Judith M. Lieu, *Christian Identity in the Jewish and Graeco-Roman World* (Oxford: Oxford University Press, 2004) 5–7.
370 Andreas Lindemann, "Paulus und die korinthische Eschatologie. Zur These von einer 'Entwicklung' im paulinischen Denken," *NTS* 37 (1991) 373–99.
371 Betz, *Galatians*, 201.
372 Weiss, *Der erste Korintherbrief*, 88–92; idem, *Primitive Christianity*, 2.460–61; Thistelton, *First Epistle*, 327–29; Mary Katherine Birge, *The Language of Belonging: A Rhetorical Analysis of Kinship Language in First Corinthians* (Leuven: Peeters, 2002) 19–22.

longs to God."³⁷³ The concept of "belonging to Christ" which comes to expression in these passages is rooted in Jewish apocalyptic expectation, classically formulated in the book of Daniel,³⁷⁴ in which the people of God in the last days are promised sovereignty over the world and a share in the resurrection.³⁷⁵

The most detailed account of Jewish messianic expectation prior to Paul is preserved in the writing known as the Psalms of Solomon, dated to the middle of the first century B.C.³⁷⁶ Here the fulfiller of Jewish hopes of deliverance is given the titles "Son of David" and "Lord Messiah" (Χριστὸς κύριος).³⁷⁷ The Messiah who is described in ch. 17 is more than the anointed king of Israel. He is the final judge of all the nations, the destroyer of the unrighteous.³⁷⁸ Yet, his power is not military, but spiritual: he exposes corruption and drives out sinners by the strength of his word; he is thoroughly imbued with holiness and embodies the highest virtues—wisdom, justice and mercy.³⁷⁹ Of special importance is the obvious interest of the author of the Psalms of Solomon in the rela-

---

373 Weiss, *Der erste Korintherbrief,* 90–92; Collins, *First Corinthians,* 166; Birge, *Language of Belonging,* 21–22.
374 Daniel 6–7; see also *4 Ezra* 6:59; Weiss, *Der erste Korintherbrief,* 89.
375 Weiss, *Der erste Korintherbrief,* 89; David W. Kuck, *Judgment and Community Conflict: Paul's Use of Apocalyptic Judgment Langauge in 1 Corinthians 3:5–4:5* (Leiden: Brill, 1992) 190–96.
376 Robert B. Wright, "Psalms of Solomon" in *The Old Testament Pseudepigrapha,* Vol. 2, ed. James H. Charlesworth (Garden City: Doubleday, 1985) 639–72, esp. 643: "There is more substance to the ideas concerning the Messiah in the Psalms of Solomon than in any other extant Jewish writing"; idem, *The Psalms of Solomon: A Critical Edition of the Greek Text* (New York: T & T Clark, 2007). On date and provenance, see also Kenneth Atkinson, "Herod the Great, Sosius, and the Siege of Jerusalem in Psalm of Solomon 17," *NovT* 38 (1996) 313–22; idem, *I Cried to the Lord: A Study of the Psalms of Solomon's Historical Background and Social Setting* (Leiden: Brill, 2004).
377 *Pss. Sol.* 17:21, 32. Cf. G. L. Davenport, "The 'Anointed of the Lord' in Psalms of Solomon 17" in *Ideal Figures in Ancient Judaism,* eds. John J. Collins and G. W. Nickelsburg (Chico: Scholars Press, 1980) 67–92; Wright, "Psalms of Solomon," 643, 646–47, 667–68; Craig A. Evans, "Messianic Hopes and Messianic Figures in Late Antiquity," *JGRChJ* 3 (2006) 20–22; Andrew Chester, *Messiah and Exaltation: Jewish Messianic and Visionary Traditions and New Testament Christology* (Tübingen: Mohr Siebeck, 2007) 340–44.
378 Wright, "Psalms of Solomon," 645; Marinus de Jonge, "Expectation of the Future in the Psalms of Solomon," *Neotestamentica* 23 (1989) 93–117.
379 *Pss. Sol.* 17:23–25; cf. Wright, "Psalms of Solomon," 643, 645; Chester, *Messiah and Exaltation,* 342–43.

tionship between the Messiah and the people for whom he is raised up.[380] The Messiah comes not only to deliver Israel from the gentile oppressor, but also to purify the people and to impart to them wisdom and righteousness.[381] Indeed, the latter aspect of the rule of the Messiah receives the greater emphasis: "He will gather a holy people whom he will lead in righteousness" (17:26); "For he shall know them that they are all children of their God" (17:27); "There will be no unrighteousness among them in his days, for all shall be holy" (17:32); "He will bless the Lord's people with wisdom and happiness" (17:35); "Faithfully and righteously shepherding the Lord's flock, he will not let any of them stumble in their pasture" (17:14); "Blessed are those born in those days!" (17:44). The persons who chanted these psalms or read them for encouragement looked forward to a future in which they would be enriched with wisdom and ennobled with righteousness by the "Lord Messiah."[382]

Such texts, and others that might have been adduced,[383] make it possible to recover an understanding of what it would have meant to "belong to Christ" prior to the redefinition of the concept by Paul in his later epistles. A modest use of historical imagination would allow us to envi-

---

380 Wright, "Psalms of Solomon," 645–46.
381 *Pss. Sol.* 17:22–23; 18:5–7; Wright, "Psalms of Solomon," 643, 645.
382 J. Schüpphaus, *Die Psalmen Salomos: Ein Zeugnis Jerusalemer Theologie und Frömmigkeit in der Mitte des vorchristlichen Jahrhunderts* (Leiden: Brill, 1977); Wright, "Psalms of Solomon," 646–47; Evans, "Messianic Hopes and Messianic Figures," 21–22; Chester, *Messiah and Exaltation*, 341–44.
383 See esp. 4 Ezra 7:27–30; 12:32–34; Michael E. Stone, "The Concept of the Messiah in 4 Ezra" in *Religions in Antiquity*, ed. J. Neusner (Leiden: Brill, 1968) 295–312; idem, *Fourth Ezra: A Commentary on the Book of Fourth Ezra*. Hermeneia (Minneapolis: Fortress Press, 1990) 207–13; idem, "The Question of the Messiah in 4 Ezra" in *Selected Studies in Pseudepigrapha and Apocrypha*, ed. M. Stone (Leiden: Brill, 1991) 317–32. On messianic figures in other Pseudepigrapha, see James H. Charlesworth, "The Concept of the Messiah in the Pseudepigrapha," *ANRW* II/19.1 (1979) 189–218; Matthew Black, "The Messianism of the Parables of Enoch: Their Date and Contributions to Christological Origins" in *The Messiah: Developments in Earliest Judaism and Christianity*, ed. J. H. Charlesworth (Minneapolis: Fortress Press, 1992) 145–68; Michael A. Knibb, "Messianism in the Pseudepigrapha in Light of the Scrolls," *Dead Sea Discoveries* 2 (1995) 165–84. On the messianism of the Dead Sea Scrolls, see John J. Collins, *The Scepter and the Star: The Messiahs of the Dead Sea Scrolls and Other Ancient Literature* (New York: Doubleday, 1995); James H. Charlesworth, Hermann Lichtenberger, and Gerbern S. Oegema, eds., *Qumran-Messianism: Studies on the Messianic Expectations in the Dead Sea Scrolls* (Tübingen: Mohr Siebeck, 1998).

sion the day on which a God-fearer, standing in the atrium or the peristyle of the house of Titius Justus, to which Paul's auditors resorted after his departure from the synagogue (Acts 18:7), would have heard, for the first time, the proclamation that "the Messiah (Χριστός) was Jesus" (Acts 18:5). Let us try to imagine the amazement with which our God-fearer would have listened as Paul witnessed that "Christ died for our sins in accordance with the scriptures" (1 Cor. 15:3), the thrill with which the announcement would have entered his consciousness that "God raised him out of the dead" (1 Thess. 1:10; 1 Cor. 15:4), the eagerness with which he would have received the exhortation "to wait for the Son from heaven—Jesus who rescues us from the coming wrath" (1 Thess. 1:10). If our God-fearer believed this "good news," and was baptized into the people of Christ (1 Cor. 12:12–13; Gal. 3:27)–what then? The texts examined above indicate that he would have experienced hope, a sense of entitlement, a feeling of sovereignty, the possession of wisdom and righteousness, happiness. An explanation of this emotional response would necessitate a separate essay in ancient social psychology—and more than one such essay! But the sources leave no doubt of the reality of a new sense of identity and community associated with the experience of "belonging to Christ."[384]

If this reconstruction of the sense of "belonging to Christ" is plausible, then the question gains urgency: Why should the Corinthian Christian whose elevated self-consciousness Paul interrogates in 2 Cor. 10:7 deny to Paul the sense of sovereignty and freedom he had come to possess as a follower of Christ? The answer to this question lies in *the new meaning which Paul had given to the death of Christ*, precisely in the course of his relationship with the church at Corinth. In that portion of the writing known to us as 1 Corinthians which preceded the composition of 2 Cor. 10–13, namely the letter now preserved in 1 Cor. 1:1–6:11,[385]

---

384 See the comments of Wright, "Psalms of Solomon," 643–46, on the "eschatological hope" and "confidence" of the psalmist; see also Weiss, *Der erste Korintherbrief*, 91, on the self-consciousness that comes to expression in 1 Cor. 3:23: "das grossartige Freiheits-und Herrschergefühl der Christen."

385 For the hypothesis that 1 Cor. 1:1–6:11 was originally an independent letter, the third in the sequence of Paul's letters to Corinth, see Weiss, *Der erste Korintherbrief*, XXXIX-XLIII; idem, *Primitive Christianity*, 1.323–41; Schenk, "Der 1. Korintherbrief als Briefsammlung," 219–43; Senft, *La première épître*, 17–25; Bünker, *Briefformular und rhetorische Disposition*, 51–59; cf. Gerhard Sellin, "Hauptprobleme des Ersten Korintherbriefes," *ANRW* II/25.4 (1987) 2940–3044.

Paul had begun to speak, for the first time in his extant letters, of his gospel as "the message about the cross" (ὁ λόγος τοῦ σταυροῦ), and had begun to focus upon a single aspect of the Christ event: "Christ crucified" (Χριστὸς ἐσταυρωμένος).[386] The reasons for this development in Paul's thought remain obscure.[387] It is possible that criticism of various aspects of Paul's person—his weakness, his lack of oratorical ability, his banausic occupation—led Paul to reflect upon his critic's assessment, and to seek justification for his existence in the shameful manner of Christ's death.[388] But whatever the origin of this development may have been, there is no mistaking its reality and novelty.

In 1 Thessalonians, Paul's earliest epistle, there is no mention of the "crucified Christ"; both the noun σταυρός and the verb σταυροῦν are missing.[389] If 1 Thess. 1:9b-10 reflects the outline of Paul's preaching in the early years of his mission,[390] then the shameful manner of Jesus' death was not emphasized. The kerygmatic formula in 1 Cor. 15:3b speaks of the death of Christ (Χριστὸς ἀπέθανεν), but not of the *manner* of his death.[391] All of this changes suddenly in 1 Cor. 1–4, where references to the "cross" and the "crucified Christ" are concentrated (1 Cor. 1:13, 17, 18, 23; 2:2, 8). The expression, ὁ λόγος τοῦ σταυροῦ ("the message about the cross"), by which Paul summarizes his gospel in 1 Cor. 1:18, is unique in the New Testament.[392] This reduction of the content of the message about Christ to a single, shameful event is stunning.[393] Paul's choice of the perfect participle, ἐσταυρωμένος (1 Cor. 1:23; 2:2), to describe the Christ whom he proclaims seems especially provocative, for the perfect tense conveys the idea that the continuing and present significance of Christ, even *after* his resurrection, consists in nothing other than the fact that he *is* "the crucified."[394] Of spe-

---

386 Schnelle, *Wandlungen im paulinischen Denken*, 49–54; Wolfgang Schrage, "Der gekreuzigte und auferweckte Herr," *ZThK* 94 (1997) 25–38.
387 Welborn, *Paul, the Fool of Christ*, 251–52.
388 Welborn, *Paul, the Fool of Christ*, 90–99, 252–53.
389 Schrage, "Der gekreuzigte und auferweckte Herr," 25–26.
390 Lüdemann, *Paul, Apostle to the Gentiles*, 107.
391 Theo K. Heckel, "Der Gekreuzigte bei Paulus," *BZ* 46 (2002) 190–210, esp. 194–95.
392 Heinz-Wolfgang Kuhn, "Jesus als Gekreuzigter in der frühchristlichen Verkündigung bis zur Mitte des 2. Jahrhunderts," *ZThK* 72 (1975) 27–41; Collins, *First Corinthians*, 101; Welborn, *Paul, the Fool of Christ*, 22–23.
393 Weiss, *Der erste Korintherbrief*, 26–27; Schrage, *Der erste Brief*, 1.165.
394 Heinz-Wolfgang Kuhn, "Kreuz," *TRE* 19 (1990) 720; Heckel, "Der Gekreuzigte bei Paulus," 196–200.

cial importance is the programmatic statement in 1 Cor. 2:2: "For I decided (ἔκρινα) not to know anything among you except Jesus Christ and him crucified (ἐσταυρωμένος)."[395] If the aorist tense of κρίνειν is to be taken seriously, Paul recollects a moment in the course of his mission work at Corinth when he "decided" to proclaim Christ as "the crucified."[396]

The consequences of this new conception of the Christ event for those who "belong to Christ" are dramatic and paradoxical: the followers of Christ must now share in the weakness, foolishness and ignominy of their crucified Lord. Paul introduces a radical explanation of the empirical fact that the majority of those who have been "called" by the gospel are persons without education, wealth, or noble birth: this is because *"God has chosen* the foolish,…the weak,…the lowborn of the world and the despised" (1 Cor. 1:26–27).[397] The consequences are most extreme for the apostles, that is, for those who have conformed their lives to the fate of the "crucified Christ" and preach "the message about the cross." Paul describes his life as an apostle in graphic and vulgar terms which associate himself and his missionary colleagues with the dregs of society, the scum of the earth: "For I suppose that God has put us apostles on show last of all, as people condemned to death, because we have become a theater-act to the world, both to angels and to human beings. We are fools on account of Christ,…we are weak,…we are dishonored;…we are hungry and thirsty, we are naked, we are beaten, we are homeless, and we toil, laboring with our own hands; we are reviled, harassed, slandered; we have become like the refuse of the world, the scum of all things, to this very day" (1 Cor. 4:9–13).[398]

How this new understanding of Christ and "belonging to Christ" appeared to the minority of Corinthian Christians who possessed education, wealth and birth (1 Cor. 1:26) we can judge from Paul's argument in 1 Cor. 1–4 and 2 Cor. 10–13, insofar as Paul's argument anticipates or reflects his readers' response.[399] The reduction of the content of the

---

395 Welborn, *Paul, the Fool of Christ*, 252.
396 Schnelle, *Wandlungen im paulinischen Denken*, 49–54.
397 Theissen, *Social Setting*, 71–73; Welborn, *Paul, the Fool of Christ*, 147.
398 Welborn, *Paul, the Fool of Christ*, 50–86, 249.
399 Jerry Sumney has warned against "mirror-reading" in reconstructions of Paul's opponents, most recently in "Studying Paul's Opponents: Advances and Challenges" in *Paul and His Opponents*, ed. Stanley E. Porter (Leiden: Brill, 2005) 7–58. But it is clear that Paul's argument in 2 Cor. 10–13 anticipates his readers' response, or reflects terms used in criticism of him, at a number of points:

gospel to a single, shameful event—Christ's death on the cross—was deemed to be "foolishness" (μωρία), a vulgar joke.[400] To speak of the "cross" at all was "shameful to a Roman citizen and a free man."[401] But to dwell upon the shameful manner of Jesus' death was simply obscene, a foolish vulgarity. Why reduce the good news about Christ to an account of his ignominious end, thereby "emptying" the gospel of its "power" (1 Cor. 1:17)?[402] Paul's willingness to embrace weakness and to accept abuse was seen as confirmation of suspicions aroused by his lack of oratorical ability and his decision to support himself by working with his hands: Paul was simply a μωρός ("fool") and a ταπεινός ("servile person") whose attitudes and behavior reflected the limitations of his social class.[403] To make no use of the divine gifts of speech and knowledge, to degrade oneself needlessly in banausic employment, to respond in a compliant and cringing manner to mistreatment, was to present the emissary of Christ to the world as ludicrous and contemptible. Most puzzling of all must have been Paul's redefinition of those who "belong to Christ" as "the foolish," "the weak," "the lowborn," "the despised," "mere nothings" (1 Cor. 1:27–28).[404] Why this impoverishment of the experience of "belonging to Christ"? What has become of the feeling of sovereignty, the possession of wisdom, the sense of entitlement, the happiness and hope associated with the coming of Christ, and which Christ brings to those who are his? That the Corinthians, or at least the upper class converts, viewed their wealth of "speech" (λόγος) and "knowledge" (γνῶσις)

---

see, e.g., the observations of Furnish (*II Corinthians*, 466) on λογίζεσθαι in 2 Cor. 10:7: "Here *logizesthai* repeats a term which the apostle's critics have apparently been using in mounting their attacks on his ministry, and which he has already turned back on them in vv. 2 and 4."

400 Weiss, *Der erste Korintherbrief*, 25–27; Welborn, *Paul, the Fool of Christ*, 22–23, 103.
401 Cicero *Rab. Post.* 5.16; cf. Varro *Ling. Lat.* 5.25.
402 On 1 Cor. 1:17 as a response to criticism of Paul's preaching, see Weiss, *Der erste Korintherbrief*, 23; Litfin, *St. Paul's Theology of Proclamation*187; Stephen M. Pogoloff, *Logos and Sophia: The Rhetorical Situation of 1 Corinthians* (Atlanta: Scholars Press, 1992) 99–127, esp. 109; Lindemann, *Der erste Korintherbrief*, 43; J. S. Vos, "Die Argumentation des Paulus in 1 Kor 1,10–3,4" in *The Corinthian Correspondence*, ed. R. Bieringer (Leuven: Leuven University Press, 1996) 96–97; Smit, "What is Apollos? What is Paul?" 236, 246–48; Welborn, *Paul, the Fool of Christ*, 103–104.
403 Georgi, *Gegner des Paulus*, 234–41; Hock, *Social Context*, 36, 63–65; Welborn, *Paul, the Fool of Christ*, 49–86, 102–103.
404 Theissen, *Social Setting*, 71; Collins, *First Corinthians*, 110–11; Welborn, *Paul, the Fool of Christ*, 147–48, 230.

as divine gifts conferred upon them by virtue of being "in Christ" is clear from Paul's thanksgiving for the Corinthians in 1 Cor. 1:4–5, despite his ironic treatment of their "enrichment."[405] And that the Corinthians, or at least the wealthy among them ("the satiated," "the rich," "the royal"),[406] were possessed of a strong sense of "sovereignty," like that which shines through Psalms of Solomon and is still reflected darkly in 4 Ezra, by virtue of "belonging to Christ," is abundantly clear from 1 Cor. 4:8, despite Paul's bitter and sarcastic critique: "Already you have all you want! Already you have become rich! Quite apart from us you reign like kings (ἐβασιλεύσατε)! Indeed, I wish that you had become kings, so that we might share the reign (συμβασιλεύσωμεν) with you!"[407] And that the Corinthians, or at least the elite among them, felt that they had been enriched and ennobled with wisdom and power and honor by virtue of being "in Christ," is clear from Paul's direct comparison of his condition with theirs in 1 Cor. 4:10, despite the bitterness of his antitheses: "We are fools on account of Christ, but you are wise in Christ (ἐν Χριστῷ). We are weak, but you are strong. You are held in honor, but we in disrepute."[408] For those who were imbued with a consciousness of wisdom, power, and honor on account of the coming of Christ, Paul's valorization of foolishness, weakness and dishonor must have seemed an incalculable loss.

---

405 Weiss, *Der erste Korintherbrief,* 7, 108–109; Lindemann, *Der erste Korintherbrief,* 30; Collins, *First Corinthians,* 62; Welborn, *Politics and Rhetoric,* 38.
406 For "satiety" (κόρος) as a characteristic of the rich, see Philo *Flacc.* 77; Dio Chrysostom *Or.* 7.17; Lucian *Merc. cond.* 8. On the connection of "satiety" with wealth, see esp. Luke 6:24–25; Dio Chrysostom *Or.* 1.67; 30.19. For other texts in this regard, see Marshall, *Enmity in Corinth,* 183–84, 188–89; John T. Fitzgerald, *Cracks in an Earthen Vessel: An Examination of the Catalogues of Hardships in the Corinthian Correspondence* (Atlanta: Scholars Press, 1988) 133–35. On Paul's characterization of some in Corinth as "royal" (ἐβασιλεύσατε), see Dale B. Martin, *Slavery as Salvation: The Metaphor of Slavery in Pauline Christianity* (New Haven: Yale University Press, 1990) 210 n.13, who observes that "king" is the client's term for a rich patron: see, e.g., Horace *Ep.* 1.7.37–38; Juvenal *Sat.* 5.14, 130, 137, 161; 7.45; 10.161.
407 On the irony of this passage, see Weiss, *Der erste Korintherbrief,* 105–108; Plank, *Paul and the Irony of Affliction,* 48–52; Welborn, *Paul, the Fool of Christ,* 115–16.
408 Weiss, *Der erste Korintherbrief,* 110; Theissen, *Social Setting,* 70–73; Plank, *Paul and the Irony of Affliction,* 47; H. Merklein, *Der erste Brief an die Korinther. Kapitel 1–4* (Gütersloh: Gütersloher Verlagshaus Mohn, 1992) 313–14; Welborn, *Paul, the Fool of Christ,* 128.

Paul disputes this understanding of his gospel with an argument as bold and innovative as any in his epistles (1 Cor. 1:18–2:16).[409] Paul insists, paradoxically, that the message about the cross does not empty the gospel of Christ of its power (1 Cor. 1:17), but rather discloses the hidden source of the gospel's strength, its power to save (1 Cor. 1:18, 30; 2:7). To "the low and despised of the world" (1 Cor. 1:28), to whose ranks belong the majority of the Corinthian Christians (1 Cor. 1:26), and to any others who are "called," both Jews and Greeks, the "crucified Christ" is a figure of divine empowerment. Paul reassures his Corinthian readers: "He [God] is the source of your life in Christ Jesus (ἐξ αὐτοῦ δὲ ὑμεῖς ἐστε ἐν Χριστῷ Ἰησοῦ), for us wisdom from God, and righteousness and sanctification and redemption" (1 Cor. 1:30).[410] Here all of the spiritual riches attendant upon the coming of the Messiah in Jewish eschatology are predicated of the *crucified* Christ and the people who belong to him—"the low and despised of the world, the nobodies" (1 Cor. 1:28)![411] In a supreme paradox, Paul asserts that the foolish message about the crucified Christ is actually the highest wisdom.[412] But this wisdom is incomprehensible to the rulers of this age (1 Cor. 2:6–8).[413] Paul discloses this "hidden" wisdom only to those who are able to receive

---

409 R. A. Humphries, "Paul's Rhetoric of Argumentation in 1 Corinthians 1–4," GTU Ph.D. Dissertation (Berkeley, 1979); Plank, *Paul and the Irony of Affliction*, 34–42; Schrage, *Der erste Brief*, 1.165; Alexandra R. Brown, *The Cross and Human Transformation: Paul's Apocalyptic Word in 1 Corinthians* (Minneapolis: Fortress Press, 1995) 12; Raymond Pickett, *The Cross in Corinth: The Social Significance of the Death of Jesus* (Sheffield: Sheffield Academic Press, 1997) 61; Vos, "Die Argumentation des Paulus," 104–105; Thistelton, *First Epistle*, 147–48; Welborn, *Paul, the Fool of Christ*, 115, 164–65.
410 Weiss, *Der erste Korintherbrief*, 38–43; Schrage, *Der erste Brief*, 1.213–16; Thiselton, *First Epistle*, 188–92; Welborn, *Paul, the Fool of Christ*, 230, 233.
411 Heinrici, *Der erste Brief*, 79; Theissen, *Social Setting*, 71–72; Collins, *First Corinthians*, 110–11; Welborn, *Paul, the Fool of Christ*, 147–48.
412 Weiss, *Der erste Korintherbrief*, 25, 27–29, 34; Schrage, *Der erste Brief*, 1.175; Welborn, *Paul, the Fool of Christ*, 161.
413 The identity of "the rulers of this age" (οἱ ἄρχοντες τοῦ αἰῶνος τούτου) has long been a subject of dispute, with some interpreters equating "the rulers" with spiritual, demonic powers, i.e., Martin Dibelius, *Die Geisterwelt im Glauben des Paulus* (Göttingen: Vandenhoeck & Ruprecht, 1909); Conzelmann, *1 Corinthians*, 61, and others suggesting that "the rulers" are earthly, political authorities, i.e., J. Schniewind, "Die Archonten des Äons, 1 Kor. 2,6–8" in *Nachgelassene Reden und Aufsätze*, ed. E. Kähler (Berlin: Töpelmann, 1952) 104–109; A. Wesley Carr, "The Rulers of This Age—1 Cor. ii.6–8," *NTS* 23 (1976) 20–35. Cf. Thistelton, *First Epistle*, 333–39.

it—"the initiates," "the mature" (1 Cor. 2:6–7).[414] That Paul has not yet been able to lead the Corinthians to this deeper understanding of the gospel is because they are still "infants in Christ" (1 Cor. 3:1). But Paul will not allow that any loss of sovereignty or transcendence has occurred as a result of his preaching of the crucified Christ: "All things are yours," Paul assures the Corinthians, "whether the world or life or death, whether things present or things to come; all things are yours!" (1 Cor. 3:21–22). Paul clearly believes that he has discovered the hidden meaning of the Christ event, the source of the gospel's power. Paul's pedagogical purpose, evident at several points in 1 Cor. 1–4, is to lead the Corinthians into a deeper understanding of what it means to "belong to Christ."[415]

Paul signals the continuation of his pedagogical purpose by the way in which he introduces his apostrophe of the wrongdoer in 2 Cor. 10:7, summoning him, and all of the Corinthians, to reconsider the meaning of Χριστοῦ εἶναι: "Look at what is before your face" (τὰ κατὰ πρόσωπον βλέπετε). This phrase is best understood as a directive,[416] construing βλέπετε as an imperative, as it is virtually everywhere in Paul.[417] The emphatic position of the object before the verb alerts the reader to the importance of the words τὰ κατὰ πρόσωπον: "there is something 'before your eyes' that you have failed to see; if you look again, you may comprehend it!"[418] In looking again, the reader cannot fail to notice the recapitulation of the highly charged emotional vocabulary of 10:1-2–κατὰ πρόσωπον, πεποίθησις, λογίζεσθαι: Paul thus takes the reader back in thought to the scene in which he was humiliated, while his adversary

---

414 On the τέλειοι in 1 Cor. 2:6, see Weiss, *Der erste Korintherbrief,* 52–54, 73–74; Gerhard Delling, "τέλειος," *TDNT* 8 (1972) 75–76; Lindemann, *Der erste Korintherbrief,* 62; Sigurd Grindheim, "Wisdom for the Perfect: Paul's Challenge to the Corinthian Church (1 Corinthians 2.6–16)," *JBL* 121 (2002) 689–702.

415 E.g., 1 Cor. 1:30; 2:6–16; 3:23. With special reference to Paul's pedagogical purpose in 2:6–16, see Ulrich Wilkens, "Zu 1 Kor 2,1–16" in *Theologia Crucis—Signum Crucis,* ed. C. Andresen and G. Klein (Tübingen: Mohr Siebeck, 1979) 501–37, esp. 513; Gerhard Sellin, "Das 'Geheimnis' der Weisheit und das Rätsel der 'Christuspartei' (zu 1 Kor 1–4)," *ZNW* 73 (1982) 69–96, esp. 81; Nicholas Wolter, "Verborgene Weisheit und Heil für die Heiden," *ZThK* 84 (1987) 297–319, esp. 304; Schrage, *Der erste Brief,* 1.240; Merklein, *Der erste Brief,* 224; Grindheim, "Wisdom for the Perfect," 694–97.

416 Windisch, *Der zweite Korintherbrief,* 300; Bachmann, *Der zweite Brief,* 347; Allo, *Saint Paul,* 246; Furnish, *II Corinthians,* 465; Wolff, *Der zweite Brief,* 200.

417 1 Cor. 8:9; 10:18; 16:10; Gal. 5:15; Phil. 3:2; deutero-Pauline, Col. 2:8; 4:17; Eph. 5:15. Cf. Barrett, *Second Epistle,* 256; Furnish, *II Corinthians,* 465.

418 Windisch, *Der zweite Korintherbrief,* 300; Furnish, *II Corinthians,* 465.

stood forth as confident. But by subtle shifts in the meaning of each term, Paul guides his readers toward a deeper and amended perception. Thus, πεποίθησις is given the pejorative sense of "unfounded certainty,"[419] problematizing the wrongdoer's "confidence" of "belonging to Christ"—perhaps his confidence is not rightly grounded. λογίζεσθαι is given a cognitive sense, relocated, by the qualifying phrase ἐφ' ἑαυτοῦ, within the mind of the subject: rather than calculating and evaluating on the basis of external criteria, the wrongdoer is challenged to reflect, to ponder, to dwell upon the matter in thought.[420] Most significant of all is the shift in meaning of the phrase κατὰ πρόσωπον. The reader cannot have forgotten that this phrase designated the context in which Paul appeared to be ταπεινός before the Corinthians—that is, when he was "face to face" with them (10:2).[421] But the word πρόσωπον carries the figurative meaning of "role" from the language of theater.[422] Epictetus uses the phrase κατὰ πρόσωπον in precisely this sense to describe the role that a man must play in the various circumstances of life in order to preserve his own "proper character."[423] Epictetus contrasts decisions that are made on the basis of that which is in keeping with "one's proper character" (τὸ κατὰ πρόσωπον) with "estimates of the value of external things."[424] In light of the number and vividness of the theatrical metaphors employed by Paul in 1 Cor. 1–4,[425] and especially in the "fool's speech" of 2 Cor. 11:1–12:10,[426] it seems likely that Paul intends a reference to the "roles" that he and the wrongdoer played respectively in their con-

---

419 Windisch, *Der zweite Korintherbrief*, 294, 301, 302; cf. Betz, *Der Apostel Paulus*, 68; Thrall, *Second Epistle*, 2.619, n.173.
420 Windisch, *Der zweite Korintherbrief*, 301; Thrall, *Second Epistle*, 2.623, n.205.
421 Wolff, *Der zweite Brief*, 200.
422 Philodemus *Rhet.* 1.199; Cicero *Att.* 13.19.3; Epictetus *Diatr.* 1.29.45, 57; LSJ 1533 s.v. πρόσωπον III.2.
423 Epictetus *Diatr.* 1.2; cf. Windisch, *Der zweite Korintherbrief*, 300; Robert F. Dobbins, *Epictetus. Discourses Book I; Translated with an Introduction and Commentary* (Oxford: Clarendon Press, 1998).
424 Epictetus *Diatr.* 1.2.7, 14, 28, 30; 2.10.7–8. On the influence of the Stoic Panaetius on Epictetus' concept of "one's proper character," and on Cicero's use of the term *persona* to designate various social roles, see A. Bonhöffer, *Die Ethik des Stoikers Epictet* (Stuttgart: Ferdinand Enke, 1894) 10–11; P. A. Brunt, "Stoicism and the Principate," *Papers of the British School at Rome* 43 (1975) 7–39, esp. 32–35; Dobbins, *Epictetus*, 78–82.
425 Welborn, *Paul, the Fool of Christ*, 50–101.
426 L. L. Welborn, "The Runaway Paul: A Character in the Fool's Speech, 2 Cor. 11:1–12:10," *HTR* 92 (1999) 115–63.

frontation before the Corinthians by his use of κατὰ πρόσωπον, and that he cleverly exploits this meaning of the phrase. Thus, by the summons to "look!" (βλέπετε), and by the strategic repetition of key vocabulary with an altered sense, Paul stages a scene of reconsideration in which the Corinthians, and especially the wrongdoer, are invited to "think again" (λογιζέσθω πάλιν), in the hope that they will come to a deeper understanding of what it means to "belong to Christ" and a truer appreciation of whose behavior is Christ-like.

Before turning away from 2 Cor. 10:7, we should not fail to notice what is before our *own* eyes with respect to the unnamed individual whom Paul addresses indirectly in regard to his claim to "belong to Christ": this person (in our view, the wrongdoer) is possessed of a fervent consciousness of "belonging to Christ," and is perplexed at the apparent loss of this confidence by Paul. It is necessary to emphasize this point, because, in the history of scholarship, the opponents of Paul in 2 Corinthians have been portrayed as theological epigone, focused on the surface level and preoccupied with external things, whether they are identified as Judaizers or Gnostics.[427] But if our reconstruction of the meaning of Χριστοῦ εἶναι is correct, then the individual whom Paul apostrophizes in 2 Cor. 10:7 understands the meaning of the Christ event in a way that is entirely consistent with the early preaching of the apostles, including Paul, and his sense of empowerment with wisdom and righteousness by virtue of "belonging to Christ" furnishes a window into the experience of being a Christian in the decades following the death of Jesus. It is noteworthy that Paul does not deny the wrongdoer's claim to "belong to Christ." Paul's rejoinder does not take the form, "I alone belong to Christ in full measure, while you do not," but rather, "Just as you belong to Christ, so do I," asserting an equality of relationship.[428] Our analysis of the claim of "someone" to "belong to Christ" in 2 Cor. 10:7 has opened a positive perspective on the consciousness of this individual. Whatever "wrong" he has done, it did not diminish his confidence of "belonging to Christ."

We come, now, in 2 Cor. 10:10, to an explicit quotation that embodies an evaluation of Paul, contrasting the powerful impression made by his letters with his weak appearance in person. The verse is, thus, an expository parallel to 10:1b which, like the earlier judgment, is formulated

---

427 Sumney, *Identifying Paul's Opponents*, 15–48.
428 Windisch, *Der zweite Korintherbrief*, 300, with further reference to 2 Cor. 11:5; 12:11

as a sharp antithesis consisting of two balanced and opposing clauses.[429] But in 10:10, we are provided with the substantive detail that constituted the basis for the earlier judgment, in the form of an assessment of Paul as a letter-writer and as a speaker. The criticism of Paul's qualities in these areas is of the highest value and interest, because it is the oldest such assessment that we possess.[430] Paul relates the following comment: "'The letters,' he says, 'are weighty and strong, but the bodily presence is weak and the speech is contemptible'" (αἱ ἐπιστολαὶ μέν, φησίν, βαρεῖαι καὶ ἰσχυραί, ἡ δὲ παρουσία τοῦ σώματος ἀσθενὴς καὶ ὁ λόγος ἐξουθενημένος).

Once again, it is necessary to state our reasons for regarding the evaluation of 10:10 as the words of a specific individual, rather than a generalization, as the judgment of a Corinthian, rather than an outsider, and, what is just as important, as a *literal quotation* of what someone has said, rather than a hypothetical criticism. First, the argument that 10:10 reports the words of a particular person. The verb φησίν, customarily translated "they say,"[431] is, in fact, a third person singular—literally, "he says," "he is saying."[432] (The variant φασίν is poorly attested,[433] and should be regarded as an ameliorating correction).[434] To be sure, φησί can be used in an impersonal sense to mean "it is said" or "one says,"[435] and this usage is

---

429 Windisch, *Der zweite Korintherbrief*, 305.
430 Windisch, *Der zweite Korintherbrief*, 305; Furnish, *II Corinthians*, 468; Barnett, *Second Epistle*, 475 n.42. For other early assessments, see Polycarp *Phil.* 3:2; 2 Peter 3:15–16. For later comments on Paul's epistles, see Edwin A. Judge, "Paul's Boasting in Relation to Contemporary Professional Practice," *AusBR* 16 (1968) 38–41, repr. in idem, *Social Distinctives of the First Christians*, 57–60.
431 Thus, the KJV, NRSV, along with some commentaries, e.g., Hughes, *Paul's Second Epistle*, 361, and monographs, e.g., Marshall, *Enmity in Corinth*, 323; Sumney, *Identifying Paul's Opponents*, 149.
432 So translated by A. Menzies, *The Second Epistle of the Apostle Paul to the Corinthians* (London: Macmillan, 1912) 73; Barrett, *Second Epistle*, 260; Martin, *2 Corinthians*, 311; Roetzel, *2 Corinthians*, 100.
433 B lat sy. Cf. Windisch, *Der zweite Korintherbrief*, 305 n.1; Hughes, *Paul's Second Epistle*, 362 n.19; Furnish, *II Corinthians*, 468; Barnett, *Second Epistle*, 475 n.42; Thrall, *Second Epistle*, 2.629 n.244; Harris, *Second Epistle*, 665–66.
434 Barrett, *Second Epistle*, 260. Suggesting a scribal error: Plummer, *Second Epistle*, 282; Thrall, *Second Epistle*, 2.629, n.244.
435 BDAG 1053 s.v. φημί 1c; Plummer, *Second Epistle*, 282; Windisch, *Der zweite Korintherbrief*, 305; Allo, *Saint Paul*, 248; Furnish, *II Corinthians*, 468.

common in Koine Greek.[436] Thus it is possible that Paul intends to summarize a widely held view: "this is what is being said in Corinth."[437] But Paul's references to "someone" (τις) and "such a person" (ὁ τοιοῦτος) in 10:7 and 10:11 strongly suggest that the words quoted in 10:10 are those of a specific individual.[438] We noted above the numerous, stylistic features by which Paul personalizes the opinion reflected in 10:7. Nothing in the intervening verses indicates that the subject who speaks in 10:10 is anyone other than the individual whom Paul apostrophizes in 10:7. Indeed, the paragraph that encompasses 10:7 and 10:11 is given closure by the pronouns referring to an unnamed individual: the paragraph thus stages a second-hand debate between Paul and a certain person which the Corinthians are able to overhear, indeed, which they are invited to observe. The most natural construction of φησίν in this context is as a report of an utterance by the same individual whom Paul addresses indirectly in 10:7 and 10:11.

Next, our reasons for regarding the words of 10:10 as the verdict of a local Corinthian, rather than an outsider, an itinerant apostle. Once more, the placement of the quotation in one of the opening paragraphs of the letter suggests that the speaker belongs to the principal addressees; he is one of the Corinthians who are directly addressed in 10:8 (ὑμῶν) and 10:9 (ὑμᾶς). Moreover, the person who is quoted here has read Paul's epistles, and, as we shall see, has read them with genuine appreciation. His estimation of Paul's presence and discourse involves an assess-

---

436 E.g., Epictetus *Diatr.* 3.9.15; 4.1.11, 151, 158; 9.6.7; *Ench.* 24, 2; Maximus of Tyre 5, 4a; cf. BDAG 1053 s.v. φημί 1.c; BDF §130(3); Furnish, *II Corinthians*, 468.
437 Plummer, *Second Epistle*, 279, 282; Furnish, *II Corinthians*, 468; Vegge, *2 Corinthians*, 325.
438 Barrett, *Second Epistle*, 260; Watson, "Paul's Painful Letter," 345–46; Martin, *2 Corinthians*, 311; Peterson, *Eloquence and the Proclamation of the Gospel*, 50; Thrall, *Second Epistle*, 2.629. Against the argument of Furnish (*II Corinthians*, 468) that it is usual, in such cases of the use of φησίν, for the person to be named in the immediate context (adducing Epictetus *Diatr.* 4.8.17, 25 as examples), see the rebuttal of Thrall, *Second Epistle*, 2.630, n.249: "But since the φησίν here [in 2 Cor. 10:10] is resumed by the following τοιοῦτος [in 10;11] this is not a necessary conclusion: in 2 Cor. 2.5–7 Paul uses the anonymous ὁ τοιοῦτος where it is clear that he has a particular individual in view." See, more recently, Mitchell, "The Corinthian Correspondence and the Birth of Pauline Hermeneutics" 30 n.33: "the subject of φησίν in 10:10, who can be seen, then, as identical to ὁ ἀδικήσας of 7:12, the man who "has caused the grief" [λελύπηκεν] in 2:5."

ment of his "rhetorical delivery" (ὑπόκρισις),[439] which presupposes first-hand experience of Paul's preaching. While it is possible that these observations might have been made in passing by one of Paul's missionary rivals,[440] it is more likely that they reflect the personal and repeated experience of one of Paul's Corinthian converts who had opportunities to peruse his epistles and to hear him speak.[441]

Last, the grounds for inferring that 10:10 preserves a literal quotation of what someone in Corinth has said, rather than a possible opinion that Paul attributes to an interlocutor. That the words of 10:10 are a quotation is placed beyond doubt by the marker ὅτι and by the verb φησίν.[442] Indeed, the terms used in evaluation of Paul are so exact that we must assume that Paul was present when they were uttered, or that Titus or one of Paul's other emissaries has brought him a report. Yet several scholars argue that Paul adopts the style of the diatribe and places in the mouth of a spokesman for his critics a hypothetical comment: "says my opponent."[443] But this proposal does not take sufficient account of the context; for vs. 11 makes clear that Paul is reacting to something that has actually been said, not anticipating a potential criticism.[444] Paul responds to the assessment of his letters and discourse: "This (τοῦτο) let such a person consider, that (ὅτι) what sort of persons (οἷοι) we are in word through epistles when absent, such persons (τοιοῦτοι) we are also when present in action" (10:11). Several aspects of this sentence indicate that Paul is vigorously refuting the charge of inconsistency implicit in his critic's as-

---

439 That the criticism of Paul in 2 Cor. 10:10b presupposes an experience of Paul's rhetorical delivery (ὑπόκρισις), see Winter, *Paul Among the Sophists*, 204–23.
440 As assumed by Windisch, *Der zweite Korintherbrief*, 305; Bachmann, *Der zweite Brief*, 353; Betz, *Der Apostel Paulus*, 44; Barrett, *Second Epistle* 260, an assumption made explicit by Thrall, *Second Epistle*, 2.630, who attributes the criticism to "a representative of the rival mission," and adds: "This would probably require us to suppose that the man was present in Corinth at the time of Paul's interim visit."
441 König, "Verkehr," 514; Weiss, *Primitive Christianity*, 1.342–43; Watson, "Paul's Painful Letter," 345–46; Peterson, *Eloquence and the Proclamation of the Gospel*, 72; Roetzel, *2 Corinthians*, 100.
442 Windisch, *Der zweite Korintherbrief*, 305; Betz, *Der Apostel Paulus*, 44; Bultmann, *Der zweite Brief*, 192; Thrall, *Second Epistle*, 2.629.
443 Rudolf Bultmann, *Der Stil der paulinischen Predigt und die kynisch-stoische Diatribe* (Göttingen: Vandenhoeck & Ruprecht, 1910) 10, 67; C. F. D. Moule, *An Idiom Book of New Testament Greek* (Cambridge: Cambridge University Press, 1953) 29, appealing to BDF §130(3); Bultmann, *Der zweite Brief*, 192.
444 Barrett, *Second Epistle*, 260; Thrall, *Second Epistle*, 2.629.

sessment: the neuter demonstrative pronoun τοῦτο, which summarizes the adverse opinion of 10:10, is drawn forward to the beginning of the sentence for emphasis; the conjunction ὅτι, which might have been omitted, is repeated in resumption of the foregoing critique; the addition of the relative pronoun οἷοι conveys a bitter tinge of irony in response to the evaluation.[445] All of these features are appropriate as reactions to a statement that has actually been made, but are overdone in representation of a hypothetical dialogue. Further examination of the vocabulary used in evaluation of Paul's letters and speeches (βαρύς, ἰσχυρός, ἀσθενής, ἐξουθενημένος) will strengthen the impression that 10:10 is a verbatim citation of what someone in Corinth has said.

Before investigating the terms that are used in 2 Cor. 10:10 to evaluate Paul's qualities as a speaker and a writer, we may venture a few observations on the style of the assessment quoted in 10:10, for this provides preliminary insight into the mind of Paul's critic. First, the sentence quoted is obviously an antithesis: Paul's critic employs an elementary rhetorical device to express the discrepancy he has noted between Paul's letters and speeches, carefully marking the parts of the contrast by means of a μέν...δέ construction.[446] Second, the two adjectives describing the qualities of Paul's letters in the first half of the antithesis are set opposite the two predicates attached to Paul's discourse in the second half by means of a chiasmus: thus ἰσχυρός ("strong") correlates with ἀσθενής ("weak"), while βαρύς ("impressive") pairs with ἐξουθενημένος ("contemptible").[447] The crosswise arrangement of contrasted pairs gives emphasis to each of the terms utilized.[448] The employment of such a device gives evidence of the rhetorical training of Paul's critic, and of a rather fine style. Finally, the subjects of assessment in the sentence are the products of Paul's activity or aspects of his self-presentation, rather than the person of Paul himself: thus αἱ ἐπιστολαί ("the epistles"), ἡ παρουσία τοῦ σώματος ("the bodily presence"), and ὁ λόγος ("the discourse"). The abstract quality of the evaluation is obscured in English translations

---

445 Plummer, *Second Epistle*, 283; Furnish, *II Corinthians*, 469; cf. Winter, *Paul Among the Sophists*, 210.
446 Windisch, *Der zweite Korintherbrief*, 305.
447 Heinrici, *Der zweite Brief*, 329–30; Plummer, *Second Epistle*, 282; Windisch, *Der zweite Korintherbrief*, 306.
448 J. D. Denniston, *Greek Prose Style* (Oxford: Clarendon Press, 1952) 74–77; Herbert Weir Smyth, *Greek Grammar* (Cambridge, MA: Harvard University Press, 1956) 677 §3020.

by the repeated introduction of the possessive pronoun "his."⁴⁴⁹ But no such pronouns appear in the Greek sentence that Paul quotes. The focus of the sentence upon products and qualities lends a cool objectivity to the assessment and conveys a dispassionate impartiality on the part of Paul's critic.

We turn now to the terms by which the qualities of Paul's letters are described—βαρύς and ἰσχυρός. Georg Heinrici pointed out long ago that these words have a technical usage in literary criticism.⁴⁵⁰ This insight was expanded and deepened by the research of Peter Marshall.⁴⁵¹ We shall first consider the meaning of the term βαρύς and its cognate βάρος. The evidence is drawn mainly from the critical essays of Dionysius of Halicarnassus. In his general treatise "On Literary Composition," Dionysius analyzes the ingredients of "beautiful style" (καλὴ λέξις) as follows: "elevation (ἡ μεγαλοπρέπεια), gravity (τὸ βάρος), impressiveness (ἡ σεμνολογία), dignity (τὸ ἀξίωμα), and mellowness (ὁ πίνος)."⁴⁵² Although Dionysius does not define what is meant by τὸ βάρος in this context, he makes clear that "gravity" is a primary constituent of good style. Reflecting upon the elements in his list, Dionysius observes: "These seem to me the most important, heading the list, so to speak."⁴⁵³ A more nuanced definition of τὸ βάρος emerges from Dionysius' discussions of individual authors. In his essay on Demosthenes, Dionysius judges that the great Athenian orator was "superior to the exponents of the plain, simple and unemphatic manner of expression by the intensity (ὁ τόνος), gravity (τὸ βάρος) and close texture (ἡ στριφνότης) of his style and his general pungency (τὸ πικραίνειν) of expression."⁴⁵⁴ From the terms with which βάρος is associated here, one may form some impression of the style of discourse that "weightiness" would have complemented: namely, one that was forceful, concise, astringent, even biting. An additional, important aspect of the stylistic feature τὸ βάρος is supplied by Dionysius' analysis of Thucydides. Commenting on the style of the historians who preceded Thucydides,

---

449 Furnish, *II Corinthians*, 468.
450 Heinrici, *Das zweite Sendschreiben*, 427; idem, *Der zweite Brief*, 329–30; Windisch, *Der zweite Korintherbrief*, 306 n.1. See also Wettstein, *Novum Testamentum Graece*, Vol. 2, p. 203.
451 Marshall, *Enmity in Corinth*, 384–93; see further, Winter, *Paul Among the Sophists*, 204–21.
452 Dionysius of Halicarnassus *Comp.* 11; my translation slightly modifies that of the LCL.
453 Dionysius of Halicarnassus *Comp.* 11; cf. Marshall, *Enmity in Corinth*, 386.
454 Dionysius of Halicarnassus *Dem.* 34.

Dionysius concludes: "Thus the style of each of them has all the essential virtues, being sufficiently pure, clear and concise...But the ancillary virtues, which reveal most clearly the orator's special ability, are neither all present nor fully developed individually, but are found sparsely and in diluted form—I am referring to sublimity, eloquence, dignity and grandeur. Nor is there any intensity (τόνος), any gravity (βάρος), or any emotion (πάθος) to arouse the mind, nor any robust and combative spirit (τὸ ἐρρωμένον καὶ ἐναγώνιον πνεῦμα), all of which are essential to what is called 'forcefulness' (δεινότης)."[455] Here βάρος is a component of rhetorical skill conveying the impression of formidable force, drawing its strength from the passions and an agonistic spirit.

A similar technical usage of ἰσχύς is made by Dionysius. In his essay on Thucydides, Dionysius suggests to students of political oratory that they take Demosthenes as their guide: "They should imitate those specimens of his composition in which his brevity (βραχύτης), rhetorical power (δεινότης), force (ἰσχύς), intensity (τόνος) elevation (μεγαλοπρέπεια) and other related virtues are plain for all to see."[456] Here ἰσχύς has replaced βάρος in the list of stylistic virtues that contribute to the overwhelming intensity of Demosthenes' oratory, and almost seems to be the latter's synonym. In his letter to Pompeius, Dionysius draws a comparison between Thucydides and Herodotus, and judges Thucydides to be superior in "those excellences whose powers of expression include force (ἰσχύς), intensity (τόνος) and similar qualities."[457]

What is the status of Dionysius' stylistic categories with respect to the description of Paul's letters as βαρεῖαι καὶ ἰσχυραί? Peter Marshall questions whether the standards employed by Paul's critic could have been the same as those of Dionysius of Halicarnassus.[458] The reason for Marshall's hesitation lies in the well known fact that Dionysius was the principal exponent of an Attic revival and a fierce opponent of the popular Asianic rhetoric.[459] Paul's letters are held, on the authority of the rhetori-

---
455 Dionysius of Halicarnassus *Thuc.* 23; my translation slightly modifies that of the LCL.
456 Dionysius of Halicarnassus *Thuc.* 55; cf. Marshall, *Enmity in Corinth*, 386; Winter, *Paul Among the Sophists*, 209.
457 Dionysius of Halicarnassus *Pomp.* 3; cf. Marshall, *Enmity in Corinth*, 386.
458 Marshall, *Enmity in Corinth*, 390.
459 William K. Pritchett, *Dionysius of Halicarnassus. On Thucydides* (Berkeley: University of California Press, 1975) xxvi; cf. Glen W. Bowersock, *Augustus and the Greek World* (Oxford: Clarendon Press, 1965) 130; Simon Swain, *Hellenism and*

cally trained Greek church fathers, to have fallen short of the standards of Attic purity.[460] Hence, Marshall doubts that the categories of Dionysius' analysis could have been applied to Paul. Abstracting ourselves for a moment from the controversial question of how to adjudicate Paul's epistolary style,[461] we might ask whether the coincidence of stylistic terminology between Dionysius of Halicarnassus and Paul's Corinthian critic does not warrant the opposite hypothesis: namely, that Paul's critic shares Dionysius' literary standards; that his admiration for a style that is "weighty and strong" reflects his response to the cultural challenge of being Greek under Rome, as it did for Dionysius, whose hopes for an Attic revival lay in the preference of the Roman upper class for a rhetoric that was dignified and vigorous.[462] There is something undeniably "Roman" about the combination βαρὺς καὶ ἰσχυρός. It is no surprise that the closest parallel to

---

Empire: Language, Classicism, and Power in the Greek World, AD 50–250 (Oxford: Oxford University Press, 1996) 23–27.

460 Marshall, *Enmity in Corinth*, 390, appealing to Edwin A. Judge, "Paul's Boasting in Relation to Contemporary Professional Practice," *AusBR* 16 (1968) 41–42; idem, "St. Paul and Classical Society," *JAC* 15 (1972) 35.

461 On this issue, with special reference to 2 Cor. 10–13, see Betz, *Der Apostel Paulus*, 13–42; Zmijewski, *Der Stil der paulinischen 'Narrenrede'*; Christopher Forbes, "Comparison, Self-Praise and Irony: Paul's Boasting and the Conventions of Hellenistic Rhetoric," *NTS* 32 (1986) 1–30; John T. Fitzgerald, "Paul, the Ancient Epistolary Theorists, and 2 Corinthians 10–13: The Purposes and Literary Genre of a Pauline Letter" in *Greeks, Romans, and Christians: Essays in Honor of Abraham J. Malherbe*, eds. D. Balch, E. Ferguson, and W. Meeks (Minneapolis: Fortress Press, 1990) 190–200. With reference to Galatians, see Janet Fairweather, "The Epistle to the Galatians and Classical Rhetoric," *TynBul* 45 (1994) 1–38, 213–44; Margaret M. Mitchell, "Reading Rhetoric with Patristic Exegetes: John Chrysostom on Galatians" in *Antiquity and Humanity: Essays on Ancient Religion and Philosophy presented to Hans Dieter Betz on his 70th Birthday*, eds. A. Y. Collins and M. M. Mitchell (Tübingen: Mohr Siebeck, 2001) 333–55; Malcolm Heath, "John Chrysostom, rhetoric and Galatians," *Biblical Interpretation* 12 (2004) 369–400. Generally, Anderson, *Rhetorical Theory and Paul*; Aida Besacon Spencer, *Paul's Literary Style* (Washington, D.C.: University Press of America, 2007).

462 Swain, *Hellenism and Empire*, 25–26: "We would in fact do better to take note of Dionysius' political motives in advocating pure style…It was Rome's role to be the particular 'cause and origin of such a change' by showing through the example of her own excellent taste—which her empire made influential—that Attic style was proper to a properly run city. The explicit political slant is striking. Dionysius' invocation of Rome here is certainly as a conservative member of the Greek elite who understood well the political benefits the Empire accorded his class."

this description of the style of Paul's letters is found in Cicero, who values the employment of an oratory that is "powerful and weighty" (*vis et gravitas*).[463]

The extant treatises in literary criticism from the period of the early Empire reserve the highest praise for the "forceful" style, and see in the formidable Demosthenes the paramount model of oratory.[464] The term that is used by the Greek critics for the stylistic quality that is so highly prized in Demosthenes is δεινότης, which is a certain "concentrated force" or "awe-inspiring power," like the *vis et gravitas* of Cicero.[465] Dionysius, whose substantial essay on Demosthenes is devoted to analysis of the orator's δεινότης, attributes Demosthenes' power to move the reader, even after the passage of centuries, to the fact that the great orator "spoke from the heart, and laid bare his inmost feelings and the promptings of his soul."[466] The sophisticated critic who wrote the treatise "On the Sublime," wrongly attributed to Longinus,[467] couples δεινότης with δύναμις in seeking to capture the nature of Demosthenes' genius, and glosses these terms with the expressions "sublime intensity" (ὑψηγορίας τόνος) and "living emotion" (ἔμψυχα πάθη).[468] The author of the tract "On Style," ascribed to a certain Demetrius, makes "the forcible style now in vogue" (ἡ νῦν κατέχουσα δεινότης) the special goal of his analysis, and adduces examples of Demosthenes' oratory in illustration of this type.[469] The popularity of the forceful style persisted in the second century, as demonstrated by the textbook on "Types of Style" by Hermogenes of Tarsus, for whom "forcefulness" (δεινότης) is the greatest stylistic ach-

---

463 Cicero *De or.* 2.82.334; cf. Marshall, *Enmity in Corinth*, 386–87. See also Quintilian *Inst.* 8.3.3.
464 Demetrius *Eloc.* 240–304; Dionysius of Halicarnassus *Dem.*; Longinus *Subl.*, esp. 34. See the discussion in W. Rhys Roberts, "Demetrius on Style" in *Aristotle XXIII* (Cambridge, MA: Harvard University Press, 1973) 264–68.
465 Demetrius *Eloc.* 8, 245, 283; Dionysius of Halicarnassus *Dem.* 21, 22; Longinus *Subl.* 34; cf. Pritchett, *Dionysius of Halicarnassus*, 108 n.4; Roberts, "Demetrius on Style," 265–67.
466 Dionysius of Halicarnassus *Dem.* 22.
467 See the discussion of authorship in W. Rhys Roberts, *Longinus on the Sublime* (Cambridge: Cambridge University Press, 1899) 1–23.
468 Longinus *Subl.* 34.4. Cf. G. M. A. Grube, *The Greek and Roman Critics* (Toronto: University of Toronto Press, 1968) 347–49.
469 Demetrius *Eloc.* 245, 248, 253, 270, 280. Cf. Roberts, "Demetrius on Style," 266–67; Grube, *Greek and Roman Critics*, 118.

ievement and the principal ingredient in the perfection of Demosthenes.[470]

It is in the context of the valorization of the "forceful style" by Greek critics who served Roman interests that we must seek to understand the description of Paul's letters as "weighty and strong." Far from being a pejorative comment, as Bruce Winter suggests,[471] the evaluation of Paul's epistles as βαρεῖαι καὶ ἰσχυραί is the highest praise! Paul's critic judges that his letters are written in a style that conveys "gravity and force." This description probably also implies the terms with which βάρος and ἰσχύς are repeatedly associated in literary criticism, "intensity" (τόνος) and "concision" (βραχύτης). And such a description also evokes the wellsprings of emotion (πάθος) from which rhetorical force was drawn, the reservoir of "a robust and combative spirit," as Dionysius would have it. In sum, Paul's critic attributes to his letters the pre-eminent quality of δεινότης.

Evidence in support of the view that the terms βαρύς and ἰσχυρός used in description of Paul's epistolary style embody aesthetic norms like those applied by Dionysius in his critical essays is found in the preceding verse of chapter 10, where Paul refutes the impression that he seeks "to terrify" (ἐκφοβεῖν) the Corinthians "through the epistles" (διὰ τῶν ἐπιστολῶν). The strong verb ἐκφοβεῖν,[472] found only here in the New Testament,[473] also belongs to the report of what was said by Paul's Corinthian critic, because the brachylogical assertion of vs. 9 serves as a

---

470 Hermogenes Περὶ ἰδεῶν 2.9; English trans. by Cecil W. Wooten, *Hermogenes. On Types of Style* (Chapel Hill: University of North Carolina Press, 1987) 101–108. Cf. D. Hagedorn, *Zur Ideenlehre des Hermogenes* (Göttingen: Vandenhoeck & Ruprecht, 1964); Donald A. Russell, *Criticism in Antiquity* (Berkeley: University of California Press, 1981) 143–47.
471 Winter, *Paul Among the Sophists*, 212, while allowing for the possibility that Paul's critics were saying that his letters were rhetorically impressive. Disputing any allusion to Paul's rhetoric in the terms βαρύς and ἰσχυρός, Anderson, *Ancient Rhetorical Theory and Paul*, 278 n.7.
472 BDAG 312; Plummer, *Second Epistle*, 281: "The compound verb has a strong meaning, 'to scare you out of your senses'"; Barrett, *Second Epistle*, 259: "lest I should seem as if I were frightening you to death"; Furnish, *II Corinthians*, 468. On the structure of vs. 9, see Moule, *Idiom Book*, 152, who observes that ἵνα μὴ δόξω ὡς ἂν ἐκφοβεῖν ὑμᾶς "looks like a conflation of ἵνα μὴ δόξω ἐκφοβεῖν ὑμᾶς ("lest I should seem to frighten you") and ἵνα μὴ δόξω ὡς ἐὰν ἐκφοβεῖν ὑμᾶς βούλομαι ("lest I should seem as if I wished to frighten you")."
473 Windisch, *Der zweite Korintherbrief,* 305; Plummer, *Second Epistle*, 281; Furnish, *II Corinthians*, 468.

defensive introduction to the quotation in vs. 10.⁴⁷⁴ Now in Dionysius and Demetrius, τὸ φοβερόν ("the terrifying") and τὸ δεινόν ("the forceful") are frequently coupled as virtually synonymous terms.⁴⁷⁵ Longinus describes the rhetorical force (δεινότης) of Demosthenes as "frightening" (φοβεῖσθαι) in its effect.⁴⁷⁶ The association of δεινότης with "fear" was facilitated by the root meaning of the word δεινός—"fearful," "terrible," "awful," "uncanny."⁴⁷⁷ That the literary critics had this primitive association in mind when they spoke of δεινότης and its ancillary qualities is well illustrated by Longinus' comparison of Hypereides and Demosthenes: "But nevertheless I feel that the beauties of Hypereides, as many as they are, yet lack grandeur; they are dispassionate, born of sober sense, and do not trouble the peace of the audience. No one, for instance, is panic-stricken (φοβεῖται) while reading Hypereides. But Demosthenes no sooner 'takes up the tale' than he shows the merits of great genius in their most consummate form, sublime intensity, living emotion, redundance, readiness, speed—where speed is in season—and his own unapproachable vehemence (δεινότης) and power (δύναμις): snatching into his arms all the wealth of those mighty, heaven-sent gifts—it would be impious to call them human—he thus, by those beauties that he has, invariably defeats all comers, and to make up for those he lacks, he seems to dumbfounder the world's orators with his thunder and lightning. You could sooner open your eyes to the descent of a thunderbolt than face unblinking his repeated outbursts of emotion."⁴⁷⁸ When Paul's critic suggests that Paul seeks "to terrify" the Corinthians by means of his letters, he draws the proper inference regarding the emotional effect of a style that is "weighty and strong."

Although it lies beyond the scope of the present essay to evaluate Paul's epistolary style, we need not suppress the observation that a number of passages in the writing known to us as 1 Corinthians seem to war-

---

474 Windisch, *Der zweite Korintherbrief*, 305; Menzies, *Second Epistle*, 73: "the charge that he terrorized his converts by his Epistles. This phrase appears to be quoted from an adversary"; Hughes, *Paul's Second Epistle*, 361 n.17; Barrett, *Second Epistle*, 259–60.
475 Roberts, "Demetrius on Style," 267; cf. Marshall, *Enmity in Corinth*, 388 n.179.
476 Longinus *Subl*. 34.4; Roberts, *Longinus on the Sublime*, 196.
477 Roberts, "Demetrius on Style," 266, on the Greek critics of the early Empire: "They do not, as a rule, use δεινός simply in the more or less colloquial sense of δεινὸς λέγειν. They hark back to the primitive and literal associations of the word with 'fear' (cf. Plato *Lach*. 198B; Aristotle *Eth. nic*. 1115a24–26)."
478 Longinus *Subl*. 34.4; Roberts, *Longinus on the Sublime*, 130–33.

rant the judgment of Paul's Corinthian critic. The description "impressive and forceful" seems especially apt for the letter now preserved in 1 Cor. 1:1–6:11, which, in our view, almost immediately preceded the composition of 2 Cor. 10–13.[479] Consider the extraordinary elevation and skillful construction of the section that stretches from 1 Cor. 1:18 to 2:16. In the six verses, 1:20–25, Paul employs the following figures of speech: *repetitio, anaphora, isocolon, homoioteleuton, paronomasia, oxymoron, chiasmus, litotes,* and *synkrisis*.[480] Paul's use of parallelism and antithesis in the paragraph 1:26–31 is so masterful that it moved the classical philologist Friedrich Blass to observe: "From any Greek orator the artistry of this passage would have called forth the utmost admiration."[481] At points, the elocution is sonorous and the structure poetic: "What no eye has seen, nor ear heard, nor human heart conceived, what God has prepared for those who love him" (2:9), a passage rightly printed in strophic form in the Nestle-Aland text.[482] Or consider the biting irony of the apostrophe in 4:8, "Already you are satiated! Already you are enriched! Quite apart from us you reign as kings!", in which the particle ἤδη, which introduces the first two exclamations, has a taunting, sneering quality that is impossible to convey in English.[483] Hermogenes reminds us that "the method of the indignant style is through irony" (μέθοδος μέντοι βαρύτητος αὕτη ἡ διὰ τῆς εἰρωνείας).[484] Or consider the pathos of Paul's grim account of the sufferings of the apostles of Christ in 4:9–13: "For I suppose that God has put us apostles on show last of all, as people condemned to death, because we have become a theater-act to the world, both to angels and to human beings. We are fools on account of Christ, but you are wise in Christ. We are weak, but you are strong. You are held in honor, but we are dishonored. To the present hour we

---

479 Following the literary analysis of Weiss, *Primitive Christianity*, 1.349–57; accordingly, only the letter now preserved in 2 Cor. 8 intervened between 1 Cor. 1:1–6:11 and 2 Cor. 10–13.
480 Weiss, *Der erste Korintherbrief*, 27, 29; Collins, *First Corinthians*, 103–104, 108.
481 BDF 260.
482 Nestle-Aland, *Novum Testamentum Graece*, 27th ed., 443. The origin of the saying Paul quotes in 1 Cor. 2:9 is uncertain. Origen (*PG* 13, 1769) asserts that the citation derives from the *Apocalypse of Elijah*, but extant Greek and Coptic fragments of the apocalypse do not contain the saying; cf. D. A. Koch, *Die Schrift als Zeuge des Evangeliums. Untersuchungen zur Verwendung und zum Verständnis der Schrift bei Paulus* (Tübingen: Mohr Siebeck, 1986) 37–41.
483 Weiss, *Der erste Korintherbrief*, 106–108.
484 Hermogenes Περὶ ἰδεῶν 2.8. See the discussion of this passage in relation to 2 Cor. 10–13 by Forbes, "Paul's Boasting and Hellenistic Rhetoric," 12–13.

are hungry and thirsty, we are naked, we are beaten, we are homeless, and we toil, laboring with our own hands. When reviled, we bless; when harassed, we endure; when slandered, we speak kindly. We have become like the refuse of the world, the scum of all things, to this very day."[485] The verdict of New Testament scholars and Classicists alike is divided with respect to the quality of Paul's style.[486] But it is worthwhile to remind ourselves that John Chrysostom, who was trained in rhetoric, was an unabashed admirer of Paul's compositional technique.[487] Indeed, Malcolm Heath has recently demonstrated that the terms in which Chrysostom expressed his admiration for Paul's style are similar to those found in commentaries on Demosthenes originating in the schools of rhetoric.[488] It would be a promising piece of research to analyze 1 Cor. 1:1–6:11 and 2 Cor. 10–13 in terms of the compositional features and rhetorical figures required of "the forcible style" (ὁ δεινότης χαρακτήρ) by Demetrius.[489]

---

485 Welborn, *Paul, the Fool of Christ*, 50–86, 249.
486 For the debate over the literary quality of Paul's letters in earlier scholarship, see Eduard Norden, *Die antike Kunstprosa*, 2 vols. (Leipzig: Teubner, 1898; Darmstadt: Wissenschaftliche Buchgesellschaft, 1958) 2.451–510; Heinrici, "Zum Hellenismus des Paulus" in idem, *Der zweite Brief*, 436–58; Johannes Weiss, "Beiträge zur paulinischen Rhetorik" in *Theologische Studien*, Bernhard Weiss zu seinem 70. Geburtstag dargebracht (Göttigen: Vandenhoeck & Ruprecht, 1897) 165–247. The debate has been renewed, with special focus on Paul's rhetoric, by Hans Dieter Betz, *Galatians: A Commentary on Paul's Letter to the Churches in Galatia*, Hermeneia (Philadelphia; Fortress Press, 1979); Mitchell, *Paul and the Rhetoric of Reconciliation*; C. J. Classen, "Paulus und die antike Rhetorik," *ZNW* 82 (1991) 1–33; Anderson, *Ancient Rhetorical Theory and Paul*.
487 Margaret M. Mitchell, *The Heavenly Trumpet: John Chrysostom and the Art of Pauline Interpretation* (Tübingen: Mohr Siebeck, 2000); L. Thurén, "John Chrysostom as a Rhetorical Critic: The Hermeneutics of an Early Father," *Biblical Interpretation* 9 (2001) 180–218; Malcolm Heath, "John Chrysostom, rhetoric and Galatians," *Biblical Interpretation* 12 (2004) 369–400.
488 Heath, "John Chrysostom, rhetoric," 395–98.
489 Such an analysis would move research beyond the antithesis of "Asian" and "Attic" style, already critically examined by Ulrich von Wilamowitz-Moellendorf, "Asianismus und Atticismus," *Hermes* 35 (1900) 1–52, repr. idem, *Kleine Schriften III* (Berlin: Akademie Verlag, 1969) 223–73; Laurent Pernot, *La rhétorique de l'éloge dans le monde gréco-romain*, 2 vols. (Paris: Institut d'Etudes Augustiniennes, 1993) 1.379; Swain, *Hellenism and Empire*, 24–25. In so doing, one would build upon the insights of Weiss, "Beiträge zur paulinischen Rhetorik"; idem, *Der erste Korintherbrief*, esp. 25, 27, 30, 35–36; Windisch, *Der zweite Kor-*

For purposes of our investigation, it suffices to have shown that the evaluation of Paul's epistles in 2 Cor. 10:10 echoes, in phrasing and content, the categories of stylistic analysis employed by Greek critics under the early Empire. Evidently, Paul's critic in Corinth shares the literary tastes of Dionysius and Demetrius, a finding that is hardly surprising, given the vogue of the "forceful style" in the first century.[490] We may allow for some hyperbole in the expression of admiration for Paul's letters: the force of the antithesis depends upon the height of the contrast; the sharper the contrast, the more unbearable the inconsistency. Yet, on the principle that an exaggeration always embodies the thing exaggerated, we may acknowledge that Paul's critic expresses a genuine appreciation for Paul's letters. We may further suggest that his admiration is not merely for the external form of Paul's letters, but also for the content. In praise of Demosthenes, the literary critics consistently discuss what the "subject matter" contributes to his "forcible style."[491] It is necessary to emphasize this point, because Paul's Corinthian opponents have been portrayed in the history of scholarship as focused on superficial things.[492] We have discovered that the individual who speaks in 10:10 (in our view, the wrongdoer) fully acknowledges the "gravity and force" of Paul's letters.

By contrast with his approving assessment of Paul's letters, the person quoted in 2 Cor. 10:10 finds that "the bodily presence is weak and the speech is contemptible" (ἡ δὲ παρουσία τοῦ σώματος ἀσθενὴς καὶ ὁ λόγος ἐξουθενημένος). What is the point of the epithets ἀσθενής and ἐξουθενημένος applied here in evaluation of Paul? Commentators sometimes refer the term ἀσθενής ("weak") to Paul's physical condition, on account of his illness, his "thorn in the flesh" (2 Cor. 12:7).[493] Other interpreters regard ἀσθενής as a judgment upon Paul's banausic occupation, expressing contempt for the status of a simple handworker.[494] It is certain-

---

intherbrief, 8–9, 290–425 *passim*; Vielhauer, *Geschichte der urchristlichen Literatur*, 58–70.
490 Roberts, "Demetrius on Style," 266–68.
491 Dionysius of Halicarnassus *Dem.*, esp. 8, 22; Demetrius *Eloc.* 245, 246, 248, 250, 253, 263, 268–73, 277–80; Longinus *Subl.* 12.4; 14.1, 2; 34.1–4.
492 See the overview in R. Bieringer, "Die Gegner des Paulus im 2. Korintherbrief" in *Studies on 2 Corinthians* (Leuven: Peeters, 1994)181–221; Thrall, *Second Epistle*, 2.926–45; recently, C. K. Barrett, "Sectarian Diversity at Corinth" in *Paul and the Corinthians: Studies on a Community in Conflict. Essays in Honour of Margaret Thrall*, eds. T. J. Burke and J. K. Elliott (Leiden: Brill, 2003) 297–302.
493 So, e.g., Furnish, *II Corinthians*, 478–79, 547–50; Martin, *2 Corinthians*, 312.
494 Windisch, *Der zweite Korintherbrief*, 306; Hock, *Social Context*, 35, 60; Furnish, *II Corinthians*, 479; Thrall, *Second Epistle*, 2.631–32.

ly the case that Paul elsewhere uses the term ἀσθένεια ("weakness") to refer to his physical ailment (Gal. 4:13). Nor is there any doubt that ἀσθενής is a status marker describing the social condition of the poor in general, including the working poor.[495] Paul himself uses ἀσθενής in this sense to describe his social status in 1 Cor. 4:10.[496] But certain features of the sentence quoted in 2 Cor. 10:10 indicate that, in this case, ἀσθενής describes Paul's appearance as a speaker.[497] First, the two clauses in 10:10b are coordinate; thus, the weakness of Paul's bodily presence and the contemptible character of his discourse are aspects of the same phenomenon. Second, ἀσθενής is the counterpart of ἰσχυρός within the chiasmus constructed by the parts of 10:10; as ἰσχυρός identifies a quality of Paul's style, so ἀσθενής names a characteristic of Paul's presence.[498] Third, the noun παρουσία ("presence") connotes "coming" or "arrival," the manner in which the orator makes his appearance.[499] Thus, ἀσθενής should be taken as a description of Paul's presentation of himself as a speaker.

In the rhetorical handbooks, the way in which a speaker presents himself by voice and gesture is known as "delivery" (ὑπόκρισις, *pronuntiatio* or *actio*).[500] Writers on the art of rhetoric leave no doubt about the importance of delivery for the success of an orator. Aristotle, who first theorized the subject, declares that delivery possesses the "greatest power" (δύναμις μεγίστη) in regard to speech.[501] The *auctor ad Herennium* introduces his discussion of delivery with the observation: "Many have said that the fac-

---

495 Plato *Resp.* 364 A; Xenophon *Cyr.* 8.1.30; Philo *Somn.* 155; see Christopher Forbes, "'Strength' and 'Weakness' as Terminology of Status in St. Paul: The Historical and Literary Roots of a Metaphor, with Special Reference to 1 and 2 Corinthians" (Honors Thesis, Macquarie University, 1978); Theissen, *Social Setting*, 72.
496 Welborn, *Paul, the Fool of Christ*, 58.
497 So, already, Menzies, *Second Epistle*, 73; more recently, Winter, *Paul Among the Sophists*, 204, 221–23.
498 Plummer, *Second Epistle*, 282–83; Windisch, *Der zweite Korintherbrief*, 306.
499 BDAG 780 s.v. παρουσία 2; Barrett, *Second Epistle*, 260–61; Winter, *Paul Among the Sophists*, 204, 213–23.
500 Richard Volkmann, *Die Rhetorik der Griechen und Römer* (Hildesheim: Georg Olms, 1963) 573–80; Josef Martin, *Antike Rhetorik. Technik und Methode* (Munich: Beck, 1974) 351–56; Bruce Winter, "Philodemus and Paul on Rhetorical Delivery (ὑπόκρισις)," in *Philodemus and the New Testament World*, eds. John T. Fitzgerald, Dirk Orbink, Glenn S. Holland (Leiden: Brill, 2004) 323–42.
501 Aristotle *Rhet.* 3.1, 1403b; see F. Solmsen, "The Aristotelian Tradition in Ancient Rhetoric" in *Rhetorika: Schriften zur aristotelischen und hellenistischen Rhetorik*, ed. P. Steinmetz (Hildesheim: Georg Olms, 1968) 322–23.

ulty of greatest use to the speaker and the most valuable for persuasion is delivery."[502] Quintilian acknowledges that delivery "has an extraordinarily powerful effect in oratory" (*Habet miram quondam in orationibus vim ac potestatem*),[503] and explains that "the speech that we have composed within our minds is not so important as the manner in which we produce it, since the emotion of each member of our audience will depend on the impression made upon his hearing."[504]

While the rhetoricians emphasize the importance of delivery and find in delivery the basis of the "power" (δύναμις, *vis, potestas*) of a speech, there does not seem to be an established vocabulary for referring to a deficiency in this capacity or skill. For the most part, the rhetoricians are content to speak of the lack of those faculties that contribute to good delivery, or to list the defects that are incompatible with effective oratory, without designating an abstract quality that embodies the deficiency. Quintilian stipulates that "good delivery is impossible for one who cannot remember what he has written, or lacks the quick facility of speech required by sudden emergencies, or is hampered by incurable impediments of speech."[505] Focusing on defects of voice and gesture, Quintilian explains: "physical uncouthness (*corporis deformitas*) may be such that no art can remedy it, while a feeble voice (*vox exilis*) is incompatible with first-rate excellence in delivery. For we may employ a good, strong voice as we will; whereas one that is ugly or feeble (*mala vel imbecilla*)... forces faults upon us."[506] At one point in the treatise "On Style," Demetrius uses a form of ἀσθενέω to refer to weakness in rhetorical delivery: by using "vigorous words" (δεινὰ ὀνόματα), Theopompus "seems to be forcible" (δεινὸς δοκεῖ), though, in fact, he has "spoken weakly" (ἀσθενῶς εἰπών).[507] But other rhetoricians seem to prefer ἀδύνατος as a description of weak delivery. Thus, Hyperides contrasts "those who are powerless" (οἱ ἀδύνατοι) with "those who are able to speak" (δυνάμενοι εἰπεῖν).[508] And Aristotle pronounces the "eloquent speaker" far superior to the "incompetent speaker" (ἀδύνατος) in the matter of oratory.[509]

---

502 *Rhet. Her.* 3.11.19. Cf. also Cicero *Brut.* 37; *Or. Brut.* 17; Ps.-Plutarch *Vit. X Orat.* 845B.
503 Quintilian *Inst.* 11.3.2.
504 Quintilian *Inst.* 11.3.2; see also 11.3.5–6, 7.
505 Quintilian *Inst.* 11.3.12.
506 Quintilian *Inst.* 11.3.12–13.
507 Demetrius *Eloc.* 240.
508 Hyperides 2.10.
509 Aristotle *Rhet.* 2.2.7, 1379a2.

Even if the word ἀσθενής did not establish itself in the rhetorical tradition with the force of a technical term, it is nevertheless clear that a deficiency of rhetorical delivery is consistently portrayed as "weakness," with all of the attendant symptoms—confused head, stammering voice, trembling hands, etc. The incompetent orator was a favorite subject of ridicule in invective, satire, and comedy, where the focus is decidedly upon the signs of weakness exhibited by this stock character.[510] Thus, Cicero is ridiculed as a comic Bambalio ("stutterer") in a piece of invective attributed to Q. Fufius Calenus: "Why, you always come to court trembling, as if you were going to fight as a gladiator, and after uttering a few words in a meek and half-dead voice, you take your leave, without having remembered a word of the speech you thought out at home before you came, and without having found anything to say on the spur of the moment."[511] The brothel-keeper in Herodas' second mime-poem furnishes the most perfect example of the incompetent orator: his name, Battaros, means "stammerer"; his speech to the court is characterized by incoherence, redundancy, and obscurity; he "wears a rough coat and shuffles along in rotten shoes"; knowing who he is and from what sort of clay he is mixed, he "trembles before even the humblest of common people."[512] The "ranting" Zeus in Lucian's satire is portrayed as an incompetent orator.[513] Zeus confesses: "I am confused in the head and trembly and my tongue seems to be tied."[514] While the term ἀσθενής is not used explicitly in these or other caricatures of rhetorical delivery, it is nonetheless clear that the quality of "weakness" is attributed to the incompetent orator in all cases.

Interestingly, the term ἀσθένεια is used by Plutarch to characterize the natural defect of voice which Demosthenes had to overcome in order to become an admired orator. Plutarch relates that when Demosthenes first addressed the people, "he was interrupted by their clamors and laughed at

---

510 Demetrius *Eloc.* 153 on Sophron's Boulias; Athenaeus *Deipn.* 15.698d-699a on Hegemon of Thasos; Herodas *Mime* 2; Choricius of Gaza *Apol. Mim.* 26, 109. Cf. Hermann Reich, *Der Mimus. Ein litterar-entwickelungsgeschichtlicher Versuch* (Berlin: Weidmann, 1903) 458–75.
511 Dio Cassius 46.7.
512 Herodas *Mime* 2; cf. Otto Crusius, *Untersuchungen zu den Mimiamben des Herondas* (Leipzig: Teubner, 1892) 28–52.
513 Lucian *Jup. Trag.*; see J. Coenen, *Lukian Zeus tragodos: Überlieferungsgeschichte, Text und Kommentar* (Meisenheim am Glan: Hain, 1977) 39, on the difficulty of an adequate translation of τραγῳδός.
514 Lucian *Jupp. trag.* 14; cf. Coenen, *Lukian Zeus tragodos*, 38–39.

for his inexperience, since his discourse seemed to them confused by long periods and too harshly and immoderately tortured by formal arguments."⁵¹⁵ Plutarch adds: "He had also, as it would appear, a certain weakness of voice (φωνῆς ἀσθένεια) and indistinctness of speech (γλώττης ἀσάφεια) and shortness of breath (πνεύματος κολοβότης) which disturbed the sense of what he said by disjoining his sentences."⁵¹⁶ Here ἀσθένεια is particularly connected with the voice, and is roughly synonymous with the Latin expressions *exilis* ("thin") and *imbecilla* ("feeble"), used by Quintilian to describe one of the physical characteristics "incompatible with first-rate excellence in delivery."⁵¹⁷ It is all the more significant that this mention of the "weakness" of Demosthenes' voice belongs to Plutarch's larger account of how, after several failures and embarrassments, the struggling orator became "persuaded of how much delivery (ὑπόκρισις) lends to oratory through ornament and grace."⁵¹⁸ Consequently, Demosthenes "considered it of little or no use for a man to practice declaiming if he neglected the pronunciation (προφορά) and disposition (διάθεσις) of his words."⁵¹⁹ Acting upon this insight, Plutarch relates that Demosthenes built a subterranean study, into which he would descend every day in order to "form his delivery" (πλάττειν τὴν ὑπόκρισιν) and "cultivate his voice" (διαπονεῖν τὴν φωνήν).⁵²⁰

Although the evidence is rather slim, it seems reasonable to conclude that ἀσθενής belonged to a general vocabulary by which the defects of rhetorical delivery were customarily described, that the term would have been available to Paul's critic in this sense, and that it would have been understood by the Corinthians as a derogatory estimate of Paul's presence as a speaker, even if ἀσθενής did not attain the status of a rhetorical *terminus technicus*. But if something seems to be lacking in our explanation of the choice of this word by Paul's critic, we may suggest that the missing element is to be found closer to home than we might have expected. In 1 Cor. 2:1–5, Paul himself uses the term ἀσθένεια to describe the manner of his appearance as a speaker upon his arrival in Corinth: "When I came to you, brothers and sisters, I did not come proclaiming the mystery of God in lofty words or wisdom. For I decided

---

515 Plutarch *Dem.* 7.3.
516 Plutarch *Dem.* 7.4.
517 Quintilian *Inst.* 11.3.13.
518 Plutarch *Dem.* 7.5.
519 Plutarch *Dem.* 7.5.
520 Plutarch *Dem.* 7.6.

not to know anything among you except Jesus Christ, and him crucified. And I came to you in weakness (ἐν ἀσθενείᾳ) and in fear and in much trembling. My speech and my proclamation were not with plausible words of wisdom, but with a demonstration of the spirit and of power, so that your faith might rest not on human wisdom but on the power of God." Paul's use of a number of terms in this passage that belong to the technical vocabulary of Hellenistic rhetoricians (ὑπεροχή, πείθω, ἀπόδειξις, πίστις, δύναμις) indicates that Paul intends to contrast the manner of his proclamation with that of certain missionary rivals who have made use of the art of rhetoric.[521] Thus, "weakness" (ἀσθένεια) is Paul's own chosen term for describing the manner of his self-presentation as a speaker. And Paul grounds his choice of this form of rhetorical delivery in his decision not to proclaim anything other than "Christ crucified."[522] "Weakness," "fear," and "trembling" are the paradoxical ὑπόκρισις appropriate to "the discourse about the cross." The evidence suggests that Paul's critic took the term ἀσθενής directly from Paul! In this case, the use of the term in 2 Cor. 10:10 involves imitation and mockery. Once again, we encounter the eristic tendency that surfaced in the substitution of ταπεινός for πραΰς in 10:1, and in the appropriation of the Pauline phrase κατὰ σάρκα περιπατοῦντες in 10:2—the same love of verbal combat, the same acerbity. In describing Paul's oratorical demeanor as "weak," the wrongdoer is mocking Paul's own self-characterization.

This inference regarding the proximate source of the term ἀσθενής as applied to Paul's rhetorical delivery is reinforced by consideration of the word ἐξουθενημένος ("contemptible") used to describe Paul's discourse (ὁ λόγος) in 2 Cor. 10:10. For in this case, too, the evidence suggests that the person who is quoted in 10:10 has taken the term directly from Paul. The verb ἐξουθενέω/ἐξουδενέω has a rather restricted range of usage.[523] Apart from the Septuagint and literature which the Septuagint

---

521 Edwin A. Judge, "Paul's Boasting in Relation to Contemporary Professional Practice," *AusBR* 16 (1968) 38; Lars Hartman, "Some Remarks on 1 Cor. 2.1–5," *SEÅ* 39 (1974) 117; Timothy Lim, "Not in Persuasive Words of Wisdom, but in the Demonstration of the Spirit and Power," *NovT* 29 (1987) 117; Pogoloff, *Logos and Sophia*, 131–43; Winter, *Paul Among the Sophists*, 155–64.
522 Heckel, "Der Gekreuzigte bei Paulus,"196–200; Winter, *Paul Among the Sophists*, 157.
523 LSJ 598 s.v. ἐξουθενέω, ἐξουδενέω; BDAG 352 s.v. ἐξουθενέω, ἐξουδενέω; Moulton and Milligan, *Vocabulary of the Greek Testament*, 225.

has influenced,[524] the term is found mainly in the papyri,[525] and in popular literature. A cluster of usages are found in the *Life of Aesop*, a genuine folk-book, pervaded by an anti-Hellenic bias.[526] The word appears in one of the Alexander romances attributed to Callisthenes.[527] ἐξουθενίζω or ἐξουδενίζω are used in two treatises, *De Fluviis* and *Parallela Minora*, whose style is so bad that they cannot possibly have been written by Plutarch, to whom the works are ascribed in the manuscript tradition.[528] The restriction of ἐξουθενέω to non-literary and popular texts, and the total absence of ἐξουθενέω from the canonical orators, suggest that the term was regarded as vulgar.

The proper term for "contemptible" or "despicable" is εὐκαταφρόνητος, and its simplex form καταφρόνητος.[529] Here, by contrast, the range of use is broad and includes the best authors—Antiphon, Isocrates, Aeschines, and the rest.[530] Indeed, εὐκαταφρόνητος has a specialized usage in literary criticism.[531] Analyzing the diction of various authors, Dionysius of Halicarnassus speaks of "despised and humble words" (εὐκαταφρόνητα καὶ ταπεινὰ ὀνόματα).[532] Longinus criticizes the mock-tragic style for its turbid phrasing and confused images, asserting that, when such bombast is examined in the clear light of day, "it declines, little by little, from the terrifying (τὸ φοβερόν) into the contemptible (τὸ εὐκαταφρόνητον)."[533] Demetrius argues that very short cola are out of place in prose because they produce an "arid" style which is "negligible" (εὐκαταφρόνητος) "because everything about it is minute."[534]

---

524 E.g., 1 Kgs 15:9; Ps. 72(73):22; 118(119):141; Eccl. 9:16; Mal. 2:9; Dan. 4:28; 2 Macc. 1:27; *Test. Sol.* 22:5; *Jos. Asen.* 13:10; Philo *Leg.* 2.67; *Mos.* 2.241.
525 E.g., *BGU* IV.1117,31; *PMich.* 477.23.
526 ἐξουθενέω: *Vit. Aesop.* G80 p.60; *Vit. Aesop.* W77b p.97.2; ἐξουδενέω: *Vit. Aesop.* W77b p.96.37. Cf. L. W. Daly, *Aesop without Morals* (New York: Thomas Yoseloff, 1961) 20–21.
527 Ps.-Callisthenes p.72.19.
528 Ps.-Plutarch *Mor.* 308E, 310C; Ps.-Plutarch *De Fluv.* 12.1. On the authorship of these writings, see F. C. Babbitt, *Plutarch's Moralia IV* (Cambridge, MA: Harvard University Press, 1972) 253–54.
529 Windisch, *Der zweite Korintherbrief*, 307; Bultmann, *Der zweite Brief*, 192.
530 LSJ 717 s.v. εὐκαταφρόνητος: Demosthenes 4.18; Menander *Sam.* 297; Aristotle *Pol.* 1312b24; Xenophon *Hell.* 6.4.1; 920 s.v. καταφρονέω: Antiphon 262; Aeschines 1.176; Isocrates 6.108; s.v. καταφρόνητος: Philodemus *Rhet.* 2.175.
531 LSJ 717 s.v. εὐκαταφρόνητος.
532 Dionysius of Halicarnassus *Comp.* 3.
533 Longinus *Subl.* 3.1.
534 Demetrius *Eloc.* 4.

Now, why should Paul's Corinthian critic, who has otherwise carefully chosen his words from the vocabulary of literary and rhetorical criticism, bypass the proper and established term for speech that "amounts to nothing," and employ an unorthodox and vulgar expression, especially when the use of such a word would seem to undermine the accuser's own literary judgment? Again, the answer would seem to lie in intramural conflict with Paul. For judging from the surviving texts, the ancient author who uses the verb ἐξουθενέω most frequently is Paul himself! The reason for Paul's fondness for this term may remain a matter for conjecture: perhaps Paul was influenced by the Septuagint;[535] perhaps the coarseness and strength of the term served Paul's purposes.[536] But whatever the motive, it is a fact that forms of ἐξουθενέω are found in Paul's epistles from the earliest to the latest.[537] Of immediate relevance, I would suggest, is the radical statement in 1 Cor. 1:28, which seems calculated to provoke the wealthy few in the church at Corinth: "God chose the lowborn of the world and the despised (τὰ ἐξουθενημένα), mere nothings, in order to bring to nothing the things that are." It is not difficult to understand how this novel and uncompromising dictum should have perplexed, and ultimately angered, a convert from the upper class who had experienced the empowerment of his consciousness through "belonging to Christ." The wrongdoer took the term ἐξουθενημένος from Paul in order to mock him. So imitation and ridicule are involved in the use of the term ἐξουθενημένος by Paul's critic, as in the case of ἀσθενής. Is it too much to suggest that the characterization ἐξουθενημένος was delivered by Paul's critic with an eastern Mediterranean accent? Thus a person with some rhetorical training observed the use of a colloquial expression by Paul in a controversial context, and appropriated that vulgar term as an epithet of incompetence to attach to Paul. The imitation and mockery would have made the characterization all the more devastating![538]

---

535 As implied by the references to the LXX in Plummer, *Second Epistle*, 283; Windisch, *Der zweite Korintherbrief*, 307.
536 Emphasizing the strength of the compound, Moulton and Milligan, *Vocabulary of the Greek Testament*, 225 s.v. ἐξουδενέω, ἐξουθενέω (Suidas: ἀντ' οὐδενὸς λογίζομαι).
537 1 Thess. 5:20; 1 Cor. 1:28; 6:4; 16:11; Gal. 4:14; 2 Cor. 10:10; Rom. 14:3, 10.
538 I wish to thank my friend and colleague Donald Dale Walker for correspondence on the meaning of the phrase ὁ λόγος ἐξουθενημένος.

Paul responds to the critique of his epistolary style and rhetorical delivery by denying that there is any inconsistency between his word and deed (2 Cor. 10:11). The pronoun, ὁ τοιοῦτος, used in 10:11, makes clear that Paul's response is intended, in the first instance, for the individual who has brought the criticism and has disseminated it among the Corinthians.[539] Paul does not attempt to rebut the criticism of his bodily presence and rhetorical delivery, nor can he, given the self-abasing account of his appearance as an orator in 1 Cor. 2:1–5.[540] Rather, Paul cleverly elides the contrast between his speech-making and his letter-writing by means of the phrase τῷ λόγῳ δι' ἐπιστολῶν ("in word through epistles").[541] Paul's assertion that there is no discrepancy between the sort of person he is in absence and presence employs the well known formula "in word and deed" (λόγῳ καὶ ἔργῳ).[542] It is possible that Paul's critic alleged an inconsistency in Paul's behavior by means of this formula. But the fact that the formula is found in Paul's response to the criticism quoted in 10:10 suggests that it is Paul himself who appropriates this formula in an attempt to annul the contrasting impressions of his actions by transcending the antithesis.[543]

We may now summarize what we have learned about the wrongdoer by widening the textual basis of our enquiry to include 2 Cor. 10:1–11, on the theory that this text represents the opening paragraphs of the letter to which Paul refers in 2 Cor. 2:3–4, a letter occasioned by the wrong of a certain unnamed individual. The picture that has emerged is extraordinarily rich, detailed, and colorful in respect to the values of the wrongdoer and his attitude towards Paul. Some aspects of what we have learned reinforce and augment inferences from our exegesis of 2 Cor. 1–2 and 7. Thus it is clearer than before that the wrongdoer is a member of the upper class, that he looks down upon Paul from a considerable social distance. His condescending attitude is embodied in the pungent label ταπεινός, a term expressing disdain for a social inferior. Measures of the

---

539 König, "Verkehr," 514; Menzies, *Second Epistle*, 73; Windisch, *Der zweite Korintherbrief*, 307; Barrett, "Ο ΑΔΙΚΗΣΑΣ," 115; idem, *Second Epistle*, 261; Watson, "Paul's Painful Letter," 345; Winter, *Paul Among the Sophists*, 208; Roetzel, *2 Corinthians*, 100–101.
540 Marshall, *Enmity in Corinth*, 389; Winter, *Paul Among the Sophists*, 143–44, 155–64, 227; Welborn, *Paul, the Fool of Christ*, 90–99.
541 Windisch, *Der zweite Korintherbrief*, 307; Furnish, *II Corinthians*, 469.
542 LSJ 683 s.v. ἔργον I.4; BDAG 390 s.v. ἔργον 1.a; H. Wayne Merritt, *In Word and Deed: Moral Integrity in Paul* (New York: Peter Lang, 1993) esp. 112–15, 129.
543 Merritt, *In Word and Deed*, 115.

wrongdoer's social status are the literary standards and the educational level reflected in the terms by which he evaluates Paul's epistolary style and rhetorical delivery–βαρύς, ἰσχυρός, ἀσθενής. The wrongdoer is the recipient of some rhetorical training and shares the aesthetic values of the educated elite. Moreover, we have garnered additional evidence of the overbearing influence of the wrongdoer upon the Corinthian congregation. The organization of Paul's argument reflects the assumption that the attitudes and judgments of the wrongdoer have shaped the disposition of the church toward Paul. The criticisms of Paul by this individual have instigated a general revolt of the church against its apostle, or so Paul represents the situation. Finally, we have further reason to believe that the conflict between Paul and an unnamed individual arose from an allegation of financial misconduct. This implication of Paul's use of ἀδικεῖν in 2 Cor. 7 is now reinforced by his reference to "some who reckon (λογιζομένοι) us to be acting according to human standards" in 10:2; investigation of the provenance of the verb λογίζεσθαι carried us into the realm of accounting and bookkeeping.

Other aspects of the wrongdoer's person disclosed by analysis of 2 Cor. 10:1–11 are new and could hardly have been guessed at from exegesis of 2 Cor. 1–2 and 7. First, the discovery that the individual whom Paul apostrophizes in 2 Cor. 10:7 is possessed of a lively consciousness of "belonging to Christ." To be sure, the Christian identity of the wrongdoer is given in his membership in the church at Corinth. And one might have surmised a certain depth of commitment from Paul's reference to his excessive remorse in 2 Cor. 2:7. But the robust confidence of being "of Christ" that shines through this passage is unexpected. We have sought to recover something of the nature of this experience from a close reading of Paul's earlier epistles and through consultation of texts such as the *Psalms of Solomon:* accordingly, Paul's antagonist experienced a sense of hope, entitlement, sovereignty, wisdom, righteousness, and happiness, as a result of "belonging to Christ." When we meet him in 2 Cor. 10:7, he is in full possession and enjoyment of these spiritual riches, and genuinely perplexed at the spiritual impoverishment implied in Paul's novel emphasis upon Christ as "the crucified." Second, the insight which these paragraphs afford into the wrongdoer's fondness for debate and his skill in verbal combat is altogether surprising and very intriguing. The wrongdoer exploits the nuances of Paul's vocabulary (πραΰς), appropriates Paul's jargon (κατὰ σάρκα), borrows his lingo (ἐξουθενημένος), and turns it all against him, undermining Paul's authority by mockery and imitation. Indeed, that this passage is so revealing is owing to the fact that Paul's opposite number is so nearly his equal in verbal combat.

2 Cor. 11:1–12:13

In 2 Cor. 10:12–18, Paul makes a transition to the comparison of himself with other apostles, which he presents in the ironic form of a "fool's speech" in 11:1–12:10. In this section, there are few instances of singular pronouns and singular verb-forms used in reference to a specific individual, where the context makes it likely that the individual is a Corinthian.[544] (Two possible exceptions in 11:16 and 12:6 are discussed below). For the most part, Paul's attention is focused on rival missionaries, who are represented as a group, designated by terms which emphasize their plurality–ἀπόστολοι, διάκονοι, etc.[545] It is difficult to determine whether the singular participle, ὁ ἐρχόμενος (literally, "the one who comes"), in 11:4, is a reference to a particular person, or is a generalization.[546] The evidence inclines toward seeing ὁ ἐρχόμενος as a specific in-

---

544 The gnomic quality of the statement in which Paul formulates his conviction about anyone who would engage in self-commendation in 2 Cor. 10:18 (οὐ γὰρ ὁ ἑαυτὸν συνιστάνων, ἐκεῖνός ἐστιν δόκιμος, ἀλλὰ ὃν ὁ κύριος συνίστησιν) prevents us from taking the singular pronouns and verb-forms in this verse as references to a specific individual, even if Paul's dictum is clearly aimed at the rivals who "commend themselves," and thereby show themselves to "have no understanding," in 10:12; thus, rightly, Windisch, *Der zweite Korintherbrief,* 314; Furnish, *II Corinthians,* 482; Thrall, *Second Epistle,* 2.653. In 11:20 and 11:21b, the context makes plain that Paul intends "one" or "anyone" among his apostolic rivals, rather than a local Corinthian, by the use of the singular indefinite pronoun τις: so, Windisch, *Der zweite Korintherbrief,* 347, 350; Furnish, *II Corinthians,* 497, 513; Thrall, *Second Epistle,* 2.721 n.472. The highly affective rhetorical questions in 11:29 push toward the universal ("Who is weak and I am not weak? Who is made to stumble and I do not burn with indignation?"), making it unlikely that Paul has a specific individual in mind; thus, Furnish, *II Corinthians,* 519–20; but, if so, then he must be one of Paul's apostolic rivals, rather than a Corinthian; so, M. L. Barré, "Paul as 'Eschatologic Person': a New Look at 2 Cor. 11:29," *CBQ* 37 (1975) 500–26, esp. 507–508.
545 2 Cor. 11:5, 13, 15, 18, 22, 23; 12:11. Cf. Plummer, *Second Epistle,* 289; Windisch, *Der zweite Korintherbrief,* 326; C. K. Barrett, *The Signs of an Apostle* (London: SPCK, 1970) 70; idem, *Second Epistle,* 253–54; Thrall, *Second Epistle,* 2.926–27.
546 Plummer, *Second Epistle,* 296; Windisch, *Der zweite Korintherbrief,* 325; Furnish, *II Corinthians,* 488.

dividual. The particle εἰ ("if") with the present indicative ἀνέχεσθε ("you put up with it") expresses a real condition, not just a hypothetical possibility; that is to say, Paul recalls, with bitterness, something that has actually happened in Corinth.[547] Moreover, one misses here the qualifying clause ὅστις ἐὰν ᾖ ("whoever he may be") which generalizes the reference in an otherwise similar passage in Gal. 5:10.[548] But even if Paul has a definite individual in mind in 2 Cor. 11:4, he cannot be identical with the wrongdoer, for the participle ἐρχόμενος makes clear that this person "comes" from without; he is an intruder with a "different gospel," not a resident member of the Corinthian church.[549] Although 2 Cor. 11:1 – 12:13 is focused on comparison with Paul's apostolic rivals, this passage nevertheless reveals something about the attitudes and values of the wrongdoer, since it makes clear that the apostles with whom Paul is forced to compare himself have received a ready welcome in Corinth, that their credentials as apostles are fully acknowledged, and that the substance and manner of their proclamation is admired. Hence, an examination of this portion of 2 Cor. 10 – 13 promises to enrich our portrait of the wrongdoer.

The identity of Paul's apostolic rivals in 2 Corinthians has been the subject of a long-standing debate in the history of New Testament scholarship.[550] In the nineteenth century, F. C. Baur and members of the Tübingen School identified Paul's opponents in the Corinthian correspondence as Judaizers, law-observant Jewish Christian missionaries, the same

---

547 In favor of reading the present indicative ἀνέχεσθε, rather than the variant ἀνείχεσθε, is the varied and early attestation of the former (P46, B D* 33 pc r sa), and the fact that the analogous statement in 11:20 employs the present tense; thus, Windisch, Der zweite Korintherbrief, 325 – 26; Barrett, Second Epistle, 270 n.2, 275; Furnish, II Corinthians, 489; Thrall, Second Epistle, 2.665 – 66.
548 Barrett, Second Epistle, 275.
549 Betz, Der Apostel Paulus, 13; Barrett, Second Epistle, 275; Martin, 2 Corinthians, 335.
550 For an overview of the debate in the history of scholarship, see Gerhard Friedrich, "Die Gegner des Paulus im 2. Korintherbrief" in Abraham unser Vater: Juden und Christen im Gespräch über die Bibel, eds. O. Betz, M. Hengel, and P. Schmidt (Leiden: Brill, 1963) 192 – 96; Georgi, Opponents of Paul, 7 – 16; C. K. Barrett, "Paul's Opponents in II Corinthians," NTS 17 (1971) 233 – 36; Christian Machelet, "Paulus und seine Gegner. Eine Untersuchung zu den Korintherbriefen" in Theokratia, ed. W. Dietrich (Leiden: Brill, 1973), 183 – 90; John J. Gunther, St. Paul's Opponents and Their Background: A Study of Apocalyptic and Jewish Sectarian Teachings (Leiden: Brill, 1973); Sumney, Identifying Paul's Opponents; Thrall, "Paul's Opponents in Corinth: The Evidence of 2 Corinthians" in Second Epistle, 2.926 – 45

group of teachers who challenged Paul's work in Galatia and Philippi.[551] In the twentieth century, Rudolf Bultmann and his students presented Paul's Corinthian opponents as representatives of the Gnostic movement.[552] The most thorough and nuanced reconstruction of the opposition to Paul in 2 Corinthians is that of Dieter Georgi.[553] Georgi argued that the opponents of Paul in Corinth could not be the same as the Judaizers who had disturbed Paul's churches in Galatia, since the law and circumcision are never mentioned in 2 Corinthians.[554] Nor can Paul's Corinthian opponents be described as Gnostics, because Paul does not polemicize against *gnosis*, libertinism, or possession of the spirit.[555] Taking his starting point from the honorific terms by which Paul's rivals designated themselves—διάκονοι, ἀπόστολοι, ἐργάται, Ἑβραῖοι, Ἰσραηλῖται, σπέρμα Ἀβραάμ—terms echoed by Paul in 2 Cor. 11:13 and 11:22–23, Georgi demonstrated that these missionaries took pride in their Jewish heritage, indeed, that they regarded the Christ whom they proclaimed as the fulfillment of the eschatological hopes of Israel.[556] As envoys of Christ, these missionaries believed that they enjoyed a special relationship with God: they were participants in divine power (θεῖοι ἄνδρες).[557] The missionaries manifested this power in eloquent discourses, confident, even miraculous deeds, and allegorical exegesis. In a *tour de force* of religio-historical research, Georgi demonstrated that Paul's Corinthian opponents employed apologetic methods that originated in the Hellenistic-Jewish mission to Gentiles, methods that had instructive analogues in

---

551 Ferdinand Christian Baur, "Die Christuspartei in der korinthischen Gemeinde, der Gegensatz des paulinischen und petrinischen Christentums in der ältesten Kirche, der Apostel Petrus in Rom," *Tübinger Zeitschrift für Theologie* 4 (1831) 61–206; followed by other Tübinger, such as Albert Schwegler and Adolf Hilgenfeld; see Gerd Lüdemann, *Paulus, der Heidenapostel, Band II: Antipaulinismus im frühen Christentum* (Göttingen: Vandenhoeck & Ruprecht, 1983) 13–43. The view of the opponents as Judaizers was represented in the 20th century by Oostendorp, *Another Jesus*; Barrett, "Paul's Opponents in II Corinthians," 233–54; Gunther, *St. Paul's Opponents*, esp. 299–303.
552 Anticipated by Lütgert, *Schwarmgeister in Korinth*; Rudolf Bultmann, *Exegetische Probleme des zweiten Korintherbriefes* (Uppsala: Wretmans, 1947) 20–30; Schmithals, *Gnosticism in Corinth*.
553 Georgi, *Gegner des Paulus*; English trans. with supplement, *Opponents of Paul*.
554 Georgi, *Opponents of Paul*, 2–5.
555 Georgi, *Opponents of Paul*, 7–9.
556 Georgi, *Opponents of Paul*, 27–82; anticipated by Friedrich, "Die Gegner des Paulus," 181–215.
557 Georgi, *Opponents of Paul*, 230–75.

the protreptic of Cynic-Stoic philosophers.[558] Through a close reading of 2 Cor. 3:7–18, Georgi showed that Jesus was proclaimed by these rival missionaries as a new Moses, a resplendent, spiritual Messiah who transfigures those who belong to him.[559]

For the purposes of our investigation, it is not necessary to enter further into the debate over the identity of Paul's apostolic rivals in 2 Corinthians, a debate which continues, and in which all the hypotheses of the past seem to attract present adherents.[560] It is enough to observe that the portrait of Paul's apostolic rivals which Georgi elicited from 2 Cor. 10–13 and 2:14–7:4 corresponds in important respects to the profile of the individual who is confident of "belonging to Christ" in 2 Cor. 10:7, as we have reconstructed his self-consciousness: thus, the pride in belonging to Christ's people, the sense of empowerment with divine gifts of wisdom and righteousness, the eschatological hope, answer remarkably well to the theology and proclamation of the rival missionaries with whom Paul is forced to compare himself. Indeed, the correspondence is so remarkable that we are obliged to consider that an elective affinity has been at work. Is it possible that the individual whom Paul apostrophizes in 2 Cor. 10:7 was responsible for having invoked the rival apostles as the standard by which Paul must measure himself?[561]

From Paul's ironic comparison of himself with other apostles in 2 Cor. 11:1–12:10, three aspects emerge in which the competing missionaries are admired: the *content* of their proclamation, the *manner* of their proclamation, and their *relationship* to the Corinthians. Considera-

---

558 Georgi, *Opponents of Paul*, 83–228.
559 Georgi, *Opponents of Paul*, 254–71.
560 Sellin, "Das 'Geheimnis' der Weisheit und das Rätsel der Christuspartei," 69–96; Lüdemann, *Paulus, der Heidenapostel Band II*, 127–43; Sumney, *Identifying Paul's Opponents*, 149–79; Murphy-O'Connor, *Paul*, 274–77, 280–82, 293–94, 302–304, 309–11, 317–19; Barnett, *Second Epistle*, 33–40; C. K. Barrett, "Sectarian Diversity at Corinth" in *Paul and the Corinthians: Studies on a Community in Conflict. Essays in Honour of Margaret Thrall*, eds. T. J. Burke and J. K. Elliott (Leiden: Brill, 2003) 297–302; Helmut Koester, *Paul and His World* (Minneapolis: Fortress Press, 2007) 80–85, 224–37.
561 Suggested as a possibility by Mitchell, "The Corinthian Correspondence and the Birth of Pauline Hermeneutics," 31: "other missionaries…have been invoked by a local Corinthian as the standard for apostolic authority, a comparison that set Paul's position and legitimacy in serious doubt"; similarly, idem, "Paul's Letters to Corinth,"334 n.90, postulating "an interpretive move on the part of one influential Corinthian to invoke the 'super-duper apostles' as the rhetorical standard by which Paul should be measured."

tion of each of these aspects provides insight into the values of the wrongdoer.

First, the *content* of their proclamation has met with a ready reception in Corinth. In 2 Cor. 11:4, Paul visualizes the Corinthians' response to the preaching of "the one who comes" (ὁ ἐρχόμενος), evidently the leading light among Paul's missionary rivals: "For if the one who comes proclaims another Jesus whom we did not proclaim, or you receive a different spirit which you did not receive, or you accept a different gospel which you did not accept, you put up with it well enough!"[562] This evangelist preaches "another Jesus" (ἄλλος Ἰησοῦς), with the result that the Corinthians have received a "different spirit" (πνεῦμα ἕτερον) and a "different gospel" (εὐαγγέλιον ἕτερον).[563] The nature of the contrast in christologies is here represented negatively: the Jesus whom his rival proclaims is "not the one whom we proclaimed" (ὃν οὐκ ἐκηρύξαμεν). Since Paul has related that, from a certain moment in his own mission work at Corinth, he decided (ἔκρινα) to make "Christ crucified" the exclusive content of his proclamation (1 Cor. 1:23; 2:2), we may infer that the preaching of his apostolic rival was not a "message about the cross."[564] Georgi plausibly suggests that the use of the name "Jesus," without the title "Christ," in 2 Cor. 11:4 indicates that the proclamation of Paul's rival consisted of an exposition of the powerful deeds of the earthly Jesus as they appear in the sources of the gospels.[565] On the basis of his analysis of 2 Cor. 3:7–18, Georgi also infers that Paul's missionary rivals engaged in spiritual ex-

---

562 On the text and translation of this crucial verse, see Windisch, *Der zweite Korintherbrief*, 325; Barrett, *Second Epistle*, 270 n.2, 275; Furnish, *II Corinthians*, 488–89; Thrall, *Second Epistle*, 2.665–66.

563 On the difficulties of the combination "Jesus...spirit...gospel," found nowhere else in Paul's letters, see Furnish, *II Corinthians*, 488; Thrall, *Second Epistle*, 2.667–70. A number of interpreters call attention to the formal similarity to Gal. 1:6–9: so, e.g., Bruce, *1 and 2 Corinthians*, 235; Barrett, *Second Epistle*, 275–76; Udo Borse, *Der Standort des Galaterbriefs* (Bonn: Hanstein, 1972) 84–85. But against the significance of the formal parallels, and hence, any connection of ὁ ἐρχόμενος with the Galatian Judaizers, see Windisch, *Der zweite Korintherbrief*, 327–28; Bultmann, *Der zweite Brief*, 204; Martin, *2 Corinthians*, 336. Georgi (*Opponents of Paul*, 272–73) rightly emphasizes the priority of ἄλλος Ἰησοῦς in Paul's summary of the proclamation of ὁ ἐρχόμενος: "The difference appears most of all in the Christology."

564 Georgi, *Opponents of Paul*, 273–74; Jerome Murphy-O'Connor, "Another Jesus (2 Cor. 11.4)," *RB* 97 (1990) 238–51, esp. 249–50.

565 Georgi, *Opponents of Paul*, 273–74; followed by Francis T. Fallon, *2 Corinthians* (Wilmington: Michael Glazier, 1980) 94.

egesis of scriptures such as Exodus 34, with the aim of demonstrating the surpassing glory of Christ.[566] Such a proclamation of Jesus as the embodiment of divine power, represented as the fulfillment of the hopes of Israel, would have held great attraction for one whose confidence in his new identity was shaped by the experience of "belonging to Christ."

Second, the rival apostles have won approval by the *manner* of their proclamation. This conclusion results from analysis of Paul's self-defense in 11:5–6. Having recalled, with pain, the reception which the Corinthians have given to the message of his most notorious rival (in 11:4), Paul passes,[567] in 11:5–6, to a second aspect in which comparison has revealed that his apostleship is defective—namely, his λόγος ("speech"). Paul's counter to this evaluation is introduced by an assertion of high irony and great bitterness: "For I reckon that I am in no way inferior to these super-apostles!" (λογίζομαι γὰρ μηδὲν ὑστερηκέναι τῶν ὑπερλίαν ἀποστόλων).[568] The verb λογίζεσθαι resumes the term used on three previous occasions (10:2, 7, 11) to describe the "evaluation" of Paul by his Corinthian critic.[569] Paul's ironic resumption of this verb strengthens our suspicion that the wrongdoer is responsible for having invoked the rival apostles as the standard by which Paul must be measured. The perfect infinitive ὑστερηκέναι, preceded by the emphatic μηδέν ("nothing"), suggests that the term ὑστέρημα has been used by someone in Corinth to name Paul's condition with respect to λόγος: that is, Paul's amateurish quality as a speaker has been held up to him as an irremediable "defect," on account of which he is judged to be inferior to other apostles.[570] The expression ὑπερλίαν ("superlative") is not merely ironic hyperbole,[571] but probably also mocks the idiom of the rival apostles, as Georgi has ar-

---

566 Georgi, *Opponents of Paul*, 264–71.
567 On the difficulty of the transition from 11:4 to 11:5–6, see Windisch, *Der zweite Korintherbrief*, 329. Barrett (*Second Epistle*, 277–78) finds the causal force of the particle γάρ in 11:5 in specification of the final reason for the appeal of 11:1–that the Corinthians should "put up with" Paul; similarly, Thrall, *Second Epistle*, 2.671.
568 On the irony of 11:5, see Barrett, *Second Epistle*, 278.
569 Georgi, *Opponents of Paul*, 230, 235; Bultmann, *Der zweite Brief*, 205.
570 On the force of the perfect infinitive ὑστερηκέναι in 11:5, see BDF §341; Bultmann, *Der zweite Brief*, 205; Zmijewski, *'Narrenrede'*, 115–16; Furnish, *II Corinthians*, 489. On μηδέν as emphatic, see Barrett, *Second Epistle*, 277; Furnish, *II Corinthians*, 489. That ὑστερεῖν embodies a criticism of Paul, see Betz, *Der Apostel Paulus*, 100; Martin, *2 Corinthians*, 342.
571 Betz, *Der Apostel Paulus*, 121.

gued;⁵⁷² compounds with the preposition ὑπέρ are remarkably frequent in 2 Cor. 10–13 and 2:14–7:4 (e.g., ἡ ὑπερβαλλούσῃ δόξα, "the surpassing glory" in 3:10),⁵⁷³ suggesting that the rival apostles employed such exalted language.⁵⁷⁴ In sum, the whole of 11:5 is ironic and mocking, reinforcing the impression that someone in Corinth has instigated the comparison between Paul and other apostles.

Paul's response to the unfavorable comparison takes the form of a concession, followed by an emphatic rejoinder: "But even if I am an amateur with respect to speech, I am certainly not with respect to knowledge, but in every way having manifested [this] in all things to you" (εἰ δὲ καὶ ἰδιώτης τῷ λόγῳ, ἀλλ' οὐ τῇ γνώσει, ἀλλ' ἐν παντὶ φανερώσαντες ἐν πᾶσιν εἰς ὑμᾶς). Because the description ἰδιώτης τῷ λόγῳ is found in Paul's response, Hans Dieter Betz denies that 11:6 echoes a reproach of Paul's opponents, asserting rather that the characterization belongs to Paul's self-defense.⁵⁷⁵ Betz adduces impressive parallels from the discourses of Dio Chrysostom, where the philosopher, drawing explicitly upon the example of Socrates, attacks the pretentiousness of the Sophists, conceding his "want of skill (ἀπειρία) in practically everything, but especially in speaking (περὶ τοὺς λόγους), recognizing that I am only a layman (ἰδιώτης)."⁵⁷⁶ Without doubt, Paul has formulated the contrast between his "speech" (λόγος) and "knowledge" (γνῶσις) in accordance with his own understanding in 11:6, and one senses a Socratic precedent in Paul as well. But this does not exclude the possibility that Paul's critic at Corinth had previously used the expression ἰδιώτης τῷ λόγῳ in a derogatory comparison with the rival apostles. Bruce Winter argues that this is the case, referring to uses of the term ἰδιώτης by Isocrates, Philodemus, Philo and Epictetus.⁵⁷⁷ Winter concludes that Paul's Corinthian critics employed the term ἰδιώτης in the same manner as the rhetoricians to characterize Paul as an "amateur" in public speaking who made no use of the devices of the professional orator, whatever training he may have received, and consequently appeared inarticulate in extempore dis-

---

572 Georgi, *Opponents of Paul*, 282.
573 Georgi, *Opponents of Paul*, 282; Furnish, *II Corinthians*, 490.
574 Marshall (*Enmity in Corinth*, 371–72) suggests that ὑπερλίαν ἀπόστολοι is an instance of Paul's use of innuendo to disparage rivals who have claimed "superiority."
575 Betz, *Der Apostel Paulus*, 59–69.
576 Dio Chrysostom *Or.* 42.3, cited by Betz, *Der Apostel Paulus*, 66. See already Judge, "Paul's Boasting," 37.
577 Winter, *Paul Among the Sophists*, 224–25.

course.⁵⁷⁸ To the texts cited by Winter, we may add usages of ἰδιώτης and its cognates by Dionysius of Halicarnassus and Longinus to describe the ordinary speech of the plain man.⁵⁷⁹ Thus, in his essay on Lysias, Dionysius criticizes the predecessors of the great orator who, "when they wished to add color to their speeches, abandoned the plain man's speech (τὸν ἰδιώτην) and resorted to artificial expression."⁵⁸⁰ Similarly, Longinus observes that certain phrases in Herodotus "graze the edge of vulgarity" (ταῦτα γὰρ ἐγγὺς παραξύει τὸν ἰδιώτην);⁵⁸¹ the context makes clear that by "vulgarity" Longinus means the occasional "homely expression" (ὁ ἰδιωτισμός) drawn from the language of "common life" (ἐκ τοῦ κοινοῦ βίου)."⁵⁸² By describing Paul as an ἰδιώτης τῷ λόγῳ, his Corinthian critics suggest that Paul's speech is that of the common man, lacking the refinement and polish of the orator.

Support for this interpretation is supplied by the final clause of 11:6, where Paul makes intentionally clumsy use of a rhetorical flourish, ἐν παντί...ἐν πᾶσιν.⁵⁸³ Literal-minded commentators find the last clause of 11:6 "unintelligible,"⁵⁸⁴ but, in fact, it is a master-stroke of Paul's ironic wit. By means of the pompous and vague expression ἐν παντὶ φανερώσαντες ἐν πᾶσιν εἰς ὑμᾶς ("in everything having manifested in all things to you"), Paul simultaneously mocks the ineptitude of his own delivery and undermines the rhetorical pretensions of his apostolic rivals. If this interpretation is correct, then Paul's ironic comparison of himself with his rivals in respect to the adequacy of his public speech in 11:6 is the

---

578 Winter, *Paul Among the Sophists*, 225–28; anticipated by Windisch, *Der zweite Korintherbrief*, 331. See, now, Thrall, *Second Epistle*, 2.676–77 and n.136.
579 Roberts, *Longinus on the Sublime*, 200 s.v. ἰδιώτης.
580 Dionysius of Halicarnassus *Lys.* 3.
581 Longinus *Subl.* 31.2.
582 Longinus *Subl.* 31.1. See further references in Roberts, *Longinus on the Sublime*, 200 s.v. ἰδιώτης.
583 For ἐν παντί...ἐν πᾶσιν as a rhetorical flourish, see Windisch, *Der zweite Korintherbrief*, 333; Winter, *Paul Among the Sophists*, 226.
584 So, Barrett, *Second Epistle*, 280; similarly, Bultmann, *Der zweite Brief*, 206. The sentence, as it stands, lacks an object. Commentators endeavor to supply an object, either αὐτήν or τὴν γνῶσιν, in an effort to make sense: see the suggestions in Plummer, *Second Epistle*, 300; Windisch, *Der zweite Korintherbrief*, 333; Lietzmann, *An die Korinther I/II*, 147; Barrett, *Second Epistle*, 280–81; Hughes, *Paul's Second Epistle*, 382–83; Furnish, *II Corinthians*, 491. But Bachmann (*Der zweite Brief*, 367–68) and Zmijewski ('Narrenrede', 119) suggest that Paul intentionally omitted the object, in order to accentuate the rhetorical flourish ἐν παντί...ἐν πᾶσιν.

mirror-image of the wrongdoer's scathing critique of Paul's rhetorical delivery in 10:10.[585] We are justified in concluding that Paul's critics in Corinth, among whom the wrongdoer was the chief, admired the rival apostles for the professionalism of their eloquence, and disparaged Paul for defects in his oratory.

Third, the rival apostles were well regarded in Corinth because of the nature of their *relationship* with the Corinthians, or, more precisely, with some of the Corinthians. The aspect of the relationship which stands in the foreground of 11:7–21 is that of financial support, but, as we shall see, the relationship was broader and had other dimensions, for which the proper name in the Greco-Roman context is "patronage."[586] This conclusion, once again, is an inference from the terms in which Paul defends himself in 11:7–21. In assessing the evidence of this text, we must be conscious of the force of Paul's rhetoric, since 11:7–21 is the bitterest and most sarcastic passage in the Pauline corpus, consisting, at one point, of such wild invective ("false apostles," "deceitful workers," "Satan's ministers") that one could forget, for a moment, that Paul is speaking about fellow-Christians.[587] Thus, we should not expect to find in this passage literal, much less technical descriptions of the relationships of Paul and his rivals to the Corinthians. But, fortunately, Paul's metaphors, and even his calumnies, make it possible to trace the outlines of the relationship which Paul has declined and which his rivals have accepted.

---

585 Concluding in a similar direction, Winter, *Paul Among the Sophists*, 227; Mitchell, "The Corinthian Correspondence and the Birth of Pauline Hermeneutics," 45.

586 That financial support provided to Christian teachers deserves to be understood in the context of "unequal friendship," or patronage, is an insight that has made its way into Pauline scholarship, thanks to the pioneering work of Edwin A. Judge, *The Social Pattern of the Christian Groups in the First Century: Some Prolegomena to the Study of New Testament Ideas of Social Obligation* (London: Tyndale, 1960) esp. 58–60; idem, "The Social Identity of the First Christians: A Question of Method in Religious History," *JRH* 11 (1980) 213–15; idem, "Cultural Conformity and Innovation in Paul: Some Clues from Contemporary Documents," *TynBul* 35 (1984) 12–15; followed by Marshall, *Enmity in Corinth*, 167, 220, 240; John K. Chow, *Patronage and Power: A Study of Social Networks in Corinth* (Sheffield: Sheffield Academic Press, 1992) 107–10; G. O. Kirner, "Apostolat und Patronage (II) Darstellungsteil: Weisheit, Rhetorik und Ruhm in Konflikt um die apostolischen Praxis des Paulus in der frühchristlichen Gemeinde Korinth (1 Kor. 1–4 und 9; 2 Kor. 10–13," *ZAC* 6 (2002) 27–72.

587 On invective, irony, and caricature in Paul's portrait of the rival apostles in 11:12–15, see Betz, *Der Apostel Paulus*, 100–102; Marshall, *Enmity in Corinth*, 347.

Paul begins his response to the invidious comparison with a bitter rhetorical question in 11:7: "Or (ἤ) did I commit a sin (ἁμαρτίαν ἐποίησα) in abasing myself so that you might be exalted, in that I preached the gospel of God to you as a free gift (δωρεάν)?" The form of the rhetorical question presupposes that doubts have been expressed about Paul's integrity,[588] even as the conjunction ἤ, which introduces the query, makes clear Paul's conviction that the question merits a negative response.[589] There are good reasons to conclude that, in this instance, the term ἁμαρτία derives from Paul's Corinthian critics and embodies their judgment on Paul's chosen means of subsistence.[590] This is the only place in Paul's epistles (apart from a citation of Ps. 31:1–2 LXX in Rom. 4:8) where ἁμαρτία denotes an individual sin.[591] When Paul recapitulates the defense of his relationship with the Corinthians in 12:13, he uses ἀδικία, "wrong," as a synonym of ἁμαρτία, to designate his decision not to impose a financial burden on the Corinthians.[592] This suggests that ἁμαρτία is used in a practical, rather than a religious sense in 11:7, that the phrase ἁμαρτίαν ποιεῖν should be translated "to make a mistake,"[593] and finally, that Paul's critics in Corinth have used this expression to characterize an error in judgment, a strategic misstep, that Paul made when he decided to support himself by working with his hands.

A further clue to the nature of the relationship that Paul has refused is found in the term δωρεάν ("gratis") which heads the ὅτι-clause in 11:7b, dragged forward to the beginning of the clause for emphasis.[594] As we observed above, the ὅτι-clause in 11:7b explicates, ironically, the wrongful

---

588 Heinrici, *Der zweite Brief*, 357; Plummer, *Second Epistle*, 302; Windisch, *Der zweite Korintherbrief*, 333–34; Barrett, *Second Epistle*, 281; Thrall, *Second Epistle*, 2.683.
589 Plummer, *Second Epistle*, 302; Zmijewski, *'Narrenrede'*, 123; Furnish, *II Corinthians*, 491; Thrall, *Second Epistle*, 2.682. Cf. 1 Cor. 6:9, 19; Rom. 6:3; 7:1; 11:2.
590 Plummer, *Second Epistle*, 302; Thrall, *Second Epistle*, 2.683, 704, appealing to Marshall's understanding of the affront to some wealthy Corinthians occasioned by Paul's refusal of a gift; Marshall, *Enmity in Corinth*, 221–32, esp. 246, 335.
591 Windisch, *Der zweite Korintherbrief*, 334; Furnish, *II Corinthians*, 491.
592 Windisch, *Der zweite Korintherbrief*, 334; Furnish, *II Corinthians*, 491; Harris, *Second Epistle*, 754.
593 Windisch, *Der zweite Korintherbrief*, 334; Barrett, *Second Epistle*, 281; Furnish, *II Corinthians*, 491; Ben Witherington, *Conflict and Community in Corinth: A Socio-Rhetorical Commentary on 1 and 2 Corinthians* (Grand Rapids: Eerdmans 1995) 448.
594 Heinrici, *Der zweite Brief*, 358; Plummer, *Second Epistle*, 303; Windisch, *Der zweite Korintherbrief*, 335.

act alleged against Paul: "Did I make a mistake… in that I preached the gospel of God to you as a free gift?"[595] One wonders why, in this instance, Paul did not repeat the word ἀδάπανος ("free of charge") that he had used earlier in 1 Cor. 9:18 in defense of his decision not to accept "pay" (μισθός) from the Corinthians.[596] Could it be that Paul's choice of a term in which the notion of "gift" is embedded[597] represents an aggressive counter to the Corinthians' reproach that he had departed from the norms of proper relationship in refusing to accept their "benefaction"?[598]

This inference gains color and depth from consideration of two expressions in subsequent verses of the paragraph. Reminding his readers of the conditions under which he first evangelized in Corinth, Paul asserts: "And when I was present with you and fell into want, I made myself a burden (κατενάρκησα) to no one" (11:9a). The verb καταναρκᾶν was originally a medical term meaning "to make numb."[599] Chrysostom and Theodoret take it as a synonym for βαρύνειν, thus "to weigh down," "to be a burden."[600] That Paul does not intend anything different by καταναρκᾶν is demonstrated by his use of ἀβαρής ("not burdensome") in 11:9c and καταβαρεῖν ("to lay a burden") in 12:16, in speaking of the same subject. Yet, Paul's choice of καταναρκᾶν rather than καταβαρεῖν requires some explanation. It cannot be that Paul employs καταναρκᾶν simply for the sake of variation, since the term is repeated strategically in Paul's recapitulation of his defense in 12:13, and comes up again in 12:14. So we must assume that Paul has used this unusual word intentionally, and with consciousness of its original meaning.[601] Due consider-

---

595 On the ὅτι-clause as explicative, so Windisch, *Der zweite Korintherbrief*, 334; Lietzmann, *An die Korintherbrief I/II*, 146; Bultmann, *Der zweite Brief*, 207.
596 Windisch, *Der zweite Korintherbrief*, 335; Bultmann, *Der zweite Brief*, 207; Hock, *Social Context*, 62–65.
597 BDAG 266 s.v. δωρεάν.
598 Cf. Marshall, *Enmity in Corinth*, 220 n.180; James R. Harrison, *Paul's Language of Grace in its Graeco-Roman Context* (Tübingen: Mohr Siebeck, 2003) 333.
599 LSJ 902 s.v. καταναρκάομαι, Hippocrates *De arte* 48; Moulton and Milligan, *Vocabulary of the Greek Testament*, 33 s.v. καταναρκάω; BDAG 522 s.v. καταναρκάω. Cf. Plummer, *Second Epistle*, 304–305; Windisch, *Der zweite Korintherbrief*, 336.
600 With reference to Chrysostom and Theodoret, BDAG 522 s.v. καταναρκάω; Thrall, *Second Epistle*, 2.686 n.214.
601 Windisch, *Der zweite Korintherbrief*, 336: "es ist jedenfalls wieder ein mit Absicht gewählter starker Ausdruck," appealing to the Catenae: "Nur die Cat. (=Oecumenius) glossiert es mit οὐκ ἠτόνησα (ermattete nicht) οὐδὲ ἐξέλυσα τὴν ὑπομονήν, hat also die ursprüngliche Bedeutung noch empfunden."

ation should be given to the translation preferred by Liddell and Scott, referring to 2 Cor. 11:9 and 12:13: "to be slothful towards,"[602] since this rendering captures the torpid condition embedded in the root meaning of the word.[603] The image that is thus evoked is of a person who has made himself burdensome by his sluggishness, his dormancy, his physical and mental inactivity.[604] Literary portraits of lazy household retainers populate the pages of farce and satire: such are the "lowly lazy louts" of Plautine comedy and the toady parasites of the Oxyrhynchus mime.[605] In Lucian's sketch of the lives of intellectuals who had attached themselves to the households of the wealthy, he pictures a philosopher, "pushed off into the most disregarded corner of the dining room," ignored, unentertaining, upon whom the master of the house looks with "annoyance," when he looks at him at all, because he is regarded as "sullen" and "incommodious"—all in all, a useless bore.[606]

A final expression in 11:11 completes the picture of the relationship that Paul has refused. Referring to his decision not to be a burden to anyone in Corinth, Paul asks, rhetorically: "And why? Because I do not love you? (ὅτι οὐκ ἀγαπῶ ὑμᾶς;) God knows I do!" The emergence of the question about "love," in the context of a discussion of financial support, is a clear indicator of the nature of the relationship that someone in Corinth has offered to Paul.[607] In the Greco-Roman world, the patron/client relationship was consistently described as a "friendship," exploiting the ambiguity of the terms φιλία and *amicitia*, in order to avoid the demeaning connotations inherent in the literal names.[608] The bond that held

---

602 LSJ 902 s.v. καταναρκάομαι II. Act., καταναρκᾶν τινος, "to be slothful towards."
603 Moulton and Milligan, *Vocabulary of the Greek Testament*, 330 s.v. καταναρκάω: "The subst. νάρκα (Lob. *Phryn.* p.331) = 'torpor' is found in Menander *Fragm.* p.143; cf. M. Anton. 10.9, πτοία, νάρκη, δουλεία." See also Plummer, *Second Epistle*, 305: "Galen explains νάρκη as much the same as ἀναισθησία."
604 Plummer, *Second Epistle*, 305: "The meaning here seems to be 'I crippled no man by sponging on him,' i.e. by draining him dry."
605 E.g., Plautus *Men.* 973–77; cf. Erich Segal, *Roman Laughter: The Comedy of Plautus* (Cambridge, MA: Harvard University Press, 1952) 142–43; *POxy* 413 ("Adulteress").
606 Lucian *Merc. cond.* 10, 26, 27, 30.
607 For interpretations that already move in this direction, see Hock, *Social Context*, 62–63, 65; Marshall, *Enmity in Corinth*, 225, 242–44; Thrall, *Second Epistle*, 2.690, 703–704.
608 On patronage and the language of friendship, see Saller, *Personal Patronage under the Early Empire*, 4–9, 11–15, 17–18, 24–25; idem, "Patronage and Friendship," 49–61; White, *Promised Verse*, 27–34; David Konstan, *Friendship in*

such relationships together was idealistically called "love," and was embellished with other terms of affection.[609] In a *commendatio* addressed to Lucius Verrus, the orator Fronto describes the intimacy of his relationship to his protégé Gavius Clarus: "From an early age he has attended me in a friendly fashion not only with those services by which a senator lesser in age and station properly cultivates a senator senior in rank and years, earning his goodwill; but gradually our friendship (*amicitia*) developed to the point that he is not distressed or ashamed to pay me the sort of deference which clients and faithful, hard-working freedmen yield—and not through arrogance on my part or flattery on his. But our mutual regard (*mutua caritas*) and true love (*amor verus*) have taken away from both of us all concern in restraining our services."[610] The relationship between Fronto and Clarus is an aristocratic friendship, even if the two friends are not equals; so one is not surprised to find expressions of affection.[611] But even in relations with social inferiors, "friendship" remained the stated ideal, and the language of "love" was utilized. Thus, Seneca advises wealthy patrons who lament the decline of "friendship" to learn the wisdom of the Stoic philosopher Hecaton: "to have love, they must show love themselves."[612] Even the relationship of poets and philosophers to the wealthy men upon whom their livelihood depended, a relationship that approximates what we mean by "employment," was euphemistically termed "friendship,"[613] and poor intellectuals were obliged to participate in formal expressions of affection, such as attendance at the morning sal-

---

the Classical World (Cambridge: Cambridge University Press, 1997) 135–37, 143–45. With reference to Paul's relations with certain Corinthians, see Marshall, *Enmity in Corinth*, 143–47.

609 Saller, *Personal Patronage*, 11–15, 60 n.113; idem, "Patronage and Friendship," 58–59; Konstan, *Friendship*, 122.

610 Fronto *Ad Verum* 2.7; cf. Saller, *Personal Patronage*, 9–10; idem, "Patronage and Friendship," 59.

611 Saller, *Personal Patronage*, 11–15; Konstan, *Friendship*, 49–52; Jon Hall, *Politeness and Politics in Cicero's Letters* (Oxford: Oxford University Press, 2009) 63–71.

612 Seneca *Ep.* 9.6.

613 See, e.g., Plutarch's essay "That a Philosopher Ought to Converse Especially with Men in Power," esp. *Mor.* 776B, 778 A-B; Lucian *Merc. cond.* esp. 1, 3, 20–21. On poets and philosophers as "friends" of the wealthy, see Peter White, *"Amicitia* and the Profession of Poetry in Early Imperial Rome," *JRS* 68 (1978) 74–92; T. P. Wiseman, *"Pete nobiles amicos:* Poets and Patrons in Late Republican Rome," in *Literary and Artistic Patronage in Ancient Rome* (Austin: University of Texas Press, 1982) 28–49; White, *Promised Verse*, 3–5, 13–31.

utation, accompanying the patron about the city, flattering the patron for his appearance or speech—behavior brilliantly satirized by Juvenal, Martial, and Lucian.[614] Imagining a more dignified relationship between philosopher and patron, Plutarch nevertheless allows that when a powerful man is possessed of moderation and culture, the philosopher "will not hold aloof from making him a friend and loving him" (οὐκ ἀφέξεται τοῦ φιλεῖν καὶ ἀγαπᾶν).[615]

Patronage, as defined by Richard Saller, is an asymmetrical personal relationship involving reciprocal exchange.[616] Love belongs to the reciprocity ethic as the return which a beneficiary is expected to make to one whose resources of wealth and power are greater.[617] The principles of this ethic were thoroughly analyzed by Aristotle in his discussion of the friendships of unequals.[618] Aristotle stipulates: "Now in unequal friendships, the benefits that one party receives and is entitled to claim from the other are not the same on either side…The affection rendered in these unequal friendships should also be proportionate: the better of the two parties, for instance, or the more useful or otherwise superior as the case may be, should receive more affection than he bestows (μᾶλλον φιλεῖσθαι ἢ φιλεῖν); since when the affection rendered is proportionate to desert, this produces equality in a sense between the parties, and equality is felt to be an essential element of friendship."[619] Summarizing

---

614 Juvenal *Sat.* 5, 7; Martial 2.18, 32, 55, 68; 3.30, 36, 37, 46; 10.14, 18, 70, 74, 75; 12.36; Lucian *Merc. cond.*; *Nigr.* 21–24. See also *Laus Pisonis* 104–15; Columella *De Agricultura* 1. *Praef.* 9, 12. Cf. Gilbert Highet, *Juvenal the Satirist* (Oxford: Clarendon Press, 1954) 6–8; Ludwig Friedländer, *Roman Life and Manners under the Early Empire*, 4 vols. (London: Routledge & Kegan Paul, 1968) 195–202; Phebe Lowell Bowditch, *Horace and the Gift Economy of Patronage* (Berkeley: University of California Press, 2001) 19–30.
615 Plutarch *Mor.* 778 A-B.
616 Saller, *Personal Patronage*, 1 and *passim*; idem, "Patronage and Friendship," 49; see also the superbly insightful analysis of the operation and function of patronage by Wallace-Hadrill, "Patronage in Roman society," 63–87.
617 See Aristotle's discussion of the affection (φιλία) owed to the superior party in an unequal friendship in *Eth. eud.* 7.3–5, 9–10; *Eth. nic.* 8.5–6, 7–8, 10, 14; cf. Konstan, *Friendship*, 67–82. On friendship and the reciprocity ethic in the early Empire, see Saller, *Personal Patronage*, 13–15, 24–25; Bowditch, *Gift Economy of Patronage*, 19–24.
618 Aristotle *Eth. eud.* 7.3–5, 9–10; *Eth. nic.* 8.5–6, 7–8, 10, 14; cf. Konstan, *Friendship*, 94–95; Lorraine Smith Pangle, *Aristotle and the Philosophy of Friendship* (Cambridge: Cambridge University Press, 2003) 57–64.
619 Aristotle *Eth. nic.* 8.7.2; cf. Michael Pakaluk, *Aristotle. Nicomachean Ethics Books VIII and IX* (Oxford: Clarendon Press, 1998) 92–94.

his discussion of friendship between unequals, Aristotle extracts a principle that distinguishes material benefit from moral return, and distributes the elements to the parties according to their resources, within a relationship that has reciprocity as its goal: "the superior should receive the larger share of honor, the needy one the larger share of profit; for honor is the due reward of virtue and beneficence, while need obtains the aid it requires in pecuniary gain."[620] And even more succinctly: "This principle therefore should regulate the intercourse of friends who are unequal: the one who is benefited in purse or prosperity must repay what he can, namely honor."[621]

The import of Paul's question about love, in the context of a discussion of his financial support, is now clear: Paul's refusal to accept the gift offered to him was interpreted as a lack of love for the Corinthians.[622] In drawing this conclusion, the Corinthians reflect an understanding of their relationship with Paul that is entirely consistent with the norms of unequal friendships in Greco-Roman society. Accordingly, by refusing the offer of financial support, Paul had simultaneously refused a "friendship."[623] It was only natural to infer that the motive for Paul's refusal was an unwillingness to be bound by "love," the love which a beneficiary owes to a person of superior means.

Confirmation of this interpretation is provided by the analogy of love between parents and children to which Paul has recourse in 12:14–15, when he reaffirms his determination not to be a burden to the Corinthians: "for children ought not to lay up treasure for their parents, but parents for their children. I will most gladly spend and be spent for you. If I love you more, am I to be loved less?" Aristotle, likewise, draws upon the parent-child relationship to explain the dynamics of unequal friendships: "the friendship between parents and children will be enduring and equitable, when the children render to the parents the services due to the authors of one's being, and the parents to the children those due to one's offspring."[624] In Aristotle's analysis, the father is the natural benefactor, "the source of the child's existence, which seems the greatest of all

---

620 Aristotle *Eth. nic.* 8.14.2; Pakaluk, *Aristotle. Nicomachean Ethics Books VIII and IX*, 143–44.
621 Aristotle *Eth. nic.* 8.14.3–4; Pakaluk, *Aristotle. Nicomachean Ethics Books VIII and IX*, 148.
622 Hock, *Social Context*, 63; Marshall, *Enmity in Corinth*, 233–57, esp. 244–51.
623 Marshall, *Enmity in Corinth*, 257.
624 Aristotle *Eth. nic.* 8.7.2; referenced by Marshall, *Enmity in Corinth*, 248.

goods, and of its nurture and education";⁶²⁵ the child is the beneficiary, who owes a debt that cannot be repaid in kind or equally, and hence must reciprocate as he can, with affection and honor.⁶²⁶ Seneca also adduces the parent-child relationship as an example of *beneficia:* parents almost always outdo their children, giving and continuing to give, what are considered to be "the greatest of all benefits"; children should strive to repay their parents in affection, for "not to love one's parents is unfilial."⁶²⁷ Paul's use of an established *topos* of the literature on benefits provides further confirmation of our hypothesis regarding the nature of the relationship under discussion in 11:7–21. More than this, Paul cleverly exploits the parent-child analogy to bring about a role-reversal in his relationship with the Corinthians; for in the analogy, Paul figures himself as the parental patron and the Corinthians as his filial clients.⁶²⁸

By contrast with Paul, his apostolic rivals have entered enthusiastically into clientship with the Corinthians, or, more precisely, with those in Corinth who have the resources to serve as benefactors. This situation has been an implicit assumption throughout Paul's defense of his refusal of financial support in 11:7–15, as the counter-position against which Paul's behavior has been measured and found wanting.⁶²⁹ But in 11:20, we are suddenly treated to a highly picturesque account of the deportment of one of the rival apostles in the household where he has received hospitality: "For you put up with it when someone enslaves you (εἴ τις ὑμᾶς καταδουλοῖ), when someone eats you out of house and home (εἴ τις κατεσθίει), when someone plunders you (εἴ τις λαμβάνει), when some-

---

625 Aristotle *Eth. nic.* 8.11.2; 8.12.5–6; 8.14.2–4.
626 Aristotle *Eth. nic.* 8.14.2–4.
627 Seneca *Ben.* 5.5.2; 6.24.1–2; 3.1.5; cited in connection with 2 Cor. 12:14–15 by Marshall, *Enmity in Corinth*, 248–49.
628 Windisch, *Der zweite Korintherbrief*, 399; Marshall, *Enmity in Corinth*, 249–50; Harrison, *Paul's Language of Grace*, 341–42, who rightly suggests that Paul's appropriation of the parental role in 2 Cor. 12:14–15 should be viewed against the background of benefaction ideology delineated by T. R. Stevenson, "The Ideal Benefactor and the Father Analogy in Greek and Roman Thought," *CQ* 42 (1992) 421–36.
629 That Paul's apostolic rivals in 2 Cor. 10–13 have been the recipients of financial support from certain wealthy Corinthians is widely recognized: Windisch, *Der zweite Korintherbrief*, 100–101; Käsemann, "Die Legitimitäat des Apostels," 36, 45, 48; Georgi, *Opponents of Paul*, 238–42; Oostendorp, *Another Jesus*, 76; Betz, *Der Apostel Paulus*, 100–17, esp. 102; Hock, *Social Context*, 62–63; Lüdemann, *Paulus, der Heidenapostel. Band II*, 135–36; Marshall, *Enmity in Corinth*, 175–76; Sumney, *Identifying Paul's Opponents*, 164–65.

one puts on airs (εἴ τις ἐπαίρεται), when someone strikes you in the face (εἴ τις εἰς πρόσωπον ὑμᾶς δέρει). To my shame, I say, we were too weak for that!" (11:20–21).

Several observations are in order on the style of Paul's description, before we seek to identify the character-type to which Paul has assigned his rival. First, the marker εἰ, with the present indicative, expresses a real rather than a hypothetical condition, as in 11:4; that is to say, Paul assumes that the behavior he describes has actually taken place.[630] Second, the fivefold repetition of the phrase εἴ τις ("when someone") produces a striking rhetorical effect.[631] Obviously, the emphasis created by the anaphora has greater point, if the pronoun τις refers to a specific individual. As in 11:4, Paul seems to focus on the leading light among his apostolic rivals.[632] Third, the satirical account of the behavior of a rival missionary serves not only as a foil to Paul's modest conduct, but also functions as a reproach to the Corinthians for their complaisant response to the interloper.[633] This hortatory function must be borne in mind as we seek to comprehend the roles that Paul, his rival, and the Corinthians play in the little scenario Paul has constructed. Finally, we must not fail to recognize that Paul's account of the conduct of his rival in 11:20 is an extreme caricature.[634] Indeed, Paul does not merely exaggerate the features of his rival in 11:20, but, as we shall see, assimilates the image of his rival to a social stereotype. As a result, we learn less about Paul's rival than we might have hoped from examination of the language of 11:20, but more about Paul's view of the relationship of his rival to the Corinthians.

In 11:20 Paul depicts the leading figure among his apostolic rivals as an instance of a social type so familiar and so loathsome that he was a

---

630 BDF §372; Windisch, *Der zweite Korintherbrief*, 326; Bultmann, *Der zweite Brief*, 203; Furnish, *II Corinthians*, 488, 497.
631 Windisch, *Der zweite Korintherbrief*, 347: "Jedes Glied dieser glänzenden Anapherreihe wirkt wie ein Peitschenhieb!"; Furnish, *II Corinthians*, 487.
632 Barrett (*Second Epistle*, 275, 291) rightly interprets "the one who comes" (ὁ ἐρχόμενος) in 2 Cor. 11:4 as a reference to a specific individual (even if he wrongly identifies this individual with the ἀδικήσας of 2 Cor. 7:12); cf. Betz, *Der Apostel Paulus*, 13. The alternative interpretation, which construes ὁ ἐρχόμενος in 11:4, and the singular pronouns and singular verbs in 11:20, generically (so Furnish, *II Corinthians*, 488, 497) is unconvincing.
633 Windisch, *Der zweite Korintherbrief*, 401–402; Furnish, *II Corinthians*, 511–12.
634 Rightly, Betz, *Der Apostel Paulus*, 116 n.535; Zmijewski, '*Narrenrede*', 230.

favorite subject of ridicule in comedy, mime and satire: the parasite.[635] When Greek and Roman authors wished to criticize behavior within a dependent relationship, they regularly evoked the figure of the comic parasite. The parasite is a negative reflection of the client: that is to say, "there were real people in Greco-Roman society who seemed to hostile eyes to participate in a relationship with a superior on terms comparable to the 'something-for-nothing' economy of the comic parasite and his wealthy host."[636] Cicero, Horace, Juvenal and others used the figure of the parasite to caricature the client. We may hypothesize that, like these orators and satirists, Paul evoked the parasitic type in 11:20 to serve as an unflattering portrait of the participation of his chief rival in the patronage system.

Before analyzing the language of 11:20 in detail, it is important to have the identifying features of the parasite clearly in mind, because most references to parasites outside comedy evoke the type by its distinguishing characteristics, rather than by the label παράσιτος.[637] The stock character of the parasite was distinguished, above all, by his insatiable

---

[635] The fundamental study remains that of Otto Ribbeck, *Kolax: Eine ethologische Studie*. Abhandlungen der Königl. Sächischen Gesellschaft der Wissenschaften, Phil.-hist. Klasse 9.1 (Leipzig: Teubner, 1883) 1–113; see further, M. E. Dilley, "The Parasite: A Study in Comic Development" (PhD dissertation, University of Chicago, 1924); E. Wüst, "Parasitos," *RE* 18 (1949) 1381–1405; T. B. L. Webster, *Studies in Later Greek Comedy* (Manchester: Manchester University Press, 1953) 63–65; H.-G. Nesselrath, *Lukians Parasitendialog: Untersuchungen und Kommentar* (Berlin: Walter de Gruyter, 1985); P. G. McC Brown, "Menander, Fragments 745 and 746 K-T, Menander's *Kolax*, and Parasites and Flatterers in Greek Comedy," *ZPE* 92 (1992) 91–107; Cynthia Damon, *The Mask of the Parasite: A Pathology of Roman Patronage* (Ann Arbor: University of Michigan Press, 1997); Elizabeth I. Tylawsky, *Saturio's Inheritance: The Greek Ancestry of the Roman Comic Parasite* (New York: Peter Lang, 2002); M. Fontaine, "*Parasitus colax* (Terence *Eunuchus* 30)," *Mnemosyne* 60 (2007) 483–89. My choice of the term "parasite" requires some justification. In Greek comedy until the middle of the fourth century B.C., κόλαξ was the regular term for a clever, obsequious flatterer. But the term κόλαξ was not taken up into Latin. In Roman comedy, satire, and declamation, the word *parasitus* became the established term for the hungry hanger-on. On this development, and the attempt by some scholars to analyze the genus of hanger-on into separate species, see Damon, *Mask of the Parasite*, 11–14.

[636] Damon, *Mask of the Parasite*, 8.

[637] Damon, *Mask of the Parasite*, 15, 17–18. In accordance with the etiquette of the patron-client relationship, the term *parasitus* is never used in direct address in Roman comedy.

hunger, but also by his wit, cunning, and impudence.⁶³⁸ The parasite typically ingratiated himself with the master of the house by flattery and boasting, gained a position of authority over other household members, and mistreated clients and guests.⁶³⁹ Plautus' Curculio and Terence's Phormio are supreme instances of the type—self-confident, clever, and abusive.⁶⁴⁰ In his satirical defense of the parasitic art, Lucian extols each step in the parasite's career: "friendship, that oft-lauded word, is nothing else than the first step in parasitic…knowing how to speak appropriately and to act in such a way as to become intimate and show himself extremely devoted to his patron, do you not think that this shows intelligence and highly-developed knowledge?…And at banquets, to go away with more than anybody else… do you think that can be managed without some degree of theory and wisdom?"⁶⁴¹

Evidence in support of the hypothesis that Paul intends to portray his leading rival as a parasite is provided, first of all, by analysis of the vocabulary of 11:20, for each term is drawn from comedy, or finds parallels in literature which evokes the comic type. First, Paul says "someone enslaves you." Consider the usage of καταδουλοῦν in Menander's popular play "The Hated Man" (Μισούμενος).⁶⁴² Thrasonides, a mercenary soldier, has fallen in love with a young slave girl Krateia, whom he bought, made his housekeeper, and promised freedom, to whom he gave servants, jewellery, and clothes, and whom he considered his wife,⁶⁴³ but who now "abuses" her "benefactor" because of his low pay and her extravagant expectations.⁶⁴⁴ Driven outside his own house in the dark of a stormy night, the soldier laments: "By a cheap little slave-girl I'm enslaved (καταδεδούλωκ'), who've not been by a single foe before!"⁶⁴⁵ In comedy and mime,

---

638 See the composite portraits in Ribbeck, *Kolax*, 21–76; Nesselrath, *Lukians Pasasitendialog*, 15–69; Damon, *Mask of the Parasite*, 23–36.
639 See esp. Theophrastus *Char.* 2; Lucian *Par.* Cf. Ribbeck, *Kolax*, 32–33, 43–64.
640 P. B. Corbett, *The Scurra* (Edinburgh: Scottish Academic Press, 1993) 8–10, 33, 35; Damon, *Mask of the Parasite*, 44–48, 89–101; Tylawsky, *Saturio's Inheritance*, 119, 155 n.34. See the incisive account of the figure of Phormio by David Konstan, *Roman Comedy* (Ithaca: Cornell University Press, 1983) 128–29: "the personality for whom Terence named the play is done with special brilliance and verve. Phormio is clever, bold, and ironic."
641 Lucian *Par.* 5, 22; cf. Nesselrath, *Lukians Parasitendialog*, 130–34, 191–95.
642 On the ancient celebrity of Menander's *Misoumenos*, see W. G. Arnott, *Menander II* (Cambridge, MA: Harvard University Press, 1996) 250–52.
643 Menander *Mis.* A37–40.
644 Menander *Mis.* A36, A41–98.
645 Menander *Mis.* fr. 4; text and trans. Arnott, *Menander II*, 352–53.

slaves and parasites frequently "enslave" and "clientize" their masters and patrons, by means of a saturnalian role-reversal.[646] In Plautus' *Asinaria*, for example, the clever slaves Leonida and Libanus succeed in completely reversing the master-slave relationship: the slaves begin by insisting that they be addressed as "patrons" and receive supplication; not satisfied with these verbal enhancements of status, they demand tangible signs of subservience: the master is commanded to get down and rub the knees of his slave, and even to carry the slave upon his back![647] The toady parasite in the "Adultery" mime from Oxyrhynchus joins with his mistress in a plot against his patron, and sings a parody of a dirge over his humiliated benefactor.[648]

Next, Paul observes, "someone eats you out of house and home." Hunger was the most conspicuous feature of the parasite.[649] To reveal the parasite's dependency on his patron for food, the comic poets make him insatiable.[650] Hunger is obvious in one of Alexis' parasites who complains of his tyrannical belly, "the source of all evils."[651] In Plautus' play *The Boastful Soldier*, the parasite is named Artotrogus ("Crust-muncher"); as his name would lead one to expect, Artotrogus has a strong interest in food, and the topic comes up repeatedly during his one speech on stage.[652] Plautus' parasite Gelasimus claims to be the son of Hunger: "My mother carried me in her belly for ten months, but I've been carry-

---

646 Segal, *Roman Laughter*, 103–16; William S. Anderson, *Barbarian Play: Plautus' Roman Comedy* (Toronto: Toronto University Press, 1993) 98–102; H. Wiemken, *Der griechische Mimus: Dokumente zur Geschichte des antiken Volkstheaters* (Bremen: Schünemann, 1972) 103.
647 Plautus *Asin.* 650–54, 670–702; cf. Segal, *Roman Laughter*, 104–109.
648 *POxy* 413 ("Adulteress"); cf. Wiemken, *Der griechische Mimus*, 97–105.
649 Ribbeck, *Kolax*, 34–42; Corbett, *Scurra*, 11–26; Damon, *Mask of the Parasite*, 25–26, 96–97, 99, 108–109.
650 In Greek comedy: Epicharmus 35.7; Eupolis 166; Alexis 183, 233, 263; Antiphanes 82; Aristophon 10; Axionicus 6; Diphilus 61; Epigenes 2; Eubulus 117.1–4; Sophilus 7–8; Timocles 13, 31; cf. Ribbeck *Kolax*, 34–35; Tylawski, *Saturio's Inheritance*, 14, 41, 58–59, 62–64, 78–80, 87–88, 99–100. In Latin comedy: Pomponius 151–52; Plautus *Capt.* 177, *Curc.* 309–25; *Men.* 77–109, 222–23, *Pers.* 59–60, *Stic.* 155–56, 575; Terence *Phorm.* 327–45; cf. Damon, *Mask of the Parasite*, 25, 96–97, 99. In the satirists: Horace *Sat.* 2.7, *Ep.* 1.18.10–14; Juvenal *Sat.* 5.1–11, 156–73.
651 Alexis 215; see also Diphilus 60; cf. Ribbeck, *Kolax*, 34; Damon, *Mask of the Parasite*, 25; Tylawski, *Saturio's Inheritance*, 152.
652 Plautus *Mil. glor.* 9–78, 667, 948 (*parasitum meum*); cf. Ribbeck, *Kolax*, 72; Damon, *Mask of the Parasite*, 14, 40–45.

ing her in my belly for more than ten years!"[653] The parasite in Plautus' *Captivi* is so hungry that he elevates satiety to the level of the gods, uttering an oath by "Divine Fullness,"[654] a state more often desired than achieved by comic parasites, who take the voracious Heracles as their patron deity.[655] In Terence's play *The Eunuch*, a parasitic flatterer is named Gnatho, "The Jaw."[656] Of the parasite Maenius, Horace says that he is an abyss into which one could upend the marketplace.[657] Similarly, Horace has one Mulvius confess that he is "a lightweight who is governed by his belly," a man whose head tilts way back when his nose is tracking the smell of cooking.[658] Because hunger is the parasite's defining characteristic, his organs of consumption are hypostasized. According to Plutarch (who had much to say about parasites in his treatise "How to Distinguish a Flatterer from a Friend"), the belly was more than just the focal point of the parasite's existence: "The belly is all there is to his body. It's an eye that looks high and low, a beast that creeps along on its teeth."[659] It is no wonder that the parasite's appetite is at times termed bestial: the parasite of Sophilus uses the verb χορτασθήσομαι (meaning "I'll get fattened up")—a term properly used of feeding animals—to describe his own consumption.[660] Because of his beastlike hunger, the parasite is addressed as maggot, fly, frog, caterpillar, cicada, and goose in the surviving fragments of Greek comedy.[661]

Next, Paul asserts, "someone plunders" (τις λαμβάνει). One of Horace's parasites is significantly named Pantolabus, "Take-all"; he is mentioned together with his patron, the spendthrift Nomentanus, whom

---

653 Plautus *Stic.* 159–60; cf. Damon, *Mask of the Parasite*, 25–26.
654 Plautus *Capt.* 877.
655 Cf. Diodorus 2.31; Naevius 27–29; Plautus *Curc.* 358, *Stic.* 233, 286, 395. On the special relationship between parasites and Heracles, see Athenaeus *Deipn.* 4.164b-d; Tertullian *Apol.* 15. Cf. W. G. Arnott, "Targets, Techniques, and Tradition in Plautus' *Stichus*," *Bulletin of the Institute of Classical Studies* 19 (1972) 78 n.45.
656 Ribbeck, *Kolax*, 73; Damon, *Mask of the Parasite*, 26–27. On the Menandrian original of this play, see Brown, "Menander, Fragments 745 and 746," 98–102.
657 Horace *Ep.* 1.15.26–35; cf. Damon, *Mask of the Parasite*, 111.
658 Horace *Sat.* 2.7.37–39; Damon, *Mask of the Parasite*, 108–109.
659 Plutarch *Mor.* 54B; Ribbeck, *Kolax*, 35–37; Damon, *Mask of the Parasite*, 26.
660 Sophilus 7–8; cited in Damon, *Mask of the Parasite*, 27.
661 Anaxilas 32; Antiphanes 193.7; Aristophon 10; Epigenes 2; cf. Ribbeck, *Kolax*, 34; Damon, *Mask of the Parasite*, 28 n.16.

he shamelessly plunders.⁶⁶² In Lucian's satirical defense of the parasitic art, the parasite seeks to win admiration by means of the rhetorical question: "How is it that the parasite is the only one that does not do wrong in taking (λαμβάνων) what belongs to someone else?"⁶⁶³ In Eupolis' *Flatterers*, the title characters plunder the estate of the young heir Callias, instigating the dispersal of his gold and silver utensils, fields, sheep and cattle, a race horse, one humdred drachmas, food and wine, ten talents, and napkins.⁶⁶⁴

Then, Paul adds, "someone puts on airs." The haughty behavior which Paul ascribes to his rival resembles that of the "august parasite" (σεμνοπαράσιτος) described by Alexis in *The Pilot:* this class of parasites "skillfully act the part of satraps and generals of renown in their ways of living, with eyebrows a thousand talents weight, squandering estates right and left."⁶⁶⁵ Elizabeth Tylawsky describes the distinguishing marks of the "august parasite" as "brazen confidence and self-importance": "This type of parasite took on the role of the preceptor who persuaded by sheer weight and compulsion. The heavy intonation and the repeated condescending demands for confirmation recall the instructor facing the feeble student."⁶⁶⁶ In his satirical account of the lives of intellectuals in "great houses," Lucian's alter ego extols the lives of such "august parasites": "Happy men! The elite of Rome are their friends. They dine sumptuously, and call for no reckoning. They are lodged splendidly, and travel com-

---

662 Horace *Sat.* 1.8.11; 2.1.21–22; cf. Corbett, *Scurra*, 68–69; Damon, *Mask of the Parasite*, 111–12.
663 Lucian *Par.* 21; cf. Nesselrath, *Lukians Parasitendialog*, 165.
664 Eupolis Κόλακες fr. 162–69; R. Kassel, *Poetae Comici Graeci* (Berlin: Walter de Gruyter, 1983).
665 Alexis 121 *apud* Athenaeus *Deipn.* 6.237b: "There are two classes of parasites, Nausinicus. One is the widely-prevailing kind, ridiculed on the stage, that is, we black ones. Then there lives another class, a tribe well called by the name 'august parasite,' that skillfully act the part of nabob parasites and generals of renown in their ways of living, with eyebrows a thousand talents weight, squandering estates right and left"; trans. C. B. Gulick, *Athenaeus: The Deipnosophists III* (Cambridge, MA: Harvard University Press, 1993) 67–69; cf. W. G. Arnott, *Alexis: The Fragments* (Cambridge, MA: Harvard University Press, 1996) 336. See the discussion of the "august parasite" (γένος σεμνοπαράσιτον) in Ribbeck, *Kolax*, 24; Webster, *Later Greek Comedy*, 48, 65; Nesselrath, *Lukians Parasitendialog*, 104; Tylawski, *Saturio's Inheritance*, 62.
666 Tylawski, *Saturio's Inheritance*, 62.

fortably—nay, luxuriously—with cushions at their backs, and as often as not a fine pair of creams in front of them."[667]

Paul climaxes his caricature of the behavior of his chief rival with the statement "someone strikes you in the face." Giving blows was one of the services provided by the parasite in order to win patronal approval.[668] Aristophon's parasite promises, "If someone who has drunk too much has to be tackled at the waist and thrown, you'll see me as an Argive wrestler. If there's an assault to be made upon someone's house, I'm a battering-ram. At climbing up a ladder, I am a Capaneus [one of the Seven against Thebes]. At wielding my fists, I'm a Telamon [knock-out blow]."[669] A pompous parasite in Antiphanes' *Ancestors* boasts, "at giving blows, I'm a thunderbolt, at blinding the eyes, a lightning flash, at picking a fellow up and carrying him off, a hurricane, at choking, a noose, at wrenching the bolts off a door, an earthquake…I can choke, stab, do anything that one may happen to propose—all at a moment's notice!"[670] Plautus' Curculio threatens to "pound" anyone who bars his way to his patron and his "gustatory delights": "Heads up! Friend or stranger, out of the way! Clear the street, beware my head, or chest, or elbow, or knee! I'm serious. This is urgent! Nobody has what it takes to deter me now….however intrepid—I'll chuck 'em off the sidewalk on their heads!…I'll pound a grain-fed fart out of every one of them!"[671]

Modern interpreters of Paul's caricature in 2 Cor. 11:20 may be surprised by the self-confidence, assertiveness, and abusiveness that Paul attributes to the parasitical type. But comic writers and satirists regularly portray a reversal of the asymmetrical relationship between patron and client as a warning against the dangers of the parasite. In the only surviving book of his *Satires*, Ennius describes a relation in which the parasitic guest has all the advantages and the host all the worries: "You show up happy, without a care—you've bathed, your jaws are set to attack, your arm is free for action, bright-eyed you are and standing tall, poised like a wolf to pounce—you lick your way through somebody else's fortune, and how do you think your host feels then? Miserable, by the gods! As he tries to safeguard his supplies, you swallow them down with a

---

667 Lucian *Merc. cond.* 3.
668 Damon, *Mask of the Parasite*, 30–31; Tylawski, *Saturio's Inheritance*, 64–65.
669 Aristophon 5 *apud* Athenaeus *Deipn.* 6.238b-c.
670 Antiphanes 193 *apud* Athenaeus *Deipn.* 6.238d-e.
671 Plautus *Curc.* 280–90; trans. H. Taylor, *Plautus: The Comedies I*, ed. D. Slavitt and P. Bovie (Baltimore: Johns Hopkins University Press, 1995) 345.

grin!"⁶⁷² Similarly, Terence's *Phormio* draws a boastful comparison between the parasite's complacency and the host's anxiety: "Just think of it: you come contributing nothing, perfumed and comfortable after a bath, your mind at ease, while the patron is devoured by care and expense. While everything is done to please you, he grimaces. You may smile, be helped to wine before him, take your place before him, a puzzle-meal is served to you. What in the world is a puzzle-meal? When you'd be puzzled what dish to try first. All you have to think about is what will taste best and what costs most!"⁶⁷³

Now that we have established that Paul evokes the type of the parasite by the behavior which he attributes to his chief rival in 11:20, we may look back to the first mention of this figure in 11:4, and see in the characterization, ὁ ἐρχόμενος ("the one who comes"), a foreshadowing of the type, for the verb "to come" is constantly associated with the one who "shows up" for dinner.⁶⁷⁴ The words "I'll come" are so characteristic of the parasite that they can furnish the surprise ending of one of Martial's epigrams. The addressee of *Epigram* 6.51 has stopped inviting his parasite to dinner: "You often have dinner without me, Lupercus, but I've found a way to make you smart. I'm angry, I am. Go ahead and invite me, send me a message, ask me to come. 'What will you do?' you ask. What will I do? I'll come!"⁶⁷⁵ The parasite of Martial's *Epigram* 12.82 is described at greater length, but for the denoument, one word suffices: *veni*. "Try what you may, you won't escape from Menogenes…He will praise everything, admire everything, until finally, when you've suffered through a thousand forms of tiresomeness, you say, 'Come!'."⁶⁷⁶

Paul's purpose in assimilating the image of his rival to the negative stereotype of the parasite was not merely to disenchant the Corinthians with someone whom they had welcomed into their midst, but actually to provoke revulsion against him. The assumption that the parasite will be ejected from the household as a noxious presence, once the guise of his false friendship has been penetrated, is explicitly articulated by Plutarch in his advice to philosophers on their relationships with powerful

---

672 Ennius 14–19; E. Courtney, *The Fragmentary Latin Poets* (Oxford: Oxford University Press, 1993) 12.
673 Terence *Phorm.* 339–42; trans. J. Sargeaunt, *Terence II* (Cambridge, MA: Harvard University Press, 1983) 41.
674 See already Ennius 14 (*aduenis*); Terence *Phorm.* 340 (*venire*).
675 Martial 6.51; see also *Ep.* 8.67.9–10 (*veni…veni*).
676 Martial 12.82; see the commentary on this epigram by Damon, *Mask of the Parasite*, 153–54.

men.[677] Flatterers of ordinary men are subjected to ridicule when they are found out;[678] but sycophants who batten upon the powerful, and deceive those upon whom many depend, "are driven away and punished by everyone."[679] Paul trades upon the assumption that the parasite will be driven out for the harm that he has caused, when he chooses to portray his rival as a brazen and showy parasite. Paul's rhetorical stratagem would have been more successful with an ancient than a modern audience, judging from the essays of Plutarch and Lucian. The line between the philosopher and the parasite was precariously thin: both took money for speech, as Plutarch acknowledges;[680] the difference was a matter of intention, often difficult to discern.[681] Anxiety, lest the philosopher be mistaken for a parasite, surfaces repeatedly in Plutarch's exhortation to philosophers to befriend the rich and powerful.[682]

Although Paul's account of the behavior of his chief rival in 11:20 is an outlandish caricature, we are still able to trace the outlines of a recognizable social role beneath the exaggerated features and to infer the nature of his relationship to the Corinthians. At the minimum, hospitality has been offered to this individual, room and board, interpreting κατεσθίει on the basis of Paul's reference to "eating and drinking" (φαγεῖν καὶ πιεῖν) as the prerogative claimed by certain rival apostles in 1 Cor. 9:4–14.[683] The *Digest* attests that patrons sometimes gave clients free lodgings.[684] Fronto's literary clients lived with him at points in their careers.[685] In his essay "On Salaried Posts in Great Houses," Lucian pictures the arrival of a novel intellectual in the house of a rich man, and the hospitality

---

677 Plutarch *Mor.* 778D-F.
678 Plutarch *Mor.* 778E.
679 Plutarch *Mor.* 778D-E. Plutarch continues, "Therefore, just as people laugh when the flatterers of Callias are ridiculed in comedy…the friends and intimates [of powerful men] are imprisoned, tortured, and burned, and made forever polluted and accursed, since the former did harm to one man, but the latter through one to many."
680 Plutarch *Mor.* 777B-D.
681 Plutarch *Mor.* 777E-778 A.
682 Plutarch *Mor.* 777D, 778 A, 779 A-C.
683 Windisch, *Der zweite Korintherbrief*, 347; Barrett, *Second Epistle*, 291. Cf. Theissen, *Social Setting*, 27–67.
684 *Digest* 7.8.2–3; 9.3.5; cf. Friedländer, *Roman Life and Manners*, 1.196; Saller, "Patronage and Friendship," 51. See also *Laus Pisonis* 133–37; Tacitus *Dial.* 6.2.
685 Fronto *Amic.* 1.10; cf. Saller, *Personal Patronage*, 137. For poets who took up residence in the homes of their patrons, see White, *Promised Verse*, 13.

that he is immediately accorded, the sumptuous dishes that are set before him, "until he gets tired of stuffing himself."[686]

But something more than hospitality is implied by λαμβάνει ("he takes" or "he receives"), interpreting the verb in the sense of "accept a donation," as in *Didache* 1:5.[687] In 1 Cor. 9:18, Paul refers to the financial support that his rivals have accepted and that he has declined by means of the derogatory expression μισθός, "pay" or "wages,"[688] the term used repeatedly by Lucian in his caustic exposé of philosophers who enter into "friendship" with the rich.[689] We may be sure that neither Paul's rival nor his Corinthian patrons used this socially demeaning term in reference to their gift. Nor is it likely that the donation was a regular stipend, like the scanty sum whose calculation Lucian describes in one of the more pitiable passages in his essay.[690] Rather, we should probably think of the gift that Paul's rival has accepted as a monetary reward such as was sometimes provided to valued literary protégés by admiring friends, according to Martial.[691] The gift may have been intended to enhance the evangelist's public standing in Corinthian society, or to speed him on his way to another location, or simply as a token of respect.

More important than any tangible benefit is the esteem that Paul's rival evidently enjoyed with the wealthy few in the church at Corinth. For esteem is the presupposition of the attitude and behavior which Paul caricatures under the verbs ἐπαίρεσθαι ("to put on airs") and καταδουλοῦν ("to enslave"), for which the proper name is "self-confidence." We should not assume that the self-confidence of Paul's rival was merely presumptuousness or arrogance. Rather, a display of confidence belonged to the successful function of an asymmetrical friendship between a philosopher and his patron. Plutarch encourages the philosopher-friend to believe that, in his role as the moral improver of the rich and powerful, he is himself a benefactor who "confers benefits upon many."[692] The philoso-

---

686 Lucian *Merc. cond.* 26.
687 F. Field, *Notes on the Translation of the New Testament* (Cambridge: Cambridge University Press, 1899) 184–85.
688 See the discussion in Hock, *Social Context*, 52–62; Marshall, *Enmity in Corinth*, 224; Chow, *Patronage and Power*, 106–10.
689 Lucian *Merc. cond.*, e.g., 1, ἐπὶ μισθῷ, 3, μισθοφορά, μισθός, 4, οἱ μισθοδόται, 13, μισθός.
690 Lucian *Merc. cond.* 19–20.
691 Martial 4.61; 10.11.6; cf. Friedländer, *Roman Life and Manners*, 1.196; White, *Promised Verse*, 55.
692 Plutarch *Mor.* 778D.

pher will prove a true friend to the powerful man, Plutarch explains, insofar as he "inspires confidence and thereby gives him power for affairs" (δύναμιν περὶ τὰς πράξεις ἐκ τοῦ πιστεύεσθαι δίδωσιν), since "confidence makes one willing" (βούλεσθαι δὲ ποιεῖ τὸ πιστεύειν).[693] By exuding confidence in his spiritual and rhetorical gifts, Paul's rival would have fulfilled the expectations of his role. Paul construes his rival's self-confidence as *hybris*. But, penetrating Paul's polemical caricature, we may infer that a relationship existed between Paul's rival and his Corinthian patron that approached reciprocity, because it was founded upon mutual respect.

We may now draw together the various threads of our exegesis of 11:1–21 to summarize what may be inferred about the values and attitudes of the wrongdoer, on the basis of Paul's ironic comparison of himself with certain rival apostles. We suggested, as a working hypothesis, that the wrongdoer was responsible for instigating the comparison between Paul and other evangelists, by invoking the rival apostles as the standard against which Paul must measure himself. This suggestion is supported by the flow of Paul's argument in chapters 10 and 11, which passes from an apostrophe of an individual who is confident of belonging to Christ (10:7), and who disparages Paul's rhetorical delivery (10:10), to a grudging comparison of himself with competing missionaries who are regarded as superior. Thus we are not surprised to discover a congruence between the Christology of Paul's apostolic rival, as it may be inferred from the language of 11:4, and the experience of belonging to Christ, which we reconstructed behind the claim of 10:7: Paul's rival proclaimed Jesus mighty in word and deed, the promised redeemer of Israel, and the wrongdoer was confirmed in his core belief. Something more than congruence is involved in the admiration for the professional eloquence of Paul's rival, implied in Paul's apology for his amateur oratory in 11:6, and the derogatory estimate of Paul's rhetorical delivery voiced in 10:10: here it is a case of a coincidence of aesthetic tastes between the leading figure among Paul's apostolic rivals and Paul's chief critic in Corinth. The wrongdoer esteemed the discourse of Paul's rival for its elevation, dignity, intensity, etc.—all the virtues that were cultivated in the rhetorical schools—and deemed these qualities to be appropriate to the bold proclamation of Jesus as the Messiah.

New in our emerging portrait of the wrongdoer is the inference regarding his patronal relationship with certain unnamed Christian missionaries. The wrongdoer invited one or more of Paul's rivals into a

---

693 Plutarch *Mor.* 777E-F.

"friendship" involving reciprocal exchange: the evangelist obtained material benefits—hospitality, money, status—which he recompensed with spiritual gifts—knowledge, eloquence, admonition. Paul, for reasons we have yet to explore, did not enter into this relationship, choosing, instead, to support himself by working with his hands. Much that we should like to know about this relationship is obscured by the force of Paul's rhetoric. We have endeavored to see through Paul's travesty of his rival's behavior in 11:20 by identifying the stock character to which Paul seeks to assimilate his rival's image: Paul depicts his rival as a pretentious parasite, in the hope that the Corinthians will reject him. But we have learned from our excursion into patronage that, by accepting gifts in exchange for his services, Paul's rival was acting in accordance with the norms that governed relationships between intellectuals and their social superiors.[694] Whether the relation enjoyed by the wrongdoer and the rival missionary was a "true friendship" is impossible to determine. Confident behavior may be taken as a sign of genuine amity.[695] Common values and tastes may have served to neutralize the status differences between the Christian missionary and his Corinthian patron.[696] But Paul's polemical rhetoric places the matter beyond our reach.

Even more deeply obfuscated by the rhetoric of 11:7–21 is the history of the relationship between Paul and the Corinthians with respect to financial support. The single fact that emerges from the emotional maelstrom of this passage is that Paul did not enjoy a relationship as a client with anyone in Corinth. But under what circumstances the offer of financial support was made to Paul, and the motive for Paul's refusal of the gift, remain largely unilluminated by the argument of 11:7–21. Indeed, Paul does not even state explicitly that he preferred to support himself by working with his hands,[697] although we have inferred a reference to Paul's banausic occupation in the expression ἐμαυτὸν ταπεινῶν ("demeaning myself") in 11:7.[698] Instead, recurring to the military imagery that dominated the opening paragraph of the letter, Paul insists, "I plundered (ἐσύλησα) other churches taking soldier's pay (ὀψώνιον) for the service of you"

---

694 White, *Promised Verse*, 3–5, 13–27.
695 Note the emphasis upon "confidence" in friendship in the writings of Epicurus, as illuminated by Konstan, *Friendship*, 109. See also Plutarch *Mor.* 777E-F.
696 Cicero emphasizes the role of "like sentiments" in friendship, e.g., *Fam.* 5.2.3; cf. Konstan, *Friendship*, 122–36.
697 As noted by Marshall, *Enmity in Corinth*, 176.
698 So already Plummer, *Second Epistle*, 302; Windisch, *Der zweite Korintherbrief*, 334; Hughes, *Paul's Second Epistle*, 384; Hock, *Social Context*, 64.

(11:8).⁶⁹⁹ That Paul should draw the Macedonians into the discussion (11:9), when his affection for the Corinthians was already in doubt (11:11), is best understood as a manifestation of his woundedness.⁷⁰⁰ Nor is it easy to understand Paul's vehement declaration of his determination "not to be a burden" to the Corinthians in 11:10 ("As the truth of Christ is in me, this boast of mine will not be silenced in the regions of Achaia!") as anything other than the reflex of Paul's woundedness.⁷⁰¹ Indeed, the rhetoric of 11:7–21, with its sarcastic questions, bellicose jargon, asseverations, boasts, calumnies, and caricatures, is so extreme that we may be certain that we are near the exigence of 2 Cor. 10–13 in discussion of the issue of financial support. Yet, the only reason stated in this passage for Paul's refusal to accept financial support—"not to be a burden to anyone…in any way"—is implicated so deeply in the caricature of the rival apostles as parasites that it cannot be regarded as an exhaustive account of Paul's motivation. We must wait until all of the data provided by exegesis of the texts and analysis of the relevant social conventions are available, before we seek to put forward a hypothesis regarding the origin and history of Paul's financial relationship with the Corinthians.

Finally, with respect to the patronal role that we inferred for the wrongdoer, we should make explicit the assumption that has undergirded our analysis of 11:7–21: to be able to invite Christian missionaries, whether Paul or his rivals, into a "friendship" involving hospitality, gifts and esteem, one must have sufficient resources for such a relationship.⁷⁰² This assumption is consistent with the inference drawn from exegesis of 2 Cor. 2 and 7: that the wrongdoer was a person of high social

---

699 On the military imagery of 11:8, see Windisch, *Der zweite Korintherbrief*, 335; Hughes, *Paul's Second Epistle*, 385–86; Marshall, *Enmity in* Corinth, 224; Furnish, *II Corinthians*, 492, 508; Martin, *2 Corinthians*, 346. For συλάω as "pillage," "plunder," see LSJ 1671 s.v. συλάω 2; for ὀψώνιον as "soldier's pay," see Adolf Deissmann, *Bible Studies* (Edinburgh: T & T Clark, 1923) 266; Moulton and Milligan, *Vocabulary of the Greek Testament*, 471–72 s.v. ὀψώνιον; but cf. C. Caragounis, " 'Οψώνιον: A Reconsideration of Its Meaning," *NovT* 16 (1974) 35–57.

700 Windisch, *Der zweite Korintherbrief*, 338.

701 On Paul's resort to an oath formula, or asseveration, in 11:10, see Windisch, *Der zweite Korintherbrief*, 337; Hughes, *Paul's Second Epistle*, 389; Bultmann, *Der zweite Brief*, 208.

702 Judge, *Social Pattern*, 59–60; idem, "Social Identity of the First Christians," 214; idem, "Cultural Conformity and Innovation in Paul," 15; Hock, *Social Context*, 65; Marshall, *Enmity in Corinth*, 175–77, 232–33, 240, 257; Chow, *Patronage and Power*, 109–10; Kirner, "Apostolat und Patronage (II)," 27–72.

status, capable of doing wrong with impunity and of causing pain to an entire community.[703] We also inferred high social status from the values reflected in the judgment upon Paul's behavior and occupation in 10:1, namely, that Paul is ταπεινός,[704] and from the literary standards evident in the criticism of Paul's epistolary style and rhetorical delivery in 10:10.[705] Nevertheless, one might object that Paul speaks throughout 11:7–21 to the Corinthians as a whole, when defending his refusal of financial support. How, then, are we entitled to infer a special patronal role for an individual Corinthian? This seemingly valid objection is removed by a moment's reflection upon the social realities. The majority of the Corinthian Christians lived at the subsistence level, by Paul's own admission: lacking in education, wealth and birth, they were "foolish …weak …lowborn …despised …nobodies" (1 Cor. 1:26–28).[706] Supposing that the majority of the Corinthian Christians, by the practice of renunciation (that is, by fasting),[707] had been able to offer Paul or his apostolic rivals a gift, it can scarcely have been more than symbolic, their "widow's mites."[708] Only the wealthy few in the church at Corinth would have possessed the resources for the kind of relationship under discussion in 11:7–21. This was the reality of life in a hierarchically organized society like Roman Corinth.[709] With his customary objectivity, Aristotle explains that the bestowal of benefits presupposes "the possession of more than sufficient means," or "larger means than the person benefited."[710] The

---

703 Ewald, *Sendschreiben*, 227; Weiss, *Primitive Christianity*, 1.342.
704 See above on 10:1.
705 See above on 10:10.
706 Donald W. Engels, *Roman Corinth: An Alternative Model for the Classical City* (Chicago: University of Chicago Press, 1990) 113–16; Justin J. Meggitt, *Paul, Poverty and Survival* (Edinburgh: T & T Clark, 1998) 97–100; Steven J. Friesen, "Poverty in Pauline Studies: Beyond the So-called New Consensus," *JSNT* 26 (2004) 323–61, esp. 348–53.
707 Gerd Theissen, *The Religion of the Earliest Churches* (Minneapolis: Fortress Press, 1999) 91; Meggitt, *Paul, Poverty and Survival*, 132, and his discussion of "mutualism," 157–75.
708 Roetzel, *2 Corinthians*, 48. Compare Paul's description of the "abysmal poverty" of the Macedonians in 2 Cor. 8:2, and the comments of Betz, *2 Corinthians 8 and 9*, 43. See in general, Dieter Georgi, *Remembering the Poor: The History of Paul's Collection for Jerusalem* (Nashville: Abingdon, 1992).
709 On the striking gap between the rich and the poor in Roman Corinth, see, e.g., Alciphron 3.60; with the comments of Weiss, *Der erste Korintherbrief*, x; Theissen, *Social Setting*, 69–143; Furnish, *II Corinthians*, 13. On the verticality of Roman society in general, see MacMullen, *Roman Social Relations*, 88–120.
710 Aristotle *Rhet.* 1.11.22; cf. *Eth. nic.* 8.7; *Eth. eud.* 7.8.

wrongdoer may not have been the only patron of Christian missionaries in Corinth, but he was one, and perhaps the foremost one, of the few elite Christians who played this role.

Within the long section 11:1–12:10 in which Paul is obliged to compare himself with other apostles, there are two verses, 11:16 and 12:6, where singular pronouns and singular verb-forms raise the possibility of a passing reference to the same anonymous individual who is apostrophized in 10:7 and quoted in 10:10—putatively, the wrongdoer. In both cases, it appears at first glance that Paul is speaking in a general way of what "someone" (τις) might think of him.[711] Yet in both cases, there are special features of the vocabulary and argument which suggest that the opinion of a single individual is uppermost in Paul's mind, even as he addresses all of the Corinthians. We shall see that careful examination of these passages will enrich our understanding of the attitude of the wrongdoer toward Paul.

In 11:16 Paul urges: "Again I say, let no one suppose me to be a fool; but should it be otherwise, then at least accept me as a fool, so that I too may boast a little." The injunction, μή τίς με δόξῃ ἄφρονα εἶναι ("let no one think me a fool"),[712] together with the concession, εἰ δὲ μή γε (literally, "but if not," i.e., "if one must consider me a fool"),[713] strongly suggests that "someone" (τις) in Corinth has expressed the opinion that Paul is "foolish" (ἄφρων).[714] The introduction to the verse, πάλιν λέγω ("I repeat"), looks back to 11:1, where Paul makes a similar request, and uses similar language (ἀφροσύνη, μικρόν τι).[715] This verse, which begins the "fool's speech," is loaded with a bitter irony: "If only you would put up with me in a little foolishness! But do put up with me! (Ὄφελον ἀνείχεσθέ μου μικρόν τι ἀφροσύνης· ἀλλὰ καὶ ἀνέχεσθέ μου).[716] What makes

---

711 Furnish, *II Corinthians*, 527; Harris, *Second Epistle*, 779.
712 On μή τις...δόξῃ, see 1 Cor. 16:11. Cf. Moule, *Idiom Book*, 22; Bultmann, *Der zweite Brief*, 211; Harris, *Second Epistle*, 779.
713 On the classical construction εἰ δὲ μή γε ("but if it should be otherwise"), found only here in Paul, see BDF §439(1), 480(6); Heinrici, *Der zweite Brief*, 366–67; Plummer, *Second Epistle*, 314; Barrett, *Second Epistle*, 289; Bultmann, *Der zweite Brief*, 211.
714 Plummer, *Second Epistle*, 313–14; Lietzmann, *An die Korinther I/II*, 144; Zmijewski, *'Narrenrede'*, 191. Cf. Hans-Joachim Schoeps, *Paulus* (Tübingen: Mohr Siebeck, 1959) 74.
715 Windisch, *Der zweite Korintherbrief*, 344; Furnish, *II Corinthians*, 495; Wolff, *Der zweite Brief*, 225; Thrall, *Second Epistle*, 2.709–10.
716 Windisch, *Der zweite Korintherbrief*, 315–17; Wolff, *Der zweite Brief*, 208; Furnish, *II Corinthians*, 484–85; Thrall, *Second Epistle*, 2.654.

the irony so apparent, and nearly unbearable, is the contradiction between the two wishes expressed: on the one hand, the unattainable wish, indicated by the particle ὄφελον with the past tense of the indicative (ἀνείχεσθε)—"I know that you will not bear with me in my foolishness, but if only you would!";[717] on the other hand, the admonition, taking ἀνέχεσθε as an imperative—"But do put up with me!"[718] Paul appeals for a tolerance which he simultaneously despairs of being granted!

The key to reconstructing the give-and-take behind these verses is the verb ἀνέχεσθαι ("to put up with," "to bear with," "to suffer"),[719] which, together with the term ἀφροσύνη ("foolishness"), is the rubric over the entire "foolish discourse."[720] Found only once elsewhere in Paul (1 Cor. 4:12), ἀνέχεσθαι dominates the present passage, occurring twice in 11:1, then in 11:4, 11:19, and 11:20.[721] The hypothesis that seems best warranted by the evidence is that someone in Corinth—in all likelihood, the wrongdoer—has said somewhat as follows in reference to Paul: "We are obliged to put up with a fool!" It is this sarcastic comment which has engendered the double irony of the paradoxical wish expressed in 11:1, and the forced resignation before a perception that cannot be altered in 11:16. Knowing that it cannot be otherwise (εἰ δὲ μή γε), Paul turns the expression savagely against his rivals and their Corinthian patrons: "you put up with it readily" (καλῶς ἀνέχεσθε), if someone comes and preaches a different gospel (11:4); "you gladly put up with" (ἡδέως ἀνέχεσθε) boastful fools (11:19); "you put up with" (ἀνέχεσθε) a pretentious parasite who abuses your hospitality (11:20). How did it come about that someone in Corinth said, in reference to Paul, "We are obliged to put up with a fool!"?

The answer to this question, and the cause of so much of the polemic of 2 Cor. 10–13, is to be found in the way in which Paul presents him-

---

717 BDF §359(1); Moule, *Idiom Book*, 137; Windisch, *Der zweite Korintherbrief*, 317 n.1; Bultmann, *Der zweite Brief*, 201; Furnish, *II Corinthians*, 485; Thrall, *Second Epistle*, 2.658.
718 Arguing that the imperative is more likely than the indicative in view of the context, and esp. the unambiguous imperative δέξασθε in 11:16, see Bachmann, *Der zweite Brief*, 358, 361; Allo, *Saint Paul*, 275; Héring, *Saint Paul*, 78 n.4; Barrett, *Second Epistle*, 271; Furnish, *II Corinthians*, 485; Martin, *2 Corinthians*, 327, 328; Thrall, *Second Epistle*, 2.659.
719 BDAG 78 s.v. ἀνέχω 1.
720 Windisch, *Der zweite Korintherbrief*, 317, 344; Barrett, *Second Epistle*, 271; Bultmann, *Der zweite Brief*, 200.
721 Furnish, *II Corinthians*, 485.

self and his gospel in a crucial, preceding letter. We recall that in 1 Cor. 1–4 Paul had described his gospel as "foolishness" (1:18–25) and himself and his missionary colleagues as "fools on account of Christ" (4:9–13).[722] This paradoxical manoeuvre was Paul's response to the over-valuation of "eloquent wisdom" by the elite in Corinth (1:17; 2:1, 4), and the consequent emergence of partisanship in favor of Apollos (1:12; 3:4, 5, 22; 4:6).[723] Now, it is striking that in 1 Cor. 1–4 Paul uses μωρός and μωρία to describe himself as a "fool" and his gospel as "foolishness," and nowhere either ἄφρων or ἀφροσύνη.[724] In 2 Cor. 10–13, by contrast, Paul uses ἄφρων and ἀφροσύνη exclusively, and nowhere recurs to μωρός or μωρία.[725] Although both terms belong to the rich vocabulary of "foolishness" in Greek,[726] the difference between μωρός/μωρία and ἄφρων/ἀφροσύνη is not insignificant; indeed, the difference is so pronounced that the terms can scarcely be considered synonyms. The difference consists in a social stigma that attaches to μωρός, but is not found in connection with ἄφρων.[727] The μωρός was a lower class buffoon: the "stupidity" of this social type consisted in a weakness or deficiency of intellect, generally coupled with a physical grotesqueness;[728] through association with a lower class type, μωρός eventually became "the common generic name for the mimic fool."[729] ἄφρων, by contrast, has a more abstract and intellectual quality: as an alpha-privative of the φρήν word-group, ἄφρων and ἀφροσύνη belong to the sphere of the irrational; hence, ἄφρων is "without understanding," "thoughtless," "senseless," "impudent," "crazed."[730]

---

722 Welborn, *Paul, the Fool of Christ*, 50–86, 99–101.
723 Weiss, *Der erste Korintherbrief*, xxxi-xxxiv; Murphy-O'Connor, *Paul*, 274–77; D. P. Ker, "Paul and Apollos—Colleagues or Rivals?" 75–97; Smit, "What is Apollos? What is Paul?" 231–51; Welborn, *Paul, the Fool of Christ*, 102–109.
724 Plummer, *Second Epistle*, 313; Windisch, *Der zweite Korintherbrief*, 318; Bultmann, *Der zweite Brief*, 202; Furnish, *II Corinthians*, 485. See ἄφρων in 1 Cor. 15:36.
725 Plummer, *Second Epistle*, 313; Windisch, *Der zweite Korintherbrief*, 318; Bultmann, *Der zweite Brief*, 202; Furnish, *II Corinthians*, 485.
726 Welborn, *Paul, the Fool of Christ*, 21 n.47.
727 Welborn, *Paul, the Fool of Christ*, 1–2, 32–33.
728 G. Bertram, "μωρός," *TDNT* 4 (1967) 832; Welborn, *Paul, the Fool of Christ*, 32–33, 34–48.
729 A. Nicoll, *Masks, Mimes and Miracles: Studies in the Popular Theatre* (New York: Harcourt, Brace, 1931) 28; Welborn, *Paul, the Fool of Christ*, 33 n.64.
730 LSJ 294 s.v. ἀφροσύνη, ἄφρων; Moulton and Milligan, *Vocabulary of the Greek Testament*, 99 s.v. ἄφρων; BDAG 159 s.v. ἄφρων, ἀφροσύνη. Cf. Windisch, *Der zweite Korintherbrief*, 318.

The difference between μωρός and ἄφρων may be illustrated by comparing the antics of the secondary actor in the Oxyrhynchus mime with the characteristics of the "senseless" man as delineated by Dio Chrysostom in his didactic dialogue "That the Wise Man is Fortunate." The second actor of the Oxyrhynchus mime, who is addressed as μωρέ ("O fool!"),[731] is a slave who comically mimics the chief actor and others, retorting to their words and mocking their actions, in a manner that is alternately boastful, cowardly, cunning, sacrilegious, and obscene.[732] By contrast, Dio Chrysostom demonstrates that the ἄφρων ("senseless man") is the opposite of the φρόνιμος ("sensible"): "when a man is in possession of intelligence (νοῦν ἔχων), he is just and temperate…; but when he is senseless (ἄφρων), he is dissolute and wicked."[733] Similarly, Epictetus explains that ἀφροσύνη ("folly") is the opposite of the "reasoning faculty" (φρόνησις).[734] Given the difference in the two words, the abrupt shift from μωρός to ἄφρων within Paul's Corinthian correspondence is puzzling and calls for an explanation.

There are good reasons to conclude that the substitution of ἄφρων for μωρός in the course of the Corinthian correspondence was not at the initiative of Paul himself, but of someone in Corinth. First, the structure of the sentence in 11:16—the prohibition, "let no one think me a fool (ἄφρων)," followed by the concession, "but if one does"—suggests that someone in Corinth had described Paul as "senseless," ἄφρων.[735] Second, the contrast in Paul's response to the two terms argues that ἄφρων was more closely associated with the verdict of Paul's Corinthian critic. In 1 Cor. 1–4, we recall, Paul had developed a dialectical use of μωρία and μωρός in relation to the gospel and himself, first appropriating the terms as descriptive of the message about the cross and its emissaries in the eyes of the elite (1 Cor. 1:18), then subjecting the terms to a theological analysis in order to demonstrate that God's foolishness is the true wisdom (1 Cor. 1:25), and finally accepting the role of the fool as the paradoxical form in which the apostle of the crucified Christ makes his appearance in the world (1 Cor. 3:18; 4:10).[736] But Paul is evidently unable

---

731 *POxy* 413, line 52; cf. Wiemken, *Der griechische Mimus*, 52, 60–68.
732 Wiemken, *Der griechische Mimus*, 67–68.
733 Dio Chrysostom *Or.* 73 [23].3.
734 Epictetus *Diatr.* 1.20.6.
735 Heinrici, *Der zweite* Brief, 366–67; Lietzmann, *An die Korinther I/II*, 144; Schoeps, *Paulus*, 74.
736 Weiss, *Der erste Korintherbrief*, 25; Bertram, "μωρός," *TDNT* 4 (1967) 845–47; Ulrich Wilckens, *Weisheit und Torheit: Eine exegetisch-religionsgeschichtliche Un-*

or unwilling to accept the term ἄφρων as applicable to himself, making clear from the outset of the "foolish discourse" that he is only playing a role (11:1, 17, 21), repeatedly lifting the mask and showing his face (11:21b, 23b, 30; 12:1a, 5–6, 11a), and finally placing the blame for his foolishness upon the Corinthians ("I have been a fool! You forced me to it," 12:11a).[737] How unnatural and painful Paul found the role of ἄφρων is indicated by a host of features in the text: the length and defensive tone of the prologue (11:1–21a),[738] the self-contradictions (11:1, 16),[739] the apologetic parentheses (e.g., 11:21b, ἐν ἀφροσύνῃ λέγω),[740] and the startling interruptions (e.g., 11:23a, παραφρονῶν λαλῶ) that threaten to destroy the rhetorical schema.[741] Throughout the "fool's speech" Paul undermines the aims of the discourse by ironic treatment of the materials of the genre: his accomplishments are calamities (11:23–33); his revelations are unutterable (12:1–5); his healing is inefficacious (12:7–9); his power consists in weakness (12:9–10).[742] Above all, the clear distinction that Paul maintains between "speaking as a fool" and "speaking the truth" (11:17, 21; esp. 12:6, ἐὰν γὰρ θελήσω καυχήσασθαι, οὐκ ἔσομαι ἄφρων, ἀλήθειαν γὰρ ἐρῶ), indicates his rejection of the term ἄφρων as applicable to himself.[743] In sum, the evidence strongly suggests that it was not Paul himself who was responsible for the sudden shift from μωρός to ἄφρων in his Corinthian correspondence, but someone in Corinth—the wrongdoer.

Why should someone in Corinth have substituted ἄφρων for μωρός in reference to Paul? In such cases, it is tempting to infer the motive from the effect. The effect of the substitution is clear: by replacing μωρός with ἄφρων, the terrain of the debate is shifted from the social to the cognitive. Paul is thereby deprived of the basis of his appeal to the poor and the powerless, having argued, as he did in 1 Cor. 1:26–29, that God has chosen the foolish, the weak, and the low-born of

---

tersuchung zu I. Kor. 1 und 2 (Tübingen: Mohr Siebeck, 1959) 36–37; Welborn, Paul, the Fool of Christ, 117–247.
737 Windisch, Der zweite Korintherbrief, 316; Zmijewski, 'Narrenrede', 305–306.
738 Windisch, Der zweite Korintherbrief, 317.
739 Windisch, Der zweite Korintherbrief, 344.
740 Windisch, Der zweite Korintherbrief, 350.
741 Windisch, Der zweite Korintherbrief, 353.
742 For Paul's paradoxical treatment of the material, see Betz, Der Apostel Paulus, 69–100.
743 Windisch, Der zweite Korintherbrief, 345–46, 348, 381; Betz, Der Apostel Paulus, 94–95; Zmijewski, 'Narrenrede', 361.

the world, in order to bring to nothing the wise, the powerful, and the well-born.[744] We have argued above that it was this radical assertion of the divine election of the nobodies that would have proved especially disconcerting to an upper class Christian who had experienced a new sense of empowerment, wisdom, righteousness, and hope as a result of hearing the message that the Messiah was Jesus, and coming to belong to Christ.[745] By substituting ἄφρων for μωρός in reference to Paul, someone in Corinth sought to undermine Paul's attempt to "bring the δῆμος into his faction," to use the language of ancient politics.[746]

A second, and more damaging, effect of the substitution of ἄφρων for μωρός was to call into question Paul's rationality. That Paul was cognizant of this possibility in his acceptance of the necessity of "speaking as a fool" is demonstrated by the self-conscious interruption of the "fool's speech" proper, just after it has begun (11:23), with the interjection: "I am talking like a madman!" (παραφρονῶν λαλῶ).[747] The expression παραφρονῶν λαλῶ is stronger than ἐν ἀφροσύνῃ λέγω (11:21b), and betrays Paul's mounting anxiety lest his behavior be thought to confirm the suspicion of "insanity."[748] Paul remained sensitive to the potentially disastrous consequences of having engaged in ἀφροσύνη, as we can see from the retrospective explanation of his conduct in 2 Cor. 5:13: "If we were beside ourselves (ἐξέστημεν), it was for God; if we are in our right mind (σωφρονοῦμεν), it is for you." The verb of the first sentence, ἐξίστασθαι, used as it is here in reference to God, denotes religious "ecstasy," "divine madness."[749] We should not fail to notice that Paul employs an aorist of this verb here: taken historically, ἐξέστημεν describes a condition experienced in the past.[750] While a full appreciation of the implications of this

---

744 Theissen, *Social Setting*, 70–73.
745 See above on 2 Cor. 10:7.
746 Herodotus 5.66; cf. Welborn, *Politics and Rhetoric*, 28.
747 Windisch, *Der zweite Korintherbrief*, 353.
748 Plummer, *Second Epistle*, 321; Windisch, *Der zweite Korintherbrief*, 353; Bultmann, *Der zweite Brief*, 217.
749 Cf. Philo *Ebr.* 146–47; BDAG 350 s.v. ἐξίστημι 2a. For this understanding of ἐξίστασθαι in 5:13, see Bousset, *Der zweite Brief*, 187; Windisch, *Der zweite Korintherbrief*, 179; Barrett, *Second Epistle*, 166–67; Bultmann, *Der zweite Brief*, 150–51; Martin, *2 Corinthians*, 126–27; Thrall, *Second Epistle*, 1.406. See the discussion in Hubbard Moyer, "Was Paul Out of His Mind? Re-Reading 2 Corinthians 5:13," *JSNT* 70 (1998) 39–64.
750 Bachmann, *Der zweite Brief*, 250–51; Allo, *Saint Paul*, 164. On whether the aorist ἐξέστημεν should be interpreted "historically" or as "timeless," see Plummer,

verse must await reconstruction of the history of Paul's relationship with the Corinthians, we may already suggest that, as Paul looked back upon his behavior on the occasion of his second visit to Corinth, when he was so deeply humiliated (12:20–21), and as he reflected upon his evident loss of rational control in his "letter of tears," he felt obliged to offer a theological explanation for his indulgence in ἀφροσύνη: it was a case of "divine madness."[751]

Whatever motives may have been at work in the substitution of ἄφρων for μωρός, we gain further insight into the world-view of the wrongdoer by asking about the provenance of the term ἄφρων. First, ἄφρων is used almost exclusively for "fool" in the Septuagint.[752] The many Hebrew roots meaning "fool" (אולת, כסל, סכל, נבל) are usually rendered by ἄφρων, and often with the religious sense of "ungodly."[753] The prominence of ἄφρων in the Septuagint is significant for assessing the affinities and values of the wrongdoer. We have argued above that the Christology of the individual who is interrogated by Paul in 10:7 regarding his confidence of "belonging to Christ" was rooted in Jewish messianic expectation like that found in the *Psalms of Solomon* and *4 Ezra*.[754] Moreover, we have discovered that this individual resonated with the proclamation of Paul's rival (11:4), which represented Jesus as the embodiment of divine power, the fulfiller of the hopes of Israel.[755] By substituting ἄφρων for μωρός (which is rarely used in the LXX),[756] the wrongdoer reasserts the primacy of a concept rooted in Jewish tradition as normative for evaluating the theology and praxis of Christian missionaries. The use of ἄφρων in reference to Paul may have a further, pejorative implication against the background of Septuagintal usage: it sug-

---

Second Epistle, 172; Hughes, *Second Epistle*, 191; Barrett, *Second Epistle*, 166–67; Furnish, *II Corinthians*, 308; Martin, *2 Corinthians*, 127.

751 Interpreting ἐξέστημεν as a euphemism for ἄφρων and ἀφροσύνη, Kennedy, "The Problem of Second Corinthians," 361. See also Weiss, *Primitive Christianity*, 1.343 n.74: "Perhaps II Cor. 5:13 (εἴτε ἐξέστημεν, "whether we are beside ourselves") is a reference to this [Paul's loss of personal dignity on the occasion of his second, painful visit to Corinth]. He had lost control of himself, he had acted like a madman, said his opponents, without having had either the power or the intelligence to overcome his enemies."

752 G. Bertram, "φρήν, ἄφρων, ἀφροσύνη, κτλ.," *TDNT* 9 (1974) 225.
753 Bertram, "φρήν, ἄφρων, κτλ.," *TDNT* 9 (1974) 225.
754 See above on 10:7.
755 See above on 10:7.
756 Bertram, "μωρός," *TDNT* 4 (1967) 833; W. Caspari, "Über den biblischen Begriff der Torheit," *NZK* 39 (1928) 683.

gests that Paul's attitude and behavior have foolishly disrupted the right relationship between God and man; "ungodly" is a secondary sense of ἄφρων in many occurrences of the term in Psalms and Proverbs.[757]

Potentially more illuminating of the intellectual background of the wrongdoer is the technical usage of ἄφρων/ἀφροσύνη in Stoicism. Because the life-long goal of the Stoic philosopher's striving was wisdom,[758] a great deal of attention was devoted to the definition of its opposite:[759] "Foolishness they define as ignorance of things good and evil and of what is neither good nor evil; or foolishness is ignorance of what one ought to do and what one ought not to do and of what is indifferent" (ἀφροσύνην δὲ ἄγνοιαν ἀγαθῶν καὶ κακῶν καὶ οὐδετέρων, ἢ ἄγνοιαν ὧν ποιητέον καὶ οὐ ποιητέον καὶ οὐδετέρων).[760] As the principal obstacle in epistemology, "folly" debilitates ethics, as well: ἀφροσύνη heads the list of "primary vices," followed by "injustice," "cowardice," and "profligacy."[761] Indeed, Sextus Empiricus speaks "of foolishness, which alone those of the Stoa declare to be evil" (τῆς ἀφροσύνης, ἣν μόνον φασὶν εἶναι κακὸν οἱ ἀπὸ τῆς Στοᾶς).[762] Consequently, the actions of the ἄφρων are the opposite of moral actions (κατορθώματα),[763] which establish a right relationship between the wise man and other men.[764] There is no point in exhorting a fool to right actions, "since no fool is able to live according to instructions" (κατὰ γὰρ παραγγέλματα βιοῦν μηδένα τῶν ἀφρόνων).[765] "The fool is such a type as neither to rule nor to be ruled" (οὔτε γὰρ ἄρχειν οὔτ' ἄρχεσθαι οἷος τ' ἐστὶν ὁ ἄφρων);[766] "for to fools belong neither government nor law" (ἀφρόνων γὰρ πολιτεία οὐκ ἔστιν οὐδὲ νόμος).[767] "Every

---

757 Bertram, "φρήν, ἄφρων, κτλ.," *TDNT* 9 (1974) 225.
758 J. M. Rist, *Stoic Philosophy* (Cambridge: Cambridge University Press, 1969) 97–111, esp. 100; Pierre Hadot, *What is Ancient Philosophy?* (Cambridge, MA: Harvard University Press, 2002) 49, 137–39; Troels Engberg-Pedersen, *Paul and the Stoics* (Louisville: Westminster John Knox Press, 2000) 70–73.
759 E.g., Andronicus Περὶ παθῶν in *Stoicorum Veterum Fragmenta* (=*SVF*), 4 vols., ed. Johannes von Arnim (Stuttgart: Teubner, 1979) III.19.41; Sextus Empiricus *Math.* 11.90 in *SVF* III.19.41. Cf. Rist, *Stoic Philosophy*, 81–96, esp. 82.
760 Stobaeus *Ecl.* 2.59.4 in *SVF* III.63.29.
761 Diogenes Laertius 7.92 in *SVF* III.65.18. Cf. Stobaeus *Ecl.* 2.58.5 in *SVF* III.23.33.
762 Sextus Empiricus *Math.* 11.90 in *SVF* III.19.41.
763 Sextus Empiricus *Math.* 11.207 in *SVF* III.139.25–26.
764 Cicero *Fin.* 3.24 in *SVF* III.11.
765 Stobaeus *Ecl.* 2.104.10 in *SVF* III.171.1–3.
766 Stobaeus *Ecl.* 2.102.11 in *SVF* III.158.28.
767 Philodemus *Rhet.* 2, p. 210 (Sudhaus) in *SVF* III.241.35–36.

fool is gladly joined to his own evil" (πᾶς δέ τις ἄφρων σύνεστιν ἡδέως τῇ ἑαυτοῦ κακίᾳ).⁷⁶⁸ "Fools" (ἄφρονες) are reckoned with the "vicious" (κακοί), the "unjust" (ἄδικοι), and the "faithless" (ἄπιστοι), that is, with all who are not σοφοί.⁷⁶⁹ "They say that the wise man alone is a priest; wherefore they also declare all fools to be impious (διὸ καὶ πάντας εἶναι τοὺς ἄφρονας ἀσεβεῖς)."⁷⁷⁰ The Stoics held that "every fool is an enemy to the gods" (παντ' εἶναι τὸν ἄφρονα θεοῖς ἐχθρόν).⁷⁷¹

The possibility that the thought of the wrongdoer was shaped by the categories of Stoicism is hardly surprising. Stoicism held a special attraction for practical intellectuals in Paul's day because of the rigorous account that it provided of virtue, and because of the hope that it nurtured of participating in a community of reason—powerful incentives for men who had to cope with the ambiguities and dangers of life in the early Empire.⁷⁷² In retrospect, we may now recognize that some of the values operative in the judgments passed upon Paul by his Corinthian critic seem to be shaped by a popular, moralizing Stoicism such as was embraced by Hellenistic Jews as well as educated Romans.⁷⁷³ We argued above that in the charge that Paul and his colleagues had conducted their affairs κατὰ σάρκα (10:2), someone in Corinth has taken up a phrase which was characteristic of Paul's own vocabulary, and turned it ironically against him.⁷⁷⁴ We may now suggest that this appropriation was facilitated, in terms of the value system of Paul's Corinthian critic, by the widespread use of the term σάρξ in popular Stoicism to designate the bearer of irrational

---

768 Stobaeus *Ecl.* 2.7.105 in *SVF* III.171.16.
769 Plutarch *Comm. not.* in *SVF* III.167.29–31.
770 Stobaeus *Ecl.* 2.67.20 in *SVF* III.157.4, 10–12.
771 Stobaeus *Ecl.* 2.7.105 in *SVF* III.166.15.
772 On the attraction of Stoicism, esp. the Stoic theory of the emotions, for men such as Cicero, Seneca, and Plutarch, see Harris, *Restraining Rage,* 9, 26. See also Stanley K. Stowers, "Paul and Self-Mastery" in *Paul in the Greco-Roman World,* ed. J. Paul Sampley (Harrisburg: Trinity Press International, 2003) 524–50.
773 R. Renehan, "The Greek Philosophical Background of Fourth Maccabees," *RhM* 115 (1972) 221–38; Stanley K. Stowers, "Fourth Maccabees" in *Harper's Bible Commentary* (San Francisco: Harper & Row, 1988) 924; David C. Aune, "Mastery of the Passions: Philo, 4 Maccabees and Earliest Christianity" in *Hellenization Revisited: Shaping a Christian Response within the Greco-Roman World,* ed. W. E. Helleman (New York: Lanham, 1994) 125–58; Harris, *Restraining Rage,* 26, 104–20.
774 See above on 10:2.

desires,[775] the locus of sensual pleasures,[776] the repository of passions,[777] the enslaving power which distracts and taints the mind with mortal folly[778]—sentiments expressed by Philo, the author of 4 Maccabees, and Plutarch, among others.[779] We shall have further opportunity to test our hypothesis that the values of the wrongdoer were shaped by Stoicism, when we examine the argument of Paul's "therapeutic epistle" (2 Cor. 1:1–2:13; 7:5–16) in greater detail below.[780]

The final instance of a singular pronoun in the "fool's speech" which might refer to an individual in Corinth occurs in 12:6. Reflecting upon the account of a vision which he had been forced to provide by way of self-commendation (12:1–5),[781] Paul explains: "For if I should wish to boast, I will not be a fool, for I shall be speaking the truth; but I forbear (to do this), lest someone reckon to my account more than he sees in me or hears from me" ('Εὰν γὰρ θελήσω καυχήσασθαι, οὐκ ἔσομαι ἄφρων, ἀλήθειαν γὰρ ἐρῶ· φείδομαι δέ, μή τις εἰς ἐμὲ λογίσηται ὑπὲρ ὃ βλέπει με ἢ ἀκούει [τι] ἐξ ἐμοῦ). Again, it might seem that the pronoun τις is used generally of what "anyone" might think of Paul under the circumstances.[782] But the presence of the verb λογίζεσθαι, used on previous occasions (10:7, 11) to describe the evaluation of Paul by "someone" (τις) and "such a person" (ὁ τοιοῦτος),[783] alerts us to the possibility that Paul is

---

775 Plutarch *Mor.* 135C; 1087B; 1089E; 1096C; Diogenes Laertius 10.145.
776 Philo *Deus* 143; *Gig.* 29; Plutarch *Mor.* 101B; 672E; 688D; 734 A.
777 4 Macc. 7:18; Ps.-Plutarch *Mor.* 107F; Maximus of Tyre 33.7.
778 Philo *Her.* 268; *Leg.* 2.49–50.
779 BDAG 915 s.v. σάρξ 2c; Schweizer, "σάρξ," *TDNT* 7 (1971) 102–105, 119–23.
780 See below ch. 6.
781 On the account of the vision, see Hans Dieter Betz, "Eine Christus-Aretalogie bei Paulus," *ZThK* 66 (1969) 288–305; idem, *Der Apostel Paulus*, 84–85, 89–92; Andrew T. Lincoln, "Paul the Visionary: the setting and significance of the rapture to Paradise in II Corinthians xii.1–10," *NTS* 25 (1979) 204–20; Jeremy Barrier, "Visions of Weakness: Apocalyptic Genre and the Identification of Paul's Opponents in 2 Corinthians 12:1–6," *Restoration Quarterly* 47 (2005) 33–42. On the connection of 12:6 with the preceeding account, see Windisch, *Der zweite Korintherbrief*, 381; Barrett, *Second Epistle*, 312; Zmijewski, *'Narrenrede'*, 358.
782 Furnish, *II Corinthians*, 527.
783 On λογίζεσθαι as a term used by Paul's critic(s) in 10:2, 7, 11, see Georgi, *Opponents of Paul*, 230, 232, 287 n.44; Betz, *Der Apostel Paulus*, 121; Bultmann, *Der zweite Brief*, 192; Furnish, *II Corinthians*, 456–57.

primarily concerned with the opinion of a certain individual.⁷⁸⁴ As we have seen, λογίζεσθαι is a commercial term,⁷⁸⁵ and the expression λογίζεσθαι εἴς τινα is even more clearly a *terminus technicus* of the language of commerce—"to put on someone's account," "to credit to someone," as demonstrated by the evidence of papyri and inscriptions.⁷⁸⁶ Paul's previous references to his conduct of financial affairs have been backwards glancing, retrospective justifications of his behavior in the area of accounting in general, as in 10:2,⁷⁸⁷ or defensive explanations of his refusal of financial support, as in 11:7–11.⁷⁸⁸ What is new in the present instance of Paul's use of λογίζεσθαι is the future orientation, and the unexpected connection between the self-commendation which Paul is forced to provide and the prospect that something might be "reckoned" to his account. Here we receive the first indication that something financial is at stake for Paul in the outcome of his apology in 2 Cor. 10–13. Paul is concerned lest his boasting in visions and revelations may "discredit" him in the eyes of someone in Corinth, by the perilous proximity which such accounts effect to the profile of a charlatan.⁷⁸⁹ The true import of Paul's concern will be grasped, once we have begun to explore Margaret Thrall's intuition regarding the collection as the occasion for the offence against Paul.

2 Cor. 12:14–13:10

Having completed our examination of the passages in 2 Cor. 10–13 where singular pronouns or singular verb-forms raise the question of whether Paul might be referring to the wrongdoer, we turn now, at last, to a cluster of texts in the exhortation (12:14–13:4) and peroration (13:5–10) of the letter,⁷⁹⁰ where Paul alludes to *the wrong* that was done

---

784 Barrett, "Paul's Opponents in II Corinthians," 244–45, although Barrett regards the individual as an outsider, an interloper.
785 Windisch, *Der zweite Korintherbrief*, 381; Héring, *Saint Paul*, 95; Barrett, *Second Epistle*, 305, 312; Bultmann, *Der zweite Brief*, 225; Zmijewski, 'Narrenrede', 359; Furnish, *II Corinthians*, 513, 527; Thrall, *Second Epistle*, 800, 801.
786 BDAG 597 s.v. λογίζομαι 1a; Moulton and Milligan, *Vocabulary of the Greek Testament*, 377–78 s.v. λογίζομαι. See esp. *OGIS* 595, 15; *PFay.* 21, 9.
787 See above on 10:2.
788 See above on 11:7–11.
789 Betz, *Der Apostel Paulus*, 18, 21, 95–96.
790 Compare the rhetorical analysis of Sundermann, *Der schwache Apostel*, 45.

to him on the occasion of his second visit to Corinth, and to the complicity of the Corinthians in the affair. We begin with the most explicit reference, namely that in 12:16–18. To put this final element of Paul's apology in context: Paul has concluded the foolish comparison of himself with other apostles (γέγονα ἄφρων, κτλ., 12:11–13), and now begins to prepare the Corinthians for his impending third visit.[791] That the primary obstacle to a ready reception and a successful visit lies in the area of Paul's financial conduct is already signaled by the final verse of the epilogue to the "fool's speech" (12:13), where Paul recurs to the claim that he did not "burden" (καταναρκᾶν) the Corinthians, and pleads, ironically, "Forgive me this wrong (ἀδικία)!"[792] There are further, strong indications that Paul is suspected of conniving at the Corinthians' resources in the first verse of the exhortation (12:14), in which Paul assures the Corinthians, in proverbial fashion, "I do not want what is yours (τὰ ὑμῶν) but you,"[793] and justifies his behavior by an appeal to the order of nature, "for children ought not to store up resources (θησαυρίζειν) for their parents, but parents for their children."[794] Despite the appearance of reasonableness and naturalism that Paul lends to his argument, commentators have rightly noted the tension between Paul's repeated insistence that he has not and will not "burden" the Corinthians and the assumption underlying his analogies in 12:14 that he aims at getting the Corinthians' money in some way.[795] Of course, it is Paul himself who has exposed this tension in order to resolve it. Indeed, it is difficult

---

791 On the transitional role of 12:11–13, as the "epilogue" to the "fool's speech," see Windisch, *Der zweite Korintherbrief*, 394–95, 398; Furnish, *II Corinthians*, 554, 563.

792 Windisch, *Der zweite Korintherbrief*, 398; Betz, *Der Apostel Paulus*, 102, 117; Hock, *Social Context*, 63; Furnish, *II Corinthians*, 556; Marshall, *Enmity in Corinth*, 225, 239, 244, 246. Note the use of the cognate verb ἀδικέω in 7:12!

793 Cf. Cicero *Fin.* 2.26.85, referenced by Windisch, *Der zweite Korintherbrief*, 399: "Der erste Satz V. 14aβ ist wohl die Umkehrung eines hässlichen Vorwurfes, wie er gegen alle Betrüger, Sophisten und Goëten gehoben wird, und so auch gegen Paulus erhoben worden ist: er sucht nicht euch d.i. nicht euer Heil, euere Seele, sondern euer Geld"; Bultmann, *Der zweite Brief*, 235; Thrall, *Second Epistle*, 2.844. Compare 1 Thess. 2:5.

794 Cf. Philo *Mos.* 2.245; Seneca *Ben.* 3.11.2; Plutarch *Mor.* 526 A; Plummer, *Second Epistle*, 362; Windisch, *Der zweite Korintherbrief*, 399: "Das zweite Argument V.14b ist dem νόμος φύσεως entnommen"; Bultmann, *Der zweite Brief*, 235; Furnish, *II Corinthians*, 558; Thrall, *Second Epistle*, 2.844–45.

795 Windisch, *Der zweite Korintherbrief*, 399–400; Bultmann, *Der zweite Brief*, 236; Furnish, *II Corinthians*, 565; Thrall, *Second Epistle*, 2.845–46.

to imagine that a subject so sensitive as that with which Paul deals in 12:16–18 could have been broached more skillfully under the circumstances.[796] With further assurances of his willingness to "spend and be spent" for the Corinthians,[797] and appealing to his "abundant love" (12:15),[798] Paul finally confronts the accusation: "Let it be granted that I (at least) did not burden you. Nevertheless (you say), being by nature crafty, I took you in by deceit. Surely not anyone of those whom I have sent to you—through him did I defraud you? I urged Titus (to go) and sent the brother along with him. Surely Titus did not defraud you, did he? Did we not conduct ourselves in the same spirit? Did we not walk in the same footsteps?" (12:16–18).[799]

Paul's words leave little room for doubt as to the nature of the accusation that has been made against him; indeed, there is a surprising consensus among scholars on this point.[800] In characteristically laconic fashion, C. K. Barrett summarizes the allegation: "Paul has made a great show of asking for no money, but he has instituted what purports to be a collection for the poor saints in Jerusalem, and has pocketed the proceeds himself."[801] As clear as the matter may be in general, there is more to be learned about the content of the accusation, once we have noted several features of the style of Paul's response, which are difficult to capture in translation, and which indicate Paul's attitude toward the charge against him. First, there is an incongruity about the passage, despite Paul's best efforts to integrate the matter into the argument of his exhor-

---

796 Betz, *Der Apostel Paulus*, 117.
797 Cf. Aristotle *Eth. nic.* 4.1.7, 23, 24, 29; Seneca *Ep.* 9.10; Windisch, *Der zweite Korintherbrief*, 400; Marshall, *Enmity in Corinth*, 251.
798 Cf. Aristotle *Eth. nic.* 8.7.2; Plutarch *Mor.* 143C; Windisch, *Der zweite Korintherbrief*, 401; Marshall, *Enmity in Corinth*, 251; Thrall, *Second Epistle*, 2.846–47.
799 The literal translation offered here reflects the tension and awkwardness in the syntax, particularly the anacoluthon in 12:17; see J. H. Moulton, *A Grammar of New Testament Greek*, Vol. I: *Prolegomena* (Edinburgh: T & T Clark, 1908) 144; BDF §466; Robertson, *Grammar of the Greek New Testament*, 436; Moule, *Idiom Book*, 176; Heinrici, *Der zweite Brief*, 414; Barrett, *Second Epistle*, 325; Furnish, *II Corinthians*, 559; Thrall, *Second Epistle*, 2.852.
800 Plummer, *Second Epistle*, 363–65; Windisch, *Der zweite Korintherbrief*, 402; Strachan, *Second Epistle*, 35; Hughes, *Paul's Second Epistle*, 464; Georgi, *Opponents of Paul*, 9; Barrett, *Second Epistle*, 324–25; Bultmann, *Der zweite Brief*, 237; Furnish, *II Corinthians*, 565; Betz, *2 Corinthians 8 and 9*, 76; Martin, *2 Corinthians*, 446; Barnett, *Second Epistle*, 586; Thrall, *Second Epistle*, 2.856
801 Barrett, *Second Epistle*, 324.

tation.⁸⁰² The accusation of deceit and fraud disrupts the flow of the text. The brokenness is most apparent in 12:17, where the construction of the sentence collapses: having begun the sentence with ἀπέσταλκα ("I have sent") as the main verb, Paul evidently proved unable to complete it and unwilling to rewrite it with the explosive πλεονεκτεῖν ("to defraud") as the principal predicate.⁸⁰³ Various grammatical explanations have been proposed for the resulting *anacolouthon:* a combination of two idioms,⁸⁰⁴ a Semitic way of handling the pronouns, etc.⁸⁰⁵ But the most probable explanation of the discontinuity is the emotion with which Paul writes, his instinctive recoil from the inflammatory term πλεονεκτεῖν.⁸⁰⁶ Second, there is an imploring quality to the passage that belies Paul's attempt to appear reasonable. Rhetorical questions replace argument in vss. 17–18. Nor is Paul content to await the Corinthians' response: the particles μή and μήτι, which introduce the rhetorical questions in vss. 17 and 18, presume that the only appropriate answer is "no," just as the conjunction οὐ, which introduces two further questions in vs. 18, insists that only an affirmative response is possible.⁸⁰⁷ That Paul seeks to dispose of such a dire accusation with rhetorical questions is a sign of the weakness of his position and of his vulnerability to the charge.⁸⁰⁸ Third, Paul's argument in vss. 17–18 has a circularity that robs it of the quality of a compelling de-

---

802 Windisch, *Der zweite Korintherbrief*, 402.
803 Plummer, *Second Epistle*, 364; Windisch, *Der zweite Korintherbrief*, 403; Barrett, *Second Epistle*, 325; Thrall, *Second Epistle*, 2.852.
804 Thrall, *Second Epistle*, 2.852: "It may be that it combines two idioms found elsewhere in the NT. First, the τινα...δι' αὐτοῦ is an example of a suspended noun or pronoun (i.e., a noun or pronoun unrelated grammatically to the main sentence) which is resumed (in effect repeated) by a pronoun in another case (correctly related to the main sentence). Secondly, there are two (combined and highly compressed) instances of case attraction. The full form of the phrase preceding ἀπέσταλκα would be τινὰ τούτων οὕς: the accusative case of τινά is due to the required accusative of the relative pronoun. But this pronoun has itself been attracted into the case of its implicit antecedent τούτων." Cf. Windisch, *Der zweite Korintherbrief*, 403.
805 Moule, *Idiom Book*, 176; Furnish, *II Corinthians*, 559.
806 On the emotional recoil, Barrett, *Second Epistle*, 325. On the explosive nature of the charge embodied in the verb πλεονεκτεῖν, see Gerhard Delling, "πλεονέκτης, πλεονεκτέω, πλεονεξία," *TDNT* 6 (1968) 266–74; Betz, *Der Apostel Paulus*, 116.
807 Barrett, *Second Epistle*, 325; Bultmann, *Der zweite Brief*, 238; Furnish, *II Corinthians*, 559, 560; Lambrecht, *Second Corinthians*, 214.
808 Windisch, *Der zweite Korintherbrief*, 403: "Dann ist es verwunderlich, daß er einen so abscheulichen und so verhängnisvollen Verdacht in Form einer Frage abtut."

fense; indeed, Windisch characterized the movement of Paul's thought here as a *"circulus vitiosus."*[809] Paul adduces the blamelessness of Titus as evidence of his own integrity, then seeks to ground the trustworthiness of Titus in his unanimity of purpose and conformity of conduct with Paul! Escape from this circle is blocked by Paul's inability to produce unambiguous evidence of the purity of his motives in respect to the collection.

The source of Paul's anxiety in 12:16–18 lies in the seriousness of the charge against him. A proper appreciation of the gravity of the accusation emerges from examination of two terms in particular: πανοῦργος and πλεονεκτεῖν. Again, there is surprising agreement among scholars that these words derive from Paul's Corinthian critics who have used them in an accusation which they have actually brought.[810] Support for this conclusion is found in the observation that the adjective πανοῦργος ("crafty") is used only here in the New Testament.[811] πανοῦργος, which is, literally, "capable of anything," has a bad, amoral sense from the beginning,[812] a sense which predominates later,[813] and an exclusively pejorative use in early Christian literature;[814] thus the meaning is "crafty," "sly,"

---

809 Windisch, *Der zweite Korintherbrief*, 404.
810 Plummer, *Second Epistle*, 363, on πανοῦργος, κτλ.: "He is, of course, quoting his critics' estimate of him"; Windisch, *Der zweite Korintherbrief*, 402–403; Hughes, *Paul's Second Epistle*, 464; Barrett, *Second Epistle*, 324; Bultmann, *Der zweite Brief*, 237; Furnish, *II Corinthians*, 557, 559: "Paul is citing a charge being made against him in Corinth"; Martin, *2 Corinthians*, 443; Barnett, *Second Epistle*, 586, 587, on ὑπάρχων πανοῦργος; Thrall, *Second Epistle*, 2.850–51.
811 Despite the fact that the term is frequent in the Psalms and Wisdom literature. Cf. Plummer, *Second Epistle*, 363; Windisch, *Der zweite Korintherbrief*, 403; Furnish, *II Corinthians*, 559; Thrall, *Second Epistle*, 2.850 n.605. Note Paul's use of the cognate noun πανουργία in 2 Cor. 4:2; 11:3.
812 Otto Bauernfeind, "πανουργία, πανοῦργος," *TDNT* 5 (1967) 722–27, esp. 723; BDAG 754 s.v. πανοῦργος: "first in a bad sense, and that predominately so." Esp. relevant is the negative use of the word in Old Comedy, F. Müller in *Philologus* 72 (1913) 326, 332, cited in Betz, *Der Apostel Paulus*, 104 n.433.
813 See, e.g., Philo *Det.* 165; *Mut.* 150; *Somn.* 2.66; *Sacr.* 22, 32; *Post.* 43; *Praem.* 52; *Conf.* 117; *Mos.* 2.53; *Decal.* 125, 141; *Ebr.* 223; Josephus *B.J.* 1.223, 365, 453, 468; Plutarch *Mor.* 26 A; 27 A; 28 A; 91B; 237E. Cf. Bauernfeind, "πανουργία, κτλ.," *TDNT* 5 (1967) 723; Betz, *Der Apostel Paulus*, 104.
814 BDAG 754 s.v. πανοῦργος: "in our lit. never without an unfavorable connotation"; Bauernfeind, "πανουργία, κτλ.," *TDNT* 5 (1967) 726: "The NT uses the word group only negatively."

"knavish," "villainous."[815] A survey of the uses of the term illustrates how aptly πανοῦργος was chosen in the case of Paul, for πανοῦργος resonates with the criticisms echoed in 10:2, 10:9–11, 11:7–11, 11:16, and 12:6. The association of the πανοῦργος word-group with financial misconduct is found both early and late in Greek literature: thus, in Sophocles' complaint about the power of money—"Money has shown men how to practice villainy (πανουργία)";[816] so also, the expression πανουργικὸν ξύλον in a magical spell for the detection of a thief.[817] Moreover, πανοῦργος turns up in discussions of prudence and folly.[818] In Aristotle's treatment of the faculty called "cleverness" (δεινότης), he distinguishes the types of cleverness according to their aim: "If the aim is noble, it is praiseworthy, but if base, it is mere knavery (πανουργία)," explaining, "this is how we come to speak of both prudent men (φρόνιμοι) and knaves (πανοῦργοι) as clever (δεινοί)."[819] In light of the connotations of πανοῦργος, it is instructive to recall the grudging acknowledgement by Paul's critic that his letters exhibit characteristics (βαρύς, ἰσχυρός) which define cleverness (10:10),[820] and the insinuation by the same critic that Paul's foolishness (ἀφροσύνη) is more real than feigned (11:16).[821] By applying the label πανοῦργος to Paul, someone in Corinth suggests that Paul's innate cleverness has been corrupted into knavery. In the context of a discussion of Paul's financial misconduct, the allegation that Paul is πανοῦργος implies that the force which has misdirected Paul's cleverness is money. In the same speech in which Sophocles ascribes to money the power to instruct in villainy

---

815 LSJ 1299 s.v. πανοῦργος; BDAG 754 s.v. πανοῦργος. Cf. Windisch, *Der zweite Korintherbrief*, 403: "Es hat hier die denkbar schlimmste Bedeutung."
816 Sophocles *Ant.* 300.
817 *PLond.* 46.73; cf. Moulton and Milligan, *Vocabulary of the Greek Testament*, 477 s.v. πανοῦργος; Bauernfeind, "πανουργία, κτλ.," *TDNT* 5 (1967) 723: "The expression πανουργικὸν ξύλον is an example of the way in which the negative sense is rooted in the general linguistic sense. Since it is found in a magical direction for the detection of thieves, it might suggest a piece of wood of general magical force, but what is really meant is a piece of wood from the place befitting a πανοῦργος, namely, the gallows."
818 Bauernfeind, "πανουργία, κτλ.," *TDNT* 5 (1967) 724–26.
819 Aristotle *Eth. nic.* 6.12.9. Cf. Bauernfeind, "πανουργία, κτλ.," *TDNT* 5 (1967) 724–25. Betz (*Der Apostel Paulus*, 105) emphasizes the use of the word πανοῦργος in polemic against sophists.
820 See above on 10:10.
821 See above 11:16.

(πανουργία), he observes: "money by its teaching perverts men's good minds so that they take to evil actions!"[822]

This understanding of the implications of calling Paul πανοῦργος is reinforced by other aspects of vs. 16. First, the participle ὑπάρχων, which is more than the colorless equivalent of ὤν ('being"), suggests that craftiness is a latent feature of Paul's personality.[823] Second, the verb λαμβάνειν, found in Lucian's essay on parasitism,[824] and already used by Paul in caricature of his rival in 11:20, suggests the cunning requisite to the parasitic art. Third, δόλος, "deceit" or "treachery,"[825] is associated in Greek literary tradition with the wily Odysseus;[826] indeed, the expression δόλῳ λαβεῖν ("to take by a trick") is placed on the lips of Odysseus as advice to Neoptolemus, evoking from the honorable youth the question, "Do you not think it disgraceful to tell lies (τὸ ψευδῆ λέγειν)?"[827] All in all, the picture of Paul that emerges from the charge cited in 12:16 is grotesque: Paul is a "confidence trickster"[828] whose native cleverness has been perverted into villainy by his desire for money, and who now seeks to take advantage of the Corinthians through craft and underhanded methods.

The essence of the charge against Paul is deposited in the verb πλεονεκτεῖν.[829] The repetition of πλεονεκτεῖν in rhetorical questions presupposing a negative response in 12:17–18 shows that this verb expresses the core of the allegation against Paul. Again, there is something approaching a consensus among commentators that πλεονεκτεῖν belonged

---

822 Sophocles *Ant.* 301; cf. Bauernfeind, "πανουργία, κτλ.," *TDNT* 5 (1967) 722 n.2.
823 Plummer, *Second Epistle*, 363: "In such cases ὑπάρχων is almost equivalent to φύσει"; Hughes, *Paul's Second Epistle*, 464 n.150; Thrall, *Second Epistle*, 2.850 n.602.
824 Lucian *Par.* 21; cf. Nesselrath, *Lukians Parasitendialog*, 165.
825 LSJ 443 s.v. δόλος; BDAG 256 s.v. δόλος.
826 E.g., *Od.* 9.406; 12.494. For Odysseus the trickster in comedy, see, e.g., Epicharmus fr. 99 in *Comicorum Graecorum Fragmenta*, ed. G. Kaibel (Berlin: Weidmann, 1958) 110, with the interpretation of A. W. Pickard-Cambridge, *Dithyramb, Tragedy and Comedy* (Oxford: Clarendon Press, 1927) 380–81.
827 Sophocles *Phil.* 101, 107, 108; cited in Windisch, *Der zweite Korintherbrief*, 403.
828 Barrett, *Second Epistle*, 324.
829 Windisch, *Der zweite Korintherbrief*, 403; Betz, *Der Apostel Paulus*, 116; Barrett, *Second Epistle*, 324; Furnish, *II Corinthians*, 564–65; Thrall, *Second Epistle*, 2.853, 856.

to the language used by Paul's Corinthian critics.⁸³⁰ As Thrall observes, πλεονεκτεῖν is so negative, so firmly connected with dishonest and unlawful conduct, that it is impossible to imagine that Paul would have put such an idea into his opponents' heads.⁸³¹ Paul's hypersensitivity to the charge is indicated by his invocation of an intermediate agent (Titus); in this way, Paul attempts to put a prophylactic distance between himself and a fatal suspicion. The reason for Paul's avoidance of the term lies in the detestable nature of the act so designated. πλεονεκτεῖν can describe any kind of "covetousness," including "lust for power," as well as "greed for possessions."⁸³² Because the desire to "get more than one's share" is destructive of the justice and equality upon which community depends, πλεονεξία (Latin *avaritia*) became a frequent topic in moral philosophy.⁸³³ But the context of Paul's discussion in 12:16–18 makes clear that financial matters are at issue,⁸³⁴ so that the meaning of πλεονεκτεῖν in this case is narrower and more damning: "to cheat someone in a financial transaction," "to illegally obtain money from someone by deception."⁸³⁵ It is significant, once again, that the πλεονεκτεῖν word-group consistently denotes "unlawful gain" in the Septuagint, where it translates בצע⁸³⁶

---

830 Windisch, *Der zweite Korintherbrief*, 403; Hughes, *Paul's Second Epistle*, 464; Barrett, *Second Epistle*, 324; Bultmann, *Der zweite Brief*, 237; Furnish, *II Corinthians*, 565; Martin, *2 Corinthians*, 446; Thrall, *Second Epistle*, 2.853.
831 Thrall, *Second Epistle*, 2.851, 853.
832 Delling, "πλεονέκτης, πλεονεκτέω, πλεονεξία," *TDNT* 6 (1968) 266–74, esp. 266–67; LSJ 1416 s.v. πλεονεκτέω; BDAG 824 s.v. πλεονεκτέω.
833 Delling, "πλεονέκτης, κτλ.," *TDNT* 6 (1968) 266–69. See, e.g., Aristotle *Eth. nic.* 5.2; Cicero *Tusc.*. 4.26–29; Seneca *Ep.* 90.3, 8, 36, 38, 39–40; Dio Chrysostom *Or.* 17. Cf. Betz, *Der Apostel Paulus*, 116–17.
834 Windisch, *Der zweite Korintherbrief*, 403; Hughes, *Paul's Second Epistle*, 464; Delling, "πλοενέκτης, κτλ.," *TDNT* 6 (1968) 273: "Here the context shows that financial matters are at issue"; Bultmann, *Der zweite Brief*, 237; Martin, *2 Corinthians*, 446; Betz, *2 Corinthians 8 and 9*, 97; Thrall, *Second Epistle*, 2.853, 856–57.
835 LSJ 1416 s.v. πλεονεκτέω II.2, "*defraud*," referencing Menander *Mon.* 259; 1 Thess. 4:6; 2 Cor. 12:17–18; Dio Chrysostom *Or.* 17.8; Dio Cassius 52.37; in passive, Xenophon *Mem.* 3.5.2; Demosthenes 41.25. Cf. Plummer, *Second Epistle*, 364: "'Have I ever sent anyone to you through whom you were defrauded?' This probably means that they 'got money under false pretences,' especially in connection with the Palestinian relief fund"; Windisch, *Der zweite Korintherbrief*, 403: "πλεονεκτεῖν ist hier wie 7:2; 1 Thess. 4:6 'jem. in Geldgeschäften übervorteilen, ihm wiederrechtlich Geld abnehmen." See also Betz, *2 Corinthians 8 and 9*, 97.
836 Delling, "πλεονέκτης, κτλ.," *TDNT* 6 (1968) 269–70.

Thus, in Ps. 118:36 and Prov. 1:19 πλεονεξία is "dishonest gain," and in Isa. 33:15 "unlawful gain."[837] Indeed, πλεονεξία is never used in the Septuagint where the reference is to the honest acquisition of a possession.[838] In Philo, as well, where πλεονεξία is common (40 times), the meaning is generally "covetousness," and specifically "unlawful enrichment."[839] In light of these usages, and in the context of Paul's defense of his administration of the collection, the translation of πλεονεκτεῖν that seems best warranted in 12:17–18 and most in keeping with financial parlance is "to embezzle."

An appreciation of the seriousness of the charge that was lodged against Paul by means of the term πλεονεκτεῖν may be derived both from examination of general, moralizing discussions of the corrosive effects of covetousness, and from consideration of the consequences of specific cases of embezzlement. In Dio Chrysostom's discourse "On Covetousness" (περὶ πλεονεξίας), he grounds his assertion that πλεονεξία "is the cause of the greatest evils"[840] in the observation that "greed not only injures (λυπεῖν) a man himself, but his neighbors as well."[841] As a consequence, "no one pities the covetous man or cares to instruct him, but all shun him and regard him as their enemy."[842] Seeking to bring his point home to his hearers, Dio proposes: "If, then, each of those here present wishes to know the enormity of this wickedness (πονηρία), let him consider how he feels toward those who attempt to defraud (πλεονεκτεῖν) him; for in this way he can get an idea as to how other men must feel toward him if he is that sort of man."[843]

A notorious case of embezzlement reported by Josephus illustrates the danger to which Paul was exposed by the charge of πλεονεξία. The incident is doubly relevant to Paul's situation, since monies donated for religious purposes, specifically to the temple in Jerusalem, were involved in

---

837 Delling, "πλεονέκτης, κτλ.," *TDNT* 6 (1968) 269–70.
838 Delling, "πλεονέκτης, κτλ.," *TDNT* 6 (1968) 269.
839 See esp. Philo *Spec.* 1.278; 4.5; *Mos.* 2.186; *Agr.* 83; *Leg.* 3.166; *Decal.* 155; cf. Delling, "πλεονέκτης, κτλ.," *TDNT* 6 (1968) 270.
840 Dio Chrysostom *Or.* 17.6. See the note in J. W. Cohoon, ed. and trans., *Dio Chrysostom II*, LCL (Cambridge, MA: Harvard University Press, 1977) 192 n.1: "Dio here echoes the first line of Menander, Frag. 557 (Kock): 'In the front ranks of man's woes is grasping greed' (πλεονεξία μέγιστον ἀνθρώποις κακόν)."
841 Dio Chrysostom *Or.* 17.7.
842 Dio Chrysostom *Or.* 17.7; cf. Delling, "πλεονέκτης, κτλ.," *TDNT* 6 (1968) 268.
843 Dio Chrysostom *Or.* 17.8.

the fraud. Josephus relates that a certain Jew, whom he describes as "a complete scoundrel" (πονηρὸς εἰς τὰ πάντα), was resident in Rome during the reign of Tiberius, and "pretended to be an interpreter of the wisdom of the laws of Moses."[844] Enlisting the aid of three men of like character, this teacher began to meet regularly with a woman of high rank by the name of Fulvia, who had become a Jewish proselyte. Josephus reveals that the Jewish embezzlers "urged her to send purple and gold to the temple in Jerusalem, and they, taking [the gifts] for their needs, used them for their own personal expenses (καὶ λαβόντες ἐπὶ χρείας τοῖς ἰδίοις ἀναλώμασιν αὐτὰ ποιοῦνται)."[845] Josephus infers, "it was this that had been their intention in asking for gifts from the start."[846] The swindle had disastrous consequences: when Fulvia's husband reported the affair to Tiberius, the emperor ordered the whole Jewish community to leave Rome.[847] The consuls took advantage of the general expulsion to impress four thousand Jews into military service, and deported them to Sardinia to combat the brigands.[848] Josephus concludes: "And so because of the wickedness (κακία) of four men, the Jews were banished from the city."[849]

Whether Paul actually feared that the charge of embezzlement would be reported to the Roman proconsul of Achaia or the civic magistrates of Corinth is a matter for conjecture.[850] But of greater certainty and more

---

844 Joesphus *A.J.* 18.81–82.
845 Josephus *A.J.* 18.82.
846 Josephus *A.J.* 18.82.
847 Josephus *A.J.* 18.83. The expulsion is also mentioned by Tacitus *Ann.* 2.85; Suetonius *Tib.* 36; Dio Cassius 57.18; see also Seneca *Ep.* 108.22.
848 Josephus *A.J.* 18.84. See also Tacitus *Ann.* 2.85; Suetonius *Tib.* 36. Cf. Emil Schürer, *The History of the Jewish People in the Age of Jesus Christ*, III.1, rev. and ed. by Geza Vermes, Fergus Millar and Martin Goodman (Edinburgh: T & T Clark, 1986) 75–76.
849 Josephus *A.J.* 18.84; trans. L. H. Feldman, *Josephus. Jewish Antiquities Books XVIII-XX*, LCL (Cambridge, MA: Harvard University Press, 1969) 61.
850 On the role of the provincial governor and civic magistrates in litigation in the provinces of the Roman Empire, see *SEG* 9.8, in Victor Ehrenberg and A. H. M. Jones, *Documents illustrating the Reigns of Augustus and Tiberius* (Oxford: Clarendon Press, 1976) No. 311; D. C. Braund, *Augustus to Nero: A Sourcebook on Roman History 31 B.C.-A.D. 68* (London: Croom Helm, 1985) No. 543; see the discussion in A. H. M. Jones, *The Criminal Courts of the Roman Republic and Principate* (Oxford: Blackwells, 1972) 98–100; A. N. Sherwin-White, *Roman Society and Roman Law in the New Testament* (Oxford: Clarendon Press, 1963) 14. Acts 18:12–17 represents Paul being brought before Gallio's tribunal by the Jews; for debate on the historicity of this tradition, see Gerd Lüdemann, *Early Christianity according to the Traditions in Acts: A Commentary* (Min-

immediate relevance is Paul's anxiety over the collapse of the collection, which is palpable in 12:16–18. The mention of Titus as the one through whom Paul was suspected of seeking to defraud the Corinthians in 12:18 makes it certain that the charge arose in connection with the collection for the poor saints in Jerusalem, whose organization occupied Paul's energies during the final years of his ministry.[851] Paul's statement in 2 Cor. 8:6 that Titus "had already made a beginning" (προενήρξατο) of the collection work among the Corinthians sometime in the year preceding the composition of 2 Cor. 8 (cf. 8:10–11) places the matter beyond doubt.[852] The importance of this conclusion would be heightened if Paul's mention of the sending of Titus and an unnamed brother in 12:18 were a retrospective reference to the commissioning of Titus and "our brother" as authorized agents of the collection in 8:16–24.[853] This inference, which has much to commend it, nevertheless depends upon two interrelated assumptions: that 2 Cor. 8 was originally an independent letter,[854] and that 2 Cor. 8 was composed prior to 2 Cor. 10–13.[855] This hypothesis was originally put forward by Johannes Weiss,[856]

---

neapolis: Fortress Press, 1989) 204; Rainer Riesner, *Paul's Early Period: Chronology, Mission, Strategy* (Grand Rapids: Eerdmans, 1998) 209; Gerd Lüdemann, *The Acts of the Apostles* (Amherst: Prometheus Press, 2005) 239–40.

851 Windisch, *Der zweite Korintherbrief*, 404–405; C. K. Barrett, "Titus" in *Neotestamentica et Semitica*, ed. E. E. Ellis and M. Wilcox (Edinburgh: T & T Clark, 1969) 10; repr. in idem, *Essays on Paul* (Philadelphia; Westminster Press, 1982) 127; Barrett, *Second Epistle*, 325; Bruce, *1 and 2 Corinthians*, 168–69, 251; Furnish, *II Corinthians*, 565–66.

852 The significance of Paul's choice of the double-compound verb προενάρχομαι ("to begin beforehand") is highlighted by the fact that the word is *hapax legomenon*, found only in 2 Cor. 8:6, 10; see LSJ 1478 s.v.; BDAG 868 s.v. See the discussion of the implications in Plummer, *Second Epistle*, 237; Windisch, *Der zweite Korintherbrief*, 246, 249; Betz, *2 Corinthians 8 and 9*, 54–55; Thrall, *Second Epistle*, 2.528.

853 So, Krenkel, *Beiträge*, 351–52; Drescher, "Vorgänge in Korinth," 66–67; Weiss, *Primitive Christianity*, 1.353; Windisch, *Der zweite Korintherbrief*, 404–405; Barrett, *Second Epistle*, 325; Kümmel, *Introduction*, 290: "12:18 clearly refers back to the sending of Titus and a 'brother' mentioned in 8:6, 16–18"; Furnish, *II Corinthians*, 566.

854 The hypothesis that 2 Cor. 8 was originally an independent letter goes back to Johann Salomo Semler, *Paraphrasis II. Epistolae ad Corinthios* (Halae Magdeburgicae: Hemmerde, 1776); see the detailed history of scholarship in Betz, *2 Corinthians 8 and 9*, 3–36.

855 Both assumptions are clearly identified and discussed by Windisch, *Der zweite Korintherbrief*, 404–406.

and has recently been revived by Margaret Mitchell.[857] In particular, we may call attention to the coincidence in wording and substance between 8:6, 22 and 12:18: in both passages, Paul uses the verb παρακαλεῖν with Titus as the object; in both cases, Paul mentions a "brother" whom he "sent" along with Titus.[858] The almost literal agreement between the two passages is best appreciated when set forth in parallel columns:

2 Cor. 8:6, 22	2 Cor. 12:18
παρακαλέσαι Τίτον	παρεκάλεσα Τίτον
συνεπέμψαμεν δὲ αὐτοῖς	καὶ συναπέστειλα
τὸν ἀδελφὸν ἡμῶν	τὸ ἀδελφὸν
We urged Titus	I urged Titus
and we are sending with them	and sent with [him]
our brother	the brother

---

856 Weiss, *Primitive Christianity*, 1.353: "In II Cor. 12:17 f., Paul refers to the sending of Titus and of the brother on the business of the collection for the saints, that is, to the incident of ch. 8 where this mission has just been dispatched. It follows that chs. 10–13 could not have been written before ch. 8... [which] is an entirely independent document with its conclusion cut off. It is a letter of commendation for Titus and two unnamed brethren to the church at Corinth. It must have been composed before the dispute between Paul and the church. For in 8:7 he praises the church's wealth in faith and utterance and all earnestness and in love to Paul in a more unconstrained way than would have been possible during the quarrel or even after its settlement—somewhat, in fact, in the tone of I Cor. 1:4–9." That 2 Cor. 12:16–18 refers back to 8:16–17 had already been argued by Drescher, "Vorgänge in Korinth," 67, and, still earlier, by Krenkel, *Beiträge*, 351–52, ultimately going back to a suggestion by Michael Weber, *De numero epistularum Pauli ad Corinthios rectius constituendo* (Wittenberg: University of Wittenberg, 1807) 192–94.

857 Mitchell, "Paul's Letters to Corinth," 321–35, esp. 326–27. Mitchell acknowledges that "Weiss did argue that 2 Corinthians 8 must precede the conflicts attested in the other letters in 2 Corinthians" (p. 325 n.65), nevertheless she claims originality and novelty for her own proposal: "my contribution is the virtually unprecedented argument for the placement of 2 Corinthians 8 in this succession of letters" (p. 324); "I shall focus my attention here upon my case for the novel placement and role of 2 Corinthians 8." (p. 325).

858 See, already, Windisch, *Der zweite Korintherbrief*, 405: "παρεκάλεσα Τίτον καὶ συναπέστειλα τὸν ἀδελφόν klingt wie ein Zitat aus B: εἰς τὸ παρακαλέσαι ἡμᾶς Τίτον 8:6...συνεπέμψαμεν δὲ αὐτοῖς τὸν ἀδελφὸν ἡμῶν 8:22." Cf. Mitchell, "Paul's Letters to Corinth," 326.

It is no objection to the identification of the two missions of Titus mentioned in these passages that in 12:18 Paul refers to only one brother, whereas in 8:16–24 he speaks of two.[859] For Paul takes care to distinguish between the two brothers of 2 Cor. 8 in terms of their selection and relationship to himself: the former brother was "elected by the churches" (χειροτονηθεὶς ὑπὸ τῶν ἐκκλησιῶν) as Paul's traveling companion (8:19); his assignment in relation to the collection was "to stave off the possibility that someone might complain against us in view of the large sum of money being administered by us" (8:20);[860] the latter brother, by contrast, is described as *"our* brother (ὁ ἀδελφὸς ἡμῶν) whom we have approved as being efficient in many matters at many times" (8:22).[861] Thus, only the latter brother was Paul's appointment, and only his conduct could reflect upon Paul's integrity.[862] This corresponds exactly to the situation in 12:18, where Paul appeals to the blamelessness of Titus and "the brother" as evidence of his own probity.[863]

If Paul's appeal to the conduct of Titus and an unnamed brother in 12:18 is, as it seems, a retrospective reference to the mission for which Titus and the brother were authorized in 8:16–24, then the reason for Paul's anxiety over the charge of embezzlement is all too apparent: the collapse of the collection. This far-reaching conclusion is indicated by the purpose of 2 Cor. 8 in general—which is to encourage the Corinthians to fulfill their commitment to partnership in the collection, and to mandate Paul's envoys to carry out the collection on Paul's behalf.[864] But, more particularly, the language of 8:6 and 8:11 makes clear that, in writing this letter and in commissioning Titus and the brothers, Paul aimed not merely at the continuation of the collection work in some further stage, but at the *completion* of the effort. This is the unambiguous meaning of the verb ἐπιτελεῖν, which is "to finish something

---

859 For this objection, see Thrall, *Second Epistle*, 2.854.
860 Krenkel, *Beiträge*, 352; Drescher, "Vorgänge in Korinth," 67; Weiss, *Primitive Christianity*, 1.355; Windisch, *Der zweite Korintherbrief*, 405; Furnish, *II Corinthians*, 566; Betz, *2 Corinthians 8 and 9*, 72–78.
861 Krenkel, *Beiträge*, 352; Drescher, "Vorgänge in Korinth," 67; Windisch, *Der zweite Korintherbrief*, 266; Allo, *Saint Paul*, 227; Bruce, *1 and 2 Corinthians*, 251; Barrett, *Second Epistle*, 325.
862 Krenkel, *Beiträge*, 352; Drescher, "Vorgänge in Korinth," 67; Windisch, *Der zweite Korintherbrief*, 405; Barrett, "Titus," 12; Furnish, *II Corinthians*, 566; Betz, *2 Corinthians 8 and 9*, 78.
863 Barrett, *Second Epistle*, 325; Furnish, *II Corinthians*, 566; Mitchell, "Paul's Letters to Corinth," 326.
864 Betz, *2 Corinthians 8 and 9*, 41, 70 and *passim*.

begun," "to bring to an end,"[865] a verb which has an established usage in legal and financial contexts for the execution of agreements such as deeds and contracts.[866] Moreover, the particles, νυνὶ δὲ καί ("now then"), which introduce Paul's exhortation to "complete the action" in 8:11, mark the present in which the letter is read in the church at Corinth as the moment when the Corinthians are "to finish up" what they had begun.[867] Yet the persistent suspicion of financial misconduct, which repeatedly becomes audible in 10:2, 11:7–11, 12:13, 12:14–18, makes it unlikely that the collection was completed prior to the composition of 2 Cor. 10–13. Thus the conclusion seems unavoidable: the collection, which Paul sought to complete by the composition of the administrative letter now preserved in 2 Cor. 8, and which he commissioned Titus and the brothers to retrieve on his behalf, *collapsed*, and Titus returned to Paul empty-handed! The bitter invective against Paul which reverberates throughout 2 Cor. 10–13 makes it unlikely, moreover, that the collection effort failed on account of lethargy or indifference. Rather, the conclusion that seems best warranted by the evidence is that the collection collapsed because the Corinthians, or a few Corinthians with resources and influence, *refused to contribute*. No motive for the refusal lies closer to hand than the suspicion of embezzlement, which, we must suppose, had already been insinuated.

Why should the breakdown of the collection in Corinth have been a matter of such serious concern to Paul? This is a question to which we shall devote closer attention in chapter 6, when we seek to reconstruct the history of the relationship between Paul and the Corinthians, but at this point it will serve to sketch out something of what was at stake. When one surveys Paul's references to the collection, it is clear that, from its inception at the Jerusalem conference, the legitimacy of Paul's apostleship to the Gentiles was at issue in the organization of a collection among his mission churches (Gal. 2:10).[868] Following the emergence of

---

865 BDAG 383 s.v. ἐπιτελέω 1; Gerhard Delling, "συντελέω," *TDNT* 8 (1972) 62–63; Betz, *2 Corinthians 8 and 9*, 54. See also Rom. 15:28 where the verb is also used in reference to the completion of the collection.
866 E.g., *POxy* 483.34; *BGU* IV.1062.19; Moulton and Milligan, *Vocabulary of the Greek Testament*, 247–48 s.v. ἐπιτελέω; Friedrich Preisigke, *Wörterbuch der griechischen Papyrusurkunden mit Einschluss der griechischen Inschriften, Aufschriften, Ostraka, Mumienschilder usw. aus Ägypten* (Berlin: Selbstverlag, 1924) Vol. 1, s.v. ἐπιτελέω.
867 Betz, *2 Corinthians 8 and 9*, 65.
868 K. F. Nickle, *The Collection: A Study in Paul's Strategy* (Naperville: Allenson, 1966) 40–73, esp. 59–62; Gerd Lüdemann, *Paulus, der Heidenapostel. Band*

an aggressive, Jewish-Christian opposition to Paul's ministry, it seems likely that the collection for the poor saints in Jerusalem became for Paul a tangible symbol of the unity between Jewish and Gentile Christians for which he longed (Rom. 15:25–32).[869] In Paul's final accounting of contributions to the collection in Rom. 15:25–27, there is no mention of the participation of the Galatian churches, although 1 Cor. 16:1 attests that Paul had initiated the collection among the Galatians, and had given instructions for carrying it out. The absence of any reference to a contribution from Galatia, alongside of Paul's praise for the partnership of Macedonia and Achaia (Rom. 15:26), suggests that, in the end, the Galatian churches refused to contribute.[870] To be sure, the churches of Macedonia contributed, and Paul emphasizes the voluntary nature of their cooperation (2 Cor. 8:1–5).[871] But, while praising the Macedonians' generosity, Paul acknowledges that the Macedonians gave out of "their extreme poverty" (ἡ κατὰ βάθους πτωχεία αὐτῶν, literally, "their poverty reaching down into the depths").[872] Unless Paul's description of the economic circumstances of the Macedonians is an exaggeration, their contribution could hardly have been more than symbolic.[873]

I: Studien zur Chronologie (Göttingen: Vandenhoeck & Ruprecht, 1980) 105–110; Furnish, *II Corinthians*, 410; Martin, *2 Corinthians*, 251; Stephan Joubert, *Paul as Benefactor: Reciprocity, Strategy and Theological Reflection in Paul's Collection* (Tübingen: Mohr Siebeck, 2000) 100–106; Byung-Mo Kim, *Die paulinische Kollekte* (Tübingen: Francke, 2002) 137–80.

869 Nickle, *The Collection*, 111–29; Georgi, *Remembering the Poor*, 117–20; Gerd Lüdemann, *Paulus, der Heidenapostel. Band II*, 94; Furnish, *II Corinthians*, 411–12; Jürgen Becker, *Paul: Apostle to the Gentiles* (Louisville: Westminster John Knox Press, 1993) 260; Thrall, *Second Epistle*, 2.514–15.

870 Thrall, *Second Epistle*, 2.516–17; David J. Downs, *The Offering of the Gentiles: Paul's Collection for Jerusalem in Its Chronological, Cultural, and Cultic Contexts* (Tübingen: Mohr Siebeck, 2008) 42.

871 Betz, *2 Corinthians 8 and 9*, 41–49; Thrall, *Second Epistle*, 2.520–27.

872 Betz, *2 Corinthians 8 and 9*, 43, 49–51.

873 The nuances of Paul's characterization of the Macedonians' gift in 2 Cor. 8:2–5 bear careful examination. The expression κατὰ δύναμιν in 8:3 is very common in the papyri with the meaning "in accordance with one's financial capability": Moulton and Milligan, *Vocabulary of the Greek Testament*, 171–72 s.v. δύναμις; Preisigke, *Wörterbuch der griechischen Papyrusurkunden*, Vol. 1, s.v. δύναμις; BDAG 263 s.v. δύναμις 2. Yet even this, Paul avers, was "beyond the ability" (παρὰ δύναμιν) of the Macedonians—an expression likewise attested in the papyri: Moulton and Milligan, *Vocabulary of the Greek Testament*, 171 s.v. δύναμις. Paul's emphasis upon the *personal* nature of the Macedonians' contribution in 8:5 ("on the contrary, it was their own selves that they first and foremost

If Paul's gift for the poor in Jerusalem were to be more than a token, then the generous participation of the wealthy Corinthians was essential. Indeed, Paul seems to have anticipated the crucial role that the Corinthians would play in the success of the collection on account of their wealth: at the earliest mention of the collection project in his Corinthian correspondence, Paul adds to the instructions for accumulating monies a promissory incentive: if the collection is "sufficiently large" (ἐὰν δὲ ἄξιον ᾖ), he himself will convey it to Jerusalem (1 Cor. 16:4).[874] This emphasis upon the potential size of the Corinthian contribution is reinforced by Paul's appeal to the Corinthians' "present abundance" (ἐν τῷ νῦν καιρῷ τὸ ὑμῶν περίσσευμα) in 2 Cor. 8:14.[875] If the Corinthians were to withhold their gift, the collection would make no showing at all! Then Paul's standing as an apostle and his vision of a united church would be in jeopardy.

When, despite all the precautions that Paul had taken in 2 Cor. 8:16–24,[876] the Corinthians refused to contribute to the collection, and Titus returned to Paul with the devastating report, Paul decided to visit Corinth in person. The occurrence of a second visit by Paul to Corinth, first hypothesized by Friedrich Bleek, as noted above,[877] is generally acknowledged by scholars of the New Testament, whatever their views on the unity of the writing known to us as 2 Corinthians.[878]

---

gave"), where the pronoun ἑαυτούς stands in emphatic position, politely covers the fact that the Macedonians' contribution was not primarily monetary. Cf. Plummer, *Second Epistle*, 234, who compares the Macedonians' contribution to "the widow's two mites given out of her *want*"; Betz, *2 Corinthians 8 and 9*, 47: "In fact, given the poverty of the Macedonians, Paul could hardly have hoped for substantial financial assistance from them, but he had expected to receive some."

874 For the sense of ἄξιος as "worth" or "value," see the papyri adduced by Moulton and Milligan, *Vocabulary of the Greek Testament*, 50–51 s.v. ἄξιος. For this interpretation of ἐὰν δὲ ἄξιον ᾖ in 1 Cor. 16:4, see Weiss, *Der erste Korintherbrief*, 382: "Wenn es der Mühe wert ist; also ἄξιόν ἐστι wie 2 Thess. 1:3;...nur wenn eine glänzende Sammlung zusammengekommen ist, will er es tun."

875 Betz, *2 Corinthians 8 and 9*, 68. For the hypothesis that the phrase δευτέραν χάριν in 2 Cor. 1:15 refers to Paul's request that the Corinthians contribute "twice" to the collection for the poor in Jerusalem, see Gordon Fee, "CHARIS in 2 Corinthians 1:15," *NTS* 24 (1977) 533–38.

876 Plummer, *Second Epistle*, 249–50; Betz, *2 Corinthians 8 and 9*, 76–77.

877 Bleek, "Erörterungen," 614–24; followed by Ewald, *Sendschreiben*, 220–27, who located the second visit between 1 and 2 Corinthians.

878 Paul's "interim visit" belongs to the "Minimalkonsens" that Reimund Bieringer identifies in scholarship on the Corinthian correspondence in "Zwischen Konti-

And, indeed, there is clear evidence of an intermediate visit in Paul's references to his impending "third coming" to Corinth in 2 Cor. 12:14 and 13:1, and in his retrospective explanation of his determination not to make "another painful visit" to Corinth in 2 Cor. 2:1.[879] We shall examine the arguments in support of the hypothesis that Paul visited Corinth a second time prior to the composition of 2 Cor. 10–13 in greater detail below.[880] For the moment, it suffices to suggest that it was on the occasion of this second visit to Corinth that someone in the church at Corinth did Paul "wrong" and caused Paul "pain." Our exegesis of 2 Cor. 12:16–18 leads to the conclusion that *the wrong consisted in a public accusation of embezzlement* in connection with the collection.[881] The conclusion that Paul was accused of embezzlement agrees with our earlier inference from the meaning of ἀδικεῖν in 2 Cor. 7:12: a fraudulent use of money was somehow involved in the "wrong" done to Paul. No inference is more plausible than that *the one who charged Paul with embezzlement*

---

nuität und Diskontinuität. Die beiden Korintherbriefe in ihrer Beziehung zueinander nach der neueren Forschung" in *The Corinthian Correspondence*, ed. R. Bieringer (Leuven: Leuven University Press, 1996) 11–12. See esp. Heinrich Lisco, *Die Entstehung des zweiten Korintherbriefes* (Berlin: Schneider, 1896) 1; Plummer, *Second Epistle*, xxix; Windisch, *Der zweite Korintherbrief*, 10–11; Bultmann, *Der zweite Brief*, 22; Betz, *2 Corinthians 8 and 9*, 11–12, 31–33, 34, 142–43; Thrall, *Second Epistle*, 1.49–57.

879 So, with strong exegetical arguments, Plummer, *Second Epistle*, 371; Bachmann, *Der zweite Brief*, 88, 405; Windisch, *Der zweite Korintherbrief*, 77–78, 398–99, 412–13; Allo, *Saint Paul*, 326–27, 335; Hughes, *Paul's Second Epistle*, 460; Barrett, *Second Epistle*, 323; Furnish, *II Corinthians*, 140, 557–58; Martin, *2 Corinthians*, 440; Thrall, *Second Epistle*, 1.49–50, 53–56, 163–65; 2.843, 872.

880 See below, ch. 6.

881 So, already, Betz, *2 Corinthians 8 and 9*, 77: "This is clear from 2 Cor. 12:16–18, where Paul mentioned a previous mission of Titus and a certain brother as evidence that he had not embezzled any of the money collected. Meanwhile, another mission of Titus had taken place and resulted in reconciliation. The letter of reconciliation, in which the apostle expressed his joy over the resolution of the crisis (1:1–2:13; 7:5–16; 13:11–13), states that the 'one who committed the offense' (ὁ ἀδικήσας) is no longer a problem (7:12). Paul asked that the punishment of the man be brought to an end (2:5 ff.). Thus it would appear that the offense in question was a charge of fraud made by this man against the apostle." On defamation as a form of *iniuria* in Roman law, see Kaser, *Das römische Privatrecht*, 3.520–22; J. A. Crook, *Law and Life of Rome* (London: Thames and Hudson, 1967) 252.

on his second, painful visit to Corinth *was the wrongdoer* of 2 Cor. 2:5–11 and 7:12.[882]

How Paul experienced the wrong that was done to him on the occasion of his second visit to Corinth is apparent in 2 Cor. 12:20–21: it resulted in Paul's complete humiliation. We have argued above[883] that Paul's anxious phantasy of what may happen when he returns to Corinth in 12:20–21 is constructed out of recollected elements of the painful experience of his second visit, justifying the fear that he will be again humiliated: "For I fear lest, when I come, I may find you not such persons as I wish, and indeed lest I may be found by you such a person as you do not wish; I fear lest there may be strife, jealousy, angry outbursts, intrigues, slanders, whisperings, arrogant opinions, disorders. I fear lest, when I come, my God should humiliate me again in your presence, and I may have to mourn over many who have sinned previously and have not repented of the impurity and immorality and licentiousness which they have practiced."[884] In this revealing portrait of his inner life, Paul imagines himself surrounded by beastly vices that threaten the complete destruction of his relationships, and in the center of a vast amphitheatre of discord, Paul spies himself, cringing and abject.[885] Such was Paul's experience and demeanor on the occasion of his second, "painful" visit to Corinth, when he was publicly accused of embezzlement by the wrongdoer, and found himself unable to respond, because he was so deeply humiliated.[886]

---

882 So, already, Betz, *2 Corinthians 8 and 9*, 97: "Paul's mention of the charge [of πλεονεξία] was not, therefore, mere rhetoric, but was a charge that had been formally made by someone in Corinth, in all probability by the person whom Paul called 'the offender' (ὁ ἀδικήσας) in 2 Cor. 7:12"; 143: "Finally, if the letter of reconciliation also provided for the reconciliation of the 'wrongdoer' (ὁ ἀδικήσας), we can assume that the charge that Paul wished to enrich himself by means of the collection had been advanced, above all, by the wrongdoer."

883 See above, on 2 Cor. 10:1.

884 Most commentators construe πάλιν with ταπεινώσῃ in 12:21, as a reference to a previous occasion on which Paul was "humiliated" before the Corinthians: see, e.g., Plummer, *Second Epistle*, 369–70; Allo, *Saint Paul*, 334; Barrett, *Second Epistle*, 326; Furnish, *II Corinthians*, 562; Martin, *2 Corinthians*, 451; Thrall, *Second Epistle*, 2.865–66.

885 Cf. Weiss, *Primitive Christianity*, 1.343–44.

886 A connection is perceptively inferred between the conflict recollected in 12:20–21 and the actions of the wrongdoer by Paul Barnett, "Paul, Apologist to the Corinthians" in *Paul and the Corinthians: Studies on a Community in Conflict*, ed. T. J. Burke and J. K. Elliott (Leiden: Brill, 2003) 322: "Paul engaged in a

182   Chapter Three. Inferences from Exegesis

We gain further insight into the context in which the accusation of embezzlement was made, and into the role of the wrongdoer in bringing the charge, by careful exegesis of 2 Cor. 13:1–2. Turning suddenly from recollection of what he dreads to prediction of what he will do when he comes to Corinth, Paul warns the Corinthians by citing a prescription of Deuteronomy (19:15): "By the mouth of two or three witnesses must every charge be substantiated" (ἐπὶ στόματος δύο μαρτύρων καὶ τριῶν σταθήσεται πᾶν ῥῆμα).[887] The reason for Paul's citation of this rule of judicial evidence, and its relevance to the charge of embezzlement under discussion since 12:14, have been obscured in the history of interpretation by a "highly artificial"[888] construal of the "three witnesses" of Scripture as Paul's three visits to Corinth. This interpretation, which goes back to Chrysostom and the Catena,[889] was taken over by Calvin,[890] and has established itself as the dominant explanation of the passage among modern commentators.[891] The interpretation rests upon the assumption that, since the citation immediately follows Paul's announcement, "This is the third time (τρίτον) I am coming to you" in 13a, the third visit of the announcement and the three witnesses of the scriptural citation must somehow correspond.[892] Accordingly, Paul wishes to give his third visit the status of a third witness in a judicial case: just as a (second or) third witness

---

      power struggle with one man in particular (7:12; 2:5–8). This appears to have been marked by public quarreling (12:20–13:2)."
887 On the use of στόμα in the sense of "what the mouth utters," or "testimony," see BDAG 947 s.v. στόμα 2. For the future indicative, σταθήσεται, employed to render "categorical injunctions and prohibitions in the legal language of the Old Testament," see BDF §362. For ῥῆμα as "issue" (πρᾶγμα) in the legal sense of "charge," see BDAG 905 s.v. ῥῆμα 2.
888 Windisch, *Der zweite Korintherbrief*, 413.
889 Chrysostom PG 61 col. 596 (*NPNF*, 1st ser. XII, p.411); Catena: ταῖς παρουσίαις ἀντὶ μαρτύρων ἐχρήσατο, cited in Windisch, *Der zweite Korintherbrief*, 413.
890 John Calvin, *The Second Epistle of Paul the Apostle to the Corinthians and the Epistles to Timothy, Titus and Philemon*, trans. T. A. Smail (Grand Rapids: Eerdmans, 1964) 169; originally published as *Commentaire sur la seconde épitre aux Corinthiens* (Geneve, 1547).
891 E.g., Bachmann, *Der zweite Brief*, 412; Windisch, *Der zweite Korintherbrief*, 413; Lietzmann, *An die Korinther I/II*, 160; Bruce, *1 and 2 Corinthians*, 253; Barrett, *Second Epistle*, 333; Lambrecht, *Second Corinthians*, 221; Thrall, *Second Epistle*, 2.874–76; Harris, *Second Epistle*, 908; Vegge, *2 Corinthians*, 342.
892 Windisch, *Der zweite Korintherbrief*, 413: "Das nächstliegende Annahme ist dass τρίτον und τριῶν einander entsprechen"; Barrett, *Second Epistle*, 333: "The ordinals *third* and *second* in these two verses cannot fail to be connected with the cardinals *two* and *three* in the quotation."

supplies corroborative evidence against an accused, so Paul's third visit to Corinth should silence all objections and provide the basis for a verdict.[893]

However, the assumption that Paul is speaking metaphorically in 13:1 is encumbered with difficulties, because the analogy between "visits" and "witnesses" is far from perfect. First, the three visits by Paul do not satisfy the requirements of the text that Paul quotes, since they would still constitute the testimony of only a *single* witness, Paul himself, whereas the scripture requires the evidence of two or three *different* witnesses.[894] Second, the Deuteronomic rule demands, or at least implies, the *simultaneous* appearance of two or three witnesses to sustain a charge, while Paul's visits to Corinth follow one after another, separated by temporal intervals.[895] Third, it is difficult to imagine how Paul could have regarded his initial, "foundation" visit, devoted to the proclamation of the gospel, and attended by a number of conversions (Acts 18:10), as a *witness against* the Corinthians.[896]

Interpreters are, naturally, conscious of these defects in the analogy and seek to remedy them. Thus, Wilhelm Bousset suggests that Paul applies the Deuteronomic ruling loosely, "with a certain whimsy."[897] This suggestion is unlikely, given the threatening tone of the passage.[898] Windisch concedes that Paul's choice of Deut. 19:15 is "unfortunate" from a modern point of view, but opines, condescendingly, that such a contrived analogy is what one might expect of a Rabbinical student like Paul.[899] Recognizing that Paul's foundation visit cannot qualify as a witness against the Corinthians, Bultmann supposes that Paul is thinking of the present letter, 2 Cor. 10–13, as the second of the three witnesses.[900] But this suggestion only complicates an already strained analogy.[901] In an effort to shore up the metaphorical interpretation, Hendrik van Vliet proposes that Paul must have been familiar with the development of the idea

---

893 Bachmann, *Der zweite Brief*, 412; Windisch, *Der zweite Korintherbrief*, 413; Barrett, *Second Epistle*, 333.
894 Windisch, *Der zweite Korintherbrief*, 413; Furnish, *II Corinthians*, 575.
895 Meyer, *Der zweite Brief*, 501; Windisch, *Der zweite Korintherbrief*, 413.
896 Allo, *Saint Paul*, 335–36; Bultmann, *Der zweite Brief*, 243; Furnish, *II Corinthians*, 575.
897 Bousset, *Der zweite Brief*, 222; see also Strachan, *Second Epistle*, 38.
898 Menzies, *Second Epistle*, 100; Plummer, *Second Epistle*, 373.
899 Windisch, *Der zweite Korintherbrief*, 413–14: "nach unseren Begriffen wenig glücklich gewählten 'Spruche' Dt 19:15…Sie ist künstlich, aber einem Rabbinenschüler wie Paulus wohl zuzutrauen."
900 Bultmann, *Der zweite Brief*, 243; followed by Furnish, *II Corinthians*, 575.
901 Thrall, *Second Epistle*, 2.875–76.

of "witnesses" into that of "warnings" in Rabbinic literature; by citing the rule of judicial evidence, Paul would be reminding the Corinthians that he has given them the requisite two or three "warnings," prior to coming to exercise discipline.[902] This suggestion has the advantage of largely dissolving the untenable connection between visits and witnesses, and hence it is favored by a number of commentators.[903] Unfortunately, the reinterpretation of "witnesses" as "warnings" in Jewish legal tradition cannot be traced back into the time of Paul. The application of the rule of judicial evidence to cases of persons suspected of wrongdoing, in the sense of "warnings" before witnesses, is first attested in the Mishnah tractate on "The Suspected Adulteress" (*Sotah* 1.1–2), dated to the end of the second century C.E.[904]

With all of these difficulties, we have not yet mentioned the most serious defect to which the metaphorical interpretation of Paul's scripture citation is exposed: it assumes that Paul takes no account of the *purpose* of the Deuteronomic rule! The requirement of multiple witnesses— three, or at least two—was meant *to protect the accused* from a single malicious witness intent on doing harm.[905] But the view that Paul is speaking metaphorically of his visits as "witnesses" against the Corinthians makes Paul apply the rule of judicial evidence *against the accused.*[906] Some interpreters are sensible of this contradiction and seek to diminish the tension by loosening Paul's connection to the text of Deuteronomy. Thus, van Vliet observes that the dictum is not explicitly marked as a citation of Scripture (by an introductory formula, such as καθὼς γέγραπται), and suggests that Paul quotes the rule only as "a sort of proverb."[907] Earl Ellis explains that Paul applies the Deuteronomic rule loosely, in order "to clothe his own thoughts."[908] Hans Lietzmann dismisses the inconsis-

---

902 H. van Vliet, *No Single Testimony. A Study on the Adoption of the Law of Deut. 19:15 Par. into the New Testament* (Utrecht: Kemink & Zoon, 1958) 88, 96 n.8.
903 Barrett, *Second Epistle*, 333; Furnish, *II Corinthians*, 575; Martin, *2 Corinthians*, 470; Thrall, *Second Epistle*, 2.876; Harris, *Second Epistle*, 908.
904 H. Strack and P. Billerbeck, *Kommentar zum Neuen Testament aus Talmud und Midrasch* (Munich: Beck, 1922) 1.790–91; Jacob Neusner, *Judaism, the Evidence of the Mishnah* (Chicago: University of Chicago Press, 1981) 93.
905 For sensitivity to this tension, see Bachmann, *Der zweite Brief*, 412; Thrall, *Second Epistle*, 2.874.
906 Thrall, *Second Epistle*, 2.874.
907 van Vliet, *No Single Testimony*, 88.
908 E. E. Ellis, *Paul's Use of the Old Testament* (Edinburgh: Oliver and Boyd, 1957) 10.

tency with the observation that "Paul shows few scruples in the manipulation of citations, when the wording provides him with any sort of useful handle."⁹⁰⁹ But it seems perverse to defend an interpretation which requires us to assume that Paul used a citation of Scripture contrary to its stated purpose and without consideration of its context. Perhaps we should re-examine the assumptions of the metaphorical interpretation, even if it rests upon the authority of the church fathers.

There are good reasons to suppose that Paul was cognizant of the purpose of the Deuteronomic rule of judicial evidence, and that he used the citation here in a manner consistent with that purpose. First, the wording of 13:1b departs only slightly from the text of the Septuagint, and is essentially a literal quotation: the Septuagint repeats the phrase ἐπὶ στόματος ("by the mouth") before τριῶν μαρτύρων.⁹¹⁰ The wording of Paul's citation is even closer to that of Matt. 18:16, suggesting that Paul and Matthew used the same recension of the Greek text of the Old Testament, a recension also known to the author of the *Testament of Abraham*.⁹¹¹ Thus, the fact that Paul does not explicitly identify the rule of evidence as a citation of Scripture is insignificant;⁹¹² we must assume that Paul was aware that he was quoting Deuteronomy, and that he would not have been ignorant of the context and purpose of the legislation. Second, the Deuteronomic rule of judicial evidence enjoyed a broad currency in Palestinian Judaism and in early Christianity. In addition to the texts referenced above, the following writings cite or allude to the Deuteronomic rule, or presuppose its operation in accounts of events: CD IX.16–23; 1 Tim. 5:19; John 8:17; Heb. 10:28; Mark 14:55–59.⁹¹³ Each of the texts which cite the Deuteronomic code reflect an awareness of its purpose, and, for the most part, apply it in ways that are consistent with its original intent. This is clearest in 1 Tim. 5:19: "Never accept any accusation against an elder except on the evidence of two or three witnesses."⁹¹⁴ Even when the authors of these texts seek to lessen the stringency of the Deuteronomic requirement, in the interest of community discipline, there is consciousness of the purpose of the statute, namely, to protect the accused. In the *Damascus Rule* of the Jewish sectarians, the biblical com-

---

909 Lietzmann, *An die Korinther I/II*, 160.
910 Windisch, *Der zweite Korintherbrief*, 413; Harris, *Second Epistle*, 906–907.
911 Windisch, *Der zweite Korintherbrief*, 413; Barrett, *Second Epistle*, 333.
912 Heinrici, *Der zweite Brief*, 423.
913 van Vliet, *No Single Testimony*, 68–69; Furnish, *II Corinthians*, 569; Thrall, *Second Epistle*, 2.873.
914 Windisch, *Der zweite Korintherbrief*, 413; Thrall, *Second Epistle*, 2.873.

mandment is reinterpreted to permit a verdict in cases where an offence is witnessed by two individuals on separate occasions, or when two witnesses testify to a different offence; but the reinterpretation does not result in the suspension of the requirement of multiple witnesses in order to protect the accused.[915] The only ambiguous instance is Matt. 18:16, where it is not clear whether the witnesses serve to strengthen the brother's admonition,[916] or to protect the sinner in case the admoniser is wrong.[917] In light of the evidence of contemporary sources, it seems best to assume that Paul was cognizant of the purpose of the Deuteronomic rule and used it in a way that was consistent with that purpose.

Who, then, are the accused whom Paul seeks to protect by citing the rule of judicial evidence? A minority of interpreters suggest that the Corinthians are the ones who will have to answer charges of misconduct in a formal hearing which Paul will convene when he comes to Corinth.[918] Thus Paul cites the Deuteronomic rule to assure his Corinthian readers that he will follow due process in evaluating whatever charges may be brought against members of the congregation. This suggestion is unlikely, however, since it entails Paul asking members of the Corinthian church to testify against each other—something that could not fail to exacerbate the discord that Paul deplores in 12:20.[919] Upon reflection, it seems clear that this interpretation is the product of the atomistic approach of commentators: the mention of the "impurity, immorality, and licentiousness" which the Corinthians have practiced in 12:21 is taken to indicate that Paul plans to hold a court of inquiry into the Corinthians' misconduct.[920] It is possible, of course, that the persons who had previously committed sexual sins (12:21) were the same as those who have recently aroused discord in connection with the charge of financial misconduct against Paul (12:20). But the best explanation of the mention of sexual sins at the cli-

---

915 Geza Vermes, *The Dead Sea Scrolls in English* (Hammondsworth: Penguin Books, 1975) 80, 111.
916 Ulrich V. Luz, *Matthew 8–20: A Commentary*, Hermeneia (Minneapolis: Fortress Press, 2001) 452.
917 Luz, *Matthew 8–20*, 452.
918 Meyer, *Der zweite Brief*, 500; Menzies, *Second Epistle*, 101; Allo, *Saint Paul*, 335; Hughes, *Second Epistle*, 475; M. Delcor, "The Courts of the Church of Corinth and the Courts of Qumran" in *Paul and Qumran*, ed. J. Murphy-O'connor (London: Chapman, 1968) 76.
919 Plummer, *Second Epistle*, 372; Thrall, *Second Epistle*, 2.874.
920 With reference to the offenses mentioned in 12:20–21, Furnish, *II Corinthians*, 575; Thrall, *Second Epistle*, 2.874; Harris, *Second Epistle*, 907.

max of a paragraph in which Paul defends himself against the allegation of embezzlement and recollects the unpleasant aftermath of the charge is that Paul consistently connects sexual immorality with social disorders (1 Thess. 4:1–12; 1 Cor. 10; Rom. 1:18–32) because he believes that the passion of desire exposes the body of Christ to pollution from the outside world, as Dale Martin has shown.[921] Thus, "impurity" (ἀκαθαρσία), immorality (πορνεία), and licentiousness (ἀσελγεία)" belong with "strife (ἔρις), jealousy (ζῆλος), and anger (θυμός)" to a general complex of behaviors that threaten the church, because they derive from the polluted cosmos opposed to God.[922] In any case, we should not abstract Paul's mention of the immorality of the Corinthians in 12:21 from the broader context of his defense of his financial conduct, and his expression of anxiety lest he be humiliated again, in our search for a rationale for Paul's citation of the rule of judicial evidence. We conclude that the Corinthians were not the ones whom Paul sought to assure of legal protection by citing the Deuteronomic statute.

Paul himself is the accused who seeks protection under the Deuteronomic rule from pernicious accusation by a malicious witness. Paul cites the rule not only in self-defense, but also as a warning to the Corinthians of the punishment that will fall upon those who are complicit in the wrong done to him, should the testimony of the single witness be shown to be false, in accordance with the Deuteronomic statute. This conclusion, which is almost without precedent in the history of interpretation,[923] has the considerable advantage of taking Paul's citation of the Deuteronomic rule literally, rather than metaphorically, on the assumption that Paul applies the rule in a manner consistent with its original purpose. More importantly, this interpretation offers a coherent account of the function of the scriptural citation of 13:1 in the context of Paul's exhortation to the Corinthian church in 12:14–13:4. Having concluded the foolish self-commendation that he was forced to provide (12:11–13), Paul turns to preparations for his impending third visit (12:14). A large obstacle looms in the way of the successful completion of Paul's collection project: suspicion of fraudulent conduct. Paul endeavors to remove

---

921 Dale B. Martin, *The Corinthian Body* (New Haven: Yale University Press, 1999) 163–97.
922 Martin, *The Corinthian Body*, 170–71, 178.
923 Tasker, *Second Epistle*, 186; Roetzel, *2 Corinthians*, 118: "The appeal to this text [Deut. 19:15]…guards against unsubstantiated accusations against Paul by disciples of the 'super apostles' or homegrown opposition that may have been building since Paul wrote 1 Corinthians."

this obstacle by four arguments: 1) an assurance of the purity of his motives, representing himself as a solicitous parent and a generous patron (12:14–15); 2) an appeal to the probity of Titus' conduct in the administration of the collection, designed to expose the absurdity of the charge of embezzlement (12:16–18); 3) an admonition to prevent the recurrence of the ugly conflict which erupted on the occasion of Paul's second visit, because it was destructive of community and humiliating to Paul (12:19–21); 4) a warning of the punitive consequences, if the charge against Paul should not be substantiated, in accordance with the scriptural rule of judicial evidence (13:1–4). Only a literal interpretation of Paul's scripture citation in 13:1, which recognizes that Paul himself is the individual whose protection is in view, takes sufficient account of the fact that Paul is defending himself against the charge of financial misconduct and anticipating the likely future effects of the charge throughout the exhortation of 12:14–13:4.

A full appreciation of the relevance of the Deuteronomic rule to the situation of the embattled apostle emerges only from examination of the context of the words that Paul quotes from Deuteronomy. The paragraph "on witnesses" (in Deut. 19:15–21) opens with a restatement of the prohibition of conviction on the testimony of a single witness. The point of the restatement is to expand a principle designed to protect the accused in capital cases (Num. 35:30; Deut. 17:6) into a general rule of judicial evidence.[924] Thus: "A single witness shall not suffice to witness against a person regarding any wrong (πᾶσα ἀδικία) or any transgression (πᾶν ἁμάρτημα) or any sin (πᾶσα ἁμαρτία) which he may commit" (Deut. 19:15, LXX). The focus of the legislation on the protection of the individual from pernicious accusation is clearly indicated by a proviso which immediately follows the restatement of the rule of "two or three witnesses": "If a malicious witness (μάρτυς ἄδικος) undertakes to accuse a person of impiety, then the two parties between whom there is a dispute shall appear before the Lord and before the priests and before the judges who may be

---

924 S. R. Driver, *A Critical and Exegetical Commentary on Deuteronomy* (New York: Charles Scribner's Sons, 1895) 235; Bernard M. Levinson, *Deuteronomy and the Hermeneutics of Legal Innovation* (Oxford: Oxford University Press, 1997) 43, 121; D. L. Christensen, *Deuteronomy 1:1–21:9* (Nashville: Thomas Nelson, 2001) 430–31. On Paul and Deuteronomy in general, see Brian Rosner, "Deuteronomy in 1 and 2 Corinthians" in *Deuteronomy in the New Testament: The New Testament and the Scriptures of Israel*, ed. M. J. J. Menken and S. Moyise (London: T & T Clark, 2007) ; David Lincicum, "Paul's Engagement with Deuteronomy," *Currents in Biblical Research* 7 (2008) 37–67.

in office in those days, and the judges shall make a thorough inquiry" (Deut. 19:16–18a, LXX). In the interest of retributive justice, the Deuteronomic code then stipulates that a punishment corresponding to the harm intended for the accused shall be inflicted upon the malicious witness, should his testimony be shown to be false: "And behold, if a malicious witness (μάρτυς ἄδικος) witnessed unjust things (ἄδικα) against his brother, then you shall do to him the evil thing which he sought to do against his brother, and you shall purge the evil from your midst" (Deut. 19:18b-19, LXX). The punishment of the malicious witness is meant to have a deterrent effect upon the congregation: "And the rest shall hear and shall be afraid, and a pernicious accusation such as this (τὸ ῥῆμα τὸ πονηρὸν τοῦτο) shall never again be made among you" (Deut. 19:20, LXX). The paragraph on witnesses closes with the admonition "Do not spare" (οὐ φείσεται) in punishing the malicious witness, strengthened by invocation of the *lex talionis:* "a life for a life, an eye for an eye, a tooth for a tooth, a hand for a hand, a foot for a foot" (Deut. 19:21, LXX).

Only when the full text of the Deuteronomic statute is before us can we appreciate the skillfulness of Paul's application of the rule to his present situation. Having been accused of embezzlement by someone in Corinth, and having left Corinth in disgrace, Paul now anticipates, with anxiety, what may happen when he returns. Paul seeks a prophylaxis against a repetition of the damaging charge, and finds it in the legal regulation of Deut. 19, a text that suits his purposes in every way. First, a citation of the Jewish scriptures was calculated to impress his Corinthian critics; we have found evidence in a number of passages (e.g., 10:7; 11:4) that the Christology of Paul's Corinthian critic was shaped by conceptions rooted in Hellenistic Judaism.[925] Second, and more importantly, citation of the Deuteronomic rule represents the charge against Paul as a "pernicious accusation" (τὸ ῥῆμα τὸ πονηρόν), and casts the one who brings the charge in the role of a "malicious witness" (μάρτυς ἄδικος). Thus Paul construes himself as the victim and his Corinthian critic as the culprit. Third, the invocation of the Deuteronomic rule entails a warning for anyone familiar with the context of the statute: the evil intended for the accused will fall back upon the accuser in the form of punishment, should the charge remain unsubstantiated, and should the witness be unjust. This implication of the Deuteronomic rule explains the connection between 2 Cor. 13:1 and 13:2, the transition from Paul's in-

---

925 Georgi, *Opponents of Paul,* 246–83.

vocation of the rule to his reminder of the punishment: anyone involved in false witness against Paul is hereby warned of the punishment that awaits him. Like the congregation of Israel, the Corinthians "shall hear and be afraid."

It is significant confirmation of our interpretation of 2 Cor. 13:1–2 that Paul's vocabulary echoes so fully the language of the Deuteronomic statute on witnesses, not only in the immediate context, but elsewhere in chs. 10–13, where Paul alludes to the charge of financial misconduct, and later in 2 Cor. 7, as Paul looks back upon the harm that someone intended to do to him. In 11:7, at Paul's first explicit mention of his financial relationship with the Corinthians, he asks whether, in his decision to preach the gospel to the Corinthians "free of charge," he had committed "a sin" (ἁμαρτία). Then in 12:13, when Paul recurs to his decision not to "burden" the Corinthians financially, he exclaims, ironically, "Forgive me this wrong (ἀδικία)!" Interpreters have puzzled over the incongruity of the terms ἁμαρτία and ἀδικία as descriptions of Paul's refusal of financial support from Corinth.[926] Now we discover that precisely these terms are used in the first sentence of the Deuteronomic statute: "A single witness shall not suffice to witness against a person regarding any wrong (ἀδικία) or any sin (ἁμαρτία) which he may commit" (Deut. 19:15). Similarly, the verb φείδομαι, by which Paul threatens the Corinthians with punishment in 13:2 (οὐ φείσομαι, "I will not spare"), is the same verb used in the scriptural admonition not to be lenient in punishing the malicious witness in Deut. 19:21 (οὐ φείσεται, "Do not spare"). It strains credulity to suggest that these verbal correspondences are accidental, in light of Paul's literal citation of Deut. 19:15. Most significant of all is Paul's use of the participle ἀδικήσας in 2 Cor. 7:12 to describe the one who had given offence; an adjective of this same term—namely, ἄδικος—is found in Deut. 19:16, 18 as the description of the malicious witness, μάρτυς ἄδικος, literally "an unjust witness."[927]

---

926 Windisch, *Der zweite Korintherbrief*, 334, 398: ἁμαρτία, like ἀδικία, "führt den Vorwurf *ad adsurdum*,...εἰρωνικῶς gesprochen"; Bultmann, *Der zweite Brief*, 207, 235, who also takes Paul's use of ἁμαρτία and ἀδικία, in reference to his refusal of financial support, as instances of "Ironie." See also Betz, *Der Apostel Paulus*, 101; Barrett, *Second Epistle*, 281; Furnish, *II Corinthians*, 491, 508; Thrall, *Second Epistle*, 2.682–83, 842.

927 In reference to ἀδικία in 12:13, commentators routinely note Paul's use of the cognate verb ἀδικεῖν in 7:12, but fail to connect this with Paul's citation of the Deuteronomic statute on the μάρτυς ἄδικος in 13:1: e.g., Barrett, *Second Epistle*, 323; Furnish, *II Corinthians*, 554; Thrall, *Second Epistle*, 2.842.

The implications of our exegesis of 2 Cor. 13:1–2 for an understanding of the affair of the wrongdoer are clear and significant.[928] First, the accusation of financial misconduct against Paul, made on the occasion of his "painful" second visit to Corinth, was the testimony of a single witness. The individual whom Paul describes as ὁ ἀδικήσας rose alone in the assembly of the Corinthian Christians to accuse Paul of embezzlement in connection with the collection. We may speculate about the reasons for his singularity on that occasion. Perhaps others did not share his suspicions, or did not share them to the same degree. Perhaps others were reluctant to offend the apostle, even if they harbored doubts about Paul's motives. Perhaps the *auctoritas* of the wrongdoer was so great that he was not perceived as needing a "second," and others could afford to remain silent. But Paul's citation of the rule of "two or three witnesses" is only effective as an argument, if one assumes that the charge against Paul was the testimony of a single witness. At the time of composition of 2 Cor. 10–13, the charge of embezzlement remained uncorroborated.

Second, the venue in which the charge was brought forward was a quasi-judicial proceeding in the Christian assembly, rather than a civic court. At last, we have an answer to the question that remained open in our examination of Paul's use of ἀδικεῖν in 2 Cor. 7:12. This conclusion is made more certain by the fact that no rule requiring two or more witnesses is known in Greek or Roman jurisprudence.[929] Before the court of Roman Corinth a person might well be convicted on the testimony of a single witness.[930] Paul's application of the Deuteronomic rule to his situation presumes a legal context in which the requirement of multiple witnesses would have operated. In citing the Deuteronomic rule, Paul is not only anticipating the proceedings that he may instigate when he returns to Corinth, he is also looking back upon what was said and done on the

---

928 Only Roetzel seems to grasp the implications of Paul's appeal to the Deuteronomic statute for the affair of the wrongdoer. In his comment on 13:1 (*2 Corinthians*, 118), Roetzel calls attention to Paul's anonymous references to "someone" (τις) in 10:7 and to "this one" (ὁ τοιοῦτος) in 10:10, and asks: "Might these indefinite allusions be linked to the offending brother who was later disciplined by the reconciled community and to whom Paul would then afford to be generous (2:5–11)?"
929 van Vliet, *No Single Testimony*, 11–25.
930 van Vliet, *No Single Testimony*, 15–18, citing Valerius Maximus, among others.

occasion of his second visit, as 13:2 makes clear.[931] Ironically, the church court before which Paul was accused was probably one such as Paul himself had instructed the Corinthians to establish in 1 Cor. 6:1–11.[932]

Third, it seems likely that Paul had already invoked the Deuteronomic statute on the occasion of his second visit to Corinth. This far-reaching conclusion is based squarely upon a literal construction of Paul's warning in 13:2. The perfect tense of the verb (προείρηκα) signifies a warning which Paul had issued on a previous occasion.[933] The circumstantial participle παρὼν τὸ δεύτερον specifies the second visit to Corinth as the occasion when the warning was given.[934] The ὅτι clause formulates the actual content of what Paul said on that occasion: ἐὰν ἔλθω εἰς τὸ πάλιν οὐ φείσομαι ("If I come again, I will not spare").[935] As observed above, Paul uses the wording of Deut. 19:21 (φείδομαι) in formulating his threat. Moreover, it is more natural to regard the uses of the Deuteronomic terms ἁμαρτία and ἀδικία in 11:7 and 12:13 as echoes of a rule that Paul had already invoked than as proleptic allusions to a scripture that he will cite only several paragraphs later. We may conclude that, on the occasion of Paul's second visit to Corinth, when he was accused by the wrongdoer of the crime of embezzlement before a judicial assembly of the Corinthian Christians, as the assembly threatened to degenerate into disorder, amidst "angry outbursts, slanders, whisperings, arrogant opinions" (12:20), Paul invoked the protection of the Deuteronomic rule: "By the mouth of two or three witnesses must every charge be substantiated!"

The conclusion that Paul invoked the Deuteronomic rule on the occasion of his second visit to Corinth has two further, dramatic implications. First, Paul's interposition of the Deuteronomic rule was evidently successful in suspending a verdict. This is a necessary inference from the obvious yet highly significant fact that Paul is still defending himself and his financial conduct throughout 2 Cor. 10–13 in the hope, however tenuous, that something may yet be "reckoned to his account" (λογίζε-

---

931 The phrase παρὼν τὸ δεύτερον in 13:2 refers to the second occasion when Paul was present in Corinth; see Plummer, *Second Epistle*, 373; Allo, *Saint Paul*, 336; Furnish, *II Corinthians*, 570; Thrall, *Second Epistle*, 2.876–77. For other references to Paul's second, painful visit, see 2 Cor. 2:1–4; 12:20–21.
932 Delcor, "The Courts of the Church of Corinth," 69–70, 75–76.
933 Furnish, *II Corinthians*, 569; Thrall, *Second Epistle*, 2.876.
934 Allo, *Saint Paul*, 336; Hughes, *Paul's Second Epistle*, 475; Furnish, *II Corinthians*, 570.
935 For ὅτι-*recitativum*, see BDF §470(1).

σθαι).⁹³⁶ Up to this point, the criticisms of Paul echoed in 10:1, 2, 10; 11:7, 16, etc. have been so acerbic, and Paul's response to the criticism has been so bellicose and hyperbolic (e.g., 10:1–6; 11:16–21), that there has been little reason to hope that the conflict between Paul and his opponents in Corinth might find a happy resolution. But now we have the first, clear indication that, by invoking the rule of judicial evidence, Paul managed to escape a decision that would have terminated his relationships and squandered their potential benefits for his collection effort.

Second, and more importantly, our exegesis of 2 Cor. 13:1–2 implies that, on the occasion of his second visit to Corinth, Paul declined to demand the punishment of his accuser, which the Deuteronomic statute authorized, when the testimony of the single witness remained uncorroborated. This conclusion results, once again, from a literal construction of 13:2b, attributing to the conjunction ὅτι a recitative function, and seeing in the phrase ἐὰν ἔλθω εἰς τὸ πάλιν οὐ φείσομαι a quotation of the actual words that Paul used on taking his departure from Corinth: "If I come again, I will not spare."⁹³⁷ That is to say, Paul postponed the punishment which the Deuteronomic statute permitted him to exact. This temporary amnesty was interpreted by Paul's critics as a sign of "weakness" (13:3–4). Paul, on the other hand, regarded it as a show of "leniency," as an act of "mercy."⁹³⁸ In any case, Paul's decision to refrain from inflicting punishment on the occasion of his "painful" visit left open the possibility of reconciliation with the "unjust witness."

Looking back over our exegesis of 2 Cor. 13:1–2 and its implications, one might well ask why this interpretation is without significant precedent in the history of scholarship, given its obvious advantages: a secure foundation upon a literal construction of Paul's words, a plausible assumption that Paul was cognizant of the purpose and context of the Deuteronomic rule, and a reasonable conclusion that Paul applied the Deuteronomic statute skillfully to his own situation. And why should a metaphorical construction of Paul's words in 13:1–2 have come to dominate the history of interpretation, in spite of its acknowledged difficulties

---

936 For λογίζεσθαι in 12:5 as commercial terminology, "reckon to someone's account," see BDAG 597 s.v. λογίζομαι 1.
937 That Paul is quoting what he said on the occasion of his second visit to Corinth in 13:2b, see Plummer, *Second Epistle*, 374; Hughes, *Paul's Second Epistle*, 476; Allo, *Saint Paul*, 337; Barrett, *Second Epistle*, 334; Furnish, *II Corinthians*, 570.
938 Walker, *Paul's Offer of Leniency*, 321, 324.

and highly artificial character, including the implausible assumption that Paul took no account of the purpose or context of the Deuteronomic statute, and the unwarranted conclusion that Paul used the citation loosely to clothe his own thoughts? One suspects that the explanation of this conundrum lies in a tendency that has surfaced repeatedly in the history of interpretation of 2 Corinthians: a resistance to the recognition that the apostle suffered a profound humiliation at the hands of a Corinthian convert. We have encountered this resistance in the unwillingness of some scholars to acknowledge that Paul himself is "the one wronged" (ὁ ἀδικηθείς) in 2 Cor. 7:12.[939] We met this resistance again in the colorless accounts of what Paul experienced on the occasion of his second visit to Corinth, accounts which fail to capture the depth of shame and degradation embodied in the verb ταπεινόω in 12:21.[940] Indeed, some scholars adduce as an argument in favor of the metaphorical interpretation of 2 Cor. 13:1 that it positions Paul not only as the witness against the Corinthians, but also as the judge *over* the Corinthians![941] The minority interpretation of the passage, which views the Corinthians as the ones whose (mis)conduct will be evaluated in accordance with the Deuteronomic statute, does not differ from the dominant, metaphorical interpretation, in respect to the role that it assigns to Paul: Paul functions as the "supreme judge" over the community, like the *mebaqqer*, as described in the *Damascus Document*.[942] So difficult is it for interpreters of the Pauline tradition to imagine an apostle who was not always in control! We submit that our interpretation of 2 Cor. 13:1–2 is the most congruent with the context of Paul's defense against charges of financial misconduct, and the most natural understanding of Paul's citation of the Deuteronomic statute. But our interpretation comes at the cost of the recognition that the apostle suffered a profound humiliation at the hands of one of his own converts. We should not be surprised if this cost were too high for many interpreters to bear.

We come, finally, to a passage in the peroration of the letter (13:5–10) where Paul appeals directly to the Corinthians for self-examination,

---

939 Beyschlag, "Christuspartei," 254; Pfleiderer, *Der Paulinismus*, 106–107; Krenkel, *Beiträge*, 305–307; Zahn, *Einleitung*, 248; Windisch, *Der zweite Korintherbrief*, 238–39; Allo, *Saint Paul*, 55–56, 62, 199.
940 E.g., Allo, *Saint Paul*, 61; Hyldahl, "Die Frage nach der literarischen Einheit," 304.
941 E.g., Bachmann, *Der zweite Brief*, 412; Allo, *Saint Paul*, 335; Furnish, *II Corinthians*, 575.
942 Delcor, "The Courts of the Church of Corinth," 69–70, 75–76.

in the hope of limiting their complicity in the affair of the wrongdoer and securing their eventual participation in the collection: "Test yourselves whether you are in the faith, examine yourselves (to see if you are). Or do you not recognize about yourselves that Jesus Christ is in you?—unless indeed you fail to stand the test. And I hope that you will come to know that we do not fail to stand the test. But we pray to God that you may not do anything wrong—not so that we may appear to be approved, but that you may do what is good, even if we may seem to be unapproved. For we cannot do anything against the truth, but only for the truth. For we rejoice when we are weak, but you are strong. This is what we pray for: your restoration" (13:5–9).[943]

The relationship of this admonition to Paul's defense of his apostleship, and more particularly, to his refutation of the charge of embezzlement, is obscured by the very general terms in which Paul frames his discourse. Paul's prayer for the Corinthians in vs. 7—that they may *do nothing wrong* (μὴ ποιῆσαι κακὸν μηδέν), but rather may *do what is good* (τὸ καλὸν ποιῆτε)—is so bland and colorless as to seem almost inapposite to the difficult situation in which Paul finds himself vis-a-vis the Corinthians.[944] In the paragraph as a whole, Paul restricts himself to the most general expressions—"test" (πειράζετε), "examine" (δοκιμάζετε), "in the faith" (ἐν τῇ πίστει), "unproved" (ἀδόκιμος), "approved" (δόκιμος), "the truth" (ἡ ἀλήθεια), "weak" (ἀσθενῶμεν), "strong" (δυνατοί); the result is a kind of paraphrase of what Paul has in mind, entirely vague and indefinite.[945] Doubtless, we encounter here, as Paul bends his efforts toward mending (κατάρτισις) his relationship with the Corinthians, the first instance of that elliptical style of discourse that dominates Paul's subsequent communications with Corinth, and especially the so-called "letter of reconciliation" in 2 Cor. 1:1–2:13; 7:5–16.[946] Paul's circumspect manner of speaking makes it difficult to determine to what he is referring concretely, and for what he is appealing specifically in this instance.

In addition, commentators have consistently detected ambiguity at a number of points in the paragraph, and have struggled with Paul's mean-

---

943 The translation modifies Barrett, *Second Epistle*, 337–39.
944 Windisch, *Der zweite Korintherbrief*, 422: "der Ausdruck 'nichts Böses tun' recht allgemein gehalten, matt, ja eigentlich wenig treffend ist."
945 Windisch, *Der zweite Korintherbrief*, 422.
946 On Paul's deliberate use of circumlocutions in 2 Cor. 1:1–2:13; 7:5–16, see Georgi, *Opponents of Paul*, 339–40, and ch. 4 below.

ing.⁹⁴⁷ What is the sense of the phrase "in the faith" (ἐν τῇ πίστει) in vs. 5a?⁹⁴⁸ What is the point of the rhetorical question and apparent qualification in vs. 5b? Is the genuineness of the Corinthians' Christianity really in doubt?⁹⁴⁹ What is the grammatical function of the pronoun ὑμᾶς in vs. 7a? Is ὑμᾶς the subject or the object of the infinitive ποιῆσαι κακόν? Are the Corinthians the potential agents of wrongdoing, or the objects of punishment?⁹⁵⁰ As we shall see, there is no reason to believe that the ambiguity of this passage is intentional; rather, ambiguity seems to be the unintended consequence of Paul's evasive manner of speaking by means of circumlocutions. Nevertheless, ambiguity is an undeniable aspect of the passage, and contributes to the lack of certainty regarding the point of Paul's appeal in this climactic paragraph.

Yet, a number of features of the passage before us make clear that this exhortation, for all its studied indefiniteness and resultant ambiguity, is of utmost importance to Paul, and indeed, is the rhetorical goal of the letter of 2 Cor. 10–13, as Hans Dieter Betz has argued,⁹⁵¹ so that we are obliged to seek a more precise understanding of what Paul has in mind. First, the imperatives with which the paragraph opens—πειράζετε and δοκιμάζετε—are the only hortatory imperatives in the letter of

---

947 On the ambiguity of the paragraph 2 Cor. 13:5–9, see Thrall, *Second Epistle*, 2.888–94.
948 Interpretations vary greatly: Lietzmann, *An die Korinther I/II*, 161: "die Stimmung des neuen pneumatischen Lebens"; Barrett, *Second Epistle*, 338: "For *in the faith*...Paul means, Consider whether you truly are Christians"; Bultmann, *Der zweite Brief*, 247: "Glaubensgehorsam"; Martin, *2 Corinthians*, 478: "a new existence as Christian." For other interpretations, see Thrall, *Second Epistle*, 2.888–89.
949 For the variety of interpretations, see Thrall, *Second Epistle*, 2.890–91. The best understanding is that of Windisch, *Der zweite Korintherbrief*, 420: "Wieder könnte Ἰησοῦς Χριστὸς ἐν ὑμῖν (wie vs. 3b) ein Zitat sein, eine Anspielung auf ein selbstsicheres Urteil, das die Korinther über sich selbst gefällt hatten: Ἰησοῦς Χριστὸς ἐν ἡμῖν. Paulus wollte sie dann daran erinnern, dass nach ihrem Selbstzeugnis J. Chr. in ihrer Mitte sei, also die Selbstprüfung gut ausfallen müsse."
950 The majority of interpreters take ὑμᾶς as the subject of the infinitival clause: e. g., Windisch, *Der zweite Korintherbrief*, 422; Barrett, *Second Epistle*, 339; Furnish, *II Corinthians*, 572; Martin, *2 Corinthians*, 451; Thrall, *Second Epistle*, 2.894. However, Lietzmann (*An die Korinther I/II*, 161) interprets ὑμᾶς as the object: Paul prays that God will not need to punish the Corinthians; but against this interpretation, see Bultmann, *Der zweite Brief*, 249.
951 Betz, *Der Apostel Paulus*, 134.

2 Cor. 10–13.⁹⁵² This fact alone indicates the earnestness of the appeal that follows. Second, the emphatic position of the reflexive pronoun ἑαυτούς ("yourselves") in vs. 5, and the emphatic uses of the personal pronouns ἡμεῖς ("we") and ὑμεῖς ("you") in vss. 6 and 7 reveal how much is at stake in terms of the personal relationship between Paul and his readers.⁹⁵³ Third, the irony which inhabits both the rhetorical question, ἢ οὐκ ἐπιγινώσκετε ἑαυτοὺς ὅτι Ἰησοῦς Χριστὸς ἐν ὑμῖν; ("Or do you not recognize about yourselves that Jesus Christ is in you?") and the appended qualification, εἰ μήτι ἀδόκιμοί ἐστε ("unless indeed you fail to stand the test!") reveals the rawness of Paul's unresolved emotions toward the Corinthians, at the same time that it rouses Paul's Corinthian readers to a response by way of reproach.⁹⁵⁴ Fourth, the repeated employment of litotes (ἡμεῖς οὐκ ἐσμὲν ἀδόκιμοι for ἡμεῖς ἐσμὲν δόκιμοι, and μὴ ποιεῖν κακόν for τὸ καλὸν ποιεῖν) evokes and enlarges the shadow of what Paul is too tactful to say. Finally, Paul's avowal in vs. 7b, that he is not concerned for his own reputation so long as the Corinthians are led to do what is good, taken at face value, shows how much Paul is willing to forgo—namely, the recognition of his apostolic office—in order to ensure that his readers will respond as he hopes.⁹⁵⁵ All of this makes it an urgent matter to discover, if possible, what Paul is asking the Corinthians to do.

We may begin with two conspicuous aspects of the language by which Paul summons the Corinthians to self-examination in 13:5, for these phrases evoke the context in which Paul hopes to influence the Corinthians' behavior. First, the δοκιμή-language that dominates the paragraph (δοκιμάζειν in vs. 5, ἀδόκιμος three times in vss. 5, 6 and 7, δόκι-

---

952 Windisch, *Der zweite Korintherbrief*, 419. The synonymity of the verbs emphasizes their importance; so, Wolff, *Der zweite Brief*, 263; Thrall, *Second Epistle*, 2.888.
953 Plummer, *Second Epistle*, 375: "The pronouns are very emphatic; 'It is your own selves that you must continually test,…your own selves that you must continually prove'"; Windisch, *Der zweite Korintherbrief*, 419–20; Bachmann, *Der zweite Brief*, 415; Furnish, *II Corinthians*, 572; Thrall, *Second Epistle*, 2.888.
954 On the irony in Paul's question and the reproach in Paul's qualification, see Allo, *Saint Paul*, 339; Martin, *2 Corinthians*, 479; Thrall, *Second Epistle*, 2.892. Bultmann (*Der zweite Brief*, 247) observes, rightly, that Paul intends to provoke the Corinthians to critical self-assessment. See Judith M. Gundry Volf, *Paul and Perseverance: Staying In and Falling Away* (Tübingen: Mohr Siebeck, 1990) 219.
955 Windisch, *Der zweite Korintherbrief*, 421; Barrett, *Second Epistle*, 339: "He is not concerned for his own reputation; let him appear to be wrong, rejected, dismissed from his apostolic office, so long as his converts in Corinth are doing what is good."

μος in vs. 7) establishes an unmistakable connection between the response that Paul seeks to elicit from the Corinthians as a result of their self-examination and the verdict that hangs over Paul in the quasi-judicial proceeding in which he finds himself involved. The summons, ἑαυτοὺς δοκιμάζετε ("make a critical examination of yourselves!") in vs. 5a echoes, most immediately, the statement ἐπεὶ δοκιμὴν ζητεῖτε τοῦ ἐν ἐμοὶ λαλοῦντος Χριστοῦ ("since you seek proof that Christ speaks in me") of vs. 3.[956] In accordance with its judicial usage, δοκιμάζειν is an examination of qualifications for rendering special services to a community.[957] Paul's point in applying this δοκιμή-language to the Corinthians is to suggest that the Corinthians' own authenticity is implicated in their verdict on his integrity.[958] The Corinthians cannot support the charge of the wrongdoer, and find Paul unqualified to administer the collection, without showing themselves to be unworthy.

Second, the respect in which the Corinthians are directed to "test" themselves—namely, whether they are "in the faith" (ἐν τῇ πίστει)—summons the reader back in thought to an earlier occasion when Paul seemed to suffer a lack of confidence, and challenges the Corinthians to re-examine their assumptions about Christian existence. Owing to its generality, the phrase ἐν τῇ πίστει has given rise to a variety of interpretations: "the Christian religion,"[959] "the apostolic teaching,"[960] faithful conduct or "obedience," etc.[961] Surely the clue to Paul's intention is found in the substance of the rhetorical question that follows, with which the phrase ἐν τῇ πίστει is synonymous: "Or do you not recognize about yourselves that *Jesus Christ is in you* (ὅτι Ἰησοῦς Χριστὸς ἐν ὑμῖν)."[962] To exist "in the

---

956 Windisch, *Der zweite Korintherbrief*, 419; Furnish, *II Corinthians*, 572; Thrall, *Second Epistle*, 2.889.
957 LSJ 442 s.v. δοκιμάζω 2a: Lysias 16.3; Plato *Leg.* 759D; Aristotle *Ath. pol.* 45.3; Moulton and Milligan, *Vocabulary of the Greek Testament*, 167 s.v. δοκιμάζω: "In the inscriptions indeed the verb is almost a *term. tech.* for passing as fit for a public office." So, e.g., *OGIS* 90.3.
958 Windisch, *Der zweite Korintherbrief*, 420 n.1, adducing Marcus Aurelius 10.37; Betz, *Der Apostel Paulus*, 89, 133–34, comparing Socrates' use of irony to bring his hearers to self-examination in Plato *Charm.* 158D; *Alc. maj.*1, 124C. See also Barrett, *Second Epistle*, 338; Bultmann, *Der zweite Brief*, 247; Furnish, *II Corinthians*, 572, 577, referring to Dio Chrysostom *Or.* 4.57.
959 Barrett, *Second Epistle*, 337.
960 BDAG 820 s.v. πίστις 3; Martin, *2 Corinthians*, 478.
961 Bultmann, *Der zweite Brief*, 247; Furnish, *II Corinthians*, 577.
962 Windisch, *Der zweite Korintherbrief*, 420; Wendland, *Die Briefe an die Korinther*, 257.

faith" is to experience the indwelling of Christ.⁹⁶³ The rhetorical question, introduced by the particles, ἢ οὐκ, anticipates that the Corinthians will answer in the affirmative.⁹⁶⁴ Paul knows that the Corinthians are confident that Christ is in them.⁹⁶⁵ Indeed, the conjunction ὅτι probably marks the clause that follows as a quotation, an allusion to the self-confident declaration of the Corinthians: "Jesus Christ is in us!" (Ἰησοῦς Χριστὸς ἐν ἡμῖν).⁹⁶⁶ Thus, the language of Paul's exhortation in 13:5 leads the Corinthians back in thought to an occasion, already evoked in 10:7, when someone at Corinth expressed his robust confidence of belonging to Christ, and questioned the evident lack of such confidence on the part of Paul.⁹⁶⁷ Now, at the close of the letter, Paul summons the Corinthians to re-examine their assumptions about belonging to Christ: perhaps the Corinthians have failed to comprehend that the one in whom the crucified Christ dwells will give the impression of being "weak in him" (13:4).

The substance of what Paul is urging the Corinthians to do is embodied in the prayer of 13:7, whose disclosure has the effect of an exhortation.⁹⁶⁸ The prayer, "that you may not do anything wrong" (μὴ ποιῆσαι ὑμᾶς κακὸν μηδέν), initially formulated as a litotes, is reformulated in a positive manner later in the sentence, "but that you may do what is good" (ἀλλ' ἵνα ὑμεῖς τὸ καλὸν ποιῆτε).⁹⁶⁹ As the balance and parallelism of the clauses indicates, ποιεῖν κακόν and καλὸν ποιεῖν are complementary statements of Paul's purpose for the Corinthians.⁹⁷⁰ But that purpose remains opaque to interpreters, because, as Thrall observes, "The content of

---

963 Windisch, *Der zweite Korintherbrief*, 420; Wendland, *Die Briefe an die Korinther*, 257: "Glaube ist die Wirklichkeit der Gegenwart Christi, ist das Leben Christi in dem Glaubenden, oder: Glaube heisst in Christus sein"; Barrett, *Second Epistle*, 338.
964 Furnish, *II Corinthians*, 572; Thrall, *Second Epistle*, 2.891–92.
965 Plummer, *Second Epistle*, 376; Windisch, *Der zweite Korintherbrief*, 420; Bultmann, *Der zweite Brief*, 247.
966 Windisch, *Der zweite Korintherbrief*, 420.
967 Watson, "Paul's Painful Letter," 345–46; Klauck, *2. Korintherbrief*, 79; Aejmelaeus, *Streit und Versöhnung*, 197; Mitchell, "The Corinthian Correspondence," 34. See above on 10:7.
968 Gordon P. Wiles, *Paul's Intercessory Prayers* (Cambridge: Cambridge University Press, 1974) 247; Furnish, *II Corinthians*, 578.
969 Windisch, *Der zweite Korintherbrief*, 422; Allo, *Saint Paul*, 339; Barrett, *Second Epistle*, 339; Bultmann, *Der zweite Brief*, 249; Thrall, *Second Epistle*, 2.894.
970 Barrett, *Second Epistle*, 339.

the κακόν is left vague."⁹⁷¹ Thus commentators content themselves with general observations, i.e., that "τὸ καλόν, 'what is good' (or 'noble,' or 'right,' etc.) was a cardinal theme of Hellenistic ethics."⁹⁷²

But the veneer of generality begins to dissolve, and Paul's purpose for the Corinthians begins to show through, when one situates the language of Paul's exhortation in the context of his defense against the charge of embezzlement brought by the wrongdoer. For the expression "to do wrong" or "to do harm," usually κακῶς ποιεῖν, has an established, if not to say technical usage in ancient discussions of enmity, just as the expression "to do good," εὖ ποιεῖν, belongs to the technical language of benefaction.⁹⁷³ The code of ancient social life was embodied in the maxim: "do good to friends and harm to enemies," τοὺς φίλους εὖ ποιεῖν καὶ τοὺς ἐχθροὺς κακῶς.⁹⁷⁴ Philosophers and moralists protested against the reduction of justice involved in this precept, but were forced to concede that it represented traditional morality. Thus, Xenophon's Socrates attributes to Critobulus the popular opinion "that a man's virtue consists in surpassing his friends in doing good and his enemies in doing harm" (ὅτι ἀνδρὸς ἀρετὴν εἶναι νικᾶν τοὺς μὲν φίλους εὖ ποιοῦντα, τοὺς δ' ἐχθροὺς κακῶς).⁹⁷⁵ In his paradoxical essay on "How to Profit by One's Enemies," Plutarch acknowledges that what most people expect is "to suffer ill-treatment at the hands of their enemies" (τὸ πάσχειν ὑπὸ τῶν ἐχθρῶν κακῶς), but regard it as "honorable (καλόν) to do a good turn to a friend" (φίλον τὸ εὖ ποιεῖν).⁹⁷⁶ The latter sentiment is already found in Aristotle's *Nicomachean Ethics* in the context of discussions of the claims of friendship and liberality in giving. Aristotle states that "it is honorable (καλόν) to render a service (τὸ εὖ ποιεῖν) without seeking one in return,"⁹⁷⁷ and

---

971 Thrall, *Second Epistle*, 2.894.
972 Furnish, *II Corinthians*, 573.
973 Solon fr. 13.5; Lysias 9.20; Xenophon *Mem.* 2.6.35; *Cyr.* 1.6.28; Plato *Resp.* 331E; Aristotle *Rhet.* 1.9.24; 2.5.3–8; Plutarch *Mor.* 538E. See the discussion in Lionel Pearson, *Popular Ethics in Ancient Greece* (Stanford: Stanford University Press, 1962) 15–18, 86–89; Dover, *Greek Popular Morality*, 180–84; Marshall, *Enmity in Corinth*, 35–37, 49–51; Mary Whitlock Blundell, *Helping Friends and Harming Enemies. A Study in Sophocles and Greek Ethics* (Cambridge: Cambridge University Press, 1991) 26–59.
974 Polemarchus' account of the popular code of morality in Plato *Resp.* 331E.
975 Xenophon *Mem.* 2.6.35.
976 Plutarch *Mor.* 86D-E, 90F.
977 Aristotle *Eth. nic.* 8.13.8; cf. Pakaluk, *Aristotle. Nicomachean Ethics Books VIII and IX*, 136.

that "the liberal man therefore will give for the nobility (τὸ καλόν) of giving."⁹⁷⁸

Thus the terms by which Paul communicates his wishes to the Corinthians, for all their apparent vagueness and ambiguity, carry a specific meaning in the context of Paul's conflict with an influential member of the Corinthian church. By asking the Corinthians "not to do anything wrong" (μὴ ποιῆσαι κακὸν μηδέν), Paul is appealing to his readers to limit their involvement in the enmity of the wrongdoer. The code of friendship required that one share one's friend's enemies, as Plutarch acknowledges at the beginning of his essay: "For our very friendships, if nothing else, involve us in enmities."⁹⁷⁹ Paul foresees the danger that the Corinthians may seek to do him "harm" (κακόν) because he is now perceived to be the enemy of their influential friend. What such "harm" might entail is vividly described in Plutarch's essay. The least one could expect, under the code of κακῶς ποιεῖν, was "to be reviled and to hear oneself ill spoken of by one's enemies" (λοιδορεῖσθαι καὶ κακῶς ἀκούειν αὐτὸν ὑπὸ τῶν ἐχθρῶν).⁹⁸⁰ But Plutarch also knows of cases where "the most harmful element in enmity" was realized: where the enemy "plays the detective on your actions and digs his way into your plans and searches them through and through, using every friend and servant and acquaintance as well, so far as possible," in order to expose "the infirmities, meannesses, and untoward experiences of life."⁹⁸¹ In Paul's case, anxiety surrounded his plans for the collection. Paul seeks to forestall the possibility that the Corinthians will undermine any prospect of success that the collection might have, on account of perceived obligations of friendship with the wrongdoer. At the same time, Paul expresses the hope that the Corinthians will do what is good and honorable, by showing liberality in giving to the collection. The language of ποιεῖν κακόν and καλὸν ποιεῖν was ideally suited to Paul's purposes, since it carried a specific meaning in the context of friendship and enmity, while at the same time it preserved a tactful generality that fostered reconciliation.

We may add a coda to our analysis of Paul's purpose for the Corinthians, as expressed in 13:5–10, by highlighting an additional resonance that Paul's reference to the Corinthians' πίστις in vs. 5a would have had

---

978 Aristotle *Eth. nic.* 4.1.12; cf. C. C. W. Taylor, *Aristotle. Nicomachean Ethics Books II–IV* (Oxford: Clarendon Press, 2006) 206–207.
979 Plutarch *Mor.* 86C.
980 Plutarch *Mor.* 89B.
981 Plutarch *Mor.* 87C-D.

for readers sensitive to the vocabulary of friendship. In Greco-Roman culture, πίστις (Latin *fides*) was a key relational term designating the "fidelity" required of true friendship.⁹⁸² πίστις/*fides* was understood to be the basis of friendship;⁹⁸³ without πίστις no stable friendship was possible.⁹⁸⁴ Of course, the πίστις in respect to which Paul interrogates the Corinthians is that special "faithfulness" which characterizes life in Christ. But in the context of Paul's conflict with an influential Corinthian, and the resulting enmity, it seems likely that Paul's readers would have heard some reference to the "faithfulness" that should characterize their relationships, in the exhortation ἑαυτοὺς πειράζετε εἰ ἐστὲ ἐν τῇ πίστει (13:5). Paul's challenge to the Corinthians' πίστις implies that they have not shown him the "fidelity" that is his due as the founder of the community.⁹⁸⁵ In his discourse "On Trust" (Περὶ πιστέως), Dio Chrysostom adduces examples of notable personages of history who devoted themselves to the public good, and then were treated with ingratitude by their fellow citizens, or were ruined by unjust accusation: "For example, they say that Pericles was convicted of embezzlement in an Athenian court, the noblest and best champion the city ever had."⁹⁸⁶ In the companion discourse "On Distrust" (Περὶ ἀπιστίας), Dio concludes that one should not put trust in the ordinary run of men, because "they cannot refrain from doing wrong (κακῶς ποιεῖν) for whatever reason."⁹⁸⁷

We may now summarize the results of our exegesis of 2 Cor. 10–13 for knowledge of the individual whom Paul elsewhere describes as ὁ ἀδικήσας (2 Cor. 7:12). In retrospect, we have learned an astonishing amount, more than even the most prescient researcher might have supposed! For this wealth of information, we have the circumstances to thank—the fact that Paul wrote 2 Cor. 10–13 at the height of the con-

---

982 F. Dirlmeier, *ΦΙΛΟΣ und ΦΙΛΙΑ im vorhellenistischen Griechentum* (Diss. Munich, 1931); J. Taillardat, "ΦΙΛΟΤΗΣ, ΠΙΣΤΙΣ, und Foedus," *Révue des Études Grecques* 95 (1982) 1–14; Marshall, *Enmity in Corinth*, 21–23; Konstan, *Friendship in the Classical World*, 51, 109, 130; Lynette G. Mitchell, *Greeks Bearing Gifts: The Public Use of Private Relationships in the Greek World* (Cambridge: Cambridge University Press, 2002) 5.
983 Theognis 74, 529–30; Aristotle *Eth. nic.* 8.3.8–9; Cicero *Rosc. Amer.* 111.
984 Aristotle *Eth. eud.* 7.2.40; Cicero *Amic.* 18.65; Seneca *Quomodo amicitia continenda sit* fr. 1.
985 That the Corinthians' faith is at stake in their judgment on Paul, see already John Chrysostom *PG* 61, col. 601 (*NPNF* XII, p.414); similarly, Hughes, *Paul's Second Epistle*, 480–81; cf. Thrall, *Second Epistle*, 2.890–91.
986 Dio Chrysostom *Or.* 73.5.
987 Dio Chrysostom *Or.* 74.10–11.

flict—and Paul's own, remarkable capacity for self-disclosure.[988] We may divide what we have learned into three categories: the nature of the offence, the character of the wrongdoer, and the relationship of the wrongdoer to Paul, Paul's rivals, and other Christians at Corinth.

The most conspicuous gain in our knowledge has come in the area of the offence against Paul. We had previously found reason to believe that the wrong involved Paul and a Corinthian Christian in a legal dispute, and that a fraudulent use of money was somehow a factor—this on the basis of Paul's use of the verb ἀδικεῖν/ἀδικεῖσθαι in 2 Cor. 7:12.[989] Now we have discovered something more precise and definite: the wrong consisted in a public accusation of embezzlement in connection with the collection. This conclusion, which is as certain as any that exegesis can provide, follows from the repeated use of the verb πλεονεκτεῖν ("to defraud") to describe Paul's conduct in 12:17–18, and from the characterization of Paul as "crafty" (πανοῦργος) and a perpetrator of "deceit" (δόλος) in 12:16. Analysis of these verses reveals that Paul is echoing the wording of an accusation that was actually brought against him—an inference that is not widely disputed by scholars.[990] Paul's reference to the mission of Titus and "the brother" in 12:18 establishes, beyond a reasonable doubt, that the charge of embezzlement arose in connection with the collection work among the Corinthians.

Analysis of the three paragraphs which follow Paul's rebuttal of the charge in 12:16–18 has added rich detail to our understanding of the wrong that was done to Paul on the occasion of his second visit to Corinth. Exegesis of 13:1–2, based upon a literal construction of Paul's citation of the Deuteronomic rule, produced three highly significant results: the accusation of financial misconduct was "the testimony of a single witness"; the charge of embezzlement was brought forward in a quasi-judicial proceeding of the Christian church; Paul invoked the Deuteronomic statute for his own protection. We have argued that the scene which followed the accusation of embezzlement is painfully recollected by Paul in 12:20: the assembly dissolved in "angry outbursts, slanders,

---

988 On Paul's remarkable capacity for self-disclosure, see Eduard Schwartz's sketch of Paul in his *Characterköpfe aus der antiken Literatur* (Berlin: Weidmann, 1912).
989 See above on 7:12.
990 Plummer, *Second Epistle*, 363; Windisch, *Der zweite Korintherbrief*, 402–403; Hughes, *Paul's Second Epistle*, 464; Barrett, *Second Epistle*, 324; Bultmann, *Der zweite Brief*, 237; Furnish, *II Corinthians*, 557, 559, 565; Martin, *2 Corinthians*, 443, 446; Barnett, *Second Epistle*, 586–87; Thrall, *Second Epistle*, 2.850–51, 853, 856.

whisperings, arrogant opinions, disorders." That Paul regarded the Corinthians' behavior on this occasion as evidence of complicity in the attack of the wrongdoer, may be inferred from his reference to the Corinthians' "repentance" in 2 Cor. 7:8–12. Yet, the worst outcome was avoided: the charge of embezzlement remained uncorroborated; otherwise, we have argued, the invocation of the Deuteronomic rule, with an eye to his impending visit, would have had no point; and Paul, for his part, postponed the punishment which the Deuteronomic statute permitted him to exact, in the hope for repentance and reconciliation. Paul's concluding exhortation to the Corinthians in 13:5–10 employs the established vocabulary of friendship, in order to urge the Corinthians to renounce the bond of enmity and render a magnanimous service which will restore their relationship.

With respect to the person and character of the wrongdoer, our analysis of 2 Cor. 10–13 has brought a dramatic increase in knowledge. In 2 Cor. 1–2 and 7, Paul's circumspection was so complete that we were able to draw only a single inference: the wrongdoer was a person of status and influence, capable of doing harm with impunity, like Aristotle's businessman,[991] and capable of causing "pain" to an entire community.[992] But now, from the polemic of 2 Cor. 10–13, there emerges a clear, if rudimentary portrait of the man who made himself the critic of Paul at Corinth. The wrongdoer was indeed a person of high social status. The terms by which he evaluates Paul's behavior and person (e.g. ταπεινός) belong to the value lexicon of the upper class and give expression to his sense of superiority.[993] The wrongdoer looks down upon Paul from a considerable social distance. The aesthetic standards embodied in the only explicit quotation attributed to Paul's critic (in 10:10) are those of the educated elite of the early Empire, as evidenced by the essays of Greek literary critics.[994] The wrongdoer evidently admired Paul's rival for the professionalism of his oratory, and disparaged Paul for defects in his delivery (11:5–6; 10:10b). Several aspects of the criticism against which Paul must defend himself suggest that the wrongdoer was himself the beneficiary of a rhetorical education, such as was customary for men of his

---

991 Aristotle *Rhet.* 1.12.2.
992 See above on 2 Cor. 2:5, pp. 29–31, 34–35.
993 See above on 2 Cor. 10:1, pp. 67–72.
994 Dionysius of Halicarnassus *Comp.* 11; *Dem.* 21, 22, 34; *Thuc.* 23, 55; *Pomp* 3; Demetrius *Eloc.* 240–304; Longinus *Subl.* 34.

class.⁹⁹⁵ To the most interesting features of the profile of the wrongdoer belongs an "eristic tendency": at a number of points (10:1, 2, 10), exegesis supplied evidence that Paul's own vocabulary has been turned against him (e.g. πραΰτης, κατὰ σάρκα), in some cases involving mockery and imitation (ἀσθενής, ἐξουθενημένος).⁹⁹⁶ The wrongdoer is skilled in verbal combat, and his wit is characterized by acerbity. Yet, we should not overlook the complementary evidence of a certain dignity in the character of Paul's critic. He upholds standards of behavior which he judges that Paul has violated by his personal demeanor (10:1; 11:7) and his financial misconduct (10:2; 12:16–18).⁹⁹⁷ He is critical of Paul for transgressing the norms of friendship by his refusal of a gift (11:7–11).⁹⁹⁸ His reaction against Paul's "foolishness" (11:1, 16) suggests that he sought to govern his own life by reason, in accordance with Stoic principles.⁹⁹⁹ In sum, exegesis of 2 Cor. 10–13 has revealed that Paul's Corinthian adversary was a person of high status, with aristocratic values and cultured tastes. We may concede that there is nothing unique in this profile among men of a certain class in the early Empire. The same values and tastes are presupposed in the friends to whom Plutarch addresses his essays.¹⁰⁰⁰

It is in respect to the identity of the wrongdoer *as a Christian*, and in his relationships to other Christians—Paul, other missionaries, and other Christians at Corinth—that exegesis of 2 Cor. 10–13 has produced the most interesting results. Analysis of 10:7 revealed that Paul's principal opponent in the church at Corinth was possessed of a strong consciousness of "belonging to Christ." At a later point in the letter (11:4), Paul discloses that his Corinthian critic preferred the Christology of an un-

---

995 See above on 2 Cor. 10:10, pp. 102–121. On the education available to the provincial elite in Roman Corinth, see Robert S. Dutch, *The Educated Elite in 1 Corinthians: Education and Community Conflict in Graeco-Roman Context* (London: T & T Clark, 2005) 58–92, 168–212. See in general, Yun Lee Too, *Education in Greek and Roman Antiquity* (Leiden: Brill, 2001).
996 See above on 2 Cor. 10:1, 2, 10, pp. 77–79, 80–84, 118–19, 121.
997 See above on 2 Cor. 10:2; 12:16–18, pp. 80–84, 168–81.
998 See above on 2 Cor. 11:7–11, pp. 73–80, 133–34.
999 See above on 2 Cor. 11:16, pp. 154–63.
1000 Like the Roman friends Sextius Sulla and C. Minicius Fundanus who are the dialogue partners in *De cohibenda ira*. On these friends, see W. C. Helmbold, *Plutarch. Moralia VI*, LCL (Cambridge, MA: Harvard University Press, 1931) 92–93; C. P. Jones, *Plutarch and Rome* (Oxford: Oxford University Press, 1971) 57–58, 60. On the intellectual milieu of Plutarch's addressees and readers in general, see Robert Lamberton, *Plutarch* (New Haven: Yale University Press, 2001) 1–59.

named evangelist who has come to Corinth preaching "another Jesus" and "a different gospel." We have sought to discover how this understanding of Christ would have differed from Paul's proclamation of "Christ crucified," and have proposed that the answer is to be found in the early Christian kerygma and in Jewish texts such as the *Psalms of Solomon*, where the Messiah is presented as the longed-for redeemer who confers upon those who belong to him wisdom, righteousness, and joy.[1001] Empowered by this sense of "belonging to Christ," Paul's Corinthian critic was genuinely disconcerted by Paul's novel emphasis upon "Christ crucified," and dismayed by the consequence that Paul drew from his "cross gospel"—namely, that God has chosen the weak and the foolish and the dishonored (1 Cor. 1:26–28). However one may assess our proposal regarding the Christology of Paul's adversary, the point that should not be missed, for purposes of reconstruction of the wrongdoer's identity, is that Paul's critic at Corinth was by no means the theological epigone he is represented as being in New Testament scholarship, but was possessed of a fervent Christ-consciousness, and was unwilling to relinquish, without a struggle, the Christology that had shaped his new identity. Indeed, we may suggest that it was theological conviction, more than aesthetic sensibility, that dictated the wrongdoer's preference for the proclamation of Paul's rival, whoever he was, and that motivated the offer of friendship and financial support to this missionary, of which Paul complains so bitterly in 2 Cor. 11:20–21.

We argued above that the wrongdoer was responsible for engendering the comparison between Paul and his rivals that makes up the central section of the letter of 2 Cor. 10–13, by invoking certain missionaries, and one in particular (11:4), as the standard by which Paul must measure himself.[1002] In light of the strong theological convictions manifest in 10:7 and elsewhere, we should probably assume that the wrongdoer's attempt to provoke a comparison between Paul and other missionaries was not motivated invidiously, but was prompted by a sincere desire to understand the differences between the evangelists who were rivals for his interest.

Finally, at a number of points we have found evidence of the overbearing influence of a single individual upon the Corinthian church: it is presupposed in the structure of Paul's argument in 10:1–11, which pursues a centripetal course through a hostile community towards an

---

1001 *Pss. Sol.* 17–18. See above on 2 Cor. 10:7, pp. 84–98.
1002 See above on 2 Cor. 11:1–12:13, pp. 124–164.

arch-critic who leads the revolt; it comes to expression in the seamless alternation between the second person plural pronouns and verb forms which designate all of the Corinthian readers, and the singular pronouns τις and τοιοῦτος which denote an individual (e.g., 10:7; 11:16). We have hypothesized that the basis of the wrongdoer's influence was his elevated social status, his role as the patron of the Christian groups at Corinth.[1003] This hypothesis is consistent with the results of our exegesis of 2 Cor. 2:5–11, which found Paul exhibiting an extraordinary degree of caution in counseling the forgiveness of the one who had caused him grief.[1004] In view of the strong sense of "belonging to Christ" that comes to expression in 10:7, and the preference for a particular Christology reflected in 11:4, perhaps we should also consider that the wrongdoer's influence rested partly upon his ability to articulate his theological convictions.

Precisely because our exegetical study of 2 Cor. 10–13 has been so unexpectedly productive, it seems prudent to remind readers of the principles which have guided our investigation. In widening the textual basis of our study beyond 2 Cor. 1–2 and 7, we have embraced the hypothesis that 2 Cor. 10–13 is to be identified with the "letter of tears" mentioned by Paul in 2 Cor. 2:3–4.[1005] A number of our inferences would have seemed less valid, if this hypothesis had not been operative. But, for many interpreters of 2 Corinthians since Adolf Hausrath, the proposal that 2 Cor. 10–13 is to be identified with Paul's "letter of tears" has offered the most plausible explanation of the numerous cross-references within our so-called 2 Corinthians.[1006] This hypothesis undergirded Günther Bornkamm's reconstruction of the "pre-history" of 2 Corinthians.[1007] And this hypothesis remains crucial for Margaret Mitchell's recent attempt at an "interpretive intertwining of literary and historical" data.[1008]

1003 See above on 2 Cor. 10:1; 11:7–21, pp. 67–80.
1004 See above on 2 Cor. 2:8, 11, pp. 40–51.
1005 See above on 2 Cor. 10–13.
1006 Hausrath, *Der Vier-Capitel-Brief des Paulus*; Kennedy, *The Second and Third Epistles*; Lake, *The Earlier Epistles*, 151–60; Weiss, *Primitive Christianity*, 1.341–57; Georgi, *Opponents of Paul*, 9–14; Vielhauer, *Geschichte der urchristlichen Literatur*, 150–55; Betz, *2 Corinthians 8 and 9*, 141–44; among others.
1007 Bornkamm, *Vorgeschichte*, 7–36; repr. in idem, *Gesammelte Aufsätze*, vol. 4 = *Geschichte und Glaube. Zweiter Teil* (Munich: Kaiser, 1971) 162–90, with a *Nachtrag* on pp. 190–94.
1008 Mitchell, "Paul's Letters to Corinth," 307–38.

Second, we have limited our search for additional information about the wrongdoer to passages in 2 Cor. 10–13 where the use of singular pronouns or third-person singular verb-forms gives rise to the possibility that a specific individual is intended. Even so, we have not assumed that all such usages refer to the wrongdoer. It is naturally possible that Paul is expressing a generalization in this way—what "anyone" might think or say of him under the circumstances. Consequently, each case has been evaluated independently. In some instances, e. g., 10:18, it is clear that Paul is speaking generally, almost proverbially, though not without a polemical application to his rivals.[1009] In other instances, e. g., 11:4 and 11:20, content and context indicate that a singular participle or a singular pronoun denotes a rival apostle, rather than a local Corinthian. But in five passages—10:7, 10:10, 10:11, 11:16, and 12:6—we found evidence that a singular pronoun or singular verb-form denotes a specific individual, and that this individual is a Corinthian. The evidence which informed this conclusion consisted of: observations from the context, text-linguistic markers (ὅτι, φησίν), personalizing and subjective features (πέποιθεν ἑαυτῷ, ἐφ' ἑαυτοῦ), and a consistent vocabulary (e. g., λογίζεσθαι). More cautious interpreters might insist that some of these features could be reconciled with the supposition that Paul is speaking in generalities.[1010] Yet even the most stubborn skeptic would have to concede that our interpretation of these texts is possible. In light of the fact that a specific individual is clearly intended in 2 Cor. 2 and 7, where Paul speaks of "someone" (τις) who has caused pain, and of "such a one" (ὁ τοιοῦτος) who has been punished, it would seem reasonable to take Paul's uses of these pronouns in 2 Cor. 10–13 as references to the same individual, particularly in the five passages mentioned, where features of the text and context make clear that a specific individual is intended, and that this individual is a Corinthian. In taking Paul's uses of τις and τοιοῦτος in 2 Cor. 10:7 and 10:11 as references to the individual of whom Paul speaks in 2 Cor. 2:5–11, we stand in a tradition of interpretation which goes back to Johannes Weiss, and which includes among its contemporary representatives Francis Watson and Margaret Mitchell.[1011]

1009 See above on 2 Cor. 10:18, p. 124 n. 544.
1010 E.g., Furnish, *II Corinthians*, 466, 468, 469; Wolff, *Der zweite Brief*, 197, 199; Barnett, *Second Epistle*, 453–55, 461, 475, 477.
1011 Watson, "Paul's Painful Letter," 345–46; Mitchell, "The Corinthian Correspondence and the Birth of Pauline Hermeneutics," 34. See also Klauck, *2. Korintherbrief*, 79; Aejmelaeus, *Streit und Versöhnung*, 197.

2 Cor. 2:14–6:13; 7:2–4

We have hitherto left out of account a major section of the writing known to us as 2 Corinthians, namely 2:14–7:4. In the preface we have given our reasons for subscribing to the hypothesis, which goes back to Anton Halmel, that 2 Cor. 2:14–6:13, with 7:2–4, originally constituted an independent letter.[1012] We have also indicated why, in our view, the letter of 2 Cor. 2:14–6:13; 7:2–4 is best placed *after* 2 Cor. 10–13 in the sequence of Paul's correspondence with Corinth.[1013] At this point, it suffices to observe that there are no passages in 2 Cor. 2:14–6:13; 7:2–4 where a singular pronoun or singular verb-form suggests that Paul might be referring to a specific individual. Throughout this profound writing, in which Paul seeks to explain to the Corinthians the theological basis of his ministry, he addresses his readers as a whole, employing second person plural pronouns.[1014] Where Paul formulates a generalization, he does so unambiguously.

In 4:2, for example, Paul assures his readers: "But we have renounced the shameful things that one hides, neither conducting ourselves craftily (μὴ περιπατοῦντες ἐν πανουργίᾳ), nor falsifying (μηδὲ δολοῦντες) the word of God, but by a full disclosure of the truth (we are) recommending ourselves to every human conscience (πρὸς πᾶσαν συνείδησιν ἀνθρώπων) in the sight of God."[1015] Here it is clear that Paul represents himself to every potential reader, designated by the universalizing expression πᾶσα συνείδησις ἀνθρώπων (literally, "every conscience of human beings").[1016] The emphatic generalization is all the more interesting, in light of the fact that the vocabulary by which Paul assures his readers of his integrity

---

[1012] Anton Halmel, *Der Vierkapitelbrief im zweiten Korintherbrief des Apostel Paulus* (Essen: Baedeker, 1894); see the review of Halmel by Johannes Weiss in *ThLZ* 19 (1894) 513–14. Halmel subsequently revised his hypothesis, so that 2 Cor. 7:2–4 was recognized to be the original conclusion of the letter-fragment 2:14–6:13: idem, *Der zweite Korintherbrief des Apostel Paulus* (Halle: Niemeyer, 1904).
[1013] Following the cross-references identified by Kennedy, *The Second and Third Epistles*; idem, "The Problem of Second Corinthians," 340–67. Cf. Taylor, "The Composition and Chronology of Second Corinthians," 67–87.
[1014] E.g., 2 Cor. 3:1, 2; 5:12, 13; 7:4.
[1015] Compare the translations of Furnish, *II Corinthians*, 202; Thrall, *Second Epistle*, 1.297.
[1016] Note that πᾶσαν is brought forward for emphasis. Cf. Barrett, *Second Epistle*, 129; Furnish, *II Corinthians*, 219; Thrall, *Second Epistle*, 1.112–113: "*every kind* of conscience among men."

echoes the accusation against Paul in 12:16—that he is "crafty" (πανοῦργος) and practices "deceit" (δόλος).[1017]

Even more intriguing is the jubilant declaration which climaxes Paul's exposition of the theological basis of his ministry in 5:17. Drawing the consequences for Christian existence of his paradoxical understanding of the death of Christ,[1018] Paul exclaims: "So if anyone is in Christ (ὥστε εἴ τις ἐν Χριστῷ), there is a new creation: everything old has passed away; behold, everything has become new!" In this case, the gnomic form of the statement makes clear that a generalization is intended,[1019] even though Paul employs the indefinite pronoun τις, which designates a specific individual in 2:5, 10:7, etc. Although Paul's formulation in 5:17 is clearly general, it is impossible not to hear a resonance in relation to a particular individual, since the language of Paul's affirmation recalls the confident boast of "someone" (τις) to be "of Christ" (Χριστοῦ εἶναι) in 10:7. This resonance is augmented by the preceding verse, 5:16, which is best regarded as a parallel result-sentence with 5:17: "So from now on we regard no one according to human standards (ὥστε ἡμεῖς ἀπὸ τοῦ νῦν οὐδένα οἴδαμεν κατὰ σάρκα), etc."[1020] We recall that Paul and his coworkers had been reproached with acting "according to human standards" (κατὰ σάρκα) in 10:2.[1021] The anomalous placement of the negative result-sentence of 5:16 *before* the positive (5:17) finds its explanation in the history of the conflict which the letter of 2 Cor. 10–13 so eloquently documents.[1022]

The challenge for interpreters of 2 Cor. 2:14–6:13; 7:2–4 is to explain how such general statements as 4:2, and even such "universal" theological affirmations as 5:17, relate to and arise out of the history of Paul's conflict with the church at Corinth, and with one individual in particular. The most satisfying interpretation will succeed in mediating between the

---

1017 Bultmann, *Der zweite Brief,* 103: "μὴ περιπατοῦντες ἐν πανουργίᾳ: wie 12:18. μηδὲ δολοῦντες τὸν λόγον τοῦ θεοῦ: Verteidigung degenüber dem Vorwurf des δόλος 12:16."
1018 For 5:17 as a consequence drawn from 5:16, see Windisch, *Der zweite Korintherbrief,* 189; Barrett, *Second Epistle,* 173.
1019 Note other instances of Paul's use of this gnomic form in 1 Cor. 3:12, 17; 8:3; 11:16; 14:37, 38; 16:22; Gal. 1:9; 6:3; Rom. 8:9. Cf. Furnish, *II Corinthians,* 314.
1020 Plummer, *Second Epistle,* 179; Lietzmann, *An die Korinther I/II,* 126; Allo, *Saint Paul,* 167; Bultmann, *Der zweite Brief,* 158–59; Furnish, *II Corinthians,* 332; Thrall, *Second Epistle,* 1.424.
1021 See above on 2 Cor. 10:2, pp. 80–84. Cf. Thrall, *Second Epistle,* 1.413–14.
1022 Windisch, *Der zweite Korintherbrief,* 189; Allo, *Saint Paul,* 167.

gritty particulars of Paul's personal relationships and his boldest theological generalizations, even when, as in 5:17, the generalizations clothe themselves in the soaring, eschatological hope of Deutero-Isaiah for a "new creation."[1023] We must postpone this attempt until the final chapter of our study, when we have all of the relevant data at our disposal. Even if the letter of 2 Cor. 2:14–6:13; 7:2–4 contains no references to a particular individual, we shall discover that it played an important role in creating an openness for reconciliation with the wrongdoer.

With all that we have learned about the wrongdoer from exegesis of 2 Corinthians, we are still no closer to being able to identify this individual with any of the persons known to us from Paul's Corinthian correspondence. In this respect, the traditional identification of the wrongdoer with the incestuous man of 1 Cor. 5 still offers the greater intellectual satisfaction! Thus the time has come to confront squarely the aspect of the apostle's rhetoric which has created a barrier to identification. The problem may be stated simply: at no point in his Corinthian correspondence does Paul name his opponents, but consistently resorts to periphrastic constructions.[1024] No names are mentioned at the height of the conflict in 2 Cor. 10–13, when the polemic is fiercest. In 2 Cor. 1–2 and 7, where Paul is pursuing reconciliation, his circumspection is even greater, with the result that the case of the one who did wrong almost appears to be hypothetical![1025] Building upon the research of Peter Marshall, we shall discover that, in not mentioning the name of his enemy, Paul is following a rhetorical convention that was well established in the Greco-Roman world.[1026] When the social conventions that governed friendship, enmity, and reconciliation in Paul's world are fully understood, it will be possible to put forward a plausible hypothesis regarding the identity of the one who did Paul wrong.

1023 See esp. Isa. 43:18–19. See also 1 *En.* 72:1; 2 *Bar.* 32:6; *Jub.* 4:26; 1QS IV.25 and 1QH XI.10–14; 13.11. Cf. Peter Stuhlmacher, "Erwägungen zum ontologischen Charakter der καινὴ κτίσις bei Paulus," *EvT* 27 (1967) 1–35; Furnish, *II Corinthians*, 314–15; U. Mell, *Neue Schöpfung: Eine traditions-geschichtliche und exegetische Studie zu einem soteriologischen Grundsatz paulinischer Theologie* (Berlin: Walter de Gruyter, 1989) 47–257; Thrall, *Second Epistle*, 1.420–21.
1024 Georgi, *Opponents of Paul*, 339–40; Marshall, *Enmity in Corinth*, 341–48.
1025 Windisch, *Der zweite Korintherbrief*, 84.
1026 Marshall, *Enmity in Corinth*, 341–48.

Chapter Four
Social and Rhetorical Conventions

In the epilogue to the English edition of his influential study of Paul's opponents in 2 Corinthians (1986), Dieter Georgi called attention to the "peculiar" character of Paul's rhetoric in 2 Cor. 1:1–2:13; 7:5–16,[1] and speculated about the potential results of a thorough analysis of the style of Paul's communication for knowledge of the history of Paul's conflict with Corinth: "The problem of the ἀδικήσας in 2 Cor. 2 and 7 may yield more information…Paul's preceding negative experience, a painful visit (2 Cor. 2:1–4), is commonly understood as being an insult. But the style and form of communication are remarkable. Paul's 'evasive' approach by way of circumlocution needs to be more carefully analyzed. The results of that analysis may further clarify the conflict itself."[2]

Our exegesis of 2 Cor. 1:1–2:13; 7:5–16, and especially of the crucial paragraph 2:5–11, in which Paul counsels the forgiveness of the one who caused pain, has provided abundant confirmation of Georgi's insight into the "evasive" style of Paul's communication. Extreme caution is evident, not only in Paul's consistent refusal to name the guilty party, and his strict employment of the most indefinite expressions—"someone" (τις), "such a one" (τοιοῦτος), "him" (αὐτόν), "whom" (ᾧ)—but also in a host of subtle, rhetorical devices, whose effect is to mitigate blame and to avert scrutiny: conditional sentences ("if someone has caused pain," "if I have forgiven anything"), qualifying phrases ("to some degree," "not to exaggerate it"), avowals of higher motive ("for your sake," "so

---

1 Georgi, *Opponents of Paul*, 339, with specific reference to 2 Cor. 1:12–22: "A thorough stylistic and form-critical analysis of the peculiar discussion Paul presents is still missing. If that format were to relate itself not only to general patterns, habits, and functions but also to particular circumstances, it might assist in illuminating the latter more. Also, reasons for the terminology used here, which is unusual in the context of the Pauline correspondence at large, might intimate peculiar signals not just about the issue at stake but also about its relationship to the overall conflict."
2 Georgi, *Opponents of Paul*, 339–40.

that we might not be defrauded by Satan," "so that your zeal for us might be made known to you before God"), etc.³ To take note of such stylistic features is a first step toward a deeper appreciation of the rhetorical situation in which Paul finds himself vis-à-vis the wrongdoer. But the kind of analysis of Paul's rhetoric that could yield an hypothesis regarding the identity of the wrongdoer requires us to step outside the text of Paul's epistles into the social world that provided the controlling logic of Paul's discourse.

A significant component of such an analysis was provided by Peter Marshall in his dissertation of 1987, *Enmity in Corinth: Social Conventions in Paul's Relations with the Corinthians*.⁴ Building upon the work of his teacher, Edwin Judge,⁵ Marshall demonstrated that in Paul's authentic epistles, he never once names an enemy.⁶ Rather, in speaking of enemies, Paul consistently resorts to periphrastic constructions.⁷ By way of example, Marshall cited Paul's reference in Rom. 16:17–18 to "those who create dissensions and difficulties…; for such people (οἱ τοιοῦτοι) do not serve our Lord Christ, but their own appetites, and by smooth talk and flattery they deceive the hearts of the simple-minded"—a passage which Marshall perceptively described as "a cameo of

---

3   Special sensitivity to the rhetorical devices in 2 Cor. 2:5–11 is the hallmark of Windisch, *Der zweite Korintherbrief*, 83–92.
4   Marshall. *Enmity in Corinth*, 341–48. The book was a revision of the author's PhD thesis submitted to Macquarie University in 1980, supervised by Robert Banks and Edwin Judge. The impact of the dissertation can already be traced in the pages of Furnish's commentary.
5   Marshall makes reference to Edwin A. Judge, "The Early Christians as a Scholastic Community," *JRH* 2 (1961) 125–37, esp. 127–35; repr. in idem, *The First Christians in the Roman World: Augustan and New Testament Essays*, ed. James R. Harrison (Tübingen: Mohr Siebeck, 2008) 526–52; Edwin A. Judge, "Paul's Boasting in Relation to Contemporary Professional Practice," *AusBR* 10 (1968) 37–50, esp. 41; repr. in *Social Distinctives of the Christians in the First Century: Pivotal Essays by E. A. Judge*, ed. David M. Scholer (Peabody: Hendrickson, 2008) 57–71; Edwin A. Judge, "Augustus in the Res Gestae," *Papers of the Macquarie University Continuing Education Conference for Ancient History Teachers* (Sydney: Macquarie University, 1979) 1–43; repr. in idem, *The First Christians in the Roman World*, 182–223.
6   Marshall, *Enmity in Corinth*, 342.
7   Marshall, *Enmity in Corinth*, 342, referring to the definition of περίφρασις (Latin *circumlocutio, circumscriptio*) in Quintilian *Inst.* 8.6.59–61. Cf. Aristotle *Rhet.* 3.6.1–3, 1407b; Cicero *Or.* 3.54.207; Quintilian *Inst.* 9.1.35; 9.3.91; 9.4.124.

the situation in Corinth."⁸ Marshall showed that Paul's practice of not naming his opponents was in accordance with a standard Greco-Roman rhetorical convention. Following the lead of Judge, Marshall called attention to the brilliant use of this convention by Augustus in his *Res Gestae*, where five passages in the text appear to cry out for a name, which Augustus suppresses, indicating by periphrasis persons who would have been well known to ancient readers (Brutus, Cassius, Anthony, Lepidus, and Sextus Pompeius), while damning such persons with anonymity.⁹ On the basis of his analysis of the *Res Gestae*, Marshall detailed five characteristics of the rhetorical device of non-naming of enemies: 1) it takes the place of the name of a person who is well known to the readers; 2) it makes the person available for caricature; 3) it belongs to an exercise in comparison, usually according to the conventions of praise and blame; 4) it is always used pejoratively; 5) its intention is to shame the enemy.[10]

We may supplement the findings of Judge and Marshall by examination of additional instances of non-naming of enemies in letters and speeches which furnish closer parallels to Paul's use of this rhetorical device. Cicero's correspondence with his friends abounds with examples of non-naming of enemies, as Cicero seeks to justify the political roles that he played in various conflicts and his personal relations with other political actors.[11] In his celebrated letter to Publius Lentulus Spinther, Cicero makes reference to the clique of the extreme *optimates* who were jealous of his relationship with Pompey, but does so in a manner that avoids mentioning the names of his rivals: "But in all those measures and motions of mine which seemed to offend Pompey, the comments of certain men— you ought to suspect immediately whom I mean—were brought to my ears (*certorum hominum, quos iam debes suspicari, sermons referebantur ad me*), who though they held the same political opinions as those I acted upon, and had always held them, nevertheless declared they were delighted that I failed to satisfy Pompey and that Caesar would be my

---

8   Marshall, *Enmity in Corinth*, 311–12, 342.
9   Marshall, *Enmity in Corinth*, 342–43, appealing to Judge, "Augustus in the Res Gestae" (1979).
10 Marshall, *Enmity in Corinth*, 344.
11 J. N. Adams, "Conventions of Naming in Cicero," *CQ* 28 (1978) 145–66; David F. Epstein, *Personal Enmity in Roman Politics 218–43 BC* (London: Croom Helm, 1987); Hall, *Politeness and Politics in Cicero's Letters*.

bitterest enemy."[12] Later in the same epistle, Cicero again employs the device of non-naming to indicate his arch-rivals among the *optimates*: "And at this very time, certain men (*quidam homines*), indeed those very men whom I often hint at but do not name (*et iidem illi, quos saepe nutu significo neque appello*), though they declared that they had benefited very greatly by my outspoken manner, and that they considered that episode to be my first real restoration to the Republic as my old self again…those same people now declared that they were delighted that Crassus was at enmity with me, and that those (Pompey and Caesar) who were in the same boat with him would never be friends with me."[13]

In a speech delivered prior to his exile from his native Prusa (*Or.* 46), Dio Chrysostom protests his maltreatment by a mob which suspected him of having manipulated the grain market.[14] The outraged mob attacked the properties of Dio and a neighbor, whom Dio refuses to name. Dio demands of his fellow townsmen: "What is it, then, that makes you angry with me, and why of all the citizens have you singled out for dishonor me and what's-his-name (τὸν δεῖνα), and why do you threaten us with stoning and burning?"[15] One may infer that Dio's failure to name his neighbor reflects the fact that he is a political rival, for Dio explains in what follows, "And let no one say that I am speaking on behalf of that man (ὑπὲρ ἐκείνου)," and suggests that this man should be reckoned "among the wrongdoers" (τῶν ἀδικούντων).[16]

Dio's 45th discourse is a complex apology covering his relations with the city of Prusa following his return from exile.[17] Dio's enemies have

---

12 Cicero *Fam.* 1.9.10. For the background of this letter, see David R. Shackleton Bailey, *Cicero: Epistulae ad Familiares.* Vol. I (Cambridge: Cambridge University Press, 1977) 307; Thomas N. Mitchell, "Cicero before Luca," *TAPA* 100 (1969) 295–320, esp. 296–97, 306.
13 Cicero *Fam.* 1.9.20.
14 On the occasion of this discourse, see H. Lamar Crosby, *Dio Chrysostom IV*, LCL (Cambridge, MA: Harvard University Press, 1962) 226–27; C. P. Jones, *The Roman World of Dio Chrysostom* (Cambridge, MA: Harvard University Press, 1978) 99; Giovanni Salmeri, "Dio, Rome, and the Civic Life of Asia Minor" in *Dio Chrysostom: Politics, Letters, and Philosophy*, ed. Simon Swain (Oxford: Oxford University Press, 2000) 64.
15 Dio Chrysostom *Or.* 46.6.
16 Dio Chrysostom *Or.* 46.6. See the observation of Crosby, *Dio Chrysostom IV*, 233 n.2: "One may infer from Dio's language and from his failure to name his neighbor that they were not on good terms, possibly political rivals."
17 See the introduction to the discourse in Crosby, *Dio Chrysostom IV*, 204–205; see also Jones, *Dio Chrysostom*, 99–100, 107–108.

been critical of him for a variety of reasons: he is blamed for having failed to turn his friendship with the Emperor to the benefit of his city; he is accused of having rigged the election of members to the Council; he is faulted for having procrastinated in carrying out his announced program to enhance the beauty of the city.[18] In his defense, Dio reserves his sharpest retorts for certain rivals who appear to be men of his own social class. Near the beginning of the speech, Dio concedes that "if I were now to speak of the benevolence I experienced at the hands of the present Emperor, I would greatly annoy certain persons (σφόδρα λυπήσω τινάς)— and possibly the statement would not even seem credible, that one who met with such esteem and intimacy and friendship should have neglected all these things and have given them such scant attention, having formed a longing for the confusion and bustle here at home, to put it mildly; for all that, I did not employ that opportunity or the goodwill of the Emperor for any selfish purpose, etc...."[19] As the speech unfolds, it becomes clear that, among Dio's aristocratic rivals, there is one archenemy, a spokesman for the adversarial group, to whom Dio repeatedly alludes, and to whom Dio even attributes, ironically, words of counsel which this man should have spoken to his fellow citizens on previous occasions, when they were relying upon worthless agents who had fed Prusa on false hopes: "And yet, seeing that only trifling, yes worthless, concessions were effected by them (the worthless agents), the high-minded man (ὁ ἀνήρ ὁ γενναῖος), the man who would not be the slave of envy and malice, should have said at the time, 'You are crazy and deluded in clinging so tenaciously to men like that and in cultivating such low fellows in order to gain favors that are neither essential nor important, to say nothing of their being vague and of your having no assurance."[20] In defending himself against the charge of electoral corruption, Dio again alludes to his adversaries as "others (ἕτεροι) who put in friends of their own and schemed to have in the Council persons to aid them and to give their support to whatever they might wish to accomplish."[21] Dio singles out from this group a particular rival, and voices the conviction that "they (the electors) would have sided with me rather than with somebody else (ἢ ἄλλῳ τινί)

---

18 Dio Chrysostom *Or.* 45.2–3, 5, 7, 8, 9–10, 12–13.
19 Dio Chrysostom *Or.* 45.3; my translation modifies that found in the LCL.
20 Dio Chrysostom *Or.* 45.5; cf. Crosby, *Dio Chrysostom IV*, 212 n.1: "the personal pronoun...seems to refer to the 'high-minded' citizen, who had failed to protest against relying upon the worthless agents who for some time had fed Prusa on false hopes, but who was critical of Dio's own achievements."
21 Dio Chrysostom *Or.* 45.7.

had I so desired."²² Finally, in defending his plans to beautify the city, Dio again refers periphrastically to the opposition of a rival faction: "and if the opportunity should ever arise for the fulfillment of these projects and some god should bring them to pass, then you will see the extravagance of the hostility of certain persons and their hatred of me (τότε ὄψεσθε τὴν ὑπερβολὴν τῆς τινων ἔχθρας καὶ τοῦ πρὸς ἐμὲ μίσους), to say nothing of their hatred of you, since they will no longer be ambiguous and mild in their speech and their abuse, but open and outspoken."²³ Dio concludes his address with a parting shot at a powerful individual, "a certain one of those in office" (τῶν ἐν τέλει τις), whose opposition is to blame for the delay in executing Dio's plans to beautify the city.²⁴

In all of the above instances, Dio refuses to name his enemies, employing, in place of names, periphrastic constructions. The intent of this rhetorical strategy is, as Marshall recognized, clearly pejorative: the adversaries are damned with anonymity, while, at the same time, periphrasis makes the enemies available for derogatory comparison, even caricature. Without adducing further examples,²⁵ we may conclude that an established rhetorical convention of not-naming enemies operated in the Greco-Roman world, and that this convention provided the controlling logic of Paul's practice of not naming his opponents in 2 Corinthians.

In applying his findings to 2 Corinthians, Marshall identified five passages in which Paul's periphrastic description of his opponents exhibits the characteristics of the rhetorical device of non-naming: 2:17, οἱ πολλοὶ καπηλεύοντες τὸν λόγον τοῦ θεοῦ ("the many peddlers of God's word"); 5:12, οἱ ἐν προσώπῳ καυχώμενοι καὶ μὴ ἐν καρδίᾳ ("those who boast in outward appearance and not in the heart"); 10:12, τινες τῶν ἑαυτοὺς συνιστανόντων ("some who commend themselves"); 11:4, ὁ ἐρχόμενος ἄλλον Ἰησοῦν κηρύσσει ("the one who comes and proclaims another Jesus"); 11:12, οἱ θέλοντες ἀφορμήν, ἵνα ἐν ᾧ καυχῶνται εὑρεθῶσιν καθὼς καὶ ἡμεῖς ("those who want an opportunity to be recognized as our equals in what they boast about").²⁶ It will be recognized immediately that all of the examples of Paul's use of the device of non-naming adduced

---

22 Dio Chrysostom *Or.* 45.7; the passage continues, "No, I held that, if possible, no other man (ἕτερον μηδένα) should introduce such a practice or conduct state affairs by means of political clubs or split the city into factions."
23 Dio Chrysostom *Or.* 45.15.
24 Dio Chrysostom *Or.* 45.16.
25 E.g., Cicero *Att.* 1.13; 2.22; Caesar *Bell. civ.* 1.22.5; Plutarch *Com. Aem. Tim.* 31.5; cf. Marshall, *Enmity in Corinth*, 343 n.15.
26 Marshall, *Enmity in Corinth*, 346–47.

by Marshall refer to rival missionaries, interloping apostles, rather than local Corinthian opponents of Paul. Upon reflection, it is clear that this correlation is entirely appropriate, since it is only in Paul's treatment of the rival apostles that one encounters an overtly derogatory intent, with a tendency toward caricature, in the context of an exercise in rhetorical comparison.[27]

On the other hand, none of Paul's uses of periphrastic constructions to refer to local Corinthian opponents (e.g., 10:2), and to one opponent in particular (2:5, 6, 7, 8, 10; 7:12; 10:7, 10, 11; 11:16; 12:6), exhibit the characteristics associated with the device of non-naming as an expression of enmity toward political rivals in the *Res Gestae*, in Cicero, in Dio Chrysostom, and elsewhere—that is, the pejorative attitude, the derogatory intent, the tendency toward caricature, the invidious comparisons. In none of the passages where Paul refers to his Corinthian critic by means of the expressions τις and τοιοῦτος is there any trace of an intention to shame. Rather, Paul's argument with his Corinthian critic takes the form of an assertion of an equality of relationship ("Just as you belong to Christ, so do I," 10:7) and a consistency of practice ("Let such a person understand that what we say by letter when absent, we will also do when present," 10:11). Nor is there any shadow of irony on Paul's part in the one explicit quotation that Paul attributes to his Corinthian critic (10:10), but rather undisguised defensiveness; as we have argued above, the mockery in this quotation belongs to Paul's critic, and is mixed with sincere admiration.[28] One need only contrast the highly respectful, even deferential treatment of ὁ τοιοῦτος in 2:7–8 with the savage castigation of οἱ θέλοντες ἀφορμήν in 11:13 as "false apostles, deceitful workmen, disguising themselves as apostles of Christ."[29] We may conclude that, while Marshall has correctly identified the rhetorical convention that governed Paul's use of periphrastic constructions in reference to his apostolic rivals, he has left undiscovered the controlling logic of Paul's refusal to name his local Corinthian opponents with whom he is seeking reconciliation.

---

27 Marshall, *Enmity in Corinth*, 346–47; see also Betz, *Der Apostel Paulus*, 118–31; Forbes, "Paul's Boasting and Hellenistic Rhetoric," 1–30, esp. 16–18; Winter, *Paul Among the Sophists*, 231–39.
28 See above on 2 Cor. 10:10, pp. 102–121.
29 Cf. Windisch, *Der zweite Korintherbrief*, 84, 87–89; C. K. Barrett, "PSEUDAPOSTOLOI (2 Cor. 11:13)" in *Mélanges Biblique*, ed. A. Descamps and A. de Halleux (Gembloux: Duculot, 1970) 377–96; repr. in idem, *Essays on Paul* (Philadelphia: Westminster, 1982) 87–107.

Chapter Four. Social and Rhetorical Conventions 219

In fairness to Marshall, it should be stated that he does not discuss any of the passages in 2 Corinthians where Paul employs periphrastic constructions to avoid naming his local Corinthian opponents (2:5, 6, 7, 8, 10: 7:12; 10:2, 7, 10, 11; 11:16; 12:6), and thus did not intend his analysis of Paul's use of the device of non-naming, in respect to his treatment of apostolic rivals, to be applied universally as an explanation of all instances of not-naming. Indeed, a sensitive reading of this section of Marshall's path-breaking study finds the author puzzling over the fact that Paul does not name any of his friends and associates known to us from the pages of 1 Corinthians (Chloe, Crispus, Gaius, Stephanas, Fortunatus and Achaicus) in 2 Corinthians, where he is engaged in a protracted struggle with rivals.[30] Marshall is aware of how unusual it would be, in the context of Greco-Roman society, where enmities were expressed with unrestrained bitterness, that a man should fail to call upon such friends as he had to help him withstand the attacks of his rivals.[31] Marshall speculates that Paul fails to mention his friends in 2 Corinthians because they had been silenced by the dominant faction of his opponents,[32] or that Paul avoids naming his friends because he did not wish to involve them further in enmity with his rivals.[33] Marshall is aware, of course, that relationships evolve, and that friendship and enmity had an especially pragmatic character in Greco-Roman society.[34] Today's friends might be tomorrow's enemies, as Caesar realistically observed.[35]

---

30 Marshall, *Enmity in Corinth*, 345–46.
31 Marshall, *Enmity in Corinth*, 345.
32 Marshall, *Enmity in Corinth*, 261, 262–65, 345.
33 Marshall, *Enmity in Corinth*, 345.
34 Marshall, *Enmity in Corinth*, 18–21, 38–40, citing a maxim attributed to Bias in Aristotle *Rhet.* 2.13: "They love as if they would one day hate, and hate as if they would one day love" (καὶ φιλοῦσιν ὡς μισήσοντες καὶ μισοῦσιν ὡς φιλήσοντες). The sentiment is widely distributed, as illustrated by the variants, e.g., Demosthenes 23.122: ἄχρι τούτου καὶ φιλεῖν...χρὴ καὶ μισεῖν, μηδετέρου τὸν καιρὸν ὑπερβάλλοντας.; Cicero *Amic.* 59: *ita amare oportere, ut sit aliquando esset osurus*; Diodorus Siculus 12.20.3: οὕτω τὴν ἔχθραν...ἀναλαμβάνειν ὡς ἥξοντα πάλιν εἰς σύλλυσιν καὶ φιλίαν.; Publilius Syrus 245: *ita amicum habeas, posse amicum fieri ut inimicum putes*; Valerius Maximus 7.3: *ita...oportere homines in usu amicitiae versari, ut meminissent eam gravissimas inimicitias posse converti*; Diogenes Laertius 1.87: φιλεῖν ὡς μισήσοντας. See the discussion of this maxim in Alfons Fürst, *Streit unter Freunden: Ideal und Realität in der Freundschaftslehre der Antike* (Stuttgart: Teubner, 1996) 20–23.
35 Caesar *Bell. civ.* 1.4. On the instability of friendships as a matter of political convenience, see the observation of Sallust (*Cat.* 10.5) on the tendency of his age "to value friendships and enmities in accordance with convenience rather than on

Conversely, enemies might become friends through reconciliation.³⁶ But Marshall failed to apply this knowledge to the puzzle of Paul's refusal to name his friends in 2 Corinthians. That is to say, Marshall did not give serious consideration to the possibility that some of Paul's friends had become his enemies by the time of composition of 2 Corinthians.³⁷ Thus, Marshall did not advance beyond speculation about Paul's failure to mention his friends in 2 Corinthians to the discovery of a rhetorical convention that could explain Paul's use of periphrastic constructions in relation to his local Corinthian opponents.

Those who have been influenced by Marshall's study have drawn the conclusion that the wrongdoer of 2 Cor. 2:5–11 and 7:12 could not be among the six individuals named by Paul in 1 Corinthians (Chloe, Crispus, Gaius, Stephanas, Fortunatus and Achaicus), nor the three additional individuals mentioned in connection with Corinth in Romans 16 (Tertius, Erastus and Quartus), because, in accordance with rhetorical convention, Paul never names an enemy.³⁸ If this conclusion were justified, then our search for the identity of the wrongdoer would have arrived at a dead end. But our exegesis of 2 Cor. 2:5–11 found evidence that the wrongdoer enjoyed a close relationship, even a friendship, with the apostle prior to their painful conflict. The evidence of such a friendship consists, first of all, in Paul's repeated use of the verb λυπεῖν and the noun λύπη to describe the hurt suffered by himself and the wrongdoer.³⁹ Our research disclosed that much of the discourse about λύπη in ancient literature explores a potential inherent in friendship, because friendship was understood to entail a special vulnerability to pain.⁴⁰ Moreover, the extraordinary solicitude exhibited by Paul for the welfare of the wrongdoer in 2:7–8 points to a special relationship: Paul urges the Corinthians to

---

their own merits." See also Dio Cassius 37.39.3: "Most men's friendships and enmities depend on their own self-interest and the degree of influence others hold." Cf. Epstein, *Personal Enmity*, 5.

36 E.g., Cicero *Fam.* 1.9.20; 5.8.5. See the sentiments expressed in Philo *Virt.* 23.117–18; 28.152; Publilius Syrus 142; Seneca *Ep.* 95.63; *Quomodo amicitia continenda sit* fr. 1; Diogenes Laertius 1.91. Cf. Epstein, *Personal Enmity*, 5–11; Marshall, *Enmity in Corinth*, 42–43; Fürst, *Streit unter Freunden*, 23, 26–27, 35, 190–91.

37 Marshall, *Enmity in Corinth*, 345–46.

38 E.g., Furnish, *II Corinthians*, 49, 511; Chow, *Patronage and Power*, 88, 90; Thrall, *Second Epistle*, 2.641.

39 See above on 2 Cor. 2:1–4, 5, 7, pp. 43–52.

40 E.g., Aristotle *Rhet.* 2.2.8–9, 15; 2.3; Plutarch *Mor.* 460D, 461E, 462B, 463B, 463C.

"forgive" and "console" the wrongdoer, lest he be "drowned by excessive sorrow"; he appeals to the Corinthians to "reaffirm love for him." The conclusion that Paul enjoyed a friendship with the wrongdoer is reinforced by consideration of the genre of Paul's letter in 2 Cor. 1:1–2:13; 7:5–16: the social context of a "therapeutic epistle" is friendship, and the author of a conciliatory letter aims to "heal" (θεραπεύειν) a wounded friend.[41] Why, then, does Paul not name his "friend" anywhere among the letters and letter-fragments known to us as 2 Corinthians? The question is particularly acute with respect to crucial passages in 2 Cor. 1:1–2:13; 7:5–16, where Paul is openly pursuing reconciliation with the wrongdoer. Is there a way that leads beyond this impasse?

The key to understanding Paul's practice of not naming his alienated friend in 2 Corinthians is found in consideration of a rhetorical convention that operated in letters of the "conciliatory" type.[42] Examination of letters which belong to this apologetic genre reveals that the authors of such writings consistently avoided naming the person or persons with whom they have experienced conflict and are now seeking reconciliation, and instead substitute periphrastic constructions, such as τις and τοιοῦτος.[43] Here, then, is a second instance of the rhetorical device of not-naming, which serves a different purpose and possesses different characteristics than the use of this device to which Marshall called attention, in relation to the expression of enmity. Following Marshall's example, we may

---

41 For the suggestion that 2 Cor. 1:1–2:13; 7:5–16 bears comparison with the "conciliatory (θεραπευτική) type" of letter mentioned in the handbook of epistolary style attributed to Libanius, see Windisch, *Der zweite Korintherbrief*, 8. The aim of such a letter is "to heal someone who has been caused grief by us for some reason" (θεραπευτικὴ δι' ἧς θεραπεύομέν τινα λυπηθέντα πρὸς ἡμᾶς περί τινος), according to Ps.-Libanius *Ep. Char.* 19. See the concluding enthymeme of the sample letter in Ps.-Libanius *Ep. Char.*: "For it is my aim always to heal my friends, rather than to cause them grief" (σκοπὸς γάρ μοι θεραπεύειν ἀεὶ τοὺς φίλους ἐστὶν ἤπερ λυπεῖν); my translation modifies that in Malherbe, *Ancient Epistolary Theorists*, 68–69, 76–77. On typical social relationships as determinative of epistolary types, see Stowers, "Social Typification," 78–90.

42 Examples of conciliatory letters: Demosthenes *Ep.* 2; Cicero *Fam.* 3.8; 5.2; 5.8; Apollonius of Tyana *Ep.* 45; Marcus Aurelius in Philostratus *Vit. soph.* 2.1.562–63; Chion *Ep.* 16 in Ingmar Düring, *Chion of Heraclea: A Novel in Letters* (Gothenburg: Wettergren & Kerbers, 1951) 70–77; Ps.-Aristotle *Ep.* 5 in Hercher, *Epistolographi Graeci*, 174; Ps.-Euripides *Ep.* 5 in Hercher, *Epistolographi Graeci*, 277–79; Chairemon to Apollonius in Olsson, *Papyrusbriefe aus der frühesten Römerzeit*, no. 43 (*BGU* II.531).

43 Welborn, "A Conciliatory Convention and Paul's References to the Letter of Tears" in idem, *Politics and Rhetoric*, 87–91.

specify five characteristics of the rhetorical device of not-naming friends: 1) it takes the place of the name of a person who is well known to the readers; 2) it makes the person available for conciliation; 3) it belongs to an exercise in apology, in which the circumstances of a conflict are rationalized; 4) it is always used constructively; 5) its intention is to restore the goodwill of a friend.

Examination of several conciliatory letters and speeches will illustrate how the device of not-naming friends operated in an apologetic context. The second epistle of Demosthenes is a conciliatory apology to the Council and the Assembly of Athens appealing for the orator's restoration from exile.[44] Nowhere in the course of the apology does Demosthenes mention his opponents by name, although they are known from other contexts to be Dinarchus and Hyperides.[45] Demosthenes speaks of his accusers only as "certain members of the Council": "Since, however, you have happily become aware of the undue ascendancy which certain members of the Council (τινες τῶν ἐν τῇ βουλῇ) were contriving for themselves, and since you are now deciding the cases in light of the proofs and have found the secretiveness of these men deserving of censure (τὰ δ' ἀπόρρητα τούτων ἐπιτιμήσεως ἄξι' εὑρήκατε), I think it is my right, with your consent, to enjoy the same acquittal as those who have incurred the like accusations, and not to be the only one to be deprived on a false charge of his fatherland, his property, and the company of those who are nearest and dearest to him."[46] Demosthenes' effort to conciliate his fellow Athenians goes so far that he thanks his opponents in advance, if only they will allow the prosecution to be dropped in his case, as they have for other defendants. Demosthenes justifies his forgiveness of his accusers by representing them as agents of the people, while allowing that he may have need of further assistance, should his accusers prove to be recalcitrant. Yet even at this point, his principal opponents are not named: "Now thus far I am appealing to you all, but for those in particular who are attacking me in your presence I wish to say a word: so far as con-

---

44 On the occasion and purpose of this letter, see Jonathan Goldstein, *The Letters of Demosthenes* (New York: Columbia University Press, 1968) 37–63, 78–94, 157–66. The authenticity of the letter is defended by Goldstein. If authentic, the letter would fall in the years 324–322 B.C.E., the last two years of the orator's life.

45 Goldstein, *The Letters of Demosthenes*, 161.

46 Demosthenes *Ep* 2.2; trans. N. W. and N. J. DeWitt, *Demosthenes VII: Letters*, LCL (Cambridge, MA: Harvard University Press, 1962) 211. Cf. Goldstein, *The Letters of Demosthenes*, 158–59.

cerns all that they were doing in pursuance of the decrees passed by you in disregard of the truth, let it be allowed that these actions have been taken by them as your agents, and I lodge no complaint. Since, however, you have yourselves come to recognize these decrees for what they are, if they will yield in my case, just as they are allowing the prosecution to be dropped in the case of the other defendants, they shall have my thanks; but if they attempt to continue malicious, I appeal to you all to rally to my aid and not allow the enmity of these men to prevail over the gratitude due to me from you."[47]

Dio Chrysostom's 50th oration is a conciliatory apology delivered before the Council of his native Prusa.[48] Dio has done some favor for the common people—"something to ease their burden"—and is now at pains to show that his benefaction was no sign of opposition to the Council, or disregard of the prerogatives of that body.[49] Dio takes care not to mention the name of his principal critic, but refers only to what "someone has said" and what "someone will ask": "'What has happened,' someone will say (φήσει τις), 'and what experience of the gentlemen have you had, that you are so extravagant in your language?'."[50] "'But did you, then,' someone will ask (φήσει τις), 'rise to your feet merely to deliver a eulogy of the Council?'."[51] Dio acknowledges only that "there has been a flood of talk of such kind" (καὶ λόγος ἐρρύη τοιοῦτος), and that "some have believed " (τινες ἔδοξαν) the charge that he blocked the assembling of the Council.[52]

Returning to Dio's 45th oration, we discover that this complex apology is not only a defense of his conduct against certain rivals who were critical of what he had accomplished since returning to Prusa, as noted above, but also aims at conciliating his fellow citizens, from whom he had become alienated during his exile.[53] Dio distinguishes between his rivals and other Prusans, in explaining the motives for his reticence in speaking about the wrongs he had suffered: "It was this, therefore, that made me keep quiet, that I might not be suspected of accusing certain

---

47 Demosthenes *Ep.* 2.26; trans. DeWitt, *Demosthenes VII: Letters*, 225. Cf. Goldstein, *The Letters of Demosthenes*, 166.
48 Crosby, *Dio Chrysostom IV*, 310–11; Jones, *Dio Chrysostom*, 95–96, 101.
49 Dio Chrysostom *Or.* 50.3; cf. *Or.* 43.7.
50 Dio Chrysostom *Or.* 50.6.
51 Dio Chrysostom *Or.* 50.9.
52 Dio Chrysostom *Or.* 50.10.
53 Jones, *Dio Chrysostom*, 52, 98–100, 107; Salmeri, "Dio and the Civic Life of Asia Minor," 67.

persons (τινες), or of maligning the city and, in general, that I might not be too irritating (λυπηρότερος) to anyone (μηδενί) at Prusa."⁵⁴ Seeking reconciliation with his fellow Prusans, Dio employs periphrastic constructions in taking up the delicate subject of restitution for losses that he had suffered during his exile: "And again, when now for the first time, the question of financial administration had been brought up, though I had been wronged by many men in many matters (πολλὰ ὑπὸ πολλῶν ἠδικημένος)—as indeed it was to be expected that a man should be who had come home after so many years of exile—and although with regard to some (καὶ πρὸς ἐνίους) I did not even need to go to law, but rather to speak to them and remind them of what was being held in their possession, nevertheless I did not mention these matters to anyone or make any statement (πρὸς οὐδένα οὔτ' ἐμνήσθην οὔτε λόγον ἐποιησάμην οὐδένα), although so many slaves had run away and obtained freedom, so many persons had defrauded me of money (τοσούτων δὲ χρήματα ἀπεστερηκότων), so many were occupying lands of mine, since there was no one to prevent such things."⁵⁵ Dio climaxes his account of what he suffered at the hands of his countrymen with an extended comparison of himself with Odysseus, and asks, "was it not to be expected that I should have suffered many such wrongs at the hands of many men (ἐμὲ δὲ οὐκ ἦν εἰκὸς ὑπὸ πολλῶν πολλὰ τοιαῦτα πεπονθέναι)?"⁵⁶ Turning finally to his controversial plans to beautify the city, Dio acknowledges the reservations of some of his fellow citizens, employing, as elsewhere, periphrastic constructions, while excusing his indiscretion on this matter by comparing his talk of benefactions with intimate conversations between lovers: "However, being acquainted with the views of some of the people here (οὐ μὴν ἀλλ' ἐπιστάμενός γε τὰς διανοίας τῶν ἐνθάδε ἀνθρώπων ἐνίων), as well as with my own limitations and responsibilities…I neither undertook anything too ambitious nor entertained any such expectations, only I could not control my thoughts, but, just as lovers when alone together expatiate on such things as they most desire, so I too would often mention those things which I did believe it would profit the city to have, etc."⁵⁷

In his conciliatory epistle to his friend and former teacher Herodes Atticus, Marcus Aurelius takes care not to mention the names of persons

---

54 Dio Chrysostom *Or.* 45.9
55 Dio Chrysostom *Or.* 45.10
56 Dio Chrysostom *Or.* 45.11.
57 Dio Chrysostom *Or.* 45.14.

in Herodes' household who, as Marcus chooses to represent it, have been the cause of conflict between them.[58] Rather, Marcus speaks only of "the offences of some of your household" (τινας τῶν σῶν πλημμελοῦντας).[59] Moreover, Marcus assures Herodes that he has chastised the offenders with a punishment "as mild as possible" (ὡς οἷόν τε ἐπιεικεῖ).[60]

Although we might pursue further examples, we may conclude that an established rhetorical convention of not-naming friends operated in apologetic contexts where the authors of letters and speeches attempted to conciliate wounded associates. In every case examined above, periphrastic constructions replaced the names of persons who were well known to the readers (e.g., Dinarchus and Hyperides), indeed persons who were themselves members of the community. The effect of not-naming is to avoid the possibility of "rubbing salt into an open wound," so to speak, by explicitly identifying persons connected with the cause of strife. But periphrasis also makes the person or persons available for conciliation: improvement in the image or attitude of the offender is typically achieved by generalizing the distress, as when Dio refers to what all exiles suffer,[61] or by construing the offender as the representative of the majority, as Demosthenes does in the case of Dinarchus and Hyperides.[62] In every case, the aim of the device is conciliatory—to mend a broken relationship, to heal a wounded friend.

We should observe that the necessity for this rhetorical convention and, at the same time, the condition for its successful operation, are given in the nature of Greek letters, which were "messages of public interest, even when addressed to individuals."[63] By contrast, the correspondence of Cicero furnishes few examples of the device of not-naming friends, because of its private character.[64] Even so, Cicero follows other

---

58 Philostratus *Vit. soph.* 2.1.559–63 should be read as background. Cf. G. H. R. Horsley, "An Imperial Appeal for Reconciliation" in *NewDocs*, Vol. 4, no. 20, pp. 83–87.
59 Philostratus *Vit. soph.* 2.1.562; the translation slightly modifies that of the LCL.
60 Philostratus *Vit. soph.* 2.1.562.
61 Dio Chrysostom *Or.* 45.10, 11–13.
62 Demosthenes *Ep.* 2.26.
63 N. W. and N. J. DeWitt, *Demosthenes VII: Letters*, 196. On the Greek letter in general, Sykutris, "Epistolographie," 185–220; H. Koskenniemi, *Studien zur Idee und Phraseologie des griechischen Briefes bis 400 n. Chr.* (Helsinki: Suomalainen Tiedeakatemian, 1956).
64 Although many of Cicero's letters were of a "private" nature, intended only for the recipients, others evidently circulated among a group of friends and acquaintances, and may be categorized as "semipublic." For a good discussion of the sub-

conventions of the conciliatory genre. In his letter to Crassus, for example, Cicero avoids description of the substance of their quarrel, referring only to "certain infringements which have affected our relations": these differences, he asserts, are "surmised rather than real"; they are "mere figments of the imagination"; Cicero exhorts, "Let them be utterly eradicated from our memories and our lives."[65] Cicero's treatment of the conflict is controlled by his conciliatory purpose: "Between two men such as you are and I desire to be, I would hope that alliance and friendship will conduce to the credit of both."[66]

Turning now to Paul, it is impressive how closely Paul adheres to the convention of not-naming friends in the various apologetic letters and letter-fragments that make up our 2 Corinthians. Paul consistently avoids naming any of the Corinthians with whom he has experienced conflict, employing the standard substitutes τινες, τις, τοιοῦτος, and other periphrastic constructions.[67] In the overtly conciliatory letter of 2 Cor. 1:1–2:13; 7:5–16, Paul mitigates the harshness of blame on the wrongdoer by employing qualifying phrases—"to some degree," "not to exaggerate it" (2:5). In the interest of forgiveness and reconciliation, Paul "improves" the image of the wrongdoer by dramatizing the "excessive sorrow" which now threatens to "overwhelm" him (2:7). Paul generalizes the distress caused by the wrongdoer by reminding the Corinthians of their complicity in the matter, as

---

ject, see John Nicholson, "The Delivery and Confidentiality of Cicero's Letters," *CJ* 90 (1994) 33–63.

65 Cicero *Fam.* 5.8.3; text in *Cicero: Epistulae ad Familiares*, Vol. 1, ed. David R. Shackleton Bailey (Cambridge: Cambridge University Press, 1977) 86–88, with commentary, 327–29; trans. in David R. Shackleton Bailey, *Cicero's Letters to His Friends* (Atlanta: Scholars Press, 1988) 69–71. For the strains in the relationship between Cicero and Crassus, see *Fam.* 1.9.20. See the helpful summary of the context of the letter in Bruce A. Marshall, *Crassus: A Political Biography* (Amsterdam: Hakkert, 1976) 173–74. See the nuanced analysis in Hall, *Politeness and Politics in Cicero's Letters*, 71–75.

66 Cicero *Fam.* 5.8.3. On the conciliatory purpose of the letter, see Epstein, *Personal Enmity,* 5. Cicero's conciliatory purpose is more impressive given his general dislike of Crassus, for which see *Fam.* 4.13.2; *Off.* 1.109; 3.75; cf. Dio Cassius 39.10.

67 2 Cor. 10:2, ἐπί τινας τοὺς λογιζομένους ἡμᾶς ὡς κατὰ σάρκα περιπατοῦντας; 10:7, εἴ τις πέποιθεν ἑαυτῷ Χριστοῦ εἶναι; 10:10, ὅτι αἱ ἐπιστολαὶ μέν, φησίν, βαρεῖαι καὶ ἰσχυραί, κτλ.; 10:11, τοῦτο λογιζέσθω ὁ τοιοῦτος; 11:16, μή τίς με δόξῃ ἄφρονα εἶναι; 12:6, μή τις εἰς ἐμὲ λογίσηται ὑπὲρ ὃ βλέπει με ἢ ἀκούει ἐξ ἐμοῦ; 2:5, εἰ δέ τις λελύπηκεν, κτλ.; 2:6, ἱκανὸν τῷ τοιούτῳ; 2:7, μή πως τῇ περισσοτέρᾳ λύπῃ καταποθῇ ὁ τοιοῦτος; 7:12, ἄρα εἰ καὶ ἔγραψα ὑμῖν, οὐχ ἕνεκεν τοῦ ἀδικήσαντος, κτλ.

evidenced by their remorse (7:7b, 8–9). Like the authors of the conciliatory epistles, Paul effaces himself from the conflict insofar as possible; note especially Paul's skillful use of conditional clauses—"if someone has caused pain, he has caused it not to me" (2:5); "if I have forgiven anything" (2:10). Moreover, Paul adopts a highly objective form of self-reference, ὁ ἀδικηθείς, "the one who was wronged," when the offence is finally mentioned in 7:12, just as Demosthenes speaks not of "me," but of "such a person," ὁ τοιοῦτος, when he refers to himself as the object of mistreatment.[68] Even the structure of Paul's argument in 7:12 ("it was *not on account of* the one who did the wrong, *nor on account of* the one who was wronged, *but in order that* your zeal for us might be made known to you before God") has a striking parallel in the summation of Dio's 45th oration: *"it is not that* you the Assembly desired the improvements, but a certain one of the officials opposed them, *nor yet that*, while no one opposed them, none was found enthusiastically in favor of them and ready to cooperate, *but on the contrary,* one and all, believing that the undertaking was fine and for the city's good, were ready not only to vote for it but also to contribute to it."[69] This parallel suggests that an avowal of higher motive, which functioned to lift the readers' gaze above the recent incidence of strife, was a standard tactic of conciliatory apologies. Beyond these general characteristics, it is striking how much of the vocabulary of 2 Cor. 1:1–2:13; 7:5–16 is shared with conciliatory letters and speeches which utilize the device of not-naming friends: e. g. λυπεῖν, ἐπιβαρεῖν, ἐπιτιμία, ἀδικεῖν/ἀδικεῖσθαι.[70]

We may conclude that Paul's refusal to mention the name of the individual who had done him wrong and caused him pain in 2 Cor. 2 and 7 was controlled by a rhetorical convention that was well established in the Greco-Roman world: one who wished to conciliate an alienated friend

---

68 Demosthenes *Ep.* 2.8; cf. Goldstein, *The Letters of Demosthenes*, 162: "A further mitigation was the use of the impersonal 'such a person' instead of 'me'."
69 Dio Chrysostom *Or.* 45.16; my translation modifies that of the LCL.
70 E.g., Demosthenes *Ep.* 2.2, τὰ δ᾽ ἀπόρρητα τούτων ἐπιτημήσεως ἄξι᾽ εὑρήκατε; Dio Chrysostom *Or.* 45.3, ἐγὼ δὲ ἂν λέγω νῦν, σφόδρα λυπήσω τινάς; 45.9, τοῦτο οὖν ἦν τὸ ποιῆσαν ἐμὲ τὴν ἡσυχίαν ἄγειν, ἵνα μὴ δοκῶ κατηγορεῖν τινων μηδὲ διαβάλλειν τὴν πόλιν μηδ᾽ ὅλως λυπηρότερος ᾧ τῶν ἐνθάδε μηδενί; 45.10, πολλὰ ὑπὸ πολλῶν δικημένος; 46.6, ἴσως μὲν γὰρ ἐπ᾽ οὐδένα οὐδὲ τῶν ἀδικούντων οὕτως ἔδει παροξύνεσθαι; Marcus Aurelius *apud* Philostratus *Vit. soph.* 2.1.563, μηδὲ ἡγεῖσθαι ἀδικεῖσθαι,…εἰ δέ τι λελύπηκα σε ἢ λυπῶ, κτλ. See also Chairemon to Apollonius, *BGU* II.531, 18–22; Ps.-Euripides *Ep.* 5.2, 6; Ps.-Aristotle *Ep.* 5.10–13.

avoided mentioning the name of the offender in apologetic contexts, and instead employed periphrastic constructions. Thus we cannot exclude the possibility that the wrongdoer of 2 Cor. 2:5–11 and 7:12 was among the individuals who are named by Paul in 1 Corinthians and in Romans 16 in connection with Corinth, as scholars influenced by Marshall have mistakenly assumed.[71] On the contrary, it is precisely among the group of Paul's friends at Corinth that we must look for the wrongdoer, since, in accordance with rhetorical convention, Paul does not name his wounded friend. Indeed, in the search for the identity of the wrongdoer, the weightier suspicion falls upon those individuals who can be shown to have enjoyed the closest relationships to Paul.

We may now recapitulate what we have learned about Paul's use of the rhetorical device of not-naming in 2 Corinthians and its implications for our understanding of Paul's relationships, both with his friends and with his enemies. In the earliest portions of the Corinthian correspondence, Paul mentions the names of several Corinthians (Chloe, Crispus, Gaius, Stephanas, Fortunatus and Achaicus) and three fellow-apostles (Cephas, Apollos and Barnabas).[72] From the fact that names are freely given, we may infer that enmity had not yet erupted, despite the fact that Paul represents the Corinthian Christians as having formed factions around himself, Apollos and Cephas (1 Cor. 1:12), and despite the evidence that Paul had been criticized, both with respect to the means of his subsistence (1 Cor. 9),[73] and the "foolishness" of his proclamation (1 Cor. 1:18–4:21).[74] Yet, Paul is still confident that his position as the founder and spiritual father of the community will be respected (1 Cor. 3:10–17; 4:14–21), and even threatens to come and restore discipline (1 Cor. 4:18–21).[75] By the time that Paul composes the letter now preserved in 2 Cor. 10–13, the situation has changed and is obviously more conflicted. From the fact that Paul names no one in 2 Cor. 10–13, neither rival apostles nor local Corinthians, we must assume that persons in both categories have come to be regarded as "ene-

---

71 Marshall, *Enmity in Corinth*, 345–46; Furnish, *II Corinthians*, 49, 511; Chow, *Patronage and Power*, 88, 90; Thrall, *Second Epistle*, 2.641
72 1 Cor. 1:11 (Chloe); 1:14 (Crispus and Gaius); 1:15 (Stephanas); 16:15–18 (Stephanas, Fortunatus and Achaicus); 1:12 (Apollos, Cephas); 3:4–6 (Apollos); 3:22 (Apollos, Cephas); 4:6 (Apollos); 16:12 (Apollos).
73 Theissen, "Legitimation and Subsistence" in idem, *Social Setting*, 27–67, esp. 40–54; Hock, *Social Context*, 59–62.
74 Welborn, *Paul, the Fool of Christ*, esp. 102–16.
75 Schrage, *Der erste Brief*, 363–65.

mies." Indeed, there is evidence of collusion between opponents of Paul in the two groups; we argued above that someone in Corinth invoked the rival apostles as the standard by which Paul must measure himself.[76] Thus, in defending the legitimacy of his apostleship in 2 Cor. 10–13, Paul rigorously applies the rhetorical device of not-naming, both against the rival apostles, and with respect to Corinthian opponents. But in Paul's application of this device, one marks a difference of emphasis, in accordance with Paul's purposes—that is, whether his aim is derogatory or conciliatory. With respect to his apostolic rivals, Paul employs the device of not-naming with the clear intention to shame, as Marshall demonstrated: the rival apostles are damned with anonymity, while periphrasis makes the missionaries available for pitiless invective (11:13–15) and outrageous caricature (11:19–21). With respect to his Corinthian critics, however, Paul's purpose is ultimately conciliatory, even in 2 Cor. 10–13, where only the subtle addition of the phrase ἐφ' ἑαυτοῦ ("by his own lights" or "on his own merits") to the directive τοῦτο λογιζέσθω πάλιν in 10:7 is mildly derogatory, as noted above.[77] Otherwise, Paul treats his Corinthian critic with respect, even in the midst of heated debate. The device of not-naming and the use of periphrastic substitutes make it possible for Paul to engage his critic and to defend his apostleship without further alienating his former friend. Paul's use of the device of not-naming in 2 Cor. 10–13, with respect to two groups, and with different purposes, is necessitated by the complexity of the rhetorical situation. In this respect, the 45th oration of Dio Chrysostom furnishes a useful analogy: here, too, the device of not-naming is deployed against rivals with derogatory intent, and is employed with friends for a conciliatory purpose, within a single communication, because of the complexity of the rhetorical exigence.[78]

In the conciliatory apology of 2 Cor. 1:1–2:13; 7:5–16, the rival apostles are no longer in view, and Paul forthrightly pursues reconciliation with the Corinthians. In accordance with social convention, Paul takes care not to mention the name of the wrongdoer and employs a number of subtle rhetorical devices with the aim of healing his wounded friend. Throughout all the stages of the conflict, Paul observes the standard rhetorical conventions that governed friendship, enmity, and recon-

---

76 See above on 2 Cor. 11:1–12:13, pp. 124–64; similarly, Mitchell, "The Corinthian Correspondence and the Birth of Pauline Hermeneutics," 31.
77 See above on 2 Cor. 10:7, pp. 84–101.
78 Crosby, *Dio Chrysostom IV*, 204–205.

ciliation in the Greco-Roman world. Thus, we may conclude that the individual with whom Paul has experienced conflict and whom Paul is careful not to name in 2 Cor. 2 and 7 must be looked for among the persons mentioned in 1 Corinthians or Romans 16, because he was one of Paul's former friends.

Nine individuals are mentioned by Paul in 1 Corinthians and Romans 16 in connection with Corinth: Chloe, Crispus, Gaius, Stephanas, Fortunatus, Achaicus, Tertius, Erastus and Quartus.[79] In every case, the evidence suggests that these individuals are to be identified as Christians, and are members of, or are closely associated with, the Christian *ekklesia* in Corinth.[80] Some scholars have expressed doubts whether Chloe resided in Corinth,[81] and whether she herself was a Christian,[82] but on insufficient grounds in both respects. The fact that Paul mentions her name to readers in Corinth without introduction (in 1 Cor. 1:11) indicates that Chloe and her "people" were well known to Christians there.[83]

---

79 Chloe (1 Cor. 1:11); Crispus (1 Cor. 1:14); Gaius (1 Cor. 1:14; Rom. 16:23); Stephanas (1 Cor. 1:16; 16:15–18); Fortunatus (1 Cor. 16:17); Achaicus (1 Cor. 16:17); Tertius (Rom. 16:22); Erastus (Rom. 16:23); Quartus (Rom. 16:23). Although a thorough prosopography of early Christianity at Corinth is wanting, these nine individuals are treated *inter alia*, and under different aspects, by William R. Ramsay, "A Historical Commentary on the Epistles to the Corinthians," *The Expositor* 1 (1900) 91–111; Judge, "The Early Christians as a Scholastic Community," in *The First Christians in the Roman World*, 526–52, esp. 544–45; Theissen, "Social Stratification in the Corinthian Community" in idem, *Social Setting*, 69–119; Abraham Malherbe, *Social Aspects of Early Christianity* (Philadelphia: Fortress Press, 1983) 71–84; Meeks, *The First Urban Christians*, 16, 27, 55–59, 67–69, 118–19, 123, 137, 143, 147, 151; Chow, *Patronage and Power*, 88–100; Craig Steven de Vos, *Church and Community Conflicts: The Relationship of the Thessalonian, Corinthian, and Philippian Churches with Their Wider Civic Communities* (Atlanta: Scholars Press, 1999) 197–202; Edwin A. Judge, "The Roman Base of Paul's Mission," *TynBul* 56 (2005) 103–17; repr. in idem, *The First Christians in the Roman World*, 553–67; Steven J. Friesen, "Prospects for a Demography of the Pauline Mission: Corinth among the Churches" in *Urban Religion in Roman Corinth*, ed. David N. Schowalter and Steven J. Friesen (Cambridge, MA: Harvard University Press, 2005) 351–70.
80 Judge, "Scholastic Community" in idem, *The First Christians in the Roman World*, 544–45; Theissen, *Social Setting*, 55–56, 73–75, 83, 87, 92–94.
81 Fee, *First Epistle*, 54; Chow, *Patronage and Power*, 91; Florence Gillman, *Women Who Knew Paul* (Collegeville: Liturgical Press, 1992) 38–39.
82 Barrett, *First Epistle*, 42; Conzelmann, *1 Corinthians*, 32; Fee, *First Epistle*, 54; Chow, *Patronage and Power*, 91–92.
83 Theissen, *Social Setting*, 92–93; Meeks, *First Urban Christians*, 59.

The expression οἱ Χλόης (literally, "those of Chloe"), without the partitive ἐκ used by Paul in other cases,[84] probably implies that Chloe's entire household was Christian.[85] In any case, one might ask, who but a Christian would have been so well-informed about dissensions in the Christian community at Corinth? The other individuals named by Paul in 1 Corinthians are clearly marked as Christians, by references to their "baptism," in the case of Crispus, Gaius and Stephanas (1 Cor. 1:14, 16), or to their status as "first-fruits" (ἀπαρχή) of Paul's missionary work in Achaia, as in the case of Fortunatus and Achaicus (1 Cor. 16:15–18), the traveling-companions of Stephanas (assuming that Fortunatus and Achaicus are members of Stephanas' "household").[86] That these persons resided in Corinth is evident from the context of Paul's remarks. Three additional individuals whose names are found in Rom. 16—Tertius, Erastus and Quartus—also merit our attention, because Paul's Epistle to the Romans was written from Corinth on the occasion of Paul's final visit;[87] Paul conveys their greetings in connection with those of Gaius, Paul's "host" in Corinth (Rom. 16:23).[88] That Tertius, the amanuensis who copied Paul's letter to the Romans, was also a Christian is indicated by the phrase ἐν κυρίῳ ("in the Lord") which Tertius appended to his own greeting in Rom. 16:22, to make clear that he regarded his scribal work as a Chris-

---

84 Phil. 4:22: οἱ ἐκ τῆς Καίσαρος οἰκίας; Rom. 16:10: οἱ ἐκ τῶν Ἀριστοβούλου; Rom. 16:11: οἱ ἐκ τῶν Ναρκίσσου οἱ ὄντες ἐν κυρίῳ.
85 Theissen, *Social Setting*, 93; Meeks, *First Urban Christians*, 217 n.54.
86 Ernst von Dobschütz, *Christian Life in the Primitive Church* (New York: Harper, 1904) 57; James Moffatt, *The First Epistle of Paul to the Corinthians* (New York: Harper, 1938) 278; Theissen, *Social Setting*, 87; Fee, *First Epistle*, 831.
87 Rom. 16:23; Acts 20:2–3. See Wolf-Henning Ollrog, "Die Abfassungsverhältnisse von Röm 16" in *Kirche*, ed. Dieter Lührmann and Georg Strecker (Tübingen: Mohr Siebeck, 1980) 221–44; Udo Schnelle, (*Einleitung in das Neue Testament* [Göttingen: Vandebhoeck & Ruprecht, 2002] 130 n.346) speaks of a "relativ grossen Forschungskonsens" on this point; Robert Jewett, *Romans: A Commentary*, Hermeneia (Minneapolis: Fortress Press, 2007) 18, 21–22: "There is conclusive evidence, drawn in part from primary evidence in the Pauline letters, that the letter to the Romans was created in Corinth." Cf. Charlotte Hartwig and Gerd Theissen, "Die Korinthische Gemeinde als Nebenadressat des Römerbriefs," *NovT* 46 (2004) 229–52.
88 There is a consensus that the Gaius of Rom. 16:23 is identical with the Gaius of 1 Cor. 1:14: see, e.g., Judge, "Scholastic Community" in idem, *The First Christians in the Roman World*, 545; Theissen, *Social Setting*, 89; Meeks, *First Urban Christians*, 57.

tian service.[89] We must assume that Erastus was a Christian, as well, since Paul conveys his greetings to the believers in Rome (Rom. 16:23);[90] Paul's description of Erastus as "the treasurer of the city" (ὁ οἰκονόμος τῆς πόλεως), reveals that he held civic office in Corinth.[91] Quartus, from whom Paul also sends greetings (Rom. 16:23), is termed "the brother" (ὁ ἀδελφός).[92]

We have left out of account Aquila and Prisca.[93] Although Paul found lodging and employment with this missionary couple on his arrival in Corinth (according to Acts 18:1–3),[94] Aquila and Prisca had relocated to Ephesus by the time that Paul wrote 1 Cor. 16, whence they, "together with the church in their house," send greetings to the Corinthian Christians (1 Cor. 16:19).[95] We have also omitted from consideration Lucius, Jason and Sosipater, whose greetings Paul extends to the Romans in Rom. 16:21.[96] Although these "compatriots" (συγγενεῖς) were present with Paul in Corinth when he wrote his Epistle to the Romans,[97] they

---

[89] Heinrich Schlier, *Der Römerbrief* (Freiburg: Herder, 1977) 451; Leon Morris, *The Epistle to the Romans* (Grand Rapids: Eerdmans, 1988) 543; Jewett, *Romans*, 979–80.

[90] Rightly, Theissen, *Social Setting*, 75–83; Malherbe, *Social Aspects*, 72, 74; Meeks, *First Urban Christians*, 48, 58–59, 69; James D. G. Dunn, *Romans 9–16* (Dallas: Word, 1988) 910–11; Jewett, *Romans*, 981–83. For the suggestion that Erastus was not a Christian, but an interested outsider, see Gerd Theissen, "The Social Structure of Pauline Communities: Some Critical Remarks on J. J. Meggitt, *Paul, Poverty and Survival*," *JSNT* 84 (2001) 79–80

[91] Theissen, *Social Setting*, 75–83; Meeks, *First Urban Christians*, 48, 58–59.

[92] Dunn, *Romans 9–16*, 911. Cf. 1 Cor. 1:1, Σωσθένης ὁ ἀδελφός.

[93] On Prisca and Aquila, see Judge, "Scholastic Community" in idem, *The First Christians in the Roman World*, 544, 547; Meeks, *First Urban Christians*, 59; Peter Lampe, "Prisca/Priscilla," *ABD* 5 (1992) 467; Jewett, *Romans*, 955–57.

[94] Lüdemann (*Early Christianity according to the Traditions in Acts*, 198, 201–202) finds the account of Acts 18:2–3 "untendentious" and, ultimately, "historical." Cf. Ernst Haenchen, *The Acts of the Apostles: A Commentary* (Philadelphia: Westminster Press, 1971) 533–34; C. K. Barrett, *A Critical and Exegetical Commentary on the Acts of the Apostles*. Vol. 2: *Acts 15–28* (London: T & T Clark, 2004) 860–64.

[95] Collins, *First Corinthians*, 608–609.

[96] John Gillman, "Lucius," *ABD* 4 (1992) 397; Florence Morgan Gillman, "Jason," *ABD* 3 (1992) 649; Florence Morgan Gillman, "Sosipater," *ABD* 6 (1992) 160; Jewett, *Romans*, 977–78.

[97] On the meaning of συγγενεῖς in this context, see Wilhelm Michaelis, "συγγενής, συγγένεια," *TDNT* 7 (1971) 741: "the narrower sense of relatives may be ruled out, since it is most improbable that there would have been six members of Paul's immediate family among those mentioned in Rom. 16"; Jewett, *Romans*, 978:

were not Corinthians, but delegates of Paul's churches in Macedonia, who had joined Paul in Corinth in order to accompany him on the journey to Jerusalem to deliver the collection.[98] Finally, we have excluded Titius Justus, a God-fearing Gentile, in whose house at Corinth Paul preached after his withdrawal from the synagogue (according to Acts 18:7).[99] There is no reason to doubt the historicity of the account in Acts,[100] although Titius Justus is not mentioned in any of Paul's epistles.[101] Perhaps Justus left Corinth sometime after Paul's first visit, and before the commencement of Paul's correspondence with Corinth; or perhaps Justus ceased to be associated with the Christian community.[102] Whatever the case may be, the fact that Justus is mentioned only in Acts excludes him from consideration as the wrongdoer of 2 Corinthians.

Thus, we have nine individuals in 1 Corinthians and Romans 16 who are demonstrably Corinthian Christians, all of whom are putatively friends or associates of Paul, to one degree or another. Since we have discovered that Paul adheres closely to the social convention of not-naming friends with whom he is seeking reconciliation, we must look for the wrongdoer of 2 Cor. 2 and 7 among the nine individuals of 1 Cor. 16 and Rom. 16. The criteria by which we must evaluate these suspects are those which emerged from our detailed exegesis of the letters and letter-fragments that make up 2 Corinthians: accordingly, the wrongdoer should be a person of high status and influence, capable of causing pain to an entire community; he looks down upon Paul the artisan from a considerable social distance; he is possessed of a robust confidence of "belonging to Christ," and has a preference for the ennobling Christology of a rival missionary; he enjoys a relatively high level of education, which

---

"All three are identified as Paul's συγγενεῖς, which has the connotation of fellow Jews, as in 9:3; 16:7 and 11."

98 Ollrog, *Paulus und seine Mitarbeiter*, 58; Georgi, *Remembering the Poor*, 122–23; Jewett, *Romans*, 977–78.

99 Haenchen, *Acts of the Apostles*, 535; Barrett, *Acts 15–28*, 868. For the limited sense in which one may use "Luke's" term "God-fearers," see Judith Lieu, "The Race of the God-fearers," *JTS* 46 (1995) 483–501; repr. in idem, *Neither Jew Nor Greek? Constructing Early Christianity* (London: T & T Clark, 2005) 49–68.

100 Lüdemann, *Early Christianity according to Acts*, 203.

101 Contra Edgar J. Goodspeed, "Gaius Titius Justus," *JBL* 69 (1950) 382–83, who harmonizes Acts 18:7 with Rom. 16:23, in order to identify Titius Justus with Gaius. For critique of this conjecture, see below.

102 Meeks, *First Urban Christians*, 63: "Acts does not say explicitly whether Titius Justus became a Christian."

qualifies him to be critical of Paul's oratorical ability; he has played a patronal role in relation to one or more of Paul's apostolic rivals; etc. Moreover, there must be a certain presumption in favor of identifying the wrongdoer with persons who are known to have been converts of Paul on the occasion of his first visit to Corinth, for only in this case can we posit a pre-existing relationship consistent with Paul's treatment of the wrongdoer as an alienated friend in 2 Cor. 2:5–11 and 7:12, in accordance with established social conventions.

We may begin by clearing Chloe of suspicion. To be sure, Chloe was a person of some financial means, as demonstrated by the fact that she was able to provision members of her household, whether slaves or former slaves,[103] to travel to Ephesus, where they reported to Paul about the troubles in Corinth (1 Cor. 1:11).[104] Nor is there any reason to doubt that Chloe was well disposed toward Paul, since her "people" evidently sought to arouse Paul's concern about the outbreak of faction in the Christian community.[105] Yet, it is safe to assume that a woman would not be denoted by Paul's consistent use of masculine pronouns (τις, ὁ τοιοῦτος, αὐτός) and a masculine participle (ὁ ἀδικήσας) in reference to the individual who has done him wrong and caused him pain.

We may also eliminate from consideration Fortunatus and Achaicus, the two traveling companions of Stephanas (1 Cor. 16:17). Both names probably indicate servile origins.[106] "Fortunatus" ("fortunate," "lucky") was a common name, appropriate to a freedman.[107] A *cognomen* such as "Achaicus"

---

103 Theissen, *Social Setting*, 93: "Who were 'Chloe's people'?…Within the Pauline letters themselves the closest parallel would be groups of slaves addressed summarily (Rom. 16:10, 11; Phil. 4:22)"; Meeks, *First Urban Christians*, 59: "'Chloe's people' (*hoi Chloēs*, 1 Cor. 1:11) are slaves or freedmen or both."
104 Theissen, *Social Setting*, 91.
105 Nils Dahl, "Paul and the Church at Corinth according to 1 Cor. 1:10–4:21" in *Christian History and Interpretation*, ed. W. R. Farmer, C. F. D. Moule, and R. R. Niebuhr (Cambridge: Cambridge University Press, 1967) 323; Theissen, *Social Setting*, 57; Chow, *Patronage and Power*, 94–95.
106 Ramsay, "A Historical Commentary on the Epistles to the Corinthians," 101; Weiss, *Der erste Korintherbrief*, 386; A. Robertson and A. Plummer, *A Critical and Exegetical Commentary on the First Epistle of St. Paul to the Corinthians* (Edinburgh: T & T Clark, 1914) 296; L. R. Taylor, "Freedmen and Freeborn in the Epitaphs of Imperial Rome," *American Journal of Philology* 82 (1961) 125; Judge, "The Roman Base of Paul's Mission" in *The First Christians in the Roman World*, 562.
107 Moulton and Milligan, *Vocabulary of the Greek Testament*, 675 s.v. Φορτουνᾶτος; Heikki Solin, *Die stadtrömischen Sklavennamen: Ein Namenbuch* (Stuttgart:

("from Achaia" or "the Achaian"), derived from a place name or an *ethnos*, was generally associated with slaves or freedmen.[108] The mention of Fortunatus and Achaicus along with Stephanas, following Paul's laudatory reference to Stephanas' "household" (in 1 Cor. 16:15–16), suggests that Fortunatus and Achaicus were Stephanas' dependants, whether as slaves or freedmen clients.[109] Thus, neither Fortunatus nor Achaicus would have possessed the status and influence which we have predicated of the wrongdoer.[110]

Next, we may set aside Tertius, the Christian scribe of the Epistle to the Romans (Rom. 16:22).[111] The Latin name Tertius means "third," and was often used as a name for slaves.[112] The fact that Tertius' profession was that of scribe also indicates slave status, since amanuenses were often slaves.[113] Because Paul was a guest in the house of Gaius in Corinth when he wrote the Epistle to the Romans (Rom. 16:23), we should probably infer that Tertius was a slave of Gaius.[114] The self-assurance with which Tertius speaks in the greeting which he inserts into the letter itself, rather than attaching it as a note at the end, is eloquent testimony to the sense of equality "in Christ" enjoyed by this member of the Pauline community, as Robert Jewett has observed.[115] Nevertheless, it is clear that Ter-

---

Franz Steiner, 1996) s.v. Fortunatus. Cf. Barnett, *Second Epistle*, 7; Thiselton, *First Epistle*, 1340 n.124.

108 Meeks, *First Urban Christians*, 56–57, 216 n.30: "The use of a place name as a cognomen probably indicates servile origins, although that depends upon the circumstances under which the nickname was given." See also Héring, *First Epistle*, 186; Thiselton, *First Epistle*, 1340.

109 Dobschütz, *Primitive Church*, 57; Moffatt, *First Epistle*, 278; Meeks, *First Urban Christians*, 56–57; Fee, *First Epistle*, 831.

110 Meeks, *First Urban Christians*, 56–57; Chow, *Patronage and Power*, 91.

111 Theissen, *Social Setting*, 92; Meeks, *First Urban Christians*, 57; Jewett, *Romans*, 978–80.

112 Solin, *Die stadtrömischen Sklavennamen*, 152–53, with many examples of Tertius as a slave name; Judge, "The Roman Base of Paul's Mission" in *The First Christians in the Roman World*, 562. Cf. Otto Michel, *Der Brief an die Römer* (Göttingen: Vandenhoeck & Ruprecht, 1978) 483; Jewett, *Romans*, 978.

113 E.g., *ILS* 1514 in Robert Kenneth Sherk, *The Roman Empire: Augustus to Hadrian* (Cambridge: Cambridge University Press, 1988) 237; G. H. R. Horsley, "The Distribution of a Deceased Man's Slaves," *NewDocs*, Vol. 1, 69–70. Cf. Richard N. Longenecker, "Ancient Amanuenses and the Pauline Epistles" in Richard N. Longenecker and M. C. Tenney, *New Dimensions in New Testament Study* (Grand Rapids: Eerdmans, 1974) 281–97; Jewett, *Romans*, 978.

114 Theissen, *Social Setting*, 55; Welborn, *Politics and Rhetoric*, 26; Murphy-O'Connor, *Paul*, 268.

115 Jewett, *Romans*, 980.

tius lacked the wealth and status that would qualify him for consideration as the wrongdoer.

Little can be said with certainty about the social status of Quartus, mentioned last among those who send greetings in Rom. 16:23.[116] The Latin name Quartus means "fourth."[117] Like Tertius, it was a common name among slaves and freedmen.[118] The designation of Quartus as "the brother" (ὁ ἀδελφός) would illuminate the social level of this individual, only if the suggestion of Robert Jewett were adopted, that the article has the force of a weak possessive, and should be translated "his";[119] then Quartus would share the social status of Erastus, his brother.[120] Otherwise, the expression ὁ ἀδελφός in Rom. 16:23 would function, as it does elsewhere in Paul (1 Cor. 1:1; 16:12; 2 Cor. 1:1; Phil. 2:25; Phlm. 1), to identify Quartus as a Christian "brother" with a particular function or worthy of special honor.[121]

That leaves Crispus, Gaius, Stephanas and Erastus. About these four individuals, considerably more is known, either because they are mentioned more than once in the Epistles and Acts, or because additional details are provided regarding their offices, services, and relationships to Paul. We shall discover that each of these individuals was possessed of sufficient resources and exercised sufficient influence to have played the role that we have inferred for the wrongdoer in relation to Paul, his rivals, and the Corinthian community, although there are perceptible differences of social status between them. Moreover, we shall see that each of these men was demonstrably a friend or associate of Paul, although, again, there are discernible variations in the quality of their relationships.

In 1 Cor. 1:14, Paul names Crispus as one of the few individuals whom he personally baptized at the beginning of his proclamation of the gospel in Corinth.[122] Acts 18:8 relates that "Crispus, the ruler of

---

116 John Gillman, "Quartus," *ABD* 5 (1992) 583.
117 Glare, *Oxford Latin Dictionary*, 1542–43, s.v. quartus.
118 Solin, *Die stadtrömischen Sklavennamen*, 154; Judge, "The Roman Base of Paul's Mission" in *The First Christians in the Roman World*, 562.
119 Jewett, *Romans*, 983, appealing to Smyth, *Greek Grammar*, §1121.
120 Jewett, *Romans*, 984.
121 Dunn, *Romans 9–16*, 911.
122 On the context of Paul's mention of Crispus, see Weiss, *Der erste Korintherbrief*, 19–21. For attestations of the name Crispus in the papyri, see Peter Arzt-Grabner, Ruth Elisabeth Kritzer, Amphilochios Papathomas, Franz Winter, *1. Korinther. Papyrologische Kommentare zum Neuen Testament* (Göttingen: Vandenhoeck & Ruprecht, 2006) 74. For an estimate of the "social impressiveness" of

the synagogue, believed in the Lord, together with all his household." Because it is hardly possible to doubt the identity of the Crispus of Acts 18:8 with the man named in 1 Cor. 1:14,[123] the information of Acts that Crispus was "the ruler of the synagogue" (ὁ ἀρχισυνάγωγος) prior to his conversion would be crucial for establishing the status and influence of Crispus,[124] if the information could be shown to be historically reliable. Gerd Lüdemann has subjected the account of Acts to careful analysis, and has concluded that the tradition that makes Crispus the synagogue president is "historically credible," adducing in support of this conclusion aspects of both 1 Cor. 1:14 and Acts 18:8: the exception which Paul makes to his usual practice of not personally baptizing converts in the case of Crispus, and the effect which the news of Crispus' conversion had upon others ("and many of the Corinthians, when the heard [of it], believed and had themselves baptized," Acts 18:8b).[125] These aspects find a ready explanation in the position of Crispus as "ruler of the synagogue."[126]

As the former ἀρχισυνάγωγος,[127] Crispus would have had considerable wealth, since the position entailed responsibility for the upkeep of

---

the cognomen Crispus, see Judge, "The Roman Base of Paul's Mission" in *The First Christians in the Roman World*, 561–62.

123 The identity is assumed by Judge, "Scholastic Community" in *The First Christians in the Roman World*, 544–45; Theissen, *Social Setting*, 73–74; Malherbe, *Social Aspects*, 72; Meeks, *First Urban Christians*, 57; Anthony J. Blasi, *Early Christianity as a Social Movement* (Toronto: Peter Lang, 1988) 56–59; "almost surely," according to Schrage, *Der erste Brief*, 1.155; Thiselton, *First Epistle*, 140.

124 The importance of this datum for establishing the status of Crispus is widely recognized: e.g., Theissen, *Social Setting*, 73–74; Meeks, *First Urban Christians*, 57; Murphy-O'Connor, *St. Paul's Corinth*, 267. Meggitt (*Paul, Poverty and Survival*, 142–43) attempts to diminish the significance of Crispus' office of ἀρχισυνάγωγος; but see the counterarguments of Theissen, "The Social Structure of the Pauline Communities," 81–82. It is puzzling that Crispus is omitted from the economic profile of Paul's assemblies in Friesen, "Poverty in Pauline Studies," 348–58, esp. 357.

125 Lüdemann, *Early Christianity according to Acts*, 203–204.

126 Theissen, *Social Setting*, 73: "From Acts 18:8 we learn that Crispus, one of the first Christians, was a synagogue ruler. His conversion to Christianity was probably of great significance for the founding of the community, setting off a small wave of conversions."

127 Acts 18:17 suggests that Crispus was replaced as synagogue ruler by Sosthenes. On the office of ἀρχισυνάγωγος, see Emil Schürer, *The History of the Jewish People in the Age of Jesus Christ*, II, rev. and ed. Geza Vermes, Fergus Millar and Matthew Black (Edinburgh: T & T Clark, 1979) 433–36; Jean-Baptiste Frey, *Corpus Inscriptionum Judaicarum: Jewish Inscriptions from the Third Century B.C. to the Sev-

the synagogue.¹²⁸ Gerd Theissen adduces inscriptions which illustrate the expenses undertaken by the ἀρχισυνάγωγος and permit inferences about the kind of person entrusted with this office.¹²⁹ In the Italian town of Porto, an ἀρχισυνάγωγος made repairs to the side entrance of a synagogue building "out of his own resources" (ἐκ τῶν ἰδίων).¹³⁰ In Aegina, not far from Corinth, an ἀρχισυνάγωγος named Theodorus rebuilt a synagogue from the ground up, over a period of four years.¹³¹ Theodorus evidently supplemented the funds of the community with his own contributions.¹³² The best known synagogue inscription is that of Theodotus at Jerusalem.¹³³ Theodotus, who describes himself not only as "ruler of the synagogue" (ἀρχισυνάγωγος), but also as the "son of a ruler of the synagogue" and "son's son of a ruler of the synagogue," records that he "built the synagogue (ᾠκοδόμησε τὴν συναγωγήν) for reading of the law and for teaching of the commandments."¹³⁴ In addition to the synagogue building, Theodotus constructed "the strangers' lodging and the chambers and the conveniences of waters for an inn for them that need it from abroad."¹³⁵ These and other inscriptions make clear that the role of the

---

enth Century A.D. 2 vols. (New York: KTAV Publishing, 1975) xcvii–xcix; Tessa Rajak and David Noy, "Archisynagogoi: Office, Title and Social Status in the Greco-Jewish Synagogue," *JRS* 83 (1993) 75–93; repr. in Tessa Rajak, *The Jewish Dialogue with Greece and Rome: Studies in Cultural and Social Interaction* (Leiden: Brill, 2002) 393–430.

128 Theissen, *Social Setting*, 74; Rajak, "Archisynagogoi as benefactors" and "Archisynagogoi as patrons" in idem, *The Jewish Dialogue with Greece and Rome*, 416–19.

129 Theissen, *Social Setting*, 74–75; see also Rajak, "Appendix I: Archisynagogoi as donors" in idem, *The Jewish Dialogue with Greece and Rome*, 424–26.

130 Frey, *Corpus Inscriptionum Judaicarum*, no. 548; Theissen, *Social Setting*, 74.

131 Frey, *Corpus Inscriptionum Judaicarum*, no. 722; Rajak, "Appendix I: Archisynagogoi as donors" no. 17 in idem, *The Jewsih Dialogue with Greece and Rome*, 424.

132 Cf. Baruch Lifschitz, *Donateurs et fondateurs dans les synagogues juives* (Paris: Gabalda, 1967) no. 1.

133 Frey, *Corpus Inscriptionum Judaicarum*, no. 1404; Lifschitz, *Donateurs*, no. 79; Rajak, "Appendix I: Archisynagogoi as donors" no. 25 in idem, *The Jewish Dialogue with Greece and Rome*, 425–26. Cf. Adolf Deissmann, "Appendix V: The Synagogue Inscription of Theodotus of Jerusalem" in *Light from the Ancient East: The New Testament Illustrated by Recently Discovered Texts of the Graeco-Roman World* (Grand Rapids: Baker Book House, 1980) 439–41; Theissen, *Social Setting*, 74.

134 Frey, *Corpus Inscriptionum Judaicarum*, no. 1404; the trans. follows Deissmann, *Light from the Ancient East*, 440.

135 Frey, *Corpus Inscriptionum Judaicarum*, no. 1404; see the notes in Deissmann, *Light from the Ancient East*, 440.

ἀρχισυνάγωγος was that of benefactor and patron of the Jewish community, and entailed significant financial responsibilities.[136] That an ἀρχισυνάγωγος would have enjoyed esteem beyond the boundaries of the Jewish community is possible.[137] Theissen adduces a funerary inscription of one Staphylus of Rome, *archon et archisynagogus*, who evidently also held offices in the city.[138] In practice, the influence of an ἀρχισυνάγωγος would have depended upon the network of his friends and associates. In the case of Crispus, his influence may have been considerable, if, once again, the tradition preserved in Acts is deemed to be historically reliable, for it speaks of "many of the Corinthians" (πολλοὶ τῶν Κορινθίων) who believed and had themselves baptized "when they heard [of it]"—that is, of Crispus' conversion (Acts 18:8b).[139]

As for Crispus' relationship to Paul, it would seem a positive indicator that Paul departed from his usual custom of not baptizing, and personally administered baptism to Crispus (1 Cor. 1:14).[140] If the report of Acts is trustworthy, that Crispus' conversion served as a catalyst to others (Acts 18:8), then one must assume that Paul, who once confessed himself willing to "become all things to all people, so that by any means I might save some" (1 Cor. 9:22), would have known how to value a man whose conversion had such ramifications. Yet, the manner in which Paul names Crispus, along with Gaius, as exceptions to his practice of not baptizing is strangely negative, and has rightly puzzled interpreters: "I thank God that I baptized none of you except Crispus and Gaius, so that no one

---

136 Theissen, *Social Setting*, 74, 75; Rajak, "Archisynagogoi as benefactors" in *The Jewish Dialogue with Greece and Rome*, 416: "*Archisynagogoi* are found as donors of whole synagogue buildings, restorers of buildings, or donors of parts of buildings: mosaic floors, a chancel screen, columns. These Jewish benefactors operate essentially like Greco-Roman benefactors within a 'euergistic' framework of giving benefits and receiving honors."
137 Haenchen, *Acts of the Apostles*, 535; Theissen, *Social Setting*, 74; Meeks, *First Urban Christians*, 57; Rajak, *The Jewish Dialogue with Greece and Rome*, 417: "The *archisynagogos* was a patronal figure. With his wealth, his standing, and the advantage of a title which the outside world could recognize instantly, he had the wherewithal to act as mediator for the community."
138 Theissen, *Social Setting*, 74–75; Frey, *Corpus Inscriptionum Judaicarum*, 265; Rajak, "Appendix I: Epitaphs of Archisynagogoi," no. 1 in idem, *The Jewish Dialogue with Greece and Rome*, 421–22.
139 G. Schneider, *Die Apostelgeschichte*. 2 vols. (Freiburg: Herder, 1982) 2.251; Theissen, *Social Setting*, 73; Lüdemann, *Early Christianity according to Acts*, 204.
140 Meeks, *First Urban Christians*, 57; Fee, *First Epistle*, 62; Chow, *Patronage and Power*, 89; Collins, *First Corinthians*, 83.

might say that you were baptized in my name" (1 Cor. 1:14–15).[141] As Johannes Weiss observed, there is an audible sigh of relief behind this statement, whose force might be best captured: "I am just glad that God arranged it so that I baptized none of you except...etc."[142] How *can* the apostle give thanks to God that he baptized only a few persons in Corinth? There is an unmistakable note of irony in Paul's thanksgiving in 1 Cor. 1:14.[143] The puzzlement deepens when one observes how Paul continues: catching himself, as if he had momentarily forgotten something, Paul adds, "But I did also baptize the household of Stephanas," and finally concedes, as if his memory can no longer be trusted, that there may have been others: "besides these, I do not know whether I baptized anyone else" (1 Cor. 1:16).[144] It is scarcely possible that Paul could have forgotten, even for a moment, the household of Stephanas, whom Paul himself praises as the "first-fruits of Achaia" (1 Cor. 16:15), especially as Stephanas and members of his household had recently visited Paul in Ephesus and had "refreshed" his spirit (1 Cor. 16:17–18).[145] It is clear that, in Paul's treatment of the individuals whom he had personally baptized, he is employing a rhetorical figure, which Weiss, with his customary penetration, characterized as "feigned indifference":[146] it is a matter of little importance to Paul whether he baptized someone personally; Paul wishes to make clear that he is no "baptizer" (1 Cor. 1:17a), like Apollos, the sometime disciple of John the Baptist (Acts 18:25), around whom a faction had formed in the church at Corinth (1 Cor. 1:12; 3:4).[147] Thus, Paul's strangely negative way of speaking about the baptism of Crispus and Gaius was shaped by his polemic against the outbreak of factions in the church.[148] One cannot suppress the suspicion that Crispus and Gaius are named first in this regard because they have been involved in the conflict. This suspicion is strengthened by the observation that Paul separates Crispus and Gaius in his ironical thanksgiving from Ste-

---

141 Weiss, *Der erste Korintherbrief*, 20; Lindemann, *Der erste Korintherbrief*, 41.
142 Weiss, *Der erste Korintherbrief*, 20.
143 Conzelmann, *1 Corinthians*, 36; Joseph Fitzmyer, *First Corinthians: A New Translation with Introduction and Commentary* (New Haven: Yale University Press, 2008) 146.
144 Weiss, *Der erste Korintherbrief*, 20; Lindemann, *Der erste Korintherbrief*, 42.
145 Weiss, *Der erste Korintherbrief*, 20; Lindemann, *Der erste Korintherbrief*, 42.
146 Weiss, *Der erste Korintherbrief*, 20: "gesuchte Nachlässigkeit"; Lindemann, *Der erste Korintherbrief*, 42.
147 Weiss, *Der erste Korintherbrief*, 19–20.
148 Weiss, *Der erste Korintherbrief*, 20.

phanas, his strongest supporter in Corinth (as we shall see), by the device of a feigned lapse of memory.

We may now summarize what we have learned about Crispus from Paul's reference to his baptism in 1 Cor. 1:14 and from the account of his conversion in Acts. Crispus was a person of considerable financial resources and significant personal influence, sufficient in both respects to have played the role which our exegesis has assigned to the wrongdoer. Crispus must have been closely associated with Paul during his first visit to Corinth. But by the time that Paul wrote the letter now preserved in 1 Cor. 1:1–6:11, there is evidence of tension in their relationship caused, it would seem, by Crispus' involvement in the formation of factions.

Gaius, who is mentioned in the same breath with Crispus in 1 Cor. 1:14, also must have been among the converts made by Paul on his first visit to Corinth.[149] In Rom. 16:23, Paul sends greetings from a Gaius whom he describes as "my host and the host of the whole church."[150] Although "Gaius" (Latin *Caius*) was a common Roman *praenomen*,[151] especially common at Corinth owing to the history of the colony,[152] there is no reason to doubt the identity of the two Gaii mentioned

---

149 Meeks, *First Urban Christians*, 57; Fee, *First* Epistle, 62; Thiselton, *First Epistle*, 27.
150 Judge, "Scholastic Community" in *The First Christians in the Roman World*, 545; Theissen, *Social Setting*, 55, 89; Malherbe, *Social Aspects*, 73; Meeks, *First Urban Christians*, 57; Andrew D. Clarke, *Secular and Christian Leadership in Corinth: A Socio-Historical and Exegetical Study of 1 Corinthians 1–6* (Leiden: Brill, 1993) 46.
151 Heikki Solin, "Names, personal, Roman," *OCD*, 3rd ed., Simon Hornblower and Anthony Spawforth, eds. (Oxford: Oxford University Press, 2003) 1024–26, esp. 1024; H. Rix, *Römische Personennamen: Namenforschung: Ein internationals Handbuch zur Onomastik I* (Berlin: Walter de Gruyter, 1995) 724–32; Olli Salomies, *Die römischen Vornamen: Studien zur römischen Namengebung* (Helsinki: Societas Scientiarum Fennica, 1987). It is possible that Gaius is a *praenomen* functioning as a *cognomen* in a Greek context; on this phenomenon, see Heikki Solin, "Latin Cognomina in the Greek East" in *The Greek East in the Roman Context*, ed. Olli Salomies (Helsinki: The Finnish Institute at Athens, 2001) 189–202, esp. 191, 194–96; Iiro Kajanto, *The Latin Cognomina* (Helsinki: Societas Scientiarum Fennica, 1965) 39–41, 172–75. But, as we shall see, the use of *praenomina* as *cognomina* did not become common until the second century, and then only in the less Romanized areas.
152 Corinth was re-founded as a Roman colony by Gaius Julius Caesar in 44 B.C. Many of the colonists were Caesar's freedmen, and would have borne his *praenomen*. See Appian *Punica* 136; Strabo 8.6.23; Plutarch *Caes.* 57.5; Dio Cassius

in 1 Cor. 1:14 and Rom. 16:23.¹⁵³ For the evaluation of the social status of Paul's Gaius, Paul's description of him as "my host and the host of the whole church" (ὁ ξένος μου καὶ ὅλης τῆς ἐκκλησίας) is of the utmost importance.¹⁵⁴ The term ξένος is used of parties giving or receiving hospitality;¹⁵⁵ mostly it is applied to the "guest,"¹⁵⁶ less frequently to the "host."¹⁵⁷ The context and manner of Paul's usage in Rom. 16:23 make clear that the role of "host" is intended.¹⁵⁸ Craig de Vos suggests that Paul uses ξένος in Rom. 16:23 in the general sense of a "friend,"¹⁵⁹ as a polite term for "patron";¹⁶⁰ but this does not exclude the meaning "host," since the provision of hospitality is rooted in the term ξένος and characterizes all relevant instances.¹⁶¹ What Gaius' hospitality to Paul entailed concretely is not specified; but we must assume that Gaius provided Paul with accommodation, at the minimum.¹⁶² The proximity of the greetings of Tertius the scribe to those of Gaius suggests that other services may have been generously included in the hospitality which

---

43.50.3–5; Pausanias 2.1.2. Cf. Edward T. Salmon, *Roman Colonization under the Republic* (Ithaca: Cornell University Press, 1970) 135; Engels, *Roman Corinth*, 16–17, 67; Harry A. Stansbury, "Corinthian Honor, Corinthian Conflict: A Social History of Early Roman Corinth and its Pauline Community," (Ph.D. diss., University of California at Irvine, 1990) 116–22.

153 Weiss, *Der erste Korintherbrief*, 21; Schrage, *Der erste Brief*, 1.155; Fee, *First Epistle*, 62, 82; Thiselton, *First Epistle*, 140–41; Fitzmyer, *First Corinthians*, 146.

154 Rightly, Theissen, *Social Setting*, 89; Malherbe, *Social Aspects*, 73–74; Meeks, *First Urban Christians*, 57–58; Stansbury, "Corinthian Honor, Corinthian Conflict," 460–61; de Vos, *Church and Community Conflicts*, 201–202; Friesen, "Poverty in Pauline Studies," 356.

155 LSJ 1189 s.v. ξένος I.2; Gustav Stählin, "ξένος, κτλ.," *TDNT* 5 (1967) 20.

156 E.g., *Od.* 8.543; *P.Tebt.* 118.4; LSJ *Greek-English Lexicon*, 1189 s.v. ξένος I.2; Moulton and Milligan, *Vocabulary of the Greek Testament*, 433 s.v. ξένος.

157 *Il.* 15.532; Apollonius Rhodius 1.208; Xenophon *Anab.* 2.4.15; LSJ 1189 s.v. ξένος I.2; BDAG 684 2.c.

158 Dunn, *Romans 9–16*, 910–11.

159 de Vos, *Church and Community Conflicts*, 204 n.100, referencing Xenophon *Anab.* 1.1.10–11.

160 de Vos, *Church and Community Conflicts*, 204 n.100, referencing *IG* 10.2.255, where a cognate (ξενισμόν) is used to describe the hospitality which a certain Xenainetos provided for the *thiasos* of Isis and Sarapis in the home of Sosinike; cf. G. H. R. Horsley, "A 'letter from heaven'," *NewDocs*, Vol. I, no. 6, pp. 29–32.

161 LSJ 1189 s.v. ξένος; Stählin, "ξένος, κτλ.," *TDNT* 5 (1967) 3, 17–19, 20, 23; BDAG 684 s.v. ξένος 2.c; cf. A. T. Robertson, *Word Pictures in the New Testament*, Vol. 4 (Grand Rapids: Baker Book House, 1931) 430.

162 Theissen, *Social Setting*, 89; Malherbe, *Social Aspects*, 73; Meeks, *First Urban Christians*, 27, 57.

Gaius showed to Paul.[163] If the report of Acts (20:3) that Paul stayed for three months in Greece on his final visit is historically reliable,[164] then the hospitality of Gaius may have extended for a considerable period.

While there is general agreement among scholars that Paul resided with Gaius on the occasion of his final visit to Corinth, and was, in this way, the recipient of Gaius' hospitality,[165] the manner in which "the whole church" was "hosted" by Gaius has been the subject of much dispute.[166] Robert Jewett represents a long line of commentators in construing Paul's reference to Gaius as "host of the whole church" as a reflection of Gaius' "reputation of extending hospitality to Christian travelers from all over the world."[167] On the other hand, Gerd Theissen speaks for a group of social historians who interpret the phrase "host of the whole church" as an indication that "the whole congregation met at Gaius' house,"[168] when the various Christian groups in Corinth assembled together. In adjudicating this debate, Paul's use of the expression ὅλη ἡ ἐκκλησία elsewhere in his epistles must be seen as the decisive evidence. In 1 Cor. 14:23, Paul asks his readers: "If, therefore, the whole church (ἡ ἐκκλησία ὅλη) comes together (συνέλθῃ) for a meeting (ἐπὶ τὸ αὐτό), and all speak in tongues, and outsiders or unbelievers enter,

---

163 Theissen, *Social Setting*, 89; Malherbe, *Social Aspects*, 74.
164 Lüdemann, *Early Christianity according to Acts*, 224.
165 Judge, "Scholastic Community" in *The First Christians in the Roman World*, 545; Theissen, *Social Setting*, 55, 89; Malherbe, *Social Aspects*, 73; Meeks, *First Urban Christians*, 27, 57; Chow, *Patronage and Power*, 90; de Vos, *Church and Community Conflicts*, 201.
166 Cf. Marie-Joseph Lagrange, *Saint Paul. Épître aux Romains* (Paris: Gabalda, 1950) 376–77; C. E. B. Cranfield, *The Epistle to the Romans* (Edinburgh: T & T Clark, 1979) 2.807; Malherbe, *Social Aspects*, 74 n.28; Meggitt, *Paul, Poverty and Survival*, 121 n.227, 128.
167 Jewett, *Romans*, 980–81, preceded by Fréderic Godet, *Commentary on St. Paul's Epistle to the Romans* (Grand Rapids: Kregel, 1977) 501; Theodor Zahn, *Der Brief des Paulus an die Römer* (Leipzig: Deichert, 1910) 614; Hans Lietzmann, *An die Römer* (Tübingen: Mohr Siebeck, 1928) 128; Schlier, *Der Römerbrief*, 451; Michel, *Der Brief an die Römer*, 483; Ernst Käsemann, *Commentary on Romans* (Grand Rapids: Eerdmans, 1980) 421; Ulrich Wilckens, *Der Brief an die Römer*, Vol. 3 (Zurich: Benziger, 1982) 146; Peter Stuhlmacher, *Paul's Letter to the Romans: A Commentary* (Louisville: Westminster/John Knox, 1994) 255.
168 Theissen, *Social Setting*, 89; Malherbe, *Social Aspects*, 73–74; Meeks, *First Urban Christians*, 57, 68, 76, 143; Clarke, *Secular and Christian leadership in Corinth*, 46; Stansbury, "Corinthian Honor, Corinthian Conflict," 460–61; Chow, *Patronage and Power*, 90; Welborn, *Politics and Rhetoric*, 23; Friesen, "Poverty in Pauline Studies," 356.

will they not say that you are out of your mind?"¹⁶⁹ Thus, we may conclude that Gaius served as "host" of the Corinthian Christians when they came together in common assembly.¹⁷⁰ As is widely recognized, the social context of Paul's use of the expression ὅλη ἡ ἐκκλησία was the existence of smaller groups of Christians within a city, organized as "house-churches": thus, "the church in the house" (ἡ κατ' οἶκον ἐκκλησία) of Aquila and Prisca (1 Cor. 16:19), and "the church in the house" (ἡ κατ' οἶκον ἐκκλησία) of Philemon (Phlm. 2).¹⁷¹ When the smaller house-churches of Corinth—namely, those comprised of the "household" (οἶκος) of Crispus (Acts 18:8), the "household of Stephanas" (ὁ Στεφανᾶς οἶκος, 1 Cor. 1:16), and others—came together as a "whole church" (ὅλη ἡ ἐκκλησία), Gaius served as their "host" (ξένος).¹⁷² The occasion of such

---

169 Collins, *First Corinthians*, 508–509; Robert Banks, *Paul's Idea of Community* (Exeter: Pater Noster Press, 1980) 38; Meeks, *First Urban Christians*, 75. Cf. Theissen, "The Social Structure of Pauline Communities," 83: "The assumption that he [Gaius] is only the host on behalf of the congregation for missionaries and brothers on journeys does not do justice to his characterization as ὁ ξένος μου καὶ ὅλης τῆς ἐκκλησίας (Rom. 16:23). For this interpretation we would have to understand the first genitive (μου) in a different way than the second genitive (τῆς ἐκκλησίας): first Gaius would be the host of a guest, then the host on behalf of the whole church. If we treat the two genitives analogously, we have to infer that the whole congregation met in his house (cf. also 1 Cor. 14:23)."

170 Theissen, *Social Setting*, 89; Malherbe, *Social Aspects*, 74 n.28; Meeks, *First Urban Christians*, 75.

171 Banks, *Paul's Idea of Community*, 38–39; Murphy-O'Connor, *St. Paul's Corinth*, 158; Hans-Josef Klauck, *Hausgemeinde und Hauskirche im frühen Christentum* (Stuttgart: Katholisches Bibelwerk, 1981) 39; Meeks, *First Urban Christians*, 75: "The phrase *kat' oikon* does not designate merely the place where the *ekklēsia* met. Rather, Paul probably uses *kat' oikon* to distinguish these individual household-based groups from 'the whole church' (*holē hē ekklēsia*), which could also assemble on occasion (1 Cor. 14:23; Rom. 16:23; cf. 1 Cor. 11:20). The *kat' oikon ekklēsia* is thus the 'basic cell' of the Christian movement, and its nucleus was often an existing household."; Eva Ebel, *Die Attraktivität früher christlicher Gemeinden: Die Gemeinde von Korinth im Spiegel griechisch-römischer Vereine* (Tübingen: Mohr Siebeck, 2004) 153.

172 Theissen, *Social Setting*, 89: "Returning to Gaius, it is interesting to observe that in his case Paul speaks not of a 'house-congregation' (as in Phlm. 2) but of the 'whole congregation.' From this it could be concluded that the congregation also met at other places, but in smaller groups. The Christians at Cenchreae, for example, would have met at Phoebe's house. In any event, the whole congregation met at Gaius's." Similarly, Malherbe, *Social Aspects*, 74 n.28; Meeks, *First Urban Christians*, 76, 143, 147; David Balch, "Paul, Families, and Households" in *Paul in the Greco-Roman World*, ed. Paul Sampley (Harrisburg: Trinity Press International, 2003) 260.

common assembly was, in the first instance, the "Lord's Supper" (κυριακὸν δεῖπνον). This inference is strongly commended by the language of 1 Cor. 11:17–22, which has many elements in common with the vocabulary of Rom. 16:23 and 1 Cor. 14:23.[173] Paul's description of Gaius as "host of the whole church" supports this conclusion, since the term ξένος refers specifically to a dinner-host (or dinner-guest).[174]

The conclusion that Gaius served as "host" of all the Christian groups at Corinth when they assembled to eat the Lord's Supper—a conclusion that is, in fact, widely held among scholars—does not, however, settle debate about the nature of the hospitality extended by Gaius to the ὅλη ἐκκλησία, for there remains the question of the place where Gaius hosted the "whole church," whether in his own house or in a meeting-hall of some kind. The majority of interpreters assume that Gaius placed his own residence at the disposal of the Christian community.[175] Scholars generally recognize what this assumption implies about the size of Gaius' house: Gaius must have had ample space to accommodate all of the Corinthians known to have been associated with the ἐκκλησία in Corinth.[176] Evidence suggests that the author of Acts was not exaggerating when he described the Corinthian Christians as a λαὸς πολύς (Acts 18:10).[177] The evidence consists of a reasonable calculation of totals, based upon the individuals named in 1 Corinthians and Romans 16 who can be shown to have been members of the church at Corinth at the time when Gaius was serving as "host," together with their family members and dependants.[178] Assuming that most of the named individuals were married, and allowing for a moderate number of children and slaves in the cases of those whose entire households are said to have been converted (Crispus, Stephanas), and including Chloe's "people," scholars such as Jerome Murphy-O'Connor are led to posit a base figure of 50 as

---

173 Theissen, *Social Setting*, 96; Meeks, *First Urban Christians*, 67–68.
174 LSJ 1189 s.v. ξένος; Stählin, "ξένος, κτλ.," *TDNT* 5 (1967) 3, 20.
175 Among others, Theissen, *Social Setting*, 55, 89; Malherbe, *Social Aspects*, 73–74; Murphy-O'Connor, *St. Paul's Corinth*, 156, 158; Meeks, *First Urban Christians*, 57; S. C. Barton, "Paul's Sense of Place: An Anthropological Approach to Community Formation in Corinth," *NTS* 32 (1986) 225; Fee, *First Epistle*, 683–84.
176 E.g., Malherbe, *Social Aspects*, 73–74; Meeks, *First Urban Christians*, 57; Theissen, "The Social Structure of Pauline Communities," 83; Friesen, "Poverty in Pauline Studies," 356.
177 Theissen, *Social Setting*, 89.
178 Schreiber, *Die Gemeinde in Korinth*, 30–34; Theissen, *Social Setting*, 94–95; Murphy-O'Connor, *St. Paul's Corinth*, 156, 158; de Vos, *Church and Community Conflicts*, 204 n.98; Jewett, *Romans*, 980 n.54.

the number of persons who belonged to the Christian community in Corinth.[179] This number, which is a minimum estimate, and may well be too low,[180] stands in tension with what is known from archaeology about the space available in Roman houses of the Imperial period at Corinth.[181] One of the few houses of Paul's time that has been excavated at Corinth, the villa at Anaploga, has a *triclinium* that measures 5.2 meters by 9.2 meters, and an *atrium* of 5 by 6 meters.[182] Assuming that only public spaces of the house would have been used for gatherings of the Christian community,[183] a group of 50 persons would have resulted in "uncomfortable overcrowding."[184] For this reason, scholars have been motivated to search for some space other than the *domus* of Gaius in which meetings of the whole congregation might have occurred. Craig de Vos suggests that the Corinthian Christians may have met in a *schola* or meeting-hall of a guild or an association, rented by Gaius for that purpose.[185] Against this possibility speaks the distributive force of the articular noun ὁ ξένος in Rom. 16:23, which implies that Gaius hosted the Corinthian

---

179 Murphy-O'Connor, *St. Paul's Corinth*, 156, 158; similarly, Witherington, *Conflict and Community in Corinth*, 32, 243 n.9.
180 de Vos, *Church and Community Conflicts*, 203–204: "The nature and variety of the different factions and internal conflicts suggest that we are dealing with a large group. If those named in relation to the Corinthian church, as well as those Paul does not name, brought in the majority of their dependents, the usual estimate would be too low. Consequently, the church may have numbered in the order of one hundred, as many *collegia* did." Cf. Thomas Schmeller, *Hierarchie und Egalität: Eine sozialgeschichtliche Untersuchung paulinischer Gemeinden und griechisch-römischer Vereine* (Stuttgart: Katholisches Bibelwerk, 1995) 39–49. Lindemann (*Der erste Korintherbrief*, 13) judges that the Corinthian ἐκκλησία must have numbered approximately one hundred members, "weil sonst die Vielfalt der in Kap. 7 genannten Beziehungen kaum zu erklären ist."
181 Murphy-O'Connor, *St. Paul's Corinth*, 153–61; Carolyn Osiek and David L. Balch, *Families in the New Testament World: Households and House Churches* (Louisville: Westminster/John Knox, 1997) 201–203; David G. Horrell, "Domestic Space and Christian Meetings at Corinth: Imagining New Contexts and the Buildings East of the Theatre," *NTS* 50 (2004) 349–59.
182 Stella G. Miller, "A Mosaic Floor from a Roman Villa at Anaploga," *Hesperia* 41 (1972) 333.
183 Murphy-O'Connor, *St. Paul's Corinth*, 156.
184 Murphy-O'Connor, *St. Paul's Corinth*, 158.
185 de Vos, *Church and Community Conflicts*, 204; similarly, Matthias Klinghardt, *Gemeinschaftsmahl und Mahlgemeinschaft: Soziologie und Liturgie frühchristlicher Mahlfeiern* (Tübingen: Francke Verlag, 1996) 326.

Christians in the same place where Paul enjoyed his hospitality.[186] Nor need we adjust our estimate of the size of the Christian community in Corinth so that it fits comfortably within the walls of the villa at Anaploga.[187] The archaeology of Campanian houses demonstrates that significantly more space was available in some houses than was provided by the Anaploga villa.[188] The House of the Vettii at Pompeii, for example, with its *atrium* and large peristyle garden, would have accommodated large numbers.[189] It is a methodological error to permit the archaeological record of Roman Corinth, where so few houses have been excavated, to determine conclusions about the size of the Christian community at Corinth, and hence the size of the house of Gaius, when these conclusions are based upon careful exegesis and prosopography of Paul's epistles.[190] In any case, the fact that Gaius served as "host of the whole church" at Corinth, whether in his own house or in a rented club-room, suggests that Gaius was among the wealthiest individuals in the Corinthian church.[191]

A final indication of the social status of Gaius is the companionship which he evidently enjoyed with men of substance, such as Crispus and Erastus. The fact that Gaius is mentioned in the same breath with Crispus in 1 Cor. 1:14 implies an association between them.[192] We have inferred that Crispus must have disposed of surplus resources in order to fulfill his responsibilities as ἀρχισυνάγωγος.[193] It seems reasonable to assume that Gaius was a man of the same social class. Erastus, whose

---

186 Cf. Theissen, "The Social Structure of the Pauline Communities," 83, with reference to Paul's characterization of Gaius as ὁ ξένος μου καὶ ὅλης τῆς ἐκκλησίας (Rom. 16:23): "If we treat the two genitives [μου and τῆς ἐκκλησίας] analogously, we have to infer that the whole congregation met in his [Gaius's] house."
187 Rightly, Osiek and Balch, *Households and House Churches*, 201–203.
188 Andrew Wallace-Hadrill, *Houses and Society in Pompeii and Herculaneum* (Princeton: Princeton University Press, 1994).
189 Wallace-Hadrill, *Houses and Society*, 39, 41, 51, 58.
190 Balch, "Paul, Families, and Households," 259–60; David L. Balch, "Rich Pompeiian Houses, Shops for Rent, and the Huge Apartment Building in Herculaneum as Typical Spaces for Pauline House Churches," *JSNT* 27 (2004) 28–29.
191 Meeks, *First Urban Christians*, 143, 221 n.7; Theissen, "The Social Structure of Pauline Communities," 83; Ekkehard and Wolfgang Stegemann, *Urchristliche Sozialgeschichte: Die Anfänge im Judentum und die Christusgemeinden in der mediterranen Welt* (Stuttgart: Kohlhammer, 1995), 254; Friesen, "Poverty in Pauline Studies," 356; Stephen J. Chester, *Conversion at Corinth: Perspectives on Conversion in Paul's Theology and the Corinthian Church* (London: T & T Clark, 2003) 250 n.92.
192 Weiss, *Der erste Korintherbrief*, 20–21.
193 See above on Crispus. Cf. Theissen, *Social Setting*, 74–75.

greetings are conveyed along with those of Gaius in Rom. 16:23, is described by Paul as ὁ οἰκονόμος τῆς πόλεως. We have not yet attempted to determine what office is denoted by the title οἰκονόμος τῆς πόλεως, whether that of "city treasurer" or "city steward."[194] In the former case, Erastus would be an elected official, an *aedile* of Corinth, and hence a member of the true upper class.[195] In the latter, Erastus would be a minor civil servant, and probably a slave.[196] But even slaves who filled the post of city steward might possess sufficient resources to make public dedications, such as statues and columns.[197] In either case, Erastus would not have been among the poor who, on Paul's account, made up the majority of the Christian community at Corinth (1 Cor. 1:26–28).[198] The association of Gaius with Crispus and Erastus suggests that Gaius must have belonged to the small group of Corinthian Christians who enjoyed some wealth.

In respect to Gaius' relationship with Paul, everything that we have concluded above in the case of Crispus applies to Gaius as well; indeed, the picture of the relationship between Paul and Gaius which emerges from comparison of Paul's statements about Gaius in 1 Cor. 1:14 and Rom. 16:23 is more complex and interesting than in the case of Paul and Crispus, because of the greater period of time encompassed by Paul's remarks. Thus, we may infer an initially close relationship, from the fact that Gaius was one of the few to whom Paul personally administered baptism.[199] And again, we must infer a period during which tension entered into the relationship, because of the strangely negative way

---

[194] On the ambiguity of the title ὁ οἰκονόμος τῆς πόλεως, see Henry J. Cadbury, "Erastus of Corinth," *JBL* 50 (1931) 42–58; Theissen, *Social Setting*, 75–83; Meeks, *First Urban Christians*, 58; Clarke, *Secular and Christian Leadership in Corinth*, 46–56; Meggitt, *Paul, Poverty and Survival*, 135–41.

[195] Theissen, *Social Setting*, 83; Meeks, *First Urban Christians*, 59; Clarke, *Secular and Christian Leadership in Corinth*, 56.

[196] Cadbury, "Erastus of Corinth," 57–58; Meggitt, *Paul, Poverty and Survival*, 135–41; Friesen, "Poverty in Pauline Studies," 354–55.

[197] E.g., one Gaius Tryphonos from Nicomedia in *CIG* 3777; Peter Landvogt, *Epigraphische Untersuchungen über den ΟΙΚΟΝΟΜΟΣ. Ein Beitrag zum hellenistischen Beamtenwesen* (Strassburg: M. Dumont Schauberg, 1908) 26. Cf. Theissen, *Social Setting*, 78.

[198] Theissen, *Social Setting*, 83; Meeks, *First Urban Christians*, 59; Clarke, *Secular and Christian Leadership in Corinth*, 56; de Vos, *Church and Community Conflicts*, 201.

[199] Theissen, *Social Setting*, 55; Chow, *Patronage and Power*, 90; de Vos, *Church and Community Conflicts*, 201–202; Collins, *First Corinthians*, 83.

in which Paul speaks about his role in baptizing Gaius.[200] The palpable irony of Paul's "thanksgiving" in 1 Cor. 1:14 suggests that Gaius had some culpability in the formation of factions.[201]

At what point in the history of early Christianity at Corinth, Gaius became the "host of the whole church" is not certain. Acts 18:7 reports that Paul went to the house of Titius Justus after he encountered opposition to his preaching in the synagogue at Corinth.[202] Unfortunately, the author of Acts does not relate how long Paul made the house of Justus the venue for his proclamation. We are tempted to infer that Justus' house remained the place of assembly for the Christian community throughout the time of Paul's first missionary visit in Corinth, a period of "a year and six months" (Acts 18:11).[203] But this would be a precarious inference, because of the compositional tendency of the author of Acts: "Luke" weaves all the traditions relating to Paul in a particular city into a coherent narrative, leaving the impression that all the events which he relates occurred on the occasion of a single visit.[204] The fact that Titius Justus is absent from Paul's Corinthian correspondence, even in its earliest stages, permits, and perhaps requires, the inference that the Corinthian Christians had found another place for their assembly, prior to the inception of Paul's correspondence with the community. All that we can say with certainty is that at some point prior to Paul's final stay in Corinth, Gaius became the "host" of the Corinthian Christians when they gathered in common assembly. We may take it for granted that Paul would have valued this service, even if he disapproved of Gaius' role in the formation of factions, since there is no moment in Paul's correspondence with the Corinthians when his solicitude is diminished—not even at the height of the conflict, when Paul is most deeply pained (2 Cor. 11:11; 6:12; 7:2–4).

By the time that Paul comes to Corinth on his final visit, whatever tensions may have marred his relationship with Gaius have been overcome, since Paul receives the hospitality of Gaius (Rom. 16:23) and resides with him for what may have been a considerable period (Acts 20:3).

---

200 Weiss, *Der erste Korintherbrief*, 20.
201 Weiss, *Der erste Korintherbrief*, 20–21.
202 Judge, "Scholastic Community" in *The First Christians in the Roman World*, 544; Haenchen, *Acts of the Apostles*, 535; Meeks, *First Urban Christians*, 63; Barrett, *Acts 15–28*, 867–68.
203 Theodor Zahn, *Die Apostelgeschichte des Lucas* (Leipzig: Deichert, 1921) 654; Haenchen, *Acts of the Apostles*, 535–36, 539.
204 Lüdemann, *Early Christianity according to Acts*, 11.

In a place where Paul had so many friends and supporters (Stephanas, Chloe, *et al.*), more, apparently, than in any other city,²⁰⁵ it would hardly have been necessary for Paul to accept hospitality from a person with whom he had an inimical relationship. The inference that Gaius had been restored to the circle of Paul's intimate associates by the time Paul wrote the Epistle to the Romans is reinforced by the honorific term ξένος which Paul uses to introduce Gaius to his readers in Rom. 16:23, for "the ξένος is the 'friend' who is associated with the other in the beautiful reciprocity of hospitality."²⁰⁶ Paul might simply have spoken of "Gaius, with whom I am residing" (Γάϊος μετ' οὗ οἰκέω, or Γάϊος παρ' ᾧ ξενίζομαι); but by choosing to describe Gaius as ὁ ξένος μου, Paul evokes the image of all that he enjoys as a guest—*mansio et focus, panis et aqua*—and suggests the mutual trust on which the whole relationship rests.²⁰⁷

We may summarize what we have learned about Gaius from examination of Paul's references to the man in 1 Cor. 1:14 and Rom. 16:23. Gaius was among Paul's first converts in Corinth and received baptism at Paul's hands. Gaius was a person of not inconsiderable wealth, since he served as "host of the whole assembly." At some point, tension entered into Paul's relationship with Gaius, as a result of Gaius' involvement in the formation of factions. But by the time that Paul wrote his Epistle to the Romans, his friendship with Gaius had been fully restored; indeed, there is evidence of mutual respect in their enjoyment of the noble custom of ξενία, as host and guest.²⁰⁸ In sum, Gaius is as plausible a candidate for identification with the wrongdoer as Crispus, with whom he is associated.

Surely, Stephanas is among the most interesting individuals associated with the Christian *ekklesia* in Corinth.²⁰⁹ Paul mentions Stephanas twice

---

205 Judge, "Scholastic Community" in *The First Christians in the Roman World*, 544–45; Marshall, *Enmity in Corinth*, 147, 345.
206 Stählin, "ξένος, κτλ.," *TDNT* 5 (1967) 3.
207 Stählin, "ξένος, κτλ.," *TDNT* 5 (1967) 3.
208 Dunn, *Romans 9–16*, 910–11.
209 Among recent treatments of Stephanas, see Theissen, *Social Setting*, 83–87, 91–92, 94–95; Malherbe, *Social Aspects*, 73; Meeks, *First Urban Christians*, 57–58, 75, 78, 118–19, 123, 137; Chow, *Patronage and Power*, 88–89; David W. J. Gill, "In Search of the Social Elite in the Corinthian Church," *TynB* 44 (1993) 336; Bruce W. Winter, *After Paul Left Corinth: The Influence of Secular Ethics and Social Change* (Grand Rapids: Eerdmans, 2001) 184–99; Margaret Y. MacDonald, *The Pauline Churches: A Socio-Historical Study of Institutionalization in the Pauline and Deutero-Pauline Writings* (Cambridge: Cambridge University

in his Corinthian correspondence. From 1 Cor. 1:16, we learn that Paul had personally baptized Stephanas and his household. Much more information is contained in the paragraph devoted to Stephanas in 1 Cor. 16:15–18: Stephanas and his household were "the first-fruits of Achaia"; Stephanas and members of his household had "assigned themselves to the ministry to the saints"; together with Fortunatus and Achaicus, Stephanas has visited Paul in Ephesus, and has "refreshed" Paul's spirit. Paul enjoins the Corinthians to "give recognition" to Stephanas and his associates.[210]

A proper appreciation of the rich data of these passages and their implications for our assessment of the social status of Stephanas and his relationship to Paul requires us to pay close attention to the rhetorical form and style of Paul's remarks. We have noted above how Paul's feigned lapse of memory in relation to those whom he had personally baptized in 1 Cor. 1:16 serves to separate the mention of Stephanas' household from that of Crispus and Gaius.[211] That the names of Crispus and Gaius just happened to come to Paul's mind before those of the highly prized "first-fruits of Achaia" is hardly imaginable, so that the precedence of Crispus and Gaius in Paul's account of those whom he had personally baptized must be seen as strategic, rather than accidental.[212] The effect of the device of a memory-lapse is to spare Stephanas the force of the ironic thanksgiving of 1 Cor. 1:14–15. Because this stratagem belongs to Paul's larger purpose of disavowing any role in the formation of factions, we

---

Press, 2004) 57–60; Friesen, "Poverty in Pauline Studies," 352; Friedrich Wilhelm Horn, "Stephanas und sein Haus—die erste christliche Hausgemeinde in der Achaia: Ihre Stellung in der Kommunikation zwischen Paulus und der korinthischen Gemeinde" in *Paulus und die antike Welt: Beiträge zur zeit- und religionsgeschichtlichen Erforschung des paulinischen Christentums*, ed. David C. Bienert, Joachim Jeska, Thomas Witulski (Göttingen: Vandenhoeck & Ruprecht, 2008) 83–98.

210 Among commentaries on these passages, see esp. Weiss, *Der erste Korintherbrief*, 21, 385–86; Conzelmann, *1 Corinthians*, 298–99; Fee, *First Epistle*, 828–29; Collins, *First Corinthians*, 73–75, 84–85, 602–607; Lindemann, *Der erste Korintherbrief*, 42, 383–84; Thiselton, *First Epistle*, 141–42, 1337–41; Fitzmyer, *First Corinthians*, 147, 624–26. See also A. D. Clarke, "'Refresh the hearts of the saints': A Unique Pauline Context," *TynBul* 47 (1996) 275–300; Efrain Agosto, "Paul and Commendation" in *Paul in the Greco-Roman World*, ed. J. Paul Sampley (Harrisburg: Trinity Press International, 2003) 115–19.

211 See above on Crispus; cf. Weiss, *Der erste Korintherbrief*, 20–21; Dahl, "Paul and the Church at Corinth," 318; Lindemann, *Der erste Korintherbrief*, 42.

212 Lindemann, *Der erste Korintherbrief*, 42; cf. Eckhard J. Schnabel, *Der erste Brief des Paulus an die Korinther* (Wuppertal: R. Brockhaus Verlag, 2006) 100.

must infer that Paul thought of Stephanas differently in relation to the factions than Crispus and Gaius. But it is more difficult to determine, on the basis of this passage alone, in what the difference in Stephanas' position vis-à-vis the factions consisted. Johannes Weiss suggested that perhaps Stephanas' opinion of the discord at Corinth was so much the same as Paul's own, that he was exempted in Paul's mind from the erroneous tendency of those who boasted of having been baptized in someone's name (1 Cor. 1:15).[213] But the laws of group dynamics make it unlikely that an individual and his dependants could have maintained a position above the fray, however noble their principles, once the community had split up into factions.[214] Thus, we must allow for the possibility that Stephanas is mentioned separately from Crispus and Gaius because he was on the side of Paul, because he was the champion of Paul's cause in Corinth.

Even closer attention to the form and style of Paul's exhortation in 1 Cor. 16:15–18 is necessary, if we are to properly assess the information provided by this paragraph. First, we must observe that the paragraph on Stephanas and his household makes a surprising new beginning, after Paul had begun to conclude the letter in vss. 13–14 ("Be alert, stand fast in the faith, be brave, be strong! Let everything among you be done in love.").[215] Why should Paul, having begun his concluding exhortation, start anew with a special request in vss. 15–18, as if vss. 13 and 14 were not there?[216] Paul's appeal for the recognition of Stephanas can hardly be described as an "after-thought,"[217] since the use of the παρακαλῶ formula in vs. 15 lends formality to the request, and the resumption of the direct address, ἀδελφοί, communicates a sense of urgency.[218]

Commentators have called attention to numerous features which Paul's appeal for Stephanas in 1 Cor. 16:15–18 has in common with the Hellenistic letter of recommendation, as evidenced by extant papyrus

---

213 Weiss, *Der erste Korintherbrief*, 20.
214 Schreiber, *Die Gemeinde in Korinth*, 154–60.
215 Weiss, *Der erste Korintherbrief*, 385; Conzelmann, *1 Corinthians*, 297; Lindemann, *Der erste Korintherbrief*, 383.
216 Conzelmann, *1 Corinthians*, 297.
217 Lietzmann, *An die Korinther I/II*, 210.
218 Collins, *First Corinthians*, 604; Lindemann, *Der erste Korintherbrief*, 383–84.

letters,²¹⁹ and as defined in the handbook of letter writing attributed to Demetrius:²²⁰ 1) the name of the person recommended, identified more precisely by means of a subordinate clause; 2) a predicate defining the relationship between the one recommended and the recommender; 3) a request clause, commonly using the verb ἐρωτάω ("I ask") or παρακαλέω ("I request"); 4) a circumstantial clause, generally in the form "if he has need of anything from you" or "on whatever matter he comes to you"; 5) a purpose clause, constructed with either ὅπως or ἵνα.²²¹ These elements of the letter of recommendation are present in the paragraph that Paul devotes to Stephanas, in some cases employing the standard epistolographic formulae (παρακαλῶ, ἵνα),²²² and in one instance substituting a homologous structure (the reference to the assignment of Stephanas' household to the "ministry to the saints" replaces the customary circumstantial clause).²²³ Why should Paul choose to cast his appeal on behalf of Stephanas in the style of a "letter of commendation"? The question is given force by the observation that the one who is recommended by means of this style is generally *unknown* to the recipient of the letter, for whom the letter itself serves as an introduction.²²⁴ But Stephanas is one of the Corinthians themselves and, as Paul acknowledges, is well known to his readers (οἴδατε, vs. 15)! In Rom. 16:1–2, where Paul appends a recommendation to a long letter, it is in order to introduce Phoebe, a deacon of the church at Cenchreae, to readers to whom she is evidently unknown.²²⁵

The puzzle of Paul's commendation of Stephanas is not limited to the context or form of Paul's remarks, but goes down to the level of the vocabulary and syntax, where there are numerous surprises, suggestive undertones, and conflicting emphases. First, it is very odd that Paul uses the indicative οἴδατε, with the household of Stephanas as its object,

---

219 Chan-Hie Kim, *Form and Structure of the Familiar Greek Letter of Recommendation* (Missoula: Scholars Press, 1972) 5, 198, 203, 209; Collins, *First Corinthians*, 603; Lindemann, *Der erste Korintherbrief*, 384; Agosto, "Paul and Commendation," 101–33, esp. 115–19.
220 Ps.-Demetrius, *Ep. Types* 2; Malherbe, *Ancient Epistolary Theorists*, 33; Collins, *First Corinthians*, 594–95, 602.
221 Kim, *Greek Letter of Recommendation*, 38, 64; Collins, *First Corinthians*, 602.
222 Kim, *Greek Letter of Recommendation*, 71, 195, 196, 202, 213; Collins, *First Corinthians*, 602.
223 Collins, *First Corinthians*, 603.
224 Kim, *Greek Letter of Recommendation*, 126, 130, 131.
225 Kim, *Greek Letter of Recommendation*, 126; Armin Kretzer, "συνίστημι, συνιστάνω," *EDNT* 3 (1993) 308; Jewett, *Romans*, 942–43.

after the verb of request (παρακαλῶ), rather than the infinitive εἰδέναι, as in the parallel passage, 1 Thess. 5:12.[226] That the Corinthians "know" the Stephanas household goes without saying! The use of the indicative gives the opening verse of the commendation (16:15) the character of an argumentative assertion, rather than a straightforward appeal: "You know, surely, what sort of persons you have in the case of Stephanas and his family!" Then Paul immediately explicates the basis of the readers' knowledge: "they are the first-fruits of Achaia." The formulation of vs. 15 suggests an absence of respect for Stephanas, which familiarity should have engendered.

Second, Paul's demand that the Corinthians "submit" or "be subject" (ὑποτάσσησθε) to Stephanas and his household is surprising, if not to say stunning, in context.[227] Why should the other Corinthian Christians, and especially the leaders of other house-churches, men of substance such as Crispus and Gaius, subordinate themselves to Stephanas? And in what respect should they yield submission? In all respects? Sensing the offensiveness of his demand, Paul moves immediately to relativize, and then to generalize, the subject—"such persons and everyone who assists in the work and who toils" (τοῖς τοιούτοις καὶ παντὶ τῷ συνεργοῦντι καὶ κοπιῶντι, vs. 16). But the exhortation to voluntary submission retains a jarring undertone, which Paul attempts to cover up by speaking quickly of his joy at the arrival of Stephanas and his colleagues (16:17).[228] We should not fail to observe that the offensiveness of Paul's demand for submission to Stephanas would be lessened, if Paul had indicated the area in which the Corinthians were expected to acknowledge Stephanas' leadership. Careful examination of the vocabulary of the paragraph may disclose an implicit limitation upon the area of work in which Paul appeals for voluntary submission.

Third, a series of conflicting emphases, established by Paul's subtle use of the pronouns in the last two verses of the paragraph, discloses a tension between the Stephanas household and the rest of the Corinthians, the source of which is not immediately apparent. A contrast, if not to say an opposition, between Stephanas' household and the rest of the Corinthians is implied by the emphatic use of the demonstrative pronoun οὗτοι

---

[226] Weiss, *Der erste Korintherbrief*, 385–86; Lindemann, *Der erste Korintherbrief*, 384; cf. Fitzmyer, *First Corinthians*, 624.

[227] Weiss, *Der erste Korintherbrief*, 386; Lindemann, *Der erste Korintherbrief*, 384; Agosto, "Paul and Commendation," 117.

[228] Weiss, *Der erste Korintherbrief*, 386.

("these"), following the second person plural pronoun ("your") at the beginning of the ὅτι-clause in vs. 17b: "your deficiency *these* have supplied."[229] Whether one should read ὑμέτερον, with certain manuscripts (B C D F G P) or ὑμῶν, with other witnesses (P46 ℵ A Ψ K L), an objective genitive is clearly intended,[230] with the sense: "that which I lacked and did not receive from you, *these people* (Stephanas and his associates) have supplied," or *"you* left a gap, *they* have filled it."[231]

A final moment of ironic tension is created by Paul's use of the pronouns in vs. 18a, where the possessive ἐμόν is placed in studied contrast to ὑμῶν: "for they (Stephanas and his associates) refreshed my spirit, and *yours* as well!" The addition of the phrase καὶ τὸ ὑμῶν, emphatic by virtue of its position in the sentence,[232] gives a quizzical twist to Paul's statement: "I assume that it is in accordance with *your* wishes that Stephanas and his companions refreshed my spirit?!"[233] Upon this rather bitter pivot, Paul renews his exhortation: "So (if I am correct in assuming that Stephanas and his associates acted in accordance with your wishes), you should give recognition to such persons" (vs. 18b).[234]

The ambiguities of the paragraph devoted to Stephanas are so numerous and tricky that we may never achieve certainty about the context of Paul's appeal for recognition. Every attempt to gain clarity is frustrated by Paul's consciousness of the potential offensiveness of his request for submission to Stephanas, and by the underlying tension between Stephanas and other Corinthians, reflected in the peculiarities of Paul's rhetoric. Yet, the particularities of Paul's word choice at a crucial point in his appeal for Stephanas may provide a basis for a plausible hypothesis regarding the nature of Paul's request. It can hardly be a coincidence that the vocabulary by which Paul warrants his appeal for Stephanas is used elsewhere in the Corinthian correspondence in connection with the collection for the poor in Jerusalem![235] In 1 Cor. 16:15b, Paul directs his readers' attention to the fact that Stephanas and his household "have appointed themselves

---

229 Lindemann, *Der erste Korintherbrief*, 385; Horn, "Stephanas und sein Haus," 94.
230 Weiss, *Der erste Korintherbrief*, 386; Fitzmyer, *First Corinthians*, 626.
231 Ollrog, *Paulus und seine Mitarbeiter*, 97–98; Lindemann, *Der erste Korintherbrief*, 385. Cf. Gerhard Delling, "ἀναπληρόω, κτλ.," *TDNT* 6 (1968) 306; Horn, "Stephanas und sein Haus," 94.
232 BDF §274; Lindemann, *Der erste Korintherbrief*, 385.
233 Weiss, *Der erste Korintherbrief*, 386.
234 Lindemann, *Der erste Korintherbrief*, 385.
235 Theissen, *Social Setting*, 87–88; cf. Fitzmyer, *First Corinthians*, 62; Horn, "Stephanas und sein Haus," 91–93.

to the ministry to the saints" (εἰς διακονίαν τοῖς ἁγίοις ἔταξαν ἑαυτούς). In 2 Cor. 8:4 and 9:1, Paul employs the phrase ἡ διακονία ἡ εἰς τοὺς ἁγίους ("the ministry to the saints") to designate the charitable project in which the Corinthians are urged to become partners by taking up a collection (see also 2 Cor. 9:12; Rom. 15:31).[236] Moreover, the verb by which Paul describes the action of Stephanas and his household with respect to "the ministry to the saints," namely τάσσω ("assign," "appoint"), is the simplex form of διατάσσω ("order," "arrange"), used by Paul at the beginning of the chapter (1 Cor. 16:1) in giving detailed instructions concerning the collection for the saints.[237] Paul's phrase denoting the "self-appointment" of Stephanas and his people, ἔταξαν ἑαυτούς, corresponds to an established usage in relation to economic middlemen,[238] as illustrated by a well known passage from Plato's *Republic* (2.371C: ἑαυτοὺς ἐπὶ τὴν διακονίαν τάσσουσι ταύτην).[239] The importance of the verbal connections between Paul's commendation of Stephanas in 1 Cor. 16:15–18 and his instructions regarding the collection in 1 Cor. 16:1, 2 Cor. 8:4, 9:1 is enhanced when one recalls that the clause in which Paul speaks of Stephanas' devotion to the ministry to the saints (in 1 Cor. 16:15b) corresponds to the circumstantial clause of the Hellenistic letter recommendation, which specifies the matter on which the one recommended comes to the reader, or the respect in which the one recommended needs the reader's assistance.[240]

We may now venture a hypothesis regarding the situation and purpose of Paul's commendation of Stephanas in 1 Cor. 16:15–18: Stephanas and members of his household had "appointed themselves" as Paul's agents in the collection-work at Corinth.[241] Naturally, we cannot know whether Stephanas and his colleagues volunteered for this service, or

---

236 Georgi, *Remembering the Poor*, 115; Betz, *2 Corinthians 8 and 9*, 46, 90; Jewett, *Romans*, 927, 936; Horn, "Stephanas und sein Haus," 92.
237 Collins, *First Corinthians*, 587, 605; cf. Thiselton, *First Epistle*, 1338–39; Horn, "Stephanas und sein Haus," 92.
238 LSJ 1757–58 s.v. τάσσω II; BDAG 1607 s.v. τάσσω. Cf. Lindemann, *Der erste Korintherbrief*, 384.
239 Weiss, *Der erste Korintherbrief*, 386; Conzelmann, *1 Corinthians*, 298 n.1; Lindemann, *Der erste Korintherbrief*, 384; Agosto, "Paul and Commendation," 116. For further references, see Gerhard Delling, "τάσσω, κτλ.," *TDNT* 8 (1972) 27–28, 28 n.6.
240 Collins, *First Corinthians*, 603.
241 Similarly, Collins, *First Corinthians*, 587–88.

were put up to it by Paul.²⁴² The responsibilities of Stephanas and his associates may have consisted in nothing more than collecting and safeguarding the monies set aside each week by the Corinthians, from whatever extra they had earned, in accordance with Paul's instructions (1 Cor. 16:2).²⁴³ Yet, the appointment of Stephanas and his household to this ministry was evidently viewed as problematic by some in Corinth—so much is clear from the many peculiar features of Paul's commendation examined above: the odd instance of the indicative οἴδατε following the verb of request (vs. 15); the surprising demand for voluntary submission to Stephanas (vs. 16); the self-conscious generalization of the persons to whom submission is to be given (vs. 16b); the eager avowal of joy at Stephanas' arrival (vs. 17); the contrasts signaled by Paul's use of the pronouns, disclosing underlying tensions between Stephanas and his fellow Christians (vss. 17b-18); etc. In any case, Paul would not have appealed for recognition of Stephanas, if he had not assumed that the congregation, or a portion thereof, had no strong inclination to grant it.²⁴⁴ Why Stephanas' fellow Christians should have opposed his appointment to this ministry is difficult to determine: perhaps they felt that others were better qualified by status and experience; perhaps they felt that Stephanas was too closely allied with Paul to be an honest broker; perhaps they questioned the rationale for removing funds from the several house-churches and placing them in the hands of a single individual.

What inferences may we now draw concerning Stephanas, in respect to his relationship with Paul and his social status? Several factors indicate that Stephanas was Paul's strongest supporter in the church at Corinth. The title ἀπαρχὴ Ἀχαΐας (1 Cor. 16:15) is an eloquent reminder of the basis of Paul's attachment to Stephanas, for the term not only designates the members of Stephanas' household as the first converts in Achaia,²⁴⁵ but also evokes the hope which the "first-fruits" of Paul's preaching must have engendered, as the harbingers of a successful mission to

---

242 On the implications of the phrase ἔταξαν ἑαυτούς, see Schrage, *Der erste Brief IV*, 454: "Man müsste geradezu übersetzen 'sie haben sich (selbständig) selbst eingesetzt,' sind jedenfalls nicht vom Apostel oder von der Gemeinde dazu beauftragt worden."

243 Collins, *First Corinthians*, 587–88.

244 Weiss, *Der erste Korintherbrief*, 386; Dahl, "Paul and the Church at Corinth," 318; Lindemann, *Der erste Korintherbrief*, 384, 385.

245 Weiss, *Der erste Korintherbrief*, 386; Conzelmann, *1 Corinthians*, 298; Fee, *First Epistle*, 829; Lindemann, *Der erste Korintherbrief*, 383–84; Winter, *After Paul Left Corinth*, 197. Cf. Rom. 16:5.

come, in accordance with the cultic nuances of the expression ἀπαρχή in the Biblical tradition.²⁴⁶ Thus, it must have seemed only natural to Paul to entrust Stephanas with a special ministry in connection with the collection. If our hypothesis concerning the purpose of Paul's commendation of Stephanas is plausible, then Paul's appeal for recognition of Stephanas must be seen as a mark of the highest esteem,²⁴⁷ given the extraordinary importance which the collection had assumed in Paul's thinking. And that Paul should persevere in his appeal for recognition of Stephanas, despite his awareness of potential, or actual, opposition to his requests, is a further sign of Paul's commitment to this man.

A final indicator of the nature and character of the relationship between Paul and Stephanas is the term by which Paul designates the "lack" which Stephanas and his associates have alleviated by their arrival in Ephesus–ὑστέρημα.²⁴⁸ This is the same term found in Phil. 2:30 to describe financial assistance brought to Paul from Philippi by Epaphroditus, λειτουργὸς τῆς χρείας μου ("minister to my need").²⁴⁹ From this parallel in language, Gerd Theissen has inferred that "it is reasonable to assume that in Ephesus Paul has received some material support from Stephanas."²⁵⁰ It is no objection to this conclusion that Paul insists that he did not receive support from the Corinthians in 2 Cor. 11:9, for Paul qualifies the latter assertion with the phrase *"when I was with you."*²⁵¹ Evidently, Paul was only too happy to receive support when he was *away* from Corinth,²⁵² especially when the gift came from the hands of one with whom he had a close relationship.

With respect to the social status of Stephanas, our inferences must be less certain than in the case of either Crispus or Gaius. As the head of a "household" (1 Cor. 1:16; 16:15), Stephanas would have had dependants

---

246 C. Spicq, "ΑΠΑΡΧΗ. Note de lexicographie neo-testamentaire" in *The New Testament Age*, ed. W. C. Heinrich (Macon: Mercer University Press, 1984) 493–502; Collins, *First Corinthians*, 604–605.
247 Chow, *Patronage and Power*, 88.
248 BDAG s.v. ὑστέρημα; Ulrich Wilckens, "ὕστερος, κτλ.," *TDNT* 8 (1972) 598–600.
249 Joachim Gnilka, *Der Philipperbrief*, (Freiburg: Herder, 1987) 163. See also 2 Cor. 8:14, where the ὑστέρημα ("deficiency") of the Jerusalem Christians is contrasted with the περίσσευμα ("abundance") of the Corinthians; see Betz, *2 Corinthians 8 and 9*, 68.
250 Theissen, *Social Setting*, 88.
251 Windisch, *Der zweite Korintherbrief*, 336; Marshall, *Enmity in Corinth*, 173–76, 223.
252 Georgi, *Opponents of Paul*, 239.

and responsibilities.²⁵³ The household of Stephanas may have included slaves, in addition to family members; but we cannot be sure.²⁵⁴ Fortunatus and Achaicus may have been two of Stephanas' slaves;²⁵⁵ or they may have been business associates.²⁵⁶ Stephanas evidently had the resources to travel from Corinth to Ephesus.²⁵⁷ Given the tensions we have detected between Stephanas and other Corinthians, it is unlikely that the expenses of Stephanas' travel would have been paid by the Corinthian congregation.²⁵⁸ Perhaps Stephanas was traveling on business. If our inference from Paul's use of the term ὑστέρημα is valid, then Stephanas had the wherewithal to alleviate Paul's lack,²⁵⁹ although the term does not imply anything about the size of Stephanas' gift; Paul's "spirit" may have been "refreshed" by a token.²⁶⁰

In seeking to assess the social status of Stephanas, we should not fail to notice what is *not* said in his case about offices and services. Evidently, Stephanas did not hold office in the Jewish or Christian community, like Crispus, "the ruler of the synagogue." Nor was it in the house of Stephanas that the Christians of Corinth found hospitality when they met in common assembly,²⁶¹ despite the fact that Stephanas and members of his household were the first converts in Achaia, but in the house of Gaius. These observations suggest that Wayne Meeks is probably correct in placing Stephanas somewhat lower on the social scale than Crispus or Gaius.²⁶²

As a positive indicator of Stephanas' social location, we may find a tenuous clue in the verb used to describe Stephanas' "assignment" to

---

253 Theissen, *Social Setting*, 87–88; Meeks, *First Urban Christians*, 57–58; Chow, *Patronage and Power*, 88–89; Gill, "In Search of the Elite in the Corinthian Church," 336; Winter, *After Paul Left Corinth*, 197–98.
254 Theissen, *Social Setting*, 92.
255 von Dobschütz, *Primitive Church*, 57; Héring, *First Epistle*, 186; Theissen, *Social Setting*, 92; Fee, *First Epistle*, 829, 831.
256 Meeks, *First Urban Christians*, 56–57; Collins, *First Corinthians*, 603–604.
257 Theissen, *Social Setting*, 91; Meeks, *First Urban Christians*, 58; Murphy-O'Connor, *Paul*, 267.
258 Weiss, *Der erste Korintherbrief*, 386; Lindemann, *Der erste Korintherbrief*, 385. Contra Meeks, *First Urban Christians*, 58.
259 Theissen, *Social Setting*, 87–88; Meeks, *First Urban Christians*, 58.
260 Cf. Fee, *First Epistle*, 832; Collins, *First Corinthians*, 606; Schrage, *Der erste Brief* IV, 458. See the discussion of the terminology (ἀναπαύω) in Clarke, "Refresh the hearts of the saints" 275–300.
261 Friesen, "Poverty in Pauline Studies," 352.
262 Meeks, *First Urban Christians*, 58; see already Malherbe, *Social Aspects*, 73 n.27.

the ministry to the saints in 1 Cor. 16:15–τάσσω.²⁶³ In the oft-cited passage from Plato's *Republic* (371C), those who "appoint themselves to service" (ἑαυτοὺς ἐπὶ τὴν διακονίαν τάσσουσι ταύτην), "exchanging money for goods with those who wish to sell, and goods for money with those who desire to buy," belong to the class of "shopkeepers" (κάπηλοι).²⁶⁴ Perhaps Stephanas was a successful shopkeeper, or even, given his capacity for travel, a "merchant" (ἔμπορος), like Sulpicius Cinnamus and Sulpicius Faustus, two freedmen *mercatores* ("merchants"), whose lives have been illuminated by the discovery of documents revealing their business activities at Murecine, a suburb of Pompeii.²⁶⁵ Fortunatus and Achaicus would then be associates in the business upon which Stephanas travels. A set of dossiers found at Herculaneum (the "Herculaneum Tablets") demonstrates that freeborn persons, slaves, and ex-slaves formed tight-knit communities which supported one another in business activities and legal cases.²⁶⁶

We may summarize what may be said about Stephanas, with respect to the possibility that he was the wrongdoer of 2 Cor. 2 and 7. Stephanas possessed some financial resources, enough to contribute to Paul's support. But we may doubt whether the data of 1 Cor. 16:15–18 warrant the conclusion that Stephanas could have played a patronal role in relation to other apostles, as our analysis of 2 Cor. 11:1–21 suggests that the ἀδικήσας did. Stephanas enjoyed the closest relationship to Paul of any of the Corinthians: he was the fountain of Paul's hope and the reservoir of Paul's trust. If Stephanas had emerged as Paul's adversary, and had accused Paul of embezzlement before the Christian assembly, it would have been felt as the bitterest betrayal.

Lastly, we come to Erastus, whose greetings Paul conveys in Rom. 16:23: "Erastus, the financial manager of the city (ὁ οἰκονόμος τῆς πόλεως), greets you." For an assessment of the social status of Erastus, the title ὁ οἰκονόμος τῆς πόλεως is of the utmost importance. In his epigraphic investigation of οἰκονόμος, Peter Landvogt demonstrated that the term had a wide range of uses related to financial managers, both public

---

263 LSJ 1757–58 s.v. τάσσω II; BDAG 1607 s.v. τάσσω; Delling, "τάσσω, κτλ.," *TDNT* 8 (1972) 28.
264 Weiss, *Der erste Korintherbrief*, 386; Lindemann, *Der erste Korintherbrief*, 384.
265 L. Bove, *Documenti di operazioni finanziarie dall' archivio dei Sulpici* (Naples: Liguori, 1984); Wallace-Hadrill, *Houses and Society*, 175.
266 Most illuminating is the dossier from the Casa del Bicentenario: see V. Arangio-Ruiz, *Studi epigrafici e papirologici* (Naples: Liguori, 1974) 552–70; Wallace-Hadrill, *Houses and Society*, 175–78.

and private.²⁶⁷ Of the numerous instances examined by Landvogt, only those which designate public officials are relevant to the case of Erastus,²⁶⁸ because the phrase τῆς πόλεως, by which Paul qualifies οἰκονόμος, relates the office to the city.²⁶⁹ As a title for public officials in the free cities of Greece and Asia Minor, οἰκονόμος might refer to persons in one of three categories: 1) an officer of the city itself (οἰκονόμος τῆς πόλεως),²⁷⁰ 2) an officer of a political division of the city (e.g., a tribe = οἰκονόμος τῆς φυλῆς),²⁷¹ or 3) an officer of a corporate body of the city (e.g., the council = οἰκονόμος τῆς βουλῆς).²⁷² In all of these cases, the responsibilities of the οἰκονόμος were financial, that is, he defrayed the costs for the inscription of decrees, the erection of statues, the bestowal of crowns, etc.²⁷³ Landvogt summarizes: "In short, what is characteristic of the official business of the οἰκονόμος in this period [the Hellenistic age and later] is that he functioned solely as a financial officer."²⁷⁴

This determination does not clarify the social status of the οἰκονόμος, however; for the inscriptions reflect that the title might be applied to persons in a wide range of classes, embracing freeborn citizens, on the one

---

267 Peter Landvogt, *Epigraphische Untersuchungen über den OIKONOMOΣ: Ein Beitrag zum hellenistischen Beamtenwesen* (Strassburg: M. Dumont Schauberg, 1908). The importance of Landvogt's dissertation for an evaluation of the status of Erastus was already emphasized by Cadbury, "Erastus of Corinth," 47, but the work has dropped out of some recent discussions, e.g., Meggitt, *Paul, Poverty, and Survival*, 135–41; Steven J. Friesen, "The Wrong Erastus: Ideology, Archaeology, and Exegesis" in *Corinth in Context: Comparative Perspectives on Religion and Society*, ed. Steven Friesen, Daniel Schowalter, and James Walters (Leiden: Brill, 2010) 231–56. Landvogt's evidence is supplemented by the appendix on the status of *oikonomoi* in Dale B. Martin, *Slavery as Salvation: The Metaphor of Slavery in Pauline Christianity* (New Haven: Yale University, 1990) 174–77.
268 Thus we exclude from consideration the many references to οἰκονόμοι who played the role of private stewards and estate managers; Landvogt, *OIKONOMOΣ*, 9, 17–19; cf. G. H. R. Horsley, "οἰκονόμος," *NewDocs* 4, 161; Theissen, *Social Setting*, 76–77.
269 Glen Bowersock, in personal communication with the author, June 12, 2006.
270 Thus, οἰκονόμος τῆς πόλεως in Priene, Hierapolis, Philadelphia, Cos, Phrygia, and Galatia; Landvogt, *OIKONOMOΣ*, 16–17.
271 E.g., οἰκονόμος τῆς φυλῆς in Mylas; οἰκονόμος τῆς κατοικίας in Caystrostale; Landvogt, *OIKONOMOΣ*, 17.
272 E.g., οἰκονόμος τῆς βουλῆς in Aphrodisias; οἰκονόμος τῆς γερουσίας in Cos; Landvogt, *OIKONOMOΣ*, 17.
273 Landvogt, *OIKONOMOΣ*, 17; cf. Theissen, *Social Setting*, 77; Clarke, *Secular and Christian Leadership*, 51.
274 Landvogt, *OIKONOMOΣ*, 17.

hand, and public slaves, on the other.²⁷⁵ Examples of persons in the former category come from the cities of western Asia Minor, and are dated to the Roman imperial period.²⁷⁶ In Smyrna, two lists of municipal officers from the end of the second century A.D. include the title οἰκονόμος.²⁷⁷ In both cases, the names of the persons so designated, Bassos Hermogenous and Pamphilos (the younger) _____, indicate that the bearers were freeborn.²⁷⁸ The context in which the office is listed in both inscriptions makes clear that it was a high ranking position, such as would have been held by members of the upper class.²⁷⁹ In Hierapolis, two οἰκονόμοι τῆς πόλεως provided for the erection of a statue in honor of a man who had held the offices of treasurer and chief magistrate.²⁸⁰ Despite the simplicity of the names of the οἰκονόμοι, given as Tatianos and Diokles in the inscription, Landvogt judges that they must have been citizens, since the erection of a statue in honor of the chief magistrate would scarcely have been entrusted to public slaves.²⁸¹ In Aphrodisias, an inscription from the Roman period honors a certain Menander, son of Menander, οἰκονόμος of the city council (τῆς βουλῆς).²⁸² As the text of the inscription reveals, Menander was a citizen and held high office.²⁸³ In all of these instances, and in others that might have been mentioned,²⁸⁴ the term οἰκονόμος (τῆς πόλεως) refers to a high-ranking position held by a freeborn citizen.²⁸⁵

On the other hand, the inscriptions reveal that many of those who bore the title οἰκονόμος were slaves.²⁸⁶ A list of officials from Sparta of

---

275 Landvogt, *ΟΙΚΟΝΟΜΟΣ*, 12–14; Theissen, *Social Setting*, 76–79; Meeks, *First Urban Christians*, 58; Martin, *Slavery as Salvaion*, 15–17, 174–75.
276 Landvogt, *ΟΙΚΟΝΟΜΟΣ*, 14, 27–28; Theissen, *Social Setting*, 77–78; Martin, *Slavery as Salvation*, 175.
277 *CIG* 3151 and 3162 (=*I.Smyrna* 771, 772); *IGR* 4.1435.
278 Landvogt, *ΟΙΚΟΝΟΜΟΣ*, 28.
279 Landvogt, *ΟΙΚΟΝΟΜΟΣ*, 14; Martin, *Slavery as Salvation*, 175.
280 Walther Judeich, *Altertümer von Hierapolis* (Berlin: Georg Reimer, 1898) no. 35; *IGR* 4.813.
281 Landvogt, *ΟΙΚΟΝΟΜΟΣ*, 47; cf. Theissen, *Social Setting*, 77.
282 *CIG* 2811.
283 Landvogt, *ΟΙΚΟΝΟΜΟΣ*, 44; Theissen, *Social Setting*, 77; Martin, *Slavery as Salvation*, 175.
284 E.g., *I.Smyrna* 761: Διόδωρος νεώτερος οἰκονομῶν, κτλ.; cf. Louis Robert, *Hellenica 11–12* (Paris: Librairie d'Amerique et d'Orient, 1960) 230; *TAM* 5.743: ο[ἰκ]ονόμον πάσης πόλεως βουλῆ[ς] μεγίστης Φάϊνον τείμησε πατρίς, κτλ.; *CIG* 2717: διὰ Φιλοκάλου β οἰκονόμο[υ], κτλ.; cf. Martin, *Slavery as Salvation*, 175.
285 Landvogt, *ΟΙΚΟΝΟΜΟΣ*, 14, 44, 47; Theissen, *Social Setting*, 77–78.
286 Landvogt, *ΟΙΚΟΝΟΜΟΣ*, 13; Martin, *Slavery as Salvation*, 17.

the early Roman period names a Philodespotos as οἰκονόμος.²⁸⁷ The same Philodespotos is described as a "public slave" (δημόσιος) in two other inscriptions.²⁸⁸ (The name Philodespotos means "one who loves his master").²⁸⁹ Other οἰκονόμοι of servile status in the Roman period are found at Athens, Nikaia (Bithynia), Prusa and Patara.²⁹⁰ Indeed, Landvogt judges that the majority of οἰκονόμοι under the Roman Empire were taken from the slave population.²⁹¹ We should not suppose, however, that all slave οἰκονόμοι were poor. A funerary inscription from Nicomedia honors the family of Gaius Tryphonos, οἰκονόμος: originally a public slave, he was set free by the philanthropy of the citizens;²⁹² as the text of the inscription reveals, Gaius Tryphonos was prosperous.²⁹³

In about half of the inscriptions mentioning οἰκονόμοι from Greece, Macedonia, and Asia Minor, the social status of the person holding the office cannot be determined.²⁹⁴ This is the case, for example, with an inscription from Cos mentioning a Dionysios πόλεως Κώων οἰκονόμος.²⁹⁵ Similarly, the inscription for a memorial to Dionysios, "οἰκονόμος of the Chalcedonians," provides no clue to the officer's status.²⁹⁶ In cases where the name of an οἰκονόμος appears without a father's name, and where it is stipulated that the office was held for a number of years, and not as a result of annual election, Landvogt infers that the person was a slave or a freedman.²⁹⁷ So, for example, in the memorial of Philetos of Cos: Φιλήτου οἰκονόμου τῆς Κώων πόλεως οἰκον[ο]μήσαντος ἔτη κγ̄ ἀμέμπ[τ]ως.²⁹⁸ But in the majority of instances, we must admit that the social status of the person bearing the title οἰκονόμος is indeterminable.²⁹⁹

---

287 *IG* 5.1.40 (*CIG* 1276); Landvogt, *ΟΙΚΟΝΟΜΟΣ*, 23; Martin, *Slavery as Salvation*, 174.
288 *IG* 5.1.147, 153 (*CIG* 1239); Landvogt, *ΟΙΚΟΝΟΜΟΣ*, 23; cf. A. Spawforth, "The Slave Philodespotos," *ZPE* 27 (1977) 294.
289 Theissen, *Social Setting*, 78.
290 *IG* 2–3.11492 (Athens); *SEG* 28.1033, 1034 (Nikaia); *SEG* 28.1045 (Prusa); *TAM* 2.437 (Patara); *SEG* 24.496 (Stobi); cf. Martin, *Slavery as Salvation*, 174.
291 Landvogt, *ΟΙΚΟΝΟΜΟΣ*, 13; cf. Cadbury, "Erastus of Corinth," 50.
292 *CIG* 3777; *TAM* 4.276; cf. Cadbury, "Erastus of Corinth," 50.
293 Landvogt, *ΟΙΚΟΝΟΜΟΣ*, 26; Theissen, *Social Setting*, 78. See also *SEG* 24.496: Diadoumenos of Stobi and his fellow-slaves (οἱ σύνδουλοι) dedicated a statue (or perhaps an altar) to the nymphs.
294 Martin, *Slavery as Salvation*, 16.
295 *CIG* 2512; Landvogt, *ΟΙΚΟΝΟΜΟΣ*, 24; Martin, *Slavery as Salvation*, 175.
296 *CIG* 3793; Landvogt, *ΟΙΚΟΝΟΜΟΣ*, 26; Martin, *Slavery as Salvation*, 175.
297 Landvogt, *ΟΙΚΟΝΟΜΟΣ*, 12.
298 Landvogt, *ΟΙΚΟΝΟΜΟΣ*, 24; Martin, *Slavery as Salvation*, 175.

Thus, with respect to the title οἰκονόμος, we find ourselves in agreement with those scholars (Henry J. Cadbury and Gerd Theissen) who have assessed the usage of the term most carefully with respect to Paul's Erastus: "on the basis of linguistic usage alone, we cannot reach any unequivocal conclusions about Rom. 16:23."[300] Since it is apparent that Paul mentions the office of Erastus with the intention of honoring him, one might incline to view the office which Erastus holds as a high-ranking position befitting a citizen.[301] But this would be an unwarranted conclusion, since slaves, and rather poor ones at that, took pride in the title οἰκονόμος and included it in their funerary inscriptions.[302]

Nevertheless, in seeking to ascertain what civic office Erastus might have held, it does not suffice to focus exclusively upon the Greek expression οἰκονόμος τῆς πόλεως.[303] This is because Corinth was a Roman colony whose official language was Latin, as demonstrated by the great preponderance of Latin inscriptions in the period from Augustus to Hadrian.[304] Thus we must ask ourselves, what Latin title would have corresponded to the Greek οἰκονόμος τῆς πόλεως? In his useful lexicon and analysis of *Greek Terms for Roman Institutions*, Hugh J. Mason judges that οἰκονόμος could designate the Latin municipal office of aedile.[305] In support of this conclusion, Mason references the inscriptions from Hierapolis and Smyrna cited above, where it appears that the office of οἰκο-

---

299 E.g., *SEG* 39.1316; see further, Martin, *Slavery as Salvation*, 175–76.
300 Theissen, *Social Setting*, 49–50; cf. Cadbury, "Erastus of Corinth," 49–50.
301 Theissen, *Social Setting*, 76; Clarke, *Secular and Christian Leadership*, 56; Florence M. Gillman, "Erastus," *ABD* 2 (1992) 571; de Vos, *Church and Community Conflicts*, 200 n.83; Jewett, *Romans*, 982.
302 E.g., *SEG* 38.710, cited in Meggitt, *Paul, Poverty, and Survival*, 139 n.337; cf. Meeks, *First Urban Christians*, 58; Friesen, "Poverty in Pauline Studies," 355.
303 Theissen, *Social Setting*, 78–79; Bruce W. Winter, *Seek the Welfare of the City: Christians as Benefactors and Citizens* (Grand Rapids: Eerdmans, 1994) 185–92.
304 John Harvey Kent, *Corinth, Volume VIII, Part III: The Inscriptions 1926–1950* (Princeton: The American School of Classical Studies at Athens, 1966) 18–19: "It will be noted that of the 104 texts that are prior to the reign of Hadrian 101 are in Latin and only three are in Greek, a virtual monopoly for the Latin language."
305 Hugh J. Mason, *Greek Terms for Roman Institutions: A Lexicon and Analysis* (Toronto: Hakkert, 1974) 71, 145, 175–76. Mason's lexicon has proven influential, e.g., Clarke, *Secular and Christian Leadership*, 50; David W. J. Gill, "Erastus the Aedile," *TynBul* 40 (1989) 297; Winter, *Seek the Welfare of the City*, 185, 187, 191; Jewett, *Romans*, 981.

νόμος τῆς πόλεως is a high-ranking position held by citizens.[306] Mason also cites an inscription from Philadelphia honoring a sophist with a statue or stele, whose erection was cared for by a certain Antonios, ὁ οἰκονόμος τῆς πόλεως.[307] Among the examples of οἰκονόμος as an equivalent of *aedilis coloniae*, Mason adduces Paul's usage in Rom. 16:23.[308] Against the conclusion that οἰκονόμος τῆς πόλεως is Paul's translation of *aedilis*, it has become customary to observe that ἀγορανόμος is the regular Greek word for aedile.[309] This is a valid objection. But it is not always noted that the term ἀγορανόμος is not attested in Corinthian inscriptions before the second century A.D.[310] Hence it remains a possibility that Paul used

---

306 Mason, *Greek Terms for Roman Institutions*, 71 s.v. οἰκονόμος 4: *IGR* 4.813 (Hierapolis); *IGR* 4.1435 (Smyrna). Friesen's judgment ("The Wrong Erastus," 247 n. 48) that Mason's interpretation of these inscriptions is "clearly mistaken" ignores the arguments of Landvogt, *ΟΙΚΟΝΟΜΟΣ*, 14, 28, 47.
307 Mason, *Greek Terms for Roman Institutions*, 71 s.v. οἰκονόμος 4: *IGR* 4.1630 (Philadelphia). Cf. Landvogt, *ΟΙΚΟΝΟΜΟΣ*, 26–27; Theissen, *Social Setting*, 77; Gill, "Erastus the Aedile," 297; Clarke, *Secular and Christian Leadership*, 50 n.60.
308 Mason, *Greek Terms for Roman Institutions*, 71 s.v. οἰκονόμος 4.
309 Cadbury, "Erastus of Corinth," 54; Theissen, *Social Setting*, 80; Meeks, *First Urban Christians*, 58; Clarke, *Secular and Christian Leadership*, 50; Gill, "Erastus of Corinth," 297–98; Friesen, "The Wrong Erastus," 246. Cf. Winter, *Seek the Welfare of the City*, 187.
310 *IG* 4.203; Kent, *Corinth VIII.3: The Inscriptions*, no. 306, pp. 120–21: an inscription containing a list of buildings constructed or repaired by P. Licinius Priscus Juventianus at the Isthmian sanctuary "in return for his aedileship" (ὑπὲρ ἀγορανομίας); cf. Oscar Broneer, "An Official Rescript from Corinth," *Hesperia* 8 (1939) 181–90; Louis Robert, *Hellenica* 1 (1940) 43–53. The inscription has been dated "within ten years of A.D. 170" by Kent, *Corinth VIII.3: The Inscriptions*, 121, and around 110 A.D. by B. Puech, "Grand-prêtres et helladarques d'achaïe," *REA* 85 (1983) 15–43, esp. 35–41. Especially important are the observations of Daniel J. Geagan, "Notes on the Agonistic Institutions of Roman Corinth," *GRBS* 4 (1968) 75: "There is no certain instance of the title *agoranomos* being applied to a civic official or magistrate of Roman Corinth. Although the title *aedilis* is rendered *agoranomos* elsewhere, the only possible equivalent found at Corinth is *oikonomos* (Romans 16:23). Only three epigraphical references to the *agoranomia* or to an *agoranomos* are preserved from Roman Corinth: a dedication (*SEG* 9.50) indicated that 'Cn. Pompeius Zenas dedicated to Dionysos a tenth part (?) when he was *agoranomos* of Zeus.' The *agoranomos* cited in Kent no. 308 clearly belongs to a religious organization, for which this stone contains a fragment of the statues. The third (*IG* 4.203) relates the benefactions of P. Licinius Priscus to the Isthmian sanctuary. Lines 23–27 indicate that 'the same man built the stoa next to the stadium with its vaulted chambers and adornments for the sake of the *agoranomia*.' It is only logical to conclude that such gifts to the

οἰκονόμος to refer to a Corinthian aedile, particularly since Paul adds the words "of the city" (τῆς πόλεως).³¹¹ Indeed, the principal epigrapher of Roman Corinth, John H. Kent, argues that οἰκονόμος may have been an accurate description of the responsibilities of the aediles at Corinth, owing to the particularities of financial management in that city: "Corinth was a unique colony in that she controlled the management of the games which were internationally famous. She therefore administered the Isthmian festivals by means of a completely separate set of officials [the *agonothetai*], and the Corinthian aediles, thus relieved of all responsibility for public entertainment, were in effect confined in their activities to local economic matters."³¹² Thus, Kent offers the explanation: "It is possibly for this reason that St. Paul does not use the customary word ἀγορανόμος to describe a Corinthian aedile, but calls him οἰκονόμος (*Romans* XVI, 23)."³¹³ If the conclusions of Mason and Kent are valid, and Paul's Erastus was indeed an aedile of Corinth, this would have dramatic implications for our assessment of Erastus' social status: Erastus would then be a high-ranking official, one of only four annually elected magistrates,³¹⁴ and *"a fortiori,* a Roman citizen, designated, as frequently throughout the East, by *cognomen* alone."³¹⁵

Isthmian sanctuary would have been connected with an office and *not the Roman aedileship.*" See also Daniel J. Geagan, "The Isthmian Dossier of P. Licinius Priscus Juventianus," *Hesperia* 58 (1989) 349–60; cf. Winter, *Seek the Welfare of the City,* 190.

311 Glen Bowersock, personal communication, June 12, 2006. See also Gill, "Erastus the Aedile," 297; Stansbury, "Corinthian Honor, Corinthian Conflict," 322; de Vos, *Church and Community Conflicts,* 200.

312 Kent, *Corinth VIII.3: The Inscriptions,* 27. See also Gill, "Erastus the Aedile," 298; Winter, *Seek the Welfare of the City,* 189; de Vos, *Church and Community Conflicts,* 201.

313 Kent, *Corinth VIII.3: The Inscriptions,* 27; cf. Gill, "Erastus the Aedile," 298; Winter, *Seek the Welfare of the City,* de Vos, *Church and Community Conflicts,* 201.

314 Kent, *Corinth VIII.3: The Inscriptions,* 24–27, 99–100; James Wiseman, "Corinth and Rome I: 228 BC-AD 267," *ANRW* II.7.1 (Berlin: Walter de Gruyter, 1979) 398–99; Engels, *Roman Corinth,* 18; Clarke, *Secular and Christian Leadership,* 14–16; Stansbury, "Corinthian Honor, Corinthian Conflict," 157.

315 Glen Bowersock, personal communication, June 12, 2006. See in general, G. Daux, "L'onomastique romaine d'expression grecque" in *L'Onomastique latine,* eds. H. G. Pflaum and N. Duval (Paris: CNRS, 1975) 405–17; A.D. Rizakis, "Anthroponymie et société: les noms romains dans les provinces hellénophones de l'Empire" in *Roman Onomastics in the Greek East: Social and Political Aspects* (Athens: Finnish Institute, 1996) 11–30. On the name Erastus, see Judge, "The

The stakes involved in an assessment of the title and office of Paul's Erastus were greatly heightened in 1929, by the discovery of an inscription recording the gift of a pavement to the city of Corinth by a certain Erastus who served as aedile.[316] By the archaeologists who superintended the excavations, T. L. Shear and F. J. de Waele, the Erastus of the inscription was immediately hailed as identical with the Erastus mentioned by Paul in Rom. 16:23.[317] But within a year of the discovery, the classicist A. G. Roos had voiced reservations,[318] and in 1931, Henry J. Cadbury declared the identification of the two Erasti "improbable if not impossible."[319] Almost a century of heated debate has brought no consensus, though we may note that, as a general tendency, archaeologists and classicists favor identification,[320] while New Testament scholars find reasons to demur.[321] The implications of the issue are potentially so significant, not only for the social status of Paul's Erastus, but also for that of Paul's Gaius, with whom Erastus is associated in his greetings

---

Roman Base of Paul's Mission," in *The First Christians in the Roman World*, 553–68.

316 Theodore Leslie Shear,"Discoveries at the Wealthy City of the Double Sea," *The Illustrated London News* (August 17, 1929) 286; idem, "Excavations in the Theatre District and Tombs of Corinth in 1929," *AJA* 33 (1929) 515–46, esp. 525–26; F. J. de Waele, "Die Korinthischen Ausgrabungen 1928–1929," *Gnomon* 6 (1930) 52–57, esp. 54.

317 Theodore Leslie Shear, "Excavations in the Theatre District and Tombs of Corinth in 1929," *AJA* 33 (1929) 525–26; F. J. de Waele, "Erastus, oikonoom van Korinthe en vriend van St. Paulus," *Mededeelingen van het Nederlandsch Historisch Instituut te Rom* 9 (1929) 40–48. See also A. M. Woodward, "Archaeology in Greece, 1928–1929," *JHS* 49 (1929) 221.

318 A. G. Roos, "De Titulo quodam latino Corinthi nuper reperto," *Mnemosyne* 58 (1930) 160–65.

319 Cadbury, "Erastus of Corinth," 42–58, esp. 58.

320 E.g., William A. McDonald, "Archaeology and St. Paul's Journeys in Greek Lands, Part III—Corinth," *BA* 5 (1942) 36–48, esp. 46; Oscar Broneer, "Corinth, Center of St. Paul's Missionary Work in Greece," *BA* 14 (1951) 78–96, esp. 94; Kent, *Corinth VIII.3: The Inscriptions*, 99–100; Mason, *Greek Terms for Roman Institutions*, 71; Wiseman, "Corinth and Rome I," 499 n.226; Engels, *Roman Corinth*, 108.

321 E.g., Cadbury, "Erastus of Corinth," 58; Colin J. Hemer, *The Book of Acts in the Setting of Hellenistic History* (Tübingen: Mohr Siebeck, 1989) 235 n.40; Justin J. Meggitt, "The Social Status of Erastus (Rom. 16:23)," *NovT* 38 (1996) 220–21; repr. in *Christianity at Corinth: The Quest for the Pauline Church*, ed. David G. Horrell and Edward Adams (Louisville: Westminster John Knox Press, 2004) 219–25; idem, *Paul, Poverty, and Survival*, 135–41; Friesen, "Poverty in Pauline Studies," 354–55; idem, "The Wrong Erastus," 231–56.

268   Chapter Four. Social and Rhetorical Conventions

(Rom. 16:23), that we cannot forgo a discussion of the text of the famous inscription, even if we should be warned from the outset that the facts regarding the date, location, and re-use of the inscription are so uncertain that our conclusions may not advance beyond what is probable.

The crucial, central slab of the Erastus inscription was found at the entrance to a paved plaza (measuring 19 m. x 19 m.) northeast of the theater.[322] The slab, a block of grey Acrocorinthian limestone, contained cuttings for letters that were presumably of bronze, fastened in place with lead (of which traces were found in some letters and punctuation marks).[323] The inscription reads as follows:

**ERASTVS   PRO   AED
S   P   STRAVIT**

From the beginning, F. J. de Waele recognized that the inscription was not complete: the initial 'E' in the first line of the inscription had been bisected by a precise vertical cut.[324] De Waele conjectured that a slab to the left was missing, on which additional letters of the inscription would be found.[325] Shear noted that the block had been broken on the right side as well.[326] Eventually, Oscar Broneer recognized that a fragment which had been discovered by de Waele in the east parodos of the theater

---

322 Shear, "Excavations in the Theatre District," 525; photo from Shear, fig. 9.
323 Shear, "Excavations in the Theatre District," 525; Kent, *Corinth VIII.3: The Inscriptions*, no. 232, pp. 99–100. On the basis of personal communication from Ruth Siddall, Friesen identifies the medium as "white porcellanite," rather than grey limestone ("The Wrong Erastus," 9 n.18). Shear's photo shows traces of lead in the letters **'S'** and **'R'** of the word **STRAVIT**. See also de Waele, "Erastus, oikonoom," 40, 41 n.1.
324 de Waele, "Erastus, oikonoom," 41 n.1.
325 de Waele, "Erastus, oikonoom," 41 n.1; see also Kent, *Corinth VIII.3: The Inscriptions*, 100.
326 Shear, "Excavations in the Theatre District," 525.

in 1928 belonged to the missing right slab.³²⁷ A second portion of the right slab was found in the basement of a late vaulted building southwest of the theater in 1947.³²⁸ The recovery of these pieces of the right slab of the inscription confirmed a suggestion made by H. Van de Weerd in 1931, that the letters **AED** should be restored as *aedilitate*.³²⁹ On the assumption that the second line of the inscription was placed symmetrically below the first (an assumption supported by the spacing at the left edge of the second line),³³⁰ John Kent calculated that seven letters are missing before the *cognomen* Erastus: thus, the left hand slab (which has yet to be discovered) would have contained an abbreviated *praenomen* and a *nomen* consisting of five or six letters.³³¹ The complete text of the inscription may be reconstructed as follows:

**[PR.NOMEN]   ERASTVS   PRO   AEDILIT[AT]E
              S   P   STRAVIT**

*[praenomen nomen] Erastus pro aedilit[at]e
s(ua) p(ecunia) stravit*

"*praenomen nomen* Erastus in return for his aedileship
laid (the pavement) at his own expense."

In seeking to determine whether Paul's Erastus should be identified with the Erastus of the inscription, the date of the inscription is the crucial factor.³³² Unfortunately, the dating of the inscription is encumbered with difficulties—imprecision with respect to palaeography and vagaries in the history of the re-use of the fragments. Van de Weerd noted that

---

327 Richard Stillwell, *Corinth II: The Theatre* (Princeton: The American School of Classical Studies at Athens, 1952) 4; Kent, *Corinth VIII.3: The Inscriptions*, 99.
328 Kent, *Corinth VIII.3: The Inscriptions*, 99.
329 H. Van de Weerd, "Een Nieuw Opschrift van Korinthe," *Revue Belge de Philologie et d'Histoire* 10 (1931) 87–95, esp. 94; McDonald, "Archaeology and St. Paul's Journeys," 46; Stillwell, *Corinth II: The Theatre*, 4. In fact, this solution had already been proposed by Roos, "De Titulo," 163; followed by Cadbury, "Erastus of Corinth," 53.
330 Kent, *Corinth VIII.3: The Inscriptions*, 100.
331 Kent, *Corinth VIII.3: The Inscriptions*, 100.
332 The importance of the date was already recognized by de Waele, "Erastus, oikonoom," 43; followed by Van de Weerd, "Een Nieuw Opschrift," 94; recently, Meggitt, "The Social Status of Erastus" in *Christianity at Corinth*, 222; Friesen, "The Wrong Erastus," 237–45.

the letters of the inscription appear to have been chiseled with care;[333] such care is generally held to characterize inscriptions from the early Imperial period;[334] but Van de Weerd was unwilling to wager a precise conclusion about the date.[335] The fact that the language of the inscription is Latin, rather than Greek, may also point to the period before Hadrian, when the Hellenization of the city resulted in a dramatic increase in the proportion of Greek inscriptions.[336] But lettering and language provide only the roughest approximation of a date.

The principal obstacle to a precise dating of the Erastus inscription is the re-use of the inscription in other building projects in the area of the theater. As a result of re-use, none of the fragments of the inscription can be said to have been found *in situ*,[337] not even the crucial, central slab preserving the name of Erastus. In the earliest and most detailed excavation report, de Waele indicated that the block with the Erastus inscription was discovered approximately .05 m. above and to the south of the paved plaza, where it formed part of a long row of stones.[338] These stones later served as the foundation for a wall of the Byzantine era, but had been moved to their present location at an earlier period.[339] In any case, the Erastus inscription does not lie *in situ*, a point that is repeatedly emphasized by de Waele.[340]

What, then, was the original location of the Erastus inscription? The text of the inscription refers to a pavement, that is, to something "laid" (*stravit*) at the expense of the donor.[341] In a later excavation report, de Waele described the area in front of the theater as consisting of three plazas paved with thin marble slabs of which only the central and eastern

---

333 Van de Weerd, "Een Nieuw Opschrift," 95.
334 On the letter-forms of inscriptions and dating, in general, see Fergus Millar, "Epigraphy" in *Sources for Ancient History*, ed. Michael Crawford (Cambridge: Cambridge University Press, 1983) 98; cf. Kent's comments on the lettering of the Hicesius inscription in *Corinth VIII: The Inscriptions*, 99.
335 Van de Weerd, "Een Nieuw Opschrift," 95.
336 Kent, *Corinth VIII.3: The Inscriptions*, 19.
337 Contra Kent, *Corinth VIII.3: The Inscriptions*, 99; Gill, "Erastus the Aedile," 293–94; Clarke, *Secular and Christian Leadership*, 47.
338 de Waele, "Erastus, oikonoom," 41 n.1.
339 de Waele, "Erastus, oikonoom," 41 n.1, 43; see now Friesen, "The Wrong Erastus," 238, citing the excavation notebook.
340 de Waele, "Erastus, oikonoom," 41 n.1: "Gevonden 15 April 1929. Ligt niet *in situ*"; 42: "Het blok met de inscriptie ligt niet *in situ*."
341 Kent, *Corinth VIII.3: The Inscriptions*, 99.

Chapter Four. Social and Rhetorical Conventions   271

portions had been exposed.³⁴² The street that runs along the east side of the theater was also paved at the same time as the plazas, according to de Waele.³⁴³ Thus, the Erastus inscription could refer to any of these paving projects, although it is most natural to associate it with the northeast plaza,³⁴⁴ to which the inscription, in its present location, stands in closest proximity.

Thus, the date of the Erastus inscription is ultimately dependant upon the date of the paved areas near the theater. But here, too, one encounters difficulties related to the history of the repair of the plaza. De Waele recognized that certain irregularities in the pavement of the plaza give evidence of a major repair or restoration at some point after the pavement was laid.³⁴⁵ In an attempt to ascertain the date of this repair, de Waele carried out a trial dig under the pavement: within the filling of broken tiles and stones, a coin of Hadrian came to light.³⁴⁶ The coin of Hadrian demonstrated that the restoration of the plaza could not have been undertaken prior to the reign of this emperor.³⁴⁷ De Waele reasoned that the original pavement, to which the inscription refers, must have been laid before the middle of the second century.³⁴⁸ Moreover, the re-use of the inscription in the repair of the pavement suggested to de Waele that the donor, Erastus, had been dead for some time, perhaps more than a generation, when the stone was re-used.³⁴⁹ In this way, de Waele arrived at the second half of the first century as the most likely date for the Erastus inscription.³⁵⁰ It fell to Van de Weerd to point out the flaw in de Waele's logic: the Hadrianic coin provides only a *terminus a quo* for the restoration of the pavement; the repair

---

342 de Waele, "Die Korinthischen Ausgrabungen," 53, 54.
343 de Waele, "Erastus, oikonoom," 43; cf. Van de Weerd, "Een Nieuw Opschrift," 94.
344 de Waele, "Die Korinthischen Ausgrabungen," 53, 54.
345 de Waele, "Erastus, oikonoom," 41 n.1, 43.
346 de Waele, "Erastus, oikonoom," 43; cf. Van de Weerd, "Een Nieuw Opschrift," 94.
347 de Waele, "Erastus, oikonoom," 43; cf. Van de Weerd, "Een Nieuw Opschrift," 94.
348 de Waele, "Erastus, oikonoom," 43.
349 de Waele, "Erastus, oikonoom," 43; cf. Theissen, *Social Setting*, 80.
350 de Waele, "Erastus, oikonoom," 43; cf. Kent, *Corinth VIII.3: The Inscriptions*, 100: "near the middle of the first century after Christ."; similarly, Wiseman, "Rome and Corinth," 521.

might have been undertaken later, perhaps even in the third century.³⁵¹ Consequently, the coin of Hadrian loses some of its value for a determination of the date of the Erastus inscription.³⁵²

A final datum related to the identification of Paul's Erastus with the Erastus of the inscription is the rarity of the *cognomen* Erastus at Corinth. Apart from Rom. 16:23 and the inscription found northeast of the theater, the name Erastus is attested for Corinth only by a marble dedication found at Skoutela in 1960;³⁵³ but this inscription dates from the second century A.D.³⁵⁴ To be sure, Erastus is not an uncommon name in general. Several epigraphic instances come from Ephesus, of which the most relevant is Ti. Claudius Erastus from a Curetes list dated to 54–59 A.D.³⁵⁵ Four Erasti are attested in Sparta;³⁵⁶ others are found in Attica, Bithynia, Laconia and Messenia, covering a span from the third century B.C. to the third century A.D.³⁵⁷ Justin Meggitt has counted fifty-five examples of the Latin *cognomen* Erastus in the *Corpus inscriptionum latinarum*,³⁵⁸ and has discovered twenty-three examples of the Greek Ἔραστος.³⁵⁹ To these we may add a handful of literary references in Plato (*Ep.* 6.322D, 323 A), Strabo (13.608), Acts (19:22), 2 Timothy (4:20) and Diogenes Laertius (3.46).³⁶⁰ Thus the name Erastus was not as uncommon as has

---

351 Van de Weerd, "Een Nieuw Opschrift," 94–95; see now Friesen, "The Wrong Erastus," 233–34.
352 Van de Weerd, "Een Nieuw Opschrift," 95.
353 D. I. Pallas and S. P. Dantes, " Ἐπιγραφες απο την Κορινθω," *Archaiologike Ephemeris* 1977 (1979) no.. 19, pp. 75–76; *SEG* 29 (1979) no. 301; Andrew D. Clarke, "Another Corinthian Erastus Inscription," *TynBul* 42 (1991) 146–51.
354 Pallas and Dantes, " Ἐπιγραφες απο την Κορινθω," 76; Clarke, "Another Corinthian Erastus Inscription," 147; cf. Friesen, "The Wrong Erastus," 233 n.8, who suggests a fourth-century date.
355 *I.Eph. 1008.8*, cited by Hemer, *Acts in the Setting of Hellenistic History*, 235; cf. Clarke, "Another Corinthian Erastus Inscription," 149–50.
356 *CIG* 269; 1241; 1249; 6378; P. M. Fraser and E. Matthews, *A Lexicon of Greek Personal Names: Vol. III.A: The Peloponnese* (Oxford: Clarendon Press, 1997); cf. Clarke, *Secular and Christian Leadership*, 55 n.90; Friesen, "The Wrong Erastus," 233 n.8.
357 *SEG* 24.194; 25.194 (Attica); *SEG* 28.1010 (Bithynia); *SEG* 11.622 (Laconia); *SEG* 11.994 (Messenia); cf. Clarke, *Secular and Christian Leadership*, 55 n.90.
358 Meggitt, "The Social Status of Erastus" in *Christianity at Corinth*, 223 n.27; see already Van de Weerd, "Een Nieuw Opschrift," 41.
359 Meggitt, "The Social Status of Erastus" in *Christianity at Corinth*, 223 n.28.
360 For other literary references, see Clarke, "Another Corinthian Erastus Inscription," 149.

sometimes been alleged.³⁶¹ But the point of significance is *the rarity of this name* **at Corinth.**³⁶² The fact bears repeating that the Erastus mentioned by Paul in Rom. 16:23 and the Erastus who laid a pavement adjacent to the theater are the only persons of this name who are attested for Corinth in the latter half of the first century—the former dated securely to the reign of Nero, the latter less precisely to the period from Nero to Hadrian. It is highly unlikely that two *different* Corinthian office-holders should have had a name that was so uncommon at Corinth, when no other officials at Corinth are known to have borne this name in the first century.³⁶³

Although the archaeological record presents more uncertainties than an historian should wish, we may judge that the balance of the evidence inclines toward identification of the Erastus of Rom. 16:23 with the Erastus of the inscription. The points in favor of identification are not significantly different from those listed by John Kent a generation ago: 1) it is possible that the pavement was laid in the second half of the first century A.D.; 2) the *cognomen* Erastus is uncommon at Corinth, making it unlikely that two Corinthian officials bearing this name would be different individuals; 3) "Paul's word οἰκονόμος describes with reasonable accuracy the function of a Corinthian aedile."³⁶⁴ Additionally, one must assume that Paul, as a native of Tarsus, would have been familiar with the Greek civic vocabulary of his time.³⁶⁵

If the balance of the evidence inclines toward identification of Paul's Erastus with the Erastus of the inscription, why then are some scholars reluctant to draw this conclusion? For some, the ambiguity of the linguistic usage forestalls a verdict: because Paul does not employ the usual Greek equivalent ἀγορανόμος, there will always be some doubt about Paul's Erastus as aedile.³⁶⁶ For others, the uncertainty of the date of the

---

361 E.g., C. E. B. Cranfield, *A Critical and Exegetical Commentary on the Epistle to the Romans*, Vol. 2 (Edinburgh; T & T Clark, 1979) 807; Victor Paul Furnish, "Corinth in Paul's Time: What Can Archaeology Teach Us?" *Biblical Archaeology Review* 15 (1988) 20.
362 Rightly, Kent, *Corinth VIII.3: The Inscriptions*, 99; Theissen, *Social Setting*, 83; de Vos, *Church and Community Conflicts*, 200 n.83.
363 Murphy-O'Connor, *Paul*, 269; de Vos, *Church and Community Conflicts*, 200; Jewett, *Romans*, 982.
364 Kent, *Corinth VIII.3: The Inscriptions*, 99–100.
365 McDonald, "Archaeology and St. Paul's Journeys in Greek Lands," 46 n.2; A. J. S. Spawforth, cited in Gill, "Erastus the Aedile," 298 n.25.
366 Cadbury, "Erastus of Corinth," 54; Van de Weerd, "Een Nieuw Opschrift," 95; Theissen, *Social Setting*, 80; cf. Clarke, *Secular and Christian Leadership*, 50.

inscription proves an insuperable obstacle.³⁶⁷ For still others, the rarity of the *cognomen* Erastus at Corinth does not seem to count as a decisive factor.³⁶⁸ Perhaps this is all as it should be. But when one surveys the history of scholarship, and especially the contributions of New Testament scholars, it becomes apparent that two assumptions about the nature of the early Christian movement are at work, assumptions which are more powerful in blocking an identification of the two Erasti than any reasonable reservations about the inconclusive state of the evidence.

First, it is assumed that Paul's Erastus could not have been a high-ranking official, because the majority of the early Christians were from the lower class.³⁶⁹ This assumption is already audible in the early essay of Cadbury, who opines that "those commentators are probably wrong who cite Erastus as an exception to Paul's description of the first Corinthian Christians as including not many mighty, not many noble (1 Cor. 1:26)."³⁷⁰ The assumption is loudly voiced by Justin Meggitt, who insists that "Erastus' socio-economic situation was most likely *indistinguishable* from that of his fellow believers" who, like the vast majority of inhabitants of the Roman Empire, lived in "abject poverty."³⁷¹ Such scholars typically downplay the rarity of the name Erastus at Corinth, disregard the epigraphic evidence that οἰκονόμος sometimes means *aedilis*, and magnify the difficulty of dating the Erastus inscription.³⁷² By such scholars, Paul's Erastus is predictably seen as a public slave, and a rather poor one, at that.³⁷³

---

367 Van de Weerd, "Een Nieuw Opschrift," 95; Meggitt, "The Social Status of Erastus" in *Christianity at Corinth,* 222; Friesen, "The Wrong Erastus," 237–45.
368 Meggitt, "The Social Status of Erastus" in *Christianity at Corinth,* 223–24; idem, *Paul, Poverty and Survival,* 137–40; Friesen, "The Wrong Erastus," 233 n.8.
369 Cadbury, "Erastus of Corinth," 57; Meggitt, "The Social Status of Erastus" in *Christianity at Corinth,* 219–25; idem, *Paul, Poverty and Survival,* 135–41; Friesen, "Poverty in Pauline Studies," 354–55; idem, "The Wrong Erastus," 235, 255–56.
370 Cadbury, "Erastus of Corinth," 57.
371 Meggitt, "The Social Status of Erastus" in *Christianity at Corinth,* 225; idem, *Paul, Poverty and Survival,* 4, 50, 73.
372 Meggitt, "The Social Status of Erastus" in *Christianity at Corinth,* 219–25; idem, *Paul, Poverty and Survival,* 135–41; Friesen, "The Wrong Erastus," 233 n.8, 237–45.
373 Meggitt, "The Social Status of Erastus" in *Christianity at Corinth,* 223, 225; idem, *Paul, Poverty and Survival,* 139; Friesen, "Poverty in Pauline Studies," 355; idem, "The Wrong Erastus," 245–49.

To be sure, the majority of Pauline Christians *were poor*, even at Corinth.[374] Paul reminds his Corinthian readers that "not many" of them were educated, wealthy, or nobly-born (1 Cor. 1:26–28), in order to illustrate the paradoxical consequences of the gospel of the crucified Christ.[375] But for reasons that are not entirely apparent, it seems that at Corinth the Pauline mission made converts, perhaps for the first time, from among the upper class.[376] We have examined the multifarious evidence that Crispus and Gaius were persons of substance. Whatever the precise social status of Stephanas may have been, he cannot be reckoned among the poor. Many scholars would concede that a few, if only a few, of the Corinthian Christians were wealthy.[377] But the same scholars balk at the identification of Paul's Erastus with the aedile of the inscription,[378] because they recognize that this would place a Christian in the true upper class, among the *decuriones*, the elite of the cities, who were expected to meet most of the public expenditure, and who gained power and influence through their acts of beneficence.[379] Indeed, the Erastus inscription

---

374 Rightly, Meggitt, *Paul, Poverty and Survival*, 75–76, 96; Wolfgang and Ekkehard Stegemann, *The Jesus Movement: A Social History of the First Century* (Minneapolis: Augsburg Fortress Press, 1999) 291–96; Steven J. Friesen, "Prospects for a Demography of the Pauline Mission: Corinth Among the Churches" in *Urban Religion in Roman Corinth*, ed. Daniel N. Schowalter and Steven J. Friesen (Cambridge, MA: Harvard University Press, 2005) 351–70, esp. 367.

375 Gerd Theissen, "Social Conflicts in the Corinthian Community: Further Remarks on J. J. Meggitt, *Paul, Poverty and Survival*," *JSNT* 25 (2003) 375–76; Welborn, *Paul, the Fool of Christ*, 2, 7, 147, 164, 233–34.

376 On the social difference between Paul's converts in Thessalonica and Corinth, see John M. G. Barclay, "Thessalonica and Corinth: Social Contrasts in Pauline Christianity," *JSNT* 47 (1992) 49–74; de Vos, *Church and Community Conflicts*, 197–203.

377 E.g., Theissen, *Social Setting*, 71–73, 94–96; Malherbe, *Social Aspects*, 71–84; Meeks, *First Urban Christians*, 56–60; Clarke, *Secular and Christian Leadership*, 41–57; Theissen, "The Social Structure of Pauline Communities," 76–84; Friesen, "Poverty in Pauline Studies," 348–57.

378 E.g., Clarke, *Secular and Christian Leadership*, 55–56; Hemer, *Acts in the Setting of Hellenistic History*, 235; Friesen, "Poverty in Pauline Studies," 354–55.

379 Geza Alföldy, *The Social History of Rome* (London: Routledge, 1988) 106–15, 122, 127, 147; MacMullen, *Roman Social Relations*, 88–89. See also Richard Duncan-Jones, "Wealth and Munificence in Roman Africa," *Papers of the British School at Rome* 31 (1963) 168–71; idem, *The Economy of the Roman Empire* (New York: Cambridge University Press, 1982) 283–87. Cf. Friesen, "Poverty in Pauline Studies," 360–61. On the aedile as a decurion, see J. W. Kubitschek, "Aedilis," *RE* 1 (1894) 44–68.

advertises the wealth that is the prerequisite of the donor's magistracy.³⁸⁰ It is the proud class consciousness that comes to expression in the Erastus inscription which seems most incongruous with Paul's insistence that those whom God had chosen, even at Corinth, were "the nothings and the nobodies" of the world (1 Cor. 1:27–28).³⁸¹

Rather than assuming that Paul's Erastus must have been impoverished because the majority of Christians at Corinth were so, and then twisting the evidence to exclude the possibility of identification with the Erastus of the inscription, it is surely better, methodologically, to let the epigraphic, archaeological, and onomastic evidence stand, and tip the balance on identification as it will, and then sort out the implications for a sociology of early Christianity. Scholars of the New Testament might then find themselves pondering a more interesting question: Why should someone of the social class of Erastus ὁ οἰκονόμος τῆς πόλεως have been attracted to the Christian movement?³⁸² Why should Erastus have chosen to align himself with a religious group that drew most of its members from the lower class? It might turn out that the practical consciousness of the early Christians was more complex than that imputed to the group by modern historians.³⁸³

Second, it is assumed that Paul's Erastus could not have been the Corinthian aedile, because the pagan ceremonial obligations attendant upon that office would be incompatible with the exclusive claims of Christian faith.³⁸⁴ This objection to the identification of the two Erasti was already voiced by A. G. Roos in his early essay *"De Titulo quodam latino Corinthi*

---

380 The letters, presumably of bronze, fastened in place with lead, would seem to advertize the wealth of the donor. Cf. A. M. Woodward, "Archaeology in Greece, 1928–1929," *JHS* 49 (1929) 221; Shear, "Excavations in the Theatre District," 525; de Waele, "Erastus, oikonoom," 40–41. See also Winter, *Seek the Welfare of the City*, 180–81: "The lettering of the inscription would have stood out because it was in bronze. In fact, it is the largest metal lettering extant in the Corinthian inscriptions."
381 Welborn, *Paul, the Fool of Christ*, 147–48.
382 Theissen, "The Social Structure of Pauline Communities," 79–80.
383 For a more complex picture, see Dimitris J. Kyrtatas, *The Social Structure of the Early Christian Communities* (London: Verso, 1987) 184–85; Martin, *The Corinthian Body*, xvi-xviii and passim; see also Margaret Y. MacDonald, "The Shifting Centre: Ideology and the Interpretation of 1 Corinthians" in *Christianity at Corinth: The Quest for the Pauline Church*, ed. David G. Horrell and Edward Adams (Louisville: Westminster John Knox Press, 2004) 273–94, esp. 285–91.
384 Roos, "De Titulo, 160–65; Cadbury, "Erastus of Corinth," 55–56; Clarke, *Secular and Christian Leadership*, 53–54.

nuper reperto" (1930).³⁸⁵ Roos observed that civic magistrates in the Roman Empire—that is, *duoviri, aediles,* and *quaestores*—were required, upon assuming office, to swear an oath *per Iovem et divos imperatores et genium principis deosque Penates.*³⁸⁶ Roos found it inconceivable that the Erastus who was a friend of Paul could have taken a public oath by Jupiter, the divine Augusti and the gods, without compromising his identity as a Christian.³⁸⁷ Cadbury repeated this objection, arguing that "no Christian could consent to the paganism involved in holding such an office as aedile."³⁸⁸ The objection has recently been revived by Andrew Clarke in his study of *Secular and Christian Leadership at Corinth,* as a caution against certain identification of the Erastus of Rom. 16:23 with the Erastus of the inscription.³⁸⁹ One wonders whether this assumption is not also implicit in Justin Meggitt's analysis of the social status of Paul's Erastus.³⁹⁰

The problematic nature of this assumption was already identified by Cadbury, despite his attraction to Roos' objection: "The principal answer to the argument is that we have no certainty that Christians so early objected to the idolatrous associations of public office."³⁹¹ Only from the correspondence of Pliny with Trajan, three generations after Paul, do we have evidence that Christians were unwilling to invoke the Roman gods or to offer obeisance to the Roman emperor.³⁹² More recently, James B. Rives has demonstrated, in his investigation of religion and authority in Roman Carthage, that persons in cosmopolitan societies like Carthage and Corinth experienced few constraints upon private religious activities, and consequently defined their individual religious identities much as they pleased, in diverse and idiosyncratic ways, adopting practices and beliefs from other cultures, generally without a sense that their personal beliefs and practices conflicted with the collective religious iden-

---

385 Roos, "De Titulo," 164–65.
386 Roos, "De Titulo," 164–65, appealing to the Lex Malacitana 59 and the Lex Salpens 26, and referencing Theodor Mommsen, *Gesammelte Schriften* I (Berlin: Weidmann, 1905) 320–21.
387 Roos, "De Titulo," 165, drawing attention to Pliny *Ep.* 10.96.
388 Cadbury, "Erastus of Corinth," 55.
389 Clarke, *Secular and Christian Leadership,* 53–54, 55.
390 Meggitt, "The Social Status of Erastus" in *Christianity at Corinth,* 219–25; idem, *Paul, Poverty and Survival,* 135–41.
391 Cadbury, "Erastus of Corinth," 55.
392 Pliny *Ep.* 10.96: *quorum nihil posse cogi dicuntur qui sunt vera Christiani.*

tity of the group.³⁹³ Paul's Erastus might well have experienced no conflict of conscience in the discharge of ceremonial duties connected to the *sacra publica*. How Paul felt about Christian involvement in pagan rituals is another matter (cf. 1 Cor. 8)!³⁹⁴

It is the presence and operation of these problematic assumptions—pauperism and exclusivism—which gives the debate over the identity of Paul's Erastus among New Testament scholars its hyperbolic and speculative character.³⁹⁵ To the former category belongs Cadbury's pronouncement that the identification of the two Erasti is "improbable if not impossible,"³⁹⁶ as well as Steven Friesen's assertion that "the epigraphic record makes it impossible to identify Erastus the *aedile* with Erastus the *oikonomos*."³⁹⁷ To the latter category must be reckoned the preference of Cadbury and others for the Vulgate translation *arcarius civitatis*,³⁹⁸ for which title there is no inscriptional evidence at Roman Corinth,³⁹⁹ as well as Theissen's conjecture that Paul's Erastus held the junior office of *quaestor*,⁴⁰⁰ for which office, again, there is little evidence at Corinth,⁴⁰¹

---

393 J. B. Rives, *Religion and Authority in Roman Carthage from Augustus to Constantine* (Oxford: Clarendon Press, 1995) 173–93, esp. 186, 192–93; cf. James Walters, "Civic Identity in Roman Corinth and Its Impact on Early Christians" in *Urban Religion in Roman Corinth*, ed. Daniel N. Schowalter and Steven Friesen (Cambridge: Harvard University Press, 2005) 397–418. See also Winter, *Seek the Welfare of the City*, 192–95.
394 Joop F. M. Smit, *"About the Idol Offerings": Rhetoric, Social Context and Theology of Paul's Discourse in 1 Corinthians 8:1–11:1* (Leuven: Peeters, 2000); John Fotopoulos, *Food Offered to Idols in Roman Corinth: A Socio-rhetorical Reconsideration of 1 Corinthians 8:1–11:1* (Tübingen: Mohr Siebeck, 2003).
395 On the "pauperistic perspective" of Meggitt, see Bengt Holmberg, "The Methods of Historical Reconstruction in the Scholarly 'Recovery' of Corinthian Christianity" in *Christianity at Corinth*, 255–71, esp. 263, 270.
396 Cadbury, "Erastus of Corinth," 58.
397 Friesen, "The Wrong Erastus," 247.
398 So, already, Roos, "De Titulo," 164; Cadbury, "Erastus of Corinth," 51–52, 56; Friesen, "The Wrong Erastus," 248; cf. Theissen, *Social Setting*, 76.
399 McDonald, "Archaeology and St. Paul's Journeys," 46 n.2; Clarke, *Secular and Christian Leadership*, 51–52; cf. Theissen, *Social Setting*, 76; Jewett, *Romans*, 981 n.61.
400 Theissen, *Social Setting*, 82–83; followed by Meeks, *First Urban Christians*, 59; Murphy-O'Connor, *Paul*, 269; see now John K. Goodrich, "Erastus, *Quaestor* of Corinth: The Administrative Rank of ὁ οἰκονόμος τῆς πόλεως (Rom. 16:23) in an Achaean Colony," *NTS* 56 (2009) 90–115.
401 Kent, *Corinth VIII.3: The Inscriptions*, nos. 119, 125, 168, 170; but the word *quaestor* is restored by the epigrapher in each of these instances. The Greek equivalent of *quaestor* is ταμίας, but there is no evidence for the use of ταμίας at Cor-

and above all, the highly creative suggestion that the name on the inscription might have been "Eperastus," a suggestion which, when it was first offered by Van de Weerd,[402] was at least possible, but which, since the recovery of the right hand portion of the inscription, can only be maintained by means of the additional assumption that the second line of the inscription, which appears to be complete, *was not placed symmetrically* below the first line, an assumption which Meggitt is willing to make,[403] and which lends an air of desperation to Meggitt's attempt to deny any connection between the Erastus of the inscription and the Erastus of Rom. 16:23.[404]

We may now present our conclusions regarding the social status of Paul's Erastus. Understandably, our conclusions must remain tentative, given the ambiguity of the linguistic and archaeological data. If the title ὁ οἰκονόμος τῆς πόλεως refers to a minor financial office held by a public slave, as is often the case in the inscriptions,[405] then Paul's Erastus could not have belonged to the social elite in any sense. Erastus may have been as poor as Longeinos, the οἰκονόμος τῆς πόλεως of Thessalonika, whose simple epitaph for his wife was carved into recycled stone;[406] or, Erastus may have been somewhat more prosperous, like the freed slave Gaius Tryphonos of Nicomedia, whose epitaph celebrates his achievements.[407] If, however, the title οἰκονόμος refers to a high-ranking position held by a freeborn citizen, as is the case in several cities of western Asia Minor,[408] then Paul's Erastus would have been a person of wealth and influence. We have argued above that the balance of evidence inclines toward identification of Paul's Erastus with the aedile of the inscription.

---

inth in this period; see Mason, *Greek Terms for Roman Institutions*, 91; Wiseman, "Corinth and Rome I," 499; Gill, "Erastus the Aedile," 298–99; Clarke, *Secular and Christian Leadership*, 53; Winter, *Seek the Welfare of the City*, 191.

402 Van de Weerd, "Een Nieuw Opschrift," 91.
403 Meggitt, "The Social Status of Erastus" in *Christianity at Corinth*, 224–25; idem, *Paul, Poverty and Survival*, 139–40 n.345; followed by Friesen, "The Wrong Erastus," 233 n.8.
404 de Vos, *Church and Community Conflicts*, 199–200 n.82.
405 E.g., *IG* 2–3.11492; *IG* 5.1.40; *SEG* 24.496; *SEG* 28.1033; cf. Landvogt, ΟΙΚΟΝΟΜΟΣ, 13, 26; Martin, *Slavery as Salvation*, 17, 174.
406 *SEG* 38.710; cited by Meggitt, *Paul, Poverty and Survival*, 139 n.337; Friesen, "The Wrong Erastus," 247–48.
407 *TAM* 4.276; cf. Martin, *Slavery as Salvation*, 175.
408 *CIG* 2811, 3151, 3162; *IGR* 4.1435; 4.1630; Landvogt, ΟΙΚΟΝΟΜΟΣ, 14, 26–27, 28, 44; Mason, *Greek Terms for Roman Institutions*, 71; Martin, *Slavery as Salvation*, 175.

280 Chapter Four. Social and Rhetorical Conventions

If this conclusion is valid, then Paul's Erastus would belong to the true upper class, the 3 percent or so of the population who controlled the resources and who consequently exercised influence over the cities of the Roman Empire.⁴⁰⁹

An observation by John Kent regarding the lost slab to the left of the Erastus inscription permits a more precise determination of Erastus' social status: on the assumption that the second line was placed symmetrically below the first, the left hand block would have contained insufficient space for a patronymic or a tribal abbreviation.⁴¹⁰ Thus, Kent infers that "Erastus was probably a Corinthian freedman who had acquired considerable wealth in commercial activities."⁴¹¹ Erastus would then be one of the many freedmen who prospered in the new city of Roman Corinth, like his older contemporary Cn. Babbius Philinus.⁴¹² The wealth, if not to say, ostentation of Erastus is advertised by the material and height (0.18 m.) of the letters of the inscription, extraordinary in both respects.⁴¹³ The kind of beneficence with which Erastus was competing in the contest for public honor is well illustrated by an inscription found in the theater at Corinth, whose lettering shows that it dates to the first half of the first century A.D.:

---

409 Kent, *Corinth VIII.3: The Inscriptions*, 27; Meeks, *First Urban Christians*, 59; Winter, *Seek the Welfare of the City*, 196–97; Theissen, "The Social Structure of the Pauline Communities," 80; Jewett, *Romans*, 982.
410 Kent, *Corinth VIII.3: The Inscriptions*, 100.
411 Kent, *Corinth VIII.3: The Inscriptions*, 100; cf. Meeks, *First Urban Christians*, 59.
412 A. B. West, *Corinth VIII: Latin Inscriptions 1896–1926* (Cambridge, MA: Harvard University Press, 1931) no. 132; Kent, *Corinth VIII.3: The Inscriptions*, no. 155; cf. Meeks, *First Urban Christians*, 48, 59; Gill, "Erastus the Aedile," 295.
413 de Waele, "Erastus, oikonoom," 41 n.1; cf. Winter, *Seek the Welfare of the City*, 180–81.

"Hicesius the aedile built [this] at his own expense, with the official permission of the city council" (*Hicesius aed[ilis] d[e] s[ua] p[ecunia] f[ecit] d[ecreto] d[ecurionum]*).⁴¹⁴ We have no way of knowing how the expenditure for the pavement that Erastus laid compared with the cost of the building which Hicesius constructed, since Hicesius' building has not been identified.⁴¹⁵ But at least we can say that an appearance of extraordinary munificence is awakened by the large bronze letters of Erastus' pavement stone.

In regard to Paul's relationship with Erastus of Corinth, two data seem significant: first, the fact that Erastus is not mentioned anywhere in the writing known to us as 1 Corinthians; and, second, that Erastus is designated by a civic title, rather than a term which evokes his relationship to Paul, or one which describes his role in the Christian community. From the first fact, we may infer with some certainty that Erastus was not among the early converts to Christianity at Corinth.⁴¹⁶ In any case, Erastus is not named with those whom Paul recollects having baptized with his own hands in 1 Cor. 1:14–16. Indeed, the fact that Erastus does not make his appearance until the penultimate paragraph of the epistle written during Paul's final period of residence in Corinth suggests that Paul's acquaintance with Erastus was not of long standing. The fact that Erastus is not designated by his function in the Christian community, but by his office in the city, might justify the further inference that Erastus was a Christian neophyte, whose place in the community and whose contribution to its ministry had not been firmly established at the time when Paul wrote his epistle to the Romans.⁴¹⁷ All of the data

---

414 Kent, *Corinth VIII.3: The Inscriptions*, no. 231; cf. Gill, "Erastus the Aedile," 295.
415 Kent, *Corinth VIII.3: The Inscriptions*, 99; Gill, "Erastus the Aedile," 295.
416 Weiss, *Der erste Korintherbrief*, 20–21.
417 Recently, Theissen ("The Social Structure of the Pauline Communities," 79–80) has suggested that Erastus was not a Christian believer, but someone who was attracted to the Christian community. Friesen ("The Wrong Erastus," 249–55) has elaborated this suggestion with additional arguments. Theissen and Friesen call attention to the fact that Paul introduces Erastus by means of an epithet describing his function in the city, rather than his role within the church. But Paul's description of Erastus as "the administrator of the city" does not warrant the conclusion that "Erastus was not a participant in the Christian assemblies at Corinth" (Friesen). At most, this is only a possibility, as Theissen concedes. One should not fail to notice that Paul gives an attribute of each person from whom he sends greetings in Rom. 16, in some cases denoting membership or function in the Christian community ("our sister," "co-worker in Christ," "host of the

might be justified by the hypothesis that Erastus was a recent convert by an evangelist other than Paul, or, alternatively, that Erastus was led to affiliate with the Christian group at Corinth under the influence of Gaius, "the host of the whole assembly," with whom Erastus is closely associated in his greetings (Rom. 16:23).[418]

We may now extrapolate inferences with respect to the possibility that Erastus was the individual who did Paul wrong. If Paul's Erastus was an aedile of Corinth, as the linguistic usage permits, and as the archaeological and onomastic evidence suggests, then clearly he possessed the financial resources to have played the role which exegesis has assigned to the wrongdoer, that is, the would-be patron of Paul, and the patron of other Christian missionaries (2 Cor. 11:1–21). Indeed, at this point in our investigation, it appears that Erastus was the Christian of highest social standing at Corinth. Yet, the absence of Erastus from 1 Corinthians, and the way in which Erastus is identified in Rom. 16:23, raise questions whether Erastus could have enjoyed the kind of pre-existing relationship with Paul that we have inferred in the case of the wrongdoer.

Crispus, Gaius, Stephanas, and Erastus—all remain, after careful consideration, candidates for identification with the wrongdoer. Perhaps less suspicion falls upon Stephanas, because of the ambiguity of his social status, and upon Erastus, because of the absence of a pre-existing relationship with Paul. How, then, should we proceed toward identification of the wrongdoer? Is there a social convention which might allow for progress in detection, as the convention of not naming wounded friends earlier directed us to look for the wrongdoer among the persons mentioned in 1 Corinthians and Romans 16? Yes, just as social conventions operated in the conduct of enmity and in the pursuit of reconciliation, so a social convention governed the successful conclusion of reconciliation. This convention involved an act of hospitality, at the minimum a dinner, but in some cases a more extended period of residence, in which one

---

whole church"), in other cases specifying a relationship to himself ("my relative"). Yet, in every case it seems clear that the person from whom Paul sends greetings is a Christian believer. In none of Paul's other epistles does he send greetings from a non-believer. Thus, one should be chary of the conclusion that Erastus is the single exception to Paul's practice of exchanging greetings between the saints (cf. Phil. 4:21). In the case of Erastus, the appellation ὁ οἰκονόμος τῆς πόλεως politely specifies a distinguishing characteristic of someone who has been a Christian for a short time, and whose role in the community and relationship to Paul has not yet been firmly established.

418 Cf. Theissen, "The Social Structure of Pauline Communities," 80.

of the parties to the reconciliation was the guest, and the other the host.[419] The social ritual of hospitality celebrated the putting aside of enmity and the restoration of friendly relations, and publicized the reconciliation to others.[420]

There are numerous examples of the operation of this convention in Roman political history, where the pragmatic calculation of self-interest often led to reconciliation (*reditus in gratiam*).[421] Returning to the celebrated letter of Cicero to Lentulus Spinther, we learn that Cicero had been superficially reconciled to Crassus, the triumvir whom he had always hated.[422] That reconciliation had been disrupted by a fresh quarrel and bitter attacks.[423] But Pompey strove to bring about a reconciliation with Crassus (*ut cum Crasso redirem in gratiam*), and when these efforts were successful, Cicero relates that "Crassus, so that our reconciliation might be, as it were, formally announced to the people of Rome (*ut quasi testata populo Romano esset nostra gratia*), set out for his province, I might almost say, from under my very roof; for having previously arranged a day with me [literally, "asked me to name a day," that is, invited himself], he was my guest at a dinner I gave at the country house of my son-in-law Crassipes (*paene a meis laribus in provinciam est profectus. Nam cum mihi condixisset, cenavit apud me in mei generi Crassipedis hortis*)."[424] Plutarch recounts the same incident in his life of Cicero, and throws further light on the mechanics of this social ritual. Plutarch relates: "When Crassus was about to set out for Syria, wishing that Cicero would be a friend rather than an enemy (ἐβούλετο τὸν Κικέρωνα μᾶλλον αὐτῷ φίλον ἢ ἐχθρὸν εἶναι), he said to him in a friendly manner (φιλοφρονούμενος) that he wished to dine with him (βούλεσθαι δειπνῆσαι παρ' αὐτῷ);

---

419 Epstein, *Personal Enmity in Roman Politics*, 5–11, 13, 15, 18, 86; Hall, *Politeness and Politics*, 71–76.
420 Epstein, *Personal Enmity in Roman Politics*, 5; Hall, *Politeness and Politics*, 71.
421 Beryl Rawson, *The Politics of Friendship* (Sydney: Sydney University Press, 1978) 11–13; Epstein, *Personal Enmity in Roman Politics*, 5.
422 Cicero *Fam.* 1.9.20. For Cicero's intense dislike of Crassus, see *Att.* 4.13.2; *Off.* 1.109; 3.75; see also Dio Cassius 39.10. See the useful summary of the course of the relationship between Cicero and Crassus in Marshall, *Crassus*, 173–74; for more detailed evaluation, see Thomas N. Mitchell, "Cicero before Luca (September 57 – April 56 B.C.)," *TAPA* 100 (1969) 295–320.
423 Cicero *Fam.* 1.9.20. See the analysis of Cicero's account of the quarrel in Elizabeth Rawson, *Cicero: A Portrait* (London: Bristol Classical Press, 1983) 131; Hall, *Politeness and Politics*, 137–38.
424 Cicero *Fam.* 1.9.20; cf. Epstein, *Personal Enmity in Roman Politics*, 5; Hall, *Politeness and Politics*, 71.

and Cicero readily received him into his house (κἀκεῖνος ὑπεδέξατο προ-θύμως)."⁴²⁵

This social convention for concluding a reconciliation was so well established in Roman public life that it furnished Cicero with the substance of one of his famous jokes. Plutarch, again, relates that "when some friends interceded with Cicero for Vatinius, saying that the man sought reconciliation and friendship (περὶ Βατινίου φίλων τινῶν ἐντυγχανόντων ὡς μνωμένου διαλύσεις καὶ φιλίαν), for he was an enemy (ἦν γὰρ ἐχθρός), Cicero remarked: 'It surely cannot be that Vatinius also wishes to dine with me?' (οὐ δήπου καὶ Βατίνιος δειπνῆσαι παρ' ἐμοὶ βούλεται)."⁴²⁶

A dramatic instance of the operation of this social convention is preserved by Cassius Dio in his account of the reconciliation between Octavian and Anthony at Brundisium in 40 B.C.: "When they had reached this agreement, they entertained each other at banquets (εἱστίασαν ἀλλήλους), Caesar in military and Roman fashion and Anthony in Asiatic and Egyptian style."⁴²⁷ Although Dio expresses contempt for the cynical self-interest involved in such reconciliations,⁴²⁸ he duly reports the dinners which celebrated the reconciliation (κατηλλαγμένων δὲ αὐτῶν), and describes the effect of the social ritual upon those who witnessed it.⁴²⁹

The conciliatory epistles furnish further examples of the operation of this social convention in the Roman East. The conciliatory letter of Chairemon, the gymnasiarch of Arsinoe, to Apollonius, his "best and dearest," highlights the anticipated hospitality which will set aside the differences between the friends: "If the gods are willing, I will surely visit you after the feast of Souchos" (θεῶν δὲ βουλομένων πάν[τ]ως μετὰ τὰ Σουχεῖα σὲ ἀσπάσομαι), Chairemon promises.⁴³⁰ It is worth noting the role that religion plays in this reconciliation, for Chairemon and Apollonius were brothers in the cult of the Dioscuri. Chairemon assures his friend: "I swear to you by the Dioscuri whom we together worship (ὄμνυμι δέ σοι κατὰ τ[ω]ν Δ[ιο]σκ[ο]ύρων, ὧν κοινῇ σεβόμεθα)…to desire to enjoy your abodes (ἐπιθυμεῖν τῶν ἠθῶν σου ἀπολαῦσαι), all the same, it will be found perfect with respect to our cultic association, if fortune al-

---

425 Plutarch *Comp. Dem. Cic.* 26.1; cf. Epstein, *Personal Enmity in Roman Politics*, 131 n.20; Hall, *Politeness and Politics*, 228 n.133.
426 Plutarch *Comp. Dem. Cic.* 26.2.
427 Dio Cassius 48.30.1.
428 Dio Cassius 48.29.3.
429 Dio Cassius 48.30.2. See also Dio Cassius 44.34.7.
430 *BGU* I.248; Olsson, *Papyrusbriefe aus der frühesten Römerzeit*, no. 41, p. 122.

lows (ὅμως τ[έ]λειον ε[ὑ]ρήσεται τῆς τύχης ἐπιτρεπούσης περὶ τοῦ κοινοῦ)."[431]

Apollonius of Tyana sought reconciliation with his brother Hestiaeus following a dispute over money.[432] In his 44th epistle, Apollonius appeals for reconciliation, and toward the end of the letter, invites himself home as his brother's guest: Apollonius expresses his longing, like Odysseus, to return to his home and behold the sepulchers of his fathers.[433] The next letter makes clear that the overture has been accepted, a readiness for reconciliation is present. Apollonius first assures Hestiaeus of the permanence of their affections: those who are convinced that they are philosophers cannot rightly be supposed to hate their brothers.[434] What is now uppermost in Apollonius' mind is not their misunderstanding about money, which was something that they tried to despise even before they became philosophers, but the suspicion and hurt feelings that have resulted from what he wrote.[435] It was never Apollonius' intention, he asserts, to cause his brother grief.[436] The letter concludes with a reference to the hospitality which will ratify and publicize their reconciliation: "Now, indeed, this too I make known, that if heaven should perhaps consent, I will, after meeting my friends in Rhodes, shortly depart thence, and return to you towards the end of spring" (νυνὶ μέντοι καὶ τοῦτο δηλῶ, συγχωροίη γὰρ ἂν ἴσως τὸ δαιμόνιον, ὅτι συμβαλὼν τοῖς ἐν Ῥόδῳ φίλοις, μετ' ὀλίγον ἐκεῖθεν ἐπάνειμι πρὸς ὑμᾶς λήγοντος ἔαρος).[437]

A final, elegant example of the operation of the hospitality convention is furnished by the conciliatory epistle of Marcus Aurelius to his friend Herodes Atticus.[438] Marcus concludes his letter with the words: "But if I grieved you in anything or am still grieving you, demand reparation from me in the temple of Athena at the time of the Mysteries (ἀπαίτησον παρ' ἐμοῦ δίκας ἐν τῷ ἱερῷ τῆς ἐν ἄστει Ἀθηνᾶς ἐν μυστηρί-

---

431 BGU I.248; Olsson, *Papyrusbriefe aus der frühesten Römerzeit*, no. 41, p. 122.
432 Text and commentary in Penella, *The Letters of Apollonius of Tyana*, 48–51, 54–57, 62–65, 76–79, 108–109, 113–14, 118, 128. Cf. Philostratus *Vit. soph.* 1.18; 3.33; 8.2.3.
433 Apollonius *Ep.* 44; Penella, *The Letters of Apollonius of Tyana*, 113.
434 Apollonius *Ep.* 45.
435 Apollonius *Ep.* 45.
436 Apollonius *Ep.* 45: ὧν ἑκάτερον ἐπίσης ἀνιαρὸν ἀδελφοῖς τε καὶ φίλοις ἂν εἴη.
437 Apollonius *Ep.* 45.
438 Text in *Philostratus and Eunapius: Lives of the Sophists*, ed. W. C. Wright (Cambridge, MA: Harvard University Press, 1968) 174–75. For background, see Philostratus *Vit. soph.* 2.1.559–63.

οις). For I made a vow, when the war began to blaze highest, that I would be initiated, and I could wish that *you yourself* should initiate me into those rites (ηὐξάμην γάρ, ὁπότε ὁ πόλεμος μάλιστα ἐφλέγμαισε, καὶ μυηθῆναι, εἴη δὲ καὶ σοῦ μυσταγωγοῦντος)."[439] This is the conventional request for hospitality which solemnizes and publicizes a reconciliation, but with the profundity and urbanity that characterizes the utterances of the philosopher-king.

The necessity for a social ritual to provide reinforcement for reconciliation and to announce publicly that good relations had been restored was given in the antinomy between the extraordinary importance of reconciliation in Roman political life, on the one hand, and the inherent ambiguity of reconciliation, on the other. The intensely personal character of Roman political life ascribed to reconciliation a crucial function in the continuous process of forming and reforming political groups.[440] For this reason, "Roman political opinion apparently took reconciliations very seriously, and expected the terms to be scrupulously observed."[441] Cicero's letters attest how much damage a Roman could suffer to his reputation by defaulting on his promises of reconciliation.[442] Yet, reconciliations were also ambiguous, because they originated in the perception and construction of relationships.[443] Cicero's letters, again, reveal that a subtle shift in the tone of a relationship might constitute a reconciliation,[444] but that it was also possible to be in doubt whether a reconciliation had occurred.[445] This logical bind between the necessity and ambiguity of reconciliation was effectively resolved by the social ritual of hospitality, which formalized the informal overtures and publicized the private *rapprochement*.[446]

---

439 Philostratus *Vit. soph.* 2.1.562–63.
440 Rawson, *The Politics of Friendship*, 11–13; Epstein, *Personal Enmity in Roman Politics*, 5–8.
441 Epstein, *Personal Enmity in Roman Politics*, 6, citing Valerius Maximus 2.9.6; Livy 29.37.10.
442 Cicero *Fam.* 1.9.4; 1.9.19; 3.7.2; 3.8.2; 3.8.7; 3.10.1; 3.10.5; 3.10.9; 3.12.2; 3.12.4; *Quint. fratr.* 2.12.2–3. See the nuanced discussion of Cicero's strained reconciliation with Appius Claudius Pulcher in Hall, *Politeness and Politics*, 139–54.
443 Epstein, *Personal Enmity in Roman Politics*, 10–11.
444 As illustrated by Cicero's correspondence with Quintus Metellus Celer in *Fam.* 5.1; 5.2; cf. Epstein, *Personal Enmity in Roman Politics*, 11; Hall, *Politeness and Politics*, 153–60.
445 E.g., Cicero *Fam.* 5.2.5; cf. Epstein, *Personal Enmity in Roman Politics*, 11.
446 Epstein, *Personal Enmity in Roman Politics*, 5, 11.

If we assume that Paul and the wrongdoer followed the standard convention that governed reconciliation, then it is possible to formulate a plausible hypothesis regarding the identity of the wrongdoer: the wrongdoer should be the person with whom Paul is a guest on the occasion of his next visit to Corinth. It should be pointed out that this is the only assumption which our hypothesis requires, and that it is an entirely reasonable assumption to make, given the fact that Paul has adhered so closely to social and rhetorical conventions in earlier phases of his relationship with the wrongdoer. Among the greetings at the close of Paul's Epistle to the Romans, in Rom. 16:23, Paul sends greetings from "Gaius, my host, and the host of the whole church." On the occasion of his third and final visit to Corinth, Paul was a guest in the house of Gaius. If Paul and his erstwhile opponent followed the social convention that governed the successful conclusion of reconciliation, then a plausible identification of the wrongdoer can be made: the wrongdoer was Gaius.[447]

---

[447] It must be emphasized that the identification of Gaius as the wrongdoer is only an hypothesis made plausible by Paul's demonstrated adherence to the social and rhetorical conventions governing friendship, enmity, and reconciliation. It is possible that the hospitality Paul enjoyed with Gaius on the occasion of his final visit to Corinth was unrelated to the previous history of conflict and reconciliation. In this case, as in many others, the evidence falls short of historical proof. Our aim has been to articulate a framework of convention that makes possible a plausible identification.

Chapter Five
Prosopography

What can we know about Gaius on the basis of Paul's statements in 1 Cor. 1:14 and Rom. 16:23? Surprisingly, a great deal. We may begin by recapitulating what we have already learned from scrutiny of Gaius in the line-up of potential suspects. We may then proceed with a more thorough prosopography, drawing inferences from his name, his role as host of the Christian community, and his relationships with Crispus and Erastus. The depth and detail of the portrait we are able to develop will depend upon information supplied by the onomastics, epigraphy and archaeology of Roman Corinth.

From Paul's reference to the baptism of Gaius in 1 Cor. 1:14, we inferred that Gaius was among the first converts to Christianity at Corinth on the occasion of Paul's first missionary journey to the city.[1] Paul emphasizes the fact that Gaius was one of the few whom he personally baptized.[2] Since Paul goes on to explain in 1 Cor. 1:17 that it was not his usual practice to administer baptism, the fact that Gaius was one of the rare exceptions should be taken as an indication of his prominence in the community, as it is in the case of Crispus.[3] The precedence of Gaius in conversion and the exceptional status of his baptism by Paul permit us to infer that Gaius must have had a special importance to Paul.[4]

From Paul's description of Gaius as "the host of the whole church" in Rom. 16:23, we inferred that Gaius must have been a person of considerable wealth.[5] Gaius' house must have been of ample dimensions to ac-

---

1 See above, ch. 4, pp. 241, 249. Cf. Weiss, *Der erste Korintherbrief*, 20–21; Judge, "The Early Christians as a Scholastic Community" in idem, *The First Christians in the Roman World*, 545; Fee, *First Epistle*, 62; Murphy-O'Connor, *Paul*, 267; Thiselton, *First Epistle*, 27.
2 Weiss, *Der erste Korintherbrief*, 20–21; Meeks, *First Urban Christians*, 57.
3 Weiss, *Der erste Korintherbrief*, 21; Judge, ""The Social Pattern of the Christian Groups" in idem, *Social Distinctives of the Christians in the First Century*, 26.
4 Theissen, *Social Setting*, 55; Marshall, *Enmity in Corinth*, 345; Chow, *Patronage and Power*, Collins, *First Corinthians*, 83.
5 See above, ch. 4, pp. 241–48. Cf. Weiss, *Der erste Korintherbrief*, 21; Theissen, *Social Setting*, 74–75; Meeks, *First Urban Christians*, 57; Fee, *First Epistle*, 62;

commodate all of the Corinthian Christians meeting together, since a reasonable calculation of the persons associated with named Corinthians suggests that the congregation was not small (cf. Acts 18:10, a λαὸς πολύς).⁶ As the host of all the house-churches in Corinth, Gaius functioned, in the most concrete sense, as the "patron" of the Christian community.⁷ In a society structured by "benefits,"⁸ the service which Gaius provided as host would have garnered him significant influence. This aspect of Gaius' profile may be greatly enhanced by drawing upon the growing body of knowledge about patronage in Roman society.⁹

Close attention to the context in which Paul names Gaius as one of the few whom he had personally baptized revealed that Gaius must have played some role in the formation of factions in the church at Corinth.¹⁰ We recall that Gaius' involvement in the outbreak of faction was an inference from the unmistakable irony of Paul's thanksgiving in 1 Cor. 1:14, and from Paul's employment of the rhetorical figures of feigned indifference and lapse of memory in 1 Cor. 1:14–17.¹¹ Here, again, we have a feature of Gaius' portrait whose details may be enriched by careful analysis of Paul's argument against factions in 1 Cor. 1–4. We shall discover whose partisan Gaius became, and how much his support for one of Paul's rivals contributed, alongside other factors, to the alienation from Paul that is so apparent in 2 Cor. 10–13.

Horrell, *The Social Ethos of the Corinthian Correspondence*, 96; Murphy-O'Connor, *Paul*, 267; Collins, *First Corinthians*, 84; Thiselton, *First Epistle*, 27–28.

6 Floyd V. Filson, "The Significance of the Early House Churches," *JBL* 58 (1939) 105–12; Theissen, *Social Setting*, 55, 89; Malherbe, *Social Aspects*, 73–74; Meeks, *First Urban Christians*, 57; Horrell, *The Social Ethos of the Corinthian Correspondence*, 96; Murphy-O'Connor, *Paul*, 267; Collins, *First Corinthians*, 84; de Vos, *Church and Community Conflicts*, 201–202, 203–204.

7 Meeks, *First Urban Christians*, 57, 119, 221 n.7; Marshall, *Enmity in Corinth*, 345; Chow, *Patronage and Power*, 90; Kirner, "Apostolat und Patronage (II)," 55–56; Theissen, "The Social Structure of the Pauline Communities," 82–83.

8 Cicero *Off.* 1.15.47; Seneca *Ben.* 7.22.1; 7.23.3; cf. Marshall, *Enmity in Corinth*, 9–13.

9 E.g., Saller, *Personal Patronage under the Early Empire*, esp. 7–39; idem, "Patronage and Friendship in Early Imperial Rome: Drawing the Distinction" in *Patronage in Ancient Society*, ed. Andrew Wallace-Hadrill (London: Routledge, 1989) 49–62; Andrew Wallace-Hadrill, ""Patronage in Roman Society: from Republic to Empire" in *Patronage in Ancient Society*, 63–87; White, *Promised Verse*, esp. 3–34.

10 See above, ch. 4, p. 249.

11 Weiss, *Der erste Korintherbrief*, 19–21; Lindemann, *Der erste Korintherbrief*, 41–42.

Finally, we noted that Gaius is named by Paul in the same breath with two other Corinthians, Crispus and Erastus, and from these associations we inferred that Gaius must be a person of the same class as these individuals.[12] Now that we have drawn a conclusion regarding the office denoted by the title οἰκονόμος τῆς πόλεως, and hence the social status of Erastus, we shall have occasion to think further about the implications of this association for the likely position of Gaius in Corinthian society. Likewise, further reflection upon Gaius' relationship with Crispus will yield a hypothesis regarding the source and motive of Gaius' attraction to the Christian movement.

We begin our detailed prosopography with consideration of the name "Gaius." What may we infer from the fact that this man bears a good Roman *praenomen*, indeed the *praenomen* of Julius Caesar?[13] Because Corinth was re-founded as a Roman colony by order of Gaius Julius Caesar in 44 B.C.,[14] many Corinthians in the following century bore the *praenomen* Gaius, as illustrated by coins and inscriptions.[15] Perhaps Paul's Gaius was a descendant of one of the Italian freedmen or veterans with whom Caesar repopulated the city.[16] But it is also possible that Paul's

---

12 See above, ch. 4, pp. 248–49. Cf. Theissen, "The Social Structure of the Pauline Communities," 78–83.

13 Salomies, *Die römischen Vornamen*, esp. 339–45; Solin, "names, personal, Roman," *OCD* (2003) 1024. Cf. Ramsay, "A Historical Commentary on the Epistles to the Corinthians," 101–102; Weiss, *Der erste Korintherbrief*, 21; Goodspeed, "Gaius Titius Justus," 382; Meeks, *First Urban Christians*, 212 n.214; John Gillman, "Gaius," *ABD* 2 (1992) 869; Judge, "The Roman Base of Paul's Mission" in idem, *The First Christians in the Roman World*, 561; Schnabel, *Der erste Brief*, 99.

14 Appian *Punica* 136; Strabo *Geogr.* 8.4.8; 8.6.23; Plutarch *Caes.* 57.5; Dio Cassius 43.50.3–5; Pausanias 2.1.2. On Corinth as a conventional Roman colony, see Engels, *Roman Corinth*, 16–17, 62, 67, 71–73; Mary E. Hoskins Walbank, "The Foundation and Planning of Early Roman Corinth," *Journal of Roman Archaeology* 10 (1997) 95–130.

15 Benjamin Dean Meritt, *Corinth Volume VIII, Part I: Greek Inscriptions 1896–1927* (Cambridge, MA: Harvard University Press, 1931) 169–72; West, *Corinth VIII: Latin Inscriptions*, 149–50; Kent, *Corinth VIII.3: The Inscriptions*, 228–30; Michel Amandry, *Le Monnayage des Duovirs Corinthiens* (Paris: École Francaise D'Athènes, 1988) 252–53; Anthony J. S. Spawforth, "Roman Corinth: The Formation of a Colonial Elite" in *Roman Onomastics in the Greek East: Social and Political Aspects*, ed. A. D. Rizakis (Athens: Research Center for Greek and Roman Antiquity, 1996) 167–82.

16 Polystratus (*Greek Anthology* 7.297); Strabo *Geogr.* 8.6.23; Wiseman, "Corinth and Rome I," 497; Engels, *Roman Corinth*, 16, 67.

Chapter Five. Prosopography   291

Gaius belonged to one of the Greek families who immigrated to Corinth, and who co-opted Latin *praenomina* as a sign of their Romanization, or to suggest social connections which they wished they had.[17]

What may we infer from the fact that Paul's friend is designated by his *praenomen* Gaius,[18] rather than his *cognomen*, as in the case of

---

17 Compare Gaios Philodespotou at Callatis in *Bull. Epig.* (1971) 434, who is clearly not a Roman citizen. Cf. Wiseman, "Corinth and Rome I," 497; Engels, *Roman Corinth*, 68, 70; Spawforth, "Roman Corinth," 173–74; Glen W. Bowersock, personal communication, June 4, 2006. See in general Rizakis, "Anthroponymie et société" in *Roman Onomastics in the Greek East*, 11–30.

18 I regard Gaius as a true *praenomen*, rather than a *praenomen* functioning as a *cognomen* in a Greek context. Edwin Judge has urged upon me consideration of the latter possibility (personal communication, April, 2009), observing that Gaius (Gaios in its Greek spelling) occurs by itself as a Greek name, just as Lucius (Loukios in Greek) and Marcus (Markos in Greek). The prime example for Gaius by itself is the famous imperial jurist, who is known by that name and whose origins are obscure. On the process by which Latin *praenomina* passed into Greek usage, see in general W. Schulze, *Zur Geschichte lateinischer Eigennamen* (Göttingen: Vandenhoeck & Ruprecht, 1904) 506–14, esp. 506, 509; Daux, "L'onomastique romaine d'expression greque" in *L'Onomastique latine*, 405–17. On how Latin *praenomina* then turned into *cognomina*, see Solin, "Latin Cognomina in the Greek East" in *The Greek East in the Roman Context*, 189–202, on Gaius specifically, 191, 194–96; Kajanto, *The Latin Cognomina*, 39–41, 172–75. But the use of *praenomina* as *cognomina* did not become common until the second century, and then only in the less Romanized areas. See the conclusion of Salomies, *Die römischen Vornamen*, 164–65: "Der Gebrauch von Pränomina als Cognomina ist jedoch nie besonders üblich gewesen und scheint vor der Mitte des 2. Jh. kaum belegt zu sein. Ein grosser Teil der Beispiele stammt aus den am wenigsten romanisierten Provinzen, und die Träger dieser Cognomina scheinen zumeist den wenig romanisierten Bevölkerungsschichten angehört zu haben." Several examples from Laconia are catalogued by A. D. Rizakis, S. Zoumbaki, Cl. Lepenioti, *Roman Peloponnese II: Roman Personal Names in Their Social Context (Laconia and Messenia)* (Athens: Research Centre for Greek and Roman Antiquity, 2004) no. 202, *IG* 5.1.80B, line 5, Sparta [Trajanic]; no. 203, *IG* 5.1.117, line 5, Sparta [first quarter of the 2nd c. A.D.]; no. 203a, *IG* 5.1.212, line 12, Sparta [2nd half of 1st c. B.C.]; no. 204, *SEG* 11 (1950) 558 col. III, line 12, Sparta [about A.D. 100]; no. 206, *SEG* 48 919980 462, line 9, unknown provenance, now in Sparta museum [mid-2nd c. A.D.]. But only a single, doubtful example is adduced for Achaia and the Corinthia by A. D. Rizakis and S. Zoumbaki, *Roman Peloponnese I: Roman Personal Names in Their Social Context (Achaia, Arcadia, Argolis, Corinthia, and Eleia)* (Athens: Research Centre for Greek and Roman Antiquity, 2001) no. 62, *SEG* 39 (1989) 409, Patrai [ca. A.D. 250–300]: "a mosaic representing gladiators in a house of the imperial era. The letters ΓΑ can be read beside a human figure." The reason for the infrequency of *praenomina* as *cognomina* in the more Romanized areas is supplied by Salomies, *Die römischen*

Crispus? W. R. Ramsay attributed the use of the *praenomen* to the fact that Paul's Gaius was a freedman.[19] Freedmen preferred to be addressed by their *praenomina*, for it was one of their new prerogatives that they might bear a first name.[20] In one of his most skillful satires, Horace travesties a legacy hunter who seeks to flatter those who have recently gained their freedom by addressing them with their new *praenomina:* "'Good Quintus,' say, or 'Publius' (nothing endears a speaker more than this to slavish ears)."[21] The parvenu Trimalchio in Petronius' *Satyricon* is addressed by his friends and slaves as "Gaius," "our Gaius," as a mark of his new freedman status.[22] We may assume that a person who is known only by the name "Gaius" is, prima facie, a freedman using his new first name. If such a person had long possessed the citizenship, he would be more likely to be called by his *cognomen*.[23]

While this rule of nomenclature may be valid in general, we cannot conclude that it applies to Paul's Gaius specifically, because we cannot be certain that Gaius was known *only* by his *praenomen*, or that he preferred to be addressed by his first name, *only that Paul chooses to refer to him in this way*. Thus, we must seek to comprehend the logic of Pauline onomastics, before we can draw any conclusions from the fact that Gaius is called by his *praenomen*. Just at this point, we encounter difficulties, for there

---

Vornamen, 165: "Der Grund dazu ist offenbar der, dass Pränomina zumindest offiziell bis ins 3. Jh. in Gebrauch waren und dass man wenigstens in Italien und in den romanisierten Westprovinzen bis in dieser Zeit zumindest eine Ahnung davon gehabt haben muss, was ein Pränomen war, und wie es sich von einem Cognomen unterschied." Thus the recent onomastic catalogues would seem to confirm an observation made over a century ago by Ramsay, "A Historical Commentary on the Epistles to the Corinthians," 101 n. 2: "In Asia Minor a name like Gaius or Lucius was often assumed by a provincial as his single name of the Greek fashion. In such cases Gaius or Lucius is no longer a *praenomen*, but has become a non-Roman name. That custom was, however, not common in Greece at this time, but belonged rather to the less educated cities."

19 Ramsay, "A Historical Commentary on the Epistles to the Corinthians," 100–101.
20 Cf. Weiss, *Der erste Korintherbrief*, 21.
21 Horace *Sat.* 2.5.33.
22 Petronius *Satyr.* 30, 50, 62, 74. Cf. M. S. Smith, *Petronii Arbitri 'Cena Trimalchionis'* (Oxford: Oxford University Press, 1975) 62 n.3; R. Bracht Branham and Daniel Kinney, *Petronius. Satyrica* (Berkeley: University of California Press, 1996) 26 n.30.2: "Trimalchio's *praenomen* 'Gaius' is obtrusively used as a mark of his new freedman status."
23 Glen W. Bowersock, personal communication, June 11, 2006.

are obvious anomalies in Paul's use of names.[24] First, Paul never employs more than a single epithet in reference to any person in his epistles. In this respect, the author of Acts is more informative: e.g., the addition of the *nomen* (*gentilicium*) Titius in the case of Justus in Acts 18:7 permits us to infer that he is a Roman citizen.[25] Second, Paul uses *praenomina* in some cases, e.g. Titus (Gal. 2:3) and Lucius (Rom. 16:21), *nomina* in two instances, Junia (Rom. 16:7) and Julia (Rom. 16:15), and *cognomina* in many others, e.g. Aquila (1 Cor. 16:19), Clement (Phil. 4:3), Rufus (Rom. 16:13), without any evident pattern of discrimination.[26] Still more anomalous and frustrating is the fact that, where data indicative of social status exist, it seems that Paul violates, or at least ignores, the distinctions implicit in the trinomial classification system. Thus, the use of Latin *cognomina* should normally imply Roman citizenship, but not in Paul: Tertius the scribe (Rom. 16:22) is evidently a slave, while Fortunatus and Achaicus (1 Cor. 16:17) are likely slaves or freedmen.[27] On the other hand, the use of Latin *praenomina* is assumed normally to imply freedman status, but, again, not in Paul: Edwin Judge concludes, on the basis of Gaius' role as "host of the whole *ekklesia*" at Corinth, that Gaius "should be" a Roman citizen, and suggests that Lucius (Rom. 16:21) may be a Roman citizen, as well, depending upon the meaning of the term "kinsman" (συγγενής).[28] The problem of Pauline onomastics is generally recognized by those who have investigated the subject, and is nicely summarized by Edwin Judge: "Paul is extraordinarily elusive in social terms. This is precisely because he will not use conventional classifications, but devises his own epithets for people in their personal relationships, to make his new points. Although keenly interest-

---

24 E.A. Judge, "Greek Names of Latin Origin" in *NewDocs*, Vol. 2, 107; idem, "The Roman Base of Paul's Mission" in idem, *The First Christians in the Roman World*, 553–67, esp. 555.
25 Goodspeed, "Gaius Titius Justus," 382; Meeks, *First Urban Christians*, 63; Judge, "The Roman Base of Paul's Mission" in idem, *The First Christians in the Roman World*, 562.
26 Judge, "The Roman Base of Paul's Mission" in idem, *The First Christians in the Roman World*, 555, 562, 566.
27 Ramsay, "A Historical Commentary on the Epistles to the Corinthians," 101; Weiss, *Der erste Korintherbrief*, 386; Meeks, *First Urban Christians*, 56–57; Heikki Solin, *Die Stadtrömischen Sklavennamen* (Stuttgart: F. Steiner, 1996) 252–53; Jewett, *Romans*, 978; Judge, "The Roman Base of Paul's Mission" in idem, *The First Christians in the Roman World*, 562.
28 Judge, "The Roman Base of Paul's Mission" in idem, *The First Christians in the Roman World*, 561. Cf. M.-F. Baslez, *Saint Paul* (Paris: Fayard, 1991) 30–36.

ed in the obligations created by the Roman ranking system, he avoids situating people within it. This makes the phenomenon of the Latin names around Paul doubly intriguing."[29]

Is it possible to discern a principle at work, however idiosyncratic, in Paul's use of names? Perhaps Paul's own name provides a clue. Παῦλος is the Greek form of a Latin *cognomen*, Paul(l)us.[30] This is the name that Paul gives himself always and exclusively in his epistles.[31] We owe to the author of Acts the information that Paul originally bore the Israelite name of 'Sha'ul' (Greek Σαούλ or Σαοῦλος).[32] Although Paul never uses his Hebrew name, there is no reason to believe that the author of Acts invented it.[33] Paul twice relates the fact that he was a member of the tribe of Benjamin (Phil. 3:5; Rom. 11:1). The most famous Benjaminite, of course, was King Saul (1 Sam. 9:1). Hence it stands to reason that Paul should have been given the name of his regal forebear as his birth-name, in order to emphasize his descent.[34]

At what point did the change of name from Saul to Paul occur? It is possible that Paul bore a double name from the beginning, a usage that is widely attested in the papyri and inscriptions,[35] and that was employed by

---

29 Judge, "The Roman Base of Paul's Mission" in idem, *The First Christians in the Roman World*, 555.
30 BDAG 789; Hermann Dessau, "Der Name des Apostels Paulus," *Hermes* 45 (1910) 347–68; Colin J. Hemer, "The Name of Paul," *TynBul* 36 (1985) 179–83; Murphy-O'Connor, *Paul*, 42. For the infrequent instances of Paul(l)us as a *praenomen* (presumably the result of the transformation of a *cognomen* into a *praenomen*), see G. A. Harrer, "Saul Who Also is Called Paul," *HTR* 33 (1940) 27 n.24, 29.
31 1 Thess. 1:1; 1 Cor. 1:1; Gal. 1:1; 2 Cor. 1:1; Phil. 1:1; Phlm. 1, 19; Rom. 1:1. Cf. W. M. Ramsay, *St. Paul the Traveller and the Roman Citizen* (London: Hodder and Stoughton, 1897) 81–88.
32 Acts 7:58; 8:1, 3; 9:1, 8, 11, 22, 24; 11:25, 30; 12:25; 13:1–2, 7, 9. Cf. BDAG 917. For debate on the spelling of the name Saul in Greek, see Harrer, "Saul Who Also is Called Paul," 19–33, esp. 24–25; Murphy-O'Connor, *Paul*, 42; Riesner, *Die Frühzeit des Paulus*, 145; Richard Bauckham, *The Jewish World around the New Testament* (Tübingen: Mohr Siebeck, 2008) 376–78.
33 Martin Hengel, *The Pre-Christian Paul* (Philadelphia: Trinity Press International, 1991) 9; Lüdemann, *Earliest Christianity according to Acts*, 151; Murphy-O'Connor, *Paul*, 43.
34 Haenchen, *Acts of the Apostles*, 399 n.1; Hengel, *The Pre-Christian Paul*, 9; Lüdemann, *Earliest Christianity according to Acts*, 151.
35 Adolf Deissmann, "Saulus Paulus" in *Bible Studies: Contributions Chiefly from Papyri and Inscriptions to the History of the Languages, the Literature, and the Religion of Hellenistic Judaism and Primitive Christianity* (Edinburgh: T & T Clark,

Jews in this period.³⁶ But this seems unlikely in the case of Paul, because of the extreme rarity of the name Παῦλος among non-Romans in the Greek East, especially among Jews, by whom the name does not seem to have been adopted at all.³⁷

The author of Acts introduces the name "Paul" in the context of the first missionary journey of Barnabas and Saul to Cyprus, and in connection with the conversion of the Roman proconsul Sergius Paulus (Acts 13:4–12). Luke's account has given rise to the suggestion that the name Paul was taken from the proconsul whom Paul converted,³⁸ or that the change of name from Jewish Σαῦλος to Greek Παῦλος marked the transition in the apostle's field of labor from Palestine to the Gentile world.³⁹ Both of these conjectures are in keeping with Luke's purposes, and articulate the theological perspectives implicit in his narrative: Luke wished to emphasize the continuity of the new faith with Israel, and so calls the apostle Σαῦλος prior to Acts 13:9; Luke wished to emphasize the friendly relations of the new faith with Rome, and so connects the emergence of the name Παῦλος with the conversion of the Roman

---

1923) 313–17, appealing to W. Schmid, *Der Atticismus in seinen Hauptvertretern* (Stuttgart, 1893) 3.838.
36 Deissmann, "Saulus Paulus" in *Bible Studies*, 314, referencing 1 Macc. 7:5, 12, 20 ff.; 9:54 ff.; 2 Macc. 14:3; Josephus *A.J.* 12.2.4; 12.6.4; 12.9.7; 13.1.2; 13.5.1; 13.12.1; 13.16.4; 18.2.2; 20.3.3; *B.J.* 1.4.7. See also Harry J. Leon, *The Jews of Ancient Rome* (Philadelphia: Jewish Publication Society of America, 1960) 107; Lüdemann, *Earliest Christianity according to Acts*, 151. Cf. Riesner, *Die Frühzeit des Paulus,* 127.
37 Deissmann, "Saulus Paulus" in *Bible Studies*, 316: "So far as we know, there has hitherto been no evidence to show that the name Παῦλος was adopted by any other Jew." On the possible exception in a papyrus referring to the Jewish war of Trajan, cited by Ulrich Wilcken, "Ein Aktenstück zum jüdischen Kriege Trajans," *Hermes* 27 (1892) 464–70, Deissmann concedes (*Bible Studies*, 316 n.4): "The name, indeed, is mutilated in almost all the passages, so that the restoration Σαῦλος would also be possible." Riesner (*Frühzeit des Apostels Paulus*, 128) asserts that the name Paulus (Παῦλος) does not appear among Jews in Josephus, nor in the *Corpus Inscriptionum Iudaicarum*, nor in the *Corpus Papyrorum Judaicarum*; Paulinus appears for the first time in a late inscription from Beth She'arim (2ⁿᵈ–4ᵗʰ cent. A.D.).
38 Dessau, "Der Name des Apostels Paulus," 347–68; G. Kehnscherper, "Der Apostel Paulus als römischer Bürger," *Studia Evangelica* (Berlin: Akademie Verlag, 1964) 422–30; Edwin A. Judge and G. S. R. Thomas, "The Origin of the Church at Rome: A New Solution?" *Reformed Theological Review* 25 (1966) 84.
39 Henry J. Cadbury, *The Making of Luke-Acts* (New York: Macmillan, 1927) 225; Haenchen, *Acts of the Apostles*, 399–400.

proconsul.⁴⁰ But we should not fail to remind ourselves that the account of Paul's mission to Cyprus is a redactional construction, and a rather artistic one at that!⁴¹ As Martin Hengel has observed, the coincidences and connections in the Acts account derive from the narrator Luke, who knew how to arrange facts effectively, while not necessarily making them up.⁴²

Among the elements of tradition which Luke did *not* invent is the phrase relating to Paul's name in Acts 13:9, Σαῦλος, ὁ καὶ Παῦλος.⁴³ In a careful study of this phrase, Adolf Deissmann demonstrated that the formula ὁ καί, which is the Greek equivalent of the Latin *qui et*, implies that Παῦλος was a surname, and that the apostle was already known by this name before his mission to Cyprus: "When Acts 13:9 is placed in philological context, we see that it cannot mean 'Saul who was *henceforth* also called Paul'; an ancient reader could only have taken it to mean 'Saul who was *also* called Paul'."⁴⁴ While it may not be possible to know for certain when or under what circumstances the Jew Saul acquired the Roman name Paul,⁴⁵ the most plausible suggestion, in my view, is that offered by the philosopher Giorgio Agamben, on the basis of Moritz Lambertz's study of surnames in the Roman Empire: the apostle bestowed the unusual name "Paul" upon himself as a sign of his new being in Christ, at the moment when he assumed the apostolic voca-

---

40 Haenchen, *Acts of the Apostles*, 403; Walter Schmithals, *Die Apostelgeschichte des Lukas* (Zurich: Theologischer Verlag, 1982) 123; Lüdemann, *Early Christianity according to Acts*, 149.

41 Martin Hengel, *Acts and the History of Earliest Christianity* (Philadelphia: Fortress Press, 1979) 109–14. See also C. K. Barrett, *Acts 1–14: A Critical and Exegetical Commentary on the Acts of the Apostles* (London: T & T Clark, 2004) 609–10.

42 Hengel, *Acts and the History of Earliest Christianity*, 113–14; see also Martin Hengel and Anna Maria Schwemer, *Paul Between Damascus and Antioch* (Louisville: Westminster John Knox Press, 1997) 69.

43 Lüdemann, *Early Christianity according to Acts*, 151; Murphy-O'Connor, *Paul*, 42–43.

44 Deissmann, "Saulus Paulus" in *Bible Studies*, 314. Cf. Riesner, *Die Frühzeit des Paulus*, 127. On the use of double names in general, see G. H. R. Horsley, "The Use of a Double Name" in *NewDocs*, Vol. 1, 89–96.

45 For various hypotheses, see Dessau, "Der Name des Apostels Paulus," 347–68; Harrer, "Saul Who Also is Called Paul," 19–33; Cadbury, *The Book of Acts in History*, 74–76; Sherwin-White, *Roman Society and Roman Law in the New Testament*, 151–54. See the discussion in Lüdemann, *Early Christianity according to Acts*, 241; Hengel, *The Pre-Christian Paul*, 9–10; Murphy-O'Connor, *Paul*, 41–43; Sean M. McDonough, "Small Change: Saul to Paul, Again," *JBL* 125 (2006) 390–91.

tion.⁴⁶ This conjecture has the advantage of recognizing that Παῦλος functions in the epistles as a *signum* or *supernomen*,⁴⁷ even if it is a Latin *cognomen* in origin.⁴⁸ That is, Παῦλος is a self-deprecatory nickname expressing the apostle's sense of humility: "Paul" (Latin *paul[l]us*) means "small, of little significance."⁴⁹ In changing his name from *Saulos* to *Paulos*, the apostle signifies a "passage from the regal to the insignificant, from grandeur to smallness."⁵⁰ This suggestion is supported by Paul's description of himself as "the least" (ἐλάχιστος) of the apostles" (1 Cor. 15:9),⁵¹ and by Paul's repeated linking of his name to the term δοῦλος (Rom. 1:1; cf. Phil. 1:1), since the proper names of slaves were often replaced by mere *signa* conferred upon them at their owners' whim, generally descriptive of physical qualities.⁵² Agamben summarizes his insight into the thought process involved in Paul's change of name: "At the very moment when the call transforms him who is a free man into 'the slave of the Messiah,' the apostle must, like a slave, lose his

---

46 Giorgio Agamben, *The Time That Remains: A Commentary on the Letter to the Romans* (Stanford: Stanford University Press, 2005) 7–11, appealing to Moritz Lambertz, "Zur Ausbreitung der Supernomen oder Signum," *Glotta* 5 (1914) 147–56, esp. 152. As is well known, this explanation of Paul's name change goes back to Augustine, *Enarrationes in Psalmos* 72.4. Ironically, Fr. Murphy-O'Connor, OP, judges that this view, now advocated by the philosopher Agamben, "has nothing to recommend it, except as an opportunity for rhetorical piety" (*Paul*, 44).
47 Rightly, Harrer, "Saul Who Also is Called Paul," 21; see also Murphy-O'Connor, *Paul*, 43; Jewett, *Romans*, 99. See the discussion of an inscription found in Naples (*CIL* 10.3377) illustrating the use of a *supernomen* by Hemer, "The Name of Paul," 179–83, esp. 183. On the use of the surname (*supernomen*) in general, see Iiro Kajanto, *Supernomina: A Study in Latin Epigraphy* (Helsinki: Societas Scientiarum Fennica, 1966).
48 BDAG 789.
49 Glare, *Oxford Latin Dictionary*, 1313; cf. Augustine *Enarrat. Ps.* 72.4: "Paulum…minimum est."
50 Agamben, *The Time That Remains*, 9.
51 On the possibility of a play on words between Παῦλος ("the little one") and ὁ ἐλάχιστος ("the least"), see Johannes Munck, "Paulus tamquam abortivus" in *New Testament Essays: Studies in Memory of T. W. Manson*, ed. A. J. B. Higgins (Manchester: Manchester University Press, 1959) 180–93, esp. 188–90; Thorlief Boman, "Paulus abortivus (1. Kor. 15,8)," *Studia Theologica* 18 (1964) 46–50. This interpretation is supported by Augustine's exegesis. See the discussion in Thiselton, *First Epistle*, 1209–10.
52 Moritz Lambertz, "Die griechischen Sklavennamen," *Jahresbericht über das Staatsgymnasium im VIII Bezirk Wiens* 57–58 (1906–1908) 19; Solin, *Die stadtrömischen Sklavennamen*, 152–54.

name, whether it be Roman or Jewish. From this point on he must call himself by a simple surname."[53] Thus Paul's change of name was the onomastic forerunner of a principle that he would eventually apply to all those who were "called" by the gospel: "God chose the weak things of the world to confound the things which are mighty,...and things which are not, to bring to nothing the things that are" (1 Cor. 1:27–28).[54]

Should we assume that the gesture of humility implicit in the apostle's choice of a surname also operated in Paul's references to his converts and coworkers, as the principle of naming for all those with whom Paul shared the new life in Christ? Edwin Judge seems to incline to this opinion. Judge observes that Paul does not conform to the Roman convention of naming, but "devises his own epithets" for those with whom he has relationships in the messianic community.[55] Judge argues that, in naming, Paul exhibits "a quite distinctive pattern of behavior, inspired by his own humiliation understood in the light of the suffering Messiah. He expects other believers also to experience this through a kind of 'imitation'. Various obligations arise from it, sometimes converging with conventional ones. But the rejection of social status and the building of a new community strike down any naturalistic system of convention."[56]

What are the consequences of our excursus into Pauline onomastics for the designation of Gaius by his *praenomen*, rather than his *cognomen*? The most likely scenario is that Gaius was a freedman. As numerous inscriptions and Petronius' romance demonstrate, considerable wealth was not inconsistent with freedman status.[57] But Paul's unconventional pat-

---

53 Agamben, *The Time That Remains*, 11.
54 Agamben, *The Time That Remains*, 10; cf. Welborn, *Paul, the Fool of Christ*, 147–48, 250.
55 Judge, "The Roman Base of Paul's Mission" in idem, *The First Christians in the Roman World*, 555.
56 Judge, "The Roman Base of Paul's Mission" in idem, *The First Christians in the Roman World*, 566; see also E. A. Judge, "Cultural Conformity and Innovation in Paul,' *TynBul* 35 (1984) 3–24; repr. in idem, *Social Distinctives of the Christians*, 157–74.
57 E.g., Cn. Babbius Philinus of Corinth, whose lack of patronymic indicates that he was probably a freedman, in West, *Corinth VIII: Latin Inscriptions*, nos. 2, 3, 98–101, 131, 132, 155; cf. Spawforth, "Roman Corinth," 169. See the study of the social status of freedmen in the inscriptions by Mary Gordon, "The Freedman's Son in Municipal Life," *JRS* 21 (1931) 65–77, with the comments of Moses I. Finley, *The Ancient Economy* (Berkeley: University of California Press, 1973) 77. See also Stanislaw Mrozek, "Wirtschaftliche Grundlagen des Aufstiegs der Freigelassenen im römischen Reich," *Chiron* 5 (1975) 311–17.

tern of naming raises the possibility that Gaius was a Roman citizen whom Paul chose to address informally by his common Latin *praenomen*,[58] perhaps in order to avoid using a *cognomen* which would have had unmistakable aristocratic connotations for his readers, in keeping with the new Christian emphasis upon humility.[59] Thus the possibility cannot be excluded, on the basis of Paul's use of the *praenomen*, that Gaius held the citizenship.

The fact that Paul's Gaius bears a Roman *praenomen* leaves open a number of possibilities: Gaius may have been a descendant of one of the Italian settlers of the colony, or, alternatively, a Greek immigrant to the city (from the time when Greek immigration became more frequent);[60] Gaius may have been a freedman who gained wealth and a name following his manumission, or a freedman now enjoying Roman citizenship, or a freeborn citizen of higher rank.

If these possibilities cannot be narrowed on the basis of onomastics, we can, at least, dispose of two specious identifications. First, it is highly unlikely that Gaius of Corinth is the same person as any of the other men in the New Testament who bear the name Gaius: the Macedonian traveling companion of Paul who was present with Paul in Ephesus at the riot of the silversmiths (Acts 19:29); Gaius of Derbe (in Asia Minor) who accompanied Paul in delivering the collection to Jerusalem (Acts 20:4); or, the "beloved Gaius" who is the addressee of 3 John (vs. 1).[61] These identifications have nothing to commend them beyond a drive toward harmonization of New Testament characters.[62]

Equally groundless is the suggestion of Edgar J. Goodspeed,[63] adopted by a number of commentators,[64] that the Gaius whom Paul names as his host in Rom. 16:23 is to be identified with Titius Justus, in whose house next door to the synagogue at Corinth Paul preached for a time according to Acts 18:7, and whose full Roman name would then be

---

58 Compare Lucius in Rom. 16:21; BDAG 603; Judge, "The Roman Base of Paul's Mission" in idem, *The First Christians in the Roman World*, 561; Jewett, *Romans*, 977.
59 Judge, "The Roman Base of Paul's Mission" in idem, *The First Christians in the Roman World*, 566.
60 Spawforth, "Roman Corinth," 173–74.
61 Gillman, "Gaius," 869; Jewett, *Romans*, 980.
62 Rightly, Weiss, *Der erste Korintherbrief*, 21.
63 Goodspeed, "Gaius Titius Justus," 382–83.
64 E.g., F. F. Bruce, *The Letter to the Romans* (Grand Rapids: Eerdmans, 1985) 265–66; Cranfield, *Romans*, 2.807; Jewett, *Romans*, 980.

Gaius Titius Justus.⁶⁵ Goodspeed sought to enhance this identification by observing that the *nomen* of the hypothetical Gaius suggests a formal connection with the prestigious Titian *gens*, familiar from Cicero and Horace. But support for this identification crumbles upon closer inspection. In fact, the name Titius is poorly attested in the manuscript tradition (B* D² sy); codex Sinaiticus and other ancient witnesses give the name as Titus Justus,⁶⁶ while Alexandrinus and the majority of Greek manuscripts omit the name Titius altogether.⁶⁷ Moreover, the assumed basis of identity between Gaius and Titius Justus is at least partly defective: the author of Acts does *not* say that Paul *resided* in the house of Titius Justus, but only that he began to preach there, after he departed from the synagogue (Acts 18:7).⁶⁸ An unbiased reading of the account in Acts 18:1–11 would lead to the conclusion that Paul continued to live with his fellow artisans Aquila and Priscilla, even after he had begun to preach in the house of Justus.⁶⁹ In sum, the precious and tantalizing relics of tradition preserved in Acts 18 are insufficient to sustain Goodspeed's hypothesis of the identity of Paul's Gaius with Titius Justus.

Thus, the prospects for a more precise identification of Paul's Gaius on the basis of his name alone would seem to be triply frustrated: first, by the popularity of the name Gaius, which was, alongside Lucius, Marcus, Publius and Quintus, the most frequently occurring *praenomen* at all times in Roman history;⁷⁰ second, by the peculiarity of Paul's onomastic usage, who insists on referring to his converts and coworkers by a single epithet, and that, generally, the least distinctive;⁷¹ third, by the apparent disinterest of the author of Acts in supplying biographical details of the several individuals whose names had come down to him through tradition.⁷²

---

65 Goodspeed, "Gaius Titius Justus," 382; Gillman, "Gaius," 869.
66 ℵ E 36 453 945 1175 1739 1891; cf. Barrett, *Acts 15–28*, 868.
67 A B² D* Ψ; cf. Barrett, *Acts 15–28*, 868.
68 Codex Bezae (D*) of Acts 18:7 describes a change in Paul's residence, replacing ἐκεῖθεν ("from there") with ἀπὸ Ἀκύλα ("from Aquila"). But the reading ἐκεῖθεν is strongly supported; cf. Haenchen, *Acts of the Apostles*, 535: "ἐκεῖθεν means 'from the synagogue'."
69 Malherbe, *Social Aspects*, 74 n.30; Lüdemann, *Early Christianity according to Acts*, 203; Murphy-O'Connor, *Paul*, 262–63; Barrett, *Acts 15–28*, 867.
70 Solin, "Names, personal, Roman," *OCD* (2003) 1024.
71 Judge, "The Roman Base of Paul's Mission" in idem, *The First Christians in the Roman World*, 554–55, 566.
72 Meeks, *First Urban Christians*, 26, 63; Lüdemann, *Early Christianity according to Acts*, 203.

Yet, paradoxically, it might be possible to make a virtue of the seeming defect in our evidence. The fact that the *praenomen* Gaius was so common at Roman Corinth entails the existence of a significant body of epigraphic and numismatic data for purposes of illustration.[73] By surveying first-century coins and inscriptions in which the name Gaius appears, it may be possible to form an estimate of the sort of person whom Paul's Gaius may have been. It is important, however, to make clear from the outset that the value of the information which the coins and inscriptions provide is evocative, rather than probative. There is no way of demonstrating whether any of the individuals who are numismatically or epigraphically attested at Corinth with the *praenomen* Gaius might be related to that Gaius who was the host of the Christian *ekklesia* at Corinth. If, as seems likely, Paul's Gaius was a freedman, it is possible that he left no trace of himself in the archaeological record.[74] Even if Paul's Gaius had gained the citizenship, it is possible that he remained unattested, as a result of having passed his life as a *privatus*, or simply because of the lacunose state of the record.[75] Of course, it is also possible that Paul's Gaius *is* to be found among the Gaii who are memorialized in the inscriptions at Corinth. Unfortunately, a positive identification cannot be made, for the reasons given in the preceding paragraph. The aims of our excursus will be achieved, if we are able to form a more rounded portrait of the kind of person whom Paul's Gaius may have been, by examining what can be known about several Corinthians from the mid-first century who bore the *praenomen* Gaius.

Excursus A: Corinthian Persons

The first point to be made is that the number of *datable* persons with the *praenomen* Gaius (Latin Caius) at Corinth is considerably smaller than the number of those actually attested. This point may be abun-

---

73 The primary materials are inscriptions and coins bearing the name of Gaius in Meritt, *Corinth VIII.1: Greek Inscriptions*; West, *Corinth VIII: Latin Inscriptions*; Kent, *Corinth VIII.3: The Inscriptions*; Amandry, *Le Monnayage des Duovirs Corinthiens*; A. Burnett, M. Amandry and P. Ripolles, *Roman Provinical Coinage I* (London: British Museum Press, 1992).
74 Yet, the servile element is well represented in the epigraphy of Roman Corinth; see Spawforth, "Roman Corinth," 167, 169–70.
75 Kent, *Corinth VIII.3: The Inscriptions*, 17: "it is difficult to think of any other ancient site where the inscriptions are so cruelly mutilated and broken."

dantly illustrated: e.g., it is not possible to assign a date to Gaius Servilius Rufus, although he is a member of the important Corinthian family of the Servilii,[76] nor to Gaius Antonius, whose name is contained in a list of proper names in the nominative case,[77] still less to Gaius Julius Lectus and his wife Julia Polla, about whom nothing further is known.[78] In these cases, the lettering allows for a date in the first century, but the epigraphers withhold judgment, because the texts give no indication of a date.[79] In some instances, the names suggest a date during the early Empire, perhaps in the first century A.D.: e.g., an inscription recording the *hellenodikae* for one of the athletic festivals at Corinth lists Gaius Asinius, Gaius Julius and Gaius Mussidius among other men who bear distinguished Roman names; but it is impossible to identify these individuals or to date them precisely.[80] Occasionally, disagreement between the epigraphers frustrates our purposes: e.g., the memorial of Gaius Julius Marcianus: "Gaius Julius Marcianus, while still living (acquired this burial place) for himself, Terentia Julia his wife, and his daughter, who was still living, Julia Rectina."[81] All of these persons have names which are found in old Roman families, but seem to be unknown apart from this inscription.[82] Kent dates the inscription to the middle of the second century A.D., but concedes that, in the opinion of M. Mitsos, it dates from the first century B.C., or the first century after Christ.[83]

For purposes of comparison with Paul's Gaius, we may eliminate from consideration a number of Gaii who may be dated securely to the first century B.C., or the second century A.D. In the former category belong: Gaius Julius _____, *duovir* with L. Aeficius Certus in

---

76 West, *Corinth VIII.2: Latin Inscriptions*, no. 163, p. 117. On the Corinthian Servilii, see Spawforth, "Roman Corinth," 181.
77 Kent, *Corinth VIII.3: The Inscriptions*, no. 369, p. 143. On the numerous other Corinthian Antonii, see Spawforth, "Roman Corinth," 176.
78 West, *Corinth VIII.2: Latin Inscriptions*, no. 79, pp. 61–62.
79 Kent, *Corinth VIII.3: The Inscriptions*, 143; West, *Corinth VIII.2: Latin Inscriptions*, 61–62.
80 Meritt, *Corinth VIII.1: Greek Inscriptions*, no. 18, pp. 27–28. Also ambiguous are Gaius Julius Ion and Gaius Julius Flaccus, in Meritt, no. 19, pp. 28–29. Meritt dates this inscription "in the first century A.D., perhaps soon after the deification of Livia under Claudius," but notes that Gaius Julius Flaccus also appears in no. 14, dated in the year 3 A.D.
81 Kent, *Corinth VIII.3: The Inscriptions*, no. 294.
82 Kent, *Corinth VIII.3: The Inscriptions*, 116.
83 Kent, *Corinth VIII.3: The Inscriptions*, 116.

44/43 B.C.;[84] Gaius Julius Nicephorus, *duovir* with P. Tadius Chilo in 43/42 B.C.;[85] Gaius Pinnius _____, *duovir* with P. Aebutius in 37/36 B.C. (?);[86] Gaius Minutius _____, associated with M. Insteius, the *duovir* of 34/33 B.C.[87] In the latter category fall: Gaius Avidius P[_____], an official of one of the Isthmian games, from the middle of the second century;[88] Gaius Caelius Martialis, procurator of Trajan for the province of Achaia;[89] Gaius Caristanius Julianus, proconsul of Achaia under Trajan;[90] Gaius Julius Severus, proconsul of Achaia under Trajan;[91] Gaius _____ Cerialis, procurator of Hadrian for the province of Achaia;[92] Gaius Cutius Lesbicus, *duovir* during the reign of Hadrian;[93] Gaius Vibius Megetos, a physician, from the last quarter of the second century A.D.[94]

In a number of cases which may be reliably dated in the first century A.D., the floruit of the person under consideration occurs too near the beginning of the century, or too near its close, for that person to have been associated with the apostle Paul. For example, the Heii, Gaius Aristo, Gaius Pamphilus and Gaius Pollio, all probably freedmen of the same Gaius Heius,[95] served as magistrates of Corinth during the reign of Augustus,[96] and were thus too early to have been Paul's Gaius. The

---

84 Katherine N. Edwards, *Corinth VI: The Coins, 1896–1929* (Cambridge, MA: Harvard University Press, 1933) no. 16, p. 16; Amandry, *Le Monnayage des Duovirs Corinthiens*, 28–32, 120–22; Burnett, *Roman Provincial Coinage I*, no. 1116; Spawforth, "Roman Corinth," 179.
85 Edwards, *Corinth VI: The Coins*, no. 17; Amandry, *Le Monnayage des Duovirs Corinthiens*, 32–33, 113–24; Burnett, *Roman Provincial Coinage I*, no. 1117; Spawforth, "Roman Corinth," 179.
86 Edwards, *Corinth VI: The Coins*, nos. 20–31; Amandry, *Le Monnayage des Duovirs Corinthiens*, 36–38, 130–33; Burnett, *Roman Provincial Coinage I*, nos. 1124–26; Spawforth, "Roman Corinth," 180.
87 Kent, *Corinth VIII.3: The Inscriptions*, no. 345, p. 137.
88 Kent, *Corinth VIII.3: The Inscriptions*, no. 223, pp. 95–96.
89 Kent, *Corinth VIII.3: The Inscriptions*, no. 135, p. 63.
90 West, *Corinth VIII.2: Latin Inscriptions*, n.55, pp. 35–37.
91 West, *Corinth VIII.2: Latin Inscriptions*, nos. 56, 57, pp. 38–40; Kent, *Corinth VIII.3: The Inscriptions*, no. 126, p. 58.
92 Kent, *Corinth VIII.3: The Inscriptions*, no. 137, p. 64.
93 Kent, *Corinth VIII.3: The Inscriptions*, no. 198, pp. 26, 88.
94 Kent, *Corinth VIII.3: The Inscriptions*, no. 206, p. 90.
95 Spawforth, "Roman Corinth," 178–79.
96 Edwards, *Corinth VI: The Coins*, nos. 25–26, 33–34, 36–39; Amandry, *Le Monnayage des Duovirs Corinthiens*, 38–39, 43–47, 47–49, 52–55, 140–42,

same is true of Gaius Servilius Primus, *duovir* with M. Antonius Hipparchus in 2/1 B.C.,[97] Gaius Julius Hera[clanus], quinquennial *duovir* with P. Aebutius in A.D. 1/2,[98] Gaius Secundius Dinippus, *agonothete* in 3 A.D.,[99] and Gaius Mussius Priscus, *duovir* with Gaius Heius Pollio in A.D. 4/5.[100] An ambiguous case is that of Gaius Rutilius Fuscus,[101] a member of an important Corinthian family distinguished by occupancy of the highest civic offices and by major public benefactions.[102] Rutilius Fuscus served as *isagogeus* at the Claudian games when his father, L. Rutilius, was *agonothete* of the Isthmian festival in 51 A.D.[103] Because the *isagogeus* was frequently a boy or young man,[104] we may surmise that Rutilius Fuscus was not old enough to have been Paul's Gaius.[105] Similarly, Gaius O[rfidius] Benignus Juventianus seems to have been the adopted son of Gaius Orfidius Benignus, a military legate under Otho, slain in the battle at Bedriacum in 69 A.D.,[106] and thus too young to have been Paul's Gaius, if, indeed, he were resident in Corinth at all during the fifth decade of the first century.[107]

There remain four Corinthians bearing the *praenomen* Gaius who may be reliably dated to the middle of the first century A.D., and who thus merit our closer attention. We should remind ourselves, once again, of the improbability that Paul's Gaius should have been attested in the epigraphic record, particularly if he was not a Roman citizen, of the small number of datable persons with the *praenomen* Gaius, in comparison with the number of those actually attested, and of the

---

151–56; Burnett, *Roman Provincial Coinage I*, nos. 1127–28, 1132, 1133, 1139–44; Kent, *Corinth VIII.3: The Inscriptions*, nos. 150–51, pp. 67–69.
97 Edwards, *Corinth VI: The Coins*, nos. 28–29; Amandry, *Le Monnayage des Duovirs Corinthiens*, 50–51; Burnett, *Roman Provincial Coinage I*, nos. 1136–37; cf. Spawforth, "Roman Corinth," 181.
98 Edwards, *Corinth VI: The Coins*, no. 32; Amandry, *Le Monnayage des Duovirs Corinthiens*, 51–52, 148–50.
99 Kent, *Corinth VIII.3: The Inscriptions*, 30.
100 Edwards, *Corinth VI: The Coins*, nos. 36–39; Amandry, *Le Monnayage des Duovirs Corinthiens*, 52–54, 151–56.
101 West, *Corinth VIII.2: Latin Inscriptions*, no. 82, pp. 66–69; Kent, *Corinth VIII.3: The Inscriptions*, no. 251, p. 104.
102 West, *Corinth VIII.2: Latin Inscriptions*, 66; Spawforth, "Roman Corinth," 181.
103 West, *Corinth VIII.2: Latin Inscriptions*, 67–68; Kent, *Corinth VIII.3: The Inscriptions*, 30; Spawforth, "Roman Corinth," 181.
104 West, *Corinth VIII.2: Latin Inscriptions*, 67.
105 West, *Corinth VIII.2: Latin Inscriptions*, 68.
106 Kent, *Corinth VIII.3: The Inscriptions*, no. 196, pp. 87–88.
107 Kent, *Corinth VIII.3: The Inscriptions*, 88.

Isi et Sarapi v(ovit) G(aius) Julius [S]yr[us]
"Gaius Julius Syrus dedicated (this column) to Isis and Sarapis"

lacunose state of the archaeological record in general. But with these caveats in mind, we may proceed through the list of persons, proceeding in order of ascending interest.

First, Gaius Julius Syrus, who erected a column of green marble streaked with white found in the theater.[108] The inscription is broken on all sides, but enough of the text is preserved to be read as follows: On the basis of the lettering, Kent dates the inscription to the middle of the first century A.D.[109] The dedicator, Gaius Julius Syrus, is otherwise unknown. His *nomen* Julius suggests that he was a descendant of a freedman of the colony's founder. His *cognomen* Syrus is an indication of Syrian origins.[110] The expense of the dedication testifies to Syrus' wealth, perhaps the result of success in commerce.[111] Pottery made in Syria has been discovered in the "Cellar Building" located on the southwest corner of the forum of Roman Corinth.[112] There were two temples of Isis and

---

108 Kent, *Corinth VIII.3: The Inscriptions*, no. 57.
109 Kent, *Corinth VIII.3: The Inscriptions*, 33.
110 Like Publilius Syrus, the mime writer, who was brought to Rome, probably from Antioch; Pliny *NH* 35.199. See further Heikki Solin, "Three Ciceroniana," *CQ* 37 (1987) 521–23.
111 Kent, *Corinth VIII.3: The Inscriptions*, 33. For comparison with other votives to Isis and Sarapis in Corinth, see Dennis Edwin Smith, "The Egyptian Cults at Corinth," *HTR* 70 (1977) 201–31, esp. 216–21; Elizabeth J. Milleker, "Three Heads of Sarapis from Corinth," *Hesperia* 54 (1985) 121–35. For success in commerce in the cities of the Greek East of the Roman Empire in general, see H. W. Pleket, "Urban Elites and Business in the Greek Part of the Roman Empire" in *Trade in the Ancient Economy*, ed. Peter Garnsey, Keith Hopkins, and C. R. Whittaker (Berkeley: University of California Press, 1983) 131–44, 203–207.
112 Kathleen Slane Wright and R. E. Jones, "A Tiberian Pottery Deposit from Corinth," *Hesperia* 49 (1980) 135–77.

two of Sarapis in Roman Corinth, according to Pausanias.[113] However, Syrus' marble column seems to have been a private donation, and is thus an example of the way in which an individual might shape his personal religious identity in a cosmopolitan society like Roman Corinth.[114] Might such an individual have sought to enhance his identity by participation in a religious movement from the region of his origin?

Second, Gaius Novius Felix, who set up an honorific inscription for Q. Cispuleius Primus and himself.[115]

West infers that Novius Felix was connected with the family of M. Novius Bassus, *duovir* of Corinth in the reign of Augustus.[116] While Novius Felix may have been the son of Bassus, his *cognomen* suggests that he was a freedman of the family.[117] The Novii came to Corinth from Campania; the family had business interests in the East, with Delian ties, which may have included banking.[118] The freedman Cispuleius Primus,[119] with

---

113 Pausanias 2.4.6. On the Isis and Sarapis temples in Corinth, together with the "chapel" in Corinth and the sanctuaries at Kenchreai, see Smith, "The Egyptian Cults at Corinth," 201–16.
114 Compare the account of how individuals shaped their religious identities in the cities of the Roman Empire by Rives, *Religion and Authority in Roman Carthage*, 14, 173; John North, "The Development of Religious Pluralism" in *The Jews Among Pagans and Christians in the Roman Empire*, ed. Judith Lieu, John North, and Tessa Rajak (London: Routledge, 1994) 187.
115 West, *Corinth VIII.2: Latin Inscriptions*, 60–61, no. 77.
116 West, *Corinth VIII.2: Latin Inscriptions*, 61; see also Spawforth, "Roman Corinth," 180.
117 West, *Corinth VIII.2: Latin Inscriptions*, 61; similarly, Spawforth, "Roman Corinth," 180.
118 A. J. N. Wilson, *Emigration from Italy in the Republican Age of Rome* (Manchester: Manchester University Press, 1966) 119; Spawforth, "Roman Corinth," 180.

whom Novius Felix is associated in the inscription, is described as *Augustalis Ti. Caesaris Augusti*.[120] The *Augustales* were a religious and social organization whose responsibilities related to the Imperial cult, in the context of which they funded public entertainments and undertook building projects.[121] The vast majority of *Augustales* attested in inscriptions were freedmen,[122] like Trimalchio in Petronius' *Satyricon*.[123] The institution provided wealthy freedmen with opportunities for public display and prestige.[124] Thus, we may regard Gaius Novius Felix as a freedman of a family which had immigrated to Corinth, who had gained wealth in business, and who was desirous of honor. Wayne Meeks has argued that Pauline Christianity held an attraction for such aspiring freedmen, as a vehicle of resolution for the status inconsistency which they experienced.[125] Might Paul's friend and host have been such a person as Gaius Novius Felix?

---

119 West (*Corinth VIII.2: Latin Inscriptions*, 60–61) argues that Cispuleius Primus was the former slave of Q. Cispuleius Theophilus, mentioned in no. 107.
120 See the arguments of West (*Corinth VIII.2: Latin Inscriptions*, 61) for the interpretation of the abbreviation **AVG** in line 3 of the inscription as *Aug(ustali)*.
121 R. Duthoy, "La function sociale de l'Augustalité," *Epigraphica* 36 (1974) 134–54; idem, "Les *Augustales*," *ANRW* 2.16.2 (Berlin: Walter de Gruyter, 1978) 1254–1309; S. E. Ostrow, "The *Augustales* in the Augustan Scheme" in *Between Republic and Empire. Interpretations of Augustus and His Principate*, ed. K. A. Raaflaub (Berkeley: University of California Press, 1990) 364–79; A. Abramenko, *Die Munizipale Mittelschicht in kaiserzeitlichen Italien. Zu einem neuen Verständnis von Sevirat und Augustalität* (Frankfurt: Peter Lang, 1993). On the *Augustales* in Corinth, see Margaret L. Laird, "The Emperor in a Roman Town: The Base of the *Augustales* in the Forum at Corinth" in *Corinth in Context: Comparative Studies on Religion and Society*, ed. Steven J. Friesen, Daniel N. Schowalter, and James C. Walters (Leiden: Brill, 2010) 67–116, esp. 75 on C. Novius Felix.
122 R. Duthoy, "Recherches sur la repartition géographique et chronologique des termes *sevir Augustalis, Augustalis*, et *sevir* dans l'Empire romain," *Epigraphische Studien* 11 (1976) 143–214. 85–95 % of those attested in inscriptions are freedmen.
123 Petronius *Sat.* 30; see John Bodel, "Trimalchio's Underworld" in *The Search for the Ancient Novel*, ed. J. Tatum (Baltimore: Johns Hopkins University Press, 1993) 248.
124 James B. Rives, "Augustales," *OCD* (2003) 215.
125 Meeks, *First Urban Christians*, 22–23, 191. The importance of status dissonance as a factor in conversion to Pauline Christianity has been reiterated by Theissen, "The Social Structure of the Pauline Communities," 67–68, 73–74.

Third, Gaius Julius Polyaenus, *duovir* with Tiberius Claudius Optatus, whose coins are dated to 57/58 or 58/59 A.D.[126]

Polyaenus is also known from an inscribed piece of white marble revetment.[127] In origin, Polyaenus seems to have been a Sicyonian, since he also coined in Nero's honor at Sicyon.[128] Thus, Polyaenus was a *peregrinus*, or foreigner, who held citizenship in two communities: in Corinth, he was elected magistrate, yet he remained an effective member of his native Sicyon, with liabilities to perform public services there. Anthony Spawforth suggests that Polyaenus is best seen as the descendant of one of the freedmen of Caesar, the colony's founder, well-known for the number and wealth of his ex-slaves.[129] Although Polyaenus obviously gained great wealth and attained the highest office in Roman Corinth, as the grandson of a freedman and as a *peregrinus*, he may have suffered some of that personal insecurity and restlessness which social historians describe as "status dissonance."[130] Even in Roman Corinth, where freedmen were not legally barred from holding civic magistracies, control of the highest offices was largely confined to certain elite families—the Cornelii, the

---

126 Edwards, *Corinth VI: The Coins*, nos. 61–64; Amandry, *Le Monnayage des Duovirs Corinthiens*, 22–24, 24–26, 209–15; Burnett, *Roman Provincial Coinage I*, nos. 1201, 1202.
127 West, *Corinth VIII.2: Latin Inscriptions*, no. 180, p. 121.
128 Amandry, *Le Monnayage des Duovirs Corinthiens*, 21 n.51; cf. Spawforth, "Roman Corinth," 179.
129 Spawforth, "Roman Corinth," 179, referencing Appian *Bell. Civ.* 3.94.
130 Meeks, *First Urban Christians*, 22; Theissen, "The Social Structure of the Pauline Communities," 67–68.

Heii, the Rutilii, and members of the tribe Aemilia.[131] Gerd Theissen has recently reaffirmed the importance of status dissonance, caused by freedman status or alien origin, in attracting a minority of persons from the local upper class to early Christianity.[132] Might Gaius Julius Polyaenus have been one of the few individuals of affluence who discovered among the Pauline Christians a fellowship from which he had been excluded in the most privileged circles at Corinth?

Fourth, and most spectacular, is Gaius Julius Spartiaticus, whose entire public career is known to us from a Latin dedication by the tribesmen of Calpurnia recording all of his municipal and imperial offices.[133]

---

131 West, *Corinth VIII.2: Latin Inscriptions*, nos. 12, 80, 82, 106, 124; Kent, *Corinth VIII.3: The Inscriptions*, nos. 152, 156, 164, 175, 208–209, 212, 224, 237, 321, 327, pp. 24–31. Cf. Stansbury, "Corinthian Honor, Corinthian Conflict," 86–88; Spawforth, "Roman Corinth," 178–79, 181.
132 Theissen, "The Social Structure of the Pauline Communities," 67–68, 73–74.
133 West, *Corinth VIII.2: Latin Inscriptions*, no. 68, pp. 50–53; cf. L. R. Taylor and Allen B. West, "The Euryclids in Latin Inscriptions from Corinth," *AJA* 30 (1926) 389–400, esp. 393–400. See also the pedestal in Meritt, *Corinth VIII.1: Greek Inscriptions*, no. 70, pp. 53–54. For sources on Spartiaticus, see *Prosopographia Imperii Romani IV*, ed. A. Stein and L. Petersen (Berlin: Walter de Gruyter, 1952–1966) no. 587, pp. 281–82; *RP* 2 "LAC 509" and *RP* 1 "COR 353".

310   Chapter Five. Prosopography

C. Iulio, Laconis f(ilio)	Gaius Julius, son of Laco,
Euryclis n(epoti), Fab(ia tribu), Spartiati(co)	grandson of Eurycles, of the tribe Fabia, Spartiaticus,
[p]rocuratori Caesaris et Augustae Agrippinae, trib(uno) mil(itum), equo p(ublico)	procurator of Caesar and Augusta Agrippina, tribune of the soldiers, awarded a public horse
[ex]ornato a Divo Claudio, flam(ini) Divi Juli, pontif(ici), IIvir(o) quinq(ennali) iter(um),	by the deified Claudius, flamen of the deified Julius, pontifex, duovir quinquennalis twice,
agonotheti Isthmion et Caese(reon) [S]ebasteon, archieri domus Aug(ustae) [in] perpetuum primo Achaeon	agonothete of the Isthmian and Caesarean-Augustan games, high-priest of the house of Augustus in perpetuity first of the Achaeans
–ob v[i]rtutem eius et animosam f[usi]ss[im]amque erga domum divinam et erga coloniam nostr(am) munificientiam tribules tribu Calpurnia [pa]trono.	–because of his virtue and eager and all-encompassing munificence toward the divine house and munificence toward our colony, the tribesmen of the tribe Calpurnia [dedicated this] to their patron.

The inscription must be dated between A.D. 54, the year of the death of Claudius, who is called *Divus* in line 5, and A.D. 55, when Agrippina's short-lived co-regency with Nero, reflected in the title *Augusta*, came to an end.[134] The inscription is carved in cursive letter forms on a statue base of Acrocorinthian limestone.[135] Several aspects of the language reveal that the text is a translation of a document originally composed in Greek.[136]

Spartiaticus is identified as the son of Laco, about whom much is known from an inscription likewise found at Corinth,[137] and the grandson of Eurycles, about whom much will be said in what follows.[138] Spar-

---

134   West, *Corinth VIII.2: Latin Inscriptions*, 52; Taylor and West, "The Euryclids in Latin Inscriptions from Corinth," 396; K. M. T. Chrimes, *Ancient Sparta: A Reexamination of the Evidence* (Manchester: Manchester University Press, 1952) 183 n.6.
135   Taylor and West, "The Euryclids in Latin Inscriptions from Corinth," 393; West, *Corinth VIII.2: Latin Inscriptions*, 50.
136   West, *Corinth VIII.2: Latin Inscriptions*, 51.
137   West, *Corinth VIII.2: Latin Inscriptions*, no. 67, pp. 46–49; Taylor and West, "The Euryclids in Latin Inscriptions from Corinth," 389–93.
138   Chrimes, *Ancient Sparta*, 169–82; G. W. Bowersock, "Eurycles of Sparta," *JRS* 51 (1961) 112–18; *Prosopographia Imperii Romani IV*, ed. A. Stein and L. Petersen (Berlin: Walter de Gruyter, 1952–1966) no. 301, pp. 208–210; G. Steinhauer, Γάιος Ἰούλιος Εὐρυκλῆς. Συμβολὴ στὴν ἱστορία τῆς ῥωμαϊκῆς Σπάρτης (Ph.D. dissertation, University of Athens, 1989); Paul Cartledge and Antho-

tiaticus' public career began with service as a tribune of the soldiers in the Roman army.[139] He eventually inherited his father's role as "procurator" of the Imperial family, a title which is best seen as designating the stewardship of a private domain in Greece, belonging first to Claudius, and then to Nero.[140] Like his father Laco, Spartiaticus was a Corinthian magistrate, elected *duovir quinquennalis* twice, most likely in 47/48 and 52/53 A.D.,[141] and he was *agonothetes* of the Isthmian and Caesarean games,[142] a position of extraordinary prestige, since he would have been responsible for organizing and financing the games.[143] Unlike his father, Spartiaticus had been officially admitted to the equestrian order, awarded a public horse by Claudius.[144] Spartiaticus also held a number of priesthoods: he was flamen of the deified Julius,[145] pontifex,[146] and high-priest of the house of Augustus in perpetuity.[147] The last named office, which climaxes Spartiaticus' *cursus*, was a newly established position of great im-

---

ny Spawforth, *Hellenistic and Roman Sparta: A Tale of Two Cities* (London: Routledge, 2002) 97–104.
139 West, *Corinth VIII.2: Latin Inscriptions*, 51; Cartledge and Spawforth, *Hellenistic and Roman Sparta*, 103.
140 The procuratorial title is problematic. West (*Corinth VIII.2: Latin Inscriptions*, 49, 51) suggests that "the title procurator was given to Laco to regularize his position as Spartan dynast," exercising authority on behalf of the emperor. But, as Cartledge and Spawforth (*Hellenistic and Roman Sparta*, 102) observe, "the title…attached Laco to the emperor personally, rather than the province." Moreover, "it is difficult to see Sparta, a free city, as the personal property of the emperor." Thus, the best interpretation is that offered by Chrimes (*Ancient Sparta*, 184–86): Laco and Spartiaticus held a procuratorship of imperial estates in the province of Achaia. Similarly, Linda J. Piper, *Spartan Twilight* (New Rochelle, NY: Aristide D. Carazas, 1986) 165.
141 West, *Corinth VIII.2: Latin Inscriptions*, 52; Chrimes, *Ancient Sparta*, 183 n.6;184; *Prosopographia Imperii Romani IV*, 281; Kent, *Corinth VIII.3: The Inscriptions*, 25
142 West, *Corinth VIII.2: Latin Inscriptions*, 52; Kent, *Corinth VIII.3: The Inscriptions*, 31.
143 West, *Corinth VIII.2: Latin Inscriptions*, 52. On the costs of the games and the burden of the office of *agonothetes*, see Geagan, "Notes on the Agonistic Institutions of Roman Corinth," 69, 74; Kent, *Corinth VIII.3: The Inscriptions*, 30; Wiseman, "Corinth and Rome I," 500.
144 West, *Corinth VIII.2: Latin Inscriptions*, 51–52. Cf. Dio Cassius 59.9; Suetonius *Claud.* 16.
145 Taylor and West, "The Euryclids in Latin Inscriptions from Corinth," 394; West, *Corinth VIII.2: Latin Inscriptions*, 53.
146 West, *Corinth VIII.2: Latin Inscriptions*, 53.
147 Taylor and West, "The Euryclids in Latin Inscriptions from Corinth," 394–95.

portance, as demonstrated by the fact that it is the only office mentioned in a Greek inscription in Spartiaticus' honor from Athens: ἀρχιερεὺς Θεῶν Σεβαστῶν καὶ γένους Σεβαστῶν ἐκ τοῦ κοινοῦ τῆς Ἀχαΐας διὰ βίου πρῶτον τῶν ἀπ' αἰῶνος.[148] Spartiaticus was thus the first man to be chosen by the general assembly of the Achaeans as high-priest for life in the Imperial cult;[149] as such, Spartiaticus held the highest office in the province.[150]

It may seem incredible that a man such as Spartiaticus could have been attracted to the gospel of Messiah Jesus. But in Spartiaticus' case, there was a hereditary connection with Judaism. And herein lies one of the most fascinating episodes in the history of Augustan Greece.[151]

The grandfather of whom Spartiaticus shows himself so proud was one Eurycles of Sparta.[152] Eurycles makes his appearance in history as the commander of a warship on the side of Octavian in the battle of Actium.[153] A grateful Octavian rewarded Eurycles with Roman citizenship,[154] after which he became Gaius Julius Eurycles,[155] and with the gift of enormous estates on the island of Cythera.[156] The friendship of the emperor compensated Eurycles for the obscurity of his family origins.[157] Lachares, the father of Eurycles, had been executed on a charge

---

148 *IG* 3.805 = *SIG*³ 790; cf. Taylor and West, "The Euryclids in Latin Inscriptions from Corinth," 394–95; *Prosopographia Imperii Romani IV*, no. 587, p.282. See also a Spartan dedication, *IG* 5.1.463.
149 Taylor and West, "The Euryclids in Latin Inscriptions from Corinth," 394; West, *Corinth VIII.2: Latin Inscriptions*, 51.
150 Taylor and West, "The Euryclids in Latin Inscriptions from Corinth," 394; Chrimes, *Ancient Sparta*, 183 n.6.
151 Josephus *B.J.* 1.513–31; *A.J.* 16.300–10.
152 Chrimes, *Ancient Sparta*, 169–81; G. W. Bowersock, "Eurycles of Sparta," *JRS* 51 (1961) 112–18; "C. Iulius Eurycles" in *Prosopographia Imperii Romani IV*, no. 301, pp. 208–10; Piper, *Spartan Twilight*, 156–65; Cartledge and Spawforth, *Hellenistic and Roman Sparta*, 97–104.
153 Plutarch *Ant.* 67; Bowersock, "Eurycles of Sparta," 112; Cartledge and Spawforth, *Hellenistic and Romans Sparta*, 97.
154 Bowersock, "Eurycles of Sparta," 112; Piper, *Spartan Twilight*, 157.
155 *Prosopographia Imperii Romani IV*, 208; Piper, *Spartan Twilight*, 156; Cartledge and Spawforth, *Hellenistic and Roman Sparta*, 98.
156 Chrimes, *Ancient Sparta*, 172–73; Bowersock, "Eurycles of Sparta," 116; Cartledge and Spawforth, *Hellenistic and Roman Sparta*, 98–99. Cf. Dio Cassius 54.7.2; Strabo *Geogr.* 8.5.1.
157 Bowersock, "Eurycles of Sparta," 116; Cartledge and Spawforth, *Hellenistic and Roman Sparta*, 97–98.

of "piracy,"[158] and the charge against Lachares seems to have had some foundation in fact.[159]

In the years following Actium, Eurycles employed the gifts of the emperor to extend his influence.[160] Inscriptions show that he made liberal benefactions to the Laconian cities of Asopus and Gytheum.[161] Eurycles also made sizeable outlays in support of the Augustan program of religious restoration: he was the founder of Sparta's Imperial cult;[162] he was involved in the revival of the civic cults of the Dioscuri and Poseidon.[163] Thus, although Eurycles was wealthy, his spending on public works in Sparta and his benefactions to other cities and sanctuaries soon had him looking for additional sources of income.[164]

In his search for money, Eurycles looked eastwards, to Herod the Great of Judaea. The story of how Eurycles insinuated himself into Herod's court and exploited the dynastic intrigues to his own financial advantage is told by Josephus in the first book of *The Jewish War* and in the sixteenth book of the *Antiquities*.[165] Why should Eurycles have fixed upon Herod as the victim of his financial opportunism? In part, it must have been because the great wealth of Herod was well known.[166] Herod had made generous gifts to the chief cities of Greece, including Sparta itself.[167] But there is good reason to take seriously the

---

158 Plutarch *Ant.* 67; Chrimes, *Ancient Sparta*, 180 n.5.
159 Bowersock, "Eurycles of Sparta," 116; Piper, *Spartan Twilight*, 156; Cartledge and Spawforth, *Hellenistic and Roman Sparta*, 97. Cf. SIG^3 786.
160 Chrimes, *Ancient Sparta*, 179–80; Piper, *Spartan Twilight*, 157–58; Cartledge and Spawforth, *Hellenistic and Roman Sparta*, 100, 103–104.
161 *IG* 5.1.970 = *Documents Illustrating the Reigns of Augustus and Tiberius*, ed. Victor Ehrenberg and A. H. M. Jones (Oxford: Clarendon Press, 1976) no. 351, p. 157; *L'Année Épigraphique* (1929) no. 99, ll. 19–20; Ernst Kornemann, *Neue Dokumente zum lakonischen Kaiserkult* (Breslau: M. & H. Marcus, 1929) 6, 15–20; cf. Chrimes, *Ancient Sparta*, 171, 179–80; Bowersock, "Eurycles of Sparta," 116; Piper, *Spartan Twilight*, 157.
162 Cartledge and Spawforth, *Hellenistic and Roman Sparta*, 99, referencing *IG* 5.1. 1172.
163 *IG* 5.1.141–42, 206–12; cf. Cartledge and Spawforth, *Hellenistic and Roman Sparta*, 99.
164 Cartledge and Spawforth, *Hellenistic and Roman Sparta*, 100. Cf. Josephus *B.J.* 1.513.
165 Jospehus *B.J.* 1.513–31; *A.J.* 16.300–310; see the analysis in Chrimes, *Ancient Sparta*, 174–76; Bowersock, "Eurycles of Sparta," 115–16.
166 A. H. M. Jones, *The Herods of Judaea* (Oxford: Clarendon Press, 1938) ch. 3; Chrimes, *Ancient Sparta*, 175.
167 Josephus *B.J.* 1.422–25; *IG* 3.550, 551.

suggestion of Josephus that belief in a kinship between Spartans and Jews was also a factor.[168] The legend of a kinship between Jews and Spartans can be traced back to pre-Maccabean times.[169] Because of a belief in this kinship, Jason, author of the Hellenistic reform in Jerusalem, ended his life in Sparta.[170] A document in 1 Maccabees purports to record a treaty of friendship between the Jews and the Spartans concluded on the basis of their shared kinship in 145 B.C.[171] Josephus records the same document in apparent good faith in the 13th book of the *Antiquities*, treating the legend of kinship as an established fact.[172] Thus Josephus explains that Herod and his whole court were delighted to show special honor to the Spartan Eurycles, on account of his country and ancestry.[173]

At the court of Herod, Eurycles exploited Herod's suspicions of his two sons by Mariamne, revealing a supposed plot against their father on the part of Alexander and Aristobulus, and receiving as a reward fifty talents from Herod.[174] As a result, Herod's sons were imprisoned and strangled at Sebaste in 7 B.C.[175]

---

168 Chrimes, *Ancient Sparta*, 175–76; M. Pani, *Roma a il re d'oriente da Augusto a Tiberio* (Bari: Università di Bari, 1984) 123–26; Cartledge and Spawforth, *Hellenistic and Roman Sparta*, 100.
169 Arnaldo Momigliano, *Alien Wisdom: The Limits of Hellenization* (Cambridge: Cambridge University Press, 1975) 113–14. See the critical evaluation of this legend by Erich S. Gruen, *Heritage and Hellenism: The Reinvention of Jewish Tradition* (Berkeley: University of California Press, 1998) 253–68.
170 2 Macc. 5:9. Cf. Momigliano, *Alien Wisdom*, 113; Gruen, *Heritage and Hellenism*, 255, 259, 265.
171 1 Macc. 12:6–18. Momigliano (*Alien Wisdom*, 113–14) regards the letter from Jonathan to the Spartans as "probably authentic," and the letter from the Spartans to Simon as "certainly authentic," but the letter of King Areus of Sparta to the Jews as "probably forged to provide a background for the authentic correspondence of the second century." See the discussion in Jonathan A. Goldstein, *I Maccabees. A New Translation with Introduction and Commentary* (Garden City: Doubleday, 1976) 444–62; Ranon Katzoff, "Jonathan and Late Sparta," *American Journal of Philology* 106 (1985) 485–89; Gruen, *Heritage and Hellenism*, 254–60, 263–64.
172 Josephus *A.J.*13.164. Cf. Chrimes, *Ancient Sparta*, 176; Cartledge and Spawforth, *Hellenistic and Roman Sparta*, 100.
173 Josephus *B.J.* 1.515, with the comments of Chrimes, *Ancient Sparta*, 176 n.3.
174 Josephus *A.J.* 16.300–309; *B.J.* 1.516–29.
175 Josephus *B.J.* 1.536–37; Bowersock, "Eurycles of Sparta," 115–16; Piper, *Spartan Twilight*, 159; Cartledge and Spawforth, *Hellenistic and Roman Sparta*, 100.

Eurycles returned to Sparta greatly enriched, and resumed his efforts to be the first man in Sparta.[176] But the descendants of the old Spartan aristocracy united against him. Eurycles was denounced in the court of Augustus for fomenting political unrest.[177] Plutarch preserves the valuable piece of information that one of Eurycles' accusers before Augustus was a descendant of the old and distinguished family of Brasidas.[178] The aristocrat no doubt resented the fact that his ancient family still lacked Roman citizenship, while an upstart, who happened to choose the winning side at Actium, dominated Sparta.[179] The attack upon Eurycles by the prominent families of Sparta was evidently successful, for Josephus tells us that Eurycles went into exile,[180] and there, sometime before 2 B.C., Eurycles died.[181]

Eurycles' son Laco learned the folly of his father's rivalries: according to Strabo, he renounced all such "ambition."[182] Instead, Laco directed his energies into Imperial service. A Corinthian inscription tells us that Laco became the administrator ("procurator") of Imperial estates in Greece.[183] He also served as *flamen Augusti*, a further display of his loyalty to the Imperial house.[184] He sent his younger son Spartiaticus into the Roman army as an equestrian officer.[185] And he succeeded in marrying his eldest son Argolicus into the family of a Mytilenean senator highly

---

176 Josephus *B.J.* 1.531; Chrimes, *Ancient Sparta*, 175–79; Bowersock, "Eurycles of Sparta," 115–16.
177 Josephus *B.J.* 1.531; Strabo *Georg.* 8.5.5; Chrimes, *Ancient Sparta*, 179–80; Bowersock, "Eurycles of Sparta," 116.
178 Plutarch *Reg. imp. apophth.* 14 (*Mor.* 207F); Chrimes, *Ancient Sparta*, 179; Bowersock, "Eurycles of Sparta," 116.
179 H. Box, "Roman Citizenship in Laconia," *JRS* 21 (1931) 202; Bowersock, "Eurycles of Sparta," 116; Cartledge and Spawforth, *Hellenistic and Roman Sparta*, 101.
180 Josephus *B.J.* 1.531; Chrimes, *Ancient Sparta*, 180–81.
181 Strabo *Georg.* 8.5.3; Bowersock, "Eurycles of Sparta," 114–15; Cartledge and Spawforth, *Hellenistic and Roman Sparta*, 101.
182 Strabo *Georg.* 8.5.3, adopting the emendation φιλοτιμίαν proposed by Ronald Syme, cited in Bowersock, "Eurycles of Sparta," 114 n.24.
183 West, *Corinth VIII.2: Latin Inscriptions*, no. 67, pp. 47, 49; cf. Chrimes, *Ancient Sparta*, 184; Cartledge and Spawforth, *Hellenistic and Roman Sparta*, 102, noting that his filiation is given by *praenomen* (C. f.), rather than *cognomen*.
184 West, *Corinth VIII.2: Latin Inscriptions*, no. 67, pp. 47, 49.
185 West, *Corinth VIII.2: Latin Inscriptions*, no. 68, p.51; Chrimes, *Ancient Sparta*, 184; Cartledge and Spawforth, *Hellenistic and Roman Sparta*, 103.

favored by the emperor.[186] But friendship with an emperor such as Tiberius could be a dangerous thing, and it proved to be Laco's undoing. Tacitus tells us that when the Mytilenean senator Pompeius Macer, who had been an intimate of Tiberius, was disgraced in 33 A.D., Tiberius sent into exile Pompeia Macrina, the wife of Argolicus, Argolicus himself, and his father Laco.[187] Although the language of Tacitus is vague, it would appear that Laco's property was sequestrated.[188] Laco and his son Spartiaticus settled in the Roman colony of Corinth.[189] K. M. T. Chrimes has calculated that, at the time of his exile in 33 A.D., Laco would have been more than 50 years of age, while Spartiaticus cannot have been much less than 30.[190]

At the death of Tiberius, Laco recovered his fortune: the sentence of exile was revoked, and the property was restored.[191] Anthony Spawforth suggests that Caligula was responsible for the rehabilitation of the house of Eurycles, and that the hereditary connection with Judaism may have played a role, since Caligula counted among his intimate friends the Jewish prince Herod Agrippa, grandson of Herod, the host of Eurycles.[192]

The epigraphic evidence from Corinth suggests that, after reinstatement in Imperial favor, Laco and his son did not return to Sparta,[193] but continued to reside in Corinth, where they not only held citizenship, but eventually attained the highest municipal offices.[194] Given the family history, it seems entirely plausible that Spartiaticus would have been attracted to Judaism as a God-fearer, that Spartiaticus would have formed

---

186 *Prosopographia Imperii Romani IV,* no. 372, p.226; Chrimes, *Ancient Sparta,* 182; Piper, *Spartan Twilight,* 164; Cartledge and Spawforth, *Hellenistic and Roman Sparta,* 102.
187 Tacitus *Ann.* 6.18; Chrimes, *Ancient Sparta,* 182–83; Glen W. Bowersock, "Augustus and the East: the Problem of the Succession" in *Caesar Augustus. Seven Aspects,* ed. F. Millar and E. Segal (Oxford: Oxford University Press, 1984) 178–79; Cartledge and Spawforth, *Helenistic and Roman Sparta,* 102.
188 Bowersock, "Augustus and the East," 178–79; Cartledge and Spawforth, *Hellenistic and Roman Sparta,* 102.
189 West, *Corinth VIII: Latin Inscriptions,* nos. 67, 68; Chrimes, *Ancient Sparta,* 183; Spawforth, "Roman Corinth," 174.
190 Chrimes, *Ancient Sparta,* 185–87.
191 Chrimes, *Ancient Sparta,* 183–84; Cartledge and Spawforth, *Hellenistic and Roman Sparta,* 102.
192 Cartledge and Spawforth, *Hellenistic and Roman Sparta,* 102.
193 Taylor and West, "The Euryclids in Latin Inscriptions from Corinth," 397; Chrimes, *Ancient Sparta,* 183.
194 Piper, *Spartan Twilight,* 165.

a friendship with the respected ruler of the synagogue, Crispus, and that he would have responded with excitement to the message that the Messiah had appeared in the person of Jesus, and that, in all of this, Spartiaticus would not have sensed a conflict with his identity as an eminent Greek and Roman citizen, but would have viewed his interest in things Jewish as an act of filial piety to his great ancestor, Eurycles.[195]

One final, precious anecdote regarding Spartiaticus is preserved by Musonius in a comment upon the effects of exile.[196] The passage of Musonius provides a glimpse into the moral interior of a man who is otherwise known only through the ornaments of his public career. Musonius is quoted as saying that Spartiaticus was a conspicuous example of the benefits which might come from being exiled: "We even know of some who were cured of chronic ailments in exile, as for instance, in our day Spartiaticus the Lacedaemonian, who suffered for many years from a pleurisy and was often ill on account of high-living (τρυφή), but when he stopped living a life of luxury, he also ceased to be ill."[197] Chrimes convincingly argued that Spartiaticus' high-living and ill-health belonged to the period before his Corinthian career, and that the exile which put an end to his luxurious life and cured him was that which he endured with his father in about 33 A.D.[198] In his new home in Corinth, Spartiaticus experienced a reformation in his character.[199]

Reflecting upon what is known about Gaius Julius Spartiaticus and his origins, it is impossible not to notice the similarities between this man and the profile of the wrongdoer, Gaius ὁ ξένος μου καὶ ὅλης τῆς ἐκκλησίας, which has emerged from exegesis of the relevant portions of Paul's Corinthian correspondence. As the wrongdoer looked down upon Paul from a considerable social distance, embodying his disdain for Paul in potent, derogatory labels (ταπεινός, ἀσθενής, ἐξουθενημένος),[200] so Spartiaticus could only have looked down upon his contemporaries from a position of inherited wealth and eminence, and as a consequence of his own achievements and relationships.[201] As the wrongdoer

---

195 Notice that Gaius Julius Spartiaticus is called *Euryclis n.* in the honorific inscription from Corinth: West, *Corinth VIII: Latin Inscriptions*, no. 68; cf. Bowersock, "Eurycles of Sparta," 117.
196 Musonius *ap.* Stobaeus *Flor.* 40.9.
197 Trans. by Lutz, *Musonius Rufus: "The Roman Socrates,"* 70–71.
198 Chrimes, *Ancient Sparta*, 186.
199 Chrimes, *Ancient Sparta*, 186–87; Piper, *Spartan Twilight*, 165–66.
200 See above, ch. 3.
201 Cf. Chow, *Patronage and Power*, 50–51; Spawforth, "Roman Corinth," 174.

evaluated Paul's literary performance by terms which reflect the aesthetic preferences of the Roman upper class (βαρὺς καὶ ἰσχυρός),[202] so Spartiaticus, and the Euryclids in general, present a textbook case of Romanization, the gradual absorption of a Greek family into the Imperial system.[203] In each of the generations through which we have traced the Euryclids, we have noted an intense involvement in matters religious;[204] their priestly offices nurtured the connection with the Imperial house,[205] but also compensated for the dubious origins of the clan.[206] Especially intriguing is the hereditary connection of the Euryclids with Judaism, which contributed to the fortune of the family, and perhaps also to its restoration from exile.[207] From our exegesis of 2 Cor. 10–13, we inferred that the wrongdoer embraced the sense of belonging to the Messiah, and that he was influenced by Jewish-Christian opponents of Paul.[208] 1 Cor. 1:14 suggests that Gaius had a close relationship with Crispus, the former ἀρχισυνάγωγος.[209] The Corinthian inscription which provides Spartiaticus' *cursus* honors him as the patron of the Calpurnia, a tribe obviously named for Caesar's wife;[210] similarly, Paul's Gaius served as patron of the Christian group at Corinth.[211] We have found evidence that Paul's Gaius was somehow involved in the formation of factions in the church at Corinth, and have encountered numerous instances of a fondness for debate and an acerbity of expression in Gaius' critique of Paul, reflected in 2 Cor. 10–13.[212] In this connection, one cannot fail to notice the contentiousness which runs through the Euryclid family history, as if it were an

---

202 See above, ch. 3.
203 Cartledge and Spawforth, *Hellenistic and Roman Sparta*, 102–103; Spawforth, "Roman Corinth," 174; Ramsay MacMullen, *Romanization in the Time of Augustus* (New Haven: Yale University Press, 2000) 12, 20.
204 West, *Corinth VIII.2: Latin Inscriptions,* 47–48; cf. Cartledge and Spawforth, *Hellenistic and Roman Sparta*, 99, on the participation of the Euryclids in the Augustan programme of religious restoration.
205 Cartledge and Spawforth, *Hellenistic and Roman Sparta*, 102–103.
206 Chrimes, *Ancient Sparta*, 179–80; Bowersock, "Eurycles of Sparta," 116.
207 Chrimes, *Ancient Sparta*, 174–76; Cartledge and Spawforth, *Hellenistic and Roman Sparta*, 102.
208 See above, ch. 3, pp. 89–101, 127–32.
209 Weiss, *Der erste Korintherbrief,* 20–21; Lindemann, *Der erste Korintherbrief,* 42.
210 West, *Corinth VIII.2: Latin Inscriptions,* 53.
211 Meeks, *First Urban Christians,* 57, 119, 221 n.7; Chow, *Patronage and Power,* 90; Kirner, "Apostolat und Patronage (II)," 55–56; Theissen, "The Social Structure of the Pauline Communities," 82–83.
212 Weiss, *Der erste Korintherbrief,* 20–21; Lindemann, *Der erste Korintherbrief,* 42. On the acerbity of Paul's critic in 2 Cor. 10:1, 2, 7, 10, etc., see above, ch. 3.

inherited trait; this observation is particularly relevant, if Groag is correct in referring Plutarch's account of a destructive rivalry between two brothers, "the most powerful of the Greeks in my time,"[213] to Spartiaticus and his brother Cratinus.[214] Finally, Musonius' account of the moral reform of Spartiaticus in exile naturally evokes comparison with Paul's account of the remorse of the wrongdoer in 2 Cor. 2:7; in both cases, we evidently have to do with a person capable of repentance and change.

Lest we be carried away by these similarities in the direction of identification, we should sternly remind ourselves of the limitations of our knowledge. Comparison is invited by the fact that our sources are so much richer for Spartiaticus than for any other Corinthian bearing the name of Gaius. If we possessed, in the case of Julius Syrus or Novius Felix, a complete *cursus honorum*, with other inscriptions recording honors and offices, and biographical information from literary sources, as we have in the case of Spartiaticus, we might discover as many similarities between Paul's host and one of these other Corinthian Gaii, and might be drawn in a different direction. Indeed, the features which Paul's Gaius has in common with Spartiaticus might be shown to be characteristic of upper class Roman provincials in general, at least as social aspirations, judging from Plutarch's portraits of his contemporaries.[215] In Spartiaticus' profile, only the connection with Judaism is anomalous. So we should resist any temptation to make an identification, and should be content with having formed a more robust image of the kind of man whom Paul's Gaius may have been.

A final reminder of the gaps in the archaeological record, and of how much has been lost, is offered by an inscription honoring Gaius Caristanius Julianus, proconsul of Achaia under Trajan.[216] Although this man is much too late to be considered Paul's Gaius, his family connections are tantalizing to the highest degree.[217] Caristanius Julianus belonged to a

---

213 Plutarch *Mor.* 488.
214 Edmund Groag, *Die römischen Reichsbeamten von Achaia bis auf Diokletian* (Vienna: Hölder-Pichler-Tempsky, 1939) cols. 7–8; cf. Cartledge and Spawforth, *Hellenistic and Roman Sparta*, 103.
215 Lamberton, *Plutarch*, 1–26, 44–51; Rebecca Preston, "Roman Questions, Greek Answers: Plutarch and the Construction of Identity" in *Being Greek under Rome: Cultural Identity, the Second Sophistic and the Development of Empire*, ed. Simon Goldhill (Cambridge: Cambridge University Press, 2001) 86–122.
216 West, *Corinth VIII.2: Latin Inscriptions*, no. 55, pp. 35–37; cf. *Prosopographia Imperii Romani IV*, no. 426, p. 101.
217 West, *Corinth VIII.2: Latin Inscriptions*, 36.

family of Pisidian Antioch known from several inscriptions.[218] An earlier generation of scholars asserted that one of the members of this family in the first century A.D., Gaius Caristanius Fronto, married into the distinguished Roman family of the Sergii Pauli.[219] To this family belonged the Sergius Paulus who was proconsul in Cyprus at the time of Paul's visit according to Acts 13:7.[220] A recently discovered inscription from Caunus puts in question any suggestion of marriage between members of the Caristanii and the Sergii Paulli.[221] Yet, one might ask whether it is possible that one of the Caristanii, who were scattered throughout the Eastern provinces in positions of Imperial service,[222] had settled in Roman Corinth by the middle of the first century A.D.? It is interesting to note that another Caristanius, Sagaris by name, who was honored at Delphi with Julianus,[223] has a namesake who is attested in inscriptions at Corinth.[224]

---

218 *ILS* 9502, 9503, 9485; Michael Christol, Thomas Drew-Bear, and Mehmet Taslialan, "L'empereur Claude, le chevalier C. Caristanius Fronto Caesianus Iullus et le culte imperial à Antioche de Pisidie," *Tyche* 16 (2001) 1–20, the text of the inscription on pp. 1–2. Cf. Robert L. Mowery, "Paul and Caristanius at Pisidian Antioch," *Biblica* 87 (2006) 221–42.

219 On the basis of the restoration of the name Sergia Paulla in *IGR* 3.300 by Sir William Ramsay: see G. L. Cheesman, "The Family of the Caristanii at Antioch in Pisidia," *JRS* 3 (1913) 253–66, esp. 260–66; W. M. Ramsay, "Studies in the Roman Province Galatia," *JRS* 16 (1926) 201–15, esp. 202–206; West, *Corinth VIII.2: Latin Inscriptions*, 36.

220 Cheesman, "The Family of the Caristanii," 265; Ramsay, "Studies in the Roman Province Galatia," 203; West, *Corinth VIII.2: Latin Inscriptions*, 36; followed, recently, by Stephen Mitchell, *Anatolia. Land, Men, and Gods in Asia Minor II: The Rise of the Church* (Oxford: Oxford University Press, 1993) 6–7.

221 Christian Marek, *Die Inschriften von Kaunos* (Munich: Beck, 2006) no. 126. On the inscription, the wife of Gaius Caristanius Fronto is Calpurnia Paulla, not Sergia Paulla. See the discussion in Michael Christol and Thomas Drew-Bear, "Les Sergii Paulli et Antioche" in *Actes du Ier Congrès international sur Antioche de Pisidie*, ed. T. Drew-Bear, M. Taslialan and C. M. Thomas (Paris: de Boccard, 2002) 177–91, esp. 178–81. See now Alexander Weiß, "Sergius Paullus, Statthalter von Zypern," *ZPE* 169 (2009) 188–192.

222 Cheesman, "The Family of the Caristanii at Antioch in Pisidia," 253, 260, 266; Barbara Levick, *Roman Colonies in Southern Asia Minor* (Oxford: Oxford University Press, 1967) 62–64, 111–13; Christol, Drew-Bear, Taslialan, "L'empereur Claude, le chevalier C. Caristanius Fronto," 1–20; Mowery, "Paul and Caristanius," 240.

223 Émile Bourguet, *De rebus Delphicis imperatoriae aetatis capita duo* (Montepessulano: Camillus Coulet, 1905) 27; West, *Corinth VIII: Latin Inscriptions*, 37; *Prosopographia Imperii Romani IV*, 101.

224 *ILS* 1503; cf. 1504; West, *Corinth VIII: Latin Inscriptions*, 37.

Whoever Paul's Gaius may have been, with respect to his family of origin and public career, at some point near the middle of the first century, he became a Christian (1 Cor. 1:14), and then, sometime later, "the host of the whole *ekklesia*" at Corinth (Rom. 16:23).[225] As we observed above, Paul's description of Gaius as ὁ ξένος μου καὶ ὅλης τῆς ἐκκλησίας is of the utmost importance for establishing his social status.[226] To recapitulate, we argued that the noun ξένος implies the concrete provision of hospitality, both to Paul and to the Corinthians.[227] While it is possible that Gaius hosted the Christian assembly in a meeting-hall rented for that purpose,[228] the most natural construction of Paul's language suggests that Gaius placed his own house at the disposal of the Christian community: the distributive force of the articular noun ὁ ξένος implies that Gaius hosted the assembly in the same place where Paul enjoyed his hospitality.[229] As for the kind of hospitality which Gaius extended to the Christian community, Paul's use of the expression ὅλη ἡ ἐκκλησία elsewhere in the Corinthian correspondence (1 Cor. 14:23) proves determinative: Gaius hosted the Corinthian Christians when they came together in common assembly, principally and primarily, to eat the Lord's Supper (1 Cor. 11:17–22).[230] This common assembly was a larger gathering of several sub-groups or house-churches, designated by the formula "the church in the house of X."[231] This conclusion, which is widely held by scholars,[232] has significant implications for our assessment of the social status of Gaius and his relationship to his fellow Christians. As Peter

---

225 It is impossible to determine precisely when Gaius became "the host of the whole *ekklesia*" at Corinth. Meeks (*First Urban Christians*, 76) speculates, plausibly, that "Gaius, before he became "host…of the whole church" (Rom. 16:23), was probably host of one of the household groups."
226 Theissen, *Social Setting*, 89; Malherbe, *Social Aspects*, 73–74; Meeks, *First Urban Christians*, 57–58; Murphy-O'Connor, *Paul*, 267.
227 LSJ 1189 s.v. ξένος I.2; Stählin, "ξένος, κτλ.," *TDNT* 5 (1967) 20; Theissen, *Social Setting*, 89; Dunn, *Romans 9–16*, 910–11.
228 As suggested by de Vos, *Church and Community Conflicts*, 204.
229 Theissen, "The Social Structure of Pauline Communities," 83.
230 Theissen, *Social Setting*, 89, 96; Klauck, *Hausgemeinde und Hauskirche*, 34; Meeks, *First Urban Christians*, 67–68, 75; Collins, *First Corinthians*, 508–509.
231 Banks, *Paul's Idea of Community*, 38–39; Murphy-O'Connor, *St. Paul's Corinth*, 158; Klauck, *Hausgemeinde und Hauskirche*, 39; Meeks, *First Urban Christians*, 75; Ebel, *Die Gemeinde von Korinth im Spiegel griechisch-römischer Vereine*, 153.
232 E.g., Theissen, *Social Setting*, 89; Malherbe, *Social Aspects*, 74 n.28; Meeks, *First Urban Christians*, 76, 143, 147; Murphy-O'Connor, *Paul*, 267; Balch, "Paul, Families, and Households," 260.

Lampe observes, we know of only one person in the early church who hosted all the Christians of a given city in his house as a central meeting place—Gaius of Corinth.[233] Indeed, Wayne Meeks had already noted the unusual role played by Gaius in hosting "the whole church" in a given city: "Gaius's role was unusual enough for Paul to single it out when mentioning him to the Roman Christians; it may have been unique."[234] Even Steven Friesen, who places all of the Pauline Christians on a "poverty scale," acknowledges that Gaius must have had "a larger house than others, which makes him perhaps the wealthiest person we know of from Paul's assemblies."[235] Thus, we may now seek to extrapolate the further implications of Gaius' role as "host of the whole *ekklesia*," not only in terms of his social status, but also, and more importantly, with respect to his relationships with his fellow Christians, with Paul, and with other Christian missionaries.

How many persons might have enjoyed Gaius' hospitality at meetings of "the whole *ekklesia*"? The question is obviously crucial for an assessment of Gaius' status and role in the Christian community. If the total number of Christians at Corinth were small, then Gaius might have accommodated this group in domestic quarters above a workshop, or in a room in an apartment building. But if the assembly were large, then we must look to a *domus*, and a rather spacious one, at that. As observed above, consideration has been given to this question by Jerome Murphy-O'Connor, among others.[236] Our object here is merely to review the calculations of these scholars and to supplement their conclusions with inferences from exegesis.

Murphy-O'Connor identified 14 male members of the Christian community at Corinth, on the basis of names mentioned in Paul's epistles.[237] Assuming that each of these individuals was married, like Aquila,

---

233 Peter Lampe, *From Paul to Valentinus: Christians at Rome in the First Two Centuries* (Minneapolis: Fortress Press, 2003) 192 n.26; idem "Paul, Patrons, and Clients" in *Paul in the Greco-Roman World*, ed. J. Paul Sampley (Harrisburg: Trinity Press International, 2003) 496.
234 Meeks, *First Urban Christians*, 221 n.7.
235 Friesen, "Poverty in Pauline Studies," 356.
236 Murphy-O'Connor, *St. Paul's Corinth*, 156, 158; Schreiber, *Die Gemeinde in Korinth*, 30–34; Theissen, *Social Setting*, 94–95; Osiek and Balch, *Households and House Churches*, 201–203; Balch, "Paul, Families, and Households," 259–60; de Vos, *Church and Community Conflicts*, 203–204.
237 Murphy-O'Connor, *St. Paul's Corinth*, 156; cf. Theissen, *Social Setting*, 94–95.

Murphy-O'Connor reached a minimum figure of 28 persons.[238] But in the case of Crispus (Acts 18:8) and Stephanas (1 Cor. 1:16), we are told that the entire "household" was baptized along with them. The Greco-Roman household was a much larger social unit than the modern nuclear family: a household might include slaves, hired workers, freedmen, friends, and lodgers, in addition to the owner and his extended family.[239] Even the household of Stephanas, a shopkeeper or merchant, as may be, might have consisted of 10 individuals, of whom two, Fortunatus and Achaicus, are known to us by name (1 Cor. 16:17).[240] Paul's way of referring to "Chloe's people" (οἱ Χλοής) probably implies that her entire household was Christian, as well.[241] There is no reason to doubt that Gaius and Erastus would also have brought their households along with them; indeed, it is difficult to imagine that family members and dependents of men such as these could have refused to share the religious affiliation of their *paterfamilias*, given the hierarchical organization of the Roman household, and the role of religion in sustaining that hierarchy.[242] Andrew Wallace-Hadrill has emphasized the close correlation between wealth and household size: the wealthy generally maintained larger households.[243] Wallace-Hadrill pictures the wealthy householder in his atrium house with his wife, children, and slaves, "surrounded by a great penumbra of persons of varied status,...a fluctuating assortment of dependents."[244] In such cases, Wallace-Hadrill urges, it is more accurate to speak

---

238 Murphy-O'Connor, *St. Paul's Corinth*, 156.
239 Judge, *The Social Pattern of the Christian Groups in the First Century*, 30–39, repr. in idem, *Social Distinctives of the Christians*, 20–27; P. R. C. Weaver, *Familia Caesaris: A Social Study of the Emperor's Freedmen and Slaves* (Cambridge: Cambridge University Press, 1972); Malherbe, *Social Aspects*, 69; Meeks, *First Urban Christians*, 30; Wallace-Hadrill, *Houses and* Society, 91–117.
240 Meeks, *First Urban Christians*, 75, 119; Collins, *First Corinthians*, 73–75; de Vos, *Church and Community Conflicts*, 204 n.98: "In the case of both Stephanas (1 Cor. 1:16) and Crispus (Acts 18:8), their households are also said to have been 'converted'. Assuming moderate numbers of slaves, and that the bulk of the households were included in the church, a number in the order of 12–15 is possible."
241 Meeks, *First Urban Christians*, 217 n.54.
242 Meeks, *First Urban Christians*, 76; Paul Veyne, *A History of Private Life: From Pagan Rome to Byzantium* (Cambridge, MA: Harvard University Press, 1987) 27, 30–31; Richard P. Saller, "*Pietas* and *patria potestas*: obligation and power in the Roman household" in idem, *Patriarchy, Property and Death in the Roman Family* (Cambridge: Cambridge University Press, 1997) 102–32.
243 Wallace-Hadrill, *Houses and Society*, 92–117.
244 Wallace-Hadrill, *Houses and Society*, 12.

of "housefuls."[245] Accordingly, it is not unreasonable to think that the households of the wealthiest Christians at Corinth—Crispus, Gaius, and Erastus—might have consisted of 20 persons.[246] Limiting our calculation to named individuals and their dependents, it would seem that the base figure of 50 persons posited by Murphy-O'Connor is far too low.[247] Moreover, we must make allowances for a number of individuals and house-hold groups whom Paul does not mention by name.[248] A more accurate estimate of the size of the Christian community at Corinth would approach 100.[249] If this total seems surprisingly large,[250] we should remind ourselves that the membership of the Dionysiac association which Pompeia Agrippinilla established in her household in Tusculum, attested by a well-known inscription, numbered nearly 400 in all.[251]

In what sort of dwelling might Gaius have hosted meetings of "the whole *ekklesia*"? Three venues have been considered by scholars: the apartment building (*insula*), residential quarters (*cenacula*) above a workshop, and the house (*domus*).[252] The first of these may be treated briefly. Space to accommodate large assemblies existed in apartment buildings

---

245 Wallace-Hadrill, *Houses and Society*, 92.
246 *BGU* I.115, a census return from Arsinoe for the year 187 A.D.: the household consists of 20 related family members, as well as 7 other persons associated with the household; see Donald Charles Barker, "Household Patterns in the Roman Empire, with Special Reference to Egypt" (PhD diss., Macquarie University, 1994).
247 Murphy-O'Connor, *St. Paul's Corinth*, 158. See the critique of Murphy-O'Connor's estimate by Balch, "Rich Pompeiian Houses," 28.
248 de Vos, *Church and Community Conflicts*, 203–204.
249 de Vos, *Church and Community Conflicts*, 204 n.98: "a number in the order of 100 is not unreasonable"; Lindemann, *Der erste Korintherbrief*, 13: "Eine der deraus zu ziehenden Schlussfolgerungen muss wohl lauten, dass man sich die korinthische Kirche zur Zeit der Abfassung des 1 Kor als zahlenmässig nicht allzu klein vorstellen darf; die Gemeinde kann kaum weniger als etwa einhundert Mitglieder gehabt haben, weil sonst die Vielfalt der in Kap. 7 genannten Beziehungen kaum zu erklären ist."
250 Theissen, "The Social Structure of Pauline Communities," 83: "Other clubs in antiquity provide valid comparative figures. They rarely have more than 100 or less than 10 members; most of them comprise 20 to 50 members," appealing to Schmeller, *Hierarchie und Egalität*, 40.
251 *IGR* 160; Achille Vogliano, "Le grand iscrizione Bacchia del Metropolitan Musuem," *AJA* 37 (1933) 215–31; Meeks, *First Urban Christians*, 31, 205 n.143; B. H. McLean, "The Agrippinilla Inscription: Religious Associations and Early Church Formation" in idem, *Origins and Method: Towards a New Understanding of Judaism and Christianity* (Sheffield: Sheffield Academic Press, 1993) 239–70.
252 Balch, "Rich Pompeiian Houses," 27–46.

like those of Ostia and Herculaneum.[253] The *insulae* of Ostia have internal courtyards,[254] and the apartment building in Herculaneum's Insula Orientalis II has a palestra-gymnasium.[255] Robert Jewett has proposed the apartment building as a meeting place for Pauline "tenement churches" in his analysis of 2 Thessalonians 3:10.[256] It is attractive to imagine the Christians of Corinth coming, in the early evening, from the many shops and industries on the street level of an *insula*—the dye-works, the baker's shop, the fullery, etc.—and assembling in the courtyard of the building to eat the Lord's Supper. Wallace-Hadrill has argued that such dense blocks of shops and flats were valuable sources of rental income for the proprietors of the *domus*, in association with which these edifices were erected in urban neighborhoods, like the Termini quarter of Rome.[257] Might Gaius have hosted the whole *ekklesia* in the courtyard of such an apartment building? The problem with this attractive hypothesis has been clearly stated by David Horrell: "there is no archaeological evidence in Corinth for the existence of *insulae* in the sense of multi-storied blocks of five or more floors, such as are known from Rome, Ostia, and Herculaneum."[258] Evidently, the demographic pressures which led to the construction of *insulae* at Rome and elsewhere did not exist in Roman Corinth.[259]

---

253 Amedeo Maiuri, *Ercolano: I nuovi scavi (1927–1958)* (Rome: Instituto Poligrafico dello Strato, 1958) 1.113–43; J. J. Deiss, *Herculaneum: Italy's Buried Treasure* (Malibu: J. Paul Getty Museum, 1989) 114–15, 149–53.
254 James E. Packer, *The Insulae of Imperial Ostia* (Rome: American Academy in Rome, 1971); cf. Balch, "Rich Pompeiian Houses," 34.
255 Maiuri, *Ercolano*, 1.113–43, 449; Mario Pagano, *Herculaneum: A Reasoned Archaeological Itinerary* (Naples: T & M, 2000) 88–91.
256 Robert Jewett, "Tenement Churches and Communal Meals in the Early Church: The Implications of a Form-Critical Analysis of 2 Thess. 3:10," *BR* 38 (1993) 63–83.
257 Andrew Wallace-Hadrill, *"Domus* and *Insulae* in Rome: Families and Housefuls" in *Early Christian Families in Context: An Interdisciplinary Dialogue*, ed. Carolyn Osiak and David Balch (Grand Rapids: Eerdmans, 2003) 3–18.
258 Horrell, "Domestic Space and Christian Meetings at Corinth," 361; similarly, Dirk Jongkind, "Corinth in the First Century AD: The Search for Another Class," *TynBul* 52 (2001) 141–42; see further Mortimer Wheeler, *Roman Art and Architecture* (London: Thames and Hudson, 1964) 129–32; A. J. Brothers, "Urban Housing" in *Roman Domestic Buildings*, ed. Ian M. Barton (Exeter: University of Exeter Press, 1996) 33–64.
259 Mary E. Hoskins Walbank, *The Nature and Development of Roman Corinth to the End of the Antonine Period* (Ph.D. diss., Open University, London, 1986) 315; Horrell, "Domestic Space and Christian Meetings at Corinth," 361.

At Corinth, workshops seem to have provided a significant source of domestic housing for those who worked in them, either in apartments above the shop, or in the workshop itself.²⁶⁰ David Horrell has called attention to a series of contiguous shops along the east side of East Theater Street in Corinth, as possible spaces for the meeting of the Pauline *ekklesia*.²⁶¹ The archaeologist Charles K. Williams has determined that Buildings 1 and 3 in this series were constructed early in the first century A.D., and then were rebuilt and modified following the earthquake of 77 A.D.²⁶² The ground floor of both buildings seems to have been devoted to the preparation of foods, perhaps in large part for the enjoyment of theater crowds.²⁶³ The discovery of extensive fragments of collapsed frescoes amidst the debris on the floor of Building 3 led Williams to the conclusion that this shop must have had at least one upper storey in which a family resided.²⁶⁴ The well-executed scheme of frescoes consists of a series of yellow ochre panels, each framed by slender Corinthian columns, at the center of which stands a single bird on a twig facing left.²⁶⁵ Williams surmised: "The yellow-ground fresco suggests some sort of large room or, at least, a large unfenestrated wall in a room that would probably have

---

260 Jerome Murphy-O'Connor, "A City Workshop" in *St. Paul's Corinth: Texts and Archaeology*, 3ʳᵈ rev. and expanded ed. (Collegeville: Liturgical Press, 2002) 194–96; Horrell, "Domestic Space and Christian Meetings at Corinth," 361; see, in general, Simon P. Ellis, *Roman Housing* (London: Duckworth, 2000) 78–80.
261 Horrell, "Domestic Space and Christian Meetings at Corinth," 361–69.
262 Charles K. Williams and O. H. Zervos, "Corinth, 1985: East of the Theater," *Hesperia* 55 (1986) 129–75; Charles K. Williams and O. H. Zervos, "Corinth, 1987: South of Temple E and East of the Theater," *Hesperia* 57 (1988) 95–146.
263 Williams and Zervos, "Corinth, 1985: East of the Theater," 131, 132, 135, 146–48.
264 Williams and Zervos, "Corinth, 1985: East of the Theater," 134, 139–42, 147–48. Williams has evidently revised his view of the evidence for a second story above Building 3: "the wall with yellow-ground fresco decoration, which initially had been thought to have collapsed from the second floor of Building 3 in reality had decorated the north wall of a ground-floor room of Builing 5, which had been constructed above the terrace wall against which Building 3 had stood"; quoted in Daniel N. Schowalter, "Seeking Shelter in Roman Corinth: Archaeology and the Placement of Paul's Communities" in *Corinth in Context: Comparative Studies on Religion and Society*, ed. Steven J. Friesen, Daniel N. Schowalter, and James C. Walters (Leiden: Brill, 2010) 334 n.20.
265 Williams and Zervos, "Corinth, 1985: East of the Theater," 140; see also Laura M. Gadbery, "Roman wall-painting at Corinth: new evidence from east of the Theater" in *The Corinthia in the Roman Period*, ed. Timothy E. Gregory (Ann Arbor: University of Michigan Press, 1993) 47–64, esp. 49–54.

been more than a *cubiculum*."[266] In an upper storey room such as this, David Horrell has sought to picture meetings of the Pauline *ekklesia*.[267] Horrell observes how well this scenario correlates with Luke's account of a meeting at Troas in an upper-storey room (ὑπερῷον), from the window-ledge of which Eutychus fell to his death (Acts 20:9).[268]

Again, we are presented with an attractive hypothesis. Perhaps it was in such a room above their workshop that the artisans Prisca and Aquila hosted meetings of "the church in their house" (1 Cor. 16:19; Rom. 16:3–5).[269] Nor should we be surprised that a successful artisan would be able to afford the luxury of a wall-painting: frescoes adorned the walls of other shops along East Theater Street,[270] and the walls of *cenacula* above shops in Herculaneum were nicely decorated.[271] The problem with imagining a room above a workshop as the meeting place for "the whole *ekklesia*" is simply one of space. Horrell acknowledges that it would have been very crowded in the upper room of Building 3, which he calculates as measuring approximately 10 x 5 meters.[272] This is on the assumption of 50 persons as participants.[273] It would have been impossible to cram 100 persons (in our view, the more realistic figure) into the space available. Moreover, domestic space above a workshop is not easily imaginable as an architectural context for the σχίσματα that arose when the *ekklesia* came together to celebrate the Lord's Supper (1 Cor. 11:18), as Horrell, again, concedes.[274] Finally, one might ask whether the patronal role that we have inferred for the wrongdoer in relation to Paul's apostolic rivals, on the basis of our exegesis of 2 Cor. 11:7–21,[275] is really consistent with the financial resources of a shopkeeper, like the butchers of East Theater Street?[276]

---

266 Williams and Zervos, "Corinth, 1985: East of the Theater," 140.
267 Horrell, "Domestic Space and Christian Meetings at Corinth," 368–69.
268 Horrell, "Domestic Space and Christian Meetings at Corinth," 368.
269 Murphy-O'Connor, *St. Paul's Corinth*, 192–98; Horrell, "Domestic Space and Christian Meetings at Corinth," 367.
270 Gadbery, "Roman wall-painting at Corinth," 54–64; Jongkind, "Corinth in the First Century AD," 143, 147.
271 Wallace-Hadrill, *Houses and Society*, 103, 106, 108, 116, 175, 179; Balch, "Typical Spaces for Pauline House Churches," 34–37.
272 Horrell, "Domestic Space and Christian Meetings at Corinth," 365, 367–68.
273 Horrell, "Domestic Space and Christian Meetings at Corinth," 368.
274 Horrell, "Domestic Space and Christian Meetings at Corinth," 350, 367, referencing Murphy-O'Connor, *St. Paul's Corinth*, 180, 182–184.
275 See above, ch. 3, pp. 132–39.
276 Williams and Zervos, "Corinth, 1985: East of the Theater," 146–48.

So, we return to the *domus* as the most likely place in which Gaius hosted meetings of "the whole *ekklesia*." In the *domus* we find the space necessary to accommodate the numbers to which a reasonable calculation of persons and households has led us. Houses in Roman cities of the Imperial period varied greatly in size. The well preserved ruins of Pompeii permit us to form a clear image of that variety: alongside large, luxury villas are hundreds of medium-sized and smaller residences.[277] In a palatial mansion, such as the House of the Faun, with its two *atria* and two gardens, one of which is a large peristyle, hundreds of visitors could have been accommodated.[278] The house of the well-to-do freedman A. Vettius Conviva would also have provided ample space, not only in the *triclinium*, but also in the peristyle, which is surrounded by three reception rooms, one of which is large.[279] Even a *domus* of modest dimensions, such as the Casa dell' Ara Massima, might have accommodated a sizeable number of persons in the several rooms off of its colorful *atrium*, and in rooms on the upper floor.[280] As Paul Zanker observes: "If we take the houses in Pompeii as a guide, even 'middle-class' houses provided luxurious amounts of space—at least by modern standards."[281] These observations are based upon the houses of Pompeii, a medium-sized town in Italy.[282] But recent studies of Greek houses on Delos and in Pergamon reveal a similar generosity of space: houses built or remodeled in the early Roman period incorpo-

---

[277] Wallace-Hadrill, *Houses and Society*, 72–87; Paul Zanker, *Pompeii: Public and Private Life* (Cambridge, MA: Harvard University Press, 1998) 3–5, 12–20; Osiek and Balch, *Households and House Churches*, 14–17.

[278] Adolf Hoffmann and Mariette de Vos, "Casa del Fauno" in *Pompei e Mosaici*, ed. Ida Baldassare (Rome: Istituto della Enciclopedia Italiana, 1994) 5.80–141, esp. 80–82; Wallace-Hadrill, *Houses and Society*, 21, 26, 86, 107; Mark Grahame, "Public and private in the Roman house: investigating the social order of the Casa del Fauno" in *Domestic Space in the Roman World: Pompeii and Beyond*, ed. Ray Laurence and Andrew Wallace-Hadrill (Portsmouth, RI: Journal of Roman Archaeology, 1997) 137–164; Balch, "Typical Spaces for Pauline House Churches," 30.

[279] Valeria Sampaolo, "Casa dei Vettii" in *Pompei e Mosaici*, ed. Ida Baldassare (Rome: Istituto della Enciclopedia Italiana, 1994) 5.468–572; Wallace-Hadrill, *Houses and Society*, 39, 58.

[280] Klaus Stemmer, *Casa dell' Ara Massima* (Munich: Hirmer Verlag, 1992); idem, "Casa dell' Ara massima" in *Pompei e Mosaici*, ed. Ida Baldassare (Rome: Istituto della Enciclopedia Italiana, 1994) 5.847–886.

[281] Zanker, *Pompeii*, 10–11.

[282] Zanker, *Pompeii*, 4.

rated peristyle courtyards and large dining halls,[283] evidence of the influence of Roman culture upon the domestic architecture of Greece and Asia Minor.[284]

In addition to size, the flexibility of the space available within the *domus* represents an advantage over other locations, in consideration of the needs of the early Christian community, especially in the celebration of the Lord's Supper. In his study of kitchens and dining rooms at Pompeii, Pedar Foss observes that, by a simple change of furniture, many rooms might be converted into dining spaces;[285] as a result, numbers of persons might dine simultaneously.[286] A similar conclusion emerges from Katherine Dunbabin's examination of convivial spaces in the Roman villa: dining was not confined to rooms specifically designed for that purpose; moveable furniture could be set up at will, indoors and out.[287]

Moreover, a trend toward the proliferation of space devoted to dining is clearly observable in houses of the Imperial period.[288] Wallace-Hadrill quips, "Trimalchio's boast of four *cenationes* is by no means immodest to judge from the Campanian remains."[289] The Casa del Menandro in Pompeii has five major reception rooms distributed around its peristyle, the largest of which seems to have served for dining, judging from its situation on a wing of the peristyle.[290] Similarly, Roman-era houses on Delos

---

283 Monica Trümper, *Wohnen in Delos: Eine baugeschichtliche Untersuchung zum Wandel der Wohnkultur in hellenistischer Zeit* (Rahden and Westfalen: Marie Leidorf, 1998) 152–155; Ulrike Wulf-Rheidt, "The Hellenistic and Roman Houses of Pergamon" in *Pergamon, Citadel of the Gods: Archaeological Record, Literary Description, and Religious Development*, ed. Helmut Koester (Harrisburg: Trinity Press International, 1998) 301–314; cf. Balch, "Paul, Families, and Households," 262–65.
284 Trümper, *Wohnen in Delos*, 153–54; Michele George, "Domestic Architecture and Household Relations: Pompeii and Roman Ephesos," *JSNT* 27 (2004) 15–23.
285 Pedar William Foss, "Kitchens and Dining Rooms at Pompeii: The Spatial and Social Relationship of Cooking to Eating in the Roman Household" (Ph.D. diss., University of Michigan, 1994) 144–45.
286 Foss, "Kitchens and Dining Rooms at Pompeii," 86; cf. Osiek and Balch, *Households and House Churches*, 201–202.
287 Katherine M. D. Dunbabin, "Convivial spaces: dining and entertainment in the Roman villa," *Journal of Roman Archaeology* 9 (1996) 66–80, esp. 67–68.
288 Dunbabin, "Convivial spaces," 68, 70; Wallace-Hadrill, *Houses and Society in Pompeii and Herculaneum*, 52.
289 Wallace-Hadrill, *Houses and Society*, 52, citing Petronius *Sat.* 77.
290 Wallace-Hadrill, *Houses and Society*, 54.

have three or more rooms which open directly onto the courtyard, often decorated with mosaics, wall-paintings, and marble.[291] Houses in Pergamon have summer and winter *triclinia*, and a variety of smaller, adjoining rooms arrayed around the courtyard.[292]

Finally, the distribution of space within the *domus* permits us to make good sense of Paul's account of the group dynamics which developed when the whole church met to celebrate the Lord's Supper (1 Cor. 11:17–34). When Murphy-O'Connor first examined the house as a context for Christian meetings a generation ago, he readily grasped that the architectural plan of the typical Roman *domus* would have structured and heightened the class distinctions between the "haves" and the "have-nots" (1 Cor. 11:22).[293] Because only nine spaces were available in the *triclinium*,[294] the majority of the congregation—slaves and the poor—would have been obliged to find places in the *atrium* or the garden, while the host, Gaius, reclined intimately with a few social equals, as was the custom.[295] The hypothesis that the Corinthian Christians made use of a house for their assembly furnishes the best explanation of the divisions that arose when they met to celebrate the Lord's Supper.

Before we seek to imagine Gaius in his house at Corinth as host of the Christian assembly, it is important to identify two respects in which the Roman house differed dramatically from our modern houses. First, the Roman house was *public* in a way that our houses are not. Paul Zanker observes: "Our homes are private spaces, in which we live for the most part in nuclear families, screened from the public gaze in every sense…The Roman house, by contrast, was a center of social communication and a pointed demonstration of the occupants' standing."[296] Wallace-Hadrill, similarly, notices: "the Roman house was a constant focus of public life. It was where a public figure not only received his dependents

---

291 Trümper, *Wohnen in Delos*, 86, 152; cf. Balch, "Paul, Families, and Households," 262.
292 Wulf-Rheidt, "The Hellenistic and Roman Houses of Pergamon," 304, 309.
293 Murphy-O'Connor, *St. Paul's Corinth*, 158–59.
294 Katherine M. D. Dunbabin, *"Triclinium* and *Stibadium"* in *Dining in a Classical Context*, ed. W. J. Slater (Ann Arbor: University of Michigan, 1991) 121–48, esp. 127.
295 Murphy-O'Connor, *St. Paul's Corinth*, 159; followed by Peter Lampe, "Das korinthische Herrenmahl im Schnittpunkt hellenistisch-römischer Mahlpraxis und paulinischer Theologia Crucis (1 Kor 11,17–34)," *ZNW* 82 (1991) 183–213, esp. 197, 201; Osiek and Balch, *Households and House Churches*, 200–203.
296 Zanker, *Pompeii*, 10.

Chapter Five. Prosopography

and friends, but conducted business of all sorts. His house was a powerhouse; it was where the network of social contacts that provided the underpinning for his activities outside the house was generated and activated."[297] The determinants of the difference between our modern homes and the Roman house, with respect to public and private space, are clearly delineated by these quotations. First, "the Romans lacked our distinction of place of work (office, factory, etc.) from place of leisure (home). Business was regularly conducted at home."[298] Second, the Roman house advertised the social status of its occupants by the way in which it put its occupants, and especially its proprietor, on display.[299] Consequently, the houses of the elite were typically located in the center of town, rather than in the suburbs,[300] and, under ordinary circumstances, stood open to the public during the day,[301] with access controlled by a doorkeeper.[302] The architecture invited passers-by to look deeply into the interior of the house, along a visual axis that ran from the threshold of the entrance passage, over the rectangular light-well of the *atrium*, to the square opening of the *tablinum*, where the owner of the house was displayed, as if on a stage, conducting his business before an ornamental marble table, beyond which a vista opened into the peristyle garden, with its balanced columns.[303] Through the hours of the day, a crowd of callers came and went from the house: clients waited in the *atrium* for a morning audience, or came to the *tablinum* seeking the proprietor's advice or assistance; craftsmen and shopkeepers, who operated out of the workshops or taverns that

---

297 Wallace-Hadrill, *Houses and Society*, 12.
298 Wallace-Hadrill, *Houses and Society*, 47; see also Zanker, *Pompeii*, 10–11.
299 Wallace-Hadrill, *Houses and Society*, 51, 59; idem, "Patronage in Roman society; from republic to empire" in *Patronage in Ancient Society*, ed. A. Wallace-Hadrill (London: Routledge, 1989) 63–64; Zanker, *Pompeii*, 12–13; Timothy Peter Wiseman, "*Conspicui postes tectaque digna deo:* the public image of aristocratic and imperial houses in the late Republic and Early Empire" in *L'Urbs: espace urbain et histoire (1er siècle av. J.-C. – IIIe siècle ap. J.-C.)* (Rome: Ecole francaise de Rome, 1987) 393–413.
300 Wallace-Hadrill, *Houses and Society*, 118, 119, 121; Zanker, *Pompeii*, 10.
301 Wallace-Hadrill, *Houses and Society*, 5; Ray Laurence, *Roman Pompeii: Space and Society* (London: Routledge, 1994) 88; Zanker, *Pompeii*, 10; Osiek and Balch, *Households and House Churches*, 24–25.
302 Wallace-Hadrill, *Houses and Society*, 3, 39; Laurence, *Roman Pompeii*, 88; Osiek and Balch, *Households and House Churches*, 25.
303 Wallace-Hadrill, "Patronage in Roman society," 63–64; idem, *Houses and Society*, 51; Zanker, *Pompeii*, 10–13; Osiek and Balch, *Households and House Churches*, 25.

lined the street, were part of the routine business of the house; in the afternoon, friends might come to dinner in the *triclinium*, or in one of the reception rooms that surrounded the garden peristyle.[304] When one comprehends the function of the house in Roman society, the reason for its public character becomes clear: from the ability of the proprietor to exploit the openness of his house to the outside world, the householder derived his profit, power, and status.[305]

A second respect in which the Roman house differed from our modern houses was in its greater *social heterogeneity*.[306] Social diversity was especially characteristic of the large house of the *atrium*-peristyle variety.[307] Among the most alienating features of life in our post-industrial cities is the physical separation of the rich from the poor: the poor majority live crowded into small houses and apartment buildings in the slums, while a rich minority luxuriates in spacious houses in exclusive neighborhoods. But in the large Roman house, slaves and clients lived side-by-side with their wealthy patron.[308] Wallace-Hadrill concludes his study of houses and society in Pompeii and Herculaneum with the observation: "We have seen, not so much a gulf between 'rich families' and 'poor families,' but the promiscuity of the big household, in which rich and poor inhabit the same spaces, separated by social rituals rather than physical environment."[309] Consequently, the poor were to be found in great numbers in large *atrium* houses, a situation which seems paradoxical from a modern perspective.[310] Because the areas open to visitors in a Roman house offered little or no privacy, there would have been more occasions for social

---

304 Andrew Wallace-Hadrill, "Houses and Households: Sampling Pompeii and Herculaneum" in *Marriage, Divorce and Children in Ancient Rome*, ed. Beryl Rawson (Oxford: Clarendon Press, 1991) 217–18; idem, *Houses and Society*, 12; Ray Laurence, "The Temporal Logic of Space" in idem, *Roman Pompeii: Space and Society* (London: Routledge, 1994) 122–32; Zanker, *Pompeii*, 12–13.
305 Wallace-Hadrill, *Houses and Society*, 59, 118.
306 Wallace-Hadrill, *Houses and Society*, 103, 141–42, 185–86; Osiek and Balch, *Households and House Churches*, 23.
307 Wallace-Hadrill, "Houses and Households," 217–18; idem, *Houses and Society*, 117.
308 Wallace-Hadrill, "Houses and Households," 217–18; idem, *Houses and Society*, 103; Osiek and Balch, *Households and House Churches*, 23.
309 Wallace-Hadrill, *Houses and Society*, 185–86.
310 Wallace-Hadrill, *Houses and Society*, 45–47; 103, 141; cf. Balch, "Paul, Families, and Households," 259.

interchange in houses than in apartment buildings.³¹¹ Zanker observes: "In the central 'access' spaces, the *atrium* and peristyle, any of the people in the house might encounter one another. Their awareness of these comings and goings, the large number of adjacent rooms, and the varied tasks performed throughout the day inevitably turned the house of a large family into a site of intense social activity."³¹²

Given all the advantages of the *domus* as a space for meetings of the first Christians at Corinth, we must ask ourselves why scholars have moved away from the house as a venue, and have sought to imagine other contexts in which Gaius might have hosted the assembly—the meeting-hall of a guild,³¹³ or residential quarters above a workshop.³¹⁴ The answer to this question lies, for the most part, in the poverty of domestic archaeology at Corinth. In his survey of 1979, the archaeologist James Wiseman reported that only four houses of the Roman period had been excavated at Corinth: the villa at Anaploga, a house attached to Temple E, the Shear villa, and a house located against the east wall of the South Basilica along the road to Cenchreae.³¹⁵ Moreover, it is widely believed that, of the houses which have been excavated, only the villa at Anaploga dates to the time of Paul.³¹⁶ The problems of the Anaploga villa, as an example of the kind of house in which Gaius might have hosted the *ekklesia*, were already identified by Murphy-O'Connor: the space available in the "access" areas of this villa is far too small to have accommodated the whole *ekklesia*, even on a rather conservative estimate of its membership.³¹⁷ The villa at Anaploga has a *triclinium* that measures approximately 5 meters by 9 meters, and an *atrium* of 5 by 6 meters.³¹⁸ As Murphy-O'Connor observed, a gathering of 50 persons in the public spaces of the Anaploga villa would have resulted in "extremely uncom-

---

311 Wallace-Hadrill, *Houses and Society*, 12, 45–47, 60, 118; Zanker, *Pompeii*, 12; Balch, "Paul, Families, and Households," 259; Wallace-Hadrill, *"Domus* and *Insulae* in Rome," 3–18.
312 Zanker, *Pompeii*, 12.
313 de Vos, *Church and Community Conflicts*, 204–205.
314 Horrell, "Domestic Space and Christian Meetings at Corinth," 360–69.
315 Wiseman, "Corinth and Rome I," 528.
316 Wiseman, "Corinth and Rome I," 528; Murphy-O'Connor, *St. Paul's Corinth*, 178; Horrell, "Domestic Space and Christian Meetings at Corinth," 350, 354–55
317 Murphy-O'Connor, *St. Paul's Corinth*, 182–83.
318 Stella Grobel Miller, "A Mosaic Floor from a Roman villa at Anaploga," *Hesperia* 41 (1972) 333; cf. Murphy-O'Connor, *St. Paul's Corinth*, 180; Horrell, "Domestic Space and Christian Meetings at Corinth," 350 n.4.

fortable overcrowding."[319] More recently, David Horrell has called attention to studies of the city plan of Roman Corinth which suggest that "the villa at Anaploga may have lain outside the city walls in Roman times and quite probably functioned as a working farmhouse."[320] Hardly the most plausible context in which to imagine meetings of the first urban Christians!

Despite the fact that archaeology has been ongoing at Corinth for more than a century, little is known about the residential quarters of the city.[321] Excavations have concentrated on the area around the forum, in the theater district, and on the sanctuaries of Demeter and Kore and of Asclepius. As a result, only a handful of houses have been excavated (and these only partially) in a city whose population may have approached 80,000.[322] In our search for a house like that of Gaius at Corinth, we are confronted by the counterpart of a "text-hindered archaeology," lamented by J. T. Smith in his study of Roman villas,[323] namely, that of an "archaeology-hindered interpretation." But surely Carolyn Osiek and David Balch are correct in insisting that we cannot permit our conclusions regarding the size of the house of Gaius to be constrained by the neglect of domestic archaeology at Corinth.[324] If careful exegesis and prosopography of Paul's epistles leads to the conclusion that a number in the order of 100 is not unreasonable as an estimate of the membership of the Christian community at Corinth, then we must assume that a house capable of accommodating such a group existed in Corinth at the time of Paul's visit, if, indeed, we are justified in concluding that a *domus* is the most likely place in which to imagine Gaius hosting meetings of "the whole *ekklesia*." Because of the dearth of domestic archaeology at Corinth, we are obliged to look to the Campanian

---

319 Murphy-O'Connor, *St. Paul's Corinth*, 183.
320 James Wiseman, *The Land of the Ancient Corinthians* (Göteburg: Aström, 1978) 19; idem, "Corinth and Rome I," 497–528; Horrell, "Domestic Space and Christian Meetings at Corinth." 354, referencing Walbank, *The Nature and Development of Roman Corinth*, 323; eadem, "The Foundation and Planning of Early Roman Corinth," *Journal of Roman Archaeology* 10 (1997) 95–130.
321 Jongkind, "Corinth in the First Century AD," 143–44; Horrell, "Domestic Space and Christian Meetings at Corinth," 360.
322 Engels, *Roman Corinth*, 33, 84.
323 J. T. Smith, *Roman Villas: A Study in Social Structure* (London: Routledge, 1997) 6.
324 Osiek and Balch, *Households and House Churches*, 201–203; Balch, "Paul, Families, and Households," 259–60; idem, "Typical Spaces for Pauline House Churches," 28–29.

towns for analogies. The Casa del Menandro in Pompeii, for example, would have accommodated more than three times the estimated number of Corinthian Christians for simultaneous dining in its reception rooms and peristyle.³²⁵ And we must not forget that the Campanian cities, whose well-preserved ruins permit us to make such calculations, were less populous and less prosperous than Roman Corinth.³²⁶

Before we content ourselves with having established the *possibility* that houses of a sufficient size existed at Corinth to accommodate meetings of "the whole *ekklesia*," we should critically evaluate the widely held assumption that only the villa at Anaploga, among the few houses which have been excavated at Corinth, existed in the time of Paul.³²⁷ Is it really the case, as has been alleged, that "none of the other houses of the Roman period (partially) excavated at Corinth yield evidence for the period of Paul's visits to the city"?³²⁸ Is this conclusion borne out by careful examination of the excavation reports? We must pay particular attention to reports of archaeology at Corinth published since Wiseman's survey of 1979, because excavations east of the theater, conducted in the early 1980s, uncovered a large domestic structure whose initial occupation dates within the Julio-Claudian period.³²⁹ In turning our attention to the remains of actual houses at Corinth, we should be sure to state what is obvious: we are not attempting to identify the house of Gaius at Corinth. The purpose of our excursus into Corinthian houses will be served, if, as in the case of our onomastic excursus above, we are able to form a more vivid image of the kind of space in which Gaius hosted meetings of "the whole *ekklesia*."

---

325 John R. Clarke, *The Houses of Roman Italy, 100 B.C. – A.D. 250: Ritual, Space, and Decoration* (Berkeley; University of California Press, 1991) 170–93, esp. 170, 188; cf. Osiek and Balch, *Households and House Churches*, 202.

326 Zanker, *Pompeii*, 20: "Pompeii was by no means an important urban center; it was only one of many medium-sized country towns in Italy."

327 Wiseman, "Corinth and Rome I," 528; Murphy-O'Connor, *St. Paul's Corinth*, 178; Horrell, "Domestic Space and Christian Meetings at Corinth," 350-354-55; cf. Thiselton, *First Epistle*, 860.

328 Horrell, "Domestic Space and Christian Meetings at Corinth," 354–55.

329 Charles K. Williams, "Corinth, 1981: East of the Theater," *Hesperia* 51 (1982)115–63; idem, "Corinth, 1982: East of the Theater," *Hesperia* 52 (1983) 1–47. The house had been partially excavated in 1925 by Theodore Leslie Shear, "Excavations in the Theatre District and Tombs at Corinth in 1929," *American Journal of Archaeology* 33 (1929) 526–28. The omission of the house from Wiseman's survey of 1979 was already noted by Jongkind, "Corinth in the First Century AD," 143 n.26.

Excursus B: Corinthian Houses

We may proceed through the Corinthian houses in order of increasing interest for purposes of exemplification. First, the house adjacent to Temple E. Excavations conducted in 1933 revealed the marble-floored *atrium* of a large house of the early Roman period lying just outside the northwest corner of the *peribolos* of Temple E.[330]

A team of archaeologists from the University of California, under the direction of J. K. Anderson, undertook a further excavation at this site in 1965, in the hope of clarifying the relationship of the house to the temple precinct.[331] The archaeologists found that the *atrium* house stood upon foundations of heavy mortar and rubble, unlike the temple and its *peribolos*, which were built upon masonry foundations, where not supported by solid rock.[332] The different methods of construction suggested to Anderson separate building phases within the early Roman period, leading Anderson to hypothesize that the temple and its precinct were built first, and then the *atrium* house was added later "as an annex of some kind."[333] It seems reasonable to assume that the house was connected with the cult of Temple E, a temple which may have belonged to Augustus' sister Octavia, or more generally to the Imperial cult.[334] Our imagination naturally repopulates

---

330 The excavations were conducted by Sterling Dow; see J. K. Anderson, "Corinth: Temple E Northwest," *Hesperia* 36 (1967) 1, with Fig. 1.
331 J. K. Anderson, "Corinth: Temple E Northwest," *Hesperia* 36 (1967) 1–12; cf. Wiseman, "Corinth and Rome I," 528; Murphy-O'Connor, *St. Paul's Corinth*, 178.
332 Anderson, "Corinth: Temple E Northwest," 3.
333 Anderson, "Corinth: Temple E Northwest," 10.
334 The identification of the temple has been hotly debated: Mary E. Hoskins Walbank, "Pausanias, Octavia and Temple E at Corinth," *Annual of the British School at Athens* 84 (1989) 361–94; Charles K. Williams, "A Re-Evaluation of Temple E and the West End of the Forum of Corinth" in *The Greek Renaissance in the Roman Empire: Papers from the Tenth British Museum Classical Colloquium*, ed. Susan Walker and Averil Cameron (London: University of London Institute of Classical Studies, 1989) 156–62; for further literature, see Nancy Bookidis, "Religion in Corinth: 146 B.C.E. to 100 C.E." in *Urban Religion in Roman Corinth*, ed. Daniel N. Schowalter and Steven J. Friesen (Cambridge, MA: Harvard University Press, 2005) 155–56; Mary E. Hoskins Walbank, "Image and Cult: The Coinage of Roman Corinth" in *Corinth in Context: Comparative Studies on Religion and Society*, ed. Steven J. Friesen, Daniel N. Schowalter, and James C. Walters (Leiden: Brill, 2010) 151–97, esp. 157–59. For evidence of the imperial cult at Corinth in the first century A.D., see esp. Mary E. Hoskins Walbank, "Evidence for the Imperial Cult in Julio-Claudian Corinth" in *Subject and Ruler:*

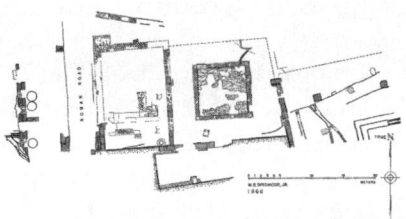

Early Roman House and Northwest Corner of *Peribolos* a Temple E

the house with a priest; but the real function of the house remains uncertain.[335]

Second, the Mosaic House, abutting on the east side of the South Basilica along the road to Cenchreae.[336] Three large rooms, paved with mosaics, were excavated here in 1934, under the direction of Charles Morgan.[337]

The position of this house relative to the South Basilica indicates that it post-dated the construction of the basilica in *circa* 40 A.D.[338] On the basis of a stylistic analysis of the mosaics, Saul Weinberg concluded that the mosaics were the products of the late Antonine or early Severan period, with the evidence favoring a date around 200 A.D.[339] The use of large and small diamond patterns, the choice of a single motif to frame individual panels, and the sharp contrast of light and dark were all features characteristic of mosaics during the Severan period.[340] Weinberg al-

---

The Cult of the Ruling Power in Classical Antiquity, ed. Alastair Small (Ann Arbor: Journal of Roman Archaeology, 1996) 201–14.

335 Anderson, "Corinth: Temple E Northwest," 1–3, 10; Henry S. Robinson, "Excavations at Corinth," *Archaiologikon Deltion* 21 (1966) 135; Jongkind, "Corinth in the First Century AD," 144; Bradley Blue, "Acts and the House Church" in *The Book of Acts in Its Graeco-Roman Setting*, ed. David W. J. Gill and Conrad Gempf (Grand Rapids: Eerdmans, 1994) 160; Horrell, "Domestic Space and Christian Meetings at Corinth," 355 n.27; Bookidis, "Religion in Corinth: 146 B.C.E. to 100 C.E.," 158 n.80.

336 Saul S. Weinberg, *Corinth, Volume I, Part 5: The Southeast Building, the Twin Basilicas, the Mosaic House* (Princeton: The American School of Classical Studies at Athens, 1960) 113–22, with pl. 55–57; cf. Wiseman, "Corinth and Rome I," 528.

337 The preliminary report was published in the *AJA* 39 (1935) 61–62, with pl. XVII.

338 Weinberg, *Corinth I.5: The Mosaic House*, 115.
339 Weinberg, *Corinth I.5: The Mosaic House*, 115.
340 Weinberg, *Corinth I.5: The Mosaic House*, 115–18, 120.

Mosaic House (Weinberg, *Corinth*, vol. 1, plate 53)

lowed that the house to which the mosaics belonged might have been erected before the mosaics were laid;³⁴¹ but, in any case, the Mosaic House is far too late for consideration as the residence of Paul's Gaius.

Third, a villa excavated in 1962–1964 in the district known as Anaploga, west and south of the agora.³⁴² This villa has been the object of exclusive attention by New Testament scholars, both those like Murphy-O'Connor who emphasize its importance for reconstructing the situation in which Gaius hosted "the whole *ekklesia*,"³⁴³ and those like David Horrell who question its plausibility as a setting for the Corinthian Lord's Supper.³⁴⁴ The interest of scholars is understandable, given the date of the villa in the first century A.D.³⁴⁵ But scholars might have taken closer notice of the characterization of the villa in the earliest report by Henry S. Rob-

---

341 Weinberg, *Corinth I.5: The Mosaic House*, 115, 122; cf. Blue, "Acts and the House Church," 161.
342 Henry S. Robinson, "Excavations at Corinth," *Archaiologikon Deltion* 18 (1963) 76–80. A full report on the villa has not been published; cf. S. E. Ramsden, "Roman Mosaics in Greece," *AJA* 83 (1979) 83; Blue, "Acts and the House Church," 157 n.148.
343 Murphy-O'Connor, *St. Paul's Corinth*, 178–82; cf. Thiselton, *First Epistle*, 860.
344 Horrell, "Domestic Space and Christian Meetings at Corinth," 350–57.
345 Robinson, "Excavations at Corinth," 78. The detailed discussion of the chronology of the villa promised by Robinson has not been published. The mosaic was dated to the last quarter of the first century by Miller, "A Mosaic Floor from a Roman Villa at Anaploga," 332, 353. Katherine M. D. Dunbabin, *Mosaics of the Greek and Roman World* (Cambridge: Cambridge University Press, 1999) 210 n.6 suggests "a late first to early second century date" for the mosaic as "more convincing." Cf. Murphy-O'Connor, *St. Paul's Corinth*, 178; Blue, "Acts and the House Church," 160; Horrell, "Domestic Space and Christian Meetings at Corinth," 350, 354.

Excursus B: Corinthian Houses   339

inson, the director of the excavation, as "a building of the first century after Christ which, while of modest size, contained one very pretentious room."³⁴⁶ We have already confronted the limitations which the dimensions of this villa's *triclinium* and *atrium* place upon the number of persons who might have been accommodated; this, together with the probable function of the villa as a working farmhouse, justify the critical questions raised by Horrell.³⁴⁷ But for the broader purpose of exemplification, the superb mosaic floor of the largest room of the villa still merits our attention.

The mosaic is composed of stone and glass *tesserae* depicting still-life scenes upon three central panels surrounded by elaborate borders.³⁴⁸ The panels represent birds plucking at fruit lying on the ground or in baskets, a motif which occurs with variations in many Campanian wall paintings of the Second and Fourth styles.³⁴⁹ The decorative scheme of the border is very complex, including an outer field of interlocked circles, a graceful rinceau enclosing centaurs, flowers and running animals, and an elaborate and colorful meander.³⁵⁰ Most striking is the range of color of the *tesserae*, augmented by the use of a great deal of glass of dark blue, turquoise, yellow and orange.³⁵¹ Stella Miller concluded that "the Anaploga mosaicist, working in the late first century of our era, was heavily influenced by western currents, specifically by the artistic style known from Campanian mosaics and paintings."³⁵² Miller suggested that the mosaicist created the floor with the aid of a sketchbook.³⁵³ For our attempt to form an impression of the kind of domestic setting in which Gaius hosted the Christian assembly, the

---

346 Robinson, "Excavations at Corinth," 78.
347 Horrell, "Domestic Space and Christian Meetings at Corinth," 353–59, raising critical questions about the date of the mosaic, the identification of the rooms, and the function of the villa.
348 Miller, "A Mosaic Floor from a Roman Villa at Anaploga," 338–43.
349 Miller, "A Mosaic Floor from a Roman Villa at Anaploga," 348.
350 Miller, "A Mosaic Floor from a Roman Villa at Anaploga," 344–47.
351 Miller, "A Mosaic Floor from a Roman Villa at Anaploga," 338–40.
352 Miller, "A Mosaic Floor from a Roman Villa at Anaploga," 353. Contrast the judgment of G. Hellenkemper Salies, "Römische Mosaiken im Griechenland," *Bonner Jahrbücher* 186 (1986) 278–79: "Aus dem späten 1. oder dem frühen 2. Jahrhundert dagegen läßt sich dem Mosaik von Anaploga nichts Vergleichbares an die Seite stellen…Es kann somit kein Zweifel bestehen, daß das Mosaik von Anaploga in die Gruppe der reich ornamentierten, sehr bunten Böden des 3. Jahrhunderts gehört, für deren Komposition und Ornamentik Parallelen zu hellenistischen Mosaiken charakteristisch sind."
353 Miller, "A Mosaic Floor from a Roman Villa at Anaploga," 354.

340   Chapter Five. Prosopography

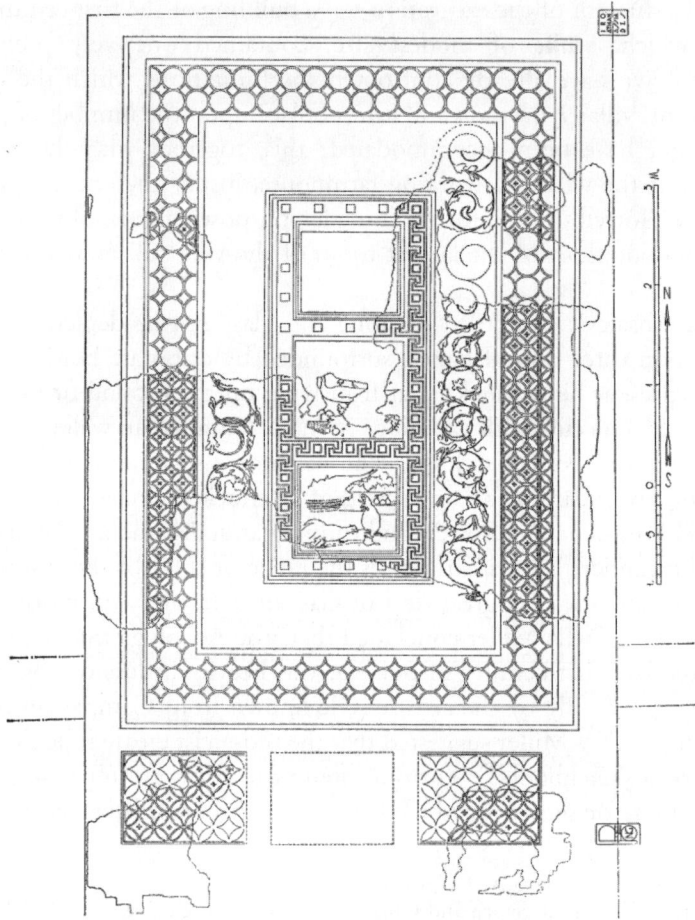

Mosaic Floor, Anaploga Villa

presence of such a fine mosaic in a house of rather modest size is highly suggestive.

The three houses we have surveyed thus far have features which limit their relevance to the situation in which Gaius hosted the Corinthian Christians—whether uncertainty of function, belatedness of construction, or modesty of size. Yet, each of the houses individually, and all of them together, contribute something to our overall conception of the kind of house in which Gaius might have hosted the Christian community: they demonstrate that large houses with marble *atria* and splendid mosaic floors were being constructed at Corinth in the early Roman period. We must remind ourselves that these houses are only partially excavated: only

Excursus B: Corinthian Houses

Anaploga Mosaic Southern Panel

three rooms of the house adjacent to Temple E have been exposed,[354] while only the northernmost rooms of the Mosaic House have been cleared, although scraps of mosaic found in trenches eastward from the remains show that the house extended to the east and the south for some distance.[355] In both cases, the archaeologists describe the houses as "large."[356]

In the cases of two additional houses, to which our attention now turns, few if any factors limit their relevance to the situation of Gaius and the Corinthian Christians: both houses date in the first century A.D., according to their excavators; both houses are large, judging from their remains, and are decorated with frescoes and mosaics; both houses enjoy favorable locations; indeed, the second of the two lies along Decumanus II North, just east of the theater.[357] One is hard-pressed to explain the neglect of these houses by New Testament scholars, except that the publication of the first is somewhat difficult of access,[358] while a detailed report of the excavation of the second was published only in the 1980s.[359]

---

354 Anderson, "Corinth: Temple E Northwest," 3.
355 Weinberg, *Corinth I.5: The Mosaic House*, 113.
356 Anderson, "Corinth: Temple E Northwest," 1; Weinberg, *Corinth I.5: The Mosaic House*, 113.
357 Charles K. Williams and H. O. Zervos, "Corinth, 1981: East of the Theater," *Hesperia* 55 (1986) 118, 128.
358 Theodore Leslie Shear, *Corinth V: The Roman Villa* (Cambridge, MA: Harvard University Press, 1930). This extraordinarily beautiful book, measuring approximately 5 x 3 feet, with copies of the mosaics made in watercolor by Nora Jenkins Shear, was published in a limited edition, accessible in only a few libraries.

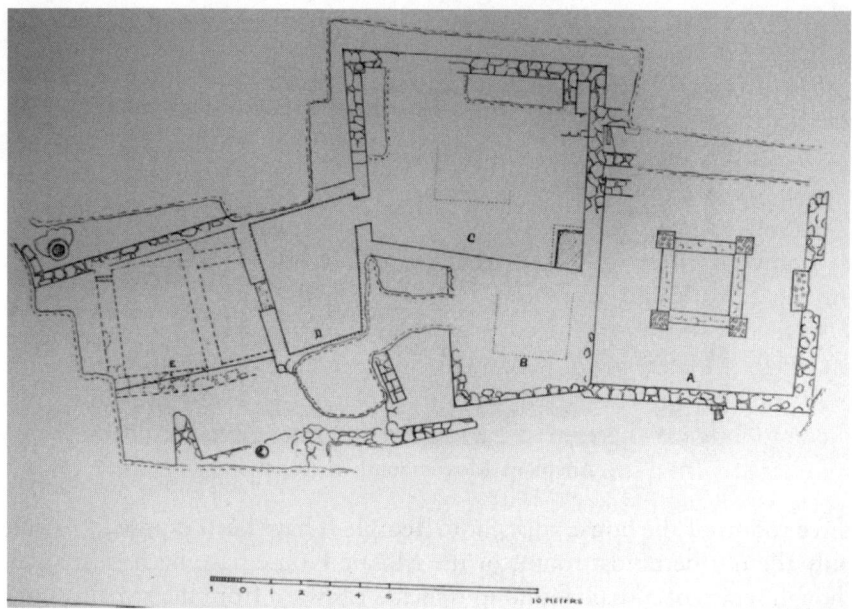

Plan of Shear Villa

The Shear Villa. A kilometer west of the theater, beside the Sicyon road, "a sumptuous Roman villa" was discovered during the excavation season of 1925.[360] Theodore Leslie Shear of Princeton University uncovered five rooms, all paved with mosaic floors of extraordinary beauty and intricacy.[361] The general orientation of the house is from east to west, though little can be said with certainty about the plan of the villa, because part of the house has been destroyed.[362]

---

359 Initial reports of the excavations were published by Theodore Leslie Shear, "Excavations at Corinth in 1925," *AJA* 29 (1925) 381–88; idem, "Excavations in the Theatre District and Tombs at Corinth in 1929," *AJA* 33 (1929) 515–36. Detailed reports awaited renewed excavations by Charles K. Williams and Orestes H. Zervos, "Corinth, 1981: East of the Theater," *Hesperia* 51 (1982) 115–63; Charles K. Williams and Orestes H. Zervos, "Corinth, 1982: East of the Theater," *Hesperia* 52 (1983) 1–47. The house is omitted in discussions by Murphy-O'Connor and Horrell.
360 Shear, "Excavations at Corinth in 1925," 391; idem, *Corinth V: The Roman Villa*, 17.
361 Shear, "Excavations at Corinth in 1925," 391.
362 Shear, *Corinth V: The Roman Villa*, 17.

The discovery of many small pieces of painted stuccoes west of Room B suggested to Shear that another room lay there,[363] while *pithoi* found outside the walls of Room E, in areas to the northwest and the south, indicated the presence of adjoining storerooms.[364] Thus Shear concluded: "It is certain that the house originally consisted of more than the five rooms that are now preserved."[365]

With respect to the function of the surviving rooms, structural and decorative features make possible several identifications. The first room on the east (Room A) Shear designated as the *atrium*, a large room, 7.15 meters square, with a square *impluvium* in its center, at each corner of which stands a column base.[366] The cement floor of the *impluvium* had originally been covered with thin plaques of colored marble, like those found elsewhere in the villa.[367] The interior walls of the room were faced with a low socle of thin marble slabs, above which the surface was covered with painted stucco, decorated in imitation of veined marble.[368] On each side of the *impluvium* lies a mosaic picture, each surrounded by a frame of guilloche pattern with an elaborate meander design.[369] The mosaic on the south side, which is perfectly preserved, shows a herdsman standing beneath an olive tree and playing a flute, while to his right are three oxen, two standing and one lying on the ground.[370]

The mosaic on the east side of the *atrium* depicts a goat reclining under a large tree with spreading branches.[371] The corners of the *atrium* consist of large mosaic squares with alternating patterns: the southeast and northwest corners have diamond shapes, while the remaining corners have circular designs.[372]

Northwest of the *atrium* lies a large room (Room C), 7.05 meters square, which Shear identified as the *triclinium*.[373] In the center of the floor is a mosaic panel depicting Europa on the bull, framed by a series

---

363 Shear, *Corinth V: The Roman Villa*, 17.
364 Shear, *Corinth V: The Roman Villa*, 17.
365 Shear, *Corinth V: The Roman Villa*, 17.
366 Shear, "Excavations at Corinth in 1925," 391.
367 Shear, "Excavations at Corinth in 1925," 391.
368 Shear, *Corinth V: The Roman Villa*, 17.
369 Shear, "Excavations at Corinth in 1925," 391.
370 Shear, "Excavations at Corinth in 1925," 391–92. On the pictorial composition of the mosaic, see Dunbabin, *Mosaics of the Greek and Roman World*, 212.
371 Shear, "Excavations at Corinth in 1925," 393.
372 Shear, "Excavations at Corinth in 1925," 393.
373 Shear, "Excavations at Corinth in 1925," 393.

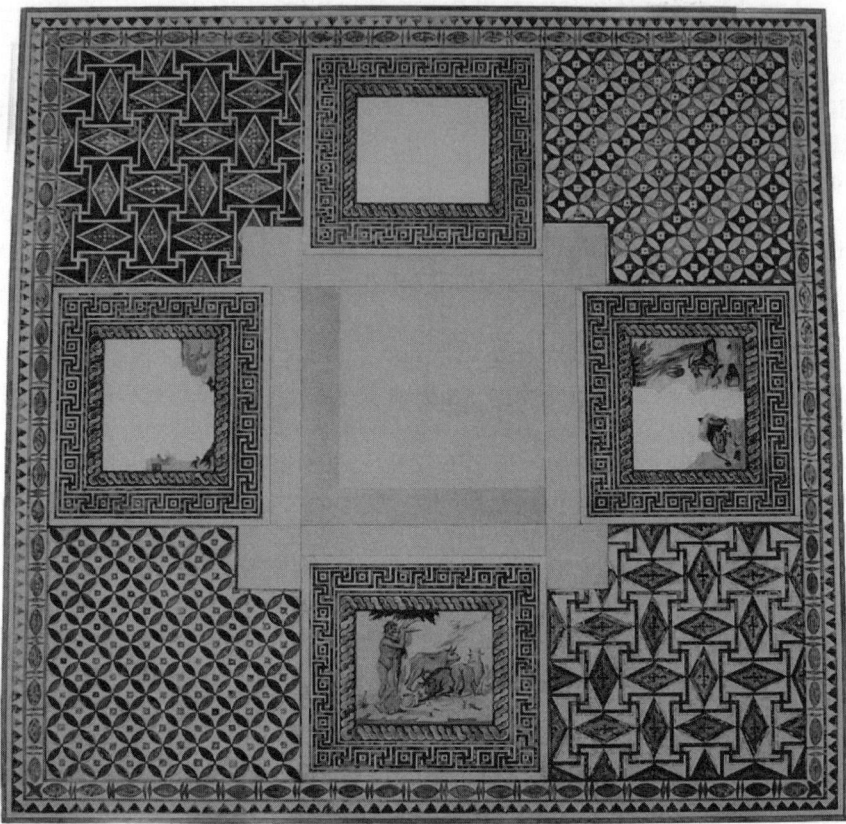

Atrium Mosaic, Shear Villa

of decorative bands. Outside the picture, a series of crescent designs covers the floor, bordered by a narrow blue band, then a broader white frame, and finally a strip of red along the walls. Shear judged that the simplicity of the border design was due to the fact that this portion of the floor was concealed by dining couches which must have been placed around the room.[374]

The large room on the west side of the house (Room E) has a plainer mosaic floor than the others in the villa, a fact which, together with evidence of adjacent storerooms, suggested to Shear that this room was used

---

374 Shear, "Excavations at Corinth in 1925," 393.

Mosaic Panel, Shear Villa

for domestic purposes.³⁷⁵ The function of the two remaining rooms is difficult to determine, although each features a stunning mosaic. The small room on the southwest side of the *atrium* (Room B), measuring 3.5 meters by 3.3 meters, displays a central mosaic panel depicting a standing figure of Dionysus holding a thyrsis, while the outside border has a series of large black crosses, with narrow red bands bisecting each bar, set on a white ground.³⁷⁶ The mosaic floor of Room D, measuring 4.4 meters by 3.4 meters, is the most impressive in the villa: a head of Dionysus, with ivy leaves in his hair, occupies a small circle in the center of a larger, circular frame of guilloche design, within which are inscribed concentric circles of pyramids, creating the impression of a flower in full bloom, by means of the skillful alternation of colors. The circle is set within a series of square frames decorated with crescents and diamonds; in each corner of the innermost frame, a cantharus is represented, with vines extending from it in both directions; the cups are colored alternately orange and grey to represent gold and silver vessels. Shear judged that

---

375 Shear, *Corinth V: The Roman Villa*, 17. Cf. Blue, "Acts and the House Church," 159.
376 Shear, "Excavations at Corinth in 1925," 394.

346   Chapter Five. Prosopography

Triclinium Mosaic, Shear Villa

"The simplicity and dignity of the head of Dionysus, the skillful representation of the eyes, the shaded flesh colors of the cheeks, and the contrasted arrangement of the green leaves and mellow fruit in the hair indicate that the mosaic craftsman was executing the conception of an artist, and place this among the best works of Greek mosaic."[377]

With respect to the date of the villa, Shear's judgment reflects the complex history of the structure. The presence of a house on this site prior to the Mummian destruction in 146 B.C. is indicated by the discovery of Attic and Corinthian pottery, and of twelve Greek coins.[378] This

---

377 Shear, "Excavations at Corinth in 1925," 394.
378 Shear, *Corinth V: The Roman Villa*, 26.

Mosaic, Shear Villa

debris was found scattered outside the walls, where it would naturally have been swept in the clearance of the ground for the erection of a new house after the resettlement of the city in 44 B.C.[379] Moreover, the walls of the house are not in structural accord with the mosaic floors, but cut some of the mosaics at odd angles.[380] The style of the mosaic pictures and patterns resembles most closely Hellenistic work at Delos which is dated in the second or third century B.C.[381] Hence, Shear concluded that the mosaic floors of the villa were made before 146 B.C., and sub-

---

379 Shear, *Corinth V: The Roman Villa*, 25.
380 Shear, *Corinth V: The Roman Villa*, 26.
381 Shear, "Excavations at Corinth in 1925," 395, 397; idem, *Corinth V: The Roman Villa*, 26. Recent commentators have argued for a date in the second century: S. E. Waywell, "Roman Mosaics in Greece," *AJA* 83 (1979) 297; Salies, "Römische Mosaiken in Griechenland," 265–66.

sequently were used in the reconstruction of the house.³⁸² Shear further judged: "It is certain that the house was occupied in the first century A.D. This fact is proved by the presence of Roman coins, of pottery of the Roman period, and of several characteristic lamps."³⁸³ These lamps, which were wheel-made of local Corinthian clay, have a characteristic shape and a square nozzle.³⁸⁴ Shear noted that the lamps from the villa "are similar to a lamp found in the well of the Athena trench in proximity to a coin of Agrippina (59 A.D.), and may be reasonably dated in the middle of the first century A.D."³⁸⁵

As attractive as the Shear Villa may be as a setting for imagining meetings of the Pauline *ekklesia*, there is another house which offers a

---

382 Shear, "Excavations at Corinth in 1925," 397; idem, *Corinth V: The Roman Villa*, 25–26.
383 Shear, *Corinth V: The Roman Villa*, 25.
384 Shear, "Excavations at Corinth in 1925," 396; idem, *Corinth V: The Roman Villa*, 25.
385 Shear, "Excavations at Corinth in 1925," 396–97. The Shear Villa is dated in the second century A.D. by Horrell, "Domestic Space and Christian Meetings at Corinth," 355 n. 27, but without giving reasons.

more plausible context, owing to its very favorable location in the city. In the course of the excavation seasons of 1928–1929, a pebble-mosaic floor was discovered in a large square room just east of the theater.[386] The house to which the mosaic belonged takes its name from a large wooden panel with a circular glass medallion set into it, found beneath collapsed debris in one of its rooms—the House of the Opus Sectile Panel.[387] The true size of the house is difficult to determine, because the eastern side of the structure lies under the dump of excavation earth upon which the modern Xenia Hotel of Corinth was built.[388] Although only the six westernmost rooms of the house have been excavated, Charles K. Williams, who resumed excavation in this area in 1981, unreservedly refers to the structure as "a large Roman building."[389] The overall north-south dimension of the house is in excess of 20 meters.[390]

With respect to the date of the house, Williams found evidence of two distinct levels of occupation, with the initial construction dating in the Julio-Claudian period, and a phase of rebuilding in the later first century A.D.[391] The two levels are clearly visible, in that house debris of the earlier phase was found packed under the ground floor of the late first-century structure.[392] The date of the earliest phase of the building was estimated by Williams within the first half of the first century A.D., on the basis of analysis of pottery that blocked a manhole adjacent to the house.[393] The date of the rebuilding was suggested by the fresco programme of a room in the southeast corner of the excavation, whose de-

---

[386] Theodore Leslie Shear, "Excavations in the Theatre District and Tombs of Corinth in 1928," *AJA* 32 (1928) 474–95; idem, "Excavations in the Theatre District and Tombs of Corinth in 1929," 516–46, esp. 526–28. The excavation is recorded in Corinth field notebook 321 (De Waele). This house is omitted from the 1979 survey of houses by Wiseman, "Corinth and Rome I," 528, and is likewise omitted by Murphy-O'Connor, *St. Paul's Corinth*, 178; Blue, "Acts and the House Church," 157; Horrell, "Domestic Space and Christian Meetings at Corinth," 354–55. The house is mentioned briefly by Jongkind, "Corinth in the First Century AD," 143–44.

[387] Charles K. Williams, "Corinth, 1981: East of the Theater," *Hesperia* 51 (1982) 133–34.

[388] Williams, "Corinth, 1981: East of the Theater," 133.

[389] Williams, "Corinth, 1981: East of the Theater," 133; similarly, Charles K. Williams, "Corinth, 1982: East of the Theater," *Hesperia* 52 (1983) 13.

[390] Williams, "Corinth, 1981: East of the Theater," 133.

[391] Williams, "Corinth, 1981: East of the Theater," 118, 133; idem, "Corinth, 1982: East of the Theater," 13–14.

[392] Williams, "Corinth, 1981: East of the Theater," 118, 133.

[393] Williams, "Corinth, 1981: East of the Theater," 129, 133.

Pebble Mosaic, House of the Opus Sectile Panel

sign reflects the influence of the Domus Aurea.[394] The second phase of occupation ended in fire and the total collapse of the structure in the middle of the third century A.D.[395]

An intriguing feature of this house is the pebble-mosaic floor, a Classical work dated to the fourth century B.C., incorporated within the later house plan by the Roman architect.[396] The floor is constructed of small black and white pebbles set in cement to form various designs. A meander border forms the outer edge of the room, within which is a large circle with a running wave pattern. The center displays a floral design with graceful palmettes and anthemia. In the corners are placed animal groups, which represent lions attacking, in one case a horse, and in another an antelope.[397] The floor of this room is at a level higher than those of

---

394 Williams, "Corinth, 1982: East of the Theater," 22–23, 23 n.15; see W. J. Th. Peters and P. G. P. Meyboom, "The Roots of Provincial Roman Painting, Results of Current Research in Nero's Domus Aurea" in *Roman Provincial Wall Painting*, ed. J. Liversidge (Oxford: Oxford University Press, 1982) 33–74.
395 Williams, "Corinth, 1981: East of the Theater," 118.
396 See the early reports of Shear, "Excavations in the Theatre District and Tombs at Corinth in 1929," 526–28, fig. 10; idem, *Corinth V: The Roman Villa*, 17; see also Charles K. Williams, "Corinth 1975: Forum Southwest," *Hesperia* 45 (1976) pl. 24; idem, "Corinth, 1976: Forum Southwest," *Hesperia* 46 (1977) 54, fig. 3; idem, "Corinth, 1981: East of the Theater," 117; idem, "Corinth, 1982: East of the Theater," 18, pl. 6c.
397 Shear, "Excavations in the Theatre District and Tombs at Corinth in 1929," 526–28; idem, *Corinth V: The Roman Villa*, 17; Williams, "Corinth, 1981: East of the Theater," 117.

the other rooms of the house.[398] Williams plausibly inferred that "the owner of the Roman house had antiquarian interests and, upon finding a pre-Roman floor in relatively good condition on the site, decided to have it used, even at the expense of awkwardness or inconvenience within the house plan."[399]

In a room to the southeast of the pebble-mosaic were found a number of frescoes.[400] The size of the room is difficult to determine, because it is partially covered by earth dumped from an earlier excavation.[401] The walls preserve their original plaster and fresco to a height of over a meter and a half; fragments of fresco were also found higher up the wall.[402] The fresco programme of the room is rather simple: a white background is bisected by a horizontal black stripe, above which the wall seems to have been divided into panels framed by red rectangles.[403] Williams judged that the room was originally furnished with a cement-bedded floor more ornate than the surface which is now exposed.[404]

North of the frescoed room and east of the room with the pebble-mosaic floor lies the room with the wood-and-glass panel from which the house takes its name. A large panel of wood decorated with a disk of *opus sectile* in various glasses was found amidst the fallen debris, along with fragmentary frescoes and a marble-veneered balustrade.[405] The burnt wood of the panel covered a large area on the floor which was otherwise free of nails and hardware, leading Williams to infer that the panel had functioned as a door which burned in a freestanding position, allowing the whole unit to fall face up.[406] The beautiful glass medallion, measuring .58 meters in diameter, is composed of two entwined squares, forming an 8-pointed star, surrounded by a band of mosaic glass.[407] The central circular disk portrays three fish

---

398 Williams, "Corinth, 1982: East of the Theater," 18.
399 Williams, "Corinth, 1982: East of the Theater," 18.
400 Williams, "Corinth, 1982: East of the Theater," 22.
401 Williams, "Corinth, 1982: East of the Theater," 22.
402 Williams, "Corinth, 1982: East of the Theater," 22.
403 Williams, "Corinth, 1982: East of the Theater," 22–23.
404 Williams, "Corinth, 1982: East of the Theater," 23.
405 Williams, "Corinth, 1981: East of the Theater," 118; idem, "Corinth, 1982: East of the Theater," 23.
406 Williams, "Corinth, 1981: East of the Theater," 133.
407 Williams, "Corinth, 1981: East of the Theater," 134. See the detailed description and analysis by Andrew Oliver, "A Glass Opus Sectile Panel from Corinth," *Hesperia* 70 (2001) 349–363.

Opus Sectile Panel

and an eel, facing alternately to either side.[408] The frescoes of this room show figured designs on brilliant red panels separated by flatly executed columns.[409]

While one might wish that more of this house had been excavated, its importance for our purposes lies not in its decoration, but in its location. The house lies just east of the theater along one of the principal streets that made up the Roman grid system.[410] This road, oriented east-west, was the artery that connected the north-south Lechaion road to the theater.[411] Because of the importance of this roadway, it was paved and colonnaded sometime during the first century A.D.[412] The road was flanked by sidewalks on both sides.[413] Along the south sidewalk, one gained access to the theater through a door in the west wall of the colonnade.[414] Beyond this gateway, one entered a paved court that lies immediately northeast of the theater.[415] From this court, one might go southwest across the theater square and descend into the orchestra, or one might turn left and

---

408 Williams, "Corinth, 1981: East of the Theater," 134; Oliver, "A Glass Opus Sectile Panel," 350–61.
409 Williams, "Corinth, 1981: East of the Theater," 134.
410 Williams, "Corinth, 1981: East of the Theater," 118, 128, 133.
411 Williams, "Corinth, 1981: East of the Theater," 128.
412 Shear, "Excavations in the Theatre District and Tombs at Corinth in 1929," 526; Stillwell, *Corinth II: The Theatre*, 14; Williams, "Corinth, 1981: East of the Theater," 128; idem, "Corinth, 1982: East of the Theater," 8, 10 fig. 3, 11.
413 Williams, "Corinth, 1981: East of the Theater," 128; idem, "Corinth, 1982: East of the Theater," 11.
414 Williams, "Corinth, 1982: East of the Theater," 11.
415 Williams, "Corinth, 1982: East of the Theater," 11.

enter the north-south street that passes along the eastern *parodos* of the theater, allowing entry to the theater from the rear, and thence up the slope to the Odeion.[416] Thus, the House of the Opus Sectile Panel stood at the center of the cultural life of Corinth, near a gate that opened into the theater court, which, in turn, gave access to the theater itself. The north exterior wall of the house served as the south wall of the colonnaded street.[417] Williams judged that the entrance of the house lay on the north side, along the beautiful east-west colonnaded street.[418]

The relationship of the house to the city block east of the theater is as intriguing as its location. Williams acknowledged the difficulty of forming a precise image of the area east of the theater, because of the vicissitudes suffered here in late Roman times, and because of the creation of an excavation dump in the modern period.[419] Nevertheless, examination of that portion of the block which has been excavated led Williams to the conclusion that "the original Roman plan seems to have been that of a domestic block with a long series of small shops."[420]

---

416 Williams, "Corinth, 1982: East of the Theater," 8, 11.
417 Williams, "Corinth, 1981: East of the Theater," 118; idem, "Corinth, 1982: East of the Theater," 11, 14.
418 Williams, "Corinth, 1981: East of the Theater," 133.
419 Williams, "Corinth, 1981: East of the Theater," 133; idem, "Corinth, 1982: East of the Theater," 11.
420 Williams, "Corinth, 1982: East of the Theater," 11.

354   Chapter Five. Prosopography

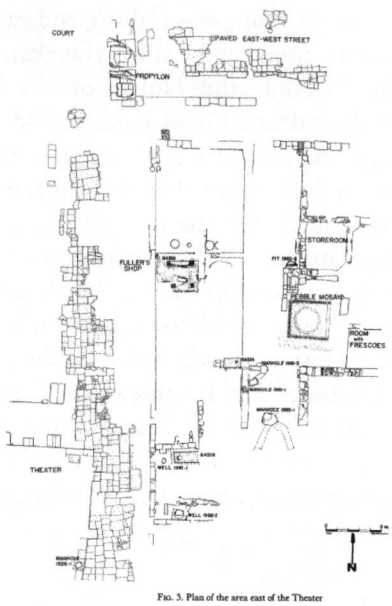

Fig. 3. Plan of the area east of the Theater

The house is separated from the row of shops to its west by a corridor or service lane, 4.8 meters wide.[421] Williams identified one of the shops as a fullery,[422] and two others as butcher shops devoted to the preparation of foods for theater-goers.[423] Was there a relationship between this row of shops and the House of the Opus Sectile Panel? In a case-study of a block in the Termini Quarter of Rome, Wallace-Hadrill infers a relationship between a rich *domus* with mosaic floors, which occupies the triangular nose of a ship-like block, and several adjacent structures—a bath which abuts against the house, and a double row of shops on the other side of the road.[424] Wallace-Hadrill suggests that the shops and the bath belonged to the proprietor of the *domus*, and were valuable sources of rental income.[425] One wonders whether we do not have a similar block of housing in the area east of the theater at Corinth: a grand house associated with a row of little shops, which were distinct units of operation, but not of ownership. Such an hypothesis accords well with the lesson of

---

421 Williams, "Corinth, 1982: East of the Theater," 13.
422 Williams, "Corinth, 1982: East of the Theater," 10.
423 Charles K. Williams, "Corinth, 1985: East of the Theater," *Hesperia* 55 (1986) 129–75, esp. 131–32, 135, 146–48.
424 Wallace-Hadrill, *"Domus* and *Insulae* in Rome," 3–18, esp. 10–14.
425 Wallace-Hadrill, *"Domus* and *Insulae* in Rome," 12.

Wallace-Hadrill's studies of Pompeii, Herculaneum and Rome: we are learning to see a Roman city "not so much as an undifferentiated sea of distinct units of housing, be they *domus* or *insulae*,...but as a series of cellular neighborhoods (*vici*),...essentially mixed in nature, between grand houses and blocks of flats and little shop units."[426]

The image that emerges from investigation of the area east of the theater is highly suggestive in the context of what is known about early Christianity at Corinth. Let us assume, for a moment, that the House of the Opus Sectile Panel was the house in which Gaius hosted meetings of "the whole *ekklesia*." Here a large group of persons might have been accommodated. The location of the house at the center of the city, along a principal east-west artery which terminates at the theater, would have facilitated access. Our imagination naturally places the artisans Aquila and Priscilla in one of the workshops belonging to this housing block. The idea is particularly attractive, if the trade which Aquila and Priscilla practiced was related to the theater, as Frederick Danker has suggested in his article on σκηνοποιός (= "maker of stage properties").[427] A plausible scenario then unfolds: Paul, who found lodging with Aquila and Priscilla because they were of the same occupation (Acts 18:3), converted the owner of the shop in which he worked and lived, the proprietor of the adjacent *domus*, a man who eventually placed his house at the disposal of the Christian community. But this is not all: our attention is drawn through the gateway at the end of the covered street into the paved plaza northeast of the theater, when we recall that it was here that the Erastus inscription was discovered. Thus does archaeology tempt us to a portrait of a movement that spread through relationships inherent in a given location, so strong is the genius of place! But even if each of the elements of this reconstruction were plausible, we should resist the aggregation, in recognition of the imperfect nature of historical evidence. Again, the purposes of our excursus will have been served, if we have formed a more robust image of the kind of house, and perhaps also the kind of neighborhood, in which Gaius hosted meetings of "the whole *ekklesia*."

---

426 Wallace-Hadrill, *"Domus* and *Insulae* in Rome," 13; idem, *Houses and Society,* 65–90. On *vici*, see further Augusto Fraschetti, *Roma e il Principe* (Rome: Laterza, 1990) 204–73; Laurence, *Roman Pompeii,* 38–50; William van Andringa, "Autels de Carrefour, organization vicinale et rapports de voisinage à Pompéi," *Rivista di Studi Pompeiani* 11 (2001) 47–86.
427 Frederick Danker in BDAG 928–29, s.v. σκηνοποιός. See also LSJ 1608, s.v. σκηνοποιός II: Pollux *Onom.* 7.189; Dio Cassius 67.2; Aristophanes *Pax* 174.

Wherever Gaius' house may have been, the role of "host" (ξένος) which Gaius played within the *domus* entailed aspects related to the function of the Roman house as an indicator of social status. The most important of these aspects were: the size of the house, the differentiation of space within the house, the social rituals by which access to various areas of the house was governed, the provision of food for guests at banquets, and the arrangement of what, in the context of convivial occasions, can only be called "entertainment." With respect to each of these aspects, the role of the proprietor of the *domus* was so firmly established by convention that we may be certain that Gaius, or whoever hosted a Christian assembly in the context of his or her home, would have been faced with such conditions, and would have been expected to behave in accordance with social etiquette.

First, the size of the house was a predictable indicator of the social status of its occupant.[428] In a familiar passage in his *De Architectura*, Vitruvius observes that "magnificent vestibules and alcoves and halls are not necessary to persons of a common fortune (*communi fortuna*), because they pay their respect by visiting among others, and are not visited by others."[429] Zanker draws the logical conclusion from Vitruvius' comments: "only the wealthy and socially prominent needed large *atria* to receive clients and large dining rooms for entertaining friends."[430] While urging moderation in residential construction, Cicero concedes: "In the home of a distinguished man, in which numerous guests must be entertained and crowds of every sort of people received, care must be taken to have it spacious."[431] The connection between house size and social status was the product of the public function of the Roman house.[432] The size of the house, and especially the dimensions of its access areas (the *vestibulum* and the *atrium*), advertised the achievements, wealth and dignity of its occupant to the public.[433] The correlation of house size and social status justifies an inference regarding Gaius' social standing: Gaius must

---

428 Wallace-Hadrill, *Houses and Society*, 4, 8–9, 12; Zanker, *Pompeii*, 12–14. On the *domus* as a status symbol, see Richard P. Saller, *"Domus* as symbol of status and family" in idem, *Patriarchy, property and death in the Roman family* (Cambridge: Cambridge University Press, 1997) 88–95.
429 Vitruvius *Arch.* 6.5.
430 Zanker, *Pompeii*, 13.
431 Cicero *Off.* 1.39.
432 Wallace-Hadrill, *Houses and Society*, 11–12, 59; Zanker, *Pompeii*, 13–14.
433 Wiseman, *"Conspicui postes tectaque digna deo,"* 393–413; Laurence, *Roman Pompeii*, 88–89; Wallace-Hadrill, *Houses and Society*, 10–12.

have belonged to the upper class, among those whose social position required greater space for large receptions, if he possessed a house capable of accommodating a large number of persons.[434] When the Christians of Corinth gathered to eat the Lord's Supper, the size of the house in which they assembled would have conveyed an unmistakable message about the wealth and influence of its owner, their "host" Gaius.

Second, the space within a Roman house was socially differentiated space.[435] Vitruvius, again, explains that certain areas of the house were open to the public, notably vestibules, halls, and peristyles, while other areas were reserved for family members, friends, and invited guests, specifically dining rooms, bedrooms, and baths.[436] Social status and relationship to the owner determined where one might be welcome within the house: thus, a poor visitor might penetrate no farther than the *atrium*, while a social equal of long acquaintance might be invited into one of the rooms in the interior.[437] Wallace-Hadrill has mapped the houses of Pompeii and Herculaneum on a conceptual grid which distinguishes public from private, and humble from grand.[438]

---

434 Malherbe, *Social Aspects*, 73–74; Meeks, *First Urban Christians*, 57, 143, 221 n.7; Murphy-O'Connor, *St. Paul's Corinth*, 182–83; Horrell, *The Social Ethos of the Corinthian Correspondence*, 96; Theissen, "The Social Structure of Pauline Communities," 82–83; Friesen, "Poverty in Pauline Studies," 356.
435 Clarke, *The Houses of Roman Italy*, 1–29; Wallace-Hadrill, *Houses and Society*, 8–16, 38–61; Osiek and Balch, *Households and House Churches*, 24–31, 183, 199; George, "Domestic Architecture and Household Relations," 7–25.
436 Vitruvius *Arch.* 6.5.
437 Wallace-Hadrill, *Houses and Society*, 38–39, 45, 47; Zanker, *Pompeii*, 12–13; George, "Domestic Architecture and Household Relations," 10.
438 Wallace-Hadrill, *Houses and Society*, 38.

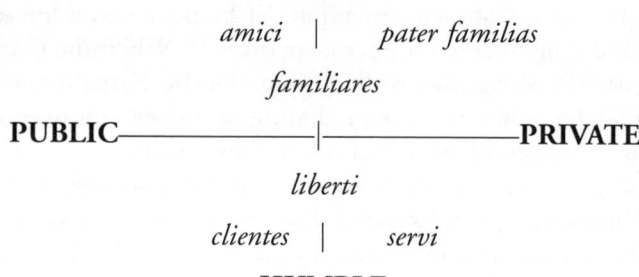

Wallace-Hadrill found that architecture and decoration served to channel the flow of persons within the house along "axes of differentiation."[439] The structure of the house directed the visitor's line of sight from the entrance-way to the *atrium* and the *tablinum*, where the owner of the house conducted his business.[440] The service areas were marginalized within the house, often accessible only down long narrow corridors.[441] The decorative schema reinforced the contrast between the seigniorial and servile areas of the house: the *atria* and *triclinia* were fitted out with fine mosaics and beautiful frescoes, while the rooms devoted to cooking, washing and working were crudely decorated, when they were decorated at all.[442] "The aim of such marginalization," Wallace-Hadrill concludes, "was to render the low-status areas 'invisible' to the visitor."[443] The social differentiation of space within the house has obvious implications for the way in which the Corinthian Christians would have encountered Gaius their "host" when they assembled to eat the Lord's Supper. It is most natural to assume that he would have presented himself to visitors in the *atrium*, where architecture and decoration would have reminded his guests of his social status. One cannot avoid the uncomfortable possibility that the "axes of differentiation" (public/private, humble/grand) would have directed Gaius' Christian visitors to different areas within the house, ac-

---

439 Wallace-Hadrill, *Houses and Society*, 8–12, 38–61.
440 Wallace-Hadrill, "Patronage in Roman Society," 63–64; idem, *Houses and Society*, 11–12, 51–52.
441 Wallace-Hadrill, *Houses and Society*, 39, with reference to the Casa del Menandro at Pompeii as an example.
442 Clarke, *The Houses of Roman Italy*, 99–101; Wallace-Hadrill, *Houses and Society*, 39, 44, 47, 50; cf. George, "Domestic Architecture and Household Relations," 10–14.
443 Wallace-Hadrill, *Houses and Society*, 44. See also Grahame, "Public and private in the Roman House," 137–61.

cording to their social status. Would a slave or freedman of another household—that of Chloe or Stephanas, let us say—have felt comfortable approaching one of the areas on the "grand" side of the household axis normally reserved for *amici* and *familiares?* And how would such a person have been received, if he had ventured near the *triclinium* or a bedroom? Wallace-Hadrill's analysis of the social differentiation of space within the *domus* reinforces Murphy-O'Connor's suggestion regarding the role of the architectural plan of a typical Roman house in heightening the divisions between the "haves" and the "have-nots" at the Lord's Supper.[444]

Third, social rituals governed access to the house and mediated movement about the internal space. The proprietor of a substantial *domus* would normally have held a *salutatio*, the traditional ritual of morning greeting, at which the crowd of persons seeking "services" paid their respects.[445] Archaeologists have called attention to stone benches outside the doors or within the vestibules for the convenience of waiting clients.[446] Within the large household, social rituals further separated those who occupied the same space, again, according to social class. Wallace-Hadrill observes: "Slaves were as important as architecture in ensuring the proper flow around the house, presenting living barriers to access to the master, from the *ostiarius* at the door to *cubicularii* and *nomenclatores* (name-callers) guarding the more intimate areas."[447] One recalls how, in Petronius' *Satyricon*, Trimalcio's slave startled the visitors with his shout as they were about to enter the dining room.[448] How would these social rituals have affected Christians who assembled at the house of Gaius? Would lower class members have been kept waiting in the ves-

---

444 Murphy-O'Connor, *St. Paul's Corinth*, 183–84; similarly, Lampe, "Das korinthische," 183–213, esp. 197, 201; Osiek and Balch, *Households and House Churches*, 200–203; Theissen, "The Social Structure of Pauline Communities," 83.
445 Saller, "Patronage and Friendship," 57–58; Veyne, *A History of Private Life I*, 90–91; Clarke, *The Houses of Roman Italy*, 4; Laurence, *Roman Pompeii*, 8, 125. See now Fabian Goldbeck, *Salutationes: Die Morgenbegrüssungen in Rom in der Republik und der frühen Kaiserzeit* (Berlin: Akademie Verlag, 2010).
446 August Mau, *Pompeii: Its Life and Art* (London: Macmillan, 1907) 248–58; Wilhelm Kroll, *Die Kultur der ciceronischen Zeit* (Leipzig: Dieterich, 1933) 187–90; Wallace-Hadrill, *Houses and Society*, 12.
447 Wallace-Hadrill, *Houses and Society*, 39. See further, Michele George, "*Servus* and *domus*: the slave in the Roman house" in *Domestic Space in the Roman World: Pompeii and Beyond*, ed. Ray Laurence and Andrew Wallace-Hadrill (Portsmouth: Journal of Roman Archaeology, 1997) 15–24.
448 Petronius *Satyr.* 30.

tibule until the master of the house was ready to receive them? Would poor congregants have been brought up short by a slave's reproof, if they had attempted to enter the *triclinium?*[449]

Fourth, the provision of food for guests at dinner was the normal expectation of a host.[450] So much is clear from the many accounts of banquets in Petronius, Plutarch, Juvenal, Martial, and the younger Pliny: the host supplied the food and drink, determined the quality and variety of what was offered, and apportioned the fare to his guests as he saw fit.[451] New Testament scholars do not usually ascribe this service to Gaius in his role as host of the Lord's Supper at Corinth. Rather, it is generally assumed that each individual Christian brought along his own provision for the meal.[452] This assumption is founded upon Paul's observation in 1 Cor. 11:21, ἕκαστος γὰρ τὸ ἴδιον δεῖπνον προλαμβάνει ἐν τῷ φαγεῖν, a

---

449 On "psychological segregation" within the Roman house, and its probable impact upon slaves, see the observations of George, "Domestic Architecture and Household Relations," 14. See further, John H. D'Arms, "Slaves at Roman Convivia" in *Dining in a Classical Context*, ed. William J. Slater (Ann Arbor: University of Michigan Press, 1991) 171–84.

450 Veyne, *A History of Private Life I*, 186–89; Dunbabin, "Convivial spaces," 66–80; John Nicols, *"Hospitium* and political friendship in the late Republic" in *Aspects of Friendship in the Graeco-Roman World*, ed. Michael Peachin (Portsmouth: Journal of Roman Archaeology, 2001) 99. See the imaginative reconstruction of a dinner party hosted by the Vettii brothers by John R. Clarke, *Roman Life 100 B.C. to A.D. 200* (New York: Abrams, 2007) 114–23.

451 Cicero *Att.* 13.52; Horace *Sat.* 2.8.7; Petronius *Satyr.* 26–74; Plutarch *Quaes. Conv.* 2.10.1; Juvenal *Sat.* 5; Martial 3.30; Pliny *Ep.* 2.6.1–4; 2.17; 5.6. Cf. Dunbabin, "Convivial spaces," 66; L. Michael White, "Paul and *Pater Familias"* in *Paul in the Greco-Roman World*, ed. J. Paul Sampley (Harrisburg: Trinity Press International, 2003) 463–64.

452 E.g., Günther Bornkamm, "Herrenmahl und Kirche bei Paulus" in idem, *Studien zu Antike und Urchristentum. Gesammelte Aufsätze II* (Munich: Kaiser, 1959) 138–76, esp. 143–44: "bei der man zusammen aß, was jeder nach Vermögen dazu beigesteuert hatte"; Theissen, *Social Setting*, 148: "the ἴδιον δεῖπνον is most likely the meal which individual Christians bring with them"; Collins, *First Corinthians*, 417–18: "The meal taken on this occasion…was one in which each participant contributed his or her own share"; Dennis E. Smith, *From Symposium to Eucharist: The Banquet in the Early Christian World* (Minneapolis: Augsburg Fortress, 2003) 178: "The householder/patron would presumably be the host. The food, however, may have been provided by everyone bringing a portion, somewhat like our potluck dinner today"; Roger W. Gehring, *House Church and Mission: The Importance of Household Structures in Early Christianity* (Peabody: Hendrickson, 2004) 173: "Everyone brought along what food he or she could for the meal."

statement which is customarily translated: "for each goes ahead with his own supper in the eating (of it)."[453] But virtually every element of this sentence, which is the descriptive core of Paul's evaluation of the Corinthian observance, is ambiguous, permitting various reconstructions of what happened at the meal.[454]

Paul's use of ἕκαστος here is just as imprecise as in other instances (cf. 1 Cor. 14:26; 1:12).[455] Surely Paul does *not* mean to say that "each and every" member of the *ekklesia* brought a sufficient provision, for he goes on to speak of some who "hunger," while others are "drunken" (11:21b). It seems best to complete the sense of ἕκαστος, as Hans-Josef Klauck suggests, by supplying "jeder, der dazu imstande ist,"[456] in which case Paul would be speaking of those who are well-off and have sufficient resources to supply their own food, or who have otherwise been apportioned food by their host.[457] The expression τὸ ἴδιον δεῖπνον is also ambiguous: it can refer to the ownership of the meal which individual Christians have brought with them, or to the manner in which the food was consumed.[458] In light of Paul's acknowledgement that some "have nothing" (11:22), it would seem best to take τὸ ἴδιον δεῖπνον in the latter sense, as a reference to the *manner* in which food was allocated and consumed, that is, "privately."[459] The verb προλαμβάνειν is likewise ambiguous: it is usually translated "to take before," giving the prefix

---

453 So, for example, Conzelmann, *1 Corinthians*, 192; Theissen, *Social Setting*, 148; Collins, *First Corinthians*, 422–23; Lindemann, *Der erste Korintherbrief*, 247, 251; Thiselton, *First Epistle*, 861–62.
454 See esp. the reconstructions of Bruce W. Winter, "The Lord's Supper at Corinth: An Alternative Reconstruction," *The Reformed Theological Review* 37 (1978) 73–82; Hans-Josef Klauck, *Herrenmahl und hellenistischer Kult. Eine religionsgeschichtliche Untersuchung zum ersten Korintherbrief* (Münster: Aschendorff, 1982) 285–332; Otfried Hofius, "Herrenmahl und Herrenmahlparadosis. Erwägungen zu 1 Kor 11,23–25," *ZThK* 85 (1988) 371–408 (English trans. "The Lord's Supper and the lord's Supper Tradition: Reflections on 1 Corinthians 11:23b-25" in *One Loaf, One Cup: Ecumenical Studies of 1 Corinthians 11 and Other Eucharistic Texts*, ed. B. F. Meyer [Macon: Mercer University Press, 1993] 75–115); Lampe, "Das korinthische Herrenmahl," 183–213.
455 Weiss, *Der erste Korintherbrief*, 28; Theissen, *Social Setting*, 148; Lindemann, *Der erste Korintherbrief*, 251.
456 Klauck, *Herrenmahl*, 293; followed by Schmeller, *Hierarchie und Egalität*, 69 n.62.
457 Theissen, *Social Setting*, 148; Schmeller, *Hierarchie und Egalität*, 67, 71.
458 Theissen, *Social Setting*, 148–51; cf. Thiselton, *First Epistle*, 862.
459 Theissen, *Social Setting*, 149.

πρo its full temporal force;⁴⁶⁰ accordingly, some at Corinth (the rich) would have begun to eat before others (slaves and the poor) arrived.⁴⁶¹ But πρo seems to have lost some of its temporal force by the first century.⁴⁶² As a result, προλαμβάνειν, in the context of eating, can mean "to take," "to get of a meal," as in an inscription from the temple of Asclepius at Epidaurus.⁴⁶³ Thus, Bruce Winter translates προλαμβάνειν in 1 Cor. 11:21 as "devour," and proposes that some in the church at Corinth selfishly ate their food while others looked on!⁴⁶⁴ Finally, the articular infinitive in the phrase ἐν τῷ φαγεῖν has caused consternation.⁴⁶⁵ It is possible that it designates "the act of eating" generally, whenever that may have occurred in relation to the Lord's Supper.⁴⁶⁶ But it is more likely that τὸ φαγεῖν looks back to the phrase κυριακὸν δεῖπνον φαγεῖν in the preced-

---

460 E.g., Bornkamm, "Herrenmahl und Kirche bei Paulus," 142' C. K. Barrett, *The First Epistle to the Corinthians* (Peabody: Hendrickson, 1993) 262; Theissen, *Social Setting*, 151; Lampe, "Das korinthische Herrenmahl," 198.
461 Bornkamm, "Herrenmahl und Kirche bei Paulus," 142: "unter den Minderbemittelten und lieblos Zurückgesetzten sind vor allem die kleinen Leute, die am Abend sich nicht so leicht aus ihrer Arbeit lösen können, also sicher vor allem Sklaven, die nicht Herren ihrer Zeit sind und zu sät kommen, ohne daß die Bemittelten Rücksicht auf sie nehmen." For a list of additional representatives of this view, see Hofius, "Herrenmahl und Herrenmahlparadosis," 383 n.26.
462 BDAG 864 s.v. προλαμβάνω: "the temporal sense…[was] felt very little." See the observation of Collins, *First Corinthians*, 422: "Paul does not stress the temporal aspect of the verb on the only other occasion that he uses it (Gal. 6:1)."
463 *SIG*³ 1170, lines 7, 9, 16; *IG* 4.126. See also Moulton and Milligan, *The Vocabulary of the Greek Testament*, 542; see further Rudolf Herzog, *Die Wunderheilungen von Epidauros* (Leipzig: Dieterich, 1931) 43–45. But cf. Lampe, "Das korinthische Herrenmahl," 191 n.28; Klauck, *Herrenmahl*, 292 n.39.
464 Winter, "The Lord's Supper at Corinth," 73–77; similarly, Hofius, "Herrenmahl und Herrenmahlparadosis," 384–91. See further Gehring, *House Church and Mission*, 174–76. But see the critique of this interpretation by Lampe, "Das korinthische Herrenmahl," 198–203.
465 Winter, "The Lord's Supper at Corinth," 77–78.
466 See the discussion of the significance of the aorist infinitive in BDF §404(2); Moulton, *A Grammar of New Testament Greek I*, 111; Ernest DeWitt Burton, *Syntax of the Moods and Tenses in New Testament Greek* (Edinburgh: T & T Clark, 1898) 50–51: the aorist articular infinitive marks "the time at which the action expressed by the principal verb takes place and simply marks in general the time of the event denoted by the principal verb, leaving the context to indicate the precise nature of the chronological relation"; Moule, *An Idiom Book of New Testament Greek*, 11; BDAG 330 s.v. ἐν 10c.

ing verse.⁴⁶⁷ Then, the greedy behavior which Paul criticizes would have taken place during the Lord's Supper itself!⁴⁶⁸

Although the majority of interpreters picture the Lord's Supper at Corinth as a kind of "potluck" to which individual Christians contributed, according to the custom of an ἔρανος,⁴⁶⁹ Thomas Schmeller offers a reconstruction which is more firmly rooted in exegesis of the text of 1 Cor. 11:17–34. In respect to the provision of food for dinner, Schmeller finds the closest analogy to the situation in the church at Corinth in the meals of cultic associations in which a single patron, or a few patrons, supplied the food and drink for a group which met in his or her house:⁴⁷⁰ e.g., the mystery cult that a certain Dionysius established in his house at Philadelphia at the beginning of the first century B.C.;⁴⁷¹ the Bacchic association over which Pompeia Agrippinilla presided as priestess in her home outside Rome.⁴⁷² If, like the patrons of these household cults,

---

467 Rightly, Theissen, *Social Setting*, 153: "The doubling of the terms 'meals' and 'eating,' δεῖπνον and φαγεῖν, is hardly mere pleonasm. Rather, φαγεῖν refers back to the phrase κυριακὸν δεῖπνον φαγεῖν of the preceding clause, while corresponding to the phrase εἰς τὸ φαγεῖν in v. 33. In both instances it is the Lord's Supper to which the verb refers. The proper meal occurs ἐν τῷ φαγεῖν, "during the Lord's Supper."
468 Winter, "The Lord's Supper at Corinth," 78–82; cf. Thiselton, *First Epistle*, 863; Gehring, *House Church and Mission*, 175–76. See in general Michael Peachin, "Friendship and abuse at the dinner table" in *Aspects of Friendship in the Graeco-Roman World*, ed. Michael Peachin (Portsmouth: Journal of Roman Archaeology, 2001) 135–44.
469 Lampe, "Das korinthische Herrenmahl," 198–200
470 Schmeller, *Hierarchie und Egalität*, 60, 71.
471 *SIG*³ 985; text in F. Sokolowski, *Lois Sacrèes de L'Asie Mineure* (Paris: École Francias d'Athènes, 1955) 53–55; text and German trans. in Schmeller, *Hierarchie und Egalität*, 96–99; English trans. in S. C. Barton and G. H. R. Horsley, "A Hellenistic Cult Group and the New Testament Churches," *JAC* 24 (1981) 9–10.
472 *CIL* 6.9148; Vogliano, "La grande iscrizione Bacchica del Metropolitan Museum, I," 215–31; Franz Cumont, "La Grande Inscription Bachique du Metropolitan Museum, II: Commentaire religieuse de l'inscription," *AJA* 37 (1933) 232–63. Cf. Ramsay MacMullen, *Paganism in the Roman Empire* (New Haven: Yale University Press, 1983) 109; Shelly Matthews, *First Converts: Rich Pagan Women and the Rhetoric of Mission in Early Judaism and Christianity* (Stanford: Stanford University Press, 2001) 26–27; Carolyn Osiek and Margaret Y. MacDonald, *A Woman's Place: House Churches in Earliest Christianity* (Augsburg Fortress Press, 2006) 208; Jörg Rüpke, *Religion of the Romans* (Cambridge: Polity Press, 2007) 214; Hubert Cancik, "Haus, Schule, Gemeinde: Zur Organisation von "fremder Religion" im Rom (1.–3. Jh. n.Chr.)" in *Gruppenreligionen im Rö-*

Gaius supplied the meal for the Christian group at Corinth, it would have been his prerogative as host to apportion the food to his guests as he saw fit.[473] The accounts of banquets in Juvenal, Martial, and Pliny reveal that social distinctions operated in the allocation of food: the host set before his friends and social equals old Falerian wine, plump goose liver, etc., while guests of lower station had to make do with meals that were "paltry and cheap."[474] Would Gaius have made such distinctions in the allocation of food for the Lord's Supper?

There is much that we do not know about Gaius' role in hosting the Lord's Supper. We do not know whether the church was assembling at the house of Gaius when Paul wrote the exhortation contained in 1 Cor. 11:17–34. Consequently, we cannot be certain whether the situation described in 1 Cor. 11:17–22 developed at Gaius' house or elsewhere. We do not know how Gaius might have responded to Paul's criticism of the inequitable distribution of food and drink at the Lord's Supper, assuming, for a moment, that Paul's censure was meant for him. One might infer that someone who was "confident of belonging to Christ" (2 Cor. 10:7) would have amended a practice that was not in keeping with the intention of the Lord Jesus in giving the meal (1 Cor. 11:23–26). But if Gaius responded to Paul's admonition constructively, so that everyone was hospitably received (1 Cor. 11:33), and hunger was alleviated, and the humiliation of unequal shares was eliminated (1 Cor. 11:22b), even then, and one might say, especially then, it would have been clear to those who had little or nothing just how dependent they were upon the largesse of their host for the provision and distribution of food.[475]

Fifth, in the Greco-Roman world, a wealthy host was expected to offer his guests entertainment over dinner.[476] The variety of such enter-

---

mischen Reich. Sozialformen, Grenzziehungen und Leistungen, ed. Jörg Rüpke (Tübingen: Mohr Siebeck, 2007) 31–48, here 35–36.

473 Kirner, "Apostolat und Patronage (II)," 55. On the role of meal hosts, see Smith, *From Symposium to Eucharist*, 33, 100–101.

474 Martial 1.20; 3.60; 4.85; 6.11; 10.49; Juvenal *Sat.* 5; Pliny *Ep.* 2.6; cited in Theissen, *Social Setting*, 157–58.

475 Theissen, *Social Setting*, 160–62; Kirner, "Apostolat und Patronage (II)," 55. Cf. James C. Walters, "Paul and the Politics of Meals in Roman Corinth" in *Corinth in Context: Comparative Studies on Religion and Society*, ed. Steven Friesen, Daniel N. Schowalter, and James C. Walters (Leiden: Brill, 2010) 358–59.

476 Christopher P. Jones, "Dinner Theater" in *Dining in a Classical Context*, ed. William J. Slater (Ann Arbor: University of Michigan Press, 1991) 185–98; Dunbabin, "Convivial spaces," 66–88.

tainment was wide: we hear most frequently of music, singing and dancing, while the more sedate and decorous preferred recitations, poetry, and story-telling.[477] The specific offering depended upon the tastes of the host and the demands of the occasion. Plutarch devotes one of his *Convivial Questions* to the subject "What are the best kind of entertainments to have during dinner?"[478] The participants in Plutarch's discussion enumerate: tragedy, comedy, mime, and poetry (to musical accompaniment on the cithara, pipe, and lyre).[479] These kinds of entertainment were evidently in vogue among cultivated circles like those of Plutarch's friends.[480] Of these entertainments, the most widely attested in the literature of the early Empire are comedy and mime.[481] We should not imagine that Gaius staged comedies for his guests at the Lord's Supper, even supposing that suitable plots could be found! But for those who were accustomed to theater at dinner, the reading of one of Paul's epistles, or the recitation of a psalm, would have fallen into the category of "entertainment." Such entertainment over dinner was normally provided by the host through the agency of a household slave.[482] Might the scribe Tertius, who was evidently a slave in the house of Gaius (Rom. 16:22–23), have "entertained" guests at the Lord's Supper by readings from the letters of Paul or other apostles? Reading for guests at dinner parties was the job of a slave *lector*.[483]

---

477 See the examples in M. Bonaria, "La musica conviviale dal mondo latino antico al medioevo" in *Spettacoli conviviali dall' antichità classica alle corti Italiane del '400* (Viterbo, 1982) 119–47; Costas Panayotakis, *Theatrum Arbitri: theatrical elements in the Satyricon of Petronius* (Leiden: Brill, 1995) 60; cf. Dunbabin, "Convival spaces," 66–67.
478 Plutarch *Quaest. conv.* 711 A-F.
479 Plutarch *Quaest. conv.* 711C.
480 Jones, "Dinner Theater," 192.
481 See, for example, Petronius *Satyr.* 53.12–13; Plutarch *Quaest. conv.* 712E; Pliny *Ep.* 3.1.9; M. Bonaria, *Romani mimi* (Rome, 1965); G. Brugnoli, "Mimi edaces" in *Spettacoli conviviali dall' antichità classica alle corti Italiane del '400* (Viterbo, 1982) 77–90; Jones, "Dinner Theater," 189, 192; Dunabin, "Convivial spaces," 67.
482 E.g., Plutarch *Quaest. conv.* 711C; cf. J. P. V. D. Balsdon, *Life and Leisure in Ancient Rome* (London: Bodley Head, 1969) 44–45; Dunbabin, "Convivial spaces," 67; Jones,"Dinner Theater," 185, 196; see in general D'Arms, "Slaves at Roman Convivia," 171–84, esp. 176–78.
483 Nepos *Att.* 14.1; Cicero *Att.* 1.12.4; *Fam.* 5.9.2; Varro *apud* Gellius *NA* 1.22.5; Martial 3.50; Pliny *Ep.* 3.5.11, 5.19.3, 9.36.4; cf. Joachim Marquardt, *Das Privatleben der Römer* (Leipzig: Hirzel, 1879) 148; Wiseman, *"Pete nobiles amicos,"* 32, 44 n.37. See further, Raymond J. Starr, "Reading Aloud: *Lectores* and Roman

As the "host" of the Lord's Supper at Corinth, Gaius was essentially the "patron," or benefactor, of the Christian group in the city.[484] One naturally wonders whether members of the group which regularly assembled at Gaius' house for dinner would have turned to their "host" for the other *beneficia* which a patron was expected to provide: legal help, a loan, advice about property or the betrothal of a daughter, a place to sit at the theater—things which, according to Cicero and Horace, friends of humbler station asked of their patron.[485] We cannot know how far the relationships and behavior of the Christians at Corinth conformed to social convention.[486] But a number of the issues dealt with in the writing known to us as 1 Corinthians—legal disputes (1 Cor. 6:1–11), marriage, divorce and betrothal (1 Cor. 7), invitations to dinner (1 Cor. 8, esp. 8:10), the benefit of free food and lodging (1 Cor. 9)—are matters which were routinely referred to a patron.[487] Conflict over these matters suggests that there was a locus of authority in the Christian community at Corinth other than Paul.[488]

If we cannot determine whether ordinary Christians would have turned to Gaius for the benefits which clients typically sought from a pa-

---

Reading," *CJ* 86 (1991) 337–43. See in general, William Shiell, *Reading Acts: The Lector and the Early Christian Audience* (Leiden: Brill, 2004).

484 For the host of a dinner party as a benefactor, see Jones, "Dinner Theater," 196. On the early Christian "house-patron," see Kirner, "Apostolat und Patronage (II)," 55: "so stellt der Hauspatron für die christlichen Versammlungen die Räumlichkeiten zur Verfügung, stiftet für gemeinsame Mahlzeiten einen Großteil des Essen und Trinkens und hatte womöglich ein offenes Ohr für die Bedürfnisse seiner ärmeren christlichen 'Mitbrüder'."

485 Cicero *De or*. 3.133; *Mur*. 70–72; Horace *Ep*. 2.1.102–107; cf. Wiseman, "Poets and Patrons," 29.

486 Judge, *The Social Pattern of the Christian Groups*, 60, repr. in idem, *Social Distinctives of the Christians*, 43 ; Chow, *Patronage and Power*, 83–112; Kirner, "Apostolat und Patronage (II)," 54–62.

487 In general, Wiseman, "Poets and Patrons," 28–30; Saller, *Personal Patronage*, 17–36, 120–34, passim. With reference to 1 Corinthians, Chow, *Patronage and Power*, 113–65; Gill, "In Search of the Social Elite," 330–37; Kirner, "Apostolat und Patronage (II)," 54–62.

488 E. A. Judge, "Christliche Gruppen in nichtchristlicher Gesellschaft: Die Sozialstruktur christlicher Gruppen im ersten Jahrhundert" in idem, *The First Christians in the Roman World*, 465; idem, "The Early Christians as a Scholastic Community" in idem, *The First Christians in the Roman World*, 530, 544–45; Welborn, "Discord in Corinth" in idem, *Politics and Rhetoric in the Corinthian Epistles*, 23–28; Chow, *Patronage and Power*, 25, 112, 166, 188–89; Carter, "'Big Men' in Corinth," 45–70; Kirner, "Apostolat und Patronage (II)," 45–70.

tron, we can be more certain about the rival apostle with whom Paul is obliged to compare himself in 2 Cor. 10:12–12:10: this unnamed evangelist has fully enjoyed (Paul would say, "thoroughly abused") the hospitality of someone at Corinth (11:4, 20).[489] The language Paul uses to describe the behavior of his rival in 2 Cor. 11:20 (καταδουλοῖ, κατεσθίει, λαμβάνει, κτλ.), even though it belongs to a savage caricature,[490] suggests the range of pleasures available to a client intellectual: being liked by his patron, being invited to dinner, and, best of all, being lodged in the patron's house, as illustrated by the careers of Archias, Lucretius, and other client intellectuals of the late Republic and the early Empire.[491] In his satirical account of the lives of intellectuals in "great houses," Lucian's alter ego exclaims: "Happy men! The elite of Rome are their friends. They dine sumptuously, and call for no reckoning. They are lodged splendidly, and travel comfortably—nay, luxuriously—with cushions at their backs, and as often as not a fine pair of creams in front of them...."[492] T. P. Wiseman has suggested another benefit which client intellectuals may have hoped to receive from their patron: publicity, that is, the provision of an audience.[493] With specific reference to the profession of poetry, Peter White observes: "In the pyramid of Roman society, wealthy men with a large following were uniquely placed to publicize the work of their poet friends."[494] Philosophers, too, sought audiences for their moral preaching, and were helped by powerful friends to get a hearing.[495] The venues for such public presentations were often porticoes attached to

---

489 See ch. 3 above.
490 L. L. Welborn, "Paul's Caricature of his Chief Rival as a Pompous Parasite in 2 Corinthians 11:20," *JSNT* 32 (2009) 39–56.
491 E.g., Cicero *Arch*. 6. Cf. Susan M. Treggiari, "Intellectuals, Poets, and their Patrons in the First Century B.C.," *Echos du monde classique: Classical News and Views* 26 (1977) 24–29, esp. 26; T. P. Wiseman, "The Two Worlds of Titus Lucretius" in idem, *Cinna the Poet, and Other Roman Essays* (Leicester: Leicester University Press, 1974) 11–43; idem, "Poets and Patrons," 31–42; Peter White, *"Amicitia* and the Profession of Poetry in Early Imperial Rome," *JRS* 68 (1978) 74–92, esp. 80, 81, 85.
492 Lucian *Merc. cond.* 3.
493 Wiseman, "Poets and Patrons," 36–38.
494 White, *"Amicitia* and the Profession of Poetry," 85.
495 Wiseman, "Poets and Patrons," 36–37, referring to Horace *Sat.* 2.3.33–34, 296; Varro *Sat. Men.* 517B; Cicero *Cael.* 41; *Fin.* 1.13, 25; 2.44, 81; *Tusc.* 2.7; 3.50; 4.6; 5.28.

scholae and *exedrae*.[496] Might Gaius have secured a lecture hall for the evangelist, about whose coming to Corinth Paul complains in 2 Cor. 11:4 and 11:20?[497] Was it in such a setting that this evangelist established his reputation for eloquence, exposing, by comparison, a defect in Paul's rhetorical delivery? This prospect is made more likely by Paul's painful acknowledgement (in 2 Cor. 11:6) that he lacked the rhetorical training of the evangelist with whom he is forced to compare himself in 2 Cor. 10:12–12:10.[498]

Paul refused the patronage offered to him by someone powerful at Corinth. So much is clear from the tortured argument of 2 Cor. 11:7–11, as we have sought to demonstrate above.[499] Indeed, Paul is already on the defensive regarding his refusal of free food and lodging in 1 Cor. 9.[500] Peter Marshall has argued that Paul's refusal of financial support was the beginning of enmity between Paul and the Corinthians, since, in a patronage society like Roman Corinth, the refusal of a gift was the refusal of a "friendship."[501] We have acknowledged the difficulty of discovering the motive for Paul's refusal of a relationship which other apostles evidently enjoyed. (cf. 1 Cor. 9:5).[502] The stated reason—"not to be a burden" (οὐ καταναρκᾶν)—is so thickly painted with the colors of Paul's caricature of his chief rival as a parasite that it cannot be regarded as a disclosure of Paul's underlying motive (2 Cor. 11:9; 12:13–14).[503] Perhaps Paul comes closer to stating his true motive in 1 Cor. 9, before his relationship with the Corinthians had become so conflicted: what

---

496 Vitruvius *Arch.* 5.11.2; Petronius *Satyr.* 90; *ILLRP* 116, 680; cf. Wiseman, "Poets and Patrons," 36.
497 See above, ch. 3. Cf. Stanley K. Stowers, "Social Status, Public Speaking and Private Teaching: The Circumstances of Paul's Preaching Activity," *NovT* 26 (1984) 59–82, esp. 66–68; Kirner, "Apostolat und Patronage (II)," 33, 60–61.
498 On Paul's rhetorical training and that of his competitors, see E. A. Judge, "Paul's Boasting in Relation to Contemporary Professional Practice," *AusBR* 16 (1968) 37–50, repr. in idem, *Social Distinctives of the Christians*, 57–71; Winter, *Paul among the Sophists*, 223–38, 231–37.
499 See ch. 3 above, pp. 132–39. So, already, Marshall, *Enmity in Corinth*, 218–58, esp. 218–19, 233, 239, 252–53.
500 Hock, *Social Context*, 59–62.
501 Marshall, *Enmity in Corinth*, 233, 257.
502 See above, ch. 3, pp. 151–52. Cf. Marshall, *Enmity in Corinth*, 222, 232, 237.
503 See above, ch. 3, pp. 132–39, 150–54. Cf. Betz, *Der Apostel Paulus*, 101–102, 115, 117, emphasizing Paul's irony in these passages.

was at stake was his "freedom" (9:1).[504] Is it too much to suggest that Paul refused the patronage of the powerful at Corinth because he had discovered the secret of the game: that patronage was a means of social control, through the manipulation of access to scarce resources?[505] Wallace-Hadrill penetrates to the core of the system when he observes: "the patron's power over the client derives not from generous and regular distribution, but from keeping him on tenderhooks with the prospect of access to resources which is never fully granted."[506] Paul sought to break free of this system by working for a living. A second motive may be disclosed by Paul's repeated attempt to cast himself in the patronal role in relation to the Corinthians (1 Cor. 9:15–18; 2 Cor. 12:14–15).[507] One might mistake this maneuver for a symptom of pride like that which leads some of Martial's client intellectuals to decline their patrons' invitations to dinner, and to send them poetic gifts, instead.[508] After all, Paul insists, "no one will deprive me of my ground for boasting!" (1 Cor. 9:15), in relation to his decision to "make the gospel free of charge" to the Corinthians (1 Cor. 9:18). But we shall discover that Paul's ultimate aim was to undermine and transform the patronage system from within.[509] A full appreciation of Paul's response to the offer of patronage must await reconstruction of the final stages of Paul's relationship with his "host" Gaius.[510]

We conclude our prosopography of Gaius by returning to the subject of Gaius' relationships with the two Corinthian Christians in connection with whom he is named in 1 Cor. 1:14 and Rom. 16:23—Crispus and Erastus. We have suggested that closer attention to these relationships will disclose further information about Gaius' attraction to the Christian movement, his affiliation within the Christian community, and his position within Corinthian society.

---

504 Cf. Marshall, *Enmity in Corinth*, 243–44, referencing Seneca *Ben.* 2.18.6–7; 5.6.2–7 emphasizing freedom from obligation.
505 See, already, E. A. Judge, "Cultural Conformity and Innovation in Paul," *TynBul* 35 (1984) 3, 23, repr. in idem, *Social Distinctives of the Christians*, 159, 173.
506 Wallace-Hadrill, "Patronage in Roman society" in idem, *Patronage in Ancient Society*, 73.
507 Marshall, *Enmity in Corinth*, 248–49; Peter Lampe, "Paul, Patrons, and Clients" in *Paul in the Greco-Roman World*, ed. J. Paul Sampley (Harrisburg: Trinity Press International, 2003) 501; Harrison, *Paul's Language of Grace*, 341–42.
508 Richard P. Saller, "Martial on Patronage and Literature," *CQ* 33 (1983) 246–57.
509 E. A. Judge, "St. Paul as a Radical Critic of Society," *Interchange* 16 (1974) 196–97; "Cultural Conformity and Innovation in Paul" in idem, *Social Distinctives of the Christians*, 106–109, 159, 173.
510 See below ch. 6.

In Paul's first mention of Gaius (1 Cor. 1:14), he is connected with Crispus in the matter of his baptism. What should we infer from this association? While it is possible that the sole basis for the association of Crispus and Gaius in this instance lies in the fact that these two received baptism from Paul's hands, this seems unlikely and insufficient, since Paul goes on to acknowledge that he had baptized others—the household of Stephanas (1 Cor. 1:16).[511] We noted earlier that the author of Acts attributes an extraordinary importance to the conversion of Crispus: "many of the Corinthians, when they heard (of it), believed and were baptized" (Acts 18:8b).[512] The conversion of Crispus evidently had a significant impact upon public opinion. "Luke" leaves no doubt about the basis of Crispus' influence, which is specified in the preceding sentence: Crispus was the ἀρχισυνάγωγος (Acts 18:8a). Because of Crispus' position as the synagogue president, his belief in the proclamation of Jesus as the Messiah served as a catalyst to the faith of others.[513] If the account of Acts is deemed to be historically reliable,[514] and if it is permissible to combine this account with Paul's report of the baptism of Crispus and Gaius in 1 Cor. 1:14, then one naturally asks whether Gaius might not have been among the "many Corinthians" who were influenced by the news of Crispus' conversion.

Moreover, the context of the account of Crispus' conversion in Acts describes Paul's preaching in the synagogue every Sabbath, where he "would try to convince Jews and Greeks" (Acts 18:4). If Luke's information is historically accurate, the synagogue at Corinth was frequented by a number of Gentile "God-fearers."[515] It is to the house of one of these "worshipers of God,"[516] Titius Justus, that Paul went when he departed from the synagogue (according to Acts 18:7).[517] This train of thought leads naturally to the inference that Gaius was a "God-fearer" (θεοσεβής)

---

511 Weiss, *Der erste Korintherbrief*, 20; Lindemann, *Der erste Korintherbrief*, 41–42; Schnabel, *Der erste Brief*, 100.
512 See above, ch. 4.
513 Theissen, *Social Setting*, 73.
514 Lüdemann, *Early Christianity according to Acts*, 203–204.
515 Haenchen, *Acts of the Apostles*, 534; Barrett, *Acts 15–28*, 864. For the limited sense in which it is appropriate to employ Luke's term "God-fearers" in reference to Gentile sympathizers of Judaism, see Judith Lieu, "The Race of the God-fearers" in idem, *Neither Jew Nor Greek? Constructing Early Christianity* (London: T & T Clark, 2002) 49–68.
516 Barrett, *Acts 15–28*, 868.
517 On the historicity of this tradition, see Lüdemann, *Early Christianity according to Acts*, 203.

before his baptism into Christ, one of the many Greeks and Romans who were attracted by the ethical monotheism of Judaism, and who associated with the synagogue.[518] The conclusion that Gaius was a "God-fearer" accords well with the results of our exegesis of 2 Corinthians: Paul's critic at Corinth had a preference for a Christology like that found in the Psalms of Solomon, which represented the Messiah as the fulfiller of the hopes of Israel (2 Cor. 10:7; 11:4).[519]

A second inference from the association of Crispus and Gaius in 1 Cor. 1:14 relates to their role in the formation of factions in the church at Corinth. We noted above the ironical quality of Paul's "thanksgiving" in 1 Cor. 1:14: Paul thanks God that he had baptized no one "except Crispus and Gaius."[520] We suggested, following Johannes Weiss,[521] that Paul's strangely negative manner of speaking about the baptism of Crispus and Gaius was conditioned by his polemic against the outbreak of faction.[522] We then hypothesized that Crispus and Gaius must have played some part in the formation of factions.[523] We found confirmation of this suspicion in Paul's use of the rhetorical device of a feigned lapse of memory in 1 Cor. 1:16, in order to separate Stephanas, whom Paul also baptized, from Crispus and Gaius.[524] By means of this stratagem, Paul sought to spare his strongest supporter at Corinth the force of the ironic thanksgiving reserved for those who had fomented discord.[525]

---

518 Barrett, *Acts 1–14*, 499–500. But note the question whether "God-fearers" would have made "good Christians" by Lieu, *Neither Jew Nor Greek?* 31–48. On the God-fearers generally, see Alf Thomas Kraabel, "The Disappearance of the God-fearers," *Numen* 23 (1981) 113–26; Max Wilcox, "The 'God-fearers' in Acts: A Reconsideration," *JSNT* 13 (1981) 102–22; Thomas M. Finn, "The God-fearers Reconsidered," *CBQ* 47 (1985) 75–84; John Gager, "Jews, Gentiles and Synagogues in the Book of Acts," *HTR* 79 (1986) 91–99; J. Andrew Overman, "The God-fearers: Some Neglected Features," *JSNT* 32 (1988) 17–26; E. A. Judge, "Jews, Proselytes and God-fearers Club Together," *NewDocs Vol. 9*, ed. S. R. Llewelyn (Grand Rapids: Eerdmans, 2002) 73–81.
519 See above, ch. 4, pp. 84–101, 128–29. For this Christology among Paul's Corinthian opponents, see already Georgi, *The Opponents of Paul*, 27–82.
520 See above, ch. 4, pp. 240–41. Cf. Lindemann, *Der erste Korintherbrief*, 42; Fitzmyer, *First Corinthians*, 146.
521 Weiss, *Der erste Korintherbrief*, 20.
522 See above, ch. 4, pp. 240–41, 249.
523 See above, ch. 4, p. 251.
524 See above, ch. 4, pp. 240–41. Cf. Weiss, *Der erste Korintherbrief*, 20; Lindemann, *Der erste Korintherbrief*, 42.
525 See above, ch. 4, p. 252. Cf. Dahl, "Paul and the Church at Corinth," 318; Lindemann, *Der erste Korintherbrief*, 42; Schnabel, *Der erste Brief*, 100.

We shall now attempt to take the next step and discover what role Gaius (along with Crispus) played in the formation of factions and whose partisan Gaius became. Careful analysis of the argumentative rhetoric of 1 Cor. 1–4 makes clear that Apollos was the one around whom a faction had formed in opposition to Paul.[526] This conclusion emerges from four aspects of Paul's argument.

First, there is the reduction in the number of factions in the course of Paul's argument: although four parties are alluded to in 1 Cor. 1:12, where Paul parodies the partisan behavior of the Corinthians, only two slogans are repeated in 1 Cor. 3:4—"I belong to Paul,"…"I belong to Apollos." From this we may conclude that the preceding apology (1 Cor. 1:18–3:4) was written with a view to the Apollos party.[527] It was evidently the adherents of Apollos who had pointed out a deficiency of σοφία λόγου in Paul's proclamation (1 Cor. 1:17; 2:4).

Second, in an important summary of his purposes in the argument, Paul states explicitly (1 Cor. 4:6): "I have applied (μετεσχημάτισα) these things to myself and Apollos for your benefit, brothers and sisters,…so that none of you may be puffed up in favor of one (ὑπὲρ τοῦ ἑνός) against the other (κατὰ τοῦ ἑτέρου)." The best way to understand the term μετεσχημάτισα in this instance is in the sense of "the application of a figure."[528] The figures of speech to which Paul makes reference are the illustrations from agriculture (1 Cor. 3:5–9), construction (1 Cor. 3:10–15), and household management (1 Cor. 4:1–5) in the preceding paragraphs.[529] The point of these illustrations is to demonstrate the collegiality of those who labor toward a common purpose as defined by God. The lessons are necessary because of the tendency of some in Corinth to become "inflated in favor of one against the other" (1 Cor. 4:6b). "The one" and "the other" refer to Apollos and Paul.[530]

Third, the figures by which Paul presents himself and Apollos as examples of harmonious relations embody subtle (and not so subtle) distinctions of status which have the effect of subordinating Apollos to

---

526 See already Ker, "Paul and Apollos—Colleagues or Rivals?" 75–97; Smit, "What is Apollos? What is Paul?" 231–51; Welborn, *Paul, the Fool of Christ*, 102–109.
527 Weiss, *Der erste Korintherbrief*, xxxiii.
528 Morna D. Hooker, "'Beyond the things which are written'? An Examination of 1 Corinthians 4:6," *NTS* 10 (1963) 127–32; J. S. Vos, "Der ΜΕΤΑΣΧΗΜΑΤΙΣΜΟΣ in 1 Kor 4,6," *ZNW* 86 (1995) 154–72.
529 Ker, "Paul and Apollos—Colleagues or Rivals?" 91–92; Welborn, *Paul, the Fool of Christ*, 106.
530 Weiss, *Der erste Korintherbrief*, 104.

Paul.[531] In the agricultural metaphor in 1 Cor. 3:5–9, it is Paul who has "planted" and Apollos who has "watered" (1 Cor. 3:6). Although both activities are necessary for growth, the one who plants has priority.[532] Apollos is, figuratively, Paul's "water-boy." The distinction is sharper in the building metaphor that follows in 1 Cor. 3:10–15, where Paul describes himself as a "skilled master-builder" (σοφὸς ἀρχιτέκτων) who has laid the foundation of the community, while Apollos is, figuratively, one of the anonymous workers who have added something to the structure.[533] Indeed, the anonymity of Apollos in this figure ("someone else is building on it," 1 Cor. 3:10) may be the clearest indication of Paul's feeling of rivalry.[534] A distinction between functions that are essential and those that are supplementary is implicit in these metaphors, and serves to diminish the contribution of Apollos to the Corinthian community.

Fourth, in light of the tension between Paul and Apollos that surfaces repeatedly in the argument of 1 Cor. 1:18–4:21, Paul's antithetical formulation of his commission as an apostle at the outset of the argument takes on a new significance in relation to Apollos: "For Christ did not send me to baptize but to proclaim the gospel, not with eloquent wisdom, so that the cross of Christ might not be emptied of its power" (1 Cor. 1:17). The negative formulation of Paul's commission ("not to baptize") distinguishes Paul from someone who was known as a "baptizer," as Apollos was, according to Acts 18:25.[535] The negative definition of the style and content of Paul's preaching ("not with eloquent wisdom") unmistakably distinguishes Paul's proclamation from that of another missionary for whom σοφία λόγου was characteristic.[536] The best explanation of the antithesis between σοφία λόγου and ὁ λόγος τοῦ σταυροῦ is that it reflects a contrast which some in Corinth have drawn between the eloquent wisdom of Apollos' preaching and the foolishness of Paul's gospel.[537]

What we learn about Apollos from the Acts of the Apostles (18:24–28) suggests that this teacher would have found an enthusiastic reception

---

531 Ker, "Paul and Apollos—Colleagues or Rivals?" 85–90; Welborn, *Paul, the Fool of Christ*, 108–109.
532 Collins, *First Corinthians*, 146.
533 Collins, *First Corinthians*, 148–50; Ker, "Paul and Apollos—Colleagues or Rivals?" 88–89.
534 Ker, "Paul and Apollos—Colleagues or Rivals?" 89.
535 Weiss, *Der erste Korintherbrief*, xxxi, 22.
536 Weiss, *Der erste Korintherbrief*, 22.
537 Smit, "What is Apollos? What is Paul?" 236, 246–48.

among those at Corinth who participated in learned culture. The author of Acts describes Apollos as "a Jew, a native of Alexandria,...an eloquent man, skilled in the exposition of Scriptures" (Acts 18:24).⁵³⁸ As a native of Alexandria,⁵³⁹ Apollos would have benefited from the rich intellectual culture of this teeming cosmopolis, to which Jews made significant contributions in the early Roman period.⁵⁴⁰ The expression ἀνὴρ λόγιος describes a person with rhetorical training, one who had mastered the art of oratory,⁵⁴¹ but also designates a "learned man" generally,⁵⁴² one who had studied philosophy and literature.⁵⁴³ The additional characterization of Apollos as δυνατός ἐν γραφαῖς probably refers to his ability to expound the deeper, allegorical meaning of religious texts through the application of a philosophical framework.⁵⁴⁴

Every mention of Apollos in the writing known to us as 1 Corinthians reveals the admiration which this Christian sophist engendered among some in Corinth⁵⁴⁵ In 1 Cor. 16:12, Paul already finds himself

---

538 On the historicity of the tradition preserved in Acts 18:24, see Lüdemann, *Early Christianity according to Acts*, 207–209.
539 On the disputed issue of whether the expression Ἀλεξανδρεὺς τῷ γένει implies that Apollos was a citizen of the Greek polis, see Winter, *Paul among the Sophists*, 175 n.142. On the political and social status of the Jews in Alexandria, see A. Kasher, *The Jews in Hellenistic and Roman Egypt: The Struggle for Equal Rights* (Tübingen: Mohr Siebeck, 1985) 197–207.
540 J. Modrzejewski, *The Jews of Egypt: From Ramses II to Emperor Hadrian* (Princeton: Princeton University Press, 1995).
541 Philo *Post.* 53 describes one engaged in σοφιστικαὶ τεχναί as a λόγιος ἀνήρ. See the definition of ἀνὴρ λόγιος in Phrynichus 198 (ὡς οἱ πολλοὶ λέγουσιν ἐπὶ τοῦ δεινοῦ εἰπεῖν καὶ ὑψηλοῦ), supported by Lobeck's citations. Cf. Field, *Notes on the Translation of the New Testament*, 129; Winter, *Paul among the Sophists*, 126.
542 Plutarch *Cic.* 49.5, where Augustus calls Cicero a λόγιος ἀνήρ. Cf. Ker, "Paul and Apollos—Colleagues or Rivals?" 77–78; Murphy-O'Connor, *Paul*, 275
543 Moulton and Milligan, *The Vocabulary of the Greek Testament*, 378; Weiss, *Der erste Korintherbrief*, xxxi n.1. Compare the curriculum of Tiberius, who studied rhetoric, philosophy and literature, and whose writings "reveal a preference for the learned and elaborate, that is, for the Alexandrian," according to Barbara Levick, *Tiberius the Politician* (London: Routledge, 1999) 15–17, esp. 16.
544 Weiss, *Der erste Korintherbrief*, xxxi n.1. Cf. Richard A. Horsley, "Wisdom of Word and Words of Wisdom at Corinth," *CBQ* 39 (1977) 224–39, esp. 232, repr. in idem, *Wisdom and Spiritual Transcendence at Corinth: Studies in First Corinthians* (Eugene: Cascade Books, 2008) 21–38, here 29.
545 Weiss, *Der erste Korintherbrief*, xxxi–xxxiv; Litfin, *St. Paul's Theology of Proclamation*, 162; Winter, *Paul among the Sophists*, 175–76; Smit, "What is Apollos? What is Paul?" 231–51.

obliged to respond to the question about when Apollos may be returning to Corinth.⁵⁴⁶ Paul's emphatic assurance that he had strongly urged (πολλὰ παρεκάλεσα) Apollos to return to Corinth should probably be seen as a reflection of the urgency which Paul sensed in the Corinthians' request.⁵⁴⁷ Indeed, according to codex D of Acts 18:27, Apollos came to Corinth on the first occasion at the invitation of "some Corinthians" (τινες Κορίνθιοι) who were visiting Ephesus and were impressed by his speech.⁵⁴⁸ In view of the role that an over-valuation of "eloquent wisdom" plays in Paul's discussion of the outbreak of faction in 1 Cor. 1–4, it would be very surprising if admiration for Apollos, the ἀνὴρ λόγιος, were not somehow involved in the problem. As Peter Richardson observes, "Apollos hovers over the difficulties in Corinth to a very much larger extent than many recent commentators allow."⁵⁴⁹ The reluctance of interpreters to acknowledge the rivalry between Paul and Apollos reflects the force of Paul's rhetoric of collegiality and unanimity in 1 Cor. 3:5–4:6.⁵⁵⁰ But we must take care to distinguish between rhetoric and reality. Thus, we may conclude that a preference for the rhetorical skill and sophistical knowledge of Apollos among some at Corinth lay at the root of the partisanship from which Paul seeks to dissuade the Corinthians in 1 Cor. 1–4.⁵⁵¹ Given the precedence of Crispus and Gaius in Paul's critique of partisanship (in 1 Cor. 1:14–15), we must also conclude that Gaius (along with Crispus) was foremost among the Corinthians who expressed their preference for Apollos over Paul. This conclusion accords well with our exegesis of 2 Cor. 10–13, which discovered at many points (especially in 10:10–11; 11:4, 5, 6) a disparagement of Paul for defects in his oratory by someone at Corinth, and a corresponding admiration by the same Corinthian critic for the professional eloquence of another apostle with whom Paul is obliged to compare him-

---

546 Weiss, *Der erste Korintherbrief,* 384–85; Robertson and Plummer, *First Epistle,* 392; Fee, *First Epistle,* 824; Winter, *Paul among the Sophists,* 141, 177; Murphy-O'Connor, *Paul,* 184.
547 Collins, *First Corinthians,* 598: "may affect an apologetic tone."
548 M.-E. Boismard and A. Lamouille, *Les Actes des deux apôtre* (Paris: Gabalda, 1990) 3.237–38; Barrett, *Acts 15–28,* 890–91.
549 Peter Richardson, "The Thunderbolt in Q and the Wise Man in Corinth" in *From Jesus to Paul,* eds. P. Richardson and J. C. Hurd (Waterloo: Laurier, 1984) 100.
550 Mitchell, *Paul and the Rhetoric of Reconciliation,* 98–99, 177–78.
551 Welborn, *Paul, the Fool of Christ,* 102–16; cf. Kirner, "Apostolat und Patronage (II)," 37–47.

self.[552] Paul represents the preference of some at Corinth for the eloquent wisdom of Apollos as the worst kind of partisanship, comparing their outspoken admiration for one apostle over another with the boisterous shouts of theater claques (in 1 Cor. 1:12), in a parody worthy of Cicero.[553] We should acknowledge how difficult it is to see beyond Paul's invective, in order to determine whether Gaius' admiration for Apollos is well described as partisanship, or would be better characterized as preference.

Finally, we turn to the connection of Gaius with Erastus. Some sort of association is implied by the fact that their greetings are conveyed in the same verse, Rom. 16:23.[554] Gerd Theissen has made the interesting observation that Erastus' greetings give the impression of being "appended" to those of Gaius, "as if he had just stopped by" Gaius' house as Paul was concluding the epistle.[555] From this insight, Craig de Vos draws the plausible inference that "Erastus' visit may have been as an *amicus cliens* to his patron who was promoting his career."[556] What this relationship suggests about the social status of Gaius depends upon one's assessment of the status of Erastus. We have acknowledged the ambiguity of the linguistic evidence pertaining to the title by which Erastus is designated, ὁ οἰκονόμος τῆς πόλεως: this title might refer to a minor financial office held by a public slave, or it might refer to a high-ranking position attained through election by a freeborn citizen.[557] If one judges that the balance of the archaeological evidence, despite its ambiguity, inclines toward identification of Paul's Erastus with the Corinthian aedile of that name,[558] then one must look for Gaius far up the social scale, among the urban elite.[559] We recall that John Kent inferred that Erastus the Corinthian aedile was a freedman, because of the lack of a patronymic.[560] As a *libertus* who had attained the lofty position of aedile, Erastus may have needed such patronage as Gaius had to offer.

---

552 See above, ch. 3, pp. 129–32.
553 Welborn, *Politics and Rhetoric*, 14–15.
554 Theissen, *Social Setting*, 89.
555 Theissen, *Social Setting*, 89.
556 de Vos, *Church and Community Conflicts*, 201–202, drawing the further inference that "Gaius was somewhat socially superior [to Erastus]."
557 See above, ch. 4, pp. 261–67.
558 See above, ch. 4, p. 274, following Kent, *Corinth VIII.3: The Inscriptions*, 99–100.
559 Cf. Gill, "In Search of the Social Elite in the Early Church," 328–30.
560 Kent, *Corinth VIII.3: The Inscriptions*, 100.

We may summarize what we have learned about Gaius on the basis of our prosopography. The fact that Gaius bears a common Roman *praenomen* leaves open a number of possibilities: Gaius may have been a descendant of one of the Italian settlers of the colony, or he may have been a Greek immigrant to the city; Gaius may have been a freedman who gained wealth following his manumission, or he may have been a freeborn citizen of higher rank. Four Corinthians bearing the *praenomen* Gaius and datable in the mid-first century were surveyed in an attempt to form a more rounded image of the kind of man whom Paul's Gaius may have been. Perhaps Paul's Gaius was a man like Julius Syrus, a descendant of a freedman of the colony's founder, a man of Eastern origin, who sought to enhance his identity by participation in a cult from the region of his birth. Perhaps Paul's Gaius was an aspiring freedman like Novius Felix, whose wealth gained in business permitted him to undertake responsibilities in a religious association. Only in the case that Paul's Gaius was a man of equestrian rank like Gaius Julius Spartiaticus would the possibilities embraced in our prosopography significantly alter our picture of the social status of the first Christians. But even this would not be entirely anomalous, since a Roman knight is among the "God-fearers" attested on inscriptions.[561]

The information that Gaius was "the host of the whole *ekklesia*" proved to be productive of more conclusive inferences regarding the status, role, and relationships of Paul's friend. Consideration of the available venues for assembly led to the conclusion that the *domus* provides the most plausible context in which Gaius would have hosted the Corinthian Christians. Moreover, because the number of Christians at Corinth was not small, and perhaps approached 100, Gaius must have possessed a substantial *domus*. As the only person in Paul's epistles who is said to have hosted all of the Christians of a given city in his house as a central meeting-place, Gaius of Corinth may well have been the wealthiest convert in the Pauline mission.[562] Despite the dearth of domestic archaeology at Corinth, a review of the excavation reports disclosed two houses of the early Roman period in which we may imagine Gaius hosting the whole

---

561 *CIJ* I.5: *Aemilio Va[l]enti eq(uiti) romano metu[e]nti q[ui vixit] an(nos) XV me(n)s(es) III die(s) XXIII*. Cf. Louis H. Feldman, "Jewish 'Sympathizers' in Classical Literature and Inscriptions," *TAPA* 81 (1950) 200–208; Laurence H. Kant, "Jewish Inscriptions in Greek and Latin," *ANRW* II.20.2 (1987) 690.
562 Lampe, "Paul, Patrons, and Clients" in *Paul in the Greco-Roman World*, 496; Friesen, "Poverty in Pauline Studies," 356.

ekklesia, especially the large house east of the theater. Analysis of the structure and function of a Roman house enabled conclusions about the social implications of Gaius' service as "host": the size of the house, the differentiation of space, the rituals by which access was governed, and expectations related to the provision of food and entertainment— all combined to enhance the status of Gaius as "host," and to cast him in the role of "benefactor." As the benefactor of the Christians at Corinth, Gaius may have been approached by members of the congregation for other *beneficia* which a patron was expected to provide: legal help, a loan, advice on domestic matters, etc. However that may be, it is clear that a rival apostle, who had come to Corinth, enjoyed the hospitality of someone in the city (2 Cor. 11:4; 11:20). This makes it likely that Gaius played the role of patron to an evangelist who preached "another Jesus" and a "different gospel."

Finally, the association of Gaius with Crispus and Erastus permitted several inferences. It is likely that Gaius was among the "many Corinthians" who were influenced by the conversion of the ἀρχισυνάγωγος, Crispus. In this case, we might infer that Gaius was a "God-fearer" before his baptism into Christ. Consideration of the ironic tone of Paul's "thanksgiving" in 1 Cor. 1:14 suggested that Crispus and Gaius were somehow involved in the formation of factions. Analysis of the argumentative rhetoric of 1 Cor. 1–4 led to the conclusion that enthusiasm for the "eloquent wisdom" of Apollos had induced some to express a preference for this teacher over Paul. No conclusion lies closer to hand than that Crispus and Gaius were foremost in their admiration for Apollos, and were, from Paul's point of view, the ringleaders of the Apollos party. Last of all, the mention of Erastus with Gaius in Rom. 16:23 led to the plausible inference that Gaius was Erastus' social superior and patron.

When we combine this prosopographical data with information derived from close reading of 2 Cor. 10–13 and 1:1–2:13; 7:5–16, the portrait of an interesting personality begins to emerge. Gaius of Corinth was a Roman provincial of considerable wealth and social status; his moral values and aesthetic standards were those of the educated elite of the early Empire; he upheld the traditional norms of friendship and sought to govern his life by reason, in accordance with Stoic principles; he had a fondness for debate and an acerbic wit; he had a strong sense of "belonging to Christ"; he was susceptible to remorse and capable of genuine repentance. All in all, he was a man worthy of Paul's friendship, capable of enmity, and amenable to reconciliation. To the story of that friendship we now turn.

Chapter Six
History of a Friendship

On the hypothesis that the wrongdoer of 2 Cor. 2 and 7 is to be identified with Paul's "host" Gaius, we may now venture to reconstruct the history of their relationship. We shall argue that "friendship" is the proper category in which to conceive of this relationship. To describe the relationship between Paul and Gaius as a friendship may seem strange from a modern point of view, in which Paul is "the apostle" and Gaius his convert, one of his spiritual "children." But we should beware of the anachronism involved in projecting an authority which Paul acquired only after his death back into the first decades of the Christian movement.[1] The conflict over the legitimacy of Paul's apostleship, to which the Corinthian epistles bear witness,[2] demonstrates that the contemporary perception of Paul by no means corresponded to the later estimation of his significance.

The relational category that would have been available to Paul and Gaius within Greco-Roman culture was that of friendship.[3] To be sure, the friendship of Paul and Gaius was a friendship of a particular sort, namely, that between social unequals.[4] Because this friendship involved "the superiority of one party over the other," the relationship would

---

1   Rightly, Kirner, "Apostolat und Patronage (II)," 58–59.
2   Käsemann, "Die Legitimität des Apostels," 42–64; Georg Strecker, "Die Legitimität des paulinischen Apostolates nach 2 Korinther 10–13," *NTS* 38 (1992) 566–86.
3   Credit for insight into the role of friendship and enmity in the relationship between Paul and the Corinthians goes to Marshall, *Enmity in Corinth,* passim, esp. 232, 245, 345. More generally, John T. Fitzgerald, "Paul and Friendship" in *Paul in the Greco-Roman World*, ed. J. Paul Sampley (Harrisburg: Trinity Press International, 2003) 319–43.
4   Marshall, *Enmity in Corinth*, 345, lists Gaius, along with four other Corinthians, as "intimates" of Paul who deserve to be "ranked among his patrons." For Gaius as friend and patron, see further White, "Paul and *Pater Familias*" in *Paul in the Greco-Roman World*, 467; Lampe, "Paul, Patrons, and Clients" in *Paul in the Greco-Roman World*, 498–99; Kirner, "Apostolat und Patronage (II)," 43. On unequal friendships in general, see Konstan, *Friendship in the Classical World*, 76–82, 135–45.

not have qualified as the "best" kind of friendship, according to Aristotle's definition.⁵ But even Aristotle concedes that social unequals are capable of friendship,⁶ while warning that, when the disparity is wide, it will be difficult for the parties to remain friends.⁷ In the case of Paul and Gaius, shared beliefs and hopes served to diminish the status differences between them, and nurtured genuine amity. A rupture eventually occurred in their relationship, when expectations were disappointed, and Gaius felt deceived.⁸ But Paul strove assiduously for reconciliation—an outcome which also belongs to the category of friendship.⁹ Thus, we shall argue that friendship, as it was understood in antiquity, is the proper category in which to conceive of the relationship between Paul and Gaius.

While a full appreciation of the propriety of this category must await the unfolding of the history of the relationship, it may be prudent here to identify the obvious features of Paul's treatment of the wrongdoer which lead us to infer a friendship. First, Paul's characterization of Gaius as "the one who did wrong" (ὁ ἀδικήσας) and of himself as "the one who was wronged" (ὁ ἀδικηθείς) in 2 Cor. 7:12 locates their interaction in the realm of friendship. Ancient literature on friendship is preoccupied with "wrong" because of the danger that "wrong" poses to the relationship. "Wrongdoing" is the first subject treated in Book 7 (on friendship) of the *Eudemian Ethics*, where Aristotle makes it constitutive of the nature of friendship: "we all say that right (τὸ δίκαιον) and wrong (τὸ ἄδικον) are chiefly displayed towards friends."¹⁰ Later, Aristotle discloses, in passing,

---

5 Aristotle *Eth. nic.* 8.7.1; Konstan, *Friendship in the Classical World*, 94–95.
6 Aristotle *Eth. nic.* 8.7.1; *Eth. eud.* 7.3.2.
7 Aristotle *Eth. nic.* 8.7.4.
8 On rupture (διάλυσις) in friendship, see, e.g., Aristotle *Eth. nic.* 8.13, 9.1.3, 9.3.2; see in general Fürst, *Streit unter Freunden*; Lorraine Smith Pangle, "Quarrels, Conflicting Claims, Dissolutions" in *Aristotle and the Philosophy of Friendship* (Cambridge: Cambridge University Press, 2003) 123–41.
9 E.g., Dionysius of Halicarnassus *Ant. rom.* 3.7.3: "mutual reconciliation is the best and the most becoming to kinsmen and friends, in which there is no remembrance of past injuries, but a general and sincere remission of everything that has been done or suffered on both sides"; Seneca *Quomodo amicitia continenda sit*, frag. 1. Cf. David L. Balch, "Political Friendship in the Historian Dionysius of Halicarnassus, *Roman Antiquities*" in *Greco-Roman Perspectives on Friendship*, ed. John T. Fitzgerald (Atlanta: Scholars Press, 1997) 124–25; Fürst, *Streit unter Freunden*, 26–27, 35, 190–91; Fitzgerald, "Paul and Paradigm Shifts," 241–62, 316–25; idem, "Paul and Friendship" in *Paul in the Greco-Roman World*, 335–37.
10 Aristotle *Eth. eud.* 7.1.3.

the deeper psychological source of concern about the effect of "wrong" upon friendship: "those who suffer harm from one another (οἱ ἀδικούμενοι) do not feel affection for one another."[11] In the *Nicomachean Ethics*, Aristotle makes "wrong" a gradient of friendship: "wrong (ἄδικα) is increasingly serious in proportion as it is done to a nearer friend."[12] Predictably, there is much talk of "wrong" in Cicero's correspondence with his friends. In an exchange between Cicero and Quintus Metellus Celer, both parties complain of "wrong": Metellus remonstrates with Cicero that their friendship had led him to expect better treatment,[13] while Cicero replies that Metellus should be content that he did not complain to him directly of "injury" (*iniuria*).[14] Surveying the conflicts between Roman friends and the incidence of enmity, David Konstan observes that when enmity between friends became unavoidable, "a speaker sought to cast himself as the injured party."[15]

Second, the term by which Paul describes the consequence of the wrong done, namely λύπη, evokes the vulnerability of friendship. We have already encountered Aristotle's explanation of the connection between "pain" and friendship: pain is worse when it comes at the hands of friends, by whom we expect to be treated well, rather than ill,[16] a sentiment echoed by Plutarch many generations later, confessing that his distress is greater the more he gives himself up to loving a person, if the relationship goes astray.[17] In the literature on friendship, a sympathetic concern with "pain" is strongly emphasized. According to Aristotle, friends wish to share one another's grief: "for a friend wishes most of all not only to feel pain with his friend, but even to feel the same pain" (βούλεται γὰρ μάλιστά τε οὐ μόνον συλλυπεῖσθαι ὁ φίλος τῷ φίλῳ ἀλλὰ καὶ τὴν αὐτὴν λύπην).[18] As a general rule of friendship, Aristotle reports that "ev-

---

11 Aristotle *Eth. eud.* 7.2.19; see also Dionysius of Halicarnassus *Ant. rom.* 8.34.1–3.
12 Aristotle *Eth. nic.* 8.9.3: "For example, it is more shocking to defraud a comrade of money than a fellow-citizen."
13 Cicero *Fam.* 5.1. Cf. Konstan, *Friendship in the Classical World*, 125; Hall, *Politeness and Politics*, 153–56.
14 Cicero *Fam.* 5.2.6. Cf. Konstan, *Friendship in the Classical World*, 126–27; Hall, *Politeness and Politics*, 156–60.
15 Konstan, *Friendship in the Classical World*, 127. See also Hall, *Politeness and Politics*, 136–38.
16 Aristotle *Rhet.* 2.2.8–9, 15, 1379a.
17 Plutarch *Mor.* 460D-464C.
18 Aristotle *Eth. eud.* 7.6.8.

eryone is reluctant to be a cause of pain (λύπη) to his friends."[19] Among the sententia attributed to Menander is the observation: "a worthy friend is a physician to your pain."[20] Cicero asserts that the sharing of adversity, and even pain, belongs to the nature of friendship.[21]

Each of these truisms on pain and friendship is echoed by Paul in 2 Cor. 1–2 and 7, as Paul seeks to conciliate the Corinthians, and especially that individual who is in danger of drowning in "excessive sorrow" (περισσοτέρα λύπη). Thus, the sharing of grief and joy between friends is asserted by Paul in a Christian sense in 2 Cor. 1:6–7: "if we are consoled, it is for your consolation, which becomes active in endurance of the same sufferings (τῶν αὐτῶν παθημάτων) which we also suffer..., for we know that as you share our sufferings, so also you share our consolation." The reluctance of a friend to be a cause of pain to his friends is affirmed by Paul in 2 Cor. 2:1–4: "So I made up my mind not to make you another painful visit (μὴ πάλιν ἐν λύπῃ πρὸς ὑμᾶς ἐλθεῖν). For if I cause you pain (εἰ γὰρ ἐγὼ λυπῶ ὑμᾶς), who is there to make me rejoice except the one who has been pained by me (καὶ τίς ὁ εὐφραίνων με εἰ μὴ ὁ λυπούμενος ἐξ ἐμοῦ)?...For I wrote to you,...not to cause you pain (οὐχ ἵνα λυπηθῆτε), but to let you know the abundant love that I have for you." The role of physician to a friend's pain is assumed by Paul in 2 Cor. 2:5–11, where he urges the Corinthians to "forgive" and "console" the remorseful wrongdoer, and to "reaffirm love" for him, "so that he may not be overwhelmed by excessive sorrow" (μή πως τῇ περισσοτέρᾳ λύπῃ καταποθῇ).

It is striking how many of the vocabulary of friendship from the relevant literature are mobilized by Paul in 2 Cor. 1:1–2:13; 7:5–16. In 2 Cor. 1:7, Paul seeks to reassure the Corinthians of the constancy of his bond with them, beyond the pain which they have mutually suffered: "And our hope is firm (βεβαία) on behalf of you, knowing that just as you are partners (κοινωνοί) of the suffering, thus also of the consolation." "Constancy" (τὸ βέβαιον) is a notable feature of Aristotle's theory of friendship: "friendship seems to be something stable (βέβαιον)";[22] "an insecure (οὐ βέβαιος) friendship is not friendship at all";[23] "bad men have

---

19 Aristotle *Eth. nic.* 9.11.4.
20 Menander *Sent.* 456, in Siegfried Jaekel, *Menandri sententiae* (Leipzig: Teubner, 1964).
21 Cicero *Amic.* 46–48. See also Lucian *Tox.* 6.
22 Aristotle *Eth. eud.* 7.2.39.
23 Aristotle *Eth. eud.* 7.5.3.

no constancy (τὸ βέβαιον) in friendship, for they do not even remain true to their own characters."²⁴ Similarly, Aristotle makes "partnership" (κοινωνία) definitive of friendship: "partnership (κοινωνία) is the essence of friendship";²⁵ "all friendship involves partnership (κοινωνία)";²⁶ "friendship is essentially a partnership" (κοινωνία γὰρ ἡ φιλία).²⁷

In the proposition (πρόθεσις) of the epistle, Paul asserts "that we have behaved in the world, and especially toward you, with simplicity and sincerity of God (ἐν ἁπλότητι καὶ εἰλικρινείᾳ τοῦ θεοῦ), and not by worldly wisdom but by the grace of God" (2 Cor. 1:12).²⁸ The demonstration of Paul's "sincerity" had become necessary, because the complex strategies employed in the previous epistles, as Paul struggled to maintain and restore his relationship, had risked the impression of dissimulation, through his assumption of a variety of roles and his rapid alteration of poses—now bellicose (2 Cor. 10:1–6), now foolish (2 Cor. 11:1–12:10), now grave (2 Cor. 4:16–5:10), now pathetic (2 Cor. 6:1–13; 7:2–4). Such changes in character posed a challenge to the ancient understanding of the basis of friendship. Employing an adjective of the same term claimed by Paul in defense of his conduct, Aristotle explains the ethical basis of "friendship between good men," in that portion of the *Eudemian Ethics* devoted to friendship: "For the good is simple (ἁπλοῦν)…and also the good man is always alike and does not change in character, whereas the wicked and the foolish (ὁ ἄφρων) are quite different in the evening from what they were in the morning."²⁹

In the first of the arguments by which Paul justifies his conduct (in 2 Cor. 1:15–22), he appeals to the constancy of his goodwill toward the Corinthians as proof of his sincerity, against the appearance of "vacillation" (ἐλαφρία).³⁰ It was a difficult argument for Paul to make, because, in fact, Paul had changed his plans, and had failed to keep his promise to

---

24 Aristotle *Eth. nic.* 8.8.5.
25 Aristotle *Eth. nic.* 8.9.1–2.
26 Aristotle *Eth. nic.* 8.12.1.
27 Aristotle *Eth. nic.* 9.12.1.
28 For 2 Cor. 1:12–14 as the *propositio* of Paul's "therapeutic epistle" in 2 Cor. 1:1–2:13; 7:5–16, see L. L. Welborn, "Paul's Appeal to the Emotions in 2 Cor. 1.1–2.13; 7.5–16," *JSNT* 82 (2001) 57. Cf. H. D. Betz, "Corinthians, Second Epistle to the," *ABD* 1 (1992) 1148–54. On ἁπλότης καὶ εἰλικρίνεια, see Windisch, *Der zweite Korintherbrief,* 54.
29 Aristotle *Eth. eud.* 7.5.2.
30 BDAG 314 s.v. ἐλαφρία. Cf. Welborn, *Politics and Rhetoric,* 139, 143–45, 177.

return to Corinth.³¹ Paul can only appeal to the "confidence" in which he formulated his plans, and ultimately, beyond the vagaries of the present situation, to the "faithfulness" of God: "In this confidence (πεποίθησις), I was wishing earlier to come to you…But God is faithful (πιστός), that our word to you has not been 'yes' and 'no'" (2 Cor. 1:15, 18). By now, it will not surprise us to discover that "confidence" was taken to be an essential characteristic of friendship, as well as a benefit of the relationship. In the *Eudemian Ethics,* Aristotle insists that "there is no stable friendship without confidence (ἄνευ πίστεως)."³² In the *Nicomachean Ethics,* Aristotle advises: "one should not admit a person to friendship or really be friends, before each has shown the other that he is worthy of friendship and has won his confidence (καὶ πιστευθῇ)."³³ Epicurus' aphorisms place a high value upon confidence or trust in friendship. One saying contrasts "utility" with "trust" as the desideratum of friendship: "We have use not so much for usefulness from our friends as for trust in their usefulness."³⁴ Another saying warns that not to rely on friends "cuts off confidence concerning the future."³⁵

Other language belonging to the friendship *topos* might easily be identified in 2 Cor. 1:1–2:13; 7:5–16, especially the highly charged emotional vocabulary that pervades the letter.³⁶ We shall examine such terms in the course of our reconstruction of the final stages of the relationship between Paul and Gaius, below. It is important to take note of the vocabulary associated with friendship in 2 Cor. 1:1–2:13; 7:5–16, because the words φιλία and φίλος do not occur, either here or elsewhere in the Pauline corpus, and one might wrongly infer, from the absence of these technical terms, that Paul had no use for friendship.³⁷ But the terms and concepts which we have briefly surveyed (ἄδικον, λύπη, βέβαιον, κοινωνία, ἁπλοῦν, πίστις) are so regularly associated with friendship in the relevant literature as to warrant the hypothesis that friendship

---

31 Halmel, *Der zweite Korintherbrief,* 43–54.
32 Aristotle *Eth. eud.* 7.2.40.
33 Aristotle *Eth. nic.* 8.3.8–9.
34 Epicurus *Vatican Saying* 34; Konstan, *Friendship in the Classical World,* 109.
35 Epicurus *Vatican Saying* 39; Konstan, *Friendship in the Classical World,* 109.
36 L. L. Welborn, "Paul and Pain: Paul's Emotional Therapy in 2 Cor. 1:1–2:13; 7:5–16 in the Context of Ancient Psychagogic Literature," *NTS* (forthcoming).
37 Judge, "St. Paul as a Radical Critic of Society," *Social Distinctives of the Christians,* 106–107; cf. Fitzgerald, "Paul and Friendship" in *Paul in the Greco-Roman World,* 331–32.

is the proper category in which to conceive of the relationship between Paul and Gaius.[38]

Beyond vocabulary, the style or genre of the letter in which Paul seeks to conciliate the wrongdoer locates his communication in the realm of friendship. On this point, we follow the suggestion of Hans Windisch, as noted above: in 2 Cor. 1:1–2:13; 7:5–16 Paul adopts the "therapeutic" or "conciliatory" style.[39] As defined by Libanius in his handbook of *Epistolary Types*, "the therapeutic style is that in which we conciliate someone who has been caused grief by us for some reason."[40] In the social situation constitutive of this letter type, the writer and the recipient are friends.[41] This assumed relationship is made explicit in the final sentence of the sample letter supplied by Libanius: "For it is my aim always to heal my friends rather than to cause them sorrow" (σκοπὸς γάρ μοι θεραπεύειν ἀεὶ τοὺς φίλους ἐστὶν ἤπερ λυπεῖν).[42]

Mention of the aim of Paul's communication raises the issue of *perspective* in friendship. Paul's vocabulary and style make clear that he sought to cast his interaction with the wrongdoer in the mold of friendship. But, would Gaius have viewed the relationship in this way, given the social disparity between them? Peter White has observed: "Whereas upper-class Romans often befriended poets and philosophers, they rarely established such connections with those artists and intellectuals whose origins and formation diverged radically from their own: musicians, actors, painters, sculptors, and even the schoolmaster-scholars known as *grammatici*."[43] Would Paul's social and educational background have qualified him for friendship with a wealthy Corinthian? Or, more to the point, would Paul's refusal of the gift of financial support when he was resident in Corinth (1 Cor. 9; 2 Cor. 11:7–10),[44] and his determination to support himself by working with his hands (1 Cor. 4:12; 9:6),[45]

---

38 See the discussion of other terminology associated with friendship in Paul by Fitzgerald, "Paul and Friendship" in *Paul in the Greco-Roman World*, 332–33.
39 Windisch, *Der zweite Korintherbrief*, 8.
40 Ps.-Libanius *Ep. Char.* 19; text and trans. in Malherbe, *Ancient Epistolary Theorists*, 68–69.
41 On social situation as constitutive of letter type, see Stowers, "Social Typification" in *The Social World of Formative Christianity and Judaism*, 78–90.
42 Ps.-Libanius *Ep. Char.* 66; Malherbe, *Ancient Epistolary Theorists*, 76–77.
43 White, *Promised Verse*, 14.
44 For Paul's refusal of a gift as a refusal of friendship, see Marshall, *Enmity in Corinth*, 246, 257, 397.
45 For Paul's banausic occupation as a barrier to elite friendship, see Hock, *Social Context*, 60–65; Welborn, *Paul, the Fool of Christ*, 109.

have rendered Paul unworthy of friendship with Gaius? Would Paul's decision to preach nothing except "Christ crucified" (1 Cor. 2:2), thus emphasizing the shameful manner of Jesus' death, have destroyed whatever ground of rapport existed with Gaius, by exposing a genuine difference of values? These questions are difficult to answer, not just because we happen to possess only Paul's side of the conversation, but rather because the greater partner in a friendship between social unequals tended to be the silent partner, while the weaker partner was more voluble, because it was with words that he sought to reciprocate more tangible benefits.[46]

To acknowledge the role of perspective in friendship is to confront the larger problem of the *definition* of "friendship."[47] The range of ties denoted by the terms φιλία and *amicitia* was vast, and the use of these terms was elastic.[48] For this reason, a number of historians question whether the concept "friendship" has much definitional force.[49] The causes of ambiguity with respect to friendship are two. First, the nature of the commitment of Roman friends to each other was "formally undefined."[50] Peter White observes: "In contrast to many other relationships into which a Roman could enter (as parent, spouse, master, soldier, or maker of a contract, for example), friendship carried no legal consequences. It could not even be translated into a definite set of rights and duties which were morally if not legally prescribed."[51] Second, the nature of the relationship between friends of different social stations would seem to be more accurately described as "patronage."[52] Richard Saller argues

---

46 White, *Promised Verse*, 20, observing that the great friends and patrons, Maecenas, Messalla, and their peers, "left little or no testimony about their relationships."
47 Peter A. Brunt, "*Amicitia* in the Late Republic," *Proceedings of the Cambridge Philological Society* 2 (1965) 1–20; Konstan, *Friendship in the Classical World*, 1, 7–8, 56–57, 68; White, *Promised Verse*, 13–14.
48 Brunt, "*Amicitia* in the Late Republic," 11, repr. in idem, *The Fall of the Roman Republic and Related Essays* (Oxford: Oxford University Press, 1988) 381; see also Konstan, *Friendship in the Classical World*, 122–24; White, *Promised Verse*, 13; Fitzgerald, "Paul and Friendship" in *Paul in the Greco-Roman World*, 329.
49 White, *Promised Verse*, 13.
50 White, *Promised Verse*, 27.
51 White, *Promised Verse*, 28
52 See the discussion in Peter White, "*Amicitia* and the profession of poetry in early imperial Rome," *JRS* 68 (1978) 74–92, esp. 81–82; Barbara K. Gold, *Literary Patronage in Greece and Rome* (Chapel Hill: University of North Carolina Press, 1987) 40, 71, 104, 134; Saller, "Patronage and Friendship," 49–62; David Konstan, "Patrons and Friends," *CP* 90 (1995) 328–42, esp. 328–29; idem, *Friendship in the Classical World*, 135–37, 143–45.

that "the status-conscious Romans subdivided their friends into categories: *superiores, pares* and *inferiores*. Each category called for an appropriate mode of behavior. Resemblances between the behavior of aristocratic *amici inferiores* and *clientes* suggest that *amici inferiores* can reasonably be analyzed under the heading of patronage."[53]

These difficulties must be countenanced by anyone who appropriates the category of "friendship" to analyze relationships in the Greco-Roman world, and they apply no less to Paul and Gaius than to Horace and Maecenas. Yet we may follow the lead of students of friendship in antiquity, by regarding these ambiguities as contextual complications of our analysis, which nevertheless do not have the effect of emptying the category "friendship" of meaning.[54] To say that friendship was "formally undefined" is to recognize that friendship represented an "open-ended commitment,"[55] particularly for the weaker party to the relationship, and that friendship operated according to "an almost completely situational ethic."[56] But this does not mean that friendship in the Greco-Roman world lacked a set of conventions—gestures and formulas—which defined the relationship, which marked its beginning and signaled its end, and which governed the conduct of enmity and the pursuit of reconciliation. It also happens to be the case that the law did not formally define patronage.[57] But who would doubt the usefulness of "patronage" as a category for analyzing relationships in the Roman world?

As for the suspicion that "friendship" was a euphemism for patronage, when applied to relationships between superiors and inferiors, we should not be too eager to dismiss the terminology with which Greeks and Romans themselves described their relationships.[58] The language of friendship was used to represent a range of relationships in Roman society, when parties spoke with each other directly, and when they spoke

---

53 Saller, "Patronage and friendship," 57, referencing Seneca *Ep.* 94.14; Pliny *Ep.* 2.6.2; 7.3.2.
54 White, *Promised Verse*, 27–34; Konstan, *Friendship in the Classical World*, 135–37, 142, 144–45; Bowditch, *Gift Economy of Patronage*, 19–30; Fitzgerald, "Paul and Friendship" in *Paul in the Greco-Roman World*, 329.
55 White, *Promised Verse*, 28.
56 White, *Promised Verse*, 28
57 Saller, "Patronage and friendship," 49; cf. Brunt, "*Amicitia* in the late Republic" in idem, *The Fall of the Roman Republic*, 440.
58 White, *Promised Verse*, 29.

about each other to third parties.[59] It is not as if there were some other vocabulary to which the language of friendship was subsidiary.[60] On the contrary, "friendship" was the name conventionally applied to attachments between wealthy Romans and the intellectuals who shared their company.[61] Our reluctance to accept the term "friendship" as descriptive of relationships between social unequals reflects our modern assumption about the nature of friendship, but is anachronistic when applied to Roman society, which was so highly stratified that "the two parties to a friendship would rarely have looked like equals."[62] As Peter White observes, "from a Roman perspective, the relationships between intellectuals and their prominent friends looked no different from a mass of other relationships in upper-class society which presented subtly compounded elements of parity and inequality. All alike go by the name of friendship."[63] Instead of devoting effort to the elaboration of a category (such as "patronage") which might be in keeping with our modern conception of unequal relationships, it is more useful to seek to understand the function of the friendship language that characterized the discourse between unequals in the Greco-Roman world. White is again insightful: "the affect-laden language which pervades their discourse is probably to be interpreted as an effort by both parties to neutralize those status differences which do still stand between them."[64] Thus, "in a Roman context, the emphasis on friendship serves to blunt the consciousness which each of the two parties has of belonging to a particular lineage, census-class, or order, and to refocus attention on particular pursuits and ideals which they share."[65]

Applying these insights to Paul and Gaius, we may conclude that "friendship" is the category which Roman society would have offered, as the evangelist and his wealthy convert moved beyond initial contact

---

59 White, *Promised Verse*, 13, 29–31; Konstan, *Friendship in the Classical World*, 144–45.
60 White, *Promised Verse*, 13.
61 White, *Promised Verse*, 13–14, 29, 31.
62 White, *Promised Verse*, 276 n.20; cf. Saller, "Patronage and friendship," 57; Konstan, *Friendship in the Classical World*, 135, 136.
63 White, *Promised Verse*, 29. See also Nicholas Horsfall, *Poets and Patron: Maecenas, Horace and the Georgics, Once More* (North Ryde: Macquarie Ancient History Association, 1981) 5, on the relationship between Horace and Maecenas: "The line between *amicus*-'friend' and *amicus*-'client' should not be drawn."
64 White, *Promised Verse*, 14; cf. Konstan, *Friendship in the Classical World*, 144.
65 White, *Promised Verse*, 14; cf. Fitzgerald, "Paul and Friendship" in *Paul in the Greco-Roman World*, 329.

to construct an ongoing relationship. Thus, the essays on friendship by Aristotle and Cicero (both of whom acknowledge the possibility of friendship between unequals),[66] and the numerous references to friendship with important persons by writers such as Horace, Propertius, and Ovid,[67] promise to throw light upon Paul's relationship with Gaius, clarifying not only the basis of their friendship, but also the conditions under which the relationship evolved, the sources of growing tension, and the causes of eventual rupture.

It suffices, at this point, to remind ourselves of what we already know and have established through exegesis about the relationship between Paul and Gaius. First, the educational level on display in the Corinthian correspondence, as in Paul's other epistles, is relatively high,[68] and would have provided a sufficient basis for friendship with a man from the upper class who had a similar education. We argued above that the evaluation of Paul's literary qualities by the anonymous critic who is quoted in 2 Cor. 10:10 is strongly positive, reflecting a convergence of aesthetic standards, in appreciation of a style that was "weighty and strong."[69] Second, the confidence of "belonging to Christ" which shines through the attitude that Paul attributes to his anonymous critic in 2 Cor. 10:7 suggests a considerable ethical congruence with the one who came to Corinth preaching that "the Messiah was Jesus" (Acts 18:5). It was upon such shared values, rather than economic parity, that partners to a friendship based their relationship, according to Cicero.[70] Finally, we have noted how scrupulously Paul observes the convention of not naming his alienated friend through all the stages by which he pursues reconcili-

---

66 Aristotle *Eth. nic.* 8.7.1; *Eth. eud.* 7.3.2; Cicero *Amic.* 19.69–20.73; White, *Promised Verse*, 276 n.20; Konstan, *Friendship in the Classical World*, 135–37.
67 Horsfall, *Poets and Patron*, 1–24; Gold, *Literary Patronage in Greece and Rome*; White, *Promised Verse*, 3–34; Elaine Fantham, *Roman Literary Culture: From Cicero to Apuleius* (Baltimore: Johns Hopkins University Press, 1996) 76–83; Bowditch, *Gift Economy of Patronage*.
68 Malherbe, "Social Level and Literary Culture" in idem, *Social Aspects*, 29–59; Ronald F. Hock, "Paul and Greco-Roman Education" in *Paul in the Greco-Roman World*, 198–227.
69 See above, ch. 3, pp. 102–14.
70 For *studia, mores* and *officia* as the basis of friendship, see Cicero *Amic.* 6.20, 9.31, 17.62–21.81; *Off.* 1.45–46; *Att.* 17.5–6; *Fam.* 3.13; cf. White, *Promised Verse*, 14, 276 n.20; Konstan, *Friendship in the Classical World*, 124–25, 130–31, 144–45. See also Horace *Sat.* 1.6.52–64; *Ep.* 1.7.22–24; *Laus Pisonis* 128–37, 218.

ation in the writing known to us as 2 Corinthians.⁷¹ In sum, if Paul uses the terminology associated with friendship in the letter by which he conciliates the wrongdoer, and if Paul's behavior toward this individual conforms to the conventions associated with friendship, enmity, and reconciliation, then we must conclude that it is proper to regard Paul and the wrongdoer (whom we have identified as Gaius) as "friends" by the standards of Roman society.

While affirming the existence of a friendship between Paul and Gaius, it is necessary to acknowledge a qualification from the outset. Evidently, Paul was not willing to accept all of the obligations of Roman friendship, because of his conception of his calling as an apostle and, more generally, because of his understanding of the "new creation" in Christ.⁷² We have already received some indication of Paul's resistance to the mechanisms of aristocratic friendship in his refusal of the gift of financial support (2 Cor. 11:7–10) proffered by someone at Corinth.⁷³ It was by means of such benefits that Roman friendships were cemented.⁷⁴ We shall discover that, in other ways, Paul re-drew the lines of the relationship into which he entered, in two instances reversing the role he was expected to play as the weaker partner to the friendship. Thus, Paul did not simply accommodate himself to the framework of Roman friendship, but shifted some of its conventional elements.⁷⁵ Drawing creatively upon forms and ideas associated with friendship, Paul transformed the tenor of the relationship from within, in accordance with a new theological principle.⁷⁶ Yet, our capacity to recognize Paul's maneuvers as innovations, and our ability to appreciate how startling some of his actions and language would have been to the upper-class friend with whom he was negotiating, depend upon the rigor of the category "friendship" in which we have chosen to interpret the relationship.

---

71 See above, ch. 4, pp. 212–30.
72 Judge, "St. Paul as Radical Critic of Society" in idem, *Social Distinctives of the Christians*, 105–107, 132–33, 167.
73 See above, ch. 3; so already Marshall, *Enmity in Corinth*, 130–64, 246, 397.
74 Cicero *Amic.* 8.26; Seneca *Ben.* 1.4.2; Marshall, *Enmity in Corinth*, 10–17, 160, 243; Judge, "The Social Identity of the First Christians" in idem, *Social Distinctives of the Christians*, 132.
75 Fitzgerald, "Paul and Paradigm Shifts," 241–62, 316–25.
76 Judge, "Cultural Conformity and Innovation in Paul" in idem, *Social Distinctives of the Christians*, 173.

So, to the story of Paul and Gaius. When Paul came to Corinth in circa 41 A.D.,[77] he found lodging with a Jew named Aquila, who had recently come to Corinth from Italy, together with his wife Priscilla, on account of the edict of Claudius banishing the Jews from Rome (Acts 18:1–2).[78] As the reason for Paul's association with this couple, the author of Acts (18:3) gives the fact that they were "of the same trade" (ὁμότεχνον).[79] We have argued elsewhere in support of Frederick Danker's proposal that the term used by "Luke" to describe Paul's occupation, σκηνοποιός, should be interpreted in reference to matters theatrical as "propmaker," rather than the traditional translation "tentmaker."[80] It is appealing to imagine Paul living and working with Aquila and Priscilla in one of the shops along East Theater Street which formed part of the residential block with the House of the Opus Sectile Panel.[81] But, in fact, we have no idea in what quarter of Corinth Paul resided.

Paul preached in the synagogue every Sabbath for an unspecified number of weeks, according to the author of Acts (18:4).[82] Significantly, "Luke" records that Greeks were among those in the synagogue with whom Paul entered into dialogue and tried to persuade.[83] The message that is placed into the mouth of Paul in Acts 18:5—"the Messiah was Jesus"—is not inconsistent with the gospel which may be reconstructed from the outline of Paul's early missionary preaching in 1 Thess. 1:9b–

---

77 I follow the early chronology established by Gerd Lüdemann, "A Chronology of Paul" in *Colloquy on New Testament Studies: A Time for Reappraisal and Fresh Approaches*, ed. B. Corley (Macon: Mercer University Press, 1983) 292, 302–303; idem, *Paul, Apostle to the Gentiles*, 6–18, 157–77; supported by Horrell, *The Social Ethos of the Corinthian Correspondence*, 73–74. See further J. J. Taylor, *Les Actes des deux apôtres, V. Commentaire historique (Act 9,1–18,22)* (Paris: Gabalda, 1994) 325–26.
78 Cf. Suetonius *Claud.* 25; Lüdemann, *Paul, Apostle to the Gentiles*, 166, 170; Wolfgang Wiefel, "The Jewish Community in Ancient Rome and the Origins of Roman Christianity" in *The Romans Debate*, ed. Karl P. Donfried (Peabody: Hendrickson, 1991) 92–93.
79 See the comments of Haenchen, *The Acts of the Apostles*, 534.
80 Welborn, *Paul, the Fool of Christ*, 11–12; BDAG 928–29 s.v. σκηνοποιός.
81 On the domestic block to which the House of the Opus Sectile Panel belonged, see Williams, "Corinth 1982: East of the Theater," 10–13.
82 On the probable historicity of Paul's preaching in the synagogue at Corinth, see Stowers, "Social Status, Public Speaking and Private Teaching," 64–65; Horrell, *The Social Ethos of the Corinthian Correspondence*, 74–75, 77. See generally, Francis Watson, *Paul, Judaism and the Gentiles: A Sociological Approach* (Cambridge: Cambridge University Press, 1986) 28–32.
83 Haenchen, *Acts of the Apostles*, 534; Barrett, *Acts 15–28*, 864.

10: in both cases, one has to do with a messianic proclamation in which there is not yet an emphasis upon the shameful manner of Jesus' death, the cross.[84]

In response to opposition from some of the Jews, Paul withdrew from the synagogue at Corinth and began preaching in the house of a "God-fearer" named Titius Justus, whose house was next door to the synagogue (Acts 18:6–7).[85] It is fair to say that "Luke" would scarcely have invented the name or person of Titius Justus.[86] Again, it is important to notice the role that "God-fearers" played in the origin of the Christian community at Corinth.

The author of Acts attributes signal importance to the conversion of the synagogue president (ἀρχισυνάγωγος) Crispus in his account of the growth of the followers of Jesus to a "large people" (Acts 18:10): "Crispus, the ruler of the synagogue, believed in the Lord, together with all of his household, and many of the Corinthians, when they heard (of it), believed and were baptized" (Acts 18:8).[87] Greater plausibility accrues to "Luke's" account of the influence of Crispus from Philo's reference to a Jewish "colony" at Corinth, which must have been of significant size and vitality, since it is one of only two Greek cities whose Jewish inhabitants Philo mentions by name.[88] That Paul made an exception to his custom of not baptizing new converts and personally admin-

---

84 Béda Rigaux, *Saint Paul: Les épitres aux Thessaloniciens* (Paris: Gabalda, 1956) 388–97; Gerhard Friedrich, "Ein Tauflied hellenistischer Judenchristen: 1 Thess. 1:9 f.," *TZ* 21 (1965) 502–16; Ernest Best, *A Commentary on the First and Second Epistles to the Thessalonians* (London: Black, 1979) 86–87; Lüdemann, *Paul, Apostle to the Gentiles*, 107; Murphy-O'Connor, *Paul*, 122; Heckel, "Der Gekreuzigte bei Paulus," 190–210, esp. 194–95.
85 Against the Western text (D), Paul did not change his residence, but only began to teach in a different location: thus, Haenchen, *Acts of the Apostles*, 535 n.2; Conzelmann, *Acts of the Apostles*, 152; Murphy-O'Connor, *Paul*, 262–63; Barrett, *Acts 15–28*, 867.
86 Lüdemann, *Early Christianity according to Acts*, 203.
87 For this interpretation, which takes the report of the conversion of Crispus as the unexpressed object of the participle ἀκούοντες, see Haenchen, *Acts of the Apostles*, 535; Schneider, *Die Apostelgeschichte*, 2.251; Lüdemann, *Early Christianity according to Acts*, 203–204; see the discussion in Murphy-O'Connor, *Paul*, 264; Barrett, *Acts 15–28*, 868–69.
88 Philo *Legat.* 281. On Jews in Corinth at this period, see further Peter Richardson, "On the Absence of 'Anti-Judaism' in 1 Corinthians" in *Anti-Judaism in Early Christianity; Vol. I. Paul and the Gospels*, ed. P. Richardson and D. Granskou (Ontario: Wilfred Laurier University Press, 1986) 59–74, esp. 60–63.

istered baptism to Crispus (1 Cor. 1:14) is further indication of the prominence of this individual.[89]

Among those who felt the impact of the conversion of the synagogue president was Gaius. This inference is justified by Paul's mention of Gaius in the same breath with Crispus, as one of the few Corinthians whom he baptized with his own hands (1 Cor. 1:14). Indeed, one can only assume that Gaius was foremost among the "many Corinthians" who were influenced by the conversion of the synagogue president (Acts 18:8). In this case, one may also infer that Gaius was a "God-fearer," one of the number of Gentiles who were attracted to Judaism by its monotheistic faith and high ethical standards,[90] and who, according to the author of Acts, made up the nucleus of the early converts to Paul's gospel.[91] With these conclusions, the stage is set for a modest act of historical imagination in regard to the conversion of Gaius.

Beyond the rational and ethical attractions of Judaism, and beyond a friendship with the influential synagogue president Crispus, we may ask: What would have motivated a Gentile "God-fearer," a man of the upper class, to respond in faith to the proclamation that "the Messiah was Jesus" (Acts 18:5) and that "God had raised Jesus out of the dead" (1 Thess. 1:9b-10)? The question finds its point in Paul's acknowledgement that the majority of those who felt the "call" of the gospel were uneducated, poor, and low-born, even in "wealthy" Corinth (1 Cor. 1:26–27).[92] Is it possible to enter, briefly, into the psychology of a man such as Gaius of Corinth?

Literature contemporary with the inception of Paul's mission at Corinth gives expression to a deepening disillusionment with the realities of Roman rule, especially in the aftermath of the Caligula crisis.[93] Making

---

89 Meeks, *First Urban Christians*, 57; Fee, *First Epistle*, 62; Collins, *First Corinthians*, 83.
90 On the "God-fearers," see the works cited above p. 373 n. 518. See also Marianne Palmer Bonz, "The Jewish Donor Inscriptions from Aphrodisias: Are They Both Third-Century, and Who Are the Theosebeis?" *HSCP* 96 (1994) 281–299.
91 Barrett, *Acts 1–14*, 500–501.
92 Theissen, *Social Setting*, 71–73; Dieter Georgi, *Theocracy in Paul's Praxis and Theology* (Minneapolis: Fortress Press, 1991) 54; Meggitt, *Paul, Poverty and Survival*, 75–76, 96.
93 Paul Allen Miller, *Subjecting Verses: Latin Love Elegy and the Emergence of the Real* (Princeton: Princeton University Press, 2004); Basil Dufallo, *The Ghosts of the Past: Latin Literature, The Dead, and Rome's Transition to a Principate* (Columbus: Ohio State University Press, 2007). On the importance of the Caligula cri-

all proper allowances for rhetorical hyperbole in Philo's invective against the Emperor Gaius,[94] it is nevertheless clear how much genuine disappointment, and later revulsion, accompanied the revelation of madness and cruelty at the center of Roman power, as Philo and his contemporaries discovered that the weight of empire could turn a young man, whose accession had aroused so much hope, into a monster:[95]

> As the author of general ruin and destruction ... you changed what gave pleasure and joy into discomfort and grief and a life which all men everywhere find unworthy of the name. And so insatiable and quenchless were your lusts that you stole all that was good and valuable whether from east or west or from all other regions of the world southwards or northwards, and in return you gave and sent them the fruits of your own bitterness and all things mischievous and hurtful that abominable and venomous souls are wont to generate... You stripped the cities of all that tends to well-being and happiness and turned them into hotbeds of what makes for confusion and tumults and the height of misery...You rained miseries untold one after the other as from perennial fountains on every part of the inhabited world.

Philo insists that knowledge of Caligula's crimes was not restricted to those who, like himself, were highly placed: "In every mouth there was common talk about these inexpiable abominations, though quietly and in undertones, since fear prevented open discussion."[96] The effect of Caligula's reign upon Jews and Jewish sympathizers must have been shattering. God had intervened to save the Jewish community of Alexandria, Philo believed, though many perished in the pogroms.[97] But Philo's confidence was broken: there is a bitter irony and a sense of hopelessness about Philo's *Legatione ad Gaium* that is not characteristic of his writings generally. Pessimism about human nature steals into Philo's thought: "We cannot escape our inborn infirmities. We creep within our covering of mortality, like snails into their shells."[98]

---

sis, see Andrew Barrett, *Caligula: The Corruption of Power* (New Haven: Yale University Press, 1990) 140–91.
94 Daniel R. Schwartz, "On Drama and Authenticity in Philo and Josephus," *Scripta Classica Israelica* 10 (1989/90) 113–29; Manuel Alexandre, *Rhetorical Argumentation in Philo of Alexandria* (Atlanta: Scholars Press, 1999).
95 Philo *Legat.* 89–90, 101.
96 Philo *Legat.* 66.
97 Philo *Legat.* 347–48.
98 Philo *Sacr.* 95.

An even darker vision of the world and human nature is found in Seneca's tragedies.[99] Here we enter a world of moral chaos, in which isolated individuals are driven to acts of violence by gigantic passions.[100] Seneca's Hercules returns from the underworld at the height of megalomania, and resolves to storm the gates of heaven; descending rapidly into madness, he slaughters his wife and children.[101] Making allowances for the nature of tragedy, it is difficult not to see the bleak world depicted in Seneca's *Hercules* as a reflection of the macabre reign of Caligula, who likewise "overstepped the bounds of human nature in his eagerness to be thought a god,"[102] descended into madness, and murdered members of his own family.[103] Amphitryon's account of the paradoxes of his world echoes the dark experiences of Seneca's own times: "Crime which prospers and flourishes is given the name of valour; good people take orders from the wicked; might is right, and laws are stifled by fear."[104] In seeking reasons for the pervasive insecurity that marks the characters of Senecan tragedy, it is worth remembering that "Seneca himself lived through and witnessed, in his own person or in the persons of those near him, almost every evil and horror that is the theme of his writings. Exile, murder, incest, the threat of poverty and a hideous death were the very texture of his career."[105]

A more thorough analysis of the psychology of the self in the mid-first century would demonstrate that the sense of a world gone wrong, which comes to expression in Philo and Seneca, was by no means idiosyncratic, but was endemic, at least among persons of a certain social class.[106]

---

99 Denis and Elisabeth Henry, *The Mask of Power: Seneca's Tragedies and Imperial Rome* (Warminster: Aris & Phillips, 1985); Cedric A. J. Littlewood, *Self-representation and Illusion in Senecan Tragedy* (Oxford: Oxford University Press, 2004); A. J. Boyle, *Roman Tragedy* (London: Routledge, 2006) 189–218.
100 J. G. Fitch and S. McElduff, "Construction of the Self in Senecan Drama," *Mnemosyne* 55 (2002) 18–40.
101 John G. Fitch, *Seneca's Hercules Furens: A Critical Text with Introduction and Commentary* (Cornell: Cornell University Press, 1987).
102 Philo *Legat.* 75.
103 Barrett, *Caligula*, 213–41.
104 Seneca *Herc. fur.* 251–53; Fitch, *Seneca's Hercules Furens*, 199–200.
105 C. J. Herrington, "Senecan Tragedy," *Arion* 5 (1966) 430.
106 Vasily Rudich, *Dissidence and Literature under Nero: the Price of Rhetoricisation* (London: Routledge, 1997); Matthew B. Roller, *Constructing Autocracy: Aristocrats and Emperors in Julio-Claudian Rome* (Princeton: Princeton University Press, 2001); Paul Veyne, *Seneca: The Life of a Stoic* (New York and London: Routledge, 2003).

The ground of this experience of disillusionment was not personal, despite Philo's fixation upon the wickedness of Caligula, but structural: the geopolitical expansion of the Roman Empire and the emergence of sole sovereignty ensured that "the actions of one man, the emperor, could indeed affect the known world."[107] And what if this one man were unable to bear the weight of Empire, and descended into paranoia, or exploded in megalomania? The family history of the Euryclids examined above demonstrates that the suspicion of a Tiberius could reach out to a provincial city such as Corinth, and result in exile and the confiscation of property.[108] In any case, the effect of the political changes of the first century upon the psyche of men such as Philo and Seneca is writ large upon their works: an increased isolation of the individual, the development of obsessive emotions, a sense of supine powerlessness.[109] We may conjecture that Paul's Gaius would have been susceptible of these emotions, even if he were less self-conscious and articulate than Seneca.

Now let us imagine the day when Gaius would have heard Paul preach for the first time at the house of Titius Justus next door to the synagogue, in the company of his friend Crispus. The announcement that God had sent the Messiah (Acts 18:5) would have signified an intervention—hoped for, but seemingly beyond hope—of divine power into a world where so much had gone awry. The message that God had raised Jesus out of the dead (1 Thess. 1:10), the very one put to death under Pontius Pilate (1 Cor. 2:8), would have signified a rupture in the chain of atrocities. The promise that the Messiah would reign, enthroned in heaven, until he has subjugated every inimical authority (1 Cor. 15:24–25) must have signified that corrupt human power over the world had been broken, shorn, and undone. If the secret of the sole sovereignty of Augustus and his successors was that it located the center of gravity in death, in utterly dependent subjecthood,[110] then Paul's message of the Messiah's resurrection must have restored the center of gravity to life, so that Gaius, in hearing Paul's gospel, would have experienced an

---

107 John G. Fitch, *Seneca VIII. Tragedies*, LCL (Cambridge: Harvard University Press, 2002) 9.
108 Chrimes, "The Family and Descendants of C. Julius Eurykles," *Ancient Sparta*, 169–204; Bowersock, "Eurycles of Sparta," 112–18.
109 Fitch, "The Self and the World," *Seneca VIII. Tragedies*, 5–10.
110 Alain Badiou, *Saint Paul: The Foundation of Universalism* (Stanford: Stanford University Press, 2003) 55–73. Cf. L. L. Welborn, "Extraction from the Mortal Site: Badiou on the Resurrection in Paul," *NTS* 55 (2009) 295–314.

upsurge, an insurrection of the self,[111] with the exhilarating sensations that attend the sudden emergence of a new subject—freedom, empowerment, hope. And in the company of others who were simultaneously experiencing and declaring the event of their faith, Gaius must have begun to sense the recovery of a community that had largely disappeared amidst the political changes of the preceding century. Naturally, we cannot know how deeply Gaius' conversion penetrated, or how many of his core values were changed. But the baptism that Gaius received at Paul's hands (1 Cor. 1:14) symbolized a death of the former self and the beginning of a new life (Rom. 6:3–4). We may assume that one who later developed a robust confidence of belonging to Christ (2 Cor. 10:7), and who eventually placed his house at the disposal of the Christian community (Rom. 16:23), must have experienced a profound transformation, as he responded to Paul's message.

We cannot know when Gaius became the "host of the whole *ekklesia*" at Corinth, whether during the year and six months of Paul's foundation visit (Acts 18:11), or later, after Paul had taken up residence in Ephesus (Acts 19). The account of Acts leads one to assume that the Christians of Corinth continued to assemble at the house of Titius Justus (Acts 18:7) during the period of Paul's initial mission. But "Luke's" account of the origins of Christianity at Corinth is meager and lacunose, and further, evinces his usual tendency toward unified composition, with the resulting consolidation of facts.[112] Thus we cannot exclude the possibility that Gaius began to host the assembly at an early date, especially if, as seems likely, Gaius possessed a larger house than other Christians.[113]

At some point during Paul's first visit to Corinth, he received an offer of financial support.[114] So much is clear from Paul's later defense of his decision to decline the offer in 1 Cor. 9:12b-18 and 2 Cor. 11:7–15.[115] In Greco-Roman context, the offer of such a gift constituted an invitation to a friendship, albeit a friendship of unequals—that is, a patron-client

---

111 Badiou, *Saint Paul*, 73.
112 Lüdemann, *Early Christianity according to Acts*, 10–12.
113 Meeks, *First Urban Christians*, 57, 76, 221 n.7; Friesen, "Poverty in Pauline Studies," 356; Theissen, "The Social Structure of Pauline Communities," 82–83; Lampe, "Paul, Patrons, and Clients" in *Paul in the Greco-Roman World*, 496.
114 Marshall, *Enmity in Corinth*, 167, 218–33, 237.
115 Georgi, *Opponents of Paul*, 238–46; Betz, *Der Apostel Paulus*, 100–17; Marshall, *Enmity in Corinth*, 173–77, 220, 222, 224, 231, 233–58.

relationship.[116] Paul's rhetoric in the above-mentioned passages makes it impossible to say by whom the offer of aid was extended. But even if support was offered in the name of the entire congregation, realistic consideration of the inequalities between persons in Roman Corinth necessitates that the gift would have drawn upon the resources of a wealthy few.[117] Thus we must allow for the possibility that Gaius was one of those who offered Paul support during his initial period of residence in Corinth.

Peter Marshall attributes great importance to Paul's refusal of the gift offered him by certain wealthy Corinthians.[118] Marshall argues that, in a society based upon *beneficia*, Paul's refusal of financial support would have been tantamount to a refusal of a friendship. Marshall infers: "This refusal gave rise to suspicion and invective and an attempt to displace Paul as the apostle in Corinth."[119] While Marshall's premises are valid, his conclusions are not justified by anything in the writing known to us as 1 Corinthians. In 1 Cor. 9, to be sure, Paul is on the defensive, forced to explain his decision to make no use of his "right" to eat and drink at the expense of the church (9:4, 6, 12b, 15). Behind Paul's spirited defense of his conduct lies the insinuation that Paul knew he was not entitled to support, because he was not really an apostle (9:1–2).[120] But questions about Paul's decision to work for a living seem to have arisen only *after* certain evangelists and apostles, who gladly accepted support from wealthy patrons, arrived in Corinth (1 Cor. 9:5).[121] It is a mistake to project the inception of enmity associated with the refusal of a gift back into the initial period of Paul's Corinthian mission. One misses throughout 1 Corinthians the bitter invective that characterizes 2 Cor. 10–13. Moreover, Paul freely names Crispus and Gaius (in 1 Cor. 1:14), the Christians of highest social standing in Corinth, and hence the ones most capable of offering Paul support—a clear indication that enmity had not yet erupted between Paul and these individuals at the time of

---

116 Judge, *The Social Pattern of the Christian Groups*, 58–60; Marshall, *Enmity in Corinth*, 167, 220, 240; Chow, *Patronage and Power*, 107–10; Kirner, "Apostolat und Patronage (II)," 27–72.
117 Marshall, *Enmity in Corinth*, 231.
118 Marshall, *Enmity in Corinth*, 233–58.
119 Marshall, *Enmity in Corinth*, 257.
120 Theissen, "Legitimation and Subsistence" in *Social Setting*, 27–68, esp. 40–54.
121 Chow, *Patronage and Power*, 102–10; Kirner, "Apostolat und Patronage (II)," 42–49.

composition of 1 Corinthians.[122] We should not forget that Paul took up residence in Corinth as a guest in the house of Aquila and Priscilla, because they were of the same trade (Acts 18:1–3). It was under these circumstances that Paul made the acquaintance of Crispus, Gaius, Stephanas, and others. Paul's decision to decline the offer of support from Gaius, whenever it came, must have occasioned consternation, as a departure from the paradigm of Greco-Roman friendship. But it need not have instigated enmity. The immediate, practical consequence of Paul's decision to continue working for a living must have been that Paul was unable to organize his life to fit the domestic routine of his would-be patron.[123] Because Paul's labor left him little time (1 Cor. 4:12; 1 Thess. 2:9),[124] he may have missed opportunities for serious conversation with his greater friend. Out of such leisurely discourse a closer relationship might have developed.[125]

In accordance with the literary-critical hypothesis adopted in this monograph, Paul's earliest written communication with Corinth would be the letter now preserved in 1 Cor. 10:1–22; 6:12–20; 10:23–11:34,[126] a letter which Paul retrospectively characterizes as a warning "not to associate with the immoral or idolaters" (1 Cor. 5:9–10). Within this early writing, devoted entirely to liminal matters, there is one issue which may have impinged upon the relationship between Paul and Gaius: the divisions at the Lord's Supper. This is especially the case if we assume that the Christians of Corinth were already assembling at the house of Gaius when Paul wrote the exhortation contained in 1 Cor. 11:17–34. The situation described in 1 Cor. 11:17–22 reveals the operation of social conventions that governed dinner parties in upper-class Greco-Roman households: like the patron of a household cult,[127] Gaius (or whoever hosted the *ekklesia*) provided the meal for the Christian group and, exercising his prerogatives as host, apportioned the fare according to the status of his guests, reserving the best food and

---

122 Theissen, *Social Setting*, 55; Chow, *Patronage and Power*, 90; de Vos, *Church and Community Conflicts*, 219.
123 On the need for the client-intellectual to organize his life so as to fit the domestic routine of his well-to-do friend, see White, *Promised Verse*, 4–6.
124 Hock, *Social Context*, 31–37.
125 Cf. *Laus Pisonis* 84–96, 133–208; Tacitus *Dial.* 5.2, 6.2; Pliny *Ep.* 3.1; White, *Promised Verse*, 23–25.
126 Weiss, *Der erste Korintherbrief*, xxxix-xliii; idem, *Primitive Christianity*, 1.343–53.
127 Schmeller, *Hierarchie und Egalität*, 26, 33–36.

wine for his social equals and intimate friends.[128] Analysis of this situation discloses an individual at its center who, in his role as host, exemplifies the values of the upper class and who, from Paul's point of view, does not evince sufficient consideration for the humiliation of the "have-nots" that resulted from his behavior (1 Cor. 11:22).

With a modest use of historical imagination, we may undertake a reconstruction of what happened at the house of Gaius when the Corinthian Christians assembled to eat the Lord's Supper. Along a well-traveled street in a good location of the city, the Christians of Corinth would have approached the house of Gaius, a substantial *domus*, not unlike the House of the Opus Sectile Panel, capable of accommodating a number of persons. The size of the house, the impression it made from the outside, and perhaps a conspicuous entrance—all combined to advertise the status of its occupant.[129] At the principal entrance, a doorkeeper[130] would have greeted those who, owing to their wealth and leisure, were able to gather before sunset—Crispus, Stephanas, Chloe, and their immediate family members.[131] A slave would have escorted the guests through the richly decorated *atrium* to the *tablinum*, where Gaius would have interrupted the business in which he was engaged, or perhaps the host would have greeted his guests in one of the reception rooms that opened off of the *peristyle*.[132] It is not difficult to imagine that Gaius and his friends would have found their way, before much time had passed, to the *triclinium* where, after a blessing over the bread, they would have begun to eat the joyful supper of the Lord. While they ate, a slave *lec-*

---

128 E.g., Juvenal *Sat.* 5; Martial 3.60; Pliny *Ep.* 2.6; see the discussion in Theissen, *Social Setting*, 153–63; Schmeller, *Hierarchie und Egalität*, 60–62, 66–73. See above, ch. 5.
129 Wiseman, "*Conspicui postes tectaque digna deo*," 393–413; Laurence, *Roman Pompeii*, 88–103.
130 Ovid *Fast.* 1.135; Plautus *Asin.* 273; Livy 5.13.6–7; K. Schneider, "Ianitor," *RE* 9 (1916) 692–93; Laurence, *Roman Pompeii*, 88; Osiek and Balch, *Households and House Churches*, 25. On access to the Roman house, see further Andrew Wallace-Hadrill, "The social structure of the Roman house," *Papers of the British School at Rome* 56 (1988) 43–97, esp. 46.
131 Bornkamm, "Herrenmahl und Kirche bei Paulus," 142; Theissen, *Social Setting*, 151–53; Lampe, "Das korinthische Herrenmahl," 198; Schmeller, *Hierarchie und Egalität*, 71; Kirner, "Apostolat und Patronage (II)," 55–59.
132 Wallace-Hadrill, *Houses and Society*, 39; George, "*Servus* and *domus*" in *Domestic Space in the Roman World*, 15–24.

tor,[133] perhaps Tertius, may have recited a messianic psalm such as Ps. 110, or perhaps Crispus and Gaius engaged the others in animated conversation about a future in which a resurrected Messiah would return and rule.

At sunset, or whenever the work day was done, the slaves and the poor, who made up the majority of the Christians at Corinth (1 Cor. 1:26–27), would have made their way to the house of Gaius. By custom, such persons would have used a side door along a service lane to gain entrance to the house,[134] and would then have walked through narrow, crudely-decorated corridors in the service areas to the *atrium* or the *peristyle*.[135] It is unlikely that humble persons, accustomed to observe the social differentiation of space within a house, would have ventured uninvited into the seigniorial areas.[136] And if slaves or the poor had approached the *triclinium*, it is uncertain how they would have been received. In any case, the couches in the *triclinium* would have been occupied by the leaders of the house-churches and their family members.[137] We cannot know what sort of food would have been provided to the crowd of poor Christians in the *atrium* and the *peristyle*—bread and wine, certainly, but perhaps little else, since Paul speaks of "hunger" (1 Cor. 11:21). From the *peristyle*, the poor would likely have been able to observe their wealthy brothers and sisters feasting sumptuously in the *triclinium*, since the *triclinia* of this period were designed to put the host and his friends on display.[138] The inequity in the distribution of food, the social differentiation of space, and the differences in hospitality and behavior would all have contributed powerfully to the humiliation of the "have-nots" (1 Cor. 11:22).

How might Gaius have responded to Paul's reproof in 1 Cor. 11:17–34? Should we conclude that the inequities were ameliorated, because we hear nothing more of divisions at the Lord's Supper in subsequent por-

---

133 E.g., Cicero *Att.* 1.12.4; *Fam.* 5.9.2; Plutarch *Quaest. conv.* 711C; Pliny *Ep.* 3.5.11, 5.19.3, 9.36.4; cf. Marquardt, *Das Privatleben der Römer*, 148; Dunbabin, "Convivial Spaces," 67; Jones, "Dinner Theater," 185, 196.
134 Wallace-Hadrill, *Houses and Society*, 39, 107, 118; Laurence, *Roman Pompeii*, 88–89; George, "Domestic Architecture and Household Relations," 10–14.
135 Clarke, *The Houses of Roman Italy*, 99–101; Wallace-Hadrill, *Houses and Society*, 39, 44, 47, 50.
136 George, "Domestic Architecture and Household Relations," 14.
137 On the limited space in a *triclinium* of traditional size, see Dunbabin, "Convivial spaces," 70.
138 Dunbabin, "Convivial spaces," 70, 78–79.

tions of the Corinthian correspondence? Gaius is still the "host of the whole *ekklesia*" in the last glimpse that Paul affords of the Christian community at Corinth (Rom. 16:23), a situation incompatible with an unamended observance. If Gaius followed Paul's advice to "wait for one another" (1 Cor. 11:34), the effect would surely have been to enhance Gaius' status as patron among those who found themselves included in the feast. Indeed, Gaius' *bona fides* as a Christian would have been demonstrated through his willingness to embrace the social and ethical implications of Jesus' intention in instituting the supper (1 Cor. 11:23–26). The image of Gaius that emerges from analysis of 1 Cor. 11:17–34 (assuming that Gaius was then the host of the *ekklesia*) is that of a man so fully shaped by the values of the upper class that he exercised his prerogatives unconsciously, without the capacity to view his behavior from the standpoint of slaves and the poor, because his ethical sensibilities were inextricably joined to the structure of the society in which he participated.[139] Yet, there is also the possibility (inferring a positive response to Paul's correction) that Gaius achieved clarity regarding his role in the solution to the crisis (1 Cor. 11:19) and altered the relations between Christians of different classes, deliberately—an outcome whose historical uniqueness and importance we should not fail to appreciate.[140]

At some point, and perhaps not long after receipt of Paul's letter, another Christian teacher visited Corinth—an Alexandrian Jew named Apollos. The paragraph devoted to Apollos in Acts, which seems to be based upon reliable tradition,[141] delineates a lively and impressive character: "an eloquent man (ἀνὴρ λόγιος), skilled in the exposition of Scriptures (δυνατὸς ἐν γραφαῖς). He had been instructed in the Way of the Lord; and he spoke with burning enthusiasm (ζέων τῷ πνεύματι ἐλάλει) and taught accurately (ἐδίδασκεν ἀκριβῶς) the things concerning Jesus" (Acts 18:24–25). The description of Apollos as an ἀνὴρ λόγιος refers to his rhetorical training, his mastery of the art of oratory.[142] The ex-

---

139 With reference to the social conscience of wealthy Corinthian Christians generally, Theissen, *Social Setting*, 162.
140 Judge, "Cultural Conformity and Innovation in Paul" in *Social Distinctives of the Christians*, 159, 173, with respect to Paul's social intentions in his exhortation to the Corinthians.
141 Haenchen, *Acts of the Apostles*, 549–50; Lüdemann, *Early Christianity according to Acts*, 208–209.
142 Philo *Post.* 53 describes one engaged in σοφιστικαὶ τεχναί as a λόγιος ἀνήρ. See also Plutarch *Cic.* 49.5. See the definition of ἀνὴρ λόγιος in Phrynichus 198: ὡς οἱ πολλοὶ λέγουσιν ἐπὶ τοῦ δεινοῦ εἰπεῖν καὶ ὑψηλοῦ. Cf. Field, *Notes on the*

pression ἀνὴρ λόγιος also designates a "learned man" generally, one who had studied philosophy and literature.[143] The observation that Apollos was δυνατός ἐν γραφαῖς evokes his ability to expound the Scriptures in order to prove that the Messiah was Jesus (Acts 18:28).[144] The characterization of Apollos' speech as ζέων τῷ πνεύματι may mark him as a pneumatic;[145] but the expression is also used of an enthusiastic orator.[146] The qualification of Apollos' teaching about Jesus as ἀκριβῶς, not only speaks of the accuracy of his gospel, but probably also suggests the conformity of the manner of his exposition to aesthetic standards.[147] All in all, there emerges from Acts a portrait of an urbane and gifted orator, a product of the rich intellectual culture of Alexandria,[148] a Christian sophist.[149] The portrait of Apollos in Acts is reinforced by attentive reading of 1 Cor. 1–4: Paul's self-conscious disavowal of "eloquent wisdom" (σοφία λόγου), in the context of the Corinthians' partisanship of Apollos, suggests that the latter exhibited an excess of these gifts and talents (1 Cor. 1:17; 2:1, 4).[150]

The majority text of Acts 18:27 speaks of Apollos wishing (βουλομένου δὲ αὐτοῦ) to pass over from Ephesus to Achaia. But Codex D relates that "certain Corinthians happened to be residing in Ephesus and hearing him urged him to go with them to their homeland."[151] Apollos

---

Translation of the New Testament, 129. See also Meeks, *First Urban Christians*, 61, 117; Winter, *Paul among the Sophists*, 178 n.172.
143 Moulton and Milligan, *Vocabulary of the Greek Testament*, 378; Weiss, *Der erste Korintherbrief*, xxxi n.1.
144 Weiss, *Der erste Korintherbrief*, xxxi n.1; Horsley, "Wisdom of Word and Words of Wisdom" in *Wisdom and Spiritual Transcendence at Corinth*, 29; Barrett, *Acts 15–28*, 887, 891.
145 Lüdemann, *Early Christianity according to Acts*, 209.
146 BDAG 426 s.v. ζέω.
147 BDAG 39 s.v. ἀκριβῶς: "strict conformity to a standard or norm," especially frequent in historical writers.
148 Christopher Haas, *Alexandria in Late Antiquity: Topography and Social Conflict* (Baltimore: Johns Hopkins University Press, 1997); Modrzejewski, *The Jews of Egypt*.
149 Winter, *Paul among the Sophists*, 176–78.
150 Weiss, *Der erste Korintherbrief*, xxxiii, 22–23; Horsley, "Wisdom of Word and Words of Wisdom" in *Wisdom and Spiritual Transcendence at Corinth*, 29–30; Lim, "Not in Persuasive Words of Wisdom," 137–49; Litfin, *St. Paul's Theology of Proclamation*, 162; Winter, *Paul Among the Sophists*, 164, 177–78.
151 Nestle-Aland, *Novum Testamentum Graece*, 378: D (with some support from P38 and the Harklensis): ἐν Ἐφέσῳ ἐπιδημοῦντές τινες Κορίνθιοι καὶ ἀκούσαντες

agreed to go, furnished with letters from the Ephesians urging the Corinthians to give him welcome.[152] It is not known where or how this tradition originated.[153] There is certainly more here than a simple attempt to explain Apollos' motivation.[154] C. K. Barrett plausibly suggests that the editor of the Western text may have had some connection with Corinth, where traditions about Apollos may have persisted into the second century.[155] We cannot know who these Corinthians were who were sojourning in Ephesus—on business?—and who invited Apollos to join them when they traveled home. Nor can we infer with whom these Corinthians had connections in their native city, that is, to whose household these persons belonged. But it is possible that here we catch a first glimpse of the preference for Apollos that later developed into partisanship by the time Paul wrote the letter preserved in 1 Cor. 1:1–6:11.

In Corinth, Apollos' forceful oratory produced sensational results. The Acts' account, again, is characterized by the kind of vocabulary that indicates the presence of reliable tradition: "for he was vigorously (εὐτόνως) confuting (διακατηλέγχετο) the Jews in public (δημοσίᾳ), demonstrating (ἐπιδεικνύς) through the Scriptures that the Messiah was Jesus" (Acts 18:28).[156] This picture of Apollos' rhetorical and dialectical skill is confirmed by Paul's references to "an excess of speech or wisdom" and "persuasive words of wisdom," in a context where Paul contrasts his own preaching with that of someone else who has visited Corinth (1 Cor. 2:1, 4).[157] In light of Paul's repeated attempts to clarify the relationship between himself and Apollos in subsequent paragraphs of the letter (1 Cor. 3:5; 4:6), it is unlikely that the "eloquent wisdom" with

---

αὐτοῦ παρεκάλουν διελθεῖν σὺν αὐτοῖς εἰς τὴν πατρίδα αὐτῶν. Cf. Barrett, *Acts 15–28*, 890.
152 Acts 18:27, D: συγκατανεύσαντος δὲ αὐτοῦ οἱ Ἐφέσιοι ἔγραψαν τοῖς ἐν Κορίνθῳ μαθηταῖς ὅπως ἀποδέξωνται τὸν ἄνδρα.
153 Bruce M. Metzger, *A Textual Commentary on the Greek New Testament* (Stuttgart: Deutsche Bibelgesellschaft, 1971) 467–68.
154 Haenchen, *Acts of the Apostles*, 551; Barrett, *Acts 15–28*, 890–91.
155 Barrett, *Acts 15–28*, 891.
156 Lüdemann, *Early Christianity according to Acts*, 208–209.
157 Weiss, *Der erste Korintherbrief*, xxxiii; Horsley, "Wisdom of Word and Words of Wisdom" in *Wisdom and Spiritual Transcendence at Corinth*, 29; Winter, *Paul Among the Sophists*, 164; Smit, ""What is Apollos? What is Paul?" 236–38, 242.

which Paul contrasts his own proclamation (1 Cor. 1:17) can have belonged to anyone other than Apollos.[158]

It is difficult to determine how long Apollos stayed in Corinth on the occasion of his first (but perhaps not only) visit (cf. 1 Cor. 16:12).[159] Acts 19:1 places Apollos in Corinth, while Paul passed through the hill country between Phrygia and Ephesus, evidently preaching as he went.[160] The Western text of Acts 18:27 also suggests an extended sojourn in Corinth by Apollos, "who, having taken up residence (ἐπιδημήσας) in Achaia, gave much support in the churches."[161] Barrett interprets this statement to mean that Apollos had his base of operation in Corinth, and traveled among the churches of the province.[162]

It seems likely that while Apollos was residing in Corinth, he accepted an offer of financial support from one or more wealthy Corinthians. This conclusion is an inference from 1 Cor. 9, where Paul is obliged to defend his practice of working for a living. Evidently, another evangelist had visited Corinth, prior to the composition of this epistle, whose willingness to "eat and drink" at the expense of the church raised questions, in retrospect, about Paul's means of subsistence. Although Paul mentions, for the sake of argument, other apostles who had made use of their "right" of support (1 Cor. 9:5), Apollos is, in fact, the only Christian teacher other than Paul who is known to have resided in Corinth at this early period.[163] In one of the closing paragraphs of the letter to which 1 Cor. 9 belongs, Paul finds it necessary to respond to the Corinthians' urgent request to know when Apollos may be returning to their city (1 Cor. 16:12).[164] Thus, it is reasonable to conclude that the evangelist whose acceptance of financial support has problematized Paul's decision to work for a living is none other than Apollos.[165]

In Greco-Roman context, an offer of financial support to a visiting sophist would normally have taken the form of an asymmetrical friend-

---

158 Heinrici, *Der erste Brief*, 12, 64; Weiss, *Der erste Korintherbrief*, 75, 104; Collins, *First Corinthians*, 145; Lindemann, *Der erste Korintherbrief*, 79–80; Welborn, *Paul, the Fool of Christ*, 102–103, 105, 109.
159 Murphy-O'Connor, *Paul*, 275–76.
160 Barrett, *Acts 15–28*, 892–93.
161 Acts 18:27, D: ὃς ἐπιδημήσας εἰς τὴν Ἀχαίαν πολὺ συνεβάλλετ ἐν ταῖς ἐκκλησίαις.
162 Barrett, *Acts 15–28*, 890.
163 Dahl, "Paul and the Church at Corinth," 90–91; Chow, *Patronage and Power*, 103; Kirner, "Apostolat und Patronage (II)," 44.
164 Fee, *First Epistle*, 823–24; Murphy-O'Connor, *Paul*, 184.
165 See already Marshall, *Enmity in Corinth*, 253.

ship, that is to say, a patron-client relationship.¹⁶⁶ The elements of this friendship would have included hospitality, that is, being lodged in the patron's house, and the pleasure of "eating and drinking" with the host, as Paul says (1 Cor. 9:4).¹⁶⁷ It is also likely that Apollos' patron would have provided a venue for his teaching.¹⁶⁸ The expression δημοσίᾳ in Acts 18:28 makes clear that Apollos' vigorous debates with the Jews of Corinth took place "in public," in view of a crowd.¹⁶⁹ Did Apollos' patron use his influence to secure access to a portico attached to a public building?¹⁷⁰ After δημοσίᾳ, the Western text (Codex E) inserts the words καὶ κατ' οἶκον. Does the editor wish to indicate various private homes, in contrast to public venues,¹⁷¹ in which Apollos preached, or does the singular denote the particular house where the Corinthian Christians regularly assembled (cf. 1 Cor. 16:19)?

While it is not possible to establish with certainty the identity of the person (or persons) who patronized Apollos in Corinth, several indicators point towards Gaius. First, there is the likelihood that Gaius was already serving as the "host of the whole *ekklesia*" at the time of Apollos' visit. As a new arrival in Corinth, it is only natural that Apollos would have found lodging with the principal benefactor of the Christian community.¹⁷² Second, the conclusion that Gaius (along with Crispus) was foremost among those who eventually expressed a preference for Apollos over Paul

---

166 White, *"Amicitia* and the Profession of Poetry in Early Imperial Rome," 74–92, esp. the conclusion on p. 92; Horsfall, *Poets and Patron*, 1, 9; Wiseman, *"Pete nobiles amicos"* in *Literary and Artistic Patronage in Ancient Rome*, 28–38; White, *Promised Verse*, 3–5, 13–16, 23–25; Konstan, *Friendship in the Classical World*, 135–37, 140–42, 143–45; A. Winterling, "Freundschaft und Klientel im kaiserzeitlichen Rom," *Historia* 57 (2008) 298–316.
167 Cf. Horace *Ep.* 1.7.61–70; Cicero *Arch.* 6; *Laus Pisonis* 68–71; Ulpian *Digest* 9.3.5.1; Lucian *Merc. cond.* 3, 20; Treggiari, "Intellectuals, Poets, and their Patrons," 26; Wiseman, "Poets and Patrons," 29–32; White, *Promised Verse*, 13. On Apollos as a recipient of hospitality from the rich patrons in Corinth, see Marshall, *Enmity in Corinth*, 253; Chow, *Patronage and Power*, 104–106.
168 Cf. Horace *Sat.* 2.3.33–34; Varro *Sat. Men.* 517B; Cicero *Cael.* 41; *Fin.* 1.13; 2.44; *Tusc.* 2.7; Wiseman, "Poets and Patrons," 36–38. See further Stowers, "Social Status, Public Speaking and Private Teaching," 59–82, esp. 65–68; Kirner, "Apostolat und Patronage (II)," 33–34.
169 BDAG 191 s.v. δημόσιος 2. Cf. Acts 16:37.
170 On such *scholae* and *exedrae* attached to public buildings, see Vitruvius *Arch.* 5.11.2; Petronius *Satyr.* 90; *ILLRP* 116, 680; Wiseman, "Poets and Patrons," 36. Cf. Kirner, "Apostolat und Patronage (II)," 33, 60–61.
171 Cf. Acts 20:20; Barrett, *Acts 15–28*, 892.
172 Cf. Lampe, "Paul, Patrons, and Clients" in *Paul in the Greco-Roman World*, 496.

(1 Cor. 1:12–15) seems to necessitate a relationship of some duration as the experiential basis for such a judgment.[173] Third, one cannot fail to be impressed by the broad affinity in education, tastes and values between the figure of Apollos, as he emerges from the relevant portions of Acts and 1 Corinthians, and the person of Gaius, as reconstructed from analysis of 1 Cor. 1:14, Rom. 16:23 and detailed exegesis of 2 Cor. 2, 7 and 10–13 (on the theory that the wrongdoer is rightly identified with Gaius).[174] Unless we are to assume that Apollos' patron remains entirely anonymous in the sources, it is difficult to imagine that anyone in Corinth could have been more receptive to Apollos, the ἀνὴρ λόγιος, than Gaius.[175]

Once again, a modest use of historical imagination will allow us to enter into the relationship between Gaius and Apollos. How must it have affected a man who valued proficiency in rhetoric (2 Cor. 10:10b-11; 11:5–6) to hear the Messiahship of Jesus expounded in accordance with the high canons of "eloquent wisdom" (1 Cor. 1:17; 2:1, 4), by an evangelist who affirmed and embodied these standards without qualification? In Apollos' preaching, Gaius finally encountered a discourse and a delivery adequate to the dignity of the subject matter! If Apollos' teaching took the form of skillful exposition of Scriptures, as Acts repeatedly asserts (18:24, 28), the appeal of such teaching to a Gentile God-fearer must have been great, reinforcing a sense of continuity in his religious development. And if Apollos' "skill" consisted in the application of a philosophical framework to the ancient texts of Judaism, so as to disclose their deeper, allegorical meaning,[176] the consonance of this hermeneutic with that of the popular Stoicism that we have predicated of Gaius must have been considerable.[177] Moreover, Apollos' willingness to accept financial support from Gaius, in conformity to the norms of classical friendship, would have confirmed Gaius in his assumption that the ethics of the Christian movement were, after all, compatible with the values of his social class, in spite of Paul's strictures. Indeed, we must allow for the possibility that friendship with the eloquent Apollos would have held

---

173 Weiss, *Der erste Korintherbrief*, 20.
174 See above, ch. 3.
175 On the supporters of Apollos as patrons of the Corinthian church, see Theissen, *Social Setting*, 97–98; Chow, *Patronage and Power*, 105; Kirner, "Apostolat und Patronage (II)," 45.
176 Weiss, *Der erste Korintherbrief*, xxx n.1; Horsley, "Wisdom of Word and Words of Wisdom" in *Wisdom and Spiritual Transcendence at Corinth*, 21–38, esp. 30.
177 See above, ch. 3.

benefits for Gaius, as well, much in the same way that friendship with the poet Martial added luster to the reputation of Pliny.[178] Nor should we underestimate the pleasure which companionship with a cultured client such as Apollos would have brought to Gaius as patron, an attraction vividly described by a notable in Tacitus' *Dialogus* who has taken up a poet and declares that "no one is more intimately linked to me both through the exercise of friendship and by constancy of association."[179] It is not difficult to imagine how much satisfaction Gaius would have derived from conversations with a skilled interpreter of Scriptures, on long walks or over dinner, in a leisure made possible by Apollos' acceptance of the offer of friendship.[180]

From the moment that Apollos entered the house of Gaius, comparisons with Paul would have been inevitable. Even if the only point explicitly mentioned in the letter that followed Apollos' visit to Corinth was Paul's unconventional means of subsistence (1 Cor. 9), the contrast between Apollos' "eloquent wisdom" and Paul's unadorned preaching would have been manifest and unavoidable. The difference in rhetorical presentation would have been especially striking, if we were to conclude that Paul's apologetic references to his "weakness," "fear," and "trembling" in 1 Cor. 2:3 do not belong to a comic self-parody,[181] but have some basis in fact.[182] It would be too much, at this stage, to speak of partisanship on behalf of Apollos, or of rivalry between Paul and Apollos, but in our calculation of the economics of friendship between Paul, Gaius, and Apollos, we would do well to remember Aristotle's insistence upon the principle of singularity in friendship, within a hierarchy of choice: "The primary friendship is not found towards *many*;…in all things it seems the mark of a sensible man to choose the *better* of two alternatives."[183] Given the realities of Roman social relations,[184] any increase in friendship

---

178 Pliny *Ep.*3.21.6; White, *Promised Verse*, 21.
179 Tacitus *Dial.* 5.2.
180 Compare Cicero *Arch.* 6; *Laus Pisonis* 68; Horace *Sat.* 1.6.47; Ovid *Trist.* 1.8.29; 3.6.19; Tacitus *Dial.* 6.2; Pliny *Ep.* 3.3; White, *Promised Verse*, 13, 23–24.
181 Welborn, *Paul, the Fool of Christ*, 90–99.
182 See the discussion in Weiss, *Der erste Korintherbrief*, 47–48; Litfin, *St. Paul's Theology of Proclamation*, 209, 302; Winter, *Paul Among the Sophists*, 158–59, 227–28.
183 Aristotle *Eth. eud.* 7.2.45–48, 1237b34, 1238a3. See the discussion of this text in Jacques Derrida, *Politics of Friendship* (London: Verso, 1997) 20–24.
184 On the tendency of client intellectuals to represent their association with the great man as an exclusive, two-party relationship, see White, *Promised Verse*,

between Gaius and Apollos would have resulted in a diminution of affection towards Paul.[185]

We cannot know how much time passed between Apollos' visit to Corinth and the composition of Paul's next epistle—the letter now preserved in 1 Cor. 7–9, 12–16.[186] As the opening words of 1 Cor. 7 reveal, the Corinthians had written Paul a letter (περὶ δὲ ὧν ἐγράψατε), seeking his advice on a number of matters: marriage, divorce and betrothal, food sacrificed to idols, spiritual gifts (especially tongues-speaking), etc. (1 Cor. 7:1; 8:1; 12:1; 16:1, 12).[187] The fact that the Corinthians should send to Paul in Asia (1 Cor. 16:19) on matters of practical importance demonstrates that Paul was still regarded as an authority by the community. Yet, several of the statements quoted by Paul from the Corinthians' letter express views that diverge sharply from Paul's own: e.g., "It is well for a man not to touch a woman" (1 Cor. 7:1); "All of us possess knowledge" (1 Cor. 8:1); "No idol in the world really exists" (1 Cor. 8:4); "Food will not bring us closer to God" (1 Cor. 8:8); etc.[188] These strongly worded opinions betray no lack of self-confidence! The group which speaks here seems to have regarded it as their duty to "build up" the consciences of "the weak" in the community, so that they would not cling to superstitious scruples (1 Cor. 8:10), so that they would strive to possess spiritual gifts (1 Cor. 14:1), etc. Dale Martin has demonstrated that the attitudes of this minority group ("the Strong") correlate with high social status and high educational level.[189] As the "host of the whole *ekklesia*" at Corinth, the strongest of "the Strong," so to speak, Gaius may have held views like those Paul attributes to this group. We may wonder how Gaius would have reacted to Paul's radical formulation of the relationship between knowledge and love in 1 Cor. 8:11–12: the proper object of religious concern is not an abstract

---

35–36. On the ranking of friends, see Konstan, *Friendship in the Classical World*, 137, 140.
185 For Paul's consciousness of being "loved less," see 2 Cor. 12:15: ἧσσον ἀγαπῶμαι;
186 Weiss, *Der erste Korintherbrief*, xxxix-xliii; idem, *History of Primitive Christianity*, 1.341.
187 Weiss, *Der erste Korintherbrief*, xlii; idem, *History of Primitive Christianity*, 1.333–34. The debate on the function of the περὶ δέ formula has been summarized by Margaret M. Mitchell, "Concerning ΠΕΡΙ ΔΕ in 1 Corinthians," *NovT* 31 (1989) 229–56.
188 Weiss, *Der erste Korintherbrief*, xxix-xxx; Horsley, *Wisdom and Spiritual Transcendence at Corinth*, 39–114.
189 Martin, *The Corinthian Body*, xv-xviii and passim.

truth about God, but "the weak brother or sister for whom Christ died." Would Gaius have accepted Paul's provocative conclusion that, by wounding the consciences of the weak, he and his enlightened associates had "sinned" against members of their own family, indeed, had "sinned against Christ" (1 Cor. 8:12)? Unfortunately, we cannot be certain which of the views attributed to "the Strong" Gaius may have held in particular instances.

Two matters which are treated in Paul's letter of response to the Corinthians pertain more directly to the relationship between Paul and Gaius. The formula περὶ δέ ("now concerning") in 1 Cor. 16:12 indicates that the Corinthians had asked about Apollos in their letter to Paul.[190] The substance of their question is embedded in Paul's response: they wished to know when Apollos would be returning to Corinth.[191] Paul's emphatic assurance that he had "often" or "earnestly" (πολλά) "exhorted" (παρακαλεῖν) Apollos to return should probably be seen as a reflection of the urgency which Paul sensed in the Corinthians' request.[192] Though Paul treats the subject as a matter of interest to the entire community, it is only natural to assume that the question had its origin with Apollos' admirers (Crispus and Gaius).[193] Given what we have learned about the economics of friendship in the Greco-Roman world, there would have been an awkwardness about the question for Paul, perhaps even the potential for insult.[194] While a number of persons might be attracted to an enlightened patron as his "friends,"[195] it is difficult to find expressions of a sense of fellowship between such client-intellectuals.[196] Peter White observes: "As far as possible, they present their association with the great man as though it were an exclusive, two-party relationship."[197] Paul's re-

---

190 Weiss, *Der erste Korintherbrief*, 384; John C. Hurd, *The Origin of I Corinthians* (Macon: Mercer University Press, 1983) 206. Cf. Collins, *First Corinthians*, 597.
191 Weiss, *Der erste Korintherbrief*, 384; Hurd, *The Origin of I Corinthians*, 207; Chow, *Patronage and Power*, 102–103.
192 Cf. Collins, *First Corinthians*, 598.
193 Cf. Marshall, *Enmity in Corinth*, 253.
194 Compare Lucian's sense of being disregarded, owing to the ready welcome given to a newcomer among the client-intellectuals gathered about the patron in *Merc. cond.* 26–27.
195 E.g., Horace *Sat.* 1.5; 2.6.41–45; *Laus Pisonis* 133–37; Tacitus *Dial.* 6.2; cf. White, *Promised Verse*, 24–25.
196 For hostility between client-intellectuals, see e.g., Horace *Sat.* 1.3, 1.9; *Ep.* 1.3.30–36, 1.18.10–20, 2.2.95–101; Juvenal *Sat.* 3.119–25; Lucian *Merc. cond.* 17, 26, 39–40.
197 White, *Promised Verse*, 35.

sponse to the question about Apollos is circumspect and ambiguous. The expression πάντως οὐκ ἦν θέλημα is as objective and impersonal as possible, leaving open the possibility of two interpretations: "he [Apollos] was not at all willing [to come]" or "it was not at all [God's] will [for him to come]."[198] Paul's final remark on the subject of Apollos, ἐλεύσεται δὲ ὅταν εὐκαιρήσῃ, may be taken as reassurance that Apollos plans to visit, but lacks only a favorable opportunity.[199] Yet, the verb εὐκαιρέω also connotes "leisure,"[200] and thus may insinuate to Apollos' Corinthian admirers that their favorite currently enjoys "leisure" provided by other friends elsewhere.[201]

The second matter which impinges upon Paul's relationship with Gaius is Paul's commendation of Stephanas in 1 Cor. 16:15–18. One will recall our hypothesis that the respect in which Paul urges submission to Stephanas is the management of the collection for the poor of Jerusalem.[202] This hypothesis is based upon Paul's use of vocabulary in describing Stephanas' appointment (εἰς διακονίαν τοῖς ἁγίοις ἔταξαν ἑαυτούς) found elsewhere in reference to the charitable project in which the Corinthians are urged to become partners (1 Cor. 16:1; 2 Cor. 8:4; 9:1, 12).[203] Moreover, the clause in which Paul mentions Stephanas' devotion to the saints corresponds to the circumstantial clause customarily employed in Greek letters of recommendation to specify the matter on which the one recommended comes to the reader in need of assistance.[204] Assuming the plausibility of our hypothesis, it is not difficult to imagine how Paul's promotion of Stephanas would have affected men of substance such as Crispus and Gaius, who were accustomed to dispose of sums of money, and who had already served in positions of leadership. Why should they submit to Stephanas in this matter? What specific qualification did Stephanas possess? Peculiar features of the rhetoric of Paul's com-

---

198 See the discussion in Heinrici, *Der erste Brief,* 517; Fee, *First Epistle,* 824; Collins, *First Corinthians,* 598; Lindemann, *Der erste Korintherbrief,* 381–82; Schrage, *Der erste Brief,* 4.447.
199 Weiss, *Der erste Korintherbrief,* 385; Collins, *First Corinthians,* 598; Schrage, *Der erste Brief,* 4.447.
200 BDAG 422.
201 Cf. Lindemann, *Der erste Korintherbrief,* 382: "ὅταν εὐκαιρήσῃ wirkt nach dem Vorangegangenen eher wie ein Euphemismus: Es mangelt ja bislang nicht an günstiger Gelegenheit, sondern am Willen (θέλημα)."
202 See above, ch. 4, pp. 256–58.
203 Cf. Theissen, *Social Setting,* 87–88; Collins, *First Corinthians,* 587–88; Fitzmyer, *First Corinthians,* 62; Horn, "Stephanas und sein Haus," 92.
204 Collins, *First Corinthians,* 603.

mendation of Stephanas, analyzed above,[205] reflect Paul's awareness of the problematic nature of his request, and disclose underlying tensions between Stephanas and his fellow Christians. We argued above that the means by which Stephanas alleviated Paul's "lack" (ὑστέρημα) was through a gift of money (1 Cor. 16:17).[206] How would Gaius have regarded Paul's willingness to accept Stephanas' gift, and, moreover, Paul's effusive praise of the "refreshment" Stephanas had brought to his spirit (1 Cor. 16:18), in light of Paul's refusal to accept an offer of financial support during the period of his initial residence in Corinth? Cicero assumes that he can discredit T. Roscius Capito by the allegation that he broke with the hospitality of a former patron, and put himself into the *fides et clientela* of a new friend, Chrysogonus.[207] We must reckon with the possibility that Paul himself contributed decisively to the outbreak of faction in the Corinthian church, and to the resulting enmity with Gaius and his supporters, by his endorsement of Stephanas generally, and by his support for Stephanas' appointment to a ministry that involved the administration of a potentially large sum of money (cf. 1 Cor. 16:4; 2 Cor. 8:20).

The next communication of the Corinthians with Paul signals the eruption of a crisis. Chloe's "people" brought news of "quarrels" (ἔριδες) among the Corinthian Christians (1 Cor. 1:11). Paul represents the dispute as an incidence of partisanship. The words λέγω δὲ τοῦτο ("But I say this" or "What I mean is this"), at the beginning of 1 Cor. 1:12, mark the slogans that follow—"I am of Paul," "But I, of Apollos!" etc.—as Paul's own formulation of the attitude and behavior of the Corinthians.[208] That is to say, Paul caricatures the Corinthians' quarrelsomeness using slogans like those shouted by the partisans of politicians in the assembly,[209] or by the fans of star performers in the amphitheater.[210] Yet, the term ἔρις that forms the substance of Chloe's report has its background in the political sphere where it is used by Greco-Roman historians to characterize conflicts between factions within city-states.[211] Unless one is prepared to conclude that Paul fundamentally misrepresents the situa-

---

205 See above, ch. 4, pp. 252–56. On criticism of Stephanas by some at Corinth, see Dahl, "Paul and the Church at Corinth," 318.
206 See above, ch. 4, pp. 258–59. See also Theissen, *Social Setting*, 88.
207 Cicero *Rosc. Amer.* 93.
208 Mitchell, *Paul and the Rhetoric of Reconciliation*, 86.
209 See the texts cited in Welborn, *Politics and Rhetoric*, 8–13.
210 Pogoloff, *Logos und Sophia*, 251 n.50; Welborn, *Politics and Rhetoric*, 14–16.
211 See the texts cited in Welborn, *Politics and Rhetoric*, 3–4.

tion, it is necessary, from this point on, to speak of "partisanship," rather than "preference," as characteristic of the relationship between the Corinthians and their apostles.

We argued above that Apollos was the focus of partisan spirit in the church at Corinth.[212] This conclusion was an inference from several conspicuous features of Paul's discourse in 1 Cor. 1–4. First, we noted the reduction in the number of the parties in the course of Paul's argument: only two slogans are repeated in 1 Cor. 3:4—"I belong to Paul,"…"I belong to Apollos"—a clear indication that the preceding apology for the "foolishness" of Paul's gospel (1 Cor. 1:17–3:4) was written with a view to the Apollos faction.[213] More importantly, Paul's summary of his purposes in the argument as a whole in 1 Cor. 4:6 takes the avoidance of partisanship on behalf of Apollos and against himself as its object: "I have applied these things to myself and Apollos for your benefit, brothers and sisters,…so that none of you may be puffed up in favor of one and against another."[214] In general, it is difficult to understand Paul's critique of "eloquent wisdom," in the context of his attempt to dissuade the Corinthians from faction, as directed at anyone other than the admirers of Apollos.[215]

Foremost among the partisans of Apollos at Corinth were Crispus and Gaius. One will recall that our conclusion regarding the role of Crispus and Gaius in the formation of factions was an inference from three unusual features of 1 Cor. 1:14–16: the anomalous precedence of Crispus and Gaius (over the "first-fruits," Stephanas) in Paul's account of conversions at Corinth; the high irony of Paul's thanksgiving that he had baptized no one except Crispus and Gaius; and the skillful use of the device of a feigned lapse-of-memory to separate Crispus and Gaius from the loyal Stephanas.[216] Because Paul's ironic comments about Crispus and Gaius follow directly upon the account of what had been "made clear" to him by Chloe's people (1 Cor. 1:11), it is necessary to infer that the report of Chloe's people contained the information that Crispus and Gaius were now quite open in declaring their admiration and support

---

212 See above, ch. 5, pp. 374–78. See also Ker, "Paul and Apollos—Colleagues or Rivals?" 75–97; Smit, "What is Apollos? What is Paul?" 231–51; Welborn, *Paul, the Fool of Christ*, 102–109.
213 See above, ch. 5, p. 374. See already Weiss, *Der erste Korintherbrief*, xxxiii.
214 Ker, "Paul and Apollos—Colleagues or Rivals?," 91–92.
215 Smit, "What is Apollos? What is Paul?" 236, 246–48.
216 See above, pp. 240–41, 249, 252, 373–74. See also Weiss, *Der erste Korintherbrief*, 20; Lindemann, *Der erste Korintherbrief*, 42.

for Apollos. Such an excess of enthusiasm for Apollos might be taken as an indication that Apollos had visited Corinth again, refreshing the impression of his wisdom and eloquence, and reinforcing the contrast with Paul. But the account of Christian origins at Corinth in Acts is so meager that we are unable to draw a conclusion on this point.

Analysis of Paul's argument in 1 Cor. 1–4 makes it likely that partisanship on behalf of Apollos went beyond expressions of admiration for the gifted Alexandrian sophist, and took the form of opinions openly derogatory of Paul. First, the negative definition of the style and content of Paul's preaching in 1 Cor. 1:17 ("not with eloquent wisdom") suggests that some in Corinth have found something wanting in Paul's proclamation, and indicates the respect in which they have found it deficient.[217] Second, the concessive manner in which Paul introduces the subject of his rhetorical self-presentation in 1 Cor. 2:1, 3, where the emphatic particle κἀγώ is adverbial in usage, and has an assentient force,[218] makes it clear that someone in Corinth has put forward a negative evaluation of Paul's preaching: *"Indeed, I did* come to you, brothers and sisters, without eloquence or wisdom (as you say)..., *Indeed, I did* come to you in weakness and fear and in much trembling..."[219] Finally, as we have argued elsewhere, the label μωρός ("fool") is so potently derogatory that it is unimaginable that the term originated with Paul himself, even if Paul proved capable of appropriating the term in a dialectical sense in the course of his argument (1 Cor. 3:18; 4:10).[220] We must conclude that the label μωρός was applied to Paul by certain members of the Christian community at Corinth to describe the impression that Paul made upon them.[221]

These conclusions are reinforced by the apologetic orientation of the entire discourse in 1 Cor. 1:17–4:21, where Paul is clearly on the defen-

---

217 Weiss, *Der erste Korintherbrief*, 22–23; Smit, "What is Apollos? What is Paul?" 236, 246–48.
218 Smyth, *Greek Grammar*, §2881–84; J. D. Denniston, *The Greek Particles* (Oxford: Clarendon Press, 1987) 396; BDF 438–39, 442.
219 Similarly, H. A. W. Meyer, *Der erste Brief an die Korinther* (Göttingen: Vandenhoeck & Ruprecht, 1839) *ad loc.*, cited in Heinrici, *Der erste Brief*, 115.
220 Welborn, *Paul, the Fool of Christ*, 50, 58, 60, 84, 90, 110, 115, 126, 128 and *passim*.
221 Welborn, *Paul, the Fool of Christ*, 102–16.

sive when speaking of the "foolishness" of his preaching.²²² The defensive tone is sharpest in those passages where Paul addresses himself in the first person singular (ἐγώ) to the Corinthians in the second person plural (ὑμεῖς), that is, in 1 Cor. 2:1–5, 3:1–4, and 4:1–5. In the latter passage (4:3), Paul explicitly rejects any judgment that the Corinthians may pass upon him. The reason for the apologetic stance of these passages may be inferred from the way in which Paul continues the discussion in 1 Cor. 3:5–15 and 4:6–7: "What then is Apollos? What is Paul?...I have applied all of this to Apollos and myself."²²³ Clearly, some in Corinth have made invidious comparisons between Apollos and Paul. It is not difficult to reconstruct what the partisans of Apollos have said: "In comparison with our learned and eloquent teacher, Paul is a fool!"

Paul's response to the report of Chloe's people takes the form of the powerful counsel of concord, now preserved in 1 Cor. 1:1–6:11, a letter that fully justifies the verdict of Paul's critic, in terms of being "weighty and strong" (2 Cor. 10:10).²²⁴ But we should not fail to recognize how much of this masterful discourse would have been shocking, and even offensive, to a member of the social elite who was also a Christian. Paul not only accepts the "fool" label,²²⁵ but expounds the ways in which his social experience as an apostle corresponds to that of a low buffoon, with an explicitness that would have been shameful to an upper-class reader: "We are fools on account of Christ, ...we are weak,...we are dishonored; we are hungry and thirsty, we are naked, we are beaten, we are homeless, and we toil, laboring with our own hands; [we are] reviled,...harassed, slandered...; we have become like the refuse of the world, the scum of all things, to this very day" (1 Cor. 4:9–13). Moreover, Paul not only accepts the characterization of his discourse as "vulgar" and "simple" (μωρία),²²⁶ but focuses upon the most scandalous element of his preaching—the cross (1 Cor. 2:2). As Cicero and Varro attest, it was this cruel and disgusting term which the cultured elite of the Roman world least

---

222 Heinrici, *Der erste Brief*, 64; Weiss, *Der erste Korintherbrief*, xxxi, 22; Winter, *Paul Among the Sophists*, 147; Smit, "What is Apollos? What is Paul?" 241–42, 250.
223 Heinrici, *Der erste Brief*, 12, 64; Smit, "What is Apollos? What is Paul?" 242.
224 On the rhetorical artistry of many passages in 1 Cor. 1–4, esp. 1:18–2:16, see BDF 260; Weiss, *Der erste Korintherbrief*, 27–36; Collins, *First Corinthians*, 90–91, 108.
225 Welborn, *Paul, the Fool of Christ*, 112–16, 248–53.
226 Welborn, *Paul, the Fool of Christ*, 1–2, 15–24, 31–33.

wanted to hear.²²⁷ The cross was an ominous lacuna at the center of public discourse.²²⁸ When the cross was mentioned at all, it was generally as the subject of jest.²²⁹ But Paul seizes upon this unspeakable word and pronounces it with a vengeance. Indeed, Paul summarizes the content of his gospel in a single phrase, ὁ λόγος τοῦ σταυροῦ ("the word of the cross"), a reduction of astonishing harshness.²³⁰ Paul's choice of the perfect participle, ἐσταυρωμένος, to describe more precisely the Christ whom he proclaims (1 Cor. 1:23; 2:2) can only be viewed as a deliberate provocation of those who hoped for a Messiah of resplendent glory: Paul insists that the continuing and present significance of Christ, even after his resurrection, consists in nothing other than the fact that he *is* "the crucified."²³¹ We argued above that Paul's explanation of the social implications of "the word of the cross" would have been especially disconcerting to a member of the educated elite.²³² Because the Messiah had been revealed as "the crucified one," Paul draws the conclusion that "God has *chosen* the foolish of the world in order to shame the wise; and God has *chosen* the weak of the world in order to shame the strong; and God has *chosen* the low-born of the world and the despised, things that are not, in order to bring to

---

227 Cicero *Rab. Post.* 5.16; Varro *De Lingua Latina* in *M. Terenti Varronis de Lingua Latina quae supersunt*, ed. G. Goetz and F. Schoell (Leipzig: Teubner, 1910) 239. See the discussion in Martin Hengel, *Crucifixion in the Ancient World and the Folly of the Message of the Cross* (Philadelphia: Fortress Press, 1977) 41–43; Welborn, *Paul, the Fool of Christ*, 21–22.
228 On the absence of references to the "cross" and "crucifixion" in Greek and Latin writers of the upper class, see Hengel, *Crucifixion in the Ancient World*, 38; Welborn, *Paul, the Fool of Christ*, 129–31.
229 As in comedy, farce, and mime: e.g., Plautus *Most.* 359–64; the *Laureolus* mime of Catullus, on which see Josephus *A.J.* 19.94; Martial *De Spect.* 7; Juvenal *Sat.* 8.187–88; Suetonius *Calig.* 57; *POxy 413* ("Adulteress"); see also Juvenal *Sat.* 6.219–23; Petronius *Satyr.* 53, 111–13. Cf. Justin Meggitt, "Laughing and Dreaming at the Foot of the Cross: Context and Reception of a Religious Symbol," *Journal for the Study of Religion, Ethics, and Society* 1 (1996) 9–14; Welborn, *Paul, the Fool of Christ*, 99–101, 132–38.
230 Heinrici, *Der erste Brief*, 66; Weiss, *Der erste Korintherbrief*, 26–27; Ulrich Wilckens, *Weisheit und Torheit: Eine exegetisch-religionsgeschichtliche Untersuchung zu 1. Kor. 1 und 2* (Tübingen: Mohr-Siebeck, 1959) 24; Collins, *First Corinthians*, 101; Lindemann, *Der erste Korintherbrief*, 43.
231 J. Schneider, "σταυρός," *TDNT* 7 (1971) 582; E. Earle Ellis, "Christ Crucified" in *Prophecy and Hermeneutic in Early Christianity* (Grand Rapids: Eerdmans, 1980) 73–74; Heinz-Wolfgang Kuhn, "Kreuz," *TRE* 19 (1990) 720; Heckel, "Der Gekreuzigte bei Paulus," 196–200.
232 See above, ch. 3, pp. 93–98.

nothing those that are" (1 Cor. 1:27–28).²³³ As Edwin Judge once observed, this remarkable dictum would have appealed very greatly to Karl Marx, another son of Israel passionately committed to showing the world a redeemed destiny for the poor and oppressed.²³⁴ Yet, for an upper-class Christian, such as Gaius, Paul's inference that God had chosen the foolish and the weak in order to bring disgrace upon the wise and the strong must have seemed a wholly unwarranted inference and an incomprehensible impoverishment of the experience of belonging to Christ.²³⁵

If Paul's attempt to dissuade certain Corinthians from partisanship of Apollos, and to defend himself against the stereotype of foolishness, had stopped with the statements we have examined thus far, however paradoxical these statements may have seemed, it is possible that Paul's relationship with Gaius might have taken a different course. A man who, despite his status in Roman society, proved capable of altering the etiquette of the communal meal, so that the "have-nots" were included more equitably in the Lord's Supper, as we have suggested above, might well have found Paul's assertion strangely compelling, that God had been mysteriously at work in the crucifixion of the Messiah by "the rulers of this age" (1 Cor. 2:6–8), with the result that the values of the age had been inverted, especially as Paul propounded this dark vision with an artistry which approached the poetical (e. g., "What no eye has seen, nor ear heard, nor human heart conceived,…etc.," 1 Cor. 2:9).²³⁶

But, as we know, Paul was not content to leave it at that. In his dismay at the outbreak of party spirit, Paul goes on to censure the wise and the strong as "fleshly" and "childlike": "Indeed, brothers, I was not able to speak to you as to spiritual people, but to fleshly, as to babies in Christ. We gave you milk to drink, not meat, for you were not yet able (to digest it). Nor are you now able, for you are still fleshly. For when there is jealously and strife among you, are you not fleshly, and do you not behave in a merely human manner? For when someone says, 'I am of Paul,' but an-

---

233 Welborn, *Paul, the Fool of Christ*, 161, 164, 234.
234 Judge, "Cultural Conformity and Innovation in Paul" in idem, *Social Distinctives of the Christians*, 159.
235 See above, ch. 3, pp. 95–98.
236 On the artistry of this passage, see Weiss, *Der erste Korintherbrief*, 30, 35; Collins, *First Corinthians*, 90–91.

Chapter Six. History of a Friendship
419

other, 'I am of Apollos,' are you not all-too human?" (1 Cor. 3:1–4).²³⁷ This characterization of those who took pride in their knowledge (1 Cor. 8:1–2; 1:5) as "infantile" could only have given offense. Still more, in a bitterly sarcastic passage, Paul mocks his critics—the wealthy friends of Apollos—as pretentious patrons: "Already you have all you want! Already you have become rich! Quite apart from us you reign like kings (ἐβασιλεύσατε)! Indeed, I wish you had become kings (ἐβασιλεύσατε), so that we might share the reign (συμβασιλεύσωμεν) with you!" (1 Cor. 4:8).²³⁸ Paul's repeated use of the expression "reign like kings" is an unmistakable allusion to the role of some as patrons.²³⁹ "King" (βασιλεύς, *rex*) was the satirist's term for a rich patron.²⁴⁰ Juvenal's hapless clients refer to the rich patrons whose largesse they pursue as "kings."²⁴¹ By styling certain persons at Corinth as "kings," Paul ridicules their pretension to patronal position and, at the same time, construes Apollos as a mere client, a parasite.²⁴² It is interesting to note that in the preceding verse, Paul suddenly switches to the second person *singular*, as if he were addressing *one patron* in particular: "For who concedes you (σε) any superiority? What do you have (ἔχεις) which you have not received (ἔλαβες)? And if you received (ἔλαβες) it, why do you boast (καυχᾶσαι) as if you had not received it?" (1 Cor. 4:7).²⁴³ Paul ironically reminds the leading figure among the Corinthian patrons that his vaunted spiritual attainments are gifts from God. Could it be that we encounter here the first use of singular verbs and pronouns which becomes so frequent in the later stages of Paul's Corinthian correspondence, as a periphrastic device for conciliating the wrongdoer?

Paul sent the powerful epistle now preserved in 1 Cor. 1:1–6:11 to Corinth by the hand of Timothy, who was charged with "reminding"

---

237 On the chiding quality of Paul's criticism of the Corinthians' spiritual defects in 1 Cor. 3:1–4, see Heinrici, *Der erste Brief*, 114–17; Weiss, *Der erste Korintherbrief*, 72–73; Fee, *First Epistle*, 102–103; Collins, *First Corinthians*, 139–41.
238 On the biting irony of this passage, see Weiss, *Der erste Korintherbrief*, 106–108; Fitzgerald, *Cracks in an Earthen Vessel*, 121, 137.
239 Martin, *Slavery as Salvation*, 210 n.13; Welborn, *Paul, the Fool of Christ*, 232.
240 E.g., Horace *Ep.* 1.7.37–38; Statius *Silvae*; cf. Gilbert Highet, "*Libertino Patre Natus*," *American Journal of Philology* 94 (1973) 279; White, *Promised Verse*, 29–30, 280 n.47.
241 Juvenal *Sat.* 5.14, 130, 137, 161; 7.45; 10.161.
242 On the implication of calling the more powerful friend "king"—namely, that the weaker friend is then likened to a client or parasite–see White, *Promised Verse*, 29.
243 Cf. Kirner, "Apostolat und Patronage (II)," 41 n.46.

the Corinthians of Paul's "ways in Messiah Jesus" (1 Cor. 4:17).²⁴⁴ Despite the polarization of the community, and the open denigration of Paul as "foolish," Paul seems to have remained confident of his ability to restore order. Indeed, Paul concludes the body of the letter with a threat to come and impose discipline (1 Cor. 4:18–21).²⁴⁵ Even if Paul's warning is imbued with an ironic consciousness of the possibility of his own discomfiture, as we have argued elsewhere,²⁴⁶ Paul writes in full assurance of his authority as apostle, as the "father" of the community (1 Cor. 4:15). Paul gives instructions for the expulsion of an incestuous man from the assembly, on the assumption that a judgment pronounced in his absence will be executed as if he were present (1 Cor. 5:3–5).²⁴⁷ Even in the apologetic portion of the epistle (1 Cor. 1:17–4:21), the tone is one of controlled excitement, a high irony that repeatedly breaks over into censure,²⁴⁸ rather than a mood of distress or grief.

Nevertheless, Paul must have sensed an urgency to bring his work among the Corinthians to a close, lest the partisanship on behalf of Apollos endanger the collection for the poor of Jerusalem,²⁴⁹ to which Paul hoped that the Corinthians would make a "considerable" contribution (1 Cor. 16:4).²⁵⁰ In this situation, it is not surprising that Paul's next communication with Corinth should have been the letter now preserved in 2 Cor. 8.²⁵¹ It is impossible to tell how much time passed between the latest portion of 1 Corinthians and the earliest portion of 2 Corinthians,

---

244 Fee, *First Epistle*, 188–89; Collins, *First Corinthians*, 196–98. On Timothy as envoy in general, see Margaret M. Mitchell, "New Testament Envoys in the Context of Greco-Roman Diplomatic and Epistolary Conventions: The Example of Timothy and Titus," *JBL* 111 (1992) 641–62.
245 Schrage, *Der erste Brief*, 1.364. Cf. G. Shaw, *The Cost of Authority: Manipulation and Freedom in the New Testament* (Philadelphia: Fortress Press, 1982) 68–69; Castelli, *Imitating Paul*, 98–111.
246 Welborn, *Paul, the Fool of Christ*, 89–90.
247 Conzelmann, *1 Corinthians*, 97–98; Meeks, *First Urban Christians*, 128.
248 Weiss, *Der erste Korintherbrief*, 25, 27, 29–30, 106; Plank, *Paul and the Irony of Affliction*, 33–70.
249 See Merklein, *Der erste Brief*, 1.331, who sees the warning of 1 Cor. 4:18–19 directed at the admirers of Apollos.
250 Weiss, *Der erste Korintherbrief*, 382. Cf. 2 Cor. 8:14, with the comments of Betz, *2 Corinthians 8 and 9*, 68.
251 For the hypothesis that 2 Cor. 8 was originally an independent letter, see Betz, *2 Corinthians 8 and 9*, 3–36 and *passim*. On the placement of 2 Cor. 8 before 2 Cor. 10–13 in the sequence of Paul's letters to Corinth, see Weiss, *Primitive Christianity*, 1.353; followed by Mitchell, "Paul's Letters to Corinth," 321–35, esp. 324–27.

but the interval cannot have been too great, because the vocabulary of 2 Cor. 8 is remarkably close to 1 Corinthians in general.[252] We have already given our reasons for placing the composition of 2 Cor. 8 before 2 Cor. 10–13: Paul's appeal to the conduct of Titus and an unnamed brother in 2 Cor. 12:18 is a retrospective reference to the mission for which Titus and the brother were authorized in 2 Cor. 8:16–24.[253] As the latter passage makes clear, Paul took extraordinary precautions to assure the Corinthians of the honesty of his administration of the collection, accepting the appointment of a "brother, elected by the churches" as an auditor "to stave off the possibility that someone might complain against us in view of the large sum of money being administered by us" (2 Cor. 8:19–20).[254] Nevertheless, as we have argued above, the Corinthians, or more precisely, those few Corinthians who possessed significant resources, refused to contribute to the collection, and Titus returned to Paul empty-handed.[255] Passages in Seneca's *De Beneficiis* aid us in forming an image of what transpired on this occasion, when Titus conveyed Paul's request for a gift. Seneca observes: "It is unpleasant and burdensome to have to say, 'I ask,' and as a man utters the words he is forced to lower his eyes."[256] Similarly, Seneca's account of a grudging benefactor may give us a glimpse of the demeanor of Gaius: he spoke with "ungraciousness, with frowning brows, and with grudging words that were scarcely audible."[257] In retrospect, the fruitless outcome of Paul's request is hardly surprising, given the tensions that Paul had created through the appointment of Stephanas as his local agent in the collection (1 Cor. 16:15–18), the emergence of partisanship on behalf of Apollos (1 Cor. 1:12; 3:4), and Paul's inflammatory critique of eloquent wisdom (in 1 Cor. 1–4). Yet, we may suggest that the final, and decisive, reason for the Corinthians' refusal to participate in the collection lay in the rad-

---

252 Krenkel, *Beiträge*, 351–54; Drescher, "Vorgänge in Korinth," 67; Weiss, *Primitive Christianity*, 1.353; Mitchell, "Paul's Letters to Corinth," 328–30.
253 See above, ch. 3. See already Weiss, *Primitive Christianity*, 1.353; Windisch, *Der zweite Korintherbrief*, 405; Mitchell, "Paul's Letters to Corinth," 226–27.
254 See the translation and commentary on these verses by Betz, *2 Corinthians 8 and 9*, 38, 74–77.
255 See above, ch. 3 on 2 Cor. 12:16–18, pp. 176–77.
256 Seneca *Ben.* 2.2.1. Cf. Miriam Griffin, "Seneca as a Sociologist: *De Beneficiis*" in *Seneca uomo politico e l'età di Claudio e di Nerone*, ed. Arturo De Vivo and Elio Lo Cascio (Bari: Edipuglia, 2003) 89–122.
257 Seneca *Ben.*1.1.6.

ical nature of Paul's argument for "equality" (ἰσότης) between Christians of different social classes in 2 Cor. 8.

Paul begins the letter now preserved in 2 Cor. 8 by calling attention to the success of the collection among the churches of Macedonia, as the occasion for requesting that the Corinthians fulfill their commitment to his charitable project. Paul emphasizes the "abysmal poverty" (ἡ κατὰ βάθους πτωχεία) of the Macedonians, which had "overflowed into the wealth (τὸ πλοῦτος) of their generosity," and praises the Macedonians for acting "on their own initiative, petitioning…for the favor of partnership in the charitable gift" (2 Cor. 8:1–5).[258] Noteworthy in this exordium is Paul's paradoxical assertion that the *poverty* of the Macedonians had become the source of *wealth* for the Jerusalem Christians.[259] Paul develops this seemingly absurd proposition in the first of three proofs, appealing to the example of Jesus Christ: "For you know the grace of our Lord Jesus Christ, that on account of you he became poor (ἐπτώχευσεν), although he was rich (πλούσιος), in order that by means of his poverty (πτωχεία) you might become rich (πλουτήσητε)" (2 Cor. 8:9). The notion that Jesus was impoverished and lived in circumstances of beggary (πτωχεία) is without parallel in the New Testament,[260] underlining the radical nature of the theory of economic relations that Paul is developing. Nowhere else in the New Testament is a soteriological function attributed to Jesus' poverty.[261]

Yet, a full appreciation of the potential offensiveness of Paul's argument can be gained only from consideration of his third, and final, proof (2 Cor. 8:13–15): an appeal to the principle of "equality" (ἰσότης).[262] Paul urges: "At the present time, your abundance should alleviate their lack, in order that their abundance may also be for your lack, so that there may be equality" (2 Cor. 8:14). The "equality" which Paul advocates is not a communism of the sort lampooned by Aristophanes in the *Ecclesiazusae*,[263] but something more radical, amounting to a total up-

---

258 Betz, *2 Corinthians 8 and 9*, 41–49. Cf. Harrison, *Paul's Language of Grace*, 315; Downs, *Offering of the Gentiles*, 131–34.
259 Betz, *2 Corinthians 8 and 9*, 43–44.
260 Betz, *2 Corinthians 8 and 9*, 62.
261 Betz, *2 Corinthians 8 and 9*, 62.
262 For 2 Cor. 8:13–15 as the third and final proof of the letter, see Betz, *2 Corinthians 8 and 9*, 67–70. On the concept of ἰσότης, see Georgi, *Remembering the Poor*, 84–91.
263 Kenneth S. Rothwell, *Politics and Persuasion in Aristophanes' Ecclesiazusae* (Leiden: Brill, 1990).

ending of the traditional notion of the basis of friendship in equality.²⁶⁴ Quoting the proverb, "Amity is equality" (ἰσότης ἡ φιλότης), Aristotle explains that "there are two sorts of equality," corresponding to the two species of friendship.²⁶⁵ In a friendship between equals, whether in wealth or virtue, equality is "numerical" (κατ' ἀριθμόν), "as it is measured by the same standard."²⁶⁶ But in a friendship between unequals, such as that between benefactor and beneficiary, equality must be "proportional" (κατ' ἀναλογίαν), "since it is just for superior and inferior to have not the same share but proportional shares."²⁶⁷ That is, between two unequal persons, justice divides benefits in proportion to their deserts, so that the two shares are not equal to each other, but each equal to its recipient's merits.²⁶⁸ In the Aristotelian calculus, this means that "the superior party claims by inverse proportion—the contribution of the inferior to stand in the same ratio to his own as he himself stands to the inferior, his attitude being that of ruler to subject."²⁶⁹ Thus, in order to restore balance and secure equality, the inferior party must render a larger share of "honor" (τιμή) to his benefactor, "such as belongs by nature to a ruler or a god."²⁷⁰ Without the operation of this inverse proportion, Aristotle judges, "it would seem that the superior comes off worse, and friendship is a charity and not a partnership."²⁷¹

Now we are able to see how profoundly Paul contradicts the assumptions about the relations between benefactors and beneficiaries with which Gaius and other wealthy Corinthians would have read his letter. Paul is arguing that the poor Jerusalem saints are in the position of the superior party, by virtue of their spiritual wealth, which has alleviated the Corinthians' deficiency; so now, as the beneficiaries, the Corinthians are obliged, by the logic of inverse proportion, to make a considerable

---

264 For the suggestion that Paul's appeal to ἰσότης may be drawing upon conventions associated with the concept of friendship in the Greco-Roman world, see Johan C. Thom, "'Harmonious Equality': The *Topos* of Friendship in Neopythagorean Writings" in *Greco-Roman Perspectives on Friendship*, ed. John T. Fitzgerald (Atlanta: Scholars Press, 1997) 77–103; Luke Timothy Johnson, "Making Connections: The Material Expression of Friendship in the New Testament," *Interpretation* 58 (2004) 158–71, esp. 165–67.
265 Aristotle *Eth. eud.* 7.9.1; see also *Eth. nic.* 8.5.5.
266 Aristotle *Eth. eud.* 7.9.5; cf. *Eth. nic.* 8.6.7.
267 Aristotle *Eth. eud.* 7.9.5.
268 Aristotle *Eth. eud.* 7.3.2; cf. *Eth. nic.* 8.7.2.
269 Aristotle *Eth. eud.* 7.10.10.
270 Aristotle *Eth. eud.* 7.10.13.
271 Aristotle *Eth. eud.* 7.10.12.

gift to the Jerusalem Christians, in order to restore equality. This argument, which is advanced somewhat elliptically and metaphorically in 2 Cor. 8:1–15,[272] is articulated explicitly in Rom. 15:26–27, after the success of the collection was guaranteed: "for Macedonia and Achaia have been pleased to share their resources with the poor among the saints at Jerusalem. They were pleased to do this, and indeed, *they owe it to them*; for if the Gentiles have come to share in their spiritual blessings, they ought also to be of service to them in material things."[273] It is not difficult to imagine how perverse this argument must have seemed to anyone shaped by the conventional notion of obligations between benefactors and beneficiaries, when Paul first advanced it in 2 Cor. 8.

As we have argued above,[274] Paul's attempt to bring the collection at Corinth to completion through the letter now preserved in 2 Cor. 8 failed of its object. Gaius and other wealthy Corinthians (Crispus? Erastus?), upon whose surplus resources the success and magnitude of the collection depended, refused to contribute. Titus and the other delegates, commissioned and authorized by Paul in 2 Cor. 8:16–23, returned to Paul empty-handed. It is not possible to determine whether Titus' report included mention of the Corinthians' suspicion of Paul's motives. But it stands to reason that Gaius and his colleagues would have given some cause for their refusal. What is clear, in any case, is that Paul decided, at this juncture, to go to Corinth in person. Although the book of Acts is silent about Paul's second visit to Corinth, it is nevertheless certain that it took place, an inference required by Paul's references to an impending "third" visit in 2 Cor. 12:14 and 13:1.[275] That this visit was intensely "painful" to both Paul and the Corinthians is evidenced by Paul's retrospective remarks in 2 Cor. 2:1–3.[276] Through detailed exegesis of key passages in the letter that Paul wrote in the aftermath of this painful

---

272 Betz, *2 Corinthians 8 and 9*, 68.
273 See the discussion of the relationship between 2 Cor. 8:14 and Rom. 15:26–27 in Windisch, *Der zweite Korintherbrief*, 259–60; Georgi, *Remembering the Poor*, 62–67; Betz, *2 Corinthians 8 and 9*, 68–69, 124; Downs, *Offering of the Gentiles*, 137–38.
274 See above, ch. 3, pp. 176–79.
275 Bleek, "Erörterungen," 614–24; Ewald, *Sendschreiben*, 220–27; Weiss, *Primitive Christianity*, 1.343–44; Betz, *2 Corinthians 8 and 9*, 142–43; Murphy-O'Connor, *Paul*, 291–92; Thrall, *Second Epistle*, 1.49–57.
276 Windisch, *Der zweite Korintherbrief*, 76–80; Furnish, *II Corinthians*, 150–54; Thrall, *Second Epistle*, 1.163–69. Cf. David E. Fredrickson, "Paul, Hardships, and Suffering" in *Paul in the Greco-Roman World*, ed. J. Paul Sampley (Harrisburg: Trinity Press International, 2003) 172–97.

visit (2 Cor. 12:16–18, 20–21; 13:1–2), we have sought to provide a plausible reconstruction of what happened on that disastrous occasion.[277] Here we can content ourselves with a modest act of historical imagination.

Upon Paul's arrival in Corinth (by sea?), an assembly was convoked, probably in the house of Gaius. Ironically, the authorization for this quasi-judicial assembly was that earlier provided by Paul himself in his instructions for adjudicating grievances among believers (1 Cor. 6:1–6)! The atmosphere in which the group assembled must have been fraught with tension. Recollecting the fearful situation, Paul refers to "slander, gossip, and conceit" (2 Cor. 12:20).[278] Paul must have spoken first. We cannot know precisely what Paul said on this occasion. Perhaps he expressed astonishment (cf. Gal. 1:6) that the Corinthians had suddenly abandoned their generous ministry, which they had begun with such eagerness and had carried forward with diligence (cf. 2 Cor. 8:6, 10–12). Doubtless, Paul reviewed the measures he had taken to insure the integrity of the administration of the collection (2 Cor. 8:16–24). It would be very surprising if Paul had concluded his remarks without referring to the means of his subsistence while in Corinth, as proof of the probity of his conduct, since this was later represented as a strategic mistake (2 Cor. 11:7–11).[279] But perhaps this reconstruction of Paul's assembly-discourse is altogether too reasonable. Perhaps Paul spoke confusedly, with obvious loss of emotional control and personal dignity. What is certain is that Paul produced an impression of abject weakness (2 Cor. 10:1). In retrospect, Paul concedes that his discourse was amateurish (2 Cor. 11:6).

At some point during the proceedings, an individual arose in the assembly and publicly accused Paul of embezzlement in connection with the collection (2 Cor. 12:16–18; 13:1–2). We have argued in detail above that this accusation of embezzlement was the "wrong" done to Paul.[280] We have also sought to make plausible the hypothesis that the

---

277 See above, ch. 3, pp. 179–94. See already Betz, *2 Corinthians 8 and 9*, 77, 97, 142–43.
278 Cf. Weiss, *Primitive Christianity*, 1.343–44; Furnish, *II Corinthians*, 562; Martin, *2 Corinthians*, 451; Thrall, *Second Epistle*, 2.865–66; Roetzel, *2 Corinthians*, 38.
279 Windisch, *Der zweite Korintherbrief*, 333–34; Furnish, *II Corinthians*, 491; Marshall, *Enmity in Corinth*, 246, 335; Thrall, *Second Epistle*, 2.683, 704; Harris, *Second Epistle*, 754.
280 See above, ch. 3, pp. 179–81. See also Betz, *2 Corinthians 8 and 9*, 77, 97.

wrongdoer was Gaius.[281] It is not difficult to appreciate how serious the moment must have been, when the "host of the whole *ekklesia*" and, hence, the principal benefactor of the Christian groups at Corinth, leveled the accusation of embezzlement against Paul. Most likely, Paul was stunned into silence. The fate of the collection hung in the balance. Paul's rectitude and honor had suffered a crushing blow.[282] When Paul recovered his wits, he employed a skillful and entirely appropriate tactic: he invoked the Deuteronomic rule of judicial evidence—"By the mouth or two or three witnesses must every charge be substantiated!" (2 Cor. 13:1). No one rose to second Gaius' accusation. This conclusion is necessitated by the logic of Paul's statements in 2 Cor. 13:1–2, as we have shown above.[283] It is a matter of conjecture why Gaius' charge remained unsubstantiated. Perhaps the majority harbored no suspicion against Paul. Sympathy for Paul's situation must have played a significant part, if Paul's account of the "pain" experienced by the Corinthians is trustworthy (2 Cor. 2:5). Gentile converts may have had no conception of what was involved in the invocation of the Deuteronomic statute. Perhaps the *gravitas* of Gaius was such that he was not perceived as needing a second. In any case, the assembly broke up in confusion. Looking back, Paul recollects "strife, jealousy, angry outbursts, intrigues, slanders, whisperings, arrogant opinions, disorders" (2 Cor. 12:20), in expressing his fear that this scenario might be repeated if he returned to Corinth.[284] Paul departed Corinth in utter humiliation (2 Cor. 12:21). It would not be surprising if the "pain" (λύπη) that bit into Paul's soul upon the return-voyage to Ephesus and in the days that followed bordered on what we would today call depression.[285]

It is worthwhile, at this juncture, to consider the causes of the *rupture* between Paul and Gaius. How had a relationship begun with such enthusiasm and intimacy, as indicated by Paul's personal administration of bap-

---

281 See above, ch. 4, pp. 241–51, 283–88.
282 So already Weiss, *Primitive Christianity*, 1.343.
283 See above, ch. 3, pp. 182–94.
284 Cf. Windisch, *Der zweite Korintherbrief*, 407–408; Barrett, *Second Epistle*, 329; Furnish, *II Corinthians*, 568.
285 On λύπη as "psychological distress" or "depression," see Harris, *Restraining Rage*, 16–17; see further, in general, Julia Kristeva, *Black Sun: Depression and Melancholia* (New York: Columbia University Press, 1992). On Paul's λύπη in 2 Cor. 1–2 and the danger of despair, see David E. Fredrickson, "Paul's Sentence of Death (2 Corinthians 1:9)" in *God, Evil, and Suffering*, ed. T. Fretheim and C. Thompson (St. Paul: Word and World, 2000) 103–107.

tism to Gaius, devolved so utterly into distrust, accusation, pain, and recrimination? Ancient literature on friendship, and especially on the causes of "rupture" (διάλυσις) within friendship,[286] illuminates the perceptions and experiences that operated on both sides. We begin with Gaius, assuming that a man of his social class would have been formed by the values inherent in Greek and Roman proverbs on friendship, values subjected to theoretical analysis by Aristotle, Cicero, and Seneca. It is important to notice that the first clear indication of a "rupture" between Paul and Gaius occurs in connection with Paul's attempt to bring the collection to a conclusion. Although tensions and strains are evident in 1 Cor. 1:1–6:11, as a result of the partisanship of Crispus and Gaius for Apollos, Paul's willingness to mention both men by name (1 Cor. 1:14) suggests that a "rupture" had not yet occurred, such as would have been perceived as "enmity," and hence subject to the convention of "not-naming."[287] A rupture occurred in relation to Paul's request for a considerable contribution to the collection. Why?

The literature of friendship suggests that Gaius may have regarded Paul's request for money as an act that revealed the merely "utilitarian" character of Paul's friendship. In Aristotle's discussion of unequal friendships, he makes clear that a friendship based upon utility (ἡ κατὰ τὸ χρήσιμον φιλία) is the most vulnerable to rupture.[288] Aristotle observes: "Complaints and recriminations (ἐγκλήματα καὶ μέμψεις) occur solely or chiefly in friendships of utility," and explains, "for here the friends associate with each other for the sake of profit."[289] The displacement of person by profit is identified by Aristotle as the source of the instability of utilitarian friendships: "Friendships based upon utility dissolve as soon as the profits cease; for the friends did not love each other, but what they got out of each other."[290] And later, commenting on dissimilar friendships in general, Aristotle explains: "a rupture occurs (διάλυσις γίνεται) as soon as the parties cease to obtain the things for the sake of which they were friends."[291] It is not difficult to imagine how Gaius might have

---

286 E.g., Aristotle *Eth. nic.* 8.13, 9.1. See in general, Fürst, *Streit unter Freunden,* 12–13, 23–31, 36–39, 97–109, 190–91 and *passim.*
287 As analyzed by Marshall, *Enmity in Corinth,* 341–48.
288 Aristotle *Eth. nic.* 8.13–14. See the analysis and discussion by Pangle, "Quarrels, Conflicting Claims, Dissolutions" in *Aristotle and the Philosophy of Friendship,* 123–41, esp. 125–27.
289 Aristotle *Eth. nic.* 8.13.2–4.
290 Aristotle *Eth. nic.* 8.4.2.
291 Aristotle *Eth. nic.* 9.1.3.

interpreted Paul's appeal for a contribution to the collection as a revelation of the utilitarian character of Paul's friendship, especially in light of Paul's stolid refusal of a gift on term such as someone in Corinth had earlier offered (cf. 1 Cor. 9; 2 Cor. 11:7–11). Paul had made a great show of refusing the gift when it would have obligated him to reciprocate with an appropriate share of affection and honor,[292] asserting his "freedom" from such obligations as a minister of the gospel (1 Cor. 9:1–18; 2 Cor. 11:7–11).[293] Now Paul comes asking for money, and a considerable sum, at that![294] Perhaps Paul's interests were merely utilitarian from the start, and his friendship of an inferior sort. Significant confirmation of the hypothesis that Gaius came to regard Paul's friendship as utilitarian is provided by Paul's retrospective defense of his motives in the collection in 2 Cor. 12:14, "For I do not seek what is yours, but you,"[295] followed by an established *topos* of ancient literature on friendship (the parent/child analogy) in 12:15, as argued above.[296]

The theory that a rupture between Paul and Gaius was precipitated by a perception of utilitarian motives has a corollary, as indicated by the literature on friendship: deception. Analyzing the dynamics of rupture in a friendship of utility, Aristotle observes: "But when he [one of the parties to a utilitarian friendship] has been deceived by his friend's

---

292 Aristotle *Eth. nic.* 8.7.2: "The affection rendered in these various unequal friendships should also be proportionate: the better of the two parties, for instance, or the more useful or otherwise superior as the case may be, should receive more affection than he bestows; since when the affection rendered is proportionate to desert, this produces equality in a sense between the parties, and equality is felt to be an essential element of friendship"; 8.14.3: "This principle therefore should regulate the intercourse of friends who are unequal: the one who is benefitted in purse or character must repay what he can, namely honor."
293 Cf. Marshall, *Enmity in Corinth*, 233–51; Harrison, *Paul's Language of Grace*, 332–44; David J. Downs, "Is God Paul's Patron? The Economy of Patronage in Pauline Theology" in *Engaging Economics: New Testament Scenarios and Early Christian Reception*, ed. Bruce W. Longenecker and Kelly D. Liebengood (Grand Rapids: Eerdmans, 2009) 129–56, esp. 147–50.
294 Weiss, *Der erste Korintherbrief*, 382 on 1 Cor. 16:4; Betz, *2 Corinthians 8 and 9*, 68 on 2 Cor. 8:14.
295 Compare Cicero *Fin.* 2.26.85: *Me igitur ipsum ames oportet non mea, si veri amici futuri sumus* ("So you must love me myself, not my possessions, if we are to be genuine friends"); cited in Windisch, *Der zweite Korintherbrief*, 399. See also Bultmann, *Der zweite Brief*, 235.
296 See above, ch. 3 on 2 Cor. 12:14–15. See also Windisch, *Der zweite Korintherbrief*, 399; Marshall, *Enmity in Corinth*, 249–50; Harrison, *Paul's Language of Grace*, 341–42.

pretence, there is ground for complaint against the deceiver: in fact, he is a worse malefactor than those who counterfeit the coinage, inasmuch as his offence touches something more precious than money.'[297] In emphasizing the part played by deception in the dissolution of friendship, Aristotle echoes the bitter wisdom of Theognis.[298] Seeking to explain the frequent and painful experience of the end of friendship, Theognis recognizes that no one can look into the heart of another man,[299] and that one can more easily deceive (ἐξαπατᾶν) a friend than an enemy.[300] Theognis describes the betrayal of his friendship by a bad man as an act of "cleverness" (ἐπιφροσύνη).[301] We may be certain that suspicion of deceit played a role in the rupture between Paul and Gaius, because of the opinion that Paul explicitly attributes to his critic in 2 Cor. 12:16: "being tricky, I took you in by deceit."[302] In our exegesis of this passage, we discovered that the language by which Paul is characterized derives from ancient portraits of the "confidence trickster."[303]

A final, darker perception may have contributed to Gaius' judgment that the dissolution of his friendship with Paul was warranted: Paul's character was inherently "flawed," his soul "sordid." In his discussion of the types of persons who are incapable of the perfect friendship, Aristotle judges that "the friendship of utility is a thing for sordid souls" (ἡ δὲ διὰ τὸ χρήσιμον ἀγοραίων);[304] even friendship based upon pleasure is better, since the same benefit is conferred by both parties as they enjoy each other's company.[305] Among the Pythagorean precepts on friendship quoted by Iamblichus is the precept that "a great and incorrigible character flaw" (κακία μεγάλη τε καὶ ἀνεπανόρθωτος) is justifiable grounds for ending a friendship.[306] Our analysis of passages in 2 Cor. 10–13 that embody the judgment of an anonymous critic upon Paul repeatedly discov-

---

297 Aristotle *Eth. nic.* 9.3.2. Cf. Kenneth D. Alpern, "Aristotle on the Friendships of Utility and Pleasure," *Journal of the History of Philosophy* 21 (1983) 303–15.
298 Fürst, *Streit unter Freunden*, 28–31.
299 Theognis 119–28; *Théognis, Poèmes élégiaques, text établi et traduit* par J. Carrière (Paris: Bude, 1962).
300 Theognis 1219–20: ἐχθρὸν μὲν χαλεπὸν καὶ δυσμενεῖ ἐξαπατῆσαι, Κύρνε· φίλον δὲ φίλωι ῥάιδιον ἐξαπατᾶν.
301 Theognis 1097–1100.
302 Cf. Windisch, *Der zweite Korintherbrief,* 403; Betz, *Der Apostel Paulus,* 104.
303 See above, ch. 3, pp. 168–70.
304 Aristotle *Eth. nic.* 8.6.4.
305 Aristotle *Eth. nic.* 8.6.4.
306 Iamblichus *Vit. Pythag.* 102=232; *Iamblichi de vita Pythagorica liber,* ed. U. Klein (Stuttgart: Teubner, 1975). Cf. Fürst, *Streit unter Freunden,* 38–39.

ered potent and derogatory labels such as ταπεινός, ἀσθενής, and ἐξουθενημένος—terms that describe one who is submissive, cringing, abject, weak, and contemptible.³⁰⁷ It seems likely that Gaius' disappointment at the revelation of Paul's utilitarian motives led him to infer that Paul was a person of base character, incapable of true friendship.

And what of Paul? How might Paul have perceived the rupture in his relationship with Gaius? The literature on friendship potentially illuminates Paul's experience, even if Paul's perspective was not entirely shaped by the values of Greco-Roman friendship, and even if Paul did not accept all of its obligations.³⁰⁸ In his own words, Paul felt that he had been "wronged" (ἀδικηθείς, 2 Cor. 7:12). Not surprisingly, "wrong" (τὸ ἄδικον) is named first as a cause of rupture within friendship by Aristotle.³⁰⁹ In his analysis of unequal friendships, Aristotle explains: "Wrong is increasingly serious in proportion as it is done to a nearer friend."³¹⁰ More interesting for our purposes is Aristotle's insight into the reason why friends wrong each other: "Friends in some cases wrong each other, because they love things more, not the possessor of them" (Ἀδικοῦσιν οἱ φίλοι ἔνιοι ἀλλήλους, τὰ γὰρ πράγματα μᾶλλον, ἀλλ' οὐ φιλοῦσι τὸν ἔχοντα).³¹¹ Surely Paul must have drawn such a conclusion about Gaius' refusal of partnership in the collection. More than this, the accusation of embezzlement must have led Paul to question whether Gaius felt any affection for him at all. Reflecting upon the lack of mutual reciprocity of affection in utilitarian friendships, Aristotle infers: "Those who suffer harm from one another do not feel affection for one another" (οἱ δ' ἀδικούμενοι οὐ φιλοῦσι σφᾶς αὐτούς).³¹² Aristotle generalizes: "Persons wrongfully treated by one another cannot be each other's friends."³¹³ In view of the magnitude of the wrong that Paul had experienced in the accusation of embezzlement, Paul must have wrestled with the possibility that his friendship with Gaius was at an end.

---

307 See ch. 3 above.
308 Judge, "St. Paul as a Radical Critic of Society" in idem, *Social Distinctives of the First Christians*, 105–107; see also 132–33, 167.
309 Aristotle *Eth. eud.* 7.1.2–3. See also Seneca *Quomodo amicitia continenda sit*, frag, 1, portraying the results of a quarrel between friends: *non minus hic sollicitus fuit, ne fecisse videretur iniuriam, quam ille, ne accepisse.*
310 Aristotle *Eth. nic.* 8.9.3.
311 Aristotle *Eth. eud.* 7.11.7.
312 Aristotle *Eth. eud.* 7.2.19.
313 Aristotle *Eth. eud.* 7.1.2.

Thus, on both sides of the relationship between Paul and Gaius there was likely a perception of the violation of the oldest rule of friendship, as articulated by Hesiod in his *Works and Days*.[314] On how to treat a friend, Hesiod advises: "Do not wrong him first, and do not lie by grace of tongue" (μή μιν πρότερος κακὸν ἔρξαι μηδὲ ψεύδεσθαι γλώσσης χάριν).[315]

One passage in Aristotle's *Nicomachean Ethics* (8.13–14) seems to cast a special light upon the dynamics of disappointment between Paul and Gaius, because of the realism with which Aristotle confronts the characteristic mixture of motives in utilitarian friendships. Aristotle explains that "ethical" friendships of a utilitarian sort are more "prone to complaints" than simple commercial transactions because the premises of such relationships are submerged and unstated: thus one begins by offering a gift or service "as if to a friend," and ends by expecting an equal or greater return, "as though it had not been a gift but a loan"; because the relationship ends in a different spirit than it began, there are complaints.[316] One can readily imagine Paul formulating a complaint against Gaius in this way: "He began by offering a gift (χάρις) for the ministry to the saints, and boasted of his willingness (προθυμία) since last year (cf. 2 Cor. 8:1,4,10–12); now he accuses me of embezzlement in this regard, as though it had not been a gift, but entrusted money!" In *Eth. nic.* 8.14, Aristotle goes on to examine more closely the "balance sheets" of unequal friendships, and why such relationships often end in rupture: "Each claims to be more worthy than the other, and whenever this happens, the friendship is ruptured."[317] Thus, the one in a friendship who is more "useful" (ὠφελιμώτερος), by virtue of his superior resources, thinks that he is entitled to a greater share of "honor" (τιμή), and that otherwise his friendship with a needy partner ceases to be a friendship at all and becomes a λειτουργία, a public service or charity.[318] Such thoughts about Paul's request for a gift, outside the bonds of a patron/client rela-

---

314 Fürst, *Streit unter Freunden*, 24.
315 Hesiod *Op.* 707–708. On the ambiguous phrase γλώσσης χάριν, see the debate in Ulrich von Wilamowitz-Moellendorf, *Hesiodos Erga* (Berlin: Weidmann, 1928) 122; Hermann Fränkel, *Dichtung und Philosophie des frühen Griechentums* (Munich: Beck, 1993) 142 n.26; M. L. West, *Hesiod, Works and Days, with Prolegomena and Commentary* (Oxford: Oxford University Press, 1978) 330–31.
316 Aristotle *Eth. nic.* 8.13.7–8; cf. Pangle, *Aristotle and the Philosophy of Friendship*, 125–26.
317 Aristotle *Eth. nic.* 8.14.1.
318 Aristotle *Eth. nic.* 8.14.1. Cf. Pangle, *Aristotle and the Philosophy of Friendship*, 129.

tionship, may have fueled Gaius' dissatisfaction and precipitated rupture. The rejoinder that Aristotle places into the mouth of the inferior friend is one that Gaius might have attributed to Paul: "The needy or inferior person maintains that it is the part of a good friend to assist those in need; what is the use (he argues) of being friends with the great if one is to get nothing out of it?"[319]

Although Paul painfully recalls the scene that ensued in the assembly at Corinth, following the public rupture of his friendship with Gaius ("angry outbursts, slanders, whisperings, arrogant opinions, etc.," 2 Cor. 12:20), and although Paul makes no attempt to conceal the emotional affect of the wrong perpetrated against him by the charge of embezzlement ("humiliation," 2 Cor. 12:21; "pain," 2 Cor. 2:5), Paul left no account of the actual moment of conflict, when he looked into the eyes of his accuser, and knew that their friendship was broken. Paul's silence about this agonizing moment is in keeping with the conventions that governed his pursuit of conciliatory purposes, as we have argued above.[320] But the lacuna in our knowledge may be partially filled by a remarkable, if fragmentary, text of Seneca, *Quomodo amicitia continenda sit*, a small pearl of the ancient literature on friendship, in which Seneca describes the moment of rupture in a friendship and the effect of personal intervention in bringing about reconciliation.[321] Seneca's account is focused upon strategies for maintaining friendship in the face of the frequent and painful conflicts to which friendship is susceptible.[322] But if we reverse the outcomes at crucial points, we approximate a portrait of the moment of rupture in the relationship between Paul and Gaius. The first fragment of Seneca's treatise records an encounter between

---

319 Aristotle *Eth. nic.* 8.14.1.
320 See above, ch. 4, pp. 219–30.
321 Text in W. Studemund, *L. Annaei Seneca librorum Quomodo amicitia continenda sit et De vita patris reliquiae quae supersunt*, in O. Rossbach, *De Seneca philosophi librorum recensione et emendation* (Hildesheim: Olms, 1969) I-XXXII. The text of the fragments is reprinted in Winfried Trillitzsch, *Seneca im literarischen Urteil der Antike. Darstellung und Sammlung der Zeugnisse* (Amsterdam: Hakkert, 1971) 2.417–19; text and German translation in Fürst, *Streit unter Freunden*, 190, 242–44.
322 Ernst Bickel, "Zu Senecas Schrift über die Freundschaft," *RhM* 60 (1905) 190–201; Trillitzsch, *Seneca im literarischen Urteil der Antike*, 1.220–21, 265; Fürst, *Streit unter Freunden*, 188–91.

friends in the immediate aftermath of a rupture, and then proceeds to offer advice for healing a wounded friendship:[323]

> He accosts me with an unusually gloomy (*tristior*) countenance! He has already broken faith (*fides*) with me, out of which one seeks remedial measures against contrarieties. One word soothes him whom discord troubles, by a single step is his anger (*ira*) abated. The one is not able to hold out against the glance of the other or to endure his intractability and hardness (*intractabilem durumque*). A true friend is not one who comes to complain, but one who engages in self-criticism and gives satisfaction to the one who has shown satisfaction to him. Not less was this one in sorrow (*sollicitus*) as the perpetrator of a wrong (*iniuria*) than the other who was the victim of it. But surely nothing was left in reserve that could have secretly poisoned [the friendship]. Rather, each spoke his mind openly to the other regarding what had offended him, and each stated clearly to the other what was latent. A dispute between close friends does not require a judge, but rather an arbitrator. Nothing can be achieved if the friends do not meet personally; nor can every quarrel be entrusted to letters. And when one has not looked into the face of the other, in whose features the inner disposition of the soul manifests itself, it remains uncertain how deeply hidden the anger is, how firmly it is rooted. Whoever would be a friend must endeavor to judge in the manner he assumes his friend would judge were he present, and draw his conclusions in the interests of the absent friend. Whoever wishes to achieve reconciliation does not conceal his countenance. Much can be achieved when the friends meet personally. How many things insolently spring up in darkness which are prohibited by the light! So, that which irritates and incites those who are absent from each other plays no role with those who are present to each other. Even if a grave negligence has crept in (*neclegentius praetermissum est*), a degrading act has been committed (*inhumanius factum*), a base calculation has been made (*sordidius conputatum*), or an arrogant word has been spoken (*superbius dictum*), it is best to postpone all of this until a point in time when the reproaches can be refuted, or what cannot be refuted can be forgiven. A wounded friendship must be treated in such a way that it heals without leaving a scar.

How much that must have passed between Paul and Gaius in the fateful moment is captured by this remarkable text: the grim, severe countenances, suspicion of deep-seated anger, the shattering recognition of a breach of trust, anxiety at having been a party to wrong, grief over what had been lost! And how poignant, in light of Seneca's advice, to reflect upon what

---

323 Studemund, *L. Annaei Senecae librorum Quomodo amicitia continenda sit*, XXVI-XXVIII.

did *not* transpire on that occasion: the missed opportunity for reconciliation, as one friend looked into the other's face!

In Ephesus,[324] to which Paul retreated following his humiliating experience in Corinth, grief bit into the apostle's soul (cf. 2 Cor. 2:1). Paul has left a hyperbolical account[325] of his "affliction which occurred in Asia" in 2 Cor. 1:8–9: "we were so utterly, unbearably crushed that we despaired of life itself; indeed, we felt within ourselves that we had received the sentence of death…"[326] Scholars have debated the precise nature of Paul's "affliction" (θλῖψις).[327] The majority posit a severe persecution,[328] perhaps an imprisonment that Paul anticipated would end in death.[329] Others suggest a grave illness that Paul feared might prove fatal.[330] But serious consideration should be given to the proposal of David Fredrickson, that here Paul reveals[331] to the Corinthians how much anguish he suffered following his painful experience at Corinth.[332] Fredrickson draws upon

---

324 So the majority of commentators, e.g., Plummer, *Second Epistle*, 16–17; Barrett, *Second Epistle*, 7; Furnish, *II Corinthians*, 55, 143; but cf. Thrall, *Second Epistle*, 1.114.
325 Frank W. Hughes, "The Rhetoric of Reconciliation: 2 Cor. 1:1–2:13; 7:5–8:24" in *Persuasive Artistry*, ed. Duane F. Watson (Sheffield: Sheffield Academic Press, 1991) 246–61, esp. 251; Fredricksen, "Paul, Hardships, and Suffering" in *Paul in the Greco-Roman World*, 181.
326 On the pathos evoked by Paul's use of the expressions καθ' ὑπερβολὴν, ὑπὲρ δύναμιν, ἐβαρήθημεν, ἐξαπορηθῆναι καὶ τοῦ ζῆν, see L. L. Welborn, "Paul's Appeal to the Emotions in 2 Corinthians 1.1–2.13; 7.5–16," *JSNT* 82 (2001) 31–60. For the progressive, confirmatory sense of ἀλλά (in 1:9) as "indeed," see Furnish, *II Corinthians*, 108, 113.
327 See the summary of the various proposals in Thrall, *Second Epistle*, 1.115–17.
328 E.g., Bousset, *Der zweite Brief*, 169; Bachmann, *Der zweite Brief*, 38; Barnett, *Second Epistle*, 83–84.
329 Furnish, *II Corinthians*, 122–23; Thrall, *Second Epistle*, 1.116–17.
330 Allo, *Saint Paul*, 11–12, 15–19; Murray J. Harris, "2 Corinthians 5:1–10: Watershed in Paul's Eschatology?" *TynBul* 22 (1971) 57; Barrett, *Second Epistle*, 64. Cf. A. E. Harvey, *Renewal through Suffering: A Study of 2 Corinthians* (Edinburgh: T & T Clark, 1996) 1–31.
331 On the phrase οὐ γὰρ θέλομεν ὑμᾶς ἀγνοεῖν as a "disclosure formula" in accordance with a widespread epistolary convention, see Terrence Y. Mullins, "Disclosure: A Literary Form in the New Testament," *NovT* 7 (1964) 44–50; John L. White, "Introductory Formulae in the Body of the Pauline Letter," *JBL* 90 (1971) 91–97. Cf. Barnett, *Second Epistle*, 83: "His disclosure formula indicates that new information is about to be given, or, more probably, in this case, a new perspective about the seriousness of that 'affliction'."
332 Fredrickson, "Paul's Sentence of Death (2 Corinthians 1:9)" in *God, Evil, and Suffering*, 103–107; idem, "Paul, Hardships, and Suffering" in *Paul in the*

the research of R. L. Fowler into the "rhetoric of desperation," a speech-form encountered from Homer to Epictetus, whose generic components include: 1) an indication of the crushing weight of affliction borne by the speaker; 2) the impossibility of finding a way out of the dilemma (ἀπορία); 3) questioning whether life is any longer sustainable under such circumstances; 4) not knowing whether to choose life or death.[333]

Support for the hypothesis that Paul's θλῖψις in 2 Cor. 1:8–9 refers to a severe depression caused by the crisis in his relationship with the Corinthians is supplied by the recurrence of the very term θλῖψις in subsequent portions of Paul's conciliatory letter (2 Cor. 1:1–2:13; 7:5–16), where Paul is clearly describing the psychological state in which he wrote to Corinth, following the experience of his "painful" visit: "For I resolved in myself this: not again in pain to come to you. For if I cause you pain, who is the one who makes me rejoice, except the one who has been pained by me? And I wrote as I did, lest that coming I might have pain from the ones who ought to make me rejoice...For I wrote to you out of much affliction (ἐκ πολλῆς θλίψεως) and anguish of heart through many tears, not that you might be pained, but that you might know the love which I have for you so abundantly" (2 Cor. 2:1–4).[334] Moreover, Paul resumes the term θλῖψις (in participial form) in his account of the anxious state in which he awaited the arrival of his emissary Titus with news about the state of the relationship with the Corinthians: "For even when we came into Macedonia, our flesh had no relief, but we were afflicted (θλιβόμενοι) in every way—fightings without, fears within" (2 Cor. 7:5).[335] In light of the repeated and unambiguous uses of θλῖψις in 2 Cor. 1:1–2:13; 7:5–16 to describe the psychological state in which Paul found himself after the crisis at Corinth, our first inclination should be to interpret the "affliction" that Paul discloses to the Corinthians in 2 Cor. 1:8 as a reference to his spiritual anguish, rather than severe persecution or imprisonment.[336] The exegetical

---

Greco-Roman World, 181–82. For the hypothesis that Paul's "affliction" refers to a severe depression caused by Paul's humiliation at Corinth, see already Drescher, "Vorgänge in Korinth," 49–51; Gerald F. Rendall, *The Epistles of St. Paul to the Corinthians* (London: Macmillan, 1909) 49.

333 R. L. Fowler, "The Rhetoric of Desperation," *HSCP* 91 (1987) 5–38; cited by Fredrickson, "Paul, Hardships, and Suffering" in *Paul in the Greco-Roman World*, 194 n.41.
334 Similarly, Drescher, "Vorgänge in Korinth," 49.
335 So, already, Drescher, "Vorgänge in Korinth," 51.
336 Contra Thrall, *Second Epistle*, 1.115.

tradition that interprets Paul's "affliction" in 2 Cor. 1:8 as an experience of severe persecution stands under the influence of Acts (e.g. Acts 19:23–40),[337] and reflects a tendency to harmonize Acts with the epistles, in order to supply the missing details of Pauline autobiography, rather than attending closely to the rhetorical *topoi* of Paul's letters. More conscious of the elements of the conciliatory style employed by Paul in 2 Cor. 1:1–2:13; 7:5–16, Fredrickson recognizes in Paul's declaration that he had passed "the death-sentence" (τὸ ἀπόκριμα τοῦ θανάτου) upon himself in 2 Cor. 1:9 a species of the "expression of regret" characteristically found in conciliatory letters,[338] in keeping with the philosophical understanding of regret as self-condemnation.[339] A later passage in Paul's therapeutic epistle confirms that the emotion he describes in 2 Cor. 1:9 is, indeed, a species of regret: "For even if I pained you with my epistle, I do not regret it (οὐ μεταμέλομαι), *even if I did regret it* (μετεμελόμην), for I see that I pained you with that epistle, but only for an hour" (2 Cor. 7:8).[340] We shall have occasion below to appreciate how skillfully Paul employs other elements of the conciliatory letter-genre in order to heal his wounded friends at Corinth. But it suffices, for the moment, to have shown that 2 Cor. 1:8–9 is most plausibly interpreted as an account of Paul's psychological distress upon his return to Asia, and so provides a window into Paul's grieving soul in the aftermath of the rupture of his friendship with Gaius.

From Paul's retrospective explanation of his actions and motives in 2 Cor. 1:23–2:4, we can form a clear image of what happened next. Paul resolved not to visit Corinth again under circumstances that might prove to be mutually painful. Paul's reluctance to make the Corinthians "another painful visit" (πάλιν ἐν λύπῃ ἐλθεῖν) is in accordance with Aristotle's dictum that a man should be "reluctant to be a cause of pain (λύπη) to his friends,"[341] as we learned above. Instead, Paul decided to pursue reconciliation through letters. Recalling Seneca's warning in his treatise on friendship, that "nothing can be achieved if the friends do

---

337 Cf. Furnish, *II Corinthians*, 122.
338 Fredrickson, "Paul, Hardships, and Suffering" in *Paul in the Greco-Roman World*, 182, referencing Cicero *Quin. frat.* 1.2.12–13; Philostratus *Vit. soph.* 2.1. 562–63; Fronto *M. Caes* 5.59.
339 Fredrickson, "Paul, Hardships, and Suffering" in *Paul in the Greco-Roman World*, 181.
340 Fredrickson, "Paul, Hardships, and Suffering" in *Paul in the Greco-Roman World*, 181.
341 Aristotle *Eth. nic.* 9.11.4.

not meet personally, nor can every quarrel be entrusted to letters,"[342] Paul's decision seems risky and his strategy without much prospect of success. But Paul must have recognized the validity of his critic's observation, echoed in 2 Cor. 10:10: in person he appeared "weak" and his speech "contemptible," while his letters were acknowledged to be "weighty and strong."[343] Paul must have understood that he could accomplish through letters what he could not hope to achieve in person.

Paul describes the letter that he next wrote to Corinth in highly emotional terms: "I wrote you out of much affliction and anguish of heart, through many tears" (2 Cor. 2:4).[344] In accordance with the source-critical hypothesis embraced in this monograph, the "letter of tears" is to be identified with the writing preserved in 2 Cor. 10–13.[345] In this apologetic letter,[346] Paul not only defends the probity of his conduct in the matter of the collection against the specific charge of embezzlement (12:14–18),[347] but also refutes the general insinuation that he lacked the apostolic legitimacy (δοκιμή) to make such a request.[348] Paul's references to "comparison" (συγκρῖναι, συγκρίνοντες, 10:12) and "self-commendation" (τῶν ἑαυτοὺς συνιστανόντων, 10:12; ὁ ἑαυτὸν συνιστάνων, 10:18) reveal that Paul's critics at Corinth had demanded of him that he demonstrate his apostolic legitimacy by comparing himself with other apostles who met with the Corinthians' approval (cf. 11:5, 12; 12:11).[349] Paul makes clear that he regards the suggestion that he "commend" himself by comparing himself with others as unprincipled "boast-

---

342 Seneca *Quomodo amicitia continenda sit*, frag. 1.
343 See above, ch. 3.
344 For συνοχή as a state of high anxiety involving "distress, dismay, anguish," see the references in Bauer, *Greek-English Lexicon*, 974 s.v. συνοχή 2. On the expression διὰ τῶν δακρύων, see the excursus "Von den Tränen des Paulus und dem Tränenbrief" in Windisch, *Der zweite Korintherbrief*, 82.
345 So already, among others, Hausrath, *Der Vier-Capitel-Brief*; Kennedy, *Second and Third Epistles*; Bornkamm, *Vorgeschichte*, 172–78; Georgi, *Opponents of Paul*, 9–13; Watson, "Paul's Painful Letter," 324–46; Welborn, "The Identification of 2 Corinthians 10–13 with the 'Letter of Tears'," 138–53.
346 Rightly, Betz, *Der Apostel Paulus*, 13–42 and *passim*.
347 Betz, *Der Apostel Paulus*, 116–17.
348 On Paul's defense of his δοκιμή in 2 Cor. 10–13, see esp. Betz, *Der Apostel Paulus*, 132–37.
349 Georgi, *Opponents of Paul*, 243; Betz, *Der Apostel Paulus*, 119–20; Strecker, "Die Legitimität des paulinischen Apostolates nach 2 Korinther 10–13," 566–86. See above, ch. 3.

ing" (10:13, 15–17; 11:10, 16–18, 21, 30; 12:1, 5, 9).[350] But what was Paul to do, given that no one in Corinth was willing to commend him (2 Cor. 12:11, "Indeed I ought to have been commended by you!")?[351] It must have been especially bitter to Paul that no one in Corinth was willing to recommend him.[352] Cicero's correspondence reveals that such pledges of support were a conventional feature of negotiations within friendship,[353] even when the atmosphere was one of mutual suspicion,[354] even when "doubts prevailed regarding the reliability of one party's support for the other."[355]

From this seemingly hopeless situation, Paul found a way out. Paul hit upon an ingenious strategy: he would commend himself, as Gaius and his colleagues wanted, comparing his accomplishments and qualifications with those of other apostles, but he would speak in the role of a "fool" (2 Cor. 11:1, 16–17, 21; 12:11)! Long ago, Hans Windisch suggested that the "fool's speech" which Paul delivers in 2 Cor. 11:21b-12:10,[356] following a lengthy and apologetic prologue (in 11:1–21a),[357] was modeled upon the performances of the fools in the mime,[358] a suggestion that I have elsewhere sought to confirm by analyzing the surviving fragments of mime, as well as mime-inspired passages in satires and novels.[359] Paul's decision to play the "fool" was fraught with

---

350 Betz, *Der Apostel Paulus*, 72–75.
351 Windisch, *Der zweite Korintherbrief*, 395: "Das folgende Sätzchen v. 11b 'ich müsste (vielmehr) von euch empfohlen werden' dient zur Begründung dieses Vorwurfs, wenn man ergänzend hinzusetzt: und das habt ihr unterlassen; im Gegenteil, ihr habt Vorwürfe gegen mich geschleudert, mein ap. Recht und meine ap. Ehre angezweifelt, oder wenigstens geschwiegen, wenn Andere meine Würde anfochten. Es ist bezeichnend für den Stil des Paulus das er diese wichtigen moment unterdrückt."
352 Not even Stephanas, apparently, unless 2 Cor. 12:11 is despairing hyperbole.
353 Cicero *Fam.* 6.10B.1. See the discussion of "pledges of support" in political friendships by Hall, *Politeness and Politics*, 38–41.
354 E.g., Cicero *Fam.* 10.11.3, with the comments of Hall, *Politeness and Politics*, 39.
355 Hall, *Politeness and Politics*, 41, referring to Cicero's very formal epistolary pledges of support to M. Licinius Crassus in *Fam.* 5.8.
356 Windisch, *Der zweite Korintherbrief*, 349. Cf. Betz, *Der Apostel Paulus*, 80; Zmijewski, *Der Stil der paulinischen "Narrenrede,"* 76, 231.
357 On 2 Cor. 11:1–21a as prologue to the speech proper, see Windisch, *Der zweite Korintherbrief*, 317, 344; Bultmann, *Der zweite Brief*, 200, 214; Zmijewski, *Der Stil der paulinischen "Narrenrede,"* 76, 231; Furnish, *II Corinthians*, 498, 532.
358 Windisch, *Der zweite Korintherbrief*, 316.
359 L. L. Welborn, "The Runaway Paul: A Character in the Fool's Speech, 2 Cor. 11:21b-12:10," *HTR* 92 (1999) 115–63, following Georgi, *Opponents of*

danger, because it risked confirming the impression of Gaius and his colleagues that Paul was ταπεινός (10:1) and ἀσθενής (10:10), a vulgar type.³⁶⁰ How painful and unnatural Paul found the role is indicated by numerous features of the text: the length and defensive tone of the prologue (11:1–21a),³⁶¹ the self-contradictions (11:1, 16),³⁶² the apologetic parentheses (11:17, 21b),³⁶³ and the startling interruptions (11:23a) that threaten to destroy the rhetorical schema.³⁶⁴ Paul makes it clear that the role has been forced upon him by others (ὑμεῖς με ἠναγκάσατε, 12:11a), and places the blame for his actions upon the Corinthians (ἐγὼ γὰρ ὤφειλον ὑφ᾽ ὑμῶν συνίστασθαι, 12:11b).³⁶⁵

Nevertheless, the "fool's speech" held distinct advantages for Paul. Like other forms of satire, the "fool's speech" enabled Paul "to speak the truth, laughingly."³⁶⁶ Horace, Persius, and others adopted the role of the "fool" in order to exercise the fool's license.³⁶⁷ Moreover, by means of irony, Paul was able to establish a critical distance towards

---

Paul, 337, who called for "more attention to the genre of the 'fool's speech,' and to its background in the ancient mimus."
360 See ch. 3 above. On the social stigma attached to the role of the "fool," see Welborn, *Paul, the Fool of Christ*, 1–3 and *passim*.
361 Windisch, *Der zweite Korintherbrief*, 317, 344.
362 Windisch, *Der zweite Korintherbrief*, 344 on 11:16 in contrast to 11:1: "Der erste Gedanke, 'dass mich niemand für einen Narren halte,' besagt das gerade Gegenteil und zeigt, wie peinich und unnatürlich das nun folgende Auftreten den Apostel ist (vgl. 12:11), dass der 'Narr' für Paulus nur eine 'Rolle' ist, und das die Worte, die der Narr nun sprechen wird, doch Ernst genommen warden müssen."
363 Windisch, *Der zweite Korintherbrief*, 350: "Die entschuldigende Parenthese ἐν ἀφροσύνῃ λέγω deutet noch einmal an, das ser nun eine 'Rolle' aufnimmt, die ihm nicht genehm ist."
364 E.g., 11:23a, παραφρονῶν λαλῶ, breaking the pattern of response (κἀγώ) in 11:22; cf. Windisch, *Der zweite Korintherbrief*, 353.
365 Windisch, *Der zweite Korintherbrief*, 395, cites Plutarch *De laude* 539D, 540C, 542E to show that Paul's feeling that the Cornthians are to blame is justified, according to the principles of ancient rhetoric. See further Forbes, "Paul's Boasting and Hellenistic Rhetoric," 1–30, esp. 1–2, 8, 18–20.
366 Horace *Sat.* 1.1.23.
367 Horace *Sat.* 2.7, with the analysis and commentary of Karl Freudenberg, *The Walking Muse: Horace on the Theory of Satire* (Princeton: Princeton University Press, 1993) 225–26. Persius *Sat.* 1, with the observations of J. C. Relihan, "The Confessions of Persius," *Illinois Classical Studies* 14 (1984) 145–67, esp. 148. See also the account of Decimus Laberius in the role of a fool in a mime that he played before Julius Caesar, described in Macrobius *Sat.* 2.7.2; 2.7.6–7, with the comments of R. Till, "Laberius und Caesar," *Historia* 24 (1975) 260–86, esp. 278.

the role that he was forced to play.[368] In a series of "asides" that punctuate the discourse (11:21b, 23b, 30; 12:1a, 5–6, 11a), Paul lifts the "mask" and shows his face, lest his hearers become so engrossed in the performance that they forget his true attitude.[369] Throughout the "fool's speech," Paul undermines the values of his critics and the norms of his rivals by ironic treatment of the materials of the genre: his accomplishments are calamities (11:23–29); his revelations are unutterable (12:1–4); his healing is inefficacious (12:7–9); his power consists in weakness (12:5, 9–10).[370] Paul's performance is virtuosic, by any standard.[371] Paul combines elements of several types of "fools" in his speech, playing the "leading slave" in 11:21b-23, acting the "braggart warrior" in 11:24–27, evoking the "anxious old man" in 11:28–29, dramatizing the feckless "runaway" in 11:30–33, portraying the "learned impostor" in 12:1–4, and miming the "quack doctor" in 12:7–9.[372] The evocation of several types of "fools" in the portrait of a single individual is not unique to Paul. In *Sat.* 2.7, Horace permits his slave Davus to portray him as an adulterer, a leading slave, a braggart warrior, a learned impostor, a parasite, and a runaway—all parts played by the fool in the mime.[373] Seneca treats the foolish Claudius in the same manner in the *Apocolocyntosis*, depicting him first as a harmless old fellow, then as a boastful hero, now as an officious slave, again as a confused antiquarian.[374] Although Paul's "foolish discourse" is concise, it approximates the length of a recitation

---

368 Windisch, *Der zweite Korintherbrief*, 316; Betz, *Der Apostel Paulus*, 72–75, 96; Forbes, "Paul's Boasting and Hellenistic Rhetoric," 10–13; Glen S. Holland, "Speaking Like a Fool: Irony in the Letters of Paul" in *Rhetoric and the New Testament*, ed. Thomas Olbricht (Sheffield: Sheffield Academic Press, 1993) 250–64, esp. 256–57.
369 Cf. Windisch, *Der zweite Korintherbrief*, 316.
370 For Paul's paradoxical treatment of the material, see esp. Betz, *Der Apostel Paulus*, 69–100.
371 See the evaluation of Windisch, *Der zweite Korintherbrief*, 316.
372 Welborn, "The Runaway Paul: A Character in the Fool's Speech," 137–59.
373 Horace *Sat.* 2.7.46–67 (adulterer), 2.7.68–72 (leading slave), 2.7.83–87 (braggart warrior), 2.7.95–101 (learned impostor), 2.7.102–11 (parasite), 2.7.111–15 (runaway). In *Sat.* 2.7.39–40, Davus asserts that the terms "weak" (*imbecillus*), "lazy" (*iners*) and "parasite" (*popino*) apply to Horace, employing terms that were regularly associated with the fool in the mime. For a similar interpretation of Horace *Sat.* 2.7, see Freudenberg, *The Walking Muse*, 225–26.
374 See the comments of Otto Weinreich, *Senecas Apocolocyntosis. Die Satire auf Tod/ Himmel und Höllenfahrt des Kaisers Claudius* (Berlin: Weidmann, 1923) 6–8; P. T. Eden, *Seneca. Apocolocyntosis* (Cambridge: Cambridge University Press, 1993) 13–17, 64, 95.

by a solo performer, judging from the *mimiambi* of Herondas.³⁷⁵ As an ironic defense of the legitimacy of Paul's apostleship, Paul's "foolish discourse" must be judged a complete success. Hans Windisch conveys the polemical power of Paul's dissimulation: "With his argument and his self-defense costumed in this surprising manner, Paul strikes the opponents perhaps a more deadly blow than with the preceding, correct presentation of the facts of the case and the points of disagreement. On the following pages stands the most sublime and most devastating thing which Paul achieved in the 'ironic' art of polemic. The destructive power of Paul's 'play-acting' consists in this: that under the 'mask' not one single untruth, not one exaggeration, nor one 'extravagance' is uttered, but on the contrary, the pure, complete truth, and the opponents are crushed by the presentation of the complete reality."³⁷⁶

Throughout Paul's "apology" in 2 Cor. 10–13, he employs the rhetorical device of "not-naming," in order to conciliate his alienated friends at Corinth. Like the authors of other conciliatory apologies,³⁷⁷ Paul consistently avoids naming any of the Corinthians with whom he had experienced conflict, employing the standard substitutes, τινες, τις, τοιοῦτος, and other periphrastic constructions. In five of the passages examined above—10:7, 10:10, 10:11, 11:16, 12:6—we found evidence that a singular pronoun or singular verb-form denoted a specific individual, and that this individual was a Corinthian (rather than an interloping apostle).³⁷⁸ We further argued that the Corinthian critic denoted by the periphrastic constructions in 2 Cor. 10–13 is the same individual whom Paul describes as the "one who caused pain" and "the one who did wrong" in 2 Cor. 2 and 7, employing the same circumlocutions, τις and τοιοῦτος.³⁷⁹ Because we have analyzed these passages in detail above, we may content ourselves here with a summary, focusing upon the contribution of each text to the conciliation of Paul's friendship with Gaius.

---

375 For discussion of the length and method of presentation of Herondas' mime-poems, see Ian C. Cunningham, review of Giuseppe Mastromarco, *Il Pubblico di Eronda* (1979) in *JHS* 101 (1981) 161.
376 Windisch, *Der zweite Korintherbrief*, 316.
377 E.g., Demosthenes *Ep.* 2.2, 8; Dio Chrysostom *Or.* 45.10, 11, 14; 50.3, 6, 9, 10; Marcus Aurelius *apud* Philostratus *Vit. soph.* 2.1.562–63. Cf. Welborn, "A Conciliatory Convention and Paul's References to the 'Letter of Tears'" in *Politics and Rhetoric*, 77–94.
378 See ch. 3 above.
379 See ch. 3 above, pp. 84–86, 102–105, 122, 154, 163–64, 208.

In each of the instances in 2 Cor. 10–13 in which Paul employs a periphrastic construction to engage the criticisms of Gaius, the context is apologetic, but Paul's aim is conciliatory, in keeping with the rhetorical device of not-naming, as analyzed above.[380] That is to say, Paul uses circumlocutions in order to make his alienated friend available for conciliation. As Seneca advised in his essay on the maintenance of friendship,[381] Paul seeks to remove the reproaches that threaten to poison the relationship. Indeed, as Seneca counseled, Paul does not attempt to conceal the displeasure of his countenance.[382]

To counter the impression that he is "cringing" and "abject" (ταπεινός, 10:1), Paul portrays himself as Christ's general, besieging, destroying, taking captive, and court-martialing the rebellious (10:3–6).[383] It was essential that Paul establish that whatever "meekness" the Corinthians had detected in his behavior did not emanate from cowardice, since ancient thought on friendship generally acceded to the demand, concisely formulated by Theognis, that one adopt a critical stance toward a friend who had shown himself to be δειλός ("cowardly").[384] Further, Paul takes pains to counter the impression that he conducted himself "according to human standards" (κατὰ σάρκα, 10:2–3), that he was "crafty" (πανοῦργος) and took the Corinthians in "by deceit" (δόλῳ, 12:16).[385] The importance of Paul's demonstration on this point is highlighted by Theognis' description of the "faithful friend" (πιστὸς ἑταῖρος) as one "in whom there's no deceit" (ὅτῳ μή τις ἔνεστι δόλος).[386] In his diatribe on friendship, Epictetus asks: "Do you think that the man who has been deceived about someone can be his friend?—No, indeed!"[387] Next, Paul contests the insinuation that somehow (doubtless owing to his cross-centered gospel) he had lost his "confidence" of belonging to Christ (10:7).[388] It was crucial that Paul re-establish his spiritual congruence with one who was "confident of belonging to Christ" (10:7). Cicero, reflecting a broad consensus, insists that one should choose as a friend one

---

380 See ch. 4 above.
381 Seneca *Quomodo amicitia continenda sit*, frag. 1.
382 Seneca *Quomodo amicitia continenda sit*, frag. 1.
383 Brink, "A General's Exhortation to His Troops," 192–99; 50 (2006) 74–89.
384 Theognis 1080: οὐδὲ μὲν αἰνήσω δειλὸς ἐόντα φίλον. Cf. Fürst, *Streit unter Freunden*, 31.
385 See above, ch. 3, pp. 80–84, 168–70.
386 Theognis 416; see also, lines 119–28.
387 Epictetus *Diatr.* 2.22.8.
388 See above, ch. 3, pp. 99–101.

whose ideals and values parallel one's own.³⁸⁹ Then, Paul seeks diligently to correct the impression of inconsistency between his words and deeds: that he is forceful, even intimidating, by letter when absent, but weak and ineffectual in person when present (10:9–11).³⁹⁰ As a strategy for restoring a broken friendship, Paul's proof of his consistency was of utmost importance. We have already encountered the emphasis on "constancy" (τὸ βέβαιον) in friendship which is a prominent feature of Aristotle's theory.³⁹¹ More pertinent to the present point is Theognis' repeated insistence that consistency of "word and deed" is required of a true friend: e.g., "A man who is friend in word but not in deed is not my friend" (μή μοι ἀνὴρ εἴη γλώσσηι φίλος, ἀλλὰ καὶ ἔργωι).³⁹² Finally, Paul counters the mistaken inference that his "foolishness" is to be taken literally, that his "foolishness" is more real than feigned (11:16).³⁹³ The necessity of such a clarification, within an attempt to restore a broken friendship, is illuminated by the premise of Epictetus' diatribe on friendship: namely, that the "fool" (ἄφρων) does not have the same capacity to love as the "wise man" (φρονιμός).³⁹⁴ Paul had good reason to be concerned about the affect of his foolish discourse upon the friend whom he sought to conciliate. Plutarch advised those who employed frank speech in order to correct a friend to "purge away, as it were, and eliminate from our frankness all wantonness, laughter, jesting, and buffoonery, which are the unwholesome seasoning of free speech."³⁹⁵

From what Paul says later, in 2 Cor. 7:8–12, we learn that Paul was anxious about the outcome of the letter of 2 Cor. 10–13. He knew that the letter was "severe," that it would cause "grief" (λύπη).³⁹⁶ Indeed, statements such as those found in 11:7–11 could not have done anything else! (Note especially Paul's loud asseveration that his "boast" of not having accepted support from the Corinthians "will not be silenced in the

---

389 Cicero *Amic.* 15, 61–81; see also *Off.* 1.45–46. See further Horace *Sat.* 1.6.52–64; *Ep.* 1.7.22–24; 2.1.245–47; *Laus Pisonis* 128–37, 218.
390 See above, ch. 3, p. 122.
391 Aristotle *Eth. eud.* 7.2.39; 7.5.3; *Eth. nic.* 8.8.5. See also Epictetus *Diatr.*. 2.22.25: οὐκ ἔστι πιστὸν τὸ τοῦ φαύλου ἡγεμονικόν· ἀβέβαιον εστιν, κτλ.
392 Theognis 979; see also 87–92, 93–94, 851–52, 1082c-f. Cf. Fürst, *Streit unter Freunden*, 30.
393 See above, ch. 3, pp. 154–63.
394 Epictetus *Diatr.* 2.22.3–4.
395 Plutarch *Adul. amic.* 27 (=*Mor.* 67E). Cf. Fürst, *Streit unter Freunden*, 196–97.
396 Cf. 2 Cor. 2:1–4.

regions of Achaia!" in 11:10).³⁹⁷ Moreover, Paul remained embarrassed about having engaged in "self-commendation" in 11:1–12:10, despite the cover provided by the paradoxical form of the "fool's speech," as the backward glancing disavowals of further exercises in "self-commendation" in 3:1 (ἀρχόμεθα πάλιν ἑαυτοὺς συνιστάνειν;) and 5:12 (οὐ πάλιν ἑαυτοὺς συνιστάνομεν ὑμῖν, κτλ.) clearly reveal.³⁹⁸ Finally, Paul was concerned about the impression produced by his "foolish discourse" and, in general, by his unrestrained display of powerful emotions such as anger and grief (cf. 2:4). Might not such displays be adduced by Paul's critics as the clearest proof of his failure to achieve the "self-mastery" (ἐγκράτεια) characteristic of a wise man,³⁹⁹ as evidence that Paul was "beside himself" (ἐκστῆναι),⁴⁰⁰ as he later concedes that he appeared to be in 5:13 (ἐξέστημεν)?⁴⁰¹ Such an apparent loss of emotional control might be taken to indicate how far Paul fell short of the ideal σώφρων. Paul's "distress" (λύπη) might seem to demonstrate that his "foolishness" (ἀφροσύνη) was more real than feigned.⁴⁰²

In his anxiety over the outcome of his "painful epistle," Paul sent Titus as his envoy to Corinth (cf. 2 Cor. 2:12–13; 7:5–6, 15).⁴⁰³

---

397 Windisch, *Der zweite Korintherbrief*, 337–38.
398 So, already, Hausrath, *Der Vier-Capitel-Brief des Paulus*, 22; Schmiedel, *Die Briefe an die Korinther*, 61.
399 See in general Stowers, "Paul and Self-Mastery" in *Paul in the Greco-Roman World*, 524–50.
400 BDAG 350 s.v. ἐξίστημι 2a. For Chrysippus' view that those who are in the grip of emotions are "beside themselves," see Galen *De placitis Hippocratis et Platonis* 4.6.24 (=*SVF* 3.475): διὸ καὶ ἐπὶ τῶνδε τῶν ἐμπαθῶν ὡς περὶ ἐξεστηκότων ἔχομεν καὶ ὡς πρὸς παρηλλαχότας ποιούμεθα τὸν λόγον καὶ οὐ παρ' ἑαυτοῖς οὐδ ἐν αὑτοῖς ὄντας ("Therefore we behave in the case of these persons who are in a state of emotion as we do towards persons who are out of their minds and we speak to them as to persons who are twisted and are not in their right minds or in control of themselves"). On the sense of the antithesis ἐξέστημεν–σωφρονοῦμεν in 5:13, see Windisch, *Der zweite Korintherbrief*, 178–79.
401 For 5:13 as a reference back to passages such as 11:21b (ἐν ἀφροσύνῃ λέγω) and 11:23b (παραφρονῶν λαλῶ), and esp. 12:1–6, see Hausrath, *Der Vier-Capitel-Brief des Paulus*, 23; Schmiedel, *Die Briefe an die Korinther*, 61; Kennedy, "The Problem of Second Corinthians," 361.
402 For the view that the wise man is not subject to "distress" (λύπη), but rather the "fool" (ἄφρων), see, e.g., Cicero *Tusc.* 4.6.14; Epictetus *Diatr.* 2.22.6–7.
403 Weiss, *Primitive Christianity*, 1. 345. See in general, C. K. Barrett, "Titus" in *Neotestamentica et Semitica*, ed. E. E. Ellis and M. Wilcox (Edinburgh: T & T Clark, 1968) 1–14; repr. in diem, *Essays on Paul* (Philadelphia: Westminster Press, 1982); Mitchell, "New Testament Envoys in the Context of Greco-Roman Diplomatic and Epistolary Conventions," 641–62, esp. 653–62.

Paul's retrospective comments upon Titus' mission to Corinth in 2 Cor. 7:5–16 reveal that Titus was charged with discerning the quality of the Corinthians' response to the polemical letter of 2 Cor. 10–13.[404] When Titus arrived in Corinth, he found the Corinthians in a state of heightened anxiety, as a result of the "severe epistle" of 2 Cor. 10–13. This inference is justified by Paul's recollection (in 2 Cor. 7:15) that Titus was "received" by the Corinthians "with fear and trembling" (μετὰ φόβου καὶ τρόμου).[405]

In keeping with the literary-critical hypothesis embraced in this monograph, we suggest that Paul did not send Titus on this delicate mission empty-handed, but with the letter now preserved in 2 Cor. 2:14–7:4 (minus the interpolated passage in 6:14–7:1).[406] One will recall our reasons for assigning 2 Cor. 2:14–7:4 to the place after 2 Cor. 10–13 in the sequence of Paul's correspondence with Corinth: namely, the cross-references that connect 2:14–7:4 with 10–13, conspicuously in 3:1 and 5:12, where Paul refers back to instances of "self-commendation" in 2 Cor. 11 and 12,[407] and equally in 5:13, where Paul alludes to previ-

---

404 Weiss, *Primitive Christianity*, 1.345–46.
405 König, "Verkehr," 533; Weiss, *Primitive Christianity*, 1.345, correcting the usual view that the "painful epistle" of 2 Cor. 10–13 was brought to Corinth by the hand of Titus: "This is nowhere stated and it even seems to be excluded by 2 Cor. 7:15, for the insubordinate church cannot have felt 'fear and trembling' in the presence of the bearer of a letter even before they had read the letter. No, the submissive reception of Titus was due to the fact that they had shortly before received Paul's letter of reproof; it had already had its effect, and this, Titus could then confirm."
406 For the hypothesis that 2 Cor. 2:14–7:4 was originally an independent letter, see Halmel, *Der Vierkapitelbrief im zweiten Korintherbrief des Apostels Paulus*, with the review of Weiss in *TLZ* 19 (1894) 513–14; Halmel, *Der zweite Korintherbrief des Apostels Paulus*; Weiss, *Primitive Christianity* 1.345–53; Bornkamm, *Vorgeschichte*, 21–23; Georgi, *Die Gegner des Paulus*, 16–24. For the hypothesis that 2 Cor. 6:14–7:1 is an interpolation, probably non-Pauline in origin, see Emmerling, *Epistola Pauli ad Corinthios posterior*, 77; Ewald, *Sendschreiben*, 231, 241; Krenkel, *Beiträge*, 332–33; Fitzmyer, "Qumran and the Interpolated Paragraph in 2 Cor. 6:14–7:1," 271–80; Betz, "2 Cor. 6:14–7:1: An Anti-Pauline Fragment?" 88–108; recently, Hultgren, "2 Cor. 6:14–7:1 and Rev. 21:3–8," 39–56. For the placement of 2 Cor. 2:14–6:13; 7:2–4 after 2 Cor. 10–13, cf. Taylor, "The Composition and Chronology of Second Corinthians," 67–87.
407 Hausrath, *Der Vier-Capitel-Brief des Paulus*, 22; Schmiedel, *Die Briefe an die Korinther*, 61; Kennedy, "The Problem of Second Corinthians," 350–51, calling attention to the use of the word πάλιν in 3:1 and 5:12: "The word πάλιν implies

ous moments when he appeared to be "beside himself," as in 11:21b and 11:23b,[408] but also, less conspicuously, in the numerous instances of "softening" in 2 Cor. 2:14–7:4, where Paul deliberately reprises words and phrases, such as καύχησις and πεποίθησις, terms used in a harsh and uncomplimentary fashion in 2 Cor. 10–13, but upon which Paul now confers a new, conciliatory sense, a strategy analyzed with subtle insight by James H. Kennedy.[409]

The letter that Titus carried, now preserved in 2 Cor. 2:14–6:13; 7:2–4, is also an "apology": that is to say, Paul is still defending the legitimacy of his apostleship and the conduct of his ministry.[410] But Paul's tone is far more conciliatory than in the apology of 2 Cor. 10–13. In keeping with his conciliatory strategy, Paul focuses upon the theoretical basis of his ministry in 2 Cor. 2:14–6:13; 7:2–4, deepening and intensifying his insight into the paradox of "power made perfect in weakness" (2 Cor. 12:9) that formed the climax of his "letter of tears" (cf. 2 Cor. 13:3–4).[411] Breaking through the sea-floor of his own being, so to speak, Paul now expounds an extreme form of the paradox of his apostolic ministry, indeed, as Paul understands it, the paradox of Christian existence as such—life made manifest in death:

> But we have this treasure in earthen vessels, in order that it may be clear that the surpassing power belongs to God and does not come from us. We are afflicted in every way, but not crushed; perplexed, but not driven to despair; persecuted, but not forsaken; struck down, but not destroyed; always bearing about in the body the death of Jesus, in order that the life of Jesus may be made manifest in our bodies. For while we live, we are always being

---

that Paul has done on a recent occasion that very thing which he now assures them that he will do no more."

408 Hausrath, *Der Vier-Capitel-Brief des Paulus*, 23; Schmiedel, *Die Briefe an die Korinther*, 61; Kennedy, "The Problem of Second Corinthians," 361, calling attention to the past tense of ἐξέστημεν in 5:13.

409 Kennedy, "The Problem of Second Corinthians," 340–46; followed by Lake, *Earlier Epistles*, 161; Plummer, *Second Epistle*, xxxi.

410 For 2 Cor. 2:14–6:13; 7:2–4 as an "apologetic" letter, see Bornkamm, *Vorgeschichte*, 22–23; Georgi, *Gegner des Paulus*, 16–24; J-F. Collange, *Enigmes de la deuxième épître de Paul aux Corinthiens. Etude exégétique de 2 Cor. 2:14–7:4* (Cambridge: Cambridge University Press, 1972) 6 and *passim*; Fallon, *2 Corinthians*, 4 and *passim*; Roetzel, *2 Corinthians*; among others.

411 Cf. C. H. Dodd, "The Mind of Paul," *New Testament Studies* (Manchester: Manchester University Press, 1953) 67–128; Sze-Kar Wan, *Power in Weakness: Conflict and Rhetoric in Paul's Second Letter to the Corinthians* (Harrisburg: Trinity Press International, 2000).

given up to death on account of Jesus, in order that the life of Jesus may be manifest in our mortal flesh. So death is at work in us, but life in you (4:7–12).[412]

The source of Paul's mysterious capacity to endure his paradoxical existence is not the concentrated inwardness of the Stoic, who has made himself invulnerable to life's adversities,[413] nor "a psychic disposition gained through remaining aloof from bodily life,"[414] like a Platonic dualist,[415] but rather Paul's "death" to himself and to self-interest, accomplished through his participation in the death of Messiah Jesus.[416] As Paul goes on to explain, those who have been grasped by the love of Christ have "died" with him, and no longer live for themselves: "For the love of Christ constrains us, because we are convinced of this–that one died for all, and therefore all died. And he died for all, so that those who

---

412 See the insightful commentary on this passage by Rudolf Bultmann, *The Second Letter to the Corinthians* (Minneapolis: Augsburg, 1985) 110–20.
413 Bultmann, *Second Letter*, 114, distinguishing Paul's conception of Christian existence from the superficially comparable attitude of the Stoic, as evidenced by Epictetus *Diatr.* 2.19.24, or Seneca *Ep.* 41.4: "If you see a man who is unterrified in the midst of dangers, untouched by desires, happy in adversity, peaceful amid the storm, who looks down upon men from a higher plane, and views the gods on a footing of equality, will not a feeling of reverence for him steal over you? Will you not say: 'This quality is too great and too lofty to be regarded as resembling this petty body in which it dwells?...'"
414 Bultmann, *Second Letter*, 118.
415 E.g., Plato *Phaed.* 66E-67 A: "For, if pure knowledge is impossible while the body is with us, one of two things must follow, either it cannot be acquired at all, or only when we are dead; for then the soul will be by itself apart from the body, but not before. And while we live, we shall, I think, be nearest to knowledge when we avoid, so far as possible, intercourse and communion with the body, except what is absolutely necessary, and are not filled with its nature, but keep ourselves pure from it until God himself sets us free. And in this way, freeing ourselves from the foolishness of the body and being pure, we shall, I think, be with the pure and shall know of ourselves all that is pure, and that is, perhaps, the truth...the true philosophers practice the art of dying." See also Philo *Gig.* 14: "These last, then, are the souls of those who have given themselves to genuine philosophy, who from first to last study to die to the life in the body, that a higher existence, immortal and incorporeal, in the presence of Him who is himself immortal and uncreated, may be their portion."
416 Bultmann, *Second Letter*, 119 on 2 Cor. 4:11, defining the παραδιδόναι εἰς θάνατον as "an event which allows for the experience of θάνατος as a sharing in the death of Jesus. In any case, the meaning is not 'so that I witness to him,' but either 'because we share in Jesus' death' or 'so that we obtain a share in Jesus' death'."

live might live no longer for themselves, but for him who for their sake died and was raised" (5:14–15).[417] The one who has been set free from the tyranny of self-interest is a "new creation," who has been "reconciled" to God, and who is the recipient of a "ministry of reconciliation" (5:17–19).[418] Paul's concluding defense of his apostolic ministry in 2 Cor. 6:3–10 is a passionate and poetic self-portrait, in which endurance, love, and truth break through all suspicion and doubt to provide a sincere and authentic self-commendation:[419]

> We are putting no obstacle in anyone's way, so that no fault may be found with our ministry, but as servants of God we have commended ourselves in every way: through great endurance, in afflictions, hardships, calamities, beatings, imprisonments, riots, labors, sleepless nights, hunger; by purity, knowledge, patience, kindness, holiness of spirit, genuine love, truthful speech, and the power of God; with the weapons of righteousness for the right hand and the left; in honor and dishonor, in ill repute and good repute. We are treated as impostors, and yet are true; as unknown, and yet are known; as dying, and see—we are alive; as punished, and yet not killed; as sorrowful, yet always rejoicing; as poor, yet making many rich; as having nothing, and yet possessing everything.[420]

The peroration of this profound epistle is the most direct and emotionally charged in the Pauline corpus:[421]

> Our mouth is open to you, Corinthians, our heart is wide. You are not restricted in us, but are restricted in your own affections. In return—I speak as to children—open wide your hearts also. Make room (in your hearts) for us; we have wronged no one (οὐδένα ἠδικήσαμεν), we have corrupted no one (οὐδένα ἐφθείραμεν), we have defrauded no one (οὐδένα ἐπλεονεκτήσαμεν). I do not say this to condemn you, for I said before that you are in our hearts, to die together and to live together. Great is my boldness (παρρησία) toward you, great is my boast (καύχησις) on your behalf! I am filled with consolation. I overflow with joy in all our affliction. (6:11–13; 7:2–4).

---

417 Bultmann, *Second Letter*, 150–53.
418 Cilliers Breytenbach, *Versöhnung: Eine Studie zur paulinischen Soteriologie* (Neukirchen-Vluyn: Neukirchener Verlag, 1989) 125–32 and passim.
419 Bultmann, *Second Letter*, 168, rightly perceiving that all the predicates in 6:4b-10 are dependent upon the participial phrase συνιστάνοντες ἑαυτούς in 6:4a.
420 Windisch, *Der zweite Korintherbrief*, 203–209; Bultmann, *Second Letter*, 168–175; Fitzgerald, *Cracks in an Earthen Vessel*.
421 Windisch, *Der zweite Korintherbrief*, 210.

Chapter Six. History of a Friendship 449

How did the letter of 2 Cor. 2:14–6:13; 7:2–4 function in Paul's attempt to conciliate the wrongdoer? It is crucial that we form as clear an understanding of this process as possible, given the circumspect quality of Paul's rhetoric. Because it was *this* letter, in accordance with our reconstruction of the sequence of events and epistles, that produced remorse and repentance in the wrongdoer (2:7), and among the Corinthians generally (7:9), whereas the "painful epistle" of 2 Cor. 10–13 had only produced "fear and trembling" (7:15).[422]

It is here that we encounter the first major shift in the paradigm of Greco-Roman friendship: *as "the one who had been wronged"* (ὁ ἀδικηθείς), *as the injured party, Paul took the initiative in reconciliation*. In an illuminating essay, John Fitzgerald has demonstrated that the standard paradigm of reconciliation dictated that the one who had done wrong and created conflict would take the initiative in ending strife and restoring peace: "According to the paradigm, it is the offending party's responsibility to seek the offer of reconciliation."[423] In illustration of this convention, Fitzgerald adduces several papyrus letters from the second century A.D.[424] In *PMich*. VIII.502, a soldier named Valerius Gemellus writes to his estranged brother urging him, "In response to my entreaty, brother, be reconciled to me (παρα]κληθείς, ἄδελφε, διαλλάγηθί μοι), so that I may enjoy your confidence (παρρησία) also while I am in service," observing that "there is no other hope like the candid intercourse (παρρησία) of brothers and one's own people."[425] Similarly, in *BGU* III.846, one Antonius Longinus appeals to his estranged mother for reconciliation: "I beseech you, mother, be reconciled to me (παρακα[λ]ῶ σαι, μῆτηρ, δ[ι]αλάγητί μοι). Furthermore I know what I have brought upon myself. I have been taught a fitting lesson. I know that I have done wrong (οἶδα ὅτι ἡμάρτηκα)."[426] Finally, in a very touching letter (*PGiss*. 17), a female

---

422 König, "Verkehr," 533; Weiss, *Primitive Christianity*, 1.345.
423 Fitzgerald, "Paul and Paradigm Shifts," 248–49. Fitzgerald rightly asserts (320 n.37) that the paradigm is attested early in Greek literature, already appearing in Hesiod *Op.* 707–14; on this passage, see also John T. Fitzgerald, "Friendship in the Greek World Prior to Aristotle" in *Greco-Roman Perspectives on Friendship*, 32.
424 Fitzgerald, "Paul and Paradigm Shifts," 249–51.
425 Text and translation in Herbert C. Youtie and John G. Winter, *Papyri and Ostraca from Karanis* (Ann Arbor: University of Michigan Press, 1951) 121–23.
426 Text and translation in George Milligan, *Selections from the Greek Papyri* (Cambridge: Cambridge University Press, 1910) 93–95; Deissmann, *Light from the Ancient East*, 186–92; John L. White, *Light from Ancient Letters* (Philadelphia: Fortress Press, 1986) 181–82; translation slightly modified.

slave named Tays, who has been estranged from her master Apollonius, beseeches him to "send for us," lamenting that "we are dying because we do not see you every day." Expressing the wish that she "were able to fly" to him, and emphasizing her distress, she appeals for reconciliation: "So, be reconciled to us (ὥστε διαλλάγηθι ἡμεῖν) and send for us."[427]

We may supplement Fitzgerald's collection with two examples from Cicero's correspondence with his friends. The spirited exchange of letters between Cicero and Quintus Metellus Celer in January, 62 B.C. represents the culmination of political and personal tensions that had been growing between the men for some time.[428] Celer's blunt letter to Cicero (*Fam.* 5.1.1) complains of mocking comments that Cicero had made against him in the senate and of Cicero's unfair attacks upon his brother Metellus Nepos.[429] Cicero's highly rhetorical response in *Fam.* 5.2 is a calculated piece of political gamesmanship.[430] Nevertheless, as the one who had given offense, Cicero complies with convention and asks for forgiveness, even if his request has an ironic edge: "If in any matter I have opposed your brother on behalf of the republic, I ask you to forgive me (*ut mihi ignoscas*)."[431]

Cicero's only surviving letter to Marcus Licinius Crassus (*Fam.* 5.8) is an appeal for reconciliation, following a long period during which goodwill between the men had deteriorated.[432] Cicero acknowledges his role in creating estrangement, while deftly attributing the wrongdoing to unnamed third parties: "Certain poisonous individuals estranged you from me more than once, and at times changed my attitude toward you."[433] Cicero then asks that past grievances be forgiven: "If in the meanwhile certain infringements, surmised rather than real, have affected

---

427 Text in L. Mitteis and U. Wilcken, *Grundzüge und Chrestomathie der Papyruskunde* (Leipzig: Teubner, 1912) 1.566 (Nr. 481); translation in George Milligan, *Here and There among the Papyri* (London: Hodder & Stoughton, 1923) 98.
428 Stanley E. Hoffer, "Cicero's 'Friendly Disagreement' with Metellus Celer (*Fam.* 5.1–2)," *Scripta Classica Israelica* 22 (2003) 93–101.
429 Hoffer, "Cicero's 'Friendly Disagreement' with Metellus Celer," 94–95; Hall, *Politeness and Politics*, 153.
430 See the rhetorical analysis of Hoffer, "Cicero's 'Friendly Disagreement' with Metellus Celer," 97–101, with the insightful comments of Hall, *Politeness and Politics in Cicero's Letters*, 156–58.
431 Hoffer, "Cicero's 'Friendly Disagreement' with Metellus Celer," 98; Hall, *Politeness and Politics*, 158.
432 Marshall, *Crassus*, 173–74; Hall, *Politeness and Politics*, 71–76. Cf. *Fam.* 1.9.20 on the accumulation of strains in the relationship.
433 *Fam.* 5.8.2.

our relations, since they were both mistaken and without substance, let them be utterly eradicated from our memories and our lives (*sint evulsa ex omni memoria vitaque nostra*)."[434] However many polite fictions may operate in this letter, in order to conceal unpleasant truths,[435] Cicero's appeal presupposes the standard paradigm: the offending party takes responsibility for extending the offer of reconciliation.[436]

Paul's decision to take the initiative in seeking reconciliation represents a striking departure from one of the norms of Greco-Roman friendship.[437] Paul not only felt that he had been "wronged" (7:12) and "pained" (2:5), he had been publically accused of embezzlement (12:16–18) and humiliated before the Corinthians (12:20–21).[438] As "the one who had been wronged" (ὁ ἀδικηθείς), Paul should have been the *recipient* of an appeal for reconciliation. Instead, Paul represents himself as the agent of reconciliation, emphatically appealing to the Corinthians for a resumption of friendship: "We are therefore Christ's ambassadors; it is as if God was making his appeal (παρακαλοῦντος) to you through us. As representatives of Christ we appeal (δεόμεθα) to you to accept the offer of friendship (καταλλάγητε) that God is making to you" (5:20).[439]

Paul's reversal of roles would have been more conspicuous because of his studied use of language belonging to the reconciliation paradigm: first, the verb καταλλάσσω (5:18, 19, 20) which, like the equivalent term διαλλάσσω, has the basic meaning "to change from enmity to friendship";[440] then, the words of entreaty παρακαλέω (5:20; 6:1) and δέομαι

---

434 *Fam.* 5.8.3.
435 Hall, *Politeness and Politics*, 74–75.
436 Further examples might be adduced, e.g., Demosthenes *Ep.* 2.1.
437 Fitzgerald, "Paul and Paradigm Shifts," 252–257.
438 See ch. 3 above, pp. 170–81.
439 The translation is that of William Barclay, *The New Testament: A New Translation*, 2 vols. (London: Collins, 1968–69) 2.72; cited by Fitzgerald, "Paul and Paradigm Shifts," 259.
440 LSJ 401 s.v. διαλλάσσω III and 899 s.v. καταλλάσσω II; BDAG 232 s.v. διαλλάσσομαι and 521 s.v. καταλλάσσω b. See also C. S. Spicq, *Theological Lexicon of the New Testament*, 3 vols. (Peabody: Hendrickson, 1994) 2.262: "For pagans and Christians alike, *reconciliation* is the action of reestablishing friendship between two persons who are on bad terms, to replace hostility with peaceful relations." Cf. Breytenbach, *Versöhnung*, 23, 47, 52–53, 61, 180, 223; Fitzgerald, "Paul and Paradigm Shifts," 258, 324 n.84.

(5:20), which appear regularly in appeals for reconciliation;[441] finally, the confidence expression παρρησία (3:12; 7:4), which finds its counterpart in the papyrus letters cited above.[442]

A further shift in the paradigm is apparent in respect to the psychological motivation of the role that Paul has chosen to play in the process of reconciliation. Paul explains his decision to take the initiative in extending the offer of reconciliation as a consequence of his "death" to himself and to self-interest, through participation in the death of Christ: constrained by the love of the "one" who "died for all," Paul now lives for the one who died for others (5:14–15).[443] By contrast, in his diatribe on friendship, Epictetus insists upon a clear-eyed recognition of the power of self-interest: "For universally, be not deceived, every animal is attached to nothing so much as to its own interest. Whatever then appears to it an impediment to this interest, whether this be a brother, or a father, or a child, or a beloved, or lover, it hates, spurns, curses; for its nature is to love nothing so much as its own interest; this is father, and brother, and kinsman, and country, and God."[444] Epictetus' solution to this dilemma is not to counsel the extinction of self-interest, but to urge the identification of self-interest with integrity: "to maintain the character of fidelity, of modesty, of patience, of abstinence, of active cooperation."[445] In the conciliatory letters examined above, reconciliation is repeatedly warranted by an appeal to mutual self-interest. For example, Cicero concludes his letter to Crassus with the argument: "Between two men such as you are and I desire to be, I would hope that alliance and friendship will conduce to the credit of both."[446]

A final shift in the paradigm relates to the role Paul assigns to God in the process of reconciliation. With radical consistency, Paul makes God the one who takes the initiative in reconciliation with human beings: "All this is from God, who reconciled us to himself through Christ (τὰ δὲ πάντα ἐκ τοῦ θεοῦ τοῦ καταλλάξαντος ἡμᾶς ἑαυτῷ διὰ Χριστοῦ)...; that is, in Christ, God was reconciling the world to himself (ὡς ὅτι θεὸς ἦν ἐν Χριστῷ κόσμον καταλλάσσων ἑαυτῷ), not counting their trespasses against them...We are therefore Christ's ambassadors, since God is

---

441 E.g., *PMich.* VIII.502, 7–8; *BGU* III.846; *PGiss.* 17, 7–8; *Vit. Aesopi* W 100, 6–7 P : δέομαι σου, δέσποτα, διαλλάγγηθι.
442 E.g., *PMich.* VIII.502, 8–9.
443 Bultmann, *Second Letter*, 150–53.
444 Epictetus *Diatr.* 2.22.
445 Epictetus *Diatr.* 2.22.
446 Cicero *Fam.* 5.8.3.

making his appeal through us; we entreat you on behalf of Christ, be reconciled (καταλλάγητε) to God" (5:18–20). This is a momentous and, evidently, unprecedented change in the understanding of God.⁴⁴⁷ In the Greco-Roman world, including Judaism, human beings appealed to God to be reconciled through prayers and sacrifices.⁴⁴⁸ Fitzgerald adduces an exemplary text from the *Roman Antiquities* of Dionysius of Halicarnassus: "For the gods themselves...are disposed to forgive the offenses of men and are easily reconciled (εὐδιάλλακτοι); and there have been many before now who, though greatly sinning against them, have appeased their anger by prayers and sacrifices."⁴⁴⁹ In keeping with this understanding, Chairemon invokes the gods in support of the reconciliation which he offers to his wounded friend Apollonius in a papyrus letter examined above: "If the gods are willing (θεῶν δὲ βουλομένων), I will certainly visit you after the Soucheia festival. I swear to you by the Dioscuri whom we worship in common...(ὄμνυμι δὲ σοι κατὰ τ[ῶ]ν Δ[ιο]σκ[ο]ύρων, ὧν κοινῇ σεβόμεθα...).⁴⁵⁰ Paul's account of God as the one who takes the initiative in offering reconciliation would seem to be a *novum* in the theology of antiquity.

As we observed above,⁴⁵¹ there are no passages in 2 Cor. 2:14–6:13; 7:2–4 where the use of a singular pronoun or a singular verb-form unambiguously suggests that Paul might be referring to a specific individual—the wrongdoer. Indeed, Paul maximizes the conciliatory strategy of construing his critic as the representative of the majority, thus generalizing the distress which the wrongdoer has caused, a strategy that we also encountered in the letters of Demosthenes and the speeches of Dio Chrysostom.⁴⁵² Nevertheless, it is impossible not to think that Gaius

---

447 So, Fitzgerald, "Paul and Paradigm Shifts," 253.
448 Sophocles *Aj.* 744; Plato *Menex.* 244 A; 2 Macc. 1:5; 8:29; 3 Macc. 5:13; Josephus *B.J.* 5.415; all texts cited by Fitzgerald, "Paul and Paradigm Shifts," 252–53.
449 Dionysius of Halicarnassus *Ant. rom.* 8.50.4; Fitzgerald, "Paul and Paradigm Shifts," 253.
450 *BGU* I.248; Olsson, *Papyrusbriefe*, 122–23. For the context of Chairemon's friendship with Apollonius, and his apology for an offense given by what he wrote in a previous letter, see *BGU* II.531. Other examples might be adduced, e.g., Marcus' letter to Herodes in Philostratus *Vit. soph.* 2.1.563: Marcus invokes the gods in support of his offer of reconciliation, expressing the wish that Herodes should initiate him into the Eleusinian rites. See further, Apollonius of Tyana *Ep.* 45: συγχωροίη γὰρ ἂν ἴσως τὸ δαιμόνιον.
451 See above, ch. 3, pp. 209–11.
452 See above, ch. 4, pp. 222–28.

would have heard himself addressed directly in 5:17, "So if anyone is in Christ—a new creation!" (ὥστε εἴ τις ἐν Χριστῷ, καινὴ κτίσις), even if Paul deliberately formulates the statement as a generalization.⁴⁵³ The indefinite pronoun τις and the expression ἐν Χριστῷ recall the confident boast of "someone" to be "of Christ" (Χριστοῦ εἶναι) in 10:7. By invoking Gaius' own confession at the jubilant climax of his argument, Paul embraces the Christology of his critic within his new, paradoxical conception of participation in the death of Christ (cf. 5:14–15).

A final and highly effective moment in the conciliatory strategy of this letter is Paul's declaration of innocence in 7:2, formulated as a tripartite anaphora: "We have wronged no one, we have corrupted no one, we have defrauded no one" (οὐδένα ἠδικήσαμεν, οὐδένα ἐφθείραμεν, οὐδένα ἐπλεονεκτήσαμεν).⁴⁵⁴ Although Paul's denials are formulated generally, it is impossible not to hear a resonance in relation to a particular individual, since the language echoes the charges against Paul in 12:16–18. Indeed, Hans Windisch asserts that Paul's use of the singular pronoun οὐδείς in 7:2 indicates that the accusations implicit in Paul's denials have been made by a particular individual, or individuals, supported by other members of the Corinthian community: "οὐδένα zeigt, dass die Beschwerden von einzelnen Gemeindegliedern ausgingen, mit denen die Gemeinde sich solidarisch fühlte."⁴⁵⁵ By resuming the language in which Gaius made his accusation (πλεονεκτεῖν), Paul not only provides a forceful recapitulation of his apologetic argument, he also, and more importantly, signals his determination to place their relationship beyond the stage of attack and defense.⁴⁵⁶ Paul's intention is clarified by the following verse (7:3a): "I do not say this to condemn you" (πρὸς κατάκρισιν οὐ λέγω).⁴⁵⁷ κατάκρισις is "a judicial verdict involving a penalty," "condemnation."⁴⁵⁸ Paul seeks to relocate their intercourse from the forensic arena to the chambers of the heart: "You are in our hearts, to die together and to live together" (7:3b).

---

453 Cf. Furnish, *II Corinthians*, 314.
454 For stylistic parallels, see Epictetus *Diatr.* 1.28.10: οὐδενὶ ὀργισθήσεται, οὐδενὶ χαλεπανεῖ, οὐδένα λοιδορήσει, οὐδένα μέμψεται, οὐ μισήσει, οὐ προσκόψει οὐδενί, and 2.2.9, quoting Socrates: οὐδὲν οὐδέποτ' ἄδικον οὔτ' ἰδίᾳ οὔτε δημοσίᾳ ἔπραξα.
455 Windisch, *Der zweite Korintherbrief*, 221.
456 Windisch, *Der zweite Korintherbrief*, 221–22.
457 Windisch, *Der zweite Korintherbrief*, 221–22.
458 BDAG 519 s.v. κατάκρισις

Chapter Six. History of a Friendship 455

We do not know in what venue Titus presented the conciliatory apology of 2 Cor. 2:14–7:4, but on the assumption that Gaius was then serving as "the host of the whole *ekklesia*," it seems likely to have been in the house of Gaius himself! Fortunately, we do not need to speculate about the affect of this letter upon Gaius and the Corinthians, since Paul reflects rather fulsomely upon the report that Titus brought back from Corinth. Titus reported the "longing" (ἐπιπόθησις), "mourning" (ὀδυρμός), and "zeal" (ζῆλος) of the Corinthians on behalf of Paul (7:7). These strong emotions are all aspects of the Corinthians' "grief" (λύπη), a "grief" that is mentioned no less than eight times in the paragraph which Paul devotes to Titus' report (7:8–13a).[459] Paul makes no attempt to conceal the fact that the cause of the grief that Titus encountered in Corinth was the rupture of Paul's relationship with one Corinthian in particular. In 2:5 Paul concedes that all of the Corinthians, and not himself alone (οὐκ ἐμὲ...ἀλλὰ...πάντας ὑμᾶς),[460] have been grieved by an unnamed individual. Equally, in 7:8 Paul acknowledges that the letter which he wrote in response to the wrongdoing had caused grief to the Corinthians.

Among the Corinthians, the one who felt the sharpest pain and experienced the deepest remorse was the wrongdoer, Gaius. This is a necessary inference from Paul's account of the "excessive grief" (περισσοτέρᾳ λύπῃ) that threatened to "overwhelm" (καταποθῇ) this individual in 2:7, unless Paul's account is regarded as hyperbolic. As we observed above,[461] the verb καταπίνειν is frightful in its force: in the passive voice which Paul uses here, καταπίνειν means "to be swallowed up by waters," "to be drowned."[462] The image that Paul's language evokes is that of a man

---

459 For ἐπιπόθησις as "yearning" and "deep desire," see BDAG 377 s.v.; cf. Furnish, *II Corinthians*, 386. For ὀδυρμός as "mourning" and "lamentation," see the texts cited in LSJ 1199 s.v.; BDAG 692 s.v.; see esp. *Tab. Cebes* 10, where one who stands under "retribution" (τιμωρία) is afflicted by "grief" (λύπη), "sorrow" (ὀδύνη) and "lamentation" (ὀδυρμός); cf. Windisch, *Der zweite Korintherbrief*, 228. For ζῆλος as a subcategory of "pain" (λύπη), see Aristotle *Rhet.* 2.11.1–7; Welborn, "Paul's Appeal to the Emotions," 54–57.
460 On the sense of the expression οὐκ ἐμὲ...ἀλλὰ...πάντας ὑμᾶς as "not *only* to me...but...to you all," see Windisch, *Der zweite Korintherbrief*, 84–85; Furnish, *II Corinthians*, 389. See also ch. 3 above.
461 See above ch. 3, pp. 39–40.
462 BDAG 524 s.v. καταπίνω 1b. Note esp. the transferred sense, in reference to mental and emotional states, in Philo *Gig.* 13; *Deus* 181. Cf. Hughes, *Paul's Second Epistle*, 67 n.12: "The intensive force of the compound καταπίνειν should be brought out: 'to swallow up completely' or 'to engulf'."

being drowned in his own tears.⁴⁶³ Paul intensifies the portrait of the wrongdoer's grief by adding the comparative adjective περισσότερος, functioning as an elative superlative—"excessive."⁴⁶⁴ An illuminating parallel to Paul's account of the grief of the wrongdoer is found in Demosthenes' apology for his excessive sorrow, at the conclusion of his conciliatory epistle to the council and assembly of Athens. Acknowledging that he had committed "some slight offence,"⁴⁶⁵ and appealing at length for forgiveness and restoration, the orator seeks to excuse his excess of grief: "Let not one of you think, men of Athens, that through lack of manhood or from any other base motive I give way to my grief (ὀδύρεσθαι) from the beginning to the end of this letter. Not so, but every man is ungrudgingly indulgent to the feelings of the moment, and those that now beset us—if only this had never come to pass!—are sorrows and tears (λῦπαι καὶ δάκρυα), longing (πόθος) both for my country and for you, and pondering over the things which I have suffered, all of which cause me to grieve (ὀδύρεσθαι)."⁴⁶⁶

The psychagogic literature of antiquity, and especially some of Plutarch's essays, permit us to form a more robust conception of the "remorse" and "regret" attendant upon Gaius' wrongdoing and the complicity of certain Corinthians. In the *Tabula* of Cebes, the one who "commits all that is injurious," and is delivered to "Retribution" (Τιμωρία), is described as living with "Grief" (Λύπη) and "Sorrow" (Ὀδύνη), personified as "ugly, filthy women dressed in rags," as well as "Lamentation" (Ὀδυρμός) and his sister "Despondency" (Ἀθυμία), portrayed as "deformed, emaciated, and naked"; eventually the wrongdoer is thrown into the house of "Unhappiness" (Κακοδαιμονία), "and here he spends the rest of his life in total unhappiness," unless he is rescued by "Repentance" (Μετάνοια).⁴⁶⁷ In Plutarch's essay on delays in the divine vengeance, he speaks of "the intervening sufferings, terrors, forebodings, and pangs of remorse to which every wrongdoer, once he has done evil, is prey" (τὰ δ' ἐν μέσῳ παθήματα καὶ φόβους καὶ προσδοκίας καὶ μεταμελείας οἷς ἀδι-

---

463 Furnish, *II Corinthians*, 156; Thrall, *Second Epistle*, 1.177; Clarence Glad, *Paul and Philodemus: Adaptability in Epicurean and Early Christian Psychagogy* (Leiden: Brill, 1995) 316.
464 BDAG 806 s.v. περισσότερος a: "excessive." Cf. Harris, *Second Epistle*, 229: "τῇ περισσοτέρᾳ λύπῃ means 'by excessive sorrow' or 'by excess of grief'."
465 Demosthenes *Ep.* 2.1.
466 Demosthenes *Ep.* 2.25.
467 *Tab. Cebes* 10 ; text and translation in John T. Fitzgerald and L. Michael White, *The Tabula of Cebes* (Chico: Scholars Press, 1983) 76–79.

κήσας ἕκαστος ἐνέχεται τῶν πονηρῶν παραλείπομεν).[468] In his essay on vice as the cause of unhappiness, Plutarch pictures the psychological suffering of a man who does evil: "vice…, when it has joined itself to the soul, crushes and overthrows it, and fills the man with grief and lamentation, dejection and remorse" (κακία…,τῇ ψυχῇ συνελθοῦσα συνέτριψε καὶ κατέβαλε, λύπης ἐνέπλησε θρήνων βαρυθυμίας μεταμελείας τὸν ἄνθρωπον).[469]

The psychagogic literature is also helpful in comprehending the movement from "remorse" to "repentance" implicit in Paul's account of the response of the Corinthians in 7:7b-11. Plutarch attributes a crucial role to the consciousness of wrongdoing. In his essay on tranquility of mind, Plutarch invokes "the conscience (ἡ σύνεσις)" of someone who "knows he has done a dreadful deed," and continues with a simile: "like an ulcer in the flesh, [the knowledge of wrong] leaves behind it in the soul regret (μεταμέλεια) which ever continues to wound and prick it."[470] Similarly, in his treatise on delays in the divine vengeance, Plutarch explains: "the thought that the soul of every wicked man revolves within itself and dwells upon is this: how it might escape from the memory of its wrongdoings (ἡ μνήμη τῶν ἀδικημάτων), drive out of itself the consciousness (τὸ συνειδός) of guilt, regain its purity, and begin its life anew."[471]

In sum, what Titus reported to Paul regarding the response of the Corinthians, and the wrongdoer in particular, was remorse and repentance (7:7b-11). As Hans Windisch observed, "in μετάνοια is summarized in one word what Paul emphasizes in vs. 7b from the report of Titus: the expressions of longing, mourning and zeal on behalf of Paul were the welcome signs of a 'change of mind' that the community had experienced."[472] Paul emphasizes the "repentance" (μετάνοια) of Gaius and the Corinthians because a fundamental "change of attitude" was understood to be the only way out of deadly remorse, the interim stage

---

468 Plutarch *Mor.* 554E-F; cf. Fredrickson, "Paul, Hardships and Suffering" in *Paul in the Greco-Roman World*, 173.
469 Plutarch *Mor.* 498D; cf. Fredrickson, "Paul, Hardships and Suffering" in *Paul in the Greco-Roman World*, 173.
470 Plutarch *Mor.* 476E; cf. Windisch, *Der zweite Korintherbrief*, 232.
471 Plutarch *Mor.* 556 A. See also the definition of "regret" (μεταμέλεια) in Ps.-Andronicus Περὶ Παθων 2.44: μεταμέλεια δὲ λύπη ἐπὶ ἁμαρτήμασι πεπραγμένοις ὡς δι' αὐτοῦ γεγονόσιν, in A. Glibert-Thirry, *Pseudo-Andronicus de Rhodes "ΠΕΡΙ ΠΑΘΩΝ"* (Leiden: Brill, 1977) 227.
472 Windisch, *Der zweite Korintherbrief*, 231.

along the path from "pain" (λύπη) to salvation (σωτηρία) (7:10). In the *Tabula* of Cebes, when "Repentance" (Μετάνοια) encounters a man in the grip of despondency, "she releases him from his ills and introduces him to another Opinion (Δόξα), who leads him to true Education (Παιδεία)."[473] Plutarch explains the psychological process: "For the other pangs (λύπαι) reason does away with, but repentance (μετάνοια) is caused by reason itself, since the soul, together with its feeling of shame, is stung and chastised by itself."[474] Titus' report inspired Paul to hope that the repentance of Gaius and the Corinthians was genuine and lasting, a confidence expressed by the elegant oxymoron μετάνοια ἀμεταμέλητος ("repentance not to be regretted") in 7:10.[475]

At some point during Titus' visit to Corinth, whether at the meeting when Titus presented Paul's conciliatory apology, or on some later occasion, the *ekklesia* resolved to discipline the wrongdoer. It is this action to which Paul clearly refers in 2:6: "Sufficient for such a one is this punishment by the majority" (ἱκανὸν τῷ τοιούτῳ ἡ ἐπιτιμία αὕτη ἡ ὑπὸ τῶν πλειόνων).[476] We argued above that the wording of 2:6 discloses a contrast, not only between two groups, "the majority" and "the minority," but also between two verdicts: the minority, loyal supporters of Paul, wished for a severer treatment of the offender than the majority had voted.[477] Paul speaks to this dissatisfied minority in 2:7: "so, on the contrary rather (τοὐναντίον μᾶλλον), you should forgive and console."[478] The adverbial expression τοὐναντίον μᾶλλον, following ἱκανόν (in 2:6), indicates that there were still some who felt that the punishment was insuf-

---

473 *Tab. Cebes* 11.
474 Plutarch *Mor.* 476E.
475 Construing ἀμεταμέλητον with μετάνοιαν, rather than σωτηρίαν: so, Plummer, *Second Epistle*, 221; Windisch, *Der zweite Korintherbrief*, 232; Furnish, *II Corinthians*, 388; Thrall, *Second Epistle*, 1.492 n.42.
476 Krenkel, *Beiträge*, 302.
477 See ch. 3 above: the two verdicts are emphasized by the demonstrative pronoun αὕτη and the repetition of the article in the phrase ἡ ἐπιτιμία αὕτη ἡ ὑπὸ τῶν πλειόνων ("this punishment, namely the one [decided upon] by the majority"), which has as its counterpart ἡ ἐπιτιμία ἐκείνη ἡ ὑπὸ τῶν ἐλασσόνων, thus following Krenkel, *Beiträge*, 301. See further Kennedy, *Second and Third Corinthians*, 100–109; Lake, *Earlier Epistles*, 170–72; Plummer, *Second Epistle*, 58; Windisch, *Der zweite Korintherbrief*, 86–88; Furnish, *II Corinthians*, 155–56, 391; Thrall, *Second Epistle*, 1.174–76; among others.
478 Krenkel, *Beiträge*, 302; Kennedy, *Second and Third Corinthians*, 106–107; Windisch, *Der zweite Korintherbrief*, 86, 88; Barrett, *Second Epistle*, 215; Furnish, *II Corinthians*, 156, 391.

ficient, and who had hitherto refused to forgive.⁴⁷⁹ The resolution that carried the day, namely, that of the majority, may have been ratified with some formality. Formality is reflected in the technical language of Paul's counterproposal in 2:8—that the Corinthians "ratify love" (κυρῶσαι ἀγάπην) for the wrongdoer; the verb κυροῦν is used here in the technical, legal sense "to confirm an act or a decision."⁴⁸⁰ With a modest use of historical imagination, we may picture what transpired at the assembly where the wrongdoer was punished. One of Gaius' staunch supporters, perhaps Crispus, who had lighted Gaius' path into the Christian community, proposed that Gaius be formally disciplined for his public accusation of embezzlement against Paul. A minority of congregants, perhaps with Stephanas as their spokesman, expressed dissatisfaction with the verdict of the majority, and advocated a harsher punishment.

And what was the punishment imposed upon the wrongdoer? We argued above that the punishment took the form of censure—an inference from the term ἐπιτιμία in 2:6, whose specific content we derived from the verb ἐπιτιμᾶν, "to rebuke, reprove, censure."⁴⁸¹ It is possible, of course, that the assembly imposed a fine as well. The charters of guilds and cultic associations include regulations prohibiting accusations against fellow-members, and impose fines upon the disobedient. The law of the association of Zeus Hypsistos (dated between 69 and 58 B.C.) stipulates: "It shall not be permissible for any one of them…to abuse one another at the banquet or to chatter or to indict or accuse another" (καὶ μ[η]ι[δ]ενὶ αὐτῶν ἐξέστωι…κακολογ[ήσειν] ἕτερος [τὸν] ἕτερον ἐν τῶι συμποσίωι μηδὲ λαλήσειν μηδὲ ἐπ[ικα]λήσειν καὶ μὲ κατηγορή[σ]ειν τοῦ ἑτέρου), and goes onto speak of "levies" that each violator shall pay.⁴⁸² The charter of the Iobacchoi of Athens prohibits insults and abuse, described as ὕβρις and λοιδορία, and exacts a fine of 25 light drach-

---

479 Plummer, *Second Epistle*, 58; Windisch, *Der zweite Korintherbrief*, 88; Lietzmann, *An die Korinther I/II*, 106; Bultmann, *Der zweite Brief*, 53; Furnish, *II Corinthians*, 156; Harris, *Second Epistle*, 229.
480 LSJ 1014 s.v. κυρόω 1; BDAG 579 s.v. κυρόω 1, with the texts cited above, ch. 3, p. 40 n.91.
481 BDAG 384 s.v. ἐπιτιμάω: Thucydides 4.28.1; Demosthenes 1.16; *SIG* 344, 55; Sir. 11:7; Josephus *A.J.* 5.105. Cf. Krenkel, *Beiträge*, 302; Bachmann, *Der zweite Brief*, 117 n.3, 119; Barrett, *Second Epistle*, 90–91. Glad (*Paul and Philodemus*, 316) argues that the punishment administered by the majority took the form of a "harsh censure," citing Plutarch *Mor.* 825E and Diodorus Siculus 3.67.2, where such rebukes result in λύπη.
482 *P.Lond* 2710, 13–17; C. Roberts, T. C. Skeat, and A. D. Nock, "The Gild of Zeus Hypsistos," *HTR* 29 (1936) 39–88, text and trans. 40–42.

mas for violations.⁴⁸³ Yet, it is unlikely that a fine was imposed upon Gaius or any of his supporters. In 7:9, Paul clarifies his purpose: "so that in no way you might suffer loss (ζημιωθῆτε) from us." The verb ζημιόω (in the passive) appears in the ordinances of guilds and associations to describe the fines that members must pay for defaming other members, or for misconduct in general. For example, a guild charter from first-century Tebtunis specifies: "If anyone prosecutes another or defames him, let him be fined eight drachmas" (ἐάν τις τοῦ ἑτέρου κατηγορήσῃ ἢι διαβολὴν ποιήσηται, ζημιούσθω δραχμὰς η).⁴⁸⁴ How could Paul deny that the Corinthians had sustained a loss, using the same term found in the guild ordinances (ζημιοῦσθαι), if Gaius or his supporters had been punished with a fine? In any case, it stands to reason that a man such as Gaius, "the host of the whole *ekklesia*," would have been more strongly affected by a public censure than by a fine of a few drachmas.

In Troas, and then in Macedonia, Paul awaited Titus' report from Corinth. The account that Paul gives in 2:12–13 and 7:5 of the anxiety he endured while he awaited news of the Corinthians' response is calculated to awaken the pity of his readers.⁴⁸⁵ Paul vividly portrays the restlessness of his mind and body during his voluntary "exile" from Corinth, using the figure of repetition to heighten the emotional affect:⁴⁸⁶

> When I came into Troas for the gospel of Christ, and a door was opened to me in the Lord, I did not have rest in my spirit, because I did not find my brother Titus there. But having said farewell to them, I went on to Macedonia. For even when we came into Macedonia, our flesh had no rest, but we were afflicted in every way—fightings without, fears within.

---

483 *IG* 2² 1368, 72–80: μάχης δὲ ἐάν τις ἄρξηται ἢ εὑρεθῇ τις ἀκοσμῶν ἢ ἐπ' ἀλλοτρίαν κλισίαν ἐρχόμενος ἢ ὑβρίζων ἢ λοιδορῶν τινα...λεπτοῦ δρ(αχμαί), κτλ. See also *IG* 2² 1369, 40–44, with the provision to fine and expel members who have caused fights and disturbances. On disturbances in guilds and associations generally, see I. N. Arnaoutoglou, "Roman Law and *collegia* in Asia Minor," *Revue Internationale des Droits de l'Antiquité* 49 (2002) 27–44, at 43.

484 *P.Mich.* V.243 (A.D. 14–37), trans. by the editor A. E. R. Boak. See also *P.Mich.* V.244, ll. 7 and 17 (A. D. 43); *P.Mich.* V.245, ll. 25 and 28. I thank my friend Don Barker for these papyrus references. See the discussion of crimes and misdemeanors in guild charters by Philip F. Venticinque, "Family Affairs: Guild Regulations and Family Relationships in Roman Egypt," *GRBS* 50 (2010) 273–94, esp. 280–88.

485 Welborn, "Paul's Appeal to the Emotions," 45–47.

486 Welborn, "Like Broken Pieces of a Ring," 562–69.

Cicero recommends that one who appeals for pity should "deplore separation from someone, as when you are torn apart from one with whom you have lived with greatest pleasure, for example,…a brother, or intimate friend."[487] In his conciliatory epistle to the council and assembly of Athens, Demosthenes seeks to stir the pity of his readers by representing himself as deprived of the company of those who are nearest and dearest.[488] Similarly, Apollonius of Tyana compares himself to Odysseus in his longing for home in his conciliatory epistle to his estranged brother, Hestiaeus.[489] Nevertheless, there is no reason to doubt the genuineness of Paul's anxiety as he awaited Titus' report from Corinth. Seneca emphasizes the apprehensiveness of the victim, no less than the anxiety of the perpetrator, in the surviving fragment of his essay on the maintenance of friendship.[490]

Paul responded to Titus' report from Corinth with exuberant joy.[491] No less than five times in the paragraph reflective of Titus' report, Paul uses χαίρω and χαρά (7:7b, 9, 13, 16), supplemented by avowals of consolation (παρακαλεῖν and παράκλησις in 7:6, 7, 13). As Windisch observed, "The whole piece must have been written in a spirit of exultation and very soon after the first exchange of thoughts with Titus."[492] Other conciliatory epistles express pleasure at the prospect of a restoration of friendship. So, for example, Apollonius confesses to the attractions of kinship and familiarity, now that misunderstanding has been put aside, and gladly announces his intention to return to his brother towards the end of spring.[493] In a similar vein, Marcus Aurelius happily contemplates the prospect that Herodes Atticus will initiate him into the Eleusinian rites, in celebration of their restoration to friendship.[494] Yet, there is nothing in the epistolary literature of antiquity that approximates Paul's excess of joy at the prospect of reconciliation with the Corinthians.

---

487 Cicero *Inv.* 1.55.109.
488 Demosthenes *Ep.* 2.1–2, 18, 20; Goldstein, *The Letters of Demosthenes*, 157–59. Cf. Isocrates 16.48; Aristotle *Rhet.* 3.14.11.
489 Apollonius *Ep.* 44.
490 Seneca *Quomodo amicitia continenda sit*, frag. 1.
491 An observation of Aristotle illuminates Paul's transition from grief to joy. In *Rhet.* 2.3, 1380a14, Aristotle states that our anger is lessened toward those who admit that they were wrong and show that they regret it (καὶ τοῖς ὁμολογοῦσι καὶ μεταμελομένοις), for, Aristotle explains, it is as though they have paid the penalty for the pain they have caused.
492 Windisch, *Der zweite Korintherbrief*, 227.
493 Apollonius *Ep.* 44, 45.
494 Philostratus *Vit. soph.* 2.1.563.

In keeping with the literary-critical hypothesis embraced in this monograph, the letter that Paul wrote to the church at Corinth in the afterglow of Titus' report is now preserved in 2 Cor. 1:1–2:13 and 7:5–16.[495] Since the time of Günther Bornkamm, it has become customary to refer to the letter of 2 Cor. 1:1–2:13; 7:5–16 as the "letter of reconciliation" ("Versöhnungsbrief").[496] This usage may have encouraged the idea that all was now well between Paul and the Corinthians, and that Paul only needed to "set the seal" upon his conciliatory efforts, so to speak. But close reading of this epistle reveals that Paul still had work to do, in order to allay suspicions of insincerity and, above all, to heal his wounded friends at Corinth.[497] With regard to the occasion of this epistle, Johannes Weiss observed: "There is still some mistrust (2 Cor. 1:13–14). The opinion still seemed to some extent to prevail that Paul had dealt with the Corinthians with worldly subtlety and not with complete sincerity, and that mental reservations were concealed beneath the words of his letters (2 Cor. 1:12–13)."[498]

Paul's assurance of the "simplicity and sincerity" (ἁπλότης καὶ εἰλικρίνεια) of his conduct in 1:12–14 constitutes the proposition (πρόθεσις) of this epistle.[499] This is a sure indication that this letter, like the preceding

---

495 As noted above, the hypothesis that 2 Cor. 1:1–2:13; 7:5–16 was originally an independent letter goes back to Weiss, *Primitive Christianity*, 1.345–53; followed by Bultmann, *Der zweite Brief*, 20–23; Schmithals, *Gnosis in Corinth*, 63–74; Bornkamm, *Vorgeschichte*, 16–23; Georgi, *Opponents of Paul*, 9–13, 335; Vielhauer, *Geschichte der urchristlichen Literatur*, 150–55; Koester, *Introduction to the New Testament*, 2.52–53, 127–30; Betz, *2 Corinthians 8 and 9*, 150–55; Welborn, "Like Broken Pieces of a Ring," 559–83; Mitchell, "Paul's Letters to Corinth," 318–35; among others.
496 Bornkamm, *Vorgeschichte*, 16–23. But see already Loisy, "Les épîtres de Paul," 213–50, esp. 213: "letter de conciliation." In addition to the works cited in n. 494 above, see further Franz Zeilinger, *Krieg und Friede in Korinth. Kommentar zum 2. Korintherbrief des Apostels Paulus. Teil 1. Der Kampfbrief, der Versöhnungsbrief, der Bettelbrief* (Vienna: Herder, 1992); Albert Brendle, *Im Prozess der Konfliktüberwindung: Eine exegetische Studie zur Kommunikationssituation zwischen Paulus und den Korinthern in 2 Kor 1,1–2,13; 7,4–16* (Frankfurt am Main: Peter Lang, 1994); Erich Grässer, *Der zweite Brief an die Korinther, Kapitel 1,1–7,16* (Gütersloh: Gütersloher Verlaghaus, 2002).
497 For this reason, Mitchell employs the somewhat infelicitous, but more accurate designation "letter toward reconciliation" in her essay "Paul's Letters to Corinth," 335.
498 Weiss, *Primitive Christianity*, 1.346.
499 Betz, "Corinthians, Second Epistle," 1148–54; Welborn, "Paul's Appeal to the Emotions," 57.

two epistles, is still to some extent "apologetic" in character.[500] Accordingly, in the first argument (1:15 – 22),[501] Paul appeals to his volition (βούλησις) as proof of his sincerity against the charge of "foolish irresponsibility" (ἐλαφρία)[502] in his failure to keep his promise to return to Corinth.[503] In the second argument (1:23 – 2:4), Paul explains that he exercised caution (εὐλάβεια), "sparing" (φειδόμενος) the Corinthians further grief by his decision not to come to Corinth. In the third argument (2:5 – 11), Paul proves his sincere goodwill by his magnanimous treatment of the one who had caused grief, recommending that the Corinthians "forgive" and "console" him, and that they "reaffirm love." Paul next (2:12 – 13; 7:5 – 7) adduces the anxious state in which he awaited news of the outcome of Titus' mission as proof of the genuineness of his affection. Paul's final argument (7:8 – 13a) appeals to the beneficial results of his painful epistle as proof of the integrity of his conduct: the grief of the Corinthians has produced repentance, salvation, and joy.

Yet, the overarching purpose of the epistle preserved in 1:1 – 2:13; 7:5 – 16 is the healing of Paul's wounded friends at Corinth, especially the wrongdoer. The Corinthians had been doubly grieved—first, by the actions of the wrongdoer (2:5), then by Paul's severe response (7:8). So, from the first word of this epistle to the last, Paul offers consolation.[504] Paul opens the *prooemium* (1:3 – 7) with praise of God as the "God of all consolation" (θεὸς πάσης παρακλήσεως). Paul represents himself as "afflicted" (θλιβόμεθα) and "comforted" (παρακαλούμεθα) "on behalf of" (ὑπέρ) the Corinthians, so that he may be able to extend consolation to his wounded friends (εἰς δύνασθαι ἡμᾶς παρακαλεῖν τοὺς ἐν πάσῃ θλίψει διὰ τῆς παρακλήσεως ἧς παρακαλούμεθα). Equally, Paul portrays the Corinthians as the source of "consolation" and "joy" for himself and Titus: "But the God who consoles the downcast consoled us by the coming of Titus (ἀλλ' ὁ παρακαλῶν τοὺς ταπεινοὺς παρεκάλεσσεν ἡμᾶς ὁ θεὸς ἐν τῇ παρουσίᾳ Τίτου), and not only by his coming, but also by the

---

500 Windisch, *Der zweite Korintherbrief*, 8. Cf. George A. Kennedy, *New Testament Interpretation through Rhetorical Criticism* (Chapel Hill: University of North Carolina Press, 1984) 87.
501 On the disposition of Paul's argument, see already the observations of Windisch, *Der zweite Korintherbrief*, 93; Betz, "Corinthians, Second Epistle," 1152 – 53.
502 For the meaning of ἐλαφρία, see BDAG 314 s.v.; cf. Harvey, *Renewal through Suffering*, 38 – 40.
503 On this point, see esp. Weiss, *Primitive Christianity*, 1.346.
504 On the concentration of occurrences of παράκλησις and παρακαλέω in 1:3 – 7 (6 instances) and 7:5 – 16 (3 instances), see Thrall, *Second Epistle*, 1.102.

consolation by which he was consoled by you (καὶ ἐν τῇ παρακλήσει ᾗ παρεκλήθη ἐφ' ὑμῖν),[505]...so that I rejoiced" (7:6–7). The jubilant peroration of this epistle (7:13b-16) reiterates Paul's consolation and joy in response to the good report of Titus: "In addition to our own consolation (ἐπὶ δὲ τῇ παρακλήσει), we rejoiced still more at the joy of Titus, because his mind has been set at rest by you all."

The epistolary form which subsumes both the apologetic and the consolatory moments in 2 Cor. 1:1–2:13; 7:5–16 is the "therapeutic" (θεραπευτική) type of letter described in the handbook on epistolary style attributed to Libanius: "The therapeutic style is that in which we conciliate someone who has been caused grief by us for some reason" (θεραπευτικὴ δι' ἧς θεραπεύομέν τινα λυπηθέντα πρὸς ἡμᾶς περί τινος).[506] Pseudo-Libanius adds: "Some also call this the apologetic style" (ταύτην δὲ καὶ ἀπολογητικήν τινες καλοῦσιν). The author provides a concise example of the letter type:[507]

> The conciliatory letter. In addition to making the statements that I did, I went on (to put them) into action, for I most certainly did not think that they would ever cause you sorrow. But if you were upset by what was said or done, be assured, most excellent sir, that I shall most certainly no longer mention what was said. For it is my aim always to heal my friends rather than to cause them sorrow.
>
> Θεραπευτική. Ἐγὼ μὲν ἐφ' οἷς εἶπον λόγοις μετῆλθον ἔργῳ, τὸ γὰρ σύνολον οὐκ ἐνόμιζόν σέ ποτε λυπηθήσεσθαι· εἰ δ' ἐπὶ τοῖς λεχθεῖσιν ἢ πραχθεῖσιν ἠχθέσθης, ἴσθι, κράτιστε ἀνδρῶν, ὡς οὐκέτι τῶν ῥηθέντων λόγον ὅλως ποτὲ ποιήσομαι. σκοπὸς γάρ μοι θεραπεύειν ἀεὶ τοὺς φίλους ἐστὶν ἤπερ λυπεῖν.

The rudimentary nature of the sample letter in the handbook clearly reveals its structure, the principal sections marked by the μέν – δέ contrast.

---

505 On the emphatic phrase τῇ παρακλήσει ᾗ παρεκλήθη, see Thrall, *Second Epistle*, 1.488 n.18.
506 Ps.-Libanius *Ep. Char.* 19, in Malherbe, *Ancient Epistolary Theorists*, 68–69. On the authorship and date of this handbook, see H. Hinck, "Die Ἐπιστολιμαῖοι Χαρακτῆρες des Pseudo-Libanius," *Neue Jahrbücher für Philologie und Paedagogik* 99 (1869) 537–62; Koskenniemi, *Studien zur Idee und Phraseologie des griechischen Briefes*, 56. The handbook is attributed to Proclus in one stream of the manuscript tradition. Sykutris, "Proclus Περὶ ἐπιστολιμαίου χαρακτῆρος," 108–18 argues that the form ascribed to Proclus is more original.
507 Ps.-Libanius *Ep. Char.* 66, in Malherbe, *Ancient Epistolary Theorists*, 76–77. See also no. 107 (θεραπευτική) of the exampla found in certain codices of Ps.-Libanius in Weichert, *Demetrii et Libanii qui feruntur* ΤΥΠΟΙ ΕΠΙΣΤΟΛΙΚΟΙ *et* ΕΠΙΣΤΟΛΙΜΑΙΟΙ ΧΑΡΑΚΤΗΠΕΣ, 62–63.

The first section reviews what was said and done that occasioned grief, climaxed by an assurance that pain was not intended. The second section acknowledges that distress has been caused, and outlines remedial measures to be taken. The letter concludes with reassurance that the author aims at healing his friends, rather than causing them sorrow.

The agreement between the therapeutic letter in the handbook and Paul's therapeutic epistle in 2 Cor. 1:1–2:13; 7:5–16 is striking. The account of what was said and done in the sample letter (ἐγὼ μὲν ἐφ' οἷς εἶπον λόγοις μετῆλθον ἔργῳ) corresponds to the twin prongs of Paul's proposition in 1:12–14, regarding 1) his conduct towards the Corinthians (ἀνεστράφημεν ἐν τῷ κόσμῳ, περισσοτέρως δὲ πρὸς ὑμᾶς), and 2) the proper understanding of what he wrote (οὐ γὰρ ἄλλα γράφομεν ὑμῖν ἀλλ' ἢ ἃ ἀναγινώσκετε ἢ καὶ ἐπιγινώσκετε), expounded in the first and second proofs, respectively (1:15–22; 1:23–2:4). Paul then explains to the Corinthians that he had no intention of causing them sorrow (ἔκρινα γὰρ ἐμαυτῷ τοῦτο τὸ μὴ πάλιν ἐν λύπῃ πρὸς ὑμᾶς ἐλθεῖν καὶ ἔγραψα ὑμῖν...οὐχ ἵνα λυπηθῆτε, 2:1–4), just as the sample letter of the handbook recommends (τὸ γὰρ σύνολον οὐκ ἐνόμιζόν σέ ποτε λυπηθήσεσθαι). In conformity to the second division in the argument of the sample letter (marked by the δέ clause, εἰ δ' ἐπὶ τοῖς λεχθεῖσιν ἢ πραχθεῖσιν ἠχθέσθης), Paul acknowledges that distress had been caused, first by the wrongdoer (εἰ δέ τις λελύπηκεν, κτλ., 2:5), and then by his own epistle (ὅτι εἰ καὶ ἐλύπησα ὑμᾶς ἐν τῇ ἐπιστολῇ, κτλ., 7:8). Finally, Paul reassures the Corinthians that his aim had always been therapeutic, namely, to provoke the repentance that leads to salvation and brings no regret (7:9–10), just as the author of the handbook recommends. The letter of 2 Cor. 1:1–2:13; 7:5–16 is much closer to the sample letter of the handbook in form, structure, and content than any of the other conciliatory epistles surveyed in our investigation, e.g., Apollonius of Tyana *Ep.* 45, *BGU* II.531 (Chairemon to Apollonius). Only if the letter of Marcus Aurelius to Herodes Atticus, excerpted by Philostratus (in *Vit. Soph.* 2.1.562–63),[508] had survived in its entirety, might we have a more perfect example of the therapeutic type of letter than we possess in 2 Cor. 1:1–2:13; 7:5–16.

Paul's decision to write a therapeutic letter to Corinth represents a second departure from the paradigm of Greco-Roman friendship. For although Paul acknowledges that he had pained the Corinthians "for an hour" by his severe epistle (7:8), we must not forget that this letter was a defensive re-

---

508 Philostratus states that he extracts from the letter only that which bears upon his narrative.

sponse to a grave accusation. The source of grief lay with the wrongdoer, the Christian of highest social standing in Corinth, who had caused pain, not only to Paul, but to the entire community (2:5). Analysis of surviving examples of therapeutic epistles makes clear that the social relationship out of which a letter of the therapeutic type emerges is one of *inequality*. The essential elements of this letter-type are as follows: 1) the writer is more powerful than the recipient, and thus capable of inflicting the "pain" (λύπη) which is the occasion of the letter; 2) the recipient has been "grieved" (λυπηθῆναι) by the writer; 3) the writer is attempting to "heal" or "conciliate" (θεραπεύειν) the recipient, so as to restore the relationship.[509] An asymmetrical social relationship characterizes all surviving examples of therapeutic letters: thus, Chairemon conciliates his estate-manager Apollonius in respect to harsh criticism embodied in a previous letter;[510] Apollonius of Tyana conciliates his younger brother Hestiaeus in regard to their dispute over money;[511] Marcus Aurelius conciliates his former teacher Herodes Atticus in relation to grief that Marcus had caused by an unfavorable legal verdict.[512] An understanding of the social relationship that defines a letter of the therapeutic type, and an appreciation of the customary actions that took place in this context, reveal Paul's decision to write a therapeutic epistle to Gaius and the Corinthians as *a strategic attempt to rearrange the established social relations of power within Greco-Roman friendship*.

Within this shift in paradigm, a second innovation—of degree rather than kind—is observable in Paul's therapeutic epistle, in comparison with other letters of the conciliatory type: *the intensity of Paul's appeal to the emotions*. To be sure, all conciliatory epistles speak to the emotions, since the aim (σκοπός) of such writing is to heal a wounded friend.[513] Thus, Chairemon's conciliatory apology to his "dear friend" (φίλτατος) Apollonius (*BGU* II.531) is characterized by a more affectionate tone than is found in other papyrus letters.[514] Marcus Aurelius plays upon the emotions of his friend Herodes Atticus, in an attempt to establish a basis for reconciliation in the commonality of affliction: Marcus dwells

---

509 Ps.-Libanius *Ep. Char.* 19, 66. The analysis of the social situation offered here builds upon the approach of Stowers, "Social Typification and the Classification of Ancient Letters" in *The Social World of Formative Christianity*, 78–90.
510 *BGU* II.531.
511 Apollonius of Tyana *Ep.* 45.
512 Philostratus *Vit. soph.* 2.1.562–63.
513 Ps.-Libanius *Ep. Char.* 66.
514 Olsson, *Papyrusbriefe aus der frühesten Römerzeit*, 120.

upon the rigors of his military quarters, laments the recent death of his wife, and remarks upon his own bad health.[515] Yet, there is nothing in the surviving epistolary corpus that approaches Paul's preoccupation with the emotions in 2 Cor. 1:1–2:13; 7:5–16. A summary of the semantic evidence will indicate the depth of Paul's concern with the emotions in this letter.

Paul opens the exordium (1:3–7) with praise of God as "the father of pities" (ὁ πατὴρ τῶν οἰκτιρμῶν) and "God of all consolation" (θεὸς πάσης παρακλήσεως). In the verses that follow, a complex and effective rhetorical figure is created by repetition of a highly charged emotional vocabulary: θλῖψις ("affliction," "distress"), παράκλησις ("comfort," "consolation"), πάθημα ("suffering," "passion"), etc. Paul asserts that his "distress" and "comfort" are "on behalf of" the Corinthians, and voices his hope for the emergence of a community of affection in which he and the Corinthians would be "partners in the same passions" (κοινωνοὶ τῶν αὐτῶν παθημάτων). Paul grounds the possibility of a renewed community of affection with the Corinthians in the fact that "the passions of Christ overflow into us" (περισσεύει τὰ παθήματα τοῦ Χριστοῦ εἰς ἡμᾶς).

In the narration (1:8–11), Paul suppresses mention of the specific incident that caused his "affliction" (θλῖψις) in Asia, and focuses instead upon his resulting psychological condition: "We were so utterly, unbearably crushed (καθ᾿ ὑπερβολὴν ὑπὲρ δύναμιν ἐβαρήθημεν) that we despaired of life itself (ἐξαπορηθῆναι ἡμᾶς καὶ τοῦ ζῆν)." The proposition that Paul sets forth in 1:12–14 concerns the motivation of his conduct, his "simplicity" (ἁπλότης) and "sincerity" (εἰλικρίνεια); the issue of the epistle is a matter of "conscience" (συνείδησις).

In the arguments by which Paul justifies his actions (1:15–2:4), he explains that the criterion that guided his conduct towards the Corinthians was his determination to be neither the agent nor the victim of "pain" (λύπη), but rather the sponsor and recipient of "joy" (χαρά). Paul concludes the paragraph with a vivid depiction of the emotional state in which he wrote to Corinth: "much distress" (πολλὴ θλῖψις), "anguish of heart" (συνοχὴ καρδίας), "many tears" (πολλὰ δάκρυα), clear indications of the abundant "love" (ἀγάπη) that he feels for the Corinthians. Above all, Paul is concerned for the emotional well-being of the wrongdoer (2:5–11), urging the Corinthians to "forgive" (χαρίσασθαι) and "console" (παρακαλέσαι) him, and reaffirm their "love" (ἀγάπη), lest he be "drowned by excessive sorrow" (τῇ περισσοτέρᾳ λύπῃ καταποθῇ).

---

515 Philostratus *Vit. soph.* 2.1.562–63.

Paul's account of the emotional state in which he awaited news of the effect of his letter upon the Corinthians (in 2:12–13; 7:5–7) vividly portrays his anxiety: "I did not have any relief in my spirit" (οὐκ ἔσχηκα ἄνεσιν τῷ πνεύματί μου); "our flesh had no rest" (οὐδεμίαν ἔσχηκεν ἄνεσιν ἡ σάρξ ἡμῶν); "afflicted in every way" (ἐν παντὶ θλιβόμενοι); "fightings without" (ἔξωθεν μάχαι); "fears within" (ἔσωθεν φόβοι). But the arrival of Titus brought "consolation" (παράκλησις) for the "downcast" (ταπεινός) apostle. Paul's summary of what Titus reported from Corinth focuses entirely upon the Corinthians' emotional response: "yearning desire" (ἐπιπόθησις), "mourning" (ὀδυρμός), "zeal" (ζῆλος). Paul's final argument (7:8–13a) appeals to the emotional effect of his letter upon the Corinthians as proof of the integrity of his conduct. Paul acknowledges that he "grieved" (ἐλύπησα) the Corinthians by means of his epistle, and that for a time he even "regretted" (μετεμελόμην) having sent it. But second thoughts have been replaced by rejoicing (χαίρω) at the discovery that the grief that the Corinthians experienced (ἐλυπήθητε) resulted in "repentance" (μετάνοια), rather than "despair," or "spiritual death" (θάνατος).[516] Paul then asserts, remarkably, that there is such a thing as "godly grief" (ἡ κατὰ θεὸν λύπη) and that the Corinthians have experienced it, and then proceeds to analyze in extraordinary detail the stages of an emotional progress: "earnestness" (σπουδή), "eagerness to clear oneself" (ἀπολογία), "indignation" (ἀγανάκτησις), "fear" (φόβος), "yearning desire" (ἐπιπόθησις), "zeal" (ζῆλος), "retribution" (ἐκδίκησις).[517] Paul assures the Corinthians that they have proven themselves entirely "guiltless" (ἀγνοί) in the affair of the wrongdoer and pronounces himself "comforted" (παρακεκλήμεθα).

The peroration of the letter (7:13b-16), at once jubilant and circumspect, celebrates the restoration of Paul's "confidence" (θαρρέω) in the Corinthians by appealing to the "joy" (χαρά) of his envoy Titus. Once again, the content of Titus' report is completely supplanted by Paul's account of its emotional effect: "We rejoiced (ἐχάρημεν) even much more at the joy (χαρά) of Titus, because his spirit has been set at rest (ἀναπέπαυται τὸ πνεῦμα αὐτοῦ) by you all." Titus' emotional response to the Corinthi-

---

516 For θάνατος as "spiritual death" in 7:10, see BDAG 443, s.v. For overtones of "despair," see the resonance with 1:8–9, ἐκ τηλικούτου θανάτου.

517 That the series of emotions in 7:11 is not casually constructed is indicated by the fact that exactly seven terms are chosen, and that each term is highlighted by the anaphoric use of ἀλλά. Cf. Windisch, *Der zweite Korintherbrief*, 234; Thrall, *Second Epistle*, 1.493.

ans is viscerally described, fully warranting Paul's "boast" (καύχησις) in the Corinthians, so that he was not "put to shame" (κατῃσχύνθην): Titus' "bowels" (σπλάγχνα) go out to the Corinthians, as he remembers how they welcomed him with "fear and trembling" (φόβος καὶ τρόμος). The peroration climaxes with a heartfelt affirmation: "I rejoice because I have complete confidence in you!" (χαίρω ὅτι ἐν παντὶ θαρρῶ ἐν ὑμῖν).

Even a summary of the evidence already makes clear that the emotional vocabulary of this letter far exceeds the φιλοφρόνησις required to maintain or restore a relationship. What a summary cannot convey is the heightened affective atmosphere created by the repetition of key terms, such as θλῖψις, παράκλησις, πάθημα, λύπη, χαρά, and their associated verb forms,[518] and by the repeated use of hyperbolic expressions, such as πᾶς, περισσοτέρως, καθ' ὑπερβολήν, ὑπὲρ δύναμιν, etc.[519] Nor can a summary give a sense of the sonority achieved by rhetorical figures, such as *traductio*,[520] or the excitement generated by the skillful use of the particles,[521] or the caution embodied in the conditionals,[522] or the sensitivity suggested by the repeated recourse to metonymy.[523] All in all, it is difficult to imagine that there is another letter from antiquity so obsessive

---

518 For θλῖψις, see 1:4 (twice); 1:6; 1:8; 2:4; 7:5; for παράκλησις/παρακαλέω, see 1:3; 1:4 (four times); 1:5; 1:6 (three times); 2:7; 2:8; 7:6 (twice); 7:7 (twice); for πάθημα/πάσχω, see 1:5; 1:6 (twice); 1:7; for λύπη/λυπέω, see 2:1; 2:2 (twice); 2:3; 2:4; 2:5 (twice); 2:7; 7:8 (twice); 7:9 (three times); 7:10 (twice); 7:11; for χαρά/χαίρω, see 1:24; 2:3; 7:7; 7:9; 7:13 (twice); 7:16. On repetition as a figure in 2 Cor., esp. 1:3–7, see Windisch, *Der zweite Korintherbrief*, 36–43.

519 For πᾶς, see 1:3; 1:4 (twice); 2:3; 2:5; 2:9; 7:5; 7:11; 7:13; 7:15; 7:16; for περισσοτέρως, see 1:12; 2:4; 7:13; 7:15. The expressions καθ' ὑπερβολήν and ὑπὲρ δύναμιν are compounded with one another in 1:8 as modifiers of ἐβαρήθημεν. These are by no means the only examples of pleonasm in 1:1–2:13; 7:5–16: see, e.g., τηλικοῦτος in 1:10, πολλοί in 1:11 (twice). On pleonasm as a figure, see Smyth, *Greek Grammar*, 681–82.

520 In 1:3–7 and 2:1–3. On the device of *traductio* (the frequent employment of the same word, or cognate words, at short intervals), see Denniston, *Greek Prose Style*, 80–81.

521 E.g., καὶ γάρ in 7:5, ἰδοὺ γάρ in 7:11. On the use of particles to express emotion, see Demetrius *Eloc.* 57; cf. Denniston, *Greek Particles*, lxxiii, 109.

522 E.g., εἰ δέ τις in 2:5, εἴ τι in 2:10. On the caution expressed by means of these clauses, see Heinrici, *Der zweite Brief*, 93–94; Windisch, *Der zweite Korintherbrief*, 84, 90.

523 E.g., the shift from βούλομαι to βουλεύομαι in 1:15–17; on this substitution, see Halmel, *Der zweite Korintherbrief*, 53–54. Note also the subtle way in which χάρις replaces χαρά in 1:15; on this substitution, see already Bleek, "Erörterungen," 621–22.

in its concern for the emotions, so vulnerable in its disclosure of the author's emotional state, or so solicitous in its practice of what should be called "emotional therapy."

A full appreciation of the originality of Paul's appeal to the emotions in 2 Cor. 1:1–2:13; 7:5–16 requires some attention to emotional therapy as practiced by Paul's contemporaries. Among the philosophers of the Hellenistic and Roman age, a vigorous discussion arose about the nature of the emotions and their function in moral life.[524] The surviving literature, which is unfortunately fragmentary,[525] nevertheless makes clear that the philosophers aimed not only to understand the psychological basis of the emotions, but also to develop kinds of therapy to restrain, modify, or even eliminate the emotions.[526] The Stoics, in particular, elaborated a systematic theory of the emotions, in which certain terms acquired a technical meaning.[527] Λύπη, for example, which is the object of Paul's concern in his therapeutic epistle, was one of the four generic emotions, according to the Stoic doctrine, alongside "pleasure" (ἡδονή), "fear" (φόβος), and "desire" (ἐπιθυμία).[528] The therapy of λύπη, that is, the development of a dependable method of consolation, was the goal of the influential

---

[524] To mention only the most important contributions to this growing body of literature: W. W. Fortenbaugh, *Aristotle on Emotions* (London: Duckworth, 1975; second edition 2002); Martha Nussbaum, *The Therapy of Desire: Theory and Practice in Hellenistic Ethics* (Princeton: Princeton University Press, 1994); S. Braund and C. Gill (eds.), *The Passions in Roman Thought and Literature* (Cambridge: Cambridge University Press, 1997); J. Sihvola and T. Engberg-Pedersen (eds.), *The Emotions in Hellenistic Philosophy* (Dordrecht: Kluwer Academic Publishers, 1998); Richard Sorabji, *Emotion and Peace of Mind: From Stoic Agitation to Christian Temptation* (Oxford; Oxford University Press, 2000); Konstan, *The Emotions of the Ancient Greeks*; Margaret R. Graver, *Stoicism and Emotion* (Chicago: University of Chicago Press, 2007); John T. Fitzgerald (ed.), *Passions and Moral Progress in Greco-Roman Thought* (London: Routledge, 2008).

[525] The most significant loss is Chrysippus' *On Affections* (Περὶ παθῶν), preserved only in quotations embedded in books 3 and 4 of Cicero's *Tusculan Disputations*, and in Galen's great work *De placitis Hippocratis et Platonis*. See Teun Tieleman, *Chrysippus' On Affections: Reconstruction and Interpretation* (Leiden: Brill, 2003).

[526] P. L. Entralgo, *The Therapy of the Word in Classical Antiquity* (New Haven: Yale University Press, 1970) esp. 97–107; W. D. Furley, "Antiphon der Athener: Ein Sophist als Psychotherapeut," *RhM* 135 (1992) 198–216; Nussbaum, *The Therapy of Desire*; Harris, *Restraining Rage*, esp. ch. 15; Tieleman, *Chrysippus' On Affections*, 140–97; Graver, *Stoicism and Emotion*, esp. 191–211.

[527] J. Sihvola and T. Engberg-Pedersen, "Introduction" to *The Emotions in Hellenistic Philosophy*, viii; Graver, *Stoicism and Emotion*, 53–60.

[528] Tad Brennan, "The Old Stoic Theory of Emotions" in *The Emotions in Hellenistic Philosophy*, 21–70, esp. 30–31; Graver, *Stoicism and Emotion*, 53–56.

fourth book of Chrysippus' *On Affections,* which, with its special title, Θεραπευτικόν (*Therapeutics*), seems to have been read and used separately from the rest.[529] The results of the philosophers' efforts to restrain or eliminate λύπη held a special attraction for practical intellectuals, such as Cicero, as one can see from books 3 and 4 of his *Tusculan Disputations.*[530]

It is in respect to the status of λύπη that Paul's view of the emotions differs most surprisingly from the fully developed systems of his intellectual contemporaries. Among the Stoics, and those who, like Cicero and Seneca, sought to combine Stoic teaching with Platonic psychology,[531] λύπη (Latin *aegritudo*) was the most problematic emotion. Cicero gives expression to this attitude:

> Do you suppose then that there is any possibility of the wise man being overwhelmed with distress (*aegritudo*), that is to say, with wretchedness? Indeed, while every passion is wretchedness, distress (*aegritudo*) is actually being put on the rack. Appetite involves eagerness, exuberant joy involves frivolity, fear involves humiliation, but distress (*aegritudo*) involves worse things—decay, torture, torment, repulsiveness. It tears and devours the soul and completely destroys it. Unless we strip it off and cast it aside, we cannot be free from wretchedness.[532]

The problematic nature of λύπη can be seen most clearly in the total absence of a rational counterpart to λύπη from the list of "good emotions" (εὐπάθειαι) which the Stoics held to characterize the life of the sage.[533] As is well known, the Stoics advocated the complete elimination of the "pas-

---

529 Galen *De placitis Hippocratis et Platonis* 5.7.52; cf. Tieleman, *Chrysippus' On Affections,* 140–41.
530 Margaret Graver, *Cicero on the Emotions: Tusculan Disputations 3 and 4* (Chicago: University of Chicago Press, 2002) 24, 27, 34–35, 121–23, 191, 205, 219.
531 On the combination of the Stoic view of the emotions with Platoic psychology in late Hellenistic and Roman thought, see J. M. Cooper, "Posidonius on Emotions" in *The Emotions in Hellenistic Philosophy,* 71–111; Richard Sorabji, "Chrysippus – Posidonius – Seneca: A High-level Debate on Emotion" in *The Emotions in Hellenistic Philosophy,* 149–69; Andrew Erskine, "Cicero and the expression of grief" in *The Passions in Roman Thought and Literature,* 36–47; Brad Inwood, "Seneca and Psychological Dualism" in *Passions and Perceptions,* ed. J. Brunschwig and M. Nussbaum (Cambridge: Cambridge University Press, 1993) 150–83.
532 Cicero *Tusc.* 3.13.27.
533 Cicero *Tusc.* 4.6.14. Cf. Brennan, "The Old Stoic Theory of Emotions" in *The Emotions in Hellenistic Philosophy,* 35, 54–57; Graver, *Stoicism and Emotion,* 53–54.

sions" (πάθη) or "vicious emotions."[534] This "absolutist" position was popular among Greek and Roman thinkers,[535] and even with Paul's Jewish contemporaries, Philo and the author of 4 Maccabees.[536] Yet, the Stoics allowed that the sage might enjoy certain other conditions which they called "good emotions" (εὐπάθειαι), which differed from the passions in being "accurate, veridical attributions of goodness and badness" to things.[537] So, to "fear" (φόβος) there corresponded the rational emotion "caution" (εὐλάβεια), to "desire" (ἐπιθυμία) corresponded "volition" (βούλησις), and to "pleasure" (ἡδονή) corresponded "joy" (χαρά).[538] But there was no fourth εὐπάθεια: the sage could have no constructive relationship to λύπη, so destructive was this emotion of moral life, so repulsive to the man who wished to achieve self-mastery.[539] This attitude toward λύπη animates Dio Chrysostom's rhetorical questions in his discourse Περὶ λύπης: "What more abject creature is there than a man who is held in thrall to pain? (καίτοι τί μὲν ταπεινότερον ἀνδρὸς λυπουμένου;) What sight is there so shameful?"[540] Observing that "life is full of painful things," Dio adopts the Stoic therapy: "but one should tear that morbid state out of his soul completely, get a firm hold on the truth that the intelligent man ought not to feel pain about anything whatever (ὅτι μὴ λυπητέον ἐστὶ περὶ μηδενὸς τῷ νοῦν ἔχοντι), and be a free man henceforth."[541] The absence of a positive counterpart to λύπη from the Stoic system of the emotions is not accidental, but rather inheres organically in the Stoic construction of emotional life.[542] Indeed, it might be argued

---

534 Brennan, "The Old Stoic Theory of Emotions" in *The Emotions in Hellenistic Philosophy*, 34; Graver, *Stoicism and Emotion*, 55–58.
535 Harris, *Restraining Rage*, 26, 104–20.
536 Renehan, "The Greek Philosophic Background of Fourth Maccabees," 221–38; Stowers, "Fourth Maccabees" in *Harper's Bible Commentary*, 924; Aune, "Mastery of the Passions: Philo, 4 Maccabees and Earliet Christianity" in *Hellenization Revisited*, 125–58.
537 Brennan, "The Old Stoic Theory of Emotions" in *The Emotions in Hellenistic Philosophy*, 34, 54–57; Graver, *Stoicism and Emotion*, 51–55, 203–204.
538 Cicero *Tusc.* 4.6.12–14; cf. Brennan, "The Old Stoic Theory of Emotions" in *The Emotions in Hellenistic Philosophy*, 34–36; Graver, *Stoicism and Emotion*, 51–55, 203–204.
539 Cicero *Tusc.* 4.6.12–14; cf. Brennan, "The Old Stoic Theory of Emotions" in *The Emotions in Hellenistic Philosophy*, 34–36; Graver, *Stoicism and Emotion*, 51–55, 203–204.
540 Dio Chrysostom *Or.* 16.1.
541 Dio Chrysostom *Or.* 16.4.
542 Brennan, "The Old Stoic Theory of Emotions" in *The Emotions in Hellenistic Philosophy*, 35; Graver, *Stoicism and Emotion*, 53–55, 194, 204.

that the aim of the Stoic system was to make the wise man invulnerable to λύπη, however many frustrations and dangers life might hold, and that the promise of this invulnerability constituted the principal attraction of the Stoic theory to the social elites.[543]

What, then, does it mean that Paul not only acknowledges that he and the wrongdoer and, indeed, all of the Corinthians have experienced λύπη, but then goes on to dissect the experience in a detail that Cicero and Seneca might have found humiliating? Paul even asserts, astonishingly, that there is a "divine distress" (ἡ κατὰ θεὸν λύπη) which leads by certain emotional stages to "salvation" (7:9–10). Comparison with the writings of Paul's philosophical contemporaries makes clear how anomalous, even shocking, this valorization of λύπη must have seemed. Cicero, for example, states unequivocally, that those who are subject to "distress" (*aegritudo*) are "fools" (*stulti*).[544] Dio Chrysostom asserts that "accepting servitude to pain is altogether irrational and strange (τὸ δὲ λύπῃ δεδουλῶσθαι παντελῶς ἄλογον καὶ θαυμαστόν)."[545] To be sure, Paul had one influential predecessor in his strange assertion that λύπη plays a constructive role in moral life: Socrates. According to Plato, Socrates actually took pride in the fact that he had caused the Athenians λύπη by means of his philosophical activity,[546] and understood his "plaguing" (λυπεῖν) of his contemporaries as his "service to the god."[547] But this aspect of Socrates' philosophical activity proved puzzling to later thinkers, including those who adopted the psychology of Plato. Cicero relates a story in which Socrates caused "distress" (*aegritudo*) to the young aristocrat Alcibiades by convincing him that he was not the man he ought to have been, and that there was no difference, despite his high birth, between him and any manual laborer. "Alcibiades then became very upset, begging Socrates with tears to take away his shameful character and give him a virtuous one."[548] Cicero recognizes the conundrum which this tradition poses

---

543 See, e.g., Seneca *De Cons. Sap.* 2.1.3; *Ben.* 2.25.2.
544 Cicero *Tusc.* 4.6.14.
545 Dio Chrysostom *Or.* 16.1.
546 Plato *Apol.* 41E.
547 Plato *Apol.* 23B.
548 Cicero *Tusc.* 3.32.77; trans. Graver, *Cicero on the Emotions*, 35. See also Plutarch *Alc.* 4; *Adul. am.* 69E-F. The anecdote may have its origin in Plato *Symp.* 215E-216C. Compare Lucian's account of the effect of a certain Platonic philosopher Nigrinus upon an inquiring student in *Nigr.* 4: "Then I felt hurt (ἐλυπούμην) because he had criticized what was dearest to me—wealth and money and reputation—and I all but cried over their downfall."

for the Stoics, whose definition of "distress" he embraces.[549] But Cicero is not sure what to say about a Socrates who does not regard "distress" as "the greatest wretchedness."[550]

In the psychagogic literature of the late first century, one encounters sentiments on the role of pain in moral progress that provide partial parallels to Paul's conviction about the salvific purpose of λύπη. Thus, Plutarch allows that one may hurt a friend in order to help him: "One ought to hurt (λυπεῖν) a friend only to help him, and ought not by hurting him to kill friendship, but to use the stinging word as a medicine which restores and preserves health in that to which it is applied."[551] Similarly, Epictetus regards the philosophical classroom as a place for medical treatment: "Men, the lecture room of the philosopher is a hospital; you ought not to walk out of it in pleasure, but in pain."[552] In a text representing harsh Cynicism, Democritus is credited with the desire "to discover something more painful (λυπηρόν) to use against" his fellow citizens, in order to bring about moral reform.[553] But the authors of the psychagogic literature attribute only a utilitarian value to λύπη in the pursuit of moral aims. Moreover, Plutarch takes care to limit the degree of λύπη which the moral philosopher inflicts: "The smart from philosophy which sinks deep in young men of good character is healed by the very words which inflicted the hurt. For this reason, he who is taken to task must feel and suffer some smart (διὸ δεῖ πάσχειν μέν τι καὶ δάκνεσθαι), yet he should not be crushed or dispirited."[554] Among none of Paul's intellectual contemporaries does one encounter a valorization of "divine λύπη" which leads by certain emotional stages to "salvation" or psychic health (7:10–11). Having allowed that a certain kind of pain—namely, that which is suffered in accordance with God's will (κατὰ θεόν)—contributes

---

549 Cicero *Tusc.*. 3.31.74–75.
550 Cicero *Tusc.* 3.32.77; cf. 3.13.27. See the penetrating analysis of the structural problem posed for Stoicism by the "tears of Alcibiades" anecdote by Graver, *Stoicism and Emotion*, 191–211.
551 Plutarch *Adul. am.*. 55C. Glad (*Paul and Philodemus*, 317) cites other relevant texts from Plutarch: *Adul. am.* 66B; 70D-E; 73D-E; *Virt. mor.* 452C; *Tranq. an.* 476F.
552 Epictetus *Diatr.*. 3.23.30. But here the verb is ἀλγέω, rather than λυπέω. This text is cited as a parallel to 2 Cor. 2:5–11; 7:9–10 by Fredrickson, "Paul, Hardships,and Suffering" in *Paul in the Greco-Roman World*, 176.
553 Ps.-Hippocrates *Ep.* 17.45. On the probable first-century date of this letter collection, see Wesley D. Smith, *Hippocrates: Pseudepigraphic Writings* (Leiden: Brill, 1990) 21–22, 28–29, 43–44.
554 Plutarch *Rect. rat. aud.* 47 A.

positively to moral life, indeed, confers the highest good upon existence—σωτηρία—the door is open to a swarm of other emotions which the Stoics strenuously sought to exclude, such as "indignation" (ἀγανάκτησις), "fear" (φόβος), "desire" (ἐπιπόθησις), etc., for which Paul not only makes a place in Christian life, but even declares that their cumulative effect has rendered the Corinthian Christians "pure," ἁγνοί (7:11), a quality which the Stoics attributed to the wise man who had extirpated his emotions![555] What is the source of this revolution in the concept of psychic health that we see unfolding in the pages of Paul's therapeutic epistle? Early in the letter (1:5–7), Paul explains that the possibility of a community of affection among the followers of Jesus is grounded in the fact that "the passions of the Messiah overflow into us" (περισσεύει τὰ παθήματα τοῦ Χριστοῦ εἰς ἡμᾶς). Paul alludes here to his fundamental conviction that "Christ died for us," that Christ was "crucified on our behalf."[556]

We may well ask ourselves how Paul's new therapy of the emotions would have affected a man such as Gaius of Corinth, whose values and attitudes were formed by popular Stoicism (if the conclusions of our exegesis and prosopography have merit). Would Gaius have been surprised that Paul did not adopt the Chrysippean therapy, which Cicero judged "the most dependable method"?[557] Chrysippus held that "the key to consolation is to get rid of the person's belief that mourning is something he ought to do, something just and appropriate."[558] Would Gaius have been perplexed by Paul's novel idea that λύπη was not merely useful in small doses, but was a thorough-going course of treatment from which one emerged into psychic wholeness? But we should also consider the alternative scenario: perhaps Paul's valorization of λύπη gave meaning to the grief by which Gaius was engulfed (2:7), by attributing his pain to a divine origin (7:9–10). After all, Cicero acknowledged that the rational consolation of Chrysippus was "a hard method to apply in time of distress," when a person was generally unwilling to accept that his grief was merely a mistake in judgment.[559]

---

555 Diogenes Laertius 7.119.
556 See the important discussion of this idea by Cilliers Breytenbach, "'Christus starb für uns'. Zur Tradition und paulinischen Rezeption des sogenannten 'Sterbeformeln'," *NTS* 29 (2003) 447–75.
557 Cicero *Tusc.* 3.79.
558 Cicero *Tusc.* 3.76.
559 Cicero *Tusc.* 3.79.

In any case, Paul seems to have taken care to lessen the shock of his novel therapy by the way in which he portrays himself in the arguments of his therapeutic letter. Recall that Paul seeks to prove his sincerity by appealing, first, to his "volition" (βούλησις) in the formulation of his plan to come to Corinth (1:15–22: ἐβουλόμην,...βουλόμενος). Then, Paul represents himself as having exercised "caution" (εὐλάβεια), "sparing" (φειδόμενος) the Corinthians further grief, by delaying his return to Corinth (1:23–2:4). Finally, Paul dramatizes the transformation of his anxiety into "joy" (χαρά) through the arrival of Titus with his good report of a change of heart among the Corinthians (7:7, 9, 13, 16). It can hardly be a coincidence that, in a letter so preoccupied with the emotions, and so assiduous in its practice of emotional therapy, Paul should portray himself as having attained the consistencies of the wise man—volition (βούλησις), caution (εὐλάβεια), and joy (χαρά). Indeed, Paul's account of his "confidence" in prospect of renewed affection with the Corinthians (7:16, ἐν παντὶ θαρρῶ ἐν ὑμῖν) probably also belongs to the portrait of himself as one who has attained the disposition of a wise man. Margaret Graver has argued that in one stream of the Stoic tradition the eupathic response that replaces fear was "confidence," rather than "caution," appealing to a statement of Cicero in the *Tusculan Disputations*, and to an extended discussion of "caution" and "confidence" in Epictetus.[560] By demonstrating the eupathic quality of his response to the Corinthians, Paul suggests that the ethical consistency of a wise man can be attained by emotional "overflow," as well as by emotional thrift, through participation in "the passions of the Christ" (1:5–7).

A final shift in the paradigm of Greco-Roman friendship relates to the *forgiveness* which Paul urges the Corinthians to extend to the wrongdoer (2:7), and which Paul himself very tactfully grants (2:10). Correcting the desire of a minority of Corinthians to impose a harsher punishment,[561] Paul insists, in rather strong terms (τοὐναντίον μᾶλλον), that the Corinthians ought "to forgive and console" (χαρίσασθαι καὶ παρακαλέσαι) the wrongdoer (2:7).[562] Indeed, Paul insists (2:9) that the willingness of

---

560 Graver, "The Status of Confidence in Stoic Classification" in *Stoicism and Emotion*, 213–20, citing Cicero *Tusc.* 4.66 ("And just as confidence [*confidere*] is proper but fear improper, so also joy is proper and gladness improper") and Epictetus *Diatr.* 2.1.1–7.
561 Kennedy, *Second and Third Epistles*, 99–109; Lake, *Earlier Epistles*, 170–72; Krenkel, *Beiträge*, 302; Plummer, *Second Epistle*, 58.
562 Windisch, *Der zweite Korintherbrief*, 87; Barrett, *Second Epistle*, 82; Furnish, *II Corinthians*, 153.

the Corinthians to forgive the wrongdoer is a "test" of the quality of their character (δοκιμή),[563] and that forgiveness is not optional, but is a measure of their obedience (εἰ εἰς πάντα ὑπήκοοί ἐστε).[564] In a sentence composed with great circumspection (2:10), Paul makes it clear that he has already forgiven the wrongdoer (καὶ γὰρ ἐγὼ ὃ κεχάρισμαι, εἴ τι κεχάρισμαι), while intimating to the Corinthians that their forgiveness is needed to complete the process of reconciliation (ᾧ δέ τι χαρίζεσθε, κἀγώ).[565]

Paul's insistence upon forgiveness has little precedent in Greco-Roman literature on the emotions. Recent studies of forgiveness in the classical world have noted that none of the philosophical schools seems to have taken much interest in forgiveness.[566] Charles Griswold asserts that "Plato never sees it [forgiveness] as a virtue or commendable quality—certainly not one of any significance."[567] The reason for Plato's neglect of forgiveness, according to Griswold, is his assumption that a good man is invulnerable to harm, and thus has nothing to forgive. David Konstan observes that Aristotle's analysis of appeasement of anger in the *Rhetoric* focuses upon relations of power and status, and makes no mention of forgiveness.[568] Konstan further notes that the Stoics taught that a wise man would disdain a slight; but that does not mean that the wise man would be inclined to forgiveness, for that would be to ignore the claims of justice, in effect to condone the crime.[569] In his treatise on clemency, Seneca asks: "Why will a wise person not forgive (*ignoscet*)?" Seneca explains that "pardon (*venia*) is the remission of a deserved penalty." But the wise man acts according to what is due, so he will not remit the penalty for an intentional wrong.[570] Seneca allows that a sage will spare (*parcet*) an offender, and try to improve him (*corriget*); thus, "he will act as though he forgave, but he will not forgive, since

---

563 Thrall, *Second Epistle*, 1.178 n.345.
564 Windisch, *Der zweite Korintherbrief*, 90–91.
565 See the analysis of the subtle sentence by Windisch, *Der zweite Korintherbrief*, 90–91.
566 Charles Griswold, "Plato and Forgiveness," *Ancient Philosophy* 27 (2007) 269–87; David Konstan, "Remorse, Repentance and Forgiveness in the Classical World," *Phoenix* 62 (2008) 243–54.
567 Griswold, "Plato and Forgiveness," 272.
568 Konstan, "Remorse, Repentance and Forgiveness," 246.
569 Konstan, "Remorse, Repentance and Forgiveness," 247, citing *SVF* 3.395 = Stobaeus 2.91.10.
570 Seneca *Clem.* 2.7.1.

he who forgives confesses that he has failed to do something that should be done."⁵⁷¹

Two final moments in Paul's therapeutic epistle merit our attention for what they contribute to Paul's quest for reconciliation with the wrongdoer. Explaining his decision not to return to Corinth in grief, Paul asks: "For if I cause you pain, then who is there to make me glad, except the one who has been pained by me? (εἰ γὰρ ἐγὼ λυπῶ ὑμᾶς, καὶ τίς ὁ εὐφραίνων με εἰ μὴ ὁ λυπούμενος ἐξ ἐμοῦ, 2:2).⁵⁷² Paul's reference to ὁ λυπούμενος is formulated generally, so that any Corinthian who might have been saddened by Paul might hear himself addressed.⁵⁷³ But in view of the content of the following paragraph (2:5–11), in which Paul expresses his concern for one Corinthian in particular, that is, the one who is in danger of drowning in "excessive λύπη," it seems likely that Paul intended the singular participle ὁ λυπούμενος to have a special resonance for this individual.⁵⁷⁴ In a tactful way, Paul takes responsibility for the distress that Gaius has suffered and is still suffering, and anticipates a future occasion on which Gaius will be "the one who gives joy" (ὁ εὐφραίνων).

In the final clause of the narration (1:11), Paul asks for the Corinthians' cooperation in prayer: "as you also join in helping on our behalf by intercessory prayer, so that from many persons thanksgiving might be offered on our behalf for the gift granted to us through many" (συνυπουργούντων καὶ ὑμῶν ὑπὲρ ἡμῶν τῇ δεήσει, ἵνα ἐκ πολλῶν προσώπων τὸ εἰς ἡμᾶς χάρισμα διὰ πολλῶν εὐχαριστηθῇ ὑπὲρ ἡμῶν). What is "the gracious gift" (τὸ χάρισμα) that Paul hopes will be the object of the Corinthians' supplication? In the context of the immediately preceding verse (1:10), most commentators take τὸ χάρισμα to refer to the divine act of deliverance from mortal danger encountered when Paul was in Asia.⁵⁷⁵ But several features of the wording of 1:11 suggest that Paul has a future "act of grace" in mind. The purpose clause (ἵνα...εὐχαριστηθῇ) points toward a future occasion when the goal of the Corinthains' intercessory prayers will be fulfilled.⁵⁷⁶ The singular form χάρισμα suggests an event that will

---

571 Seneca *Clem.* 2.7.2.
572 On the force of the particle καί in this sentence, see Thrall, *Second Epistle*, 1.166–67.
573 Thrall, *Second Epistle*, 1.165–66.
574 Martin, *2 Corinthians*, 35.
575 Bachmann, *Der zweite Brief*, 42; Lietzmann, *An die Korinther I-II*, 101; Plummer, *Second Epistle*, 21; Barrett, *Second Epistle*, 62; Furnish, *II Corinthians*, 115.
576 Bultmann, *Der zweite Brief*, 35.

occur only once.⁵⁷⁷ The definite article implies something already known to the Corinthians.⁵⁷⁸ The phrase διὰ πολλῶν probably qualifies the immediately preceding τὸ εἰς ἡμᾶς χάρισμα, rather than the following εὐχαριστηθῇ: thus, Paul means "the χάρισμα granted us by the agency of many people."⁵⁷⁹ Therefore, serious consideration should be given to the possibility that "the gift" (τὸ χάρισμα) of 1:11 refers to Paul's collection for the poor saints in Jerusalem, and that Paul is asking the Corinthians to renew their commitment to partnership in this ministry by joining others in prayer. This interpretation is supported by Paul's repeated use of the term χάρις in reference to the collection in 2 Cor. 8,⁵⁸⁰ where it almost acquires technical status.⁵⁸¹ That Paul chooses χάρισμα rather than χάρις to denote the charitable gift in 1:11 may reflect the fact that the collection in Macedonia has come to completion, since verbal substantives in –μα "specify the *result* of the action for the most part."⁵⁸² Other terms associated with the collection in 2 Cor. 8 and 9 appear in 1:11: πρόσωπον (cf. 8:24), εὐχαριστέω (cf. 9:11, 12), διὰ πολλῶν (cf. 9:12), and δέησις (cf. 9:14). Finally, the καί preceding ὑμῶν in 1:11 implies that the Corinthians will be cooperating with others, if they respond to Paul's request for help in his "act of grace." Thus, Paul pictures the Corinthians joining many others, faces upturned to God in grateful joy,⁵⁸³ prayers rising from their lips,⁵⁸⁴ interceding for the completion of the gracious gift entrusted to Paul through many. Although Paul makes his request for intercessory prayer of all the Corinthians,

---

577 Thrall, *Second Epistle*, 1.124.
578 Thrall, *Second Epistle*, 1.124.
579 Barrett, *Second Epistle*, 57; Martin, *2 Corinthians*, 12.
580 See esp. 2 Cor. 8:4: "petitioning us in the form of a sincere request for the gift and partnership in the charitable ministry for the saints" (τὴν χάριν καὶ τὴν κοινωνίαν τῆς διακονίας τῆς εἰς τοὺς ἁγίους); 8:6: "to this purpose we appointed Titus, so that just as he had begun it beforehand, he should also bring this charitable collection to completion for your benefit" (εἰς τὸ παρακαλέσαι ἡμᾶς Τίτον, ἵνα καθὼς προενήρξατο οὕτως καὶ ἐπιτελέσῃ εἰς ὑμᾶς καὶ τὴν χάριν ταύτην); 8:7: "so that you should abound in this gift of charity also" (ἵνα καὶ ἐν ταύτῃ τῇ χάριτι περισσεύητε); 8:19: "not only this, but he was also elected by the churches as our travelling companion in association with this work of charity administered by us (σὺν τῇ χάριτι ταύτῃ τῇ διακονουμένῃ ὑφ' ἡμῶν) for the glory of the Lord and for our zeal." See also 2 Cor. 9:8, 14.
581 See the comments of Betz, *2 Corinthians 8 and 9*, 42, 58–59, 76.
582 BDF §109(2).
583 For this implication of the phrase ἐκ πολλῶν προσώπων, see Bachmann, *Der zweite Brief*, 41.
584 Plummer, *Second Epistle*, 21–22.

the request applies especially to those who have the resources to complete the gift—that is, to Crispus and Gaius.

With renewed confidence in the Corinthians, Paul wrote one final letter to the churches of Achaia, before taking leave of the Macedonians—the letter now preserved in 2 Cor. 9.[585] Among the things that Titus reported to Paul upon his arrival in Macedonia must have been the Achaians' readiness to contribute to the collection for the poor in Jerusalem (9:2).[586] Few echoes of the former conflict remain in Paul's well-calculated appeal for partnership in the collection: only the rhetorical contrast between the "gift of blessing" (εὐλογία) and "greediness" (πλεονεξία) in the provision which Paul makes for the Achaians' contribution to the collection in 9:5,[587] and the exclusion of "distress" (λύπη) and "compulsion" (ἀνάγκη) from the motives for giving in 9:7, recollect the former quarrels. Indeed, Paul portrays the Achaians as God-like in the abundance of their generosity, applying to his readers the words of Ps. 111:9: "He scattered, he gave to the poor; his righteousness remains into eternity" (9:9). Paul's final written word to the Corinthians is a prayer of thanksgiving for their anticipated contribution to the collection: "Thanks be to God for his indescribable gift!" (9:15).

In the winter of 56 A.D.,[588] Paul arrived in Corinth for his third and final visit. If the report of Acts (20:3) is to be trusted,[589] Paul remained in Corinth for three months. During this period, Paul was a guest in the house of Gaius (Rom. 16:23). We have argued above that the hospitality which Gaius extended to Paul on this occasion was not a matter of convenience, but reflected an established social convention for concluding and publicizing reconciliation between formerly alienated friends.[590]

---

585 For the hypothesis that 2 Cor. 9 was originally an independent letter, see Betz, *2 Corinthians 8 and 9*, developing a proposal that goes back to Semler. Betz's overall hypothesis has not been disproven by observations on the phrase περὶ μὲν γάρ, which introduces the letter, by Stowers, "Περὶ μὲν γάρ and the Integrity of 2 Cor. 8 and 9," 340–48. I cannot follow Betz (*2 Corinthians 8 and 9*, 91–93) in regarding 2 Cor. 9 as a letter to the churches of Achaia, excluding Corinth.
586 Cf. Windisch, *Der zweite Korintherbrief*, 270.
587 Cf. Betz, *2 Corinthians 8 and 9*, 96–97.
588 Cf. the chronology of Lüdemann, *Paul, Apostle to the Gentiles*, 263; Murphy-O'Connor, *Paul*, 316, 323.
589 See the critical analysis of this tradition by Lüdemann, *Paul, Apostle to the Gentiles*, 178–79; idem, *Early Christianity according to Acts*, 224.
590 See ch. 4 above. Cf. Epstein, *Personal Enmity in Roman Politics*, 5–11; Hall, *Politeness and Politics*, 71–76.

Chapter Six. History of a Friendship

Can we imagine the scene of reunion between Paul and Gaius? Were there tears and embraces, resolving long-standing conflicts (cf. 2 Cor. 2:4, 7)? Paul had sent "brothers" on ahead of him from Macedonia to arrange things in advance (2 Cor. 9:3, 5). Was the whole congregation of Christians at Corinth present to witness the reconciliation?

How important was Paul's reconciliation with the wrongdoer, Gaius? The importance of this development is measured by the visionary quality of Paul's thought and the ethical consistency of his actions during the period of his residence with Gaius: for it was in the house of Gaius that Paul wrote his last and greatest epistle to the Romans (Rom. 16:22–23); and it was here that Paul announced his audacious plan for a new mission in Rome and in faraway Spain (Rom. 15:23–24, 28); and it was here that Paul summoned the courage to accompany the collection to Jerusalem in person (Rom. 15:25–27), even though he knew that his life was in danger and that the collection might be rejected (Rom. 15:30–32). In sum, Paul's reconciliation with the wrongdoer Gaius created the psychological conditions for the last and most productive period in Paul's life as an apostle of Christ. For a few months in the spring of 56 A.D., Paul must have believed that all things were possible, that all God's promises to him were "Yes" (2 Cor. 1:20).

Bibliography

Reference Works

Balz, H., and G. Schneider, eds. *Exegetisches Wörterbuch zum Neuen Testament.* 3 vols. Stuttgart: Kohlhammer, 1980–1983. English trans. Grand Rapids: Eerdmans, 1990–1993.

Bauer, W. *A Greek-English Lexicon of the New Testament and Other Early Christian Literature.* Trans. and rev. W. F. Arndt, F. W. Gingrich, and F. W. Danker, 3rd ed. Chicago: University of Chicago Press, 2000.

Blass, F., and A. Debrunner. *A Greek Grammar of the New Testament and Other Early Christian Literature.* Trans. and rev. R. W. Funk, Chicago: University of Chicago Press, 1961.

Denniston, J. D. *The Greek Particles.* Oxford: Clarendon Press, 1987.

Galling, K. von, ed. *Die Religion in Geschichte und Gegenwart.* 6 vols. Tübingen: Mohr-Siebeck, 1957–1962.

Glare, P. G. W. *Oxford Latin Dictionary.* Oxford: Clarendon Press, 1982.

Hornblower, S., and A. Spawforth. *The Oxford Classical Dictionary.* Oxford: Oxford University Press, 1996.

Horsley, G. H. R. *New Documents Illustrating Early Christianity.* 7 vols. North Ryde: Macquarie University Ancient History Documentary Research Centre, 1981–2004.

Kittel, G., and G. Friedrich, eds. *Theological Dictionary of the New Testament.* 10 vols. Trans. and ed. G. W. Bromiley. Grand Rapids: Eerdmans, 1964–1976.

Klauser, T., and E. Dassmann, eds. *Reallexikon für Antike und Christentum.* 14 vols. Stuttgart: Hiersemann, 1950–.

Lampe, G. W. H. *A Patristic Greek Lexicon.* Oxford: Clarendon Press, 1961.

Liddell, H. G., and R. Scott. *A Greek-English Lexicon, with a Revised Supplement.* Rev. H. S. Jones and R. McKenzie. Oxford: Clarendon Press, 1996.

Moulton, J. H., and G. Milligan. *The Vocabulary of the Greek Testament Illustrated from the Papyri and Other Non-Literary Sources.* London: Hodder & Stoughton, 1930; repr. Grand Rapids: Eerdmans, 1976.

Preisigke, Friedrich. *Wörterbuch der griechischen Papyrusurkunden mit Einschluss der griechischen Inschriften, Aufschriften, Ostraka, Mumienschilder usw. aus Ägypten.* Berlin, 1924.

Robertson, A. T. *A Grammar of the Greek New Testament in Light of Historical Research.* New York and London: Hodder & Stoughton, 1914; repr. Nashville: Broadman Press, 1931.

Schwyzer, E. *Griechische Grammatik.* 3 vols. München: Beck, 1953.

Smyth, H. W. *Greek Grammar.* Cambridge, MA: Harvard University Press, 1956.

Spicq, C. S. *Theological Lexicon of the New Testament.* 3 vols. Peabody: Hendrickson, 1994.

Stein, A. and L. Petersen. *Prosopographia Imperii Romani*. Berlin: Walter de Gruyter, 1952–1966.
Turner, N. *A Grammar of the New Testament Greek*, Vol. 3: *Syntax*. Ed. J. H. Moulton. Edinburgh: T & T Clark, 1963.
Wissowa, G., W. Kroll, et al., eds. *Paulys Realencyclopädie der classischen Altertums-Wissenschaft*. Stuttgart: Metzler; München: Druckenmüller, 1894–1978.

Texts, Editions, Translations

Editions and translations of Greek and Latin authors are from the Loeb Classical Library unless otherwise indicated.

Acta Apostolorum Apocrypha. Ed. by R. A. Lipsius and M. Bonnet. Darmstadt: Wissenschaftliche Buchgesellschaft, 1959.
Aesopica. Ed. by B. E. Perry. New York: Arno Press, 1980.
Aesop without Morals. Trans. L. W. Daly. New York: Thomas Yoseloff, 1961.
Aeschines. Speeches. Ed. and trans. by C. D. Adams. Cambridge, MA: Harvard University Press, 1919.
Aeschylus. 3 vols. Ed. and trans. by Alan H. Sommerstein. Cambridge, MA: Harvard University Press, 2009.
The Apocrypha and Pseudepigrapha of the Old Testament. 2 vols. Ed. by R. H. Charles. Oxford: Clarendon Press, 1964.
Appian. Roman History, 4 vols. Ed. and trans. by Horace White. Cambridge, MA: Harvard University Press, 1912–1913.
Aristophanes. 5 vols. Ed. and trans. by Jeffrey Henderson. Cambridge, MA: Harvard University Press, 1998–2008.
Aristotle. Art of Rhetoric. Ed. and trans. by J. H. Freese. Cambridge, MA: Harvard University Press, 1926.
Aristotle. Athenian Constitution. Eudemian Ethics. Virtues and Vices. Ed. and trans. by H. Rackham. Cambridge, MA: Harvard University Press, 1935.
Aristotle. Nichomachean Ethics. Ed. and trans. by H. Rackham. Cambridge, MA: Harvard University Press, 1934.
Aristotle. Poetics. Ed. and trans. by S. Halliwell. Cambridge, MA: Harvard University Press, 1995.
Aristotle. Politics. Ed. and trans. by H. Rackham. Cambridge, MA: Harvard University Press, 1932.
Artemidori Daldiani Onirocriticon Libri. Ed. by R. A. Pack. Leipzig: Teubner, 1963.
Artemidorus. *The Interpretation of Dreams (Oneirocritica)*. Trans. by R. J. White. Park Ridge: Noyes Press, 1975.
Athenaeus. The Deipnosophists. Ed. and trans. by C. Gulick. Cambridge, MA: Harvard University Press, 1993.

Caesar. Civil Wars. Ed. and trans. by A. G. Peskett. Cambridge, MA: Harvard University Press, 1914.
Cicero. Letters to Atticus. 4 Vols. Ed. and trans. by D. R. Shackleton Bailey. Cambridge, MA: Harvard University Press, 1999.
Cicero. Letters to Friends. 3 vols. Ed. and trans. by D. R. Schackleton Bailey. Cambridge, MA: Harvard University Press, 2001.
Cicero. Letters to Quintus and Brutus. Ed. and trans. by D. R. Shackleton Bailey. Cambridge, MA: Harvard University Press, 2002.
Cicero. Brutus. Orator. Ed. and trans. by G. L. Hendrickson and H. M. Hubbell. Cambridge, MA: Harvard University Press, 1939.
Cicero. On Duties (De Officiis). Ed. and trans. by W. Miller. Cambridge, MA: Harvard University Press, 1913.
Cicero. On Invention. Ed. and trans. by H. M. Hubbell. Cambridge, MA: Harvard University Press, 1949.
Cicero. On Old Age. On Friendship. Ed. and trans. by W. A. Falconer. Cambridge, MA: Harvard University Press, 1923.
Cicero. Pro Milone. In Pisonem. Pro Scauro. Pro Fonteio. Pro Rabirio Postumo. Ed. and trans. N. H. Watts. Cambridge, MA: Harvard University Press, 1931.
Cicero. Tusculan Disputations. Ed. and trans. by J. E. King. Cambridge, MA: Harvard University Press, 1927.
Comicorum Atticorum Fragmenta. Ed. by T. Kock. Berlin: Teubner, 1888.
Comicorum Graecorum Fragmenta. Ed. by G. Kaibel. Berlin: Weidmann, 1958.
Comicorum Romanorum Fragmenta. Ed. by O. Ribbeck. Leipzig: Teubner, 1897.
Corpus Inscriptionum Judaicarum: Jewish Inscriptions from the Third Century B.C. to the Seventh Century A.D. 2 vols. Ed. by Jean-Baptiste Frey. New York: KTAV Publishing, 1975.
The Cynic Epistles. Ed. by A. J. Malherbe. SBLSBS 12. Missoula: Scholars Press, 1977.
Demetrius. On Style. Ed. and trans. by W. Rhys Roberts. Cambridge, MA: Harvard University Press, 1973.
Demosthenes. Orations. Vol. V. Ed. and trans. A. T. Murray. Cambridge, MA: Harvard University Press, 1939.
Demosthenes. Orations. Epistles. Vol. VII. Ed. and trans. by N. W. DeWitt and N. J. Dewitt. Cambridge, MA: Harvard University Press, 1962.
Dio Cassius. Roman History. 9 vols. Ed. and trans. by Ernest Cary and Herbert B. Foster. Cambridge, MA: Harvard University Press, 1914–1927.
Dio Chrysostom. 5 vols. Ed. and trans. by J. W. Cohoon and H. Lamar Crosby. Cambridge, MA: Harvard University Press, 1932–1951.
Diogenes Laertius. Lives of Eminent Philosophers. 2 vols. Ed. and trans. by R. D. Hicks. Cambridge, MA: Harvard University Press, 1925.
Dionysius of Halicarnassus. Critical Essays. 2 vols. Ed. and trans. by S. Usher. Cambridge, MA: Harvard University Press, 198.
Dionysius of Halicarnassus. Roman Antiquities. 6 vols. Ed. and trans. by E. Cary. Cambridge, MA: Harvard University Press, 1947.
Epictetus. 2 vols. Ed. and trans. W. A. Oldfather. Cambridge, MA: Harvard University Press, 1967.

Euripides. 6 vols. Ed. and trans. by David Kovacs. Cambridge, MA: Harvard University Press, 1994–2003.
Die Fragmente der griechischen Historiker. 3 vols. Ed. by F. Jacoby. Berlin: Weidmann, 1923–1950.
Die Fragmente der Vorsokratiker. Ed. by H. Diels. Berlin: Weidmann, 1934.
Gellius. Attic Nights. 3 vols. Ed. and trans. by J. C. Rolfe. Cambridge, MA: Harvard University Press, 1927.
The Greek Anthology. 3 vols. Ed. and trans. by W. R. Paton. Cambridge, MA: Harvard University Press, 1993.
Hermes Trismegiste. Corpus Hermeticum. 4 vols. Ed. by A. D. Nock and A. J. Festugiere. Paris: Societé d'Edition "Les Belles Lettres," 1980.
Herodas. Mimes. Ed. by I. C. Cunningham. Cambridge, MA: Harvard University Press, 1993.
Herodotus. 4 vols. Ed. and trans. by A. D. Godley. Cambridge, MA: Harvard University Press, 1920–1925.
Horace. Satires, Epistles, and Ars poetica. Ed. and trans. by H. Fairclough. Cambridge, MA: Harvard University Press, 1991.
Iamblichi de vita Pythagorica liber. Ed. by U. Klein. Stuttgart: Teubner, 1975.
Inscriptiones Graecae. 2 vols. Ed. by F. Hiller von Gaertringen. Berlin: Reimer, 1895.
Josephus. Jewish Antiquities. 10 vols. Ed. and trans. by H. St. J. Thackeray and R. Marcus. Cambridge, MA: Harvard University Press, 1988.
Josephus. The Jewish War. 3 vols. Ed. and trans. by H. St. J. Thackeray. Cambridge, MA: Harvard University Press, 1990.
Josephus. The Life, Against Apion. Ed. and trans. by H. St. J. Thackeray. Cambridge, MA: Harvard University Press, 1926.
Juvenal. Ed. and trans. by G. G. Ramsey. Cambridge, MA: Harvard University Press, 1979.
Lucian. 8 vols. Ed. and trans. by A. M. Harmon and M. D. Macleod. Cambridge, MA: Harvard University Press, 1967.
Lyrica Graeca Selectae. Ed. by D. L. Page. Oxford: Oxford University Press, 1968.
The Third and Fourth Book of Maccabees. Ed. and trans. M. Hadas. New York: KTAV Press, 1976.
Martial. Epigrams. 3 vols. Ed. and trans. by D. R. Shackleton Bailey. Cambridge, MA: Harvard University Press, 1993.
Menander. 3 vols. Ed. and trans. by W. G. Arnott. Cambridge, MA; Harvard University Press, 1996.
Menander. The Principal Fragments. Ed. and trans. by F. G. Allinson. Cambridge, MA: Harvard University Press, 1964.
Menandri sententiae. Ed. Siegfried Jaekel. Leipzig: Teubner, 1964.
Minor Attic Orators. Ed. and trans. by K. J. Maidment. Cambridge, MA: Harvard University Press, 1941.
New Testament Apocrypha. 2 vols. Ed. by E. Hennecke and W. Schneemelcher. Trans. by R. McL. Wilson. Philadelphia: Fortress Press, 1963.
Novum Testamentum Graece. 27th edition. Ed. by E. Nestle and K. Aland. Stuttgart: Deutsche Bibelgesellschaft, 2001.

Novum Testamentum Graecum. 2 vols. Ed. by J. J. Wettstein. Graz: Akademische Druck und Verlagsanstalt, 1962.
Orientis Graeci Inscriptiones Selectae. 2 vols. Ed. by W. Dittenberger. Leipzig: Hirzel, 1903–1905.
The Oxyrhynchus Papyri. Ed. by B. P. Grenfell and A. S. Hunt. London: Egypt Exploration Fund, 1903.
Papyri Graecae Magicae: Die Griechischen Zauberpapyri. Ed. by K. Preisendanz. Stuttgart: Teubner, 1973.
Pausanias. Description of Greece. 5 vols. Ed. and trans. by W. H. S. Jones. Cambridge, MA: Harvard University Press, 1918–1935.
Petronius. Satyricon. Apocolocyntosis. Ed. and trans. by Michael Heseltine and W. H. D. Rouse. Cambridge, MA: Harvard University Press, 1913.
Philo, 10 vols. Ed. and trans. F. H. Colson and G. H. Whitaker. Cambridge, MA: Harvard University Press, 1929–1962.
Philonis Alexandrini in Flaccum. Ed by H. Box. London: Oxford University Press, 1939.
Philostratus, Apollonius of Tyana, Vol. III: Letters of Apollonius. Ed. and trans. by Christopher P. Jones. Cambridge, MA: Harvard University Press, 2008.
Philostratus. Lives of the Sophists. Ed. and Trans. by W. C. Wright. Cambridge, MA: Harvard University Press, 1921.
Plato. Euthyphro, Apology, Crito, Phaedo, Phaedrus. Ed. and trans. by H. N. Fowler. Cambridge, MA: Harvard University Press, 1914.
Plato. Republic, 2 vols. Ed. and trans. by Paul Shorey. Cambridge, MA: Harvard University Press, 1930, 1935.
Plato. Statesman, Philebus, Ion. Ed. and trans. by H. N. Fowler and W. R. M. Lamb. Cambridge, MA: Harvard University Press, 1925.
Plautus. 5 vols. Ed. and trans. by Paul Nixon. Cambridge, MA: Harvard University Press, 1924–1938.
Pliny. Letters. Ed. and trans. B. Radice. Cambridge, MA: Harvard University Press, 1976.
Plutarch. Lives V. Ed. and trans. by Bernadotte Perrin. Cambridge, MA: Harvard University Press, 1917.
Plutarch. Lives VI. Ed. and trans. by Bernadotte Perrin. Cambridge, MA: Harvard University Press, 1918.
Plutarch. Lives VII. Ed. and trans. by Bernadotte Perrin. Cambridge, MA: Harvard University Press, 1919.
Plutarch. Moralia I. Ed. and trans. by F. C. Babbitt. Cambridge, MA: Harvard University Press, 1927.
Plutarch. Moralia III. Ed. and trans. by F. C. Babbitt. Cambridge, MA: Harvard University Press, 1931.
Plutarch. Moralia IV. Ed. and trans. by F. C. Babbitt. Cambridge, MA: Harvard University Press, 1972.
Plutarch. Moralia VI. Ed. and trans. by W. C. Helmbold. Cambridge, MA: Harvard University Press, 1939.
Plutarch. Moralia VII. Ed. and trans. by P. H. De Lacy and B. Einarson. Cambridge, MA: Harvard University Press, 1959.

Quintilian. The Orator's Education. 5 vols. Ed. and trans. by Donald A. Russell. Cambridge, MA: Harvard University Press, 2002.
Seneca. Ad Lucilium Epistulae Morales. Ed. and trans. by R. Gummere. Cambridge, MA: Harvard University Press, 1994.
Seneca. Moral Essays. 3 vols. Ed. and trans. by J. Basore. Cambridge, MA: Harvard University Press, 1994.
Seneca. Tragedies. Ed. and trans. by John G. Fitch. Cambridge, MA: Harvard University Press, 2002.
Septuaginta. Ed. by A. Rahlfs. Stuttgart: Deutsche Bibelgesellschaft, 1935.
Sophocles. 3 vols. Ed. and trans. by Hugh Lloyd-Jones. Cambridge, MA: Harvard University Press, 1994–1996.
Stoicorum Veterum Fragmenta. 4 vols. Ed. by J. von Arnim. Leipzig: Teubner, 1905–1924.
Suetonius. 2 vols. Ed. and trans. by J. C. Rolfe. Cambridge, MA: Harvard University Press, 1979.
Sylloge Inscriptionum Graecarum. 4 vols. Ed. by W. Dittenberger. Leipzig: Teubner, 1915–1924.
Tacitus. Annals. Ed. and trans. by J. Jackson. Cambridge: Harvard University Press, 1981.
Tacitus. Histories. Ed. and trans. by C. H. Moore and J. Jackson. Cambridge, MA: Harvard University Press, 1931.
M. Terenti Varronis de Lingua Latina quae supersunt. Ed. by G. Goetz and F. Schoell. Leipzig: Teubner, 1910.
Tertulliani Opera. Ed. by E. Dekkers. Turnholti: Typographi Brepols, 1954.
Tertullian. Quinti Septimi Florentis Tertulliani Quae Supersunt Omnia. Ed. by F. Oehler. Leipzig: Weigel, 1853.
Théognis. Poèmes élégiaques, text établi et traduit. Ed. and trans. by J. Carrière. Paris: Bude, 1962.
Theophrastus. Characters. Ed. and trans. by J. Rusten. Cambridge, MA: Harvard University Press, 2002.
Thucydides. History of the Peloponnesian War. 4 vols. Ed. and trans. by C. F. Smith. Cambridge, MA: Harvard University Press, 1919–1923.
Valerius Maximus. Memorable Doings and Sayings. 2 vols. Ed. and trans. by D. R. Shackleton Bailey. Cambridge, MA: Harvard University Press, 2000.
Varro. On the Latin Language. 2 vols. Ed. and trans. by Roland G. Kent. Cambridge, MA: Harvard University Press, 1938.
Vitruvius. On Architecture. 2 vols. Ed. and trans. by Frank Granger. Cambridge, MA: Harvard University Press, 1934.
Xenophon. Anabasis. Ed. and trans. by Carleton L. Brownson. Cambridge, MA: Harvard University Press, 1998.
Xenophon. Hiero. Agesilaus. Ed. and trans. by E. C. Marchant and G.W. Bowersock. Cambridge, MA: Harvard University Press, 1925.
Xenophon. Memorabilia. Ed. and trans. by E. C. Marchant and O. J. Todd. Cambridge, MA: Harvard University Press, 1923.

Secondary Literature

Abramanko, A. *Die Munizipale Mittelschicht in kaiserzeitlichen Italien. Zu einem neuen Verständnis von Sevirat und Augustalität.* Frankfurt: Peter Lang, 1993.
Adams, Edward and David G. Horrell, eds. *Christianity at Corinth: The Quest for the Pauline Church.* Louisville: Westminster John Knox Press, 2004.
Adams, J. N. "Conventions of Naming in Cicero." *Classical Quarterly* 28 (1978): 145–166.
Aejmelaeus, Lars. *Streit und Versöhnung. Das Problem der Zusammensetzung des 2. Korintherbriefes.* Helsinki: Finnish Exegetical Society, 1987.
Agamben, Giorgio. *The Time That Remains: A Commentary on the Letter to the Romans.* Stanford: Stanford University Press, 2005.
Agosto, Efrain. "Paul and Commendation." In *Paul in the Greco-Roman World*, ed. J. Paul Sampley, 101–133. Harrisburg: Trinity Press International, 2003.
Alexandre, Manuel. *Rhetorical Argumentation in Philo of Alexandria.* Atlanta: Scholars Press, 1999.
Alföldy, Geza. *The Social History of Rome.* London: Routledge, 1988.
Allo, E.-B. *Saint Paul: Seconde Épître aux Corinthiens.* Paris: Gabalda, 1956.
Alpern, Kenneth D. "Aristotle on the Friendships of Utility and Pleasure." *Journal of the History of Philosophy* 21 (1983): 303–315.
Amandry, Michel. *Le Monnayage des Duovirs Corinthiens.* Paris: École Francaise D'Athènes, 1988.
Amaoutoglou, I. N. "Roman Law and *collegia* in Asia Minor." *Revue Internationale des Droits de la Antiquité* 49 (2002): 27–44.
Anderson, J. K. "Corinth: Temple E Northwest." *Hesperia* 36 (1967): 1–12.
Anderson, R. Dean. *Rhetorical Theory and Paul*, 2nd ed. Leuven: Peeters, 1998.
Anderson, William S. *Barbarian Play: Plautus' Roman Comedy.* Toronto: Toronto University Press, 1993.
Andringa, William van. "Autels de Carrefour, organization vicinale et rapports de voisinage à Pompéi." *Rivista di Studi Pompeiani* 11 (2001): 47–86.
Arangio-Ruiz, V. *Studi epigrafici e papirologici.* Naples: liguori, 1974.
Arnott, W. G. "Targets, Techniques, and Tradition in Plautus' *Stichus*." *Bulletin of the Institute of Classical Studies* 19 (1972): 54–79.
——. *Alexis: The Fragments.* Cambridge, MA: Harvard University Press, 1996.
Arzt-Grabner, Peter and Ruth Elizabeth Kritzer, Amphilochios Papathomas, Franz Winter. *1. Korinther. Papyrologische Kommentare zum Neuen Testament.* Göttingen: Vandenhoeck & Ruprecht, 2006.
Atkinson, Kenneth. "Herod the Great, Sosius, and the Siege of Jerusalem in Psalm of Solomon 17." *Novum Testamentum* 38 (1996): 313–322.
——. *I Cried to the Lord: A Study of the Psalms of Solomon's Historical Background and Social Setting.* Leiden: Brill, 2004.
Aune, David C. "Mastery of the Passions: Philo, 4 Maccabees and Earliest Christianity." In *Hellenization Revisited: Shaping a Christian Response within the Greco-Roman World*, ed. W. E. Helleman, 125–158. New York: Lanham, 1994.

Aune, David E. "Corinthians, Second Letter to the." In *The Westminster Dictionary of the New Testament and Early Christian Literature*, 115–117 Louisville: Westminster John Knox, 2003.
Andrews, Scott B. "Too Weak Not to Lead: The Form and Function of 2 Cor. 11:23b-33." *New Testament Studies* 43 (1997): 263–276.
Bachmann, Philipp. *Der zweite Brief des Paulus an die Korinther.* Leipzig: Deichert, 1922.
Badiou, Alain. *Saint Paul: The Foundation of Universalism.* Stanford: Stanford University Press, 2003.
Balch, David L. "Political Friendship in the Historian Dionysius of Halicarnassus, *Roman Antiquities.*" In *Greco-Roman Perspectives on Friendship*, ed. John T. Fitzgerald, 127–143. Atlanta: Scholars Press, 1997.
——. "Paul, Families, and Households." In *Paul in the Greco-Roman World*, ed. J. Paul Sampley, 258–292. Harrisburg: Trinity Press International, 2003.
——. "Rich Pompeiian Houses, Shops for Rent, and the Huge Apartment Building in Herculaneum as Typical Spaces for Pauline House Churches." *Journal for the Study of the New Testament* 27 (2004): 27–46.
Balot, Ryan K. *Greed and Injustice in Classical Athens.* Princeton: Princeton University Press, 2001.
Balsdon, J. P. V. D. *Life and Leisure in Ancient Rome.* London: Bodley Head, 1969.
Banks, Robert. *Paul's Idea of Community.* Exeter: Pater Noster Press, 1980.
Barclay, John M. G. "Thessalonica and Corinth: Social Contrasts in Pauline Christianity." *Journal for the Study of the New Testament* 47 (1992): 49–74.
Barclay, William. *The New Testament: A New Translation.* 2 vols. London: Collins, 1968–1969.
Barker, Donald Charles. "Household Patterns in the Roman Empire, with Special Reference to Egypt." Ph.D. dissertation, Macquarie University, 1994.
Barré, M. L. "Paul as 'Eschatologic Person': a New Look at 2 Cor. 11:29." *Catholic Biblical Quarterly* 37 (1975): 500–526.
Barnett, Paul. *The Second Epistle to the Corinthians.* Grand Rapids: Eerdmans, 1997.
——. "Paul, Apologist to the Corinthians." In *Paul and the Corinthians: Studies on a Community in Conflict*, ed. T. J. Burke and J. K. Elliott, 313–326. Leiden: Brill, 2003.
Barrett, Andrew. *Caligula: The Corruption of Power.* New Haven: Yale University Press, 1990.
Barrett, C. K. "Titus." In *Neotestamentica et Semitica*, ed. E. E. Ellis and M. Wilcox, 1–14. Edinburgh: T & T Clark, 1969.
——. "Ο ΑΔΙΚΗΣΑΣ" (2 Cor. 7.12)." In *Verborum Veritas*, ed. by O. Böcher and K. Haacker, 149–157. Wuppertal: Theologischer Verlag-Brockhaus, 1970.
——. "PSEUDAPOSTOLOI (2 Cor. 11:13)." In *Mélanges Biblique*, ed. A. Descamps and A. De Halleux, 377–396. Gembloux: Duculot, 1979.
——. "Paul's Opponents in II Corinthians." *New Testament Studies* 17 (1971): 233–254.
——. *Essays on Paul.* Philadelphia: Westminster, 1982.

—. *A Commentary on the Second Epistle to the Corinthians.* New York: Harper & Row, 1973.

—. "Sectarian Diversity at Corinth." In *Paul and the Corinthians: Studies on a Community in Conflict. Essays in Honour of Margaret Thrall*, eds. T. J. Burke and J. K. Elliott, 297–302. Leiden: Brill, 2003.

—. *A Critical and Exegetical Commentary on the Acts of the Apostles.* 2 vols. London: T & T Clark, 2004.

Barrier, Jeremy. "Visions of Weakness: Apocalyptic Genre and the Identification of Paul's Opponents in 2 Corinthians 12:1–6." *Restoration Quarterly* 47 (2005): 33–42.

Barton, S. C. "Paul's Sense of Place: An Anthropological Approach to Community Formation In Corinth." *New Testament Studies* 32 (1986): 225–246.

Baslez, M.-F. *Saint Paul.* Paris: Fayard, 1991.

Bauckham, Richard. *The Jewish World around the New Testament.* Tübingen: Mohr Siebeck, 2008.

Baur, Ferdinand Christian. "Die Christuspartei in der korinthischen Gemeinde, der Gegensatz des paulinischen und petrinischen Christentums in der ältesten Kirche, der Apostel Petrus in Rom." *Tübinger Zeitschrift für Theologie* 4 (1831): 61–206.

—. *Paulus, der Apostel Jesu Christi: Sein Leben und Wirken, sein Briefe und seine Lehre, ein Beitrag zu einer kritischen Geschichte des Urchristentums* Stuttgart: Becher & Müller, 1845, ²1866.

Bauernfeind, Otto. "πανουργία, πανοῦργος." *Theological Dictionary of the New Testament* 5 (1967): 722–727.

Becker, Jürgen. *Paul, Apostle to the Gentiles.* Louisville: Westminster John Knox Press, 1993.

Behm, J. "κυρόω." *Theological Dictionary of the New Testament* 3 (1965): 1098–1099.

Bertram, G. "μωρός." *Theological Dictionary of the New Testament* 4 (1967): 830–839.

—. "φρήν, ἄφρων, ἀφροσύνη, κτλ.." *Theological Dictionary of the New Testament* 9 (1974): 220–229.

Best, Ernest. *A Commentary on the First and Second Epistles to the Thessalonians.* London: Black, 1979.

Betz, Hans Dieter. "Eine Christus-Aretalogie bei Paulus." *Zeitschrift für Theologie und Kirche* 66 (1969): 288–305.

—. *II Corinthians 10–13 and the Socratic Tradition.* Claremont: Center for Hermeneutical Studies, 1970.

—. *Der Apostel Paulus und die sokratische Tradition: Eine exegetische Untersuchung zu seiner 'Apologie' in 2 Kor 10–13.* Tübingen: Mohr-Siebeck, 1972.

—. "2 Cor. 6:14–7:1: An Anti-Pauline Fragment?" *Journal of Bibical Literature* 92 (1973): 88–108.

—. *Plutarch's Ethical Writings and Early Christian Literature.* Leiden: Brill, 1978.

—. *Galatians: A Commentary on Paul's Letter to the Galatians.* Philadelphia: Fortress Press, 1979.

———. *2 Corinthians 8 and 9: Two Administrative Letters of the Apostle Paul*, trans. by L. L. Welborn. Philadelphia: Fortress Press, 1985.
———. "Corinthians, Second Epistle to the." *Anchor Bible Dictionary* 1 (1992): 1148–1154.
Beyschlag, Willibald. "Über die Christuspartei in Korinth." *Theologische Studien und Kritiken* 38 (1865): 250–259.
———. "Zur Streitfrage über die Paulusgegner des zweiten Korintherbriefes." *Theologische Studien und Kritiken* 44 (1871): 665–680.
Bieringer, Reimund. "Die Gegner des Paulus im 2. Korintherbrief." In *Studies on 2 Corinthians*, 181–221. Leuven: Peeters, 1994.
Bickel, Ernst. "Zu Senecas Schrift über die Freundschaft." *Rheinisches Museum* 60 (1905): 190–201.
———. *The Corinthian Correspondence*. Leuven: Leuven University Press, 1996.
Birge, Mary Katherine. *The Language of Belonging: A Rhetorical Analysis of Kinship Language in First Corinthians*. Leuven: Peeters, 2002.
Bitzer, Lloyd F. "The Rhetorical Situation." *Philosophy and Rhetoric* 1 (1968): 1–14.
Bjerkelund, Carl J. *Parakalo: Form, Funktion und Sinn der parakalo-Sätze in den paulinischen Briefen*. Oslo: Universitetsforlaget, 1967.
Black, Matthew. "The Messianism of the Parables of Enoch: Their Date and Contributions to Christological Origins." In *The Messiah: Developments in Earliest Judaism and Christianity*, ed. J. H. Charlesworth, 145–168. Minneapolis: Fortress Press, 1992.
Blasi, Anthony J. *Early Christianity as a Social Movement*. Toronto: Peter Lang, 1988.
Bleek, Friedrich. "Erörterungen in Beziehung auf die Briefe Pauli an die Korinther." *Theologische Studien und Kritiken* 3 (1830): 614–632.
Blue, Bradley. "Acts and the House Church." In *The Book of Acts in Its Graeco-Roman Setting*, ed. David W. J. Gill and Conrad Gempf, 119–222. Grand Rapids: Eerdmans, 1994.
Blundell, Mary Whitlock. *Helping Friends and Harming Enemies. A Study in Sophocles and Greek Ethics*. Cambridge: Cambridge University Press, 1991.
Bodel, John. "Trimalchio's Underworld." In *The Search for the Ancient Novel*, ed. J. Tatum, 237–259. Baltimore: Johns Hopkins University Press, 1993.
Boismard, M.-E. and A. Lamouille. *Les Actes des deux apôtre*. Paris: Gabalda, 1990.
Boman, Thorlief. "Paulus abortivus (1 Kor. 15,8)." *Studia Theologica* 18 (1964): 46–50.
Bonaria, M. *Romani mimi*. Rome, 1965.
———. "La musica convivial dal mondo latino al medioevo." In *Spettacoli conviviali dall' antichità classica alle corti Italiane del' 400*, ed. M. Bonaria, 119–147. Viterbo, 1982.
Bonhöffer, A. *Die Ethik des Stoikers Epictet*. Stuttgart: Ferdinand Enke, 1984.
Bookidis, Nancy. "Religion in Corinth: 146 B.C.E to 100 C.E." In *Urban Religion in Roman Corinth*, ed. Daniel N. Schowalter and Steven J. Friesen, 141–164. Cambridge, MA: Harvard University Press, 2005.

Bornkamm, Günther. *Studien zu Antike und Urchristentum. Gesammelte Aufsätze II*. Munich: Kaiser, 1959.
——. *Die Vorgeschichte des sogenannten Zweiten Korintherbriefs*. SHAW.PH 1961, 2. Abhandlung. Heidelberg: Winter, 1961.
——. *Geschichte und Glaube II*. Munich: Kaiser, 1971.
——. *Paul*. New York: Harper & Row, 1971.
Borse, Udo. *Der Standort des Galaterbriefs*. Bonn: Hanstein, 1972.
Bourguet, Émile. *De rebus Delphicis imperatoriae aetatis capita duo*. Montepessulano: Camillus Coutel, 1905.
Bousset, Wilhelm. *Der zweite Brief an die Korinther*. Göttingen: Vandenhoeck & Ruprecht, ²1908.
Bove, L. *Documenti di operazioni finanziarie dall' archivio dei Sulpici*. Naples: Liguori, 1984.
Bowditch, Phebe Lowell. *Horace and the Gift Economy of Patronage*. Berkeley: University of California Press, 2001.
Bowersock, Glen W. "Eurycles of Sparta." *Journal of Roman Studies* 51 (1961): 112–118.
——. *Augustus in the Greek World*. Oxford: Clarendon Press, 1965.
——. "Augustus and the Greek East: the Problem of the Succession." In *Caesar Augustus. Seven Aspects*, ed. F. Millar and E. Segal, 178–188. Oxford: Oxford University Press, 1984.
Box. H. "Roman Citizenship in Laconia." *Journal of Roman Studies* 21 (1931): 200–214.
Boyle, A. J. *Roman Tragedy*. London: Routledge, 2006.
Branham, R. Bracht and Daniel Kinney. *Petronius. Satyrica*. Berkeley: University of California Press, 1996.
Braun, Herbert. *Qumran und das Neue Testament*, 2 vols. Tübingen: Mohr Siebeck, 1966.
Braund, D. C. *Augustus to Nero: A Sourcebook on Roman History 31 B.C.-A.D. 68*. (London: Croom Helm, 1985.
Braund, S. and C. Gill. *The Passions in Roman Thought and Literature*. Cambridge: Cambridge University Press, 1997
Brendle, Albert. *Im Prozess der Konfliktüberwindung: Eine exegetische Studie zur Kommunikationssituation zwischen Paulus und den Korinthern in 2 Kor. 1,1–2,13; 7,4–16*. Frankfurt am Main: Peter Lang, 1994.
Brennan, Tad. "The Old Stoic Theory of Emotions." In *The Emotions in Hellenistic Philosophy*, ed. J. Sihvola and T. Engberg-Pedersen, 21–70. Dordrecht: Kluwer Academic Publishers, 1998.
Breytenbach, Cilliers. *Versöhnung: Eine Studie zur paulinischen Soteriologie*. Neukirchen- Vluyn: Neukirchener Verlag, 1989.
——. "'Christus starb für uns'. Zur Tradition und paulinischen Rezeption des sogenannten 'Sterbeformeln'." *New Testament Studies* 29 (2003): 447–475.
Brink, Laurie. "A General's Exhortation to his Troops: Paul's Military Rhetoric in 2 Cor. 10:1–11." *Biblische Zeitschrift* 49 (2005): 191–201; 50 (2006): 74–89.
Broneer, Oscar. "An Official Rescript from Corinth." *Hesperia* 8 (1939): 181–190.

Brothers, A. J. "Urban Housing." In *Roman Domestic Buildings*, ed. Ian M. Barton, 33–64. Exeter: University of Exeter Press, 1996.
Brown, Alexandra R. *The Cross and Human Transformation: Paul's Apocalyptic Word in 1 Corinthians*. Minneapolis: Fortress Press, 1995.
Bruce, F. F. *1 and 2 Corinthians*. London: Oliphants, 1971.
———. *The Letter to the Romans*. Grand Rapids: Eerdmans, 1985.
Brugnoli, G. "Mimi edaces." In *Spettacoli conviviali dall' antichità classica alle cort Italiane del' 400*. Viterbo, 1982.
Brunt, P. A. "Stoicism and the Principate." *Papers of the British School at Rome* 43 (1975): 7–39.
———. *The Fall of the Roman Republic and Related Essays*. Oxford: Oxford University Press, 1988.
Bultmann, Rudolf. *Der Stil der paulinischen Predigt und die kynisch-stoische Diatribe*. Göttingen: Vandenhoeck & Ruprecht, 1910.
———. *Exegetische Probleme des zweiten Korintherbriefes*. Uppsala: Wretmans, 1947.
———. "λύπη." *Theological Dictionary of the New Testament* 4 (1967): 313–324.
———. *Der zweite Brief an die Korinther*, ed. E. Dinkler. Göttingen: Vandenhoeck & Ruprecht, 1976.
———. *The Second Letter to the Corinthians*. Minneapolis: Augsburg, 1985.
Bünker, Michael. *Briefformular und rhetorische Disposition im 1. Korintherbrief*. Göttingen: Vandenhoeck & Ruprecht, 1983.
Burnett, A., M. Amandry and P. Ripolles. *Roman Provincial Coinage I*. London: British Museum Press, 1992.
Burton, Ernest DeWitt. *Syntax of the Moods and Tenses in New Testament Greek*. Edinburgh: T & T Clark, 1898.
Cadbury, Henry J. *The Making of Luke-Acts*. New York: Macmillan, 1927.
———. "Erastus of Corinth." *Journal of Biblical Literature* 50 (1931): 42–58.
———. *The Book of Acts in History*. New York: Harper, 1955.
Cairns, Douglas. *"Hybris*, Dishonour, and Thinking Big." *Journal of Hellenic Studies* 116 (1996): 1–32.
Cairns, Francis. *Generic Composition in Greek and Roman Poetry*. Edinburgh: Edinburgh University Press, 1972.
Cancik, Hubert. "Haus, Schule, Gemeinde: Zur Organisation von "fremder Religion" in Rom (1.–3. Jh. n. Chr.)." In *Gruppenreligionen im römischen Reich: Sozialformen, Grenzziehungen und Leistungen*, ed. Jörg Rüpke, 31–48. Tübingen: Mohr Siebeck, 2007.
Caragounis, C. "Ὀψώνιον: A Reconsideration of Its Meaning." *Novum Testamentum* 16 (1974): 35–57.
Carr, A. Wesley. "The Rulers of This Age—1 Cor. ii.6–8." *New Testament Studies* 23 (1976): 20–35.
Carter, Timothy L. ""Big Men' in Corinth." *Journal for the Study of the New Testament* 19 (1997): 45–70.
Cartledge, Paul and Anthony Spawforth. *Hellenistic and Roman Sparta: A Tale of Two Cities*. London: Routledge, 2002.
Caspari, W. "Über den biblischen Begriff der Torheit." *Neue kirchliche Zeitschrift* 39 (1928): 680–691.

Castelli, Elizabeth. *Imitating Paul: A Discourse of Power.* Louisville: Westminster John Knox, 1991.
Charlesworth, James H. "The Concept of the Messiah in the Pseudepigrapha." In *Aufstieg und Niedergang der römischen Welt* II/19.1 (1979): 189–218.
——. *Qumran Messianism: Studies on the Messianic Expectations in the Dead Sea Scrolls.* Tübingen: Mohr Siebeck, 1998.
Classen, C. J. "Paulus und die antike Rhetorik." *Zeitschrift für die neutestamentliche Wissenschaft* 82 (1991): 1–33.
Cheesman, G. L. "The Familly of the Caristanii at Antioch in Pisidia." *Journal of Roman Studies* 3 (1913): 253–266.
Chester, Stephen J. *Conversion at Corinth: Perspectives on Conversion in Paul's Theology and the Corinthian Church.* London: T & T Clark, 2003.
Chow, John K. *Patronage and Power: A Study of Social Networks in Corinth.* Sheffield: Sheffield Academic Press, 1992.
Chrimes, K. M. T. *Ancient Sparta: A Re-examination of the Evidence.* Manchester: Manchester University Press, 1952.
Christensen, D. L. *Deuteronomy 1:1–21:9.* Nashville: Thomas Nelson, 2001.
Christol, Michael, Thomas Drew-Bear, and Mehmet Taslialan. "L'empereur Claude, le Chevalier C. Caristanius Fronto Caesainus Iullus et le culte imperial à Antioche de Pisidie." *Tyche* 16 (2001): 1–20.
Christol, Michael and Thomas Drew-Bear. "Les Sergii Paulli et Antioche." In *Actes du Ier Congrès international sur Antioche de Pisidie*, ed. T. Drew-Bear, M. Taslialan and C. M. Thomas, 177–191. Paris: de Boccard, 2002.
Clarke, Andrew D. "Another Corinthian Erastus Inscription." *Tyndale Bulletin* 42 (1991): 146–151.
——. *Secular and Christian Leadership in Corinth: A Socio-Historical and Exegetical Study of 1 Corinthians 1–6.* Leiden: Brill, 1993.
——. "'Refresh the hearts of the saints': A Unique Pauline Context." *Tyndale Bulletin* 47 (1996): 275–300.
Clarke, John R. *The Houses of Roman Italy, 100 B.C. – A.D. 250: Ritual, Space, and Decoration.* Berkeley: University of California Press, 1991.
——. *Roman Life 100 B.C. to A.D. 200.* New York: Abrams, 2007.
Clemen, Carl. *Die Einheitlichkeit der paulinischen Briefe, an Hand der bisher mit bezug auf sie Angestellten Interpolations- und Compilationshypothesen geprüft.* Göttingen: Vandenhoeck & Ruprecht, 1894.
Coenen, J. *Lukian Zeus tragodos: Überlieferungsgeschichte, Text und Kommentar.* Meisenheim am Glan: Hain, 1977.
Collange, J.-F. *Enigmes de la deuxième épître de Paul aux Corinthiens. Etude exégétique de 2 Cor. 2:14–7:4.* Cambridge: Cambridge University Press, 1972.
Collins, John J. *The Scepter and the Star: The Messiahs of the Dead Sea Scrolls and Other Ancient Literature.* New York: Doubleday, 1995.
Collins, Raymond F. *First Corinthians.* Collegeville: Michael Glazier, 1999.
——. *The Power of Images in Paul.* Minneapolis: Liturgical Press, 2008.
Conzelmann, Hans. *Geschichte des Urchristentums.* Göttingen: Vandenhoeck & Ruprecht, 1969.
——. *1 Corinthians.* Philadelphia: Fortress Press, 1975.

Cooper, J. M. "Posidonius on Emotions." In *The Emotions in Hellenistic Philosophy*, ed. J. Sihvola and T. Engberg-Pederson, 71–111. Dordrecht: Kluwer Academic Publishers, 1998.
Corbett, P. B. *The Scurra.* Edinburgh: Scottish Academic Press, 1993.
Courtney, E. *The Fragmentary Latin Poets.* Oxford: Oxford University Press, 1993.
Cranfield, C. E. B. *The Epistle to the Romans.* Edinburgh: T & T Clark, 1979.
Crook, J. A. *Law and Life of Rome.* London: Thames and Hudson, 1967.
Cumont, Franz. "La Grande Inscription Bachique du Metropolitan Museum, II: Commentaire Religieuse de l'inscription." *American Journal of Archaeology* 37 (1933): 232–263.
D'Agostino, Francesco. *Epieikeia. Il tema dell' equita nell' antichità greca.* Milan: Giuffrè, 1973.
D'Arms, John H. "Slaves at Roman Convivia." In *Dining in a Classical Context*, ed. William J. Slater, 171–184. Ann Arbor: University of Michigan Press, 1991.
Dahl, Nils. "Paul and the Church at Corinth according to 1 Cor. 1:10–4:21." In *Christian History and Interpretation*, ed. W. R. Farmer, C. F. D. Moule, and R. R. Niebuhr, 313–336. Cambridge: Cambridge University Press, 1967.
———. *Studies in Paul* (Minneapolis: Augsburg, 1977).
Daly, L. W. *Aesop without Morals.* New York: Thomas Yoseloff, 1961.
Damon, Cynthia. *The Mask of the Parasite: A Pathology of Roman Patronage.* Ann Arbor: University of Michigan Press, 1997.
Daux, G. "L'onomastique romaine d'expression grecque." In *L'Onomastique latine*, ed. H. G. Pflaum and N. Duval, 405–417. Paris: CNRS, 1975.
Davenport, G. L. "The 'Anointed of the Lord' in Psalms of Solomon 17." In *Ideal Figures in Ancient Judaism*, eds. John J. Collins and G. W. Nickelsburg, 67–92. Chico: Scholars Press, 1980.
Deiss, J. J. *Herculaneum: Italy's Buried Treasure.* Malibu: J. Paul Getty Museum, 1989.
Deissmann, Adolf. *Bible Studies: Contributions Chiefly from Papyri and Inscriptions to theHistory of the Languages, the Literature, and the Religion of Hellenistic Judaism and Primitive Christianity.* Edinburgh: T & T Clark, 1923.
———. *Light from the Ancient East: The New Testament Illustrated by Recently Discovered Texts of the Graeco-Roman World.* Grand Rapids: Baker Book House, 1980.
Delcor, M. "The Courts of the Church of Corinth and the Courts of Qumran." In *Paul and Qumran*, ed. Jerome Murphy-O'Connor, 69–84. London: Chapman, 1968.
Delling, G. "πλεονεκτέω." *Theological Dictionary of the New Testament* 6 (1968): 266–274.
———. "τέλειος, κτλ." *Theological Dictionary of the New Testament* 8 (1972): 62–76.
———. "τάσσω, κτλ." *Theological dictionary of the New Testament* 8 (1972): 26–31.
Denney, James. *The Second Epistle to the Corinthians.* London: Armstrong, 1894.
Denniston, J. D. *Greek Prose Style.* Oxford: Clarendon Press, 1952.

Dessau, Hermann. "Der Name des Apostels Paulus." *Hermes* 45 (1910): 347–368.
Dewey, Arthur J. "A Matter of Honor: A Socio-Historical Analysis of 2 Corinthians 10." *Harvard Theological Review* 78 (1985): 209–17.
Dibelius, Martin. *Die Geisterwelt im Glauben des Paulus*. Göttingen: Vandenhoeck & Ruprecht, 1909.
Dilley, M. E. "The Parasite: A Study in Comic Development." Ph.D. dissertation, University of Chicago, 1924.
Dirlmeier, F. *ΦΙΛΟΣ und ΦΙΛΙΑ im vorhellenistischen Griechentum*. Dissertation, Munich, 1931.
Dobbins, Robert F. *Epictetus. Discourses Book I; Translated with an Introduction and Commentary*. Oxford: Clarendon Press, 1998.
Dobschütz, Ernst von. *Christian Life in the Primitive Church*. New York: Harper, 1904.
Dover, Kenneth James. *Greek Popular Morality in the Time of Plato and Aristotle*. Oxford: Oxford University Press, 1974.
Downs, David J. *The Offering of the Gentiles: Paul's collection for Jerusalem in Its Chronological, Cultural, and Cultic Contexts*. Tübingen: Mohr siebeck, 2008.
———. "Is God Paul's Patron? The Economy of Patronage in Pauline Theology." In *Engaging Economics: New Testament Scenarios and Early Christian Reception*, ed. Bruce W. Longenecker and Kelly D. Liebengood, 129–156. Grand Rapids: Eerdmans, 2009.
Drescher, Richard. "Der zweite Korintherbrief und die Vorgänge in Korinth seit Abfassung des ersten Korintherbriefes." *Theologische Studien und Kritiken* 70 (1897): 43–111.
Driver, S. R. *A Critical and Exegetical Commentary on Deuteronomy*. New York: Charles Scribner's Sons, 1895.
Dufallo, Basil. *The Ghosts of the Past: Latin Literature, the Dead, and Rome's Transition to a Principate*. Columbus: Ohio State University Press, 2007.
Dunbabin, Katherine M. D. *"Triclinium* and *Stibadium*." In *Dining in a Classical Context*, ed. W. J. Slater, 121–148. Ann Arbor: University of Michigan, 1991.
———. "Convivial spaces: dining and entertainment in the Roman villa." *Journal of Roman Archaeology* 9 (1996): 66–80.
———. *Mosaics of the Greek and Roman World*. Cambridge: Cambridge University Press, 1999.
Duncan-Jones, Richard. "Wealth and Munificence in Roman Africa." In *Papers of the British School at Rome* 31 (1968): 168–171.
———. *The Economy of the Roman Empire*. New York: Cambridge University Press, 1982.
Dunn, James G. G. *Romans 9–16*. Dallas: Word, 1988.
Düring, Ingmar. *Chion of Heraclea: A Novel in Letters*. Gothenburg: Wettergren & Kerbers, 1951.
Dutch, Robert S. *The Educated Elite in 1 Corinthians: Education and Community Conflict in Graeco-Roman Context*. London: T & T Clark, 2005.
Duthoy, R. "La function sociale de l'Augustalité." *Epigraphica* 36 (1974): 134–154.

———. "Recherches sur la repartition géographique et chronologique des termes *sevir Augustalis, Augustalis,* et *sevir* dans l'Empire romain." *Epigraphische Studien* 11 (1976): 143–214.
———. "Les *Augustales.*" *Aufstieg und Niedergang der römischen Welt* 2.16.2., 1254–1309. Berlin: Walter de Gruyter, 1978.
Ebel, Eva. *Die Attraktivität früher christlicher Gemeinden: Die Gemeinde von Korinth im Spiegel griechisch-römischer Vereine.* Tübingen: Mohr Siebeck, 2004.
Eden, P. T. *Seneca. Apocolocyntosis.* Cambridge: Cambridge University Press, 1993.
Edwards, Katherine N. *Corinth, Volume VI: The Coins, 1896–1929.* Cambridge, MA: Harvard University Press, 1933.
Ehrenberg, Victor and A. H. M. Jones. *Documents illustrating the Reigns of Augustus and Tiberius.* Oxford: Clarendon Press, 1976.
Ellis, E. Earle. *Paul's Use of the Old Testament.* Edinburgh: Oliver and Boyd, 1957.
———. "Paul and his Co-Workers." *New Testament Studies* 17 (1971): 437–452.
———. *Prophecy and Hermeneutic in Early Christianity.* Grand Rapids: Eerdmans, 1980.
Ellis, Simon P. *Roman Housing.* London: Duckworth, 2000.
Emmerling, Christian. *Epistola Pauli ad Corinthios posterior.* Lipsiae: Barth, 1823.
Engberg-Pedersen, Troels. *Paul and the Stoics.* Louisville: Westminster John Knox Press, 2000.
Engels, Donald W. *Roman Corinth: An Alternative Model for the Classical City.* Chicago: University of Chicago Press, 1990.
Entralgo, P. L. *The Therapy of the Word in Classical Antiquity.* New Haven: Yale University Press, 1970.
Epstein, David F. *Personal Enmity in Roman Politics 218–43 BC.* London: Croom Helm, 1987.
Erskine, Andrew. "Cicero and the expression of grief." In *The Passions in Roman Thought and Literature,* ed. S. Braund and C. Gill, 36–47. Cambridge: Cambridge University Press, 1997.
Evans, Craig A. "Messianic Hopes and Messianic Figures in Late Antiquity." *Journal of Greco-Roman Christianity and Judaism* 3 (2006): 9–40.
Ewald, Heinrich. "Bemerkungen über die Paulus Briefe." *Jahrbücher der biblischen Wissenschaft* 2 (1850): 225–232.
Fairweather, Janet. "The Epistle to the Galatians and Classical Rhetoric." *Tyndale Bulletin* 45 (1994): 1–38.
Fallon, Francis T. *2 Corinthians.* Wilmington: Michael Glazier, 1980.
Fantham, Elaine. *Roman Literary Culture: From Cicero to Apuleius.* Baltimore: Johns Hopkins University Press, 1996.
Fee, Gordon. "CHARIS in 2 Corinthians 1:15." *New Testament Studies* 24 (1977): 530–538.
———. *The First Epistle to the Corinthians.* Grand Rapids: Eerdmans, 1987.
Feldman, Louis H. "Jewish 'Sympathizers' in Classical Literature and Inscriptions." *Transactions and Proceedings of the American Philological Association* 81 (1950): 200–208.

Field, F. *Notes on the Translation of the New Testament.* Cambridge: Cambridge University Press, 1899.
Filson, Floyd V. "The Significance of the Early House Churches." *Journal of Biblical Literature* 58 (1939): 105–112.
Finley, Moses I. *The Ancient Economy.* Berkeley: University of California Press, 1973.
Finn, Thomas M. "The God-fearers Reconsidered." *Catholic Biblical Quarterly* 47 (1985): 75–84.
Fisher, N. R. E. "Hybris and Dishonor." *Greece and Rome* 23 (1976): 177–193.
——. *Hybris. S Study of the Values of Honour and Shame in Ancient Greece.* Warminster: Aris and Phillips, 1992.
Fitch, John G. *Seneca's Hercules Furens: A Critical Text with Introduction and Commentary.* Cornell: Cornell University Press, 1987.
Fitch, John G. and S. McElduff. "Construction of the Self in Senecan Drama." *Mnemosyne* 55 (2002): 18–40.
Fitzgerald, John T. *Cracks in an Earthen Vessel: An Examination of the Catalogues of Hardships in the Corinthian Correspondence.* Atlanta: Scholars Press, 1988.
——. "Paul, the Ancient Epistolary Theorists, and 2 Corinthians 10–13." In *Greeks, Romans, and Christians*, ed. D. L. Balch, 190–200. Minneapolis: Fortress Press, 1990.
——. "Paul and Paradigm Shifts: Reconciliation and Its Linkage Group." In *Paul Beyond the Judaism/Hellenism Divide*, ed. Troels Engberg-Pedersen, 241–262. Louisville: Westminster John Knox Press, 2001.
——. "Paul and Friendship." In *Paul in the Greco-Roman World*, ed. J. Paul Sampley, 319–343. Harrisburg: Trinity Press International, 2003.
——. *Passions and Moral Progress in Greco-Roman Thought.* London: Routledge, 2008.
Fitzgerald, John T. and L. Michael White. *The Tabula of Cebes.* Chico: Scholars Press, 1983.
Fitzmyer, Joseph A. "Qumran and the Interpolated Paragraph in 2 Cor. 6:14–7:1." *Catholic Biblical Quarterly* 22 (1961): 271–280.
——. *First Corinthians: A New Translation with Introduction and Commentary.* New Haven: Yale University Press, 2008.
Fontaine, M. *"Parasitus colax* (Terence *Eunuchus* 30)." *Mnemosyne* 60 (2007): 483–489.
Forbes, Christopher. "'Strength' and 'Weakness' as Terminology of Status in St. Paul: The Historical and Literary Roots of a Metaphor, with Special Reference to 1 and 2 Corinthians." Honours Thesis, Macquarie University, 1978.
——. "Comparison, Self-Praise and Irony: Paul's Boasting and the Conventions of Hellensitic Rhetoric." *New Testament Studies* 32 (1986): 1–30.
Fortenbaugh, W. W. *Aristotle on Emotions.* London: Duckworth, 1975.
Foss, Peder William. "Kitchens and Dining Rooms at Pompeii: The Spatial and Social Relationship of Cooking to Eating in the Roman Household." Ph.D. Dissertation, University of Michigan, 1994.
Fotopoulos, John. *Food Offered to Idols in Roman Corinth: A Socio-rhetorical Reconsideration of 1 Corinthians 8:1–11:1.* Tübingen: Mohr Siebeck, 2003.

Fowler, R. L. "The Rhetoric of Desperation." *Harvard Studies in Classical Philology* 91 (1987): 5–38.
Fränkel, Hermann. *Dichtung und Philosophie des frühen Griechentums*. Munich: Beck, 1993.
Fraschetti, Augusto. *Roma e il Principe*. Rome: Laterza, 1990.
Fraser, P. M. and E. Matthews. *A Lexicon of Greek Personal Names: Vol. III.A: The Peloponnese*. Oxford: Clarendon Press, 1997.
Fredrickson, David E. "Paul's Bold Speech in the Argument of 2 Corinthians 2:12–7:16." PhD Diss., Yale University, 1991.
——. "Paul's Sentence of Death (2 Corinthians 1:9)." In *God, Evil, and Suffering*, ed. T. Fretheim and C. Thompson, 103–107. St. Paul: Word and World, 2000.
——. "Paul, Hardships, and Suffering." In *Paul in the Greco-Roman World*, ed. J. Paul Sampley, 172–197. Harrisburg; Trinity Press International, 2003.
Freudenberg, Karl. *The Walking Muse: Horace on the Theory of Satire*. Princeton: Princeton University Press, 1993.
Friedländer, Ludwig. *Roman Life and Manners under the Early Empire*. 4 vols. London: Routledge & Kegan Paul, 1968.
Friedrich, Gerhard. "Die Gegner des Paulus im 2. Korintherbrief." In *Abraham unser Vater: Juden und Christen im Gespräch über die Bibel*, eds. O. Betz, M. Hengel, and P. Schmidt, 192–196. Leiden: Brill, 1963.
——. "Ein Tauflied hellenistischer Judenchristen: 1 Thess. 1:9 f." *Theologische Zeitung* 21 (1965): 502–516.
Friesen, Steven J. "Poverty in Pauline Studies: Beyond the So-called New Consensus." *Journal for the Study of the New Testament* 26 (2004): 323–361.
——. "Prospects for a Demography of the Pauline Mission: Corinth among the Churches." In *Urban Religion in Roman Corinth*, ed. by David N. Schowalter and Steven J. Friesen, 351–370. Cambridge, MA: Harvard University Press, 2005.
——. "The Wrong Erastus: Ideology, Archaeology, and Exegesis." In *Corinth in Context: Comparative Perspectives on Religion and Society*, ed. Steven Friesen, Daniel Schowalter, and James Walters, 231–256. Leiden: Brill, 2010.
Furley, W. D. "Antiphon der Athener: Ein Sophist als Psychotherapeut." *Rheinisches Museum für Philologie* 135 (1992): 198–216.
Furnish, Victor Paul. *II Corinthians: A New Translation with Introduction and Commentary*. Garden City: Doubleday, 1984.
——. "Corinth in Paul's Time: What Can Archaeology Teach Us?" *Biblical Archaeology Review* 15 (1988): 15–27.
Fürst, Alfons. *Streit unter Freunden: Ideal und Realität in der Freundschaftslehre der Antike*. Stuttgart: Teubner, 1996.
Gadbery, Laura M. "Roman wall-painting at Corinth: new evidence from east of the Theater." In *The Corinthia in the Roman Period*, ed. Timothy E. Gregory, 47–64. Ann Arbor; University of Michigan Press, 1993.
Gager, John. "Jews, Gentiles and Synagogues in the Book of Acts." *Harvard Theological Review* 79 (1986): 91–99.
Geagan, Daniel J. "Notes on the Agonistic Institutions of Roman Corinth." *Greek, Roman and Byzantine Studies* 4 (1968): 69–80.

——. "The Isthmian Dossier of P. Licinius Priscus Juventianus." *Hesperia* 58 (1989): 349–360.
Gehring, Roger W. *House Church and Mission: The Importance of Household Structures in Early Christianity.* Peabody: Hendrickson, 2004.
George, Michele. "*Servus* and *domus:* the slave in the Roman house." In *Domestic Space in the Roman World: Pompeii and Beyond*, ed. Ray Laurence and Andrew Wallace-Hadrill, 15–24. Portsmouth: Journal of Roman Archaeology, 1997.
——. "Domestic Architecture and Household Relations: Pompeii and Roman Ephesos." *Journal for the Study of the New Testament* 27 (2004): 15–23.
Georgi, Dieter. *Die Gegner des Paulus im 2. Korintherbrief: Studien zur religiösen Propaganda in der Spätantike.* Neukirchen-Vluyn: Neukirchener Verlag, 1964.
——. *Die Geschichte der Kollekte des Paulus für Jerusalem.* Hamburg: Reich, 1965.
——. *The Opponents of Paul in Second Corinthians.* Philadelphia: Fortress Press, 1986.
——. *Theocracy in Paul's Praxis and Theology.* Minneapolis: Fortress Press, 1991.
——. *Remembering the Poor: The History of Paul's Collection for Jerusalem.* Nashville: Abingdon, 1992.
Gill, David W. J. "Erastus the Aedile." *Tyndale Bulletin* 40 (1989): 293–301.
——. "In Search of the Social Elite in the Corinthian Church." *Tyndale Bulletin* 44 (1993): 323–337.
Gillman, Florence M. *Women Who Knew Paul.* Collegeville: Liturgical Press, 1992.
——. "Erastus." *Anchor Bible Dictionary* 2 (1992): 571.
——. "Jason." *Anchor Bible Dictionary* 3 (1992): 649.
——. "Sosipater." *Anchor Bible Dictionary* 6 (1992): 160.
Gillman, John. "Lucius." *Anchor Bible Dictionary* 4 (1992): 397.
Glad, Clarence. *Paul and Philodemus: Adaptability in Epicurean and Early Christian Psychagogy.* Leiden: Brill, 1995.
Glibert-Thirry, A. *Pseudo-Andronicus de Rhodes "ΠΕΡΙ ΠΑΘΩΝ".* Leiden: Brill, 1977.
Gnilka, Joachim. *Der Philipperbrief.* Freiburg: Herder, 1987.
Godet, Fréderic. *Commentary on St. Paul's Epistle to the Romans.* Grand Rapids: Kregel, 1977.
Gold, Barbara K. *Literary Patronage in Greece and Rome.* Chapel Hill: University of North Carolina Press, 1987.
Goldstein, Jonathan A. *The Letters of Demosthenes.* New York: Columbia University Press, 1968.
——. *I Maccabees. A New Translation with Introduction and Commentary.* Garden City: Doubleday, 1976.
Golla, Eduard. *Zwischenreise und Zwischenbrief.* Freiburg: Herder, 1922.
Goodrich, John K. "Erastus, *Quaestor* of Corinth: The Administrative Rank of ὁ οἰκονόμος τῆς πόλεως (Rom. 16:23) in an Achaean Colony." *New Testament Studies* 56 (2009): 90–115.
Goodspeed, Edgar J. "Gaius Titius Justus." *Journal of Biblical Literature* 69 (1950): 382–383.

Gordon, Mary. "The Freedman's Son in Municipal Life." *Journal of Roman Studies* 21 (1931): 65–77.
Gösswein, H. U. *Die Briefe des Euripides*. Meisenheim am Glan: Hain, 1975.
Grahame, Mark. "Public and private in the Roman house: investigating the social order of the Casa del Fauno." In *Domestic Space in the Roman World: Pompeii and Beyond*, ed. Ray Laurence and Andrew Wallace-Hadrill, 137–164. Portsmouth: Journal of Roman Archaeology, 1997.
Grässer, Erich. *Der zweite Brief an die Korinther, Kapitel 1,1–7,16*. Gütersloh: Gütersloher Verlaghaus, 2002.
Graver, Margaret R. *Cicero on the Emotions: Tusculan Disputations 3 and 4*. Chicago: University of Chicago Press, 2002.
———. *Stoicism and Emotion*. Chicago: University of Chicago Press, 2007.
Griffin, Miriam. "Seneca as a Sociologist: *De Beneficiis*." In *Seneca uomo politico e l'età di Claudio e di Nerone*, ed. Arturo De Vivo and Elio Lo Cascio, 89–122. Bari: Edipuglia, 2003.
Grimaldi, William M. A. *Aristotle: "Rhetoric", Pt. 2 – A Commentary*. New York: Fordham University Press, 1988.
Grindheim, Sigurd. "Wisdom for the Perfect: Paul's Challenge to the Corinthian Church (1 Corinthians 2.6–16)." *Journal of Biblical Literature* 121 (2002): 689–709.
Griswold, Charles. "Plato and Forgiveness." *Ancient Philosophy* 27 (2007): 269–287.
Groag, Edmund. *Die römischen Reichsbeamten von Achaia bis auf Diokletian*. Vienna: Hölder-Pichler-Tempsky, 1939.
Grube, G. M. A. *The Greek and Roman Critics*. Toronto: University of Toronto Press, 1968.
Gruen, Erich S. *Heritage and Hellenism: The Reinvention of Jewish Tradition*. Berkeley: University of California Press, 1998.
Grundmann. W. "Die ΝΗΠΙΟΙ in der urchristlichen Paränese." *New Testament Studies* 5 (1958/59): 188–205.
———. "ταπεινός." *Theological Dictionary of the New Testament* 8 (1972): 1–19.
Gunther, John J. *St. Paul's Opponents and Their Background: A Study of Apocalyptic and Jewish Sectarian Teachings*. Leiden: Brill, 1973.
Haas, Christopher. *Alexandria in Late Antiquity: Topography and Social Conflict*. Baltimore: Johns Hopkins University Press, 1997.
Hadot, Pierre. *What is Ancient Philosophy?* Cambridge, MA: Harvard University Press, 2002.
Haenchen, Ernst. *The Acts of the Apostles: A Commentary*. Philadelphia: Westminster Press, 1971.
Hagedorn, D. *Zur Ideenlehre des Hermogenes*. Göttingen: Vandenhoeck & Ruprecht, 1964.
Hall, David R. "Pauline Church Discipline." *Tyndale Bulletin* 20 (1969: 3–26.
———. *The Unity of the Corinthian Correspondence*. London: T & T Clark, 2003.
Hall, Jon. *Politeness and Politics in Cicero's Letters*. Oxford: Oxford University Press, 2009.
Halmel, Anton. *Der zweite Korintherbrief des Apostels Paulus*. Halle: Niemeyer, 1904.

Harnack, Adolf von. "Sanftmut, Huld and Demut in der alten Kirche." In *Festgabe für Julius Kaftan zu seinen 70. Geburtstag*, ed. A. Titius, 113–129. Tübingen: Mohr Siebeck, 1920.
Harrer, G. A. "Saul Who Also is Called Paul." *Harvard Theological Review* 33 (1940): 19–33.
Harris, Murray J. "2 Corinthians 5:1–10: Watershed in Paul's Eschatology?" *Tyndale Bulletin* 22 (1971): 32–57.
———. *The Second Epistle to the Corinthians*. Grand Rapids: Eerdmans, 2005.
Harris, William V. *Restraining Rage: The Ideology of Anger Control in Classical Antiquity*. Cambridge, MA: Harvard University Press, 2001.
Harrison, James R. *Paul's Language of Grace in its Graeco-Roman Context*. Tübingen: Mohr Siebeck, 2003.
Hartman, Lars. "Some Remarks on 1 Cor. 2.1–5." *Svensk Exegetisk Arsbok* 39 (1974): 112–124.
Harvey, A. E. *Renewal through Suffering: A Study of 2 Corinthians*. Edinburgh: T & T Clark, 1996.
Hartwig, Charlotte and Gerd Theissen. "Die Korinthische Gemeinde als Nebenadressat des Römerbriefs." *Novum Testamentum* 46 (2004): 229–252.
Hausrath, Adolf. *Der Vier-Capitel-Brief des Paulus an die Korinther*. Heidelberg: Bassermann, 1870.
———. *Neutestamentliche Zeitgeschichte*. 4 vols. Heidelberg: Bassermann, ²1875–1879.
———. *Die Sendschreiben des Apostels Paulus*. Göttingen: Dieterich, 1857.
Heath, Malcolm. *Unity in Greek Poetics*. Oxford: Clarendon Press, 1989.
———. "John Chrysostom, Rhetoric and Galatians." *Biblical Interpretation* 12 (2004): 369–400.
Heckel, Theo K. "Der Gekreuzigte bei Paulus." *Biblische Zeitschrift* 46 (2002): 190–210.
Heiland, H. W. "λογίζομαι." *Theological Dictionary of the New Testament* 4 (1967): 284.
Heinrici, C. F. Georg. *Das zweite Sendschreiben des Apostel Paulus an die Korinther*. Berlin: Hertz, 1887.
———. *Der zweite Brief an die Korinther*. Göttingen: Vandenhoeck & Ruprecht, 1900.
Hengel, Martin. *Crucifixion in the Ancient World and the Folly of the Message of the Cross*. Philadelphia: Fortress Press, 1977.
———. *Acts and the History of Earliest Christianity*. Philadelphia; Fortress Press, 1979.
———. *The Pre-Christian Paul*. Philadelphia: Trinity Press International, 1991.
Hengel, Martin and Anna Maria Schwemer. *Paul Between Damascus and Antioch*. Louisville: Westminster John Knox Press, 1997.
Henry, Denis and Elisabeth. *The Mask of Power: Seneca's Tragedies and Imperial Rome*. Warminster: Aris & Phillips, 1985.
Hemer, Colin J. "The Name of Paul." *Tyndale Bulletin* 36 (1985): 179–183.
———. *The Book of Acts in the Setting of Hellenistic History*. Tübingen: Mohr Siebeck, 1989.
Hercher, Rudolf. *Epistolographi Graeci*. Paris: Didot, 1873.

Héring, J. *The First Epistle of Saint Paul to the Corinthians.* London: Epworth, 1962.
Héring, J. *La seconde Épître de Saint Paul aux Corinthiens.* Neuchâtel and Paris: Delachaux et Niestle, 1958.
Herrington, C. J. "Senecan Tragedy." *Arion* 5 (1966): 422–471.
Herzog, Rudolf. *Die Wunderheilungen von Epidauros.* Leipzig: Dieterich, 1931.
Highet, Gilbert. *Juvenal the Satirist.* Oxford: Clarendon Press, 1954.
——. "Libertino Patre Natus." *American Journal of Philology* 94 (1973): 268–281.
Hilgenfeld, Adolf. "Die Christusleute in Korinth." *Zeitschrift für wissenschaftliche Theologie* 3 (1865): 240–252.
——. *Historisch-kritische Einleitung in das Neue Testament.* Leipzig: Fues, 1875.
——. "Paulus und die korinthischen Wirren." *Zeitschrift für wissenschaftliche Theologie* 9 (1871): 100–114.
——. "Paulus und Korinth." *Zeitschrift für wissenschaftliche Theologie* 26 (1888): 179–194.
Hinck, H. "Die Ἐπιστολιμαῖοι Χαρακτῆρες des Pseudo-Libanius." *Neue Jahrbücher für Philologie und Paedagogik* 99 (1869): 537–562.
Hock, Ronald F. "Paul's Tentmaking and the Problem of His Social Class." *Journal of Biblical Literature* 97 (1978): 555–564.
——. *The Social Context of Paul's Ministry: Tentmaking and Apostleship.* Philadelphia: Fortress Press, 1980.
——. "Paul and Greco-Roman Education." In *Paul in the Greco-Roman World*, ed. J. Paul Sampley, 198–227. Harrisburg: Trinity Press International, 2003.
Hoffer, Stanley E. "Cicero's 'Friendly Disagreement' with Metellus Celer (*Fam.* 5.1–2)." *Scripta Classica Israelica* 22 (2003): 93–101.
Hoffmann, Adolf and Mariette de Vos. "Casa del Fauno." In *Pompei e Mosaici*, ed. Ida Baldasarre, 80–141. Rome: Instituto della Enciclopedia Italiana, 1994.
Hofius, Otfried. "Herrenmahl und Herrenmahlparadosis. Erwägungen zu 1 Kor 11,23–25." *Zeitschrift für Theologie und Kirche* 85 (1988): 371–408.
——. "The Lord's Supper and the Lord's Supper Tradition: Reflections on 1 Corinthians 11:23b-25." In *One Loaf, One Cup: Ecumenical Studies of 1 Corinthians 11 and Other Eucharistic Texts*, ed. B. F. Meyer, 75–115. Macon: Mercer University Press, 1993.
Hofmann, Johann Christian Karl von. *Die heilige Schrift neuen Testaments zusammenhängend Untersucht*, 2. Theil, 3. Abteilung: *Der zweite Brief Pauli an die Korinther.* Nördlingen: Beck, ²1877.
Holland, Glenn S. "Speaking Like a Fool: Irony in the Letters of Paul." In *Rhetoric and the New Testament*, ed. Thomas Olbricht, 250–267. Sheffield: Sheffield Academic Press, 1993.
Holmberg, Bengt. "The Methods of Historical Reconstruction in the Scholarly 'Recovery' of Corinthian Christianity." In *Christianity at Corinth: The Quest for the Pauline Church*, ed. Edward Adams and David G. Horrell, 255–271. Louisville: Westminster John Knox Press, 2004.
Holtzmann, Heinrich Julius. "Das gegenseitige Verhältnis der beiden Korintherbriefe." *Zeitschrift für wissenschaftliche Theologie* 22 (1879): 455–492.

Holsten, Carl. "Einleitung in die Korintherbriefe." *Zeitschrift für wissenschaftliche Theologie* 44 (1901): 324–369.

Hooker, Morna D. "'Beyond the things which are written'? An Examination of 1 Corinthians 4:6." *New Testament Studies* 10 (1963): 127–132.

Horn, Friedrich Wilhelm. "Stephanas und sein Haus—die erste christliche Hausgemeinde in der Achaia: Ihre Stellung in der Kommunikation zwischen Paulus und der korinthischen Gemeinde." In *Paulus und die antike Welt: Beiträge zur zeit- und Religionsgeschichtlichen Erforschung des paulinischen Christentums*, ed. David C. Bienert, Joachim Jeska, Thomas Witulski, 83–98. Göttingen: Vandenhoeck & Ruprecht, 2008.

Horrell, David G. *The Social Ethos of the Corinthian Correspondence. Interests and Ideology from 1 Corinthians to 1 Clement*. Edinburgh: T & T Clark, 1996.

——. "Domestic Space and Christian Meetings at Corinth: Imagining New Contexts and the Buildings East of the Theatre." *New Testament Studies* 50 (2004): 349–359.

Horsfall, Nicholas. *Poets and Patron: Maecenas, Horace and the Georgics, Once More*. North Ryde: Macquarie Ancient History Association, 1981.

Horsley, G. H. R. "A Hellenistic Cult Group and the New Testament Churches." *Jahrbuch für Antike und Christentum* 24 (1981): 7–41.

——. "Marcus Aurelius to the Athenians, Appeal for Reconciliation." In *New Documents Illustrating Early Christianity*. Vol 4, ed. G. H. R. Horsley. 83–87. North Ryde: Macqaurie University Ancient History Documentary Research Centre, 1991.

Horsley, Richard A. "Wisdom of Word and Words of Wisdom at Corinth." *Catholic Biblical Quarterly* 39 (1977): 224–239.

——. *Wisdom and Spiritual Transcendence at Corinth: Studies in First Corinthians*. Eugene: Cascade Books, 2008.

Hughes, Frank W. "The Rhetoric of Reconciliation: 2 Cor. 1:1–2:13; 7:5–8:24." In *Persuasive Artistry*, ed. Duane F. Watson, 246–261. Sheffield: Sheffield Academic Press, 1991.

Hughes, Philip E. *Paul's Second Epistle to the Corinthians*. Grand Rapids: Eerdmans, 1962.

Hultgren, Stephen J. "2 Cor. 6:14–7:1 and Rev. 21:3–8: Evidence for the Ephesian Redaction of 2 Corinthians." *New Testament Studies* 49 (2003): 39–56.

Humphries, R. A. "Paul's Rhetoric of Argumentation in 1 Corinthians 1–4." GTU Ph.D. Dissertation. Berkeley: University of California, 1979.

Hurd, John C. *The Origin of 1 Corinthians*. Macon: Mercer University Press, 1983.

Hyldahl, Nils. "Die Frage nach der literarischen Einheit des Zweiten Korintherbriefes." *Zeitschrift für die neutestamentliche Wissenschaft* 64 (1973): 289–306.

Inwood, Brad. "Seneca and Psychological Dualism." In *Passions and Perceptions*, ed. J. Brunschwig and M. Nussbaum, 150–183. Cambridge: Cambridge University Press, 1993.

Jewett, Robert. *Paul's Anthropological Terms. A Study of Their Use in Conflict Settings*. Leiden: Brill, 1971.

——. "The Redaction of 1 Corinthians and the Trajectory of the Pauline School." *JAARSup* 46 (1978): 389–444.
——. "Tenement Churches and Communal Meals in the Early Church: The Implications of a Form-Critical Analysis of 2 Thess. 3:10." *Biblical Research* 38 (1993): 63–83.
——. *Romans: A Commentary.* Minneapolis: Fortress Press, 2007.
Johnson, Luke Timothy. "Making Connections: The Material Expression of Friendship in the New Testament." *Interpretation* 58 (2004): 158–171.
Jones, A. H. M. *The Herods of Judaea.* Oxford: Clarendon Press, 1938.
——. *The Criminal Courts of the Roman Republic and Principate.* Oxford: Blackwells, 1972.
Jones, Christopher P. "A New Letter of Marcus Aurelius to the Athenians." *Zeitschrift für Papyrologie und Epigraphik* 8 (1971): 161–183.
——. *Plutarch and Rome.* Oxford: Oxford University Press, 1971.
——. *The Roman World of Dio Chrysostom.* Cambridge, MA: Harvard University Press, 1978.
——. "Dinner Theater." In *Dining in a Classical Context*, ed. William J. Slater, 185–198. Ann Arbor, University of Michigan Press, 1991.
Jonge, Marinus de. "Expectation of the Future in the Psalms of Solomon." *Neotestamentica* 23 (1989): 93–117.
Jongkind, Dirk. "Corinth in the First Century AD: The Search for Another Class." *Tyndale Bulletin* 52 (2001): 139–148.
Joshel, S. R. *Work, Identity, and Legal Status at Rome: A Study of the Occupational Inscriptions.* Norman: University of Oklahoma Press, 1992.
Joubert, Stephan. *Paul as Benefactor: Reciprocity, Strategy and Theological Reflection in Paul's Collection.* Tübingen: Mohr Siebeck, 2000.
Judeich, Walther. *Altertümer von Hierapolis.* Berlin: Georg Reimer, 1898.
Judge, E. A. *The Social Pattern of the Christian Groups in the First Century: Some Prolegomena to the Study of New Testament Ideas of Social Obligation.* London: Tyndale, 1960.
——. "The Early Christians as a Scholastic Community." *Journal of Religious History* 2 (1961): 125–137.
——. "Paul's Boasting in Relation to Contemporary Professional Practice." *Australian Biblical Review* 16 (1968): 38–41.
——. "St. Paul and Classical Society." *Jahrbuch für Antike und Christentum* 15 (1972): 19–36.
——. "St. Paul and Socrates.' *Interchange* 14 (1973): 106–116.
——. "St Paul as a Radical Critic of Society." *Interchange* 16 (1974): 191–203.
——. "The Social Identity of the First Christians: A Question of Method in Religious History." *Journal of Religious Studies* 11 (1980): 201–217.
——. "Greek Names of Latin Origin." In *New Documents Illustrating Early Christianity*, Vol. 2, ed. G. H. R. Horsley. 107. North Ryde: Macquarie University Ancient History Documentary Research Centre, 1982.
——. "Cultural Conformity and Innovation in Paul: Some Clues from Contemporary Documents." *Tyndale Bulletin* 35 (1984): 3–24.

—. "Jews, Proselytes and God-fearers Club Together." *New Documents Illustrating Early Christianity*, Vol. 9, ed. S. R. Llewelyn, 73–81. Grand Rapids: Eerdmans, 2002.

—. "The Roman Base of Paul's Mission." *Tyndale Bulletin* 56 (2005): 103–117.

—. *Social Distinctives of the First Christians*, ed. D. M. Scholer. Peabody: Hendrickson, 2008.

—. *The First Christians in the Roman World: Augustan and New Testament Essays*, ed. James R. Harrison. Tübingen: Mohr Siebeck, 2008.

Judge, E. A. and G. S. R. Thomas. "The Origin of the Church at Rome: A New Solution?" *Reformed Theological Review* 25 (1966): 81–94.

Kajanto, Iiro. *The Latin Cognomina*. Helsinki: Societas Scientiarum Fennica, 1965.

—. *Supernomina: A Study in Latin Epigraphy*. Helsinki: Societas Scientiarum Fennica, 1966.

Käsemann, Ernst. "Die Legitimität des Apostels. Eine Untersuchung zu II Korinther 10–13." *Zeitschrift für die neutestamentliche Wissenschaft* 41 (1942): 33–71.

—. *Commentary on Romans*. Grand Rapids: Eerdmans, 1980.

Kaser, Max. *Das römische Privatrecht*. Munich: C. H. Beck, 1955.

Kasher, A. *The Jews in Hellenistic and Roman Egypt: The Struggle for Equal Rights*. Tübingen: Mohr Siebeck, 1985.

Kassel, R. *Poetae Comici Graeci*. Berlin: Walter de Gruyter, 1983.

Katzoff, Ranon. "Jonathan and Late Sparta." *American Journal of Philology* 106 (1985): 485–489.

Kehnscherper, G. "Der Apostel Paulus als römischer Bürger." In *Studia Evangelica*, 422–430. Berlin: Akademie Verlag, 1964.

Kennedy, George A. *New Testament Interpretation through Rhetorical Criticism*. Chapel Hill: University of North Carolina Press, 1984.

Kennedy, James H. "Are There Two Epistles in 2 Corinthians?" *The Expositor* 6 (1897): 231–238, 285–304.

—. *The Second and Third Epistles of St. Paul to the Corinthians*. London: Methuen, 1900.

—. "The Problem of Second Corinthians." *Hermathena* 12 (1903): 340–367.

Kent, John Harvey. *Corinth, Volume VIII, Part III: The Inscriptions 1926–1950*. Princeton: The American School of Classical Studies at Athens, 1966.

Ker, D. P. "Paul and Apollos—Colleagues or Rivals?" *Journal for the Study of the New Testament* 77 (2000): 75–97.

Kim, Byung-Mo. *Die paulinische Kollekte*. Tübingen: Francke, 2002.

Kim, Chan-Hie. *Form and Structure of the Familiar Greek Letter of Recommendation*. Missoula: Scholars Press, 1972.

Kirner, G. O. "Apostolat und Patronage (II) Darstellungsteil: Weisheit, Rhetorik und Ruhm in Konflikt um die apostolischen Praxis des Paulus in der frühchristlichen Gemeinde Korinth (1 Kor. 1–4 und 9; 2 Kor. 10–13." *Zeitschrift für antikes Christentums* 6 (2002): 27–72.

Klauck, Hans Josef. *Hausgemeinde und Hauskirche im frühen Christentum*. Stuttgart: Katholisches Bibelwerk, 1981.

———. *Herrenmahl und hellenistischer Kult. Eine religionsgeschichtliche Untersuchung zum ersten Korintherbrief.* Münster: Aschendorff, 1982.
———. *2. Korintherbrief.* Würzburg: Echter, 1986.
———. *Ancient Letters and the New Testament.* Baylor: Baylor University Press, 2006.
Klinghardt, Matthias. *Gemeinschaftsmahl und Mahlgemeinschaft: Soziologie und Liturgie Frühchristlicher Mahlfeiern.* Tübingen: Francke Verlag, 1996.
Klöpper, Albert. *Kommentar über das zweite Sendschreiben des Apostel Paulus an die Gemeinde zu Korinth.* Berlin: Reimer, 1874.
Knibb, Michael A. "Messianism in the Pseudepigrapha in Light of the Scrolls." *Dead Sea Discoveries* 2 (1995): 165–184.
Knox, John. "Chapters in a Life of Paul." In *Colloquy on New Testament Studies*, ed. Bruce Corley, 350–361. Macon: Mercer University Press, 1983.
Koch, D. A. *Die Schrift als Zeuge des Evangeliums. Untersuchungen zur Verwendung und zum Verständnis der Schrift bei Paulus.* Tügingen: Mohr Siebeck, 1986.
Koch, L. J. *Fortolkning til Paulus' andet Brev til Korinthierne.* Copenhagen: J. Frimodts Forlag, 1958.
Koester, Helmut. *Introduction to the New Testament, Vol. 2: History and Literature of Early Christianity.* New York: Walter de Gruyter, 1987.
———. *Pergamon, Citadel of the Gods: Archaeological Record, Literary Description, and Religious Development.* Harrisburg: Trinity Press International, 1998.
———. *Paul and His World.* Minneapolis: Fortress Press, 2007.
König, Karl. "Der Verkehr des Paulus mit der Gemeinde zu Korinth." *Zeitschrift für Wissenschaftliche Theologie* 40 (1897): 481–554.
Konstan, David. *Roman Comedy.* Ithaca: Cornell University Press, 1983.
———. "Patrons and Friends." *Classical Philology* 90 (1995): 328–342.
———. *Friendship in the Classical World.* Cambridge: Cambridge University Press, 1997.
———. *The Emotions of the Ancient Greeks: Studies in Aristotle and Classical Literature.* Toronto: University of Toronto Press, 2006.
———. "Remorse, Repentance and Forgiveness in the Classical World." *Phoenix* 62 (2008): 243–254.
Kornemann, Ernst. *Neue Dokumente zum lakonischen Kaiserkult.* Breslau: M. & H. Marcus, 1929.
Koskenniemi, Heikki. *Studien zur Idee und Phraseologie des griechischen Briefes bis 400 n. Chr.* Helsinki: Suomalainen Tiedeakatemian, 1956.
Kraabel, Alf Thomas. "The Disappearance of the God-fearers." *Numen* 23 (1981): 113–126.
Krenkel, Max. *Beiträge zur Aufhellung der Geschichte und der Briefe des Apostels Paulus.* Braunschweig: Schwetschke, 1895.
Kretzer, Armin. "συνίστημι, συνιστάνω." *Exegetical Dictionary of the New Testament* 3 (1993): 308.
Kristeva, Julia. *Black Sun: Depression and Melancholia.* New York: Columbia University Press, 1992.
Kroll, Wilhelm. *Die Kultur der ciceronischen Zeit.* Leipzig: Dieterich, 1933.

Kruse, Colin G. "The Offender and the Offence in 2 Corinthians 2:5 and 7:12." *Evangelical Quarterly* 88.2 (1988): 129–139.
Kubitschek, J. W. "Aedilis." *Real-Encyclopädie der classischen Altertumswissenschaft* 1 (1894): 44–68.
Kuck, David W. *Judgment and Community Conflict: Paul's Use of Apocalyptic Judgment Language in 1 Corinthians 3:5–4:5.* Leiden: Brill, 1992.
Kuhn, Heinz-Wolfgang. "Jesus als Gekreuzigter in der frühchristlichen Verkündigung bis zur Mitte des 2. Jahrhunderts." *Zeitschrift für Theologie und Kirche* 72 (1975): 27–41.
———. "Kreuz." *Theologische Realenzyklopädie* 19 (1990): 720.
Kümmel, Werner Georg. *Introduction to the New Testament.* Nashville: Abingdon, 1975.
Kyrtatas, Dimitris. *The Social Structure of the Early Christian Communities.* London: Verso, 1987.
Lagrange, Marie-Joseph. *Saint Paul. Épître aux Romains.* Paris: Gabalda, 1950.
Laird, Margaret L. "The Emperor in a Roman Town: The Base of the *Augustales* in the Forum at Corinth." In *Corinth in Context: Comparative Studies on Religion and Society*, ed. Steven J. Friesen, Dniel N. Schowalter, and James C. Walter, 67–116. Leiden: Brill, 2010.
Lake, Kirsopp. *The Earlier Epistles of St. Paul: Their Motive and Origin*, 2nd ed. London: Rivington's, 1914.
Lamberton, Robert. *Plutarch.* New Haven: Yale University Press, 2001.
Lambertz, Moritz. "Zur Ausbreitung der Supernomen oder Signum." *Glotta* 5 (1914): 147–156.
Lambrecht, Jan. "Strength in Weakness." *New Testament Studies* 43 (1997): 285–290.
Lampe, G. W. H. "Church Discipline and the Interpretation of the Epistles to the Corinthians." In *Christian History and Interpretation*, ed. W. R. Farmer et al., 337–362. Cambridge: Cambridge University Press, 1967.
Lampe, Peter. "Das korinthische Herrenmahl im Schnittpunkt hellenistisch-römischer Mahlpraxis und paulinischer Theologia Crucis (1Kor 11,17–34)." *Zeitschrift für die neutestamentliche Wissenschaft* 82 (1991): 183–213.
———. "Prisca/Priscilla." *Anchor Bible Dictionary* 3 (1992): 649.
———. *From Paul to Valentinus: Christians at Rome in the First Two Centuries.* Minneapolis: Fortress Press, 2003.
———. "Paul, Patrons, and Clients." In *Paul in the Greco-Roman World*, ed. J. Paul Sampley, 488–523. Harrisburg: Trinity Press International, 2003.
Landvogt, Peter. *Epigraphische Untersuchungen über den ΟΙΚΟΝΟΜΟΣ. Ein Beitrag zum Hellenistischen Beamtenwesen.* Strassburg: M. Dumont Schauberg, 1908.
Lassen, E. M. "The Use of the Father Image in Imperial Propagenda in 1 Cor. 4:14–21." *Tyndale Bulletin* 42 (1991): 127–136.
Laurence, Ray. *Roman Pompeii: Space and Society.* London: Routledge, 1994.
Leivestad, R. "ΤΑΠΕΙΝΟΣ – ΤΑΠΕΙΝΟΦΡΩΝ." *Novum Testamentum* 8 (1966): 36–47.
———. "The Meekness and Gentleness of Christ. II Cor. x.1." *New Testament Studies* 12 (1966): 156–164.

Leon, Harry J. *The Jews of Ancient Rome*. Philadelphia: Jewish Publication Society of America, 1960.
Levick, Barbara. *Roman Colonies in Southern Asia Minor*. Oxford: Oxford University Press, 1967.
——. *Tiberius the Politician*. London: Routledge, 1999.
Levinson, Bernard M. *Deuteronomy and the Hermeneutics of Legal Innovation*. Oxford: Oxford University Press, 1997.
Lietzmann, Hans. *An die Korinther I-II*, 4th ed., ed. W. G. Kümmel. Tübingen: Mohr Siebeck, 1949.
——. *An die Römer*. Tübingen: Mohr Siebeck, 1928.
Lieu, Judith M. "The Race of the God-fearers." *Journal of Theological Studies* 46 (1995): 483–501.
——. *Christian Identity in the Jewish and Graeco-Roman World*. Oxford: Oxford University Press, 2004.
——. *Neither Jew Nor Greek? Constructing Early Christianity*. London: T & T Clark, 2005.
Lifschitz, Baruch. *Donateurs et fondateurs dans les synagogues juives*. Paris: Gabalda, 1967.
Lim, Timothy. "Not in Persuasive Words of Wisdom, but in the Demonstration of the Spirit and Power." *Novum Testamentum* 29 (1987): 137–149.
Lincicum, David. "Paul's Engagement with Deuteronomy." *Currents in Biblical Research* 7 (2008): 37–67.
Lincoln, Andrew T. "Paul the Visionary: the setting and significance of the rapture to paradise in II Corinthians xii.1–10." *New Testament Studies* 25 (1979): 204–220.
Lindemann, Andreas. "Paulus und die korinthische Eschatologie. Zur These von einer 'Entwicklung' im paulinischen Denken." *New Testament Studies* 37 (1991): 373–399.
——. *Der erste Korintherbrief*. Tübingen: Mohr Siebeck, 2000.
Lisco, Heinrich. *Die Entstehung des zweiten Korintherbriefes*. Berlin: Schneider, 1896.
Litfin, A. D. *St. Paul's Theology of Proclamation: 1 Corinthians 1–4 and Greco-Roman Rhetoric*. Cambridge: Cambridge University Press, 1994.
Littlewood, Cedric A. J. *Self-representation and Illusion in Senecan Tragedy*. Oxford: Oxford University Press, 2004.
Loisy, A. "Les épîtres de S. Paul." *Revue d'histoire et de literature religieuses* 7 (1921): 213–250.
Long, Frederick J. *Ancient Rhetoric and Paul's Apology: The Compositional Unity of 2 Corinthians*. Cambridge: Cambridge University Press, 2004.
Longenecker, Richard N. and M. C. Tenney. *New Dimensions in New Testament Study*. Grand Rapids: Eerdmans, 1974.
Lüdemann, Gerd. *Paulus, der Heidenapostel. Band I: Studien zur Chronologie*. Göttingen: Vandenhoeck & Ruprecht, 1980.
——. "A Chronology of Paul." *Colloquy on New Testament Studies: A Time for Reappraisal and Fresh Approaches*, ed. B. Corley, 292–203. Macon: Mercer University Press, 1983.

———. *Paul, Apostle to the Gentiles: Studies in Chronology.* Philadelphia: Fortress Press, 1984.
———. *Paulus, der Heidenapostel Band II: Antipaulinismus im frühen Christentum.* Göttingen: Vandenhoeck & Ruprecht, 1989.
———. *Early Christianity according to the Traditions in Acts: A Commentary.* Minneapolis: Fortress Press, 1989.
———. *The Acts of the Apostles.* Amherst: Prometheus Press, 2005.
Lütgert, Wilhelm. *Freiheitspredigt und Schwarmgeister in Korinth.* Gütersloh: Beryelsmann, 1908.
Lutz, Cora. *Musonius Rufus; The Roman Socrates.* New Haven: Yale University Press, 1942.
Luz, Ulrich V. *Matthew 8–20: A Commentary.* Minneapolis: Fortress Press, 2001.
MacDonald, Margaret Y. *The Pauline Churches: A Socio-Historical Study of Institutionalization in the Pauline and Deutero-Pauline Writings.* Cambridge: Cambridge University Press, 2004.
———. "The Shifting Centre: Ideology and the Interpretation of 1 Corinthians." In *Christianity at Corinth: The Quest for the Pauline Church*, ed. Edward Adams and David G. Horrell, 273–294. Louisville: Westminster John Knox Press, 2004.
MacDowell, D. M. "Hybris in Athens." *Greece and Rome* 23 (1976): 14–30.
Machelet, Christian. "Paulus und seine Gegner. Eine Untersuchung zu den Korintherbriefen." In *Theokratia*, ed. W. Dietrich, 183–190. Leiden: Brill, 1973.
Mackintosh, R. "The Brief Visit to Corinth." *Expositor* 6 (1908): 226–234.
MacMullen, Ramsay. *Roman Social Relations 50 B.C. to A.D. 284.* New Haven: Yale University Press, 1974.
———. *Paganism in the Roman Empire.* New Haven: Yale University Press, 1983.
———. *Romanization in the Time of Augustus.* New Haven: Yale University Press, 2000.
Maiuri, Amedeo. *Ercolano: I nuovi scavi (1927–1958).* Rome: Instituto Poligrafico dello Strato, 1958.
Malherbe, Abraham J. *Ancient Epistolary Theorists.* Atlanta: Scholars Press, 1988.
———. "Antisthenes and Odysseus, and Paul at War." *Harvard Theological Review* 76 (1983): 143–173.
———. *Social Aspects of Early Christianity.* Philadelphia: Fortress Press, 1983.
Manson, T. W. *Studies in the Gospels and Epistles*, ed. M. Black. Manchester: Manchester University Press, 1962.
Marek, Christian. *Die Inschriften von Kaunos.* Munich: Beck, 2006.
Marquardt, Joachim. *Das Privatleben der Römer.* Leipzig: Hirzel, 1879.
Marshall, Bruce A. *Crassus: A Political Biography.* Amsterdam: Hakkert, 1976.
Marshall, Peter. *Enmity in Corinth: Social Conventions in Paul's Relations with the Corinthians.* Tübingen: Mohr-Siebeck, 1987.
Martin, Dale B. *Slavery as Salvation: The Metaphor of Slavery in Pauline Christianity.* New Haven: Yale University Press, 1990.
———. *The Corinthian Body.* New Haven: Yale University Press, 1999.
Martin, Josef. *Antike Rhetorik. Technik und Methode.* Munich: Beck, 1974.

Martin, R. P. *2 Corinthians*. Waco: Word, 1986.
Mason, Hugh J. *Greek Terms for Roman Institutions: A Lexicon and Analysis*. Toronto: Hakkert, 1974.
Matera, Frank J. *II Corinthians*. Louisville: Westminster Press, 2003.
Matthews, Shelly. *First Converts: Rich Pagan Women and the Rhetoric of Mission in Early Judaism and Christianity*. Stanford: Stanford University Press, 2001.
Mau, August. *Pompeii: Its Life and Art*. London: Macmillan, 1907.
McDonald, William A. "Archaeology and St. Paul's Journeys in Greek Lands, Part III—Corinth." *Biblical Archaeologist* 14 (1951): 78–96.
McDonough, Sean M. "Small Change: Saul to Paul, Again." *Journal of Biblical Literature* 125 (2006): 390–391.
McLean, B. H. "The Agrippinilla Inscription: Religious Associations and Early Church Formation." In *Origins and Method: Towards a New Understanding of Judaism and Christianity*, ed. B. H. McLean, 239–270. Sheffield: Sheffiled Academic Press, 1993.
Meeks, Wayne A. *The First Urban Christians: The Social World of the Apostle Paul*. New Haven: Yale University Press, 1983.
Meggitt, Justin J. "The Social Status of Erastus (Rom. 16:23)." *Novum Testamentum* 38 (1996): 218–223.
———. "Laughing and Dreaming at the Foot of the Cross: Context and Reception of a Religious Symbol." *Journal for the Study of Religion, Ethics, and Society* 1 (1996): 9–14.
———. *Paul, Poverty and Survival*. Edinburgh: T & T Clark, 1998.
Mell, U. *Neue Schöpfung: Eine traditions-geschichtliche und exegetische Studie zu einem soteriologischen Grundsatz paulinischer Theologie*. Berlin: Walter de Gruyter, 1989.
Menzies, A. *The Second Epistle of the Apostle Paul to the Corinthians*. London: Macmillan, 1912.
Meritt, Benjamin Dean. *Corinth, Volume VIII, Part I: Greek Inscriptions 1896–1927*. Cambridge, MA: Harvard University Press, 1931.
Merklein, H. *Der erste Brief an die Korinther. Kapitel 1–4*. Gütersloh: Gütersloher Verlagshaus Mohn, 1992.
Merritt, H. Wayne. *In Word and Deed: Moral Integrity in Paul*. New York: Peter Lang, 1993.
Metzger, Bruce M. *A Textual Commentary on the Greek New Testament*. Stuttgart: Deutsche Bibelgesellschaft, 1971.
Meyer, H. A. W. *Der erste Brief an die Korinther*. Göttingen: Vandenhoeck & Ruprecht, 1839.
———. *Der zweite Brief an die Korinther*. Göttingen: Vandenhoeck & Ruprecht, 1870.
Michaelis, Wilhelm. "συγγενής, συγγένεια." *Theological Dictionary of the New Testament* 7 (1971): 740–742.
Michel, Otto. *Der Brief an die Römer*. Göttingen: Vandenhoeck & Ruprecht, 1978.
Milleker, Elizabeth J. "Three Heads of Sarapis from Corinth." *Hesperia* 54 (1985): 121–135.

Miller, Paul Allen. *Subjecting Verses: Latin Love Elegy and the Emergence of the Real.* Princeton: Princeton University Press, 1984.
Miller, Stella Grobel. "A Mosaic Floor from a Roman villa at Anaploga." *Hesperia* 41 (1972): 332–354.
Milligan, George. *Selections from the Greek Papyri.* Cambridge: Cambridge University Press, 1910.
———. *Here and There among the Papyri.* London: Hodder & Stoughton, 1923.
Mitchell, Lynette G. *Greeks Bearing Gifts: The Public Use of Private Relationships in the Greek World.* Cambridge: Cambridge University Press, 2002.
Mitchell, Margaret M. "Concerning ΠΕΡΙ ΔΕ in 1 Corinthians." *Novum Testamentum* 31 (1989): 229–256.
———. *Paul and the Rhetoric of Reconciliation: An Exegetical Investigation of theLanguage and Composition of 1 Corinthians.* Tübingen: Mohr Siebeck, 1991.
———. "New Testament Envoys in the Context of Greco-Roman Diplomatic and Epistolary Vonventions: The Example of Timothy and Titus." *Journal of Biblical Literature* 111 (1992): 641–662.
———. *The Heavenly Trumpet: John Chrysostom and the Art of Pauline Interpretation.* Tübingen: Mohr Siebeck, 2000.
———. "Reading Rhetoric with Patristic Exegetes: John Chrysostom on Galatians." In *Antiquity and Humanity: Essays on Religion and Philosophy presented to Hans Dieter Betz on his 70th Birthday*, ed. A. Y. Collins, 333–355. Tübingen: Mohr Siebeck, 2001.
———. "The Corinthian Corrspondence and the Birth of Pauline Hermeneutics." In *Paul and the Corinthians: Studies on a Community in Conflict*, ed. T. J. Burke and J. K. Elliott, 17–53. Leiden: Brill, 2003.
———. "Paul's Letters to Corinth: The Interpretive Intertwining of Literary and Historical Reconstruction." In *Urban Religion in Roman Corinth*, ed. D. N. Schowalter and S. Friesen, 307–338. Cambridge, MA: Harvard University Press, 2005.
Mitchell, Stephen. *Anatolia. Land, Men, and Gods in Asia Minor II: The Rise of the Church.* Oxford: Oxford University Press, 1993.
Mitchell, Thomas N. "Cicero before Luca." *Transactions of the American Philological Association* 100 (1969): 295–320.
Mitteis, L. and U. Wilcken. *Grundzüge und Chrestomathie der Papyruskunde.* Leipzig: Teubner, 1912.
Modrzejewski, J. *The Jews of Egypt: From Ramses II to Emperor Hadrian.* Princeton: Princeton University Press, 1995.
Moffatt, James. *The Historical New Testament.* New York: Scribner's, 1901.
———. *An Introduction to the Literature of the New Testament.* New York: Scribner's 1910.
———. *The First Epistle of Paul to the Corinthians.* New York: Harper, 1938.
Morris, Leon. *The Epistle to the Romans.* Grand Rapids: Eerdmans, 1988.
Momigliano, Arnaldo. *Alien Wisdom: The Limits of Hellenization.* Cambridge: Cambridge University Press, 1975.
Mommsen, Theodor. *Gesammelte Schriften I.* Berlin: Weidmann, 1905.
Moule, C. F. D. *An Idiom Book of New Testament Greek.* Cambridge: Cambridge University Press, 1953.

Mowery, Robert L. "Paul and Caristanius at Pisidian Antioch." *Biblica* 87 (2006): 221–242.
Moyer, Hubbard. "Was Paul Out of His Mind? Re-Reading 2 Corinthians 5:13." *Journal for the Study of the New Testament* 70 (1998): 39–64.
Mrozek, Stanislaw. "Wirtschaftliche Grundlagen des Aufstiegs der Freigelassenen im römischen Reich." *Chiron* 5 (1975): 311–317.
Mullins, Terence Y. "Disclosure: A Literary Form in the New Testament." *Novum Testamentum* 7 (1964): 44–50.
Munck, Johannes. "Paulus tamquam abortivus." In *New Testament Essays: Studies in Memory of T. W. Manson*, ed. A. J. B. Higgins, 180–193. Manchester: Manchester University Press, 1959.
Murphy-O'Connor, Jerome. "Another Jesus (2 Cor. 11:4)." *Revue biblique* 97 (1990): 238–251.
——. "Lots of God-fearers: *Theosebeis* in the Aphrodisias Inscription." *Revue biblique* 99 (1992): 418–424.
——. *Paul: A Critical Life*. Oxford: Oxford University Press, 1996.
——. *St. Paul's Corinth: Texts and Archaeology*. 3rd ed. Collegeville: Liturgical Press, 2002.
Neander, August. *Auslegung der beiden Briefe an die Korinther*. Berlin: Reimer, 1959.
Nesselrath, H.-G. *Lukians Parasitendialog: Untersuchungen und Kommentar*. Berlin: Walter de Gruyter, 1985.
Neusner, Jacob. *Judaism, the Evidence of the Mishnah*. Chicago: University of Chicago Press, 1981.
Nicholson, John. "The Delivery and Confidentiality of Cicero's Letters." *Classical Journal* 90 (1994): 33–63.
Nickle, K. F. *The Collection: A Study in Paul's Strategy*. Napersville: Allenson, 1966.
Nicoll, A. *Masks, Mimes and Miracles: Studies in the Popular Theatre*. New York: Harcourt, Brace, 1931.
Nicols, John. "*Hospitium* and political friendship in the late Republic." In *Aspects of Friendship in the Graeco-Roman World*, ed. Michael Peachin, 99–110. Portsmouth: Journal of Roman Archaeology, 2001.
Norden, Eduard. *Die antike Kunstprosa*, 2 vols. Leipzig: Teubner, 1898.
North, John. "The Development of Religious Pluralism." In *The Jews Among Pagans and Christians in the Roman Empire*, ed. Judith Lieu, John North, and Tessa Rajak, 174–193. London: Routledge, 1994.
Nussbaum, Martha. *The Therapy of Desire: Theory and Practice in Hellenistic Ethics*. Princeton: Princeton University Press, 1994.
Oliver, Andrew. "A Glass Opus Sectile Panel from Corinth." *Hesperia* 70 (2001): 349–363.
Oliver, James H. *Marcus Aurelius. Aspects of Civic and Cultural Policy in the East*. Princeton: Princeton University Press, 1970.
Ollrog, Wolf-Henning. *Paulus und seine Mitarbeiter. Untersuchungen zu Theorie und Praxis der paulinischen Mission*. Neukirchen-Vluyn: Neukirchener Verlag, 1979.

——. "die Abfassungsverhältnisse von Röm 16." In *Kirche*, ed. Dieter Lührmann and Georg Strecker, 221–244. Tübingen: Mohr Siebeck, 1980.
Olsson, Bror Hjalmar. *Papyrusbriefe aus der frühesten Römerzeit*. Uppsala: Almquist and Wiksells, 1925.
Oostendorp, D. W. *Another Jesus: A Gospel of Jewish-Christian Superiority in II Corinthians*. Kampen: Kok, 1967.
Osiek, Carolyn and David L. Balch. *Families in the New Testament World: Households and House Churches*. Louisville: Westminster John Knox Press, 1997.
Osiek, Carolyn and Margaret Y. MacDonald. *A Woman's Place: House Churches in Earliest Christianity*. Augsburg Fortress Press, 2006.
Ostrow, S. E. "The *Augustales* in the Augustan Scheme." In *Between Republic and Empire. Interpretations of Augustus and His Principate*, ed. K. A. Raaflaub, 364–379. Berkeley: University of Claifornia Press, 1990.
Overman, J. Andrew. "The God-fearers: Some Neglected Features." *Journal for the Study of the New Testament* 32 (1988): 17–26.
Packer, James E. *The Insulae of Imperial Ostia*. Rome: American Academy in Rome, 1971.
Pagano, Mario. *Herculaneum: A Reasoned Archaeological Itinerary*. Naples, T & M, 2000.
Pakaluk, Michael. *Nicomachean Ethics Books VIII and IX*. Oxford: Clarendon Press, 1998.
Pallas D. I. and S. P. Dantes. "Επιγραφες απο την Κορινθω." *Archaiologike Ephemeris* 19 (1979): 75–76.
Palmer Bonz, Marianne. "The Jewish Donor Inscriptions from Aphrodisias: Are They Both Third-Century, and Who Are the Theosebeis?" *Harvard Studies in Classical Philology* 96 (1994): 281–299.
Panayotakis, Costas. *Theatrum Arbitri: theatrical elements in the Satyricon of Petronius*. Leiden: Brill, 1995.
Pangle, Lorraine Smith. *Aristotle and the Philosophy of Friendship*. Cambridge: Cambridge University Press, 2003.
Pani, M. *Roma a il re d'oriente da Augusto a Tiberio*. Bari: Università di Bari, 1984.
Peachin, Michael. "Friendship and abuse at the dinner table." In *Aspects of Friendship in the Graeco-Roman World*, ed. Michael Peachin, 135–144. Portsmouth: Journal of Roman Archaeology, 2001.
Penella, Robert. *The Letters of Apollonius of Tyana. A Critical Text with Prolegomena, Translation and Commentary*. Leiden: Brill, 1979.
Perkins, Judith, *Roman Imperial Identities in the Early Christian Era*. London: Routledge, 2009.
Pernot, Laurent. *La rhétorique de l'éloge dans le monde gréco-romain*, 2 vols. Paris: Institut d'Etudes Augustiniennes, 1993.
Peters, W. J. Th. And P. G. P. Meyboom. "The Roots of Provncial Roman Painting, Results of Current Research in Nero's Domus Aurea." In *Roman Provinical Wall Painting*, ed. J. Liversidge, 33–74. Oxford: Oxford University Press, 1982.
Peterson, Brian K. *Eloquence and the Proclamation of the Gospel in Corinth*. Atlanta: Scholars Press, 1998.

Pfleiderer, Otto. *Das Urchristentum, seine Schriften und Lehren in geschichtlichem Zusammenhang beschrieben*. Berlin: Reimer, 1887, ²1902.
Pickett, Raymond. *The Cross in Corinth: The Social Significance of the Death of Jesus*. Sheffield: Sheffield Academic Press, 1997.
Pierson, Lionel. *Popular Ethics in Ancient Greece*. Stanford: Stanford University Press, 1962.
Piper, Linda J. *Spartan Twilight*. New Rochelle: Aristide D. Carazas, 1986.
Plank, Karl. *Paul and the Irony of Affliction*. Atlanta: Scholars Press, 1987.
Pleket, H. W. "Urban Elites and Business in the Greek Part of the Roman Empire." In *Trade in the Ancient Economy*, ed. Peter Garnsey, Keith Hopkins, and C. R. Whittaker, 131–144, 203–207. Berkeley: University of California Press, 1983.
Plezia, M. *Aristotelis epistolarum fragmenta cum testament*. Warsaw: Academia Scientiarum Polona, 1968.
Plummer, Alfred. *A Critical and Exegetical Commentary on the Second Epistle of St. Paul to the Corinthians*. Edinburgh: T & T Clark, 1915.
Pogoloff, Stephen M. *Logos and Sophia: The Rhetorical Situation of 1 Corinthians*. Atlanta: Scholars Press, 1992.
Preston, Rebecca. "Roman Questions, Greek Answers: Plutarch and the Construction of Identity." In *Being Greek under Rome: Cultural Identity, the Second Sophistic and the Development of Empire*, ed. Simon Goldhill, 86–112. Cambridge: Cambridge University Press, 2001.
Pritchett, William K. *Dionysius of Halicarnassus. On Thucydides*. Berkeley: University of California Press, 1975.
Prümm, K. *Diakonia Pneumatos I: Theologische Auslegung des zweiten Korintherbriefs*. Freiburg: Herder, 1967.
Puech, B. "Grand-prêtres et helladarques d'achaïe." *Revue des etudes anciennes* 85 (1983): 15–43.
Räbiger, Julius Ferdinand. *Kritische Untersuchungen über den Inhalt der beiden Briefe des Apostels Paulus an die korinthische Gemeinde mit Rücksicht auf die in ihr herrschenden Streitigkeiten*. Breslau: Morgenstern, 1886.
Rajak, Tessa and David Noy. "Archisynagogoi: Office, Title and Social Status in the Greco-Jewish Synagogue." *Journal of Roman Studies* 83 (1993): 75–93.
———. *The Jewish Dialogue with Greece and Rome: Studies in Cultural and Social Interaction*. Leiden: Brill, 2002.
Ramsay, William M. *St. Paul the Traveller and the Roman Citizen*. London: Hodder and Stoughton, 1897.
———. "A Historical Commentary on the Epistles to the Corinthians." *TheExpositor* 1 (1900): 91–111.
———. "Studies in the Roman Province Galatia." *Journal of Roman Studies* 16 (1926): 201–215.
Ramsden, S. E. "Roman Mosaics in Greece." *American Journal of Archaeology* 83 (1979): 80–93.
Rawson, Beryl. *The Politics of Friendship*. Sydney: Sydney University Press, 1978.
Rawson, Elizabeth. *Cicero: A Portrait*. London: Bristol Classical Press, 1983.
Reich, Hermann. *Der Mimus. Ein litterar-entwickelungsgeschichtlicher Versuch*. Berlin: Weidmann, 1903.

Relihan, J. C. "The Confessions of Persius." *Illinois Classical Studies* 14 (1984): 145–167.

Rendall, Gerald H. *The Epistles of Paul to the Corinthians.* London; Macmillan, 1909.

Renehan, R. "The Greek Philosophical Background of Fourth Maccabees." *Rheinisches Museum für Philologie* 115 (1972): 221–238.

Ribbeck, Otto. *Kolax: Eine ethologische Studie.* Abhandlungen der Königl. Sächischen Gesellschaft der Wissenschaften, Phil.-hist. Klasse 9.1. Leipzig: Teubner, 1883.

Richardson, Peter. "The Thunderbolt in Q and the Wise Man in Corinth." In *From Jesus to Paul*, ed. P. Richardson and J. C. Hurd, 91–111. Waterloo: Laurier, 1984.

——. "On the Absence of 'Anti-Judaism' in 1 Corinthians." In *Anti-Judaism in Early Christianity; Vol. I. Paul and the Gospels*, ed. P. Richardson and D. Granskou, 59–74. Ontario; Wilfred Laurier University Press, 1986.

Riesner, Rainer. *Paul's Early Period: Chronology, Mission, Strategy.* Grand Rapids: Eerdmans, 1998.

Rigaux, Béda. *Saint Paul: Les épitres aux Thessaloniciens.* Paris: Gabalda, 1956.

Rist, J. M. *Stoic Philosophy.* Cambridge: Cambridge University Press, 1969.

Rives, James B. *Religion and Authority in Roman Carthage from Augustus to Constatine.* Oxford: Clarendon Press, 1995.

——. "Augustales." *Oxford Classical Dictionary* (2003): 215.

Rix, H. *Römische Personennamen: Namenforschung: Ein Internationales Handbuch zur Onomastik I.* Berlin: Walter de Gruyter, 1995.

Rizakis, A. D. "Anthroponymie et société: les noms romains dans les provinces hellénophones de l'Empire." In *Roman Onomastics in the Greek East: Social and Political Aspects*, ed. A.D. Rizakis, 11–30. Athens: Finnish Institute, 1996.

Rizakis, A. D. and S. Zoumbaki. *Roman Peloponnese I: Roman Personal Names in Their Social Context (Achaia, Arcadia, Argolis, Corinthia, and Eleia).* Athens: Research Centre for Greek and Roman Antiquity, 2001.

Rizakis, A. D., S. Zoumbaki, Cl. Lepenioti. *Roman Peloponnese II: Roman Personal Names in Their Social Context (Laconia and Messenia).* Athens: Research Centre for Greek and Roman Antiquity, 2004.

Roberts, C., T. C. Skeat, and A. D. Nock. "The Gild of Zeus Hypsistos." *Harvard Theological Review* 29 (1936): 39–88.

Roberts, W. Rhys. *Longinus on the Sublime.* Cambridge: Cambridge University Press, 1899.

Robertson, A. T. *Word Pictures in the New Testament.* 4 vols. Grand Rapids: Baker Book House, 1931.

——. *A Grammar of the Greek New Testament in the Light of Historical Research.* New York: Hodder and Stoughton, 1914.

Robinson, Henry S. "Excavations at Corinth." *Archaiologikon Deltion* 18 (1963): 76–80.

——. "Excavations at Corinth." *Archaiologikon Deltion* 21 (1966): 134–136.

Robinson, O. F. *The Criminal Law of Ancient Rome.* London: Duckworth, 1995.

Roetzel, Calvin. *2 Corinthians.* Nashville: Abingdon, 2007.

Roller, Matthew B. *Constructing Autocracy: Aristocrats and Emperors in Julio-Claudian Rome*. Princeton: Princeton University Press, 2001.
Roos, A. G. "De Titulo quodam latino Corinthi nuper reperto." *Mnemosyne* 58 (1930): 160–165.
Rosner, Brian. "Deuteronomy in 1 and 2 Corinthians." In *Deuteronomy in the New Testament: The New Testament and the Scriptures of Israel*, ed. M. J. J. Menken and S. Moyise. London: T & T Clark, 2007.
Rothwell, Kenneth S. *Politics and Persuasion in Aristophanes' Ecclesiazusae*. Leiden: Brill, 1990.
Rudich, Vasily. *Dissidence and Literature under Nero: the Price of Rhetoricisation*. London: Routledge, 1997
Rüpke, Jörg. *Religion of the Romans*. Cambridge: Polity Press, 2007.
Sabatier, A. *L'Apôtre Paul. Esquisse d'une histoire de sa pensée*. Strasbourg: Treuttel et Wurtz, 1870.
Sampaolo, Valeria. "Casa dei Vettii." In *Pompei e Mosaici*, ed. Ida Baldassare, 468–572. Rome: Istituto della Enciclopedia Otaliana, 1994.
Salies, G. Hellenkemper. "Römische Mosaiken im Griechenland." *Bonner Jahrbücher* 186 (1986): 265–286.
Saller, Richard. *Personal Patronage under the Early Empire*. Cambridge; Cambridge University Press, 1982.
—. "Martial on Patronage and Literature." *The Classical Quarterly* 33 (1983): 246–257.
—. "Patronage and Friendship in Early Imperial Rome: Drawing the Distinction." In *Patronage in Ancient Society*, ed. A. Wallace-Hadrill, 49–61. London: Routledge, 1989.
—. *Patriarchy, Property and Death in the Roman Family*. Cambridge: Cambridge University Press, 1997.
Salmeri, Giovanni. "Dio, Rome, and the Civic Life of Asia Minor." In *Dio Chrysostom: Politics, Letters, and Philosophy*, ed. Simon Swain, 53–92. Oxford: Oxford University Press, 2000.
Salmon, Edward T. *Roman Colonization under the Republic*. Ithaca: Cornell University Press, 1970.
Salomies, Olli. *Die römischen Vornamen: Studien zur römischen Namengebung*. Helsinki: Societas Scientiarum Fennica, 1987.
Sand, Alexander. *Der Begriff "Fleisch" in den paulinischen Hauptbriefen*. Regensburg: Pustet, 1967.
Schlier, Heinrich. *Der Römerbrief*. Freiburg: Herder, 1977.
Schnelle, Udo. *Einleitung in das Neue Testament*. Göttingen: Vandenhoeck & Ruprecht, 2002.
Schmeller, Thomas. *Hierarchie und Egalität: Eine sozialgeschichtliche Untersuchung paulinischer Gemeinden und griechisch-römischer Vereine*. Stuttgart: Katholisches Bibelwerk, 1995.
Schmiedel, Paul Wilhelm. *Hand-Commentar zum Neuen Testament*. Freiburg: Mohr, Siebeck, 1891, ²1892.
Schmithals, Walter. *Die Gnosis in Korinth: Eine Untersuchung zu den Korintherbriefen*. Göttingen: Vandenhoeck & Ruprecht, 1969.

———. *Gnosticism in Corinth: An Investigation of the Letters to the Corinthians*. Nashville: Abingdon, 1971.
———. *Die Apostelgeschichte des Lukas*. Zurich: Theologischer Verlag, 1982.
Schnabel, Eckhard J. *Der erste Brief des Paulus an die Korinther*. Wuppertal: R. Brockhaus Verlag, 2006.
Schneider, Gerhard. *Die Apostelgeschichte: II Teil: Kommentar zu Kap. 9,1–28,31*. Freiburg and Vienna: Herder, 1982.
Schnelle, Udo. *Wandlungen im paulinischen Denken*. Stuttgart: Katholisches Bibelwerk, 1989.
Schniewind, J. "Die Archonten des Äons, 1 Kor. 2,6–8." In *Nachgelassene Reden und Aufsätze*, ed. E. Kähler, 104–109. Berlin: Töpelmann, 1952.
Schowalter, Daniel N. "Seeking Shelter in Roman Corinth: Archaeology and the Placement of Paul's Communities." In *Corinth in Context: Comparative Studies on Religion and Society*, ed. Steven J. Friesen, Daniel N. Schowalter, and James C. Walters, 330–344. Leiden: Brill, 2010.
Schrage, Wolfgang. *Der erste Brief an die Korinther*. 4 vols. Neukirchen-Vluyn: Neukirchener Verlag, 1991–2001.
———. "Der gekreuzigte und auferweckte Herr." *Zeitschrift für Theologie und Kirche* 94 (1997): 25–38.
Schreiber, Alfred. *Die Gemeinde in Korinth: Versuch einer gruppen-dynamischen Betrachtung der Entwicklung der Gemeinde von Korinth auf Basis des ersten Korintherbriefes*. Münster: Aschendorff, 1977.
Schrenk, Gottlob. "ἄδικος." *Theological Dictionary of the New Testament* 1 (1964): 149–150.
Schulze, W. *Zur Geschichte lateinischer Eigennamen*. Göttingen: Vandenhoeck & Ruprecht, 1905.
Schüpphaus, J. *Die Psalmen Salomos: Ein Zeugnis Jerusalemer Theologie und Frömmigkeit in der Mitte des vorchristlichen Jahrhunderts*. Leiden: Brill, 1977.
Schürer, Emil. *The History of the Jewish People in the age of Jesus Christ*. 4 vols., rev. and ed. by Geza Vermes, Fergus Millar and Martin Goodman. Edinburgh: T & T Clark, 1979–1986.
Schwartz, Daniel R. "On Drama and Authenticity in Philo and Josephus." *Scripta Classica Israelica* 10 (1989/90): 113–129.
Schwartz, Eduard. *Characterköpfe aus der antiken Literatur*. Berlin: Weidmann, 1912.
Schweizer, Eduard. "σάρξ." *Theological Dictionary of the New Testament* 7 (1971): 98–151.
———. *Church Order in the New Testament*. London: SCM Press, 1979.
Schenk, Wolfgang. "Der 1. Korintherbrief als Briefsammlung." *Zeitschrift für die neutestamentliche Wissenschaft* 60 (1969): 219–243.
Segal, Erich. *Roman Laughter: The Comedy of Plautus*. Cambridge, MA: Harvard University Press, 1952.
Sellin, Gerhard. "Das 'Geheimnis' der Weisheit und das Rätsel der 'Christuspartei' (zu 1 Kor 1–4)." *Zeitschrift für die neutestamentliche Wissenschaft* 73 (1982): 69–96.
———. "Hauptprobleme des Ersten Korintherbriefes." *Aufstieg und Niedergang der römischen Welt* II/25.4 (1987): 2940–3044.

Semler, Johann Salomo. *Paraphrasis II. Epistolae ad Corinthios.* Halae Magdeburgicae: Hemmerde, 1776.
Senft, Christophe. *La première épître de Saint Paul aux Corinthiens.* Neuchatel: Neuchatel- Delachaux, 1979.
Shackleton Bailey, D. R. *Cicero: Epistulae ad Familiares.* Vol. I. Cambridge: Cambridge University Press, 1977.
——. *Cicero's Letters to His Friends.* Atlanta: Scholars Press, 1988.
Shaw, G. *The Cost of Authority: Manipulation and Freedom in the New Testament.* Philadelphia: Fortress Press, 1982.
Shear, Theodore Leslie. "Excavations at Corinth in 1925." *American Journal of Archaeology* 29 (1925): 381–388.
——. "Excavations in the Theatre District and Tombs of Corinth in 1928." *American Journal of Archaeology* 32 (1928): 474–495.
——. "Excavations in the Theatre District and Tombs of Corinth in 1929." *American Journal of Archaeology* 33 (1929): 525–526.
——. *Corinth V: The Roman Villa.* Cambridge, MA: Harvard University Press, 1930.
Sherk, Robert Kenneth. *The Roman Empire: Augustus to Hadrian.* Cambridge: Cambridge University Press, 1988.
Sherwin-White, A. N. *Roman Society and Roman Law in the New Testament.* Oxford: Clarendon Press, 1963.
Shiell, William. *Reading Acts: The Lector and the Early Christian Audience.* Leiden: Brill, 2004.
Sickenberger, Joseph. *Die beiden Briefe des heiligen Paulus an die Korinther.* Bonn: Hanstein, 1921.
Sihvola, J. and T. Engberg-Pederson. *The Emotions in Hellenistic Philosophy.* Dordrecht: Kluwer Academic Publishers, 1998.
Smit, Joop F. M. *"About the Idol Offerings": Rhetoric, Social Context and Theology of Paul's Discourse in 1 Corinthians 8:1–11:1.* Leuven: Peeters, 2000.
——. "What is Apollos? What is Paul? In Search for the Coherence of First Corinthians 1.10–4.21." *Novum Testamentum* 44 (2002): 231–251.
Smith, Dennis Edwin. "The Egyptian Cults at Corinth." *Harvard Theological Review* 70 (1977): 210–231.
——. *From Symposium to Eucharist: The Banquet in the Early Christian World.* Minneapolis: Fortress Press, 2003.
Smith, M. S. *Petronii Arbitri 'Cena Trimalchionis'.* Oxford: Oxford University Press, 1975.
Smith, J. T. *Roman Villas: A Study in Social Structure.* London; Routledge, 1997.
Smith, Wesley D. *Hippocrates: Pseudepigraphic Writings.* Leiden: Brill, 1990.
Smyth, Herbert Weir. *Greek Grammar.* Cambridge, MA: Harvard University Press, 1956.
Sokolowski, F. *Lois Sacrèes de L'Asie Mineure.* Paris: École Francais d'Athènes, 1955.
Solin, Heikki. "Three Ciceroniana." *The Classical Quarterly* 37 (1987): 521–523.
——. *Die stadtrömischen Sklavennamen: Ein Namenbuch.* Stuttgart: Franz Steiner, 1996.

———. "Latin Cognomina in the Greek East." In *The Greek East in the Roman Context*, ed. Olli Salomies, 189–202. Helsinki: The Finnish Institute at Athens, 2001.

———. "Names, personal, Roman." *Oxford Classical Dictionary*, 3rd ed., Simon Hornblower And Anthony Spawforth, eds., 1024–1026. Oxford: Oxford University Press, 2003.

Solmsen, F. "The Aristotelian Tradition in Ancient Rhetoric." In *Rhetorika: Schriften zur aristotelischen und hellenistischen Rhetorik*, ed. P. Steinmetz, 320–335. Hildesheim: Georg Olms, 1968.

Sorabji, Richard. "Chrysippus—Posidonius—Seneca: A High-level Debate on Emotion." In *The Emotions in Hellenistic Philosophy*, ed. J. Sihvola and T. Engberg-Pedersen, 149–169. Dordrecht: Kluwer Academic Publishers, 1998.

———. *Emotion and Peace of Mind: From Stoic Agitation to Christian Temptation.* Oxford: Oxford University Press, 2000.

Spawforth, Anthony J. S. "Roman Corinth: The Formation of a Colonial Elite." In *Roman Onomastics in the Greek East: Social and Political Aspects*, ed. A. D. Rizakis, 167–182. Athens: Research Center for Greek and Roman Antiquity, 1996.

Spencer, Aida Besacon. *Paul's Literary Style*. Washington, D.C.: University Press of America, 2007.

Spicq, C. *Agape in the New Testament.* St. Louis: Herder, 1963.

———. "ΑΠΑΡΧΗ. Note de lexicographie neo-testamentaire." In *The New Testament Age*, ed. W. C. Heinrich, 493–502. Macon: Mercer University Press, 1984.

Stählin, Gustav. "ξένος, κτλ." *Theological Dictionary of the New Testament* 5 (1967): 3–23.

Starr, Raymond J. "Reading Aloud: Lectores and Roman Reading." *The Classical Journal* 86 (1991): 337–343.

Stegemann, Ekkehard W. and Wolfgang Stegemann. *Urchristliche Sozialgeschichte: Die Anfänge im Judentum und die Christusgemeinden in der mediterranen Welt.* Stuttgart: Kohlhammer, 1995.

———. *The Jesus Movement: A Social History of the First Century.* Minneapolis: Fortress Press, 1999.

Steinhauer, G. Γάιος Ἰούλοις Εὐρυκλῆς. Συμβολὴ στὴν ἱστορία τῆς ῥωμαϊκῆς Σπάρτης. Ph.D. dissertation. University of Athens, 1989.

Stemmer, Klaus. *Casa dell' Ara Massima.* Munich: Hirmer Verlag, 1992.

———. "Casa dell' Ara massima." In *Pompei e Mosaici*, ed. Ida Baldassare, 847–886. Rome: Istituto della Enciclopedia Italiana, 1994.

Stepheson, Alan M. G. "A Defense of the Integrity of 2 Corinthians." In *The Authorship and Integrity of the New Testament.* London: SPCK, 1965.

Stevenson, T. R. "The Ideal Benefactor and the Father Analogy in Greek and Roman Thought." *Classical Quarterly* 42 (1992): 421–436.

Stillwell, Richard. *Corinth II: The Theatre.* Princeton: The American School of Classical Studies at Athens, 1952.

Stone, Michael E. "The Concept of the Messiah in 4 Ezra." In *Religions in Antiquity*, ed. J. Neusner, 295–312. Leiden: Brill, 1968.

―――. *Fourth Ezra: A Commentary on the Book of Fourth Ezra*. Minneapolis: Fortress Press, 1990.
―――. "The Question of the Messiah in 4 Ezra." In *Selected Studies in Pseudepigrapha and Apocrypha*, ed. M. Stone, 317–332. Leiden: Brill, 1991.
Stowers, Stanley K. "Social Status, Public Speaking and Private Teaching: The Circumstances of Paul's Preaching Activity." *Novum Testamentum* 26 (1984): 59–82.
―――. *Letter-Writing in Greco-Roman Antiquity*. Philadelphia: Westminster, 1986.
―――. "Social typification and the Classification of Ancient Letters." In *The Social World of Formative Christianity and Judaism*, ed. P. Borgen and J. Neusner, 78–90. Philadelphia: Fortress Press, 1988.
―――. "Fourth Maccabees." In *Harper's Bible Commentary*. San Francisco: Harper & Row, 1988.
―――. "Περὶ μὲν γάρ and the Integrity of 2 Cor. 8 and 9." *Novum Testamentum* 32 (1990): 340–348.
―――. "Paul and Self-Mastery." In *Paul in the Greco-Roman World*, ed. J. Paul Sampley, 524–550. Harrisburg: Trinity Press International, 2003.
Strachan, R. H. *The Second Epistle of St. Paul to the Corinthians*. New York: Harper, 1935.
Strack, Hermann and Paul Billerbeck. *Kommentar zum Neuen Testament aus Talmud und Midrasch*. Munich: Beck, 1922.
Strecker, Georg. "Die Legitimität des paulinischen Apostolates nach 2 Korinther 10–13." *New Testament Studies* 38 (1992): 566–586.
Studemund, W. *L. Annaei Seneca librorum Quomodo amicitia continenda sit et De vita patris reliquiae quae supersunt*, in O. Rossbach, *De Seneca philosophi librorum recensione et emendation*. Hildesheim: Olms, 1969.
Stuhlmacher, Peter. "Erwägungen zum ontologischen Charakter der καινὴ κτίσις bei Paulus." *Evangelische Theologie* 27 (1967): 1–35.
―――. *Paul's Letter to the Romans: A Commentary*. Louisville: Westminster John Knox Press, 1994.
Sumney, Jerry L. *Identifying Paul's Opponents: The Question of Method in 2 Corinthians*. Sheffield: Sheffield Academic Press, 1990.
―――. "Studying Paul's Opponents: Advances and Challenges." In *Paul and His Opponents*, ed. Stanley E. Porter, 7–58. Leiden: Brill, 2005.
Sundermann, H.-G. *Der schwache Apostel und die Kraft der Rede: Eine rhetorische Analyse Von 2 Kor 10–13*. Frankfurt: Lang, 1996.
Swain, Simon. *Hellenism and Empire: Language, Classicism, and Power in the Greek World, AD 50–250*. Oxford: Oxford University Press, 1996.
Sykutris, J. "Proclus Περι ἐπιστολιμαίου χαρακτῆρος," *Byzantinisch-Neugriechische Jahrbücher* 7 (1928–1929): 108–118.
―――. "Epistolographie." *Real-Encyclopädie der classischen Altertumswissenschaft* Suppl. 5 (1931): 185–220.
Taillardat, J. "ΦΙΛΟΤΗΣ, ΠΙΣΤΙΣ, und Foedus." *Révue des Études Grecques* 95 (1982): 1–14.
Tasker, R. V. G. *The Second Epistle of Paul to the Corinthians*. London: Tyndale Press, 1958.

Taylor, C. C. W. *Aristotle. Nicomachean Ethics Books II-IV.* Oxford: Oxford University Press, 2006.
Taylor, H. *Plautus: The Comedies I*, ed. D. Slavitt and P. Bovie. Baltimore: Johns Hopkins University Press, 1995.
Taylor, J. J. *Les Actes des deux apôtres, V. Commentaire historique (Act 9,1–18,22).* Paris: Gabalda, 1994
Taylor, Lily R. "Freedmen and Freeborn in the Epitaphs of Imperial Rome." *American Journal of Philology* 82 (1961): 113–132.
Taylor, Lily R. and Allen B. West. "The Euryclids in Latin Inscriptions from Corinth." *American Journal of Archaeology* 30 (1926): 389–400.
Taylor, N. H. "The Composition and Chronology of Second Corinthians." *Journal for the Study of the New Testament* 44 (1991): 67–87.
Theissen, Gerd. *The Social Setting of Pauline Christianity: Essays on Corinth.* Philadelphia; Fortress Press, 1982.
—. *The Religion of the Earliest Churches.* Minneapolis: Fortress Press, 1999.
—. "The Social Structure of Pauline Communities: Some Critical Remarks on J. J. Meggitt, *Paul, Poverty and Survival.*" *Journal for the Study of the New Testament* 84 (2001): 65–84.
Thiselton, Anthony C. *The First Epistle to the Corinthians.* Grand Rapids: Eerdmans, 2000.
Thom, Johan C. "'Harmonious Equality': The *Topos* of Friendship in Neopythagorean Writings." In *Greco-Roman Perspectives on Friendship*, ed. John T. Fitzgerald, 77–103. Atlanta: Scholars Press, 1997.
Thrall, Margaret E. "Super-Apostles, Servants of Christ, and Servants of Satan." *Journal for The Study of the new Testament* 6 (1980): 42–57.
—. "The Offender and the Offence: A Problem of Detection in 2 Corinthians." In *Scripture: Meaning and Method*, ed. B. P. Thompson, 65–78. Pickering: Hull University Press, 1987.
—. *A Critical and Exegetical Commentary on the Second Epistle to the Corinthians*, 2 vols. Edinburgh: T & T Clark, 1994, 2004.
Thurén, L. "John Chrysostom as a Rhetorical Critic: The Hermeneutics of an Early Father." *Biblical Interpretation* 9 (2001): 180–218.
Tieleman, Teun. *Chrysippus' On Affections: Reconstruction and Interpretation.* Leiden: Brill, 2003.
Till, R. "Laberius and Caesar." *Historia* 24 (1975): 260–286.
Too, Yun Lee. *Education in Greek and Roman Antiquity.* Leiden: Brill, 2001.
Treggiari, Susan M. "Intellectuals, Poets, and Their Patrons in the First Century B.C." *Echos du monde classique: Classical News and Views* 26 (1977): 24–29.
Trillitzsch, Winfried. *Seneca im literarischen Urteil der Antike. Darstellung und Sammlung der Zeugnisse.* Amsterdam: Hakkert, 1971.
Trümper, Monica. *Wohnen in Delos: Eine baugeschichtliche Untersuchung zum Wandel der Wohnkultur in hellenistischer Zeit.* Rahden and Westfalen: Marie Leidorf, 1998.
Tylawsky, Elizabeth I. *Saturio's Inheritance: The Greek Ancestry of the Roman Comic Parasite.* New York: Peter Lang, 2002.
Van de Weerd, H. "Een Nieuw Opschrift van Korinthe." *Revue Belge de Philologie et d'Histoire* 10 (1931): 87–95.

Vegge, Ivar. *2 Corinthians, a Letter about Reconciliation: A Psychagogical, Epistolographical, and Rhetorical Analysis*. Tübingen: Mohr-Siebeck, 2008.
Venticinque, Philip F. "Family Affairs: Guild Regulations and Family Relationships in Roman Egyp." *Greek, Roman, and Byzantine Studies* 50 (2010): 273–294.
Verboven, Koenraad. *The Economy of Friends. Economic Aspects of Amicitia and Patronage in the Late Republic*. Bruxelles: Édition Latomus, 2002.
Vermes, Geza. *The Dead Sea Scrolls in English*. Hammondsworth: Penguin Books, 1975.
Veyne, Paul. *A History of Private Life: From Pagan Rome to Byzantium*. Cambridge, MA: Harvard University Press, 1987.
—. *Seneca: The Life of a Stoic*. New York and London: Routledge, 2003.
Vielhauer, Philipp. *Geschichte der urchristlichen Literatur*. Berlin: Walter de Gruyter, 1975.
Vliet, H. van. *No Single Testimony. A Study on the Adoption of the Law of Deut. 19:15 Par. into the New Testament*. Utrecht: Kemink & Zoon, 1958.
Vogliano, Achille. "Le grand iscrizione Bacchia del Metropolitan Museum." *American Journal of Archaeology* 37 (1933): 215–231.
Volkmann, Richard. *Die Rhetorik der Griechen und Römer*. Hildesheim: Georg Olms, 1963.
Vos, Craig Steven de. *Church and Community Conflicts: The Relationship of the Thessalonian, Corinthian, and Philippian Churches with Their Wider Civic Communities*. Atlanta: Scholars Press, 1999.
Vos, J. S. "Der ΜΕΤΑΣΧΗΜΑΤΙΣΜΟΣ in 1 Kor 4,6." *Zeitschrift für die neutestamentliche Wissenschaft* 86 (1995): 154–172.
—. "Die Argumentation des Paulus in 1 Kor 1,10–3,4." In *The Corinthian Correspondence*, ed. R. Bieringer, 87–119. Leuven: Leuven University Press, 1996.
Waele, F. J. de. "Erastus, oikonoom van Korinthe en vriend van St. Paulus." *Mededeelingen van het Nederlandsch Historisch Instituut te Rom* 9 (1929): 40–48.
—. "Die Korinthischen Ausgrabungen 1928–1929." *Gnomon* 6 (1930): 52–57.
Walbank, Mary E. Hoskins. "The Nature and Development of Roman Corinth to the End of the Antonine Period." Ph.D. dissertation, Open University, London, 1986.
—. "Pausanias, Octavia and Temple E at Corinth." *Annual of the British School at Athens* 84 (1989): 361–394.
—. "Evidence for the Imperial Cult in Julio-Claudian Corinth." In *Subject and Ruler: The Cult of the Ruling Power in Classical Antiquity*, ed. Alastair Small, 201–214. Ann Arbor: Journal of Roman Archaeology, 1996.
—. "The Foundation and Planning of Early Roman Corinth." *Journal of Roman Archaeology* 10 (1997): 95–130.
—. "Image and Cult: The Coinage of Roman Corinth." In *Corinth in Context: Comparative Studies on Religion and Society*, ed. Steven J. Friesen, Daniel N. Schowalter, and James C. Walters, 151–197. Leiden: Brill, 2010.
Wallace-Hadrill, Andrew. "The social structure of the Roman house." *Papers of the British School at Rome* 56 (1988): 43–97.

———. "Patronage in Roman society: from republic to empire." In *Patronage in Ancient Society*, ed. A. Wallace-Hadrill, 63–87. London: Routledge, 1990.
———. "Houses and Households: Sampling Pompeii and Herculaneum." In *Marriage, Divorce and Children in ancient Rome*, ed. Beryl Rawson, 191–228. Oxford: Clarendon Press, 1991.
———. *Houses and Society in Pompeii and Herculaneum*. Princeton: Princeton University Press, 1994.
———. "*Domus* and *Insulae* in Rome: Families and Housefuls." In *Early Christian Families in Context: An Interdisciplinary Dialogue*, ed. Carolyn Osiek and David Balch, 3–18. Grand Rapids: Eerdmans, 2003.
Walker, Donald Dale. *Paul's Offer of Leniency (2 Cor. 10:1): Populist Ideology and Rhetoric in a Pauline Letter Fragment*. Tübingen: Mohr Siebeck, 2002.
Walters, James. "Civic Identity in Roman Corinth and Its Impact on Early Christians." In *Urban Religion in Roman Corinth*, ed. Daniel N. Schowalter and Steven Friesen, 397–418. Cambridge, MA: Harvard University Press, 2005.
———. "Paul and the Politics of Meals in Roman Corinth." In *Corinth in Context: Comparative Studies on Religion and Society*, ed. Steven Friesen, Daniel N. Schowalter, and James C. Walters, 350–361. Leiden: Brill, 2010.
Wan, Sze-Kar. *Power in Weakness: Conflict and Rhetoric in Paul's Second Letter to the Corinthians*. Harrisburg: Trinity Press International, 2000.
Watson, Francis. "2 Cor. x–xiii and Paul's Painful Letter to the Corinthians." *Journal of Theological Studies* 35/2 (1984): 324–346.
———. *Paul, Judaism and the Gentiles: A Sociological Approach*. Cambridge: Cambridge University Press, 1986.
Waywell, S. E. "Roman Mosaics in Greece." *American Journal of Archaeology* 83 (1979): 290–310.
Weaver, P. R. C. *Familia Caesaris: A social Study of the Emperor's Freedmen and Slaves*. Cambridge: Cambridge University Press, 1972.
Weber, Michael. *De numero epistolarum Pauli ad Corinthios rectius constituendo*. Wittenberg: University of Wittenberg, 1807.
Webster, T. B. L. *Studies in Later Greek Comedy*. Manchester: Manchester University Press, 1953.
Weichert, V. *Demetrii et Libanii qui ferentur* ΤΥΠΟΙ ΕΠΙΣΤΟΛΙΚΟΙ *et* ΕΠΙΣΤΟΛΙΜΑΙΟΙ ΧΑΡΑΚΤΗΡΕΣ. Leipzig: Teubner, 1910.
Weinberg, Saul S. *Corinth, Volume I, Part 5: The Southeast Building, the Twin Basilicas, the Mosaic House*. Princeton: The American School of Classical Studies at Athens, 1960.
Weinrich, Otto. *Senecas Apocolocyntosis. Die Satire auf Tod/Himmel und Höllenfahrt des Kaisers Claudius*. Berlin: Weidmann, 1923.
Weiss, Johannes. "Beiträge zur paulinischen Rhetorik." In *Theologische Studien*, Bernhard Weiss zu seinem 70. Geburtstag dargebracht, 165–247. Göttingen: Vandenhoeck & Ruprecht, 1897.
———. *Der erste Korintherbrief*. Göttingen: Vandenhoeck & Ruprecht, 1910.
———. *Das Urchristentum*, ed. R. Knopf. Göttingen: Vandenhoeck & Ruprecht, 1917.
———. *The History of Primitive Christianity*. 2 vols., trans. by F. C. Grant. New York: Wilson-Erickson, 1937.

Weiß, Alexander. "Sergius Paullus, Statthalter von Zypern." *Zeitschrift für Papyrologie und Epigraphik* 169 (2009): 188–192.
Weizsäcker, Karl Heinrich von. "Paulus und die Gemeinde in Korinth." *Jahrbücher für Deutsche Theologie* 19 (1873): 604–645.
——. *Das apostolische Zeitalter der christlichen Kirche.* Freiburg: Mohr, 1886, ²1892.
Welborn, L. L. "The Identification of 2 Corinthians 10–13 with the 'Letter of Tears'." *Novum Testamentum* 37 (1995): 138–153.
——. "Like Broken Pieces of a Ring: 2 Cor. 1:1–2:13; 7:5–16 and Ancient Theories of Literary Unity." *New Testament Studies* 42 (1996): 559–583.
——. *Politics and Rhetoric in the Corinthian Epistles.* Macon: Mercer University Press, 1997.
——. "The Runaway Paul: A Character in the Fool's Speech, 2 Cor. 11:1–12:10." *Harvard Theological Review* 92 (1999): 115–163.
——. "Paul's Appeal to the Emotions in 2 Corinthians 1.1–2.13; 7.5–16." *Journal for the Study of the New Testament* 82 (2001): 31–60.
——. *Paul, the Fool of Christ: A Study of 1 Corinthians 1–4 in the Comic-Philosophic Tradition.* London: T & T Clark, 2005.
——. "Extraction from the Mortal Site: Badiou on the Resurrection in Paul." *New Testament Studies* 55 (2009): 295–314.
——. "Paul's Caricature of His Chief Rival as a Pompous Parasite in 2 Corinthians 11:20." *Journal for the Study of the New Testament* 32 (2009): 39–56.
West, A. B. *Corinth VIII: Latin Inscriptions 1896–1926.* Cambridge, MA: Harvard University Press, 1931.
West, M. L. *Hesiod, Works and Days, with Prolegomena and Commentary.* Oxford: Oxford University, 1978.
Wheeler, Mortimer. *Roman Art and Architecture.* London: Thames and Hudson, 1964.
White, John L. "Introductory Formulae in the Body of the Pauline Letter." *Journal of Biblical Literature* 90 (1971): 91–97.
——. *Light from Ancient Letters.* Philadelphia: Fortress Press, 1986.
White, Lloyd Michael. *Building God's House in the Roman World.* Baltimore: John Hopkins, 1990.
——. "Paul and *Pater Familias.*" In *Paul in the Greco-Roman World*, ed. J. Paul Sampley, 457–487. Harrisburg: Trinity Press International, 2003.
White, Peter. "*Amicitia* and the Profession of Poetry in Early Imperial Rome." *Journal of Roman Studies* 68 (1978): 74–92.
——. *Promised Verse: Poets in the Society of Augustan Rome.* Cambridge, MA: Harvard University Press, 1993.
Wiefel, Wolfgang. "The Jewish Community in Ancient Rome and the Origins of Roman Christianity." In *The Romans Debate*, ed. Karl P. Donfried, 85–101. Peabody: Hendrickson, 1991.
Wiemken, H. *Der griechische Mimus: Dokumente zur Geschichte des antiken Volkstheaters.* Bremen: Schünemann, 1972.
Wilamowitz-Moellendorf, Ulrich von. "Asianismus und Atticismus." *Hermes* 35 (1900): 1–52.
——. *Hesiodos Erga.* Berlin: Weidmann, 1928.

—. *Kleine Schriften III*. Berlin: Akademie Verlag, 1969.
Wilcken, Ulrich. "Ein Aktenstück zum jüdischen Kriege Trajans." *Hermes* 27 (1892): 464–470.
Wilckens, Ulrich. *Weisheit und Torheit: Eine exegetisch-religionsgeschichtliche Untersuchung Zu I. Kor. 1 und 2*. Tübingen: Mohr Siebeck, 1959.
—. "ὕστερος, κτλ.." *Theological dictionary of the New Testament* 8 (1972): 598–600.
—. "Zu 1 Kor 2,1–16." In *Theologia Crucis—Signum Crucis*, ed. C. Andresen, 501–537. Tübingen: Mohr Siebeck, 1979.
—. *Der Brief an die Römer*. 3 vols. Zurich: Benziger, 1982.
Wiles, Gordon P. *Paul's Intercessory Prayers*. Cambridge: Cambridge University Press, 1974.
Wilcox, Max. "The 'God-fearers' in Acts: A Reconsideration." *Journal for the Study of the New Testament* 13 (1981): 102–122.
Williams, Charles K. "Corinth, 1981: East of the Theater." *Hesperia* 51 (1982): 115–163.
—. "Corinth, 1982: East of the Theater." *Hesperia* 52 (1983): 1–47.
—. "Corinth, 1985: East of the Theater." *Hesperia* 55 (1986): 129–175.
—. "A Re-Evaluation of Temple E and the West End of the Forum of Corinth." In *The Greek Renaissance in the Roman Empire: Papers from the Tenth British Museum Classical Colloquium*, ed. Susan Walker and Averil Cameron, 156–162. London: University of London Institute of classical Studies, 1989.
Williams, Charles K. and O. H. Zervos. "Corinth, 1985: East of the Theater." *Hesperia* 55 (1986): 129–175.
—. "Corinth, 1987: South of Temple E and East of the Theater." *Hesperia* 57 (1988): 95–146.
Wilson, A. J. N. *Emigration from Italy in the Republican Age of Rome*. Manchester: Manchester University Press, 1966.
Windisch, Hans. *Der zweite Korintherbrief*. Göttingen: Vandenhoeck & Ruprecht, 1924, repr. 1970.
Winter, Bruce W. "The Lord's Supper at Corinth: An Alternative Reconstruction." *The Reformed Theological Review* 37 (1978): 73–82.
—. "Civil Litigation in Corinth: The Forensic Background of 1 Cor. 6:1–8." *New Testament Studies* 37 (1991): 559–571.
—. "Gallio's Ruling on the Legal Status of Early Christianity (Acts 18:14–15)." *Tyndale Bulletin* 50 (1999); 213–234.
—. *Seek the Welfare of the City: Christians as Benefactors and Citizens*. Grand Rapids: Eerdmans, 1996.
—. *After Paul Left Corinth: The Influence of Secular Ethics and Social Change*. Grand Rapids: Eerdmans, 2001.
—. *Philo and Paul among the Sophists: Alexandrian and Corinthian Responses to a Julio- Claudian Movement*, 2nd ed. Grand Rapids: Eerdmans, 2002.
—. "Philodemus and Paul on Rhetorical Delivery (ὑπόκρισις)" In *Philodemus and the New Testament World*, eds. John T. Fitzgerald, Dirk Orbink, Glenn S. Holland, 323–342. Leiden: Brill, 2004.
Wiseman, James. *The Land of the Ancient Corinthians*. Göteburg: Aström, 1978.

——. "Corinth and Rome I: 228 BC-AD 267." *Aufstieg und Niedergang der römischen Welt* II.7.1, 438–548. Berlin: Walter de Gruyter, 1979.
Wiseman, T. P. *Cinna the Poet, and Other Roman Essays.* Leicester: Leicester University Press, 1974.
——. "*Pete nobiles amicos:* Poets and Patrons in Late Republican Rome." In *Literary and Artistic Patronage in Ancient Rome*, ed. Barbara K. Gold, 28–49. Austin: University of Texas Press, 1982.
——. "*Conspicui postes tectaque digna deo:* the public image of aristocratic and imperial houses in the late Republic and Early Empire." In *L'Urbs: espace urbain et histoire (Ier siècle av. J.-C. – IIIe siècle ap. H.-C.)*, 393–413. Rome: Ecole francaise de Rome, 1987.
Witherington, Ben. *Conflict and Community in Corinth: A Socio-Rhetorical Commentary on 1 and 2 Corinthians.* Grand Rapids: Eerdmans, 1995.
Wolff, Christian. *Der zweite Brief des Paulus an die Korinther.* Berlin: Evangelische Verlagsanstalt, 1989.
Wolter, Nicholas. "Verborgene Weisheit und Heil für die Heiden." *Zeitschrift für Theologie und Kirche* 84 (1987): 297–319.
Woodward, A. M. "Archaeology in Greece, 1928–1929." *Journal of Hellenic Studies* 49 (1929): 220–239.
Wooten, Cecil W. *Hermogenes. On Types of Style.* Chapel Hill: University of North Carolina Press, 1987.
Wright, Katherine Slane and R. E. Jones. "A Tiberian Pottery Deposit from Corinth." *Hesperia* 49 (1980): 135–177.
Wright, Robert B. "Psalms of Solomon." In *The Old Testament Pseudepigrapha*, Vol. 2, ed. by James H. Charlesworth, 639–672. Garden City: Doubleday, 1985.
——. *The Psalms of Solomon: A Critical Edition of the Greek Text.* New York: T & T Clark, 2007.
Wulf-Rheidt, Ulrike. "The Hellenistic and Roman Houses of Pergamon." In *Pergamon, Citadel of the Gods: Archaeological Record, Literary Description, and Religious Development*, ed. Helmut Koester, 301–314. Harrisburg: Trinity Press International, 1998.
Wüst, E. "Parasitos." *Real-Encyclopädie der classischen Alterthumswissenschaft* 18 (1949): 1381–1405.
Yavetz, Zwi. *Plebs and Princeps.* London: Oxford University Press, 1969.
Young, Frances and Devid F. Ford. *Meaning and Truth in 2 Corinthians.* Grand Rapids: Eerdmans, 1987.
Young, N. H. "*Paidagogos:* The Social Setting of a Pauline Metaphor." *Novum Testamentum* 29 (1987): 150–176.
Youtie, Herbert C. and John G. Winter. *Papyri and Ostraca from Karanis.* Ann Arbor: University of Michigan Press, 1951.
Zahn, Theodor. *Introduction to the New Testament*, 3 vols. Edinburgh: T & T Clark, 1909.
——. *Der Brief des Paulus an die Römer.* Leipzig: Deichert, 1910.
——. *Die Apostelgeschichte des Lucas.* Leipzig: Deichert, 1921.
Zanker, Paul. *Pompeii: Public and Private Life.* Cambridge, MA: Harvard University Press, 1998.

Zeilinger, Franz. *Krieg und Friede in Korinth. Kommentar zum 2. Korintherbrief des Apostels Paulus. Teil 1, Der Kampfbrief, der Versöhnungsbrief, der Bettelbrief.* Vienna: Herder, 1992.

Zerwick, M. *Analysis Philologica Novi Testamenti Graeci.* Rome: Pontifical Biblical Institute, 1966.

Zmijewski, Josef. *Der Stil der paulinischen 'Narrenrede': Analyse der Sprachgestaltung in 2 Kor 11,1–12,10 als Beitrag zur Methodik von Stiluntersuchungen neutestamentlicher Texte.* Bonn; Hanstein, 1972.

Index of Ancient Sources

Old Testament

Exodus		31:1-2	133
15:4	39	44:5	79
34	129	72:22	120
		110	402
Leviticus		111:9	480
6:2-5	20, 57	118:36	172
		118:141	120
Numbers			
35:30	188	*Proverbs*	
		1:19	172
Deuteronomy			
17:6	188	*Ecclesiastes*	
19:15	182, 183, 187,	9:16	120
19:15-21	188		
19:16	190	*Isaiah*	
19:16-18	189	33:15	172
19:18	190	43:18-19	211
19:18-19	189		
19:20	189	*Daniel*	
19:21	189, 190, 192	4:28	120
		6-7	91
1 Samuel		9:27	36
9:1	294	11:33	36
		11:39	36
1 Kings		12:3	36
15:9	120		
		Zechariah	
2 Chronicles		9:9	79
32:15	85		
		Malachi	
Psalms		2:9	120

New Testament

Matthew		11:29	78
2:18	32	18:16	185, 186
6:34	37	20:13	20, 53, 57
10:20	29	23:24	39

Mark

9:37	29
14:55-59	185
15:15	37

Luke

1:52	72
6:24-25	97
10:20	29
15:28	40
18:9	85
22:38	37

John

6:32	29
6:49	30
7:16	29
8:17	185
12:44	29

Acts

7:58	294
8:1	294
8:3	294
9:1	294
9:8	294
9:11	294
9:22	294
9:24	294
11:25	294
11:30	294
12:25	294
13:1-2	294
13:4-12	295
13:7	294, 320
13:9	294, 295, 296
18:1-2	392
16:37	407
18:1-3	232, 400
18:1-11	300
18:2	71
18:3	74, 355, 392
18:4	370, 392
18:5	93, 390, 392, 394, 396, 397, 399
18:6-7	393
18:7	93, 233, 249, 293, 299, 300, 370, 398
18:8	236, 238, 239, 244, 323, 370, 393, 394
18:10	183, 245, 289, 393
18:11	249, 398
18:12-17	173
18:17	237
18:24	374, 408
18:24-25	403
18:24-28	373
18:25	241, 373, 376
18:27	375, 404, 405, 406
18:28	404, 405, 407, 408
19	398
19:1	406
19:22	272
19:23-40	436
19:29	299
20:2-3	231
20:3	243, 249, 480
20:4	299
20:9	327
20:20	407
25:10	53, 56

Romans

1:1	294, 299
1:18-32	187
2:3	86
2:19	85
4:3	84
4:4	84
4:5	84
4:9	84
4:10	84
4:22	84
4:23-24	84
6:3	133
6:3-4	398
7:1	133
8:9	66, 210
8:35	33
9:3	233
11:1	294
11:2	133
11:25	35
12:1	78
12:16	78
14:3	121

14:10	121	1:12	87, 156, 228, 240, 361, 372, 376, 413, 421
15:15	35		
15:23-24	481	1:12-15	408
15:24	35	1:13	94
15:25-27	178, 481	1:14	39, 79, 228, 230, 231, 236, 239, 240, 241, 242, 247, 248, 249, 288, 289, 290, 318, 321, 369, 370, 371, 378, 394, 398, 399, 408, 427
15:25-32	178		
15:26	178		
15:26-27	424		
15:28	177, 481		
15:30	78		
15:30-32	481	1:14-15	240, 249, 251, 375
15:31	256	1:14-16	281, 414
16	230, 231, 234, 246	1:14-17	289
16:1-2	253	1:15	228, 252
16:3-5	327	1:16	39, 230, 231, 240, 244, 251, 258, 323, 325, 370, 371, 374
16:5	257		
16:7	233, 293		
16:10	231, 234	1:17-4:21	415, 420
16:11	231, 233, 234	1:17-3:4	414
16:13	293	1:17	29, 33, 94, 96, 98, 156, 241, 288, 372, 373 376, 404, 406, 408, 415
16:15	293		
16:17-18	213		
16:21	232, 293, 299	1:18-4:21	228, 373
16:22	230, 232, 235, 293	1:18-3:4	372
16:22-23	365, 481	1:18-2:16	98, 112, 416
16:23	230, 231, 232, 233, 236, 241, 242, 244, 246, 247, 248, 249, 250, 260, 264, 265, 266, 267, 268, 277, 278, 280, 282, 287, 288, 299, 321, 369, 376, 378, 398, 403, 408, 480	1:18-25	156
		1:18	94, 98, 112, 157
		1:23	94, 128, 417
		1:25	157
		1:26	82, 95, 98, 274
		1:26-27	95, 394, 402
		1:26-28	153, 248, 275
		1:26-29	158
		1:26-31	112
1 Corinthians		1:27-28	96, 276, 298, 418
1:1-6:11	XXVII, 71, 93, 112, 113, 241, 405, 416, 419, 427	1:28	98, 121
		1:30	98, 99
1:1-4:21	XXVII, 76, 82, 87, 94, 95, 99, 100, 156, 157, 290, 372, 375, 378, 404, 414, 415, 421	2:1	156, 404, 405, 408, 415
		2:1-5	118, 122, 416
		2:2	94, 95, 128, 387, 416, 417
1:1	232, 294	2:3	409, 415
1:4-5	97	2:4	156, 372, 404, 405, 408
1:5	419	2:6	99
1:10	78	2:6-7	99
1:10-12	XXVII	2:6-8	98, 418
1:11	XXVII, 228, 230, 231, 234, 236, 413, 414	2:6-16	99
		2:7	98

2:8	94, 397	5:4	72
2:9	112, 418	5:5	13, 14
2:12	41	5:9-10	400
3:1	99	6:1	14, 52
3:1-3	83	6:1-6	425
3:1-4	416, 419	6:1-11	26, 192, 366
3:4	156, 240, 372, 414, 421	6:4	121
3:4-6	228	6:5	42
3:5-4:6	378	6:7-8	20, 53, 56, 57
3:5	156, 405	6:9	133
3:5-9	372, 373	6:9-11	42
3:5-15	416	6:12-20	XXVII, 71, 4000
3:6	373	7-9	XXVII, 410
3:10	XXVI, 373	7	366, 410
3:10-15	372, 373	7:1	XXVII, 410
3:10-17	228	7:6	78
3:12	66, 210	7:12	71
3:17	210	8	XXV, 71, 278, 366
3:18	157, 415	8:1	410
3:21-22	99	8:1-2	419
3:21-23	90	8:3	210
3:22	156, 228	8:4	410
3:23	89, 90, 99	8:8	410
4:1	XXVI, 84	8:9	99
4:1-5	372, 416	8:10	366, 410
4:6	156, 228, 372, 375, 405, 414	8:11-12	410
		8:12	411
4:6-7	416	8:13	XXVI
4:7	419	9	71, 228, 368, 370, 371, 386, 399, 406, 409, 411, 428
4:8	97, 112, 419		
4:9-13	95, 112, 156, 416		
4:10	76, 97, 115, 157, 415	9:1	XXVI, 76, 369
4:12	74, 76, 155, 386, 400	9:1-2	399
4:13	40	9:1-18	428
4:14-17	71	9:4	399, 407
4:14-21	228	9:4-14	148
4:15	XXVI, 420	9:5	368, 399, 406
4:17	26, 420	9:6	386, 399
4:17-21	XXVII	9:12	399
4:18-19	420	9:12-18	3988
4:18-21	72, 228, 420	9:15	369, 399
4:21	78	9:15-18	369
5	3, 5, 10, 12, 13, 15, 16, 23, 211	9:18	76, 134, 149, 369
		9:19	36
5:1	10, 11, 12, 14, 25	9:22	239
5:1-5	6, 9, 11, 14	9:26	XXVI
5:3	72	10	187
5:3-5	420	10:1-11:1	71

10:1-11	XXVII	16:12	228, 236, 374, 406, 408, 410, 411
10:1-22	XXVII, 400		
10:5	36	16:12-15	39
10:18	99	16:13-14	252
10:23-11:34	XXVII, 400	16:15	240, 252, 253, 254, 255, 256, 257, 258, 259, 260
11:1	XXVII		
11:16	210	16:15-16	235
11:17-22	245, 321, 364, 400	16:15-18	228, 230, 231, 251, 252, 256, 260, 412, 421
11:17-34	71, 330, 364, 366, 400, 402, 403		
		16:16	254, 257
11:18	XXVII, 327	16:17	XXVII, 230, 234, 254, 255, 257, 293, 323, 413
11:18-19	XXVII		
11:19	403	16:17-18	240, 257
11:20	244	16:18	255, 413
11:21	360, 361, 362, 402	16:19	39, 232, 244, 293, 327, 407, 410
11:22	330, 361, 364, 401, 402		
11:23-26	364, 403	16:22	210, 230
11:33	364		
11:34	403	*2 Corinthians*	
12-16	XXVII, 410	1-9	XX, XXIII
12:1-14:40	71	1:1-2:13; 7:5-16	XXVI, 7, 23-59, 49, 50, 53, 163, 180, 195, 212, 221, 226, 227, 229, 378, 383, 384, 385, 386, 435, 436, 462, 463, 464, 465, 467, 469, 470
12:1	410		
12:12-13	93		
12:14-15	369		
14:1	410		
14:18	XXVI		
14:23	243, 244, 245, 321	1-2	XXII, XXIII, 19, 28, 39, 61, 64, 122, 123, 204, 207, 211, 383
14:26	361		
14:37	210		
14:38	210	1:1	236, 294
15:1-58	71	1:3	469
15:3	93, 94	1:3-7	463, 467, 469
15:4	93	1:4	469
15:6	36	1:5	469
15:8	297	1:5-7	475, 476
15:9	297	1:6	469
15:10	XXVI	1:6-7	383
15:23	89, 90	1:7	383, 469
15:24-25	397	1:8	435,, 436, 469
15:36	156	1:8-9	434, 435, 436, 468
15:54	39	1:8-11	467
16	234	1:9	434, 436
16:1	178, 256, 257, 410, 412	1:10	469, 478
16:1-4	71	1:11	479
16:2	256, 257	1:12	384, 469
16:4	179, 413, 420	1:12-13	462
16:5-9	XXVII	1:12-14	384, 462, 465, 467
16:11	121, 154	1:12-22	212

1:13-14	462		226, 227, 319, 449, 455, 458, 469, 475, 476, 481
1:14	35		
1:15	179, 385	2:7-8	13, 23, 26, 40, 50, 218, 220
1:15-2:4	467		
1:15-16	1, 38, 50	2:8	13, 24, 40, 218, 219, 459, 469
1:15-17	469		
1:15-22	384, 463, 465, 476	2:9	XXII, 31, 469, 476
1:18	385	2:10	5, 14, 24, 25, 26, 27, 29, 30, 41, 218, 219, 227, 469, 476, 477
1:20	481		
1:23-2:4	60, 436, 463, 465, 476		
1:23	XXII, 1, 38, 50, 64	2:11	14, 41
1:24	469	2:12-13	XXI, 38, 444, 460, 463, 468
2	1, 3, 4, 5, 6, 10, 12, 13, 14, 15, 16, 24, 25, 27, 30, 31, 37, 44, 58, 60, 64, 77, 152, 208, 212, 228, 230, 234, 260, 380, 408, 441	2:13	XXI, 27
		2:14-7:4	XXI, XXII, XXIII, XXI, XXV, 127, 130, 209, 445, 446, 455
2:1	1, 4, 50, 180, 434, 469	2:14-6:13; 7:2-4	209, 210, 211, 445, 456, 449, 453
2:2	469		
2:1-2	38	2:14-6:13	XXV, XXVI, 209
2:1-3	44, 424, 469	2:14	XXI
2:1-4	29, 47, 192, 212, 385, 435, 443, 465	2:17	217
		3:1	XXIII, XXV, XXVI, 209, 444, 445
2:1-11	23		
2:2	469	3:2	209
2:3	XXII, 469	3:7-18	127, 128
2:3-4	XXII, 1, 4, 8, 38, 44, 50, 60, 122, 207	3:10	130
		3:12	452
2:4	23, 44, 60, 80, 437, 444, 469, 481	4:2	XXIV, 168, 209, 210
		4:7-12	447
2:5	1, 6, 7, 14, 24, 27, 28, 29, 30, 35, 43, 44, 46, 65, 103, 180, 210, 219, 226, 227, 426, 432, 451, 455, 463, 465, 466, 469	4:11	447
		4:16-5:10	384
		5:4	39
		5:12	XXIII, XXV, XXVI, 209, 217, 444, 445
2:5-6	23	5:13	XXIV, 159, 209, 444, 445, 446
2:5-7	34, 103		
2:5-8	182	5:14-15	448, 452, 454
2:5-11	1, 9, 11, 14, 23, 25, 27, 28, 31, 41, 46, 65, 181, 191, 207, 208, 213, 218, 220, 228, 234, 383, 463, 467, 474, 478	5:16	210
		5:17	210, 211, 454
		5:17-19	448
		5:18	451
		5:18-20	453
2:6	10, 13, 14, 24, 35, 39, 42, 65, 80, 218, 219, 226, 458, 459	5:19	451
		5:20	451, 452
		6:1	451
2:7	13, 14, 24, 37, 39, 41, 44, 46, 50, 123, 218, 219,	6:1-13	384
		6:3-10	448

Index of Ancient Sources 535

6:4	448		227, 228, 234, 381, 430, 451
6:4-10	448		
6:11-13	XXI, 448	7:13	27, 461, 469, 476
6:12	249	7:13-16	464, 468
6:14-7:1	XXI, XXII, 445	7:14	27
7	XXII, XXIII,1, 3, 4, 5, 12, 16, 19, 24, 25, 27, 28, 30, 31, 39, 44, 58, 60, 61, 64, 77, 122, 123, 152, 190, 204, 207, 208, 211, 212, 228, 230, 234, 260, 380, 383, 385, 408, 441	7:15	XX, XXVI, 444, 445, 449, 469
		7:16	XXIII, 461, 469, 476
		8	XX, XXIII, XXVI, 21, 112, 174, 176, 177, 420, 421, 422, 424, 479
		8:1	431
7:2	XXIV, 41, 53, 56, 171, 454	8:1-5	178, 422
		8:2	75, 153
7:2-4	XXI, XXV, XXVI, 249, 384, 448	8:2-5	178
		8:3	178
7:3	454	8:4	256, 412, 415, 431, 479
7:4	XXI, 209, 452	8:5	178
7:5	XXI, 38, 435, 460, 469	8:6	XXIII, 21, 26, 174, 175, 176, 425, 479
7:5-6	34, 444		
7:5-7	463, 468	8:7	479
7:5-12	1, 23, 31	8:9	422
7:5-16	445, 463	8:10	174
7:6	27, 461, 469	8:10-11	174
7:6-7	464	8:10-12	425, 431
7:7	31, 33, 34, 60, 227, 455, 457, 461, 469, 476	8:11	176, 177
		8:13-15	422
7:7-11	457	8:14	179, 258, 420, 422, 424
7:8	1, 44, 50, 52, 436, 455, 463, 465, 469	8:16	26
		8:16-18	174
7:8-9	44, 227	8:16-23	424
7:8-12	204, 443	8:16-24	174, 176, 179, 421, 425
7:8-13	455, 463	8:19	176, 479
7:9	17, 60, 70, 449, 460, 461, 469, 476	8:19-20	421
		8:20	176, 413
7:9-10	32, 60, 465, 473, 474, 475	8:22	XXIII, 175, 176
		8:23	26
		8:24	479
7:10	458, 461, 468	9	XX, XXVI, 479, 480
7:10-11	XX, 474	9:1	256, 257, 412
7:11	10, 14, 17, 31, 33, 52, 60, 65, 468, 469, 475	9:2	36, 480
		9:3	481
7:11-12	70	9:5	480, 481
7:12	1, 7, 10, 23, 24, 25, 27, 29, 30, 31, 33, 47, 60, 65, 103, 140, 165, 180, 181, 182, 190, 191, 194, 202, 203, 218, 219, 220, 226,	9:7	480
		9:8	479
		9:9	480
		9:11	479
		9:12	256, 412, 479

9:14	479	10:10	XXIV, 7, 63, 65, 67, 68, 79, 86, 102-21, 103, 104, 105, 114, 115, 119, 121, 122, 132, 150, 153, 154, 169, 191, 193, 204, 205, 208, 218, 219, 318, 390, 416, 437, 439, 441
9:15	XX, 480		
10-13	XX, XXII, XXIV, XXV, XXVI, 7, 8, 19, 38, 60-208, 60, 61, 63, 65, 66, 73, 93, 95, 108, 112, 113, 125, 127, 130, 139, 152, 155, 156, 164, 174, 177, 180, 183, 190, 191, 192, 196, 197, 202, 204, 205, 207, 208, 209, 210, 229, 289, 318, 375, 378, 399, 408, 420, 421, 429, 437, 442, 443, 445, 446, 447, 449		
		10:10-11	375, 408
		10:11	7, 62, 65, 67, 83, 103, 104, 105, 122, 129, 163, 208, 218, 219, 226, 441
		10:12-12:13	66
		10:12-12:10	367, 368
		10:12	86, 124, 217, 437
		10:12-13	61
10:1	XX, 62, 63, 66, 67, 68, 72, 77, 78, 79, 84, 102, 119, 153, 193, 205, 318, 425, 439, 442	10:12-18	124
		10:13	438
		10:15-17	438
		10:18	65, 124, 208, 437
10:1-2	XXIII, 68, 99	11:1-12:13	124, 125, 229
10:1-6	62, 66, 67, 193, 384	11:1-12:10	104, 124, 127, 154, 384, 444
10:1-10	62		
10:1-11	62, 67-124, 79, 84, 122, 123	11:1	129, 154, 155, 158, 205, 438, 439
10:2	62, 65, 66, 67, 68, 80, 81, 83, 84, 100, 119, 123, 129, 163, 164, 169, 177, 193, 205, 210, 218, 219, 226, 318	11:1-21	150, 158, 260, 282, 438, 439
		11:3	168
		11:4	65, 124, 125, 128, 129, 140, 150, 155, 160, 189, 205, 207, 208, 217, 367, 368, 371, 375, 378
10:2-3	81, 442		
10:3-5	62	11:4-6	61
10:3-6	66, 442	11:5	83, 101, 124, 129, 130, 375, 437
10:4	61		
10:5	61	11:5-6	129, 204, 408
10:6	XX, XXIII, XXVI, 62, 63, 66	11:6	130, 131, 150, 368, 375, 425
10:7	7, 61, 65, 67, 83-101, 83, 85, 86, 87, 89, 93, 96, 99, 101, 103, 123, 127, 129, 150, 154, 160, 163, 183, 189, 191, 199, 205, 207, 208, 210, 218, 219, 226, 229, 318, 364, 371, 390, 398, 441, 442, 454	11:7	68, 72, 73, 133, 151, 190, 192, 193, 205
		11:7-10	386, 391
		11:7-11	60, 61, 164, 169, 177, 205, 368, 425, 428, 443
		11:7-15	139, 398
		11:7-21	132, 139, 151, 152, 153, 327
10:7-11	65. 66, 86	11:8	152
10:8	62, 86, 103	11:8-9	75
10:9	62, 86, 103, 110, 111	11:9	134, 135, 152, 258, 368
10:9-11	169, 443		

Index of Ancient Sources

11:10	152, 438, 444	12:7-9	158, 440, 443
11:11	135, 152, 249	12:9	438, 446
11:12	217, 437	12:9-10	63, 158, 440
11:12-15	132	12:11	XXV, 61, 101, 124, 158, 437, 438, 439
11:13	88, 124, 126, 218		
11:13-15	229	12:11-13	165, 187
11:15	124	12:13	134, 135, 165, 177, 190, 192
11:16	65, 124, 154, 155, 157, 169, 193, 205, 207, 208, 218, 219, 226, 439, 441, 443	12:13-14	368
		12:14-13:10	164
		12:14-13:4	66, 164, 187
		12:14	4, 134, 165, 180, 182, 187, 424, 428
11:16-17	438		
11:16-18	438	12:14-15	138, 139, 188, 369, 428
11:16-21	60, 61, 193	12:14-18	177, 437
11:17	158, 439	12:15	166, 410, 428
11:18	124	12:16	XXIV, 134, 170, 203, 210, 429, 442
11:19	155		
11:19-21	229	12:16-18	21, 165, 166, 168, 171, 174, 180, 188, 203, 205, 421, 425, 451, 454
11:20	65, 229, 124, 139-49, 139, 140, 142, 151, 155, 170, 208, 367, 368, 378		
		12:17	166, 167
11:20-21	140	12:17-18	XXIV, 41, 167, 170, 171, 172, 203
11:21-12:10	62, 63, 438		
11:21	62, 63, 124, 158, 159, 438, 439, 440, 444, 446	12:18	XXIII, 21, 167, 174, 175, 176, 203, 421
11:21-23	440	12:19-21	188
11:22	124, 439	12:20-13:2	182
11:22-23	126	12:20	69, 70, 186, 192, 203, 425, 426, 432
11:23	88, 124, 158, 159, 439, 440, 444, 446		
		12:20-21	XX, 69, 70, 160, 181, 186, 192, 425, 451
11:23-29	440		
11:23-33	158	12:21	68, 69, 70, 181, 186, 194, 426, 432
11:24-27	440		
11:28-29	440	13:1	4, 180, 183, 185, 187-91, 424, 426
11:29	63, 124		
11:30	62, 63, 158, 438, 440	13:1-2	182, 190-94, 203, 425, 426
11:30-33	440		
12	XXIII, 445	13:1-4	62, 188
12:1	62, 158, 438, 440	13:1-10	33, 62
12:1-4	440	13:2	XXII, 62, 64, 70, 189-93
12:1-5	158, 163	13:3	61, 198
12:1-6	XXIV, 444	13:3-4	63, 193, 446
12:5	63, 193, 438, 440	13:4	199
12:5-6	62, 158, 440	13:5	196-201
12:6	65, 83, 84, 124, 154, 158, 163, 169, 208, 218, 219, 226, 441	13:5-9	195, 196
		13:5-10	62, 66, 164, 194, 201, 204
12:7	114		

13:6	197	*1 Thessalonians*	
13:7	62, 63, 195-99	1:1	294
13:9	63	1:9-10	94, 392, 394
13:10	XXII, 63	1:10	93, 397
		2:5	165
Galatians		2:9	35, 400
1:1	294	4:1-12	187
1:6	425	4:6	171
1:6-9	128	5:12	254
1:9	210	5:20	121
2:3	293		
2:10	177	*2 Thessalonians*	
2:11	72	1:3	179
3:6	84	3:8	35
3:15	40	3:10	325
3:18	41		
3:27	93	*1 Timothy*	
3:29	89, 90	5:1	40
4:12	53, 56	5:19	185
4:13	115		
4:14	121	*2 Timothy*	
5:10	125	4:20	272
5:15	99		
6:3	210	*Philemon*	
		1	236, 294
Ephesians		1-2	39
5:15	99	2	244
		9	78
Philippians		18	20, 53
1:1	294, 297	18-19	57
1:14	36	19	294
1:29	41		
2:25	236	*Hebrews*	
2:30	258	10:28	185
3:2	99	11:9	39
3:3-4	85		
3:4	66	*James*	
3:5	293	1:9-10	72
4:2-3	39		
4:3	293	*1 Peter*	
4:12	75	5:8	39
4:15	75		
4:21	282	*2 Peter*	
4:22	231, 234	3:15-16	102
Colossians		*3 John*	
2:8	99	1	299
4:17	99		

Revelation   12:6   39

Old Testament Apocrypha and Pseudepigrapha

2 Baruch
32:6   211

1 Enoch
72:1   211

4 Ezra
6:59   91
7:27-30   92
12:32-34   92

Jubilees
4:26   211

Joseph and Asenath
13:10   120

1 Maccabees
7:5   295
7:12   295
7:20   295
9:54   295
12:6-18   314

2 Maccabees
1:5   453
1:27   120
5:9   314
8:29   453
11:6   32
13:23   40
14:3   295

3 Maccabees
5:13   453

4 Maccabees
7:18   163

Psalms of Solomon
17-18   206
17   91
17:14   92
17:21   91
17:22-23   92
17:23-25   91
17:26   92
17:27   92
17:32   91, 92
17:35   92
17:44   92
18:5-7   92

Sirach
4:9   53, 56
11:7   43, 459
13:3   53, 59

Testament of Solomon
4:2   32
22:5   120

Wisdom of Solomon
3:10   42, 43

Philo

De agricultura
83   172

De confusion linguarum
117   168

De decalogo
125   168
141   168
155   172

Quod deterius potiori insidari soleat
165   168

Quod Deus sit immutabilis
181   39, 455

De ebrietate
146-47   159
223   168

In Flaccum
77   97

De gigantibus
13   39, 455
14   447

Quis rerum divinarum heres sit
268   163

Legum allegoriae
2.49-50   163
2.67   120
3.166   172

Legatio ad Gaium
66   395
75   396
89-90   395
101   395
281   393
347-48   395

De vita Mosis
2.53   168
2.186   172
2.241   120
2.245   165

De mutatione nominum
150   168

De posteritate Caini
43   168
53   374, 403

De praemiis et poenis
52   168

De sacrificiis Abelis et Caini
22   168
32   168
95   395

De somniis
2.66   168
2.155   115

De specialibus legibus
1.28   172
4.5   172
4.34   57

De virtutibus
23.117-18 220
28.152   220

Josephus

Antiquitates judaicae
2.238   32
5.105   43, 459
8.356   44
12.2.4   295
12.6.4   295
12.9.7   295
13.1.2   295
13.5.1   295
13.12.1   295
13.16.4   295

13.164   314
16.300-309   314
16.300-10   312, 313
18.81-82   173
18.82   173
18.83   173
18.84   173
19.94   417
20.3.3   296

Index of Ancient Sources

Bellum judaicum
1.223	168
1.365	168
1.453	168
1.468	168
1.312-13	69
1.422-25	313
1.513	313
1.513-31	312, 313
1.515	314
1.516-29	314
1.531	315
1.536-37	314
2.146	35
4.342	32
4.365	73
5.31	32
5.415	453

Contra Apionem
2.177	52

Dead Sea Scrolls

1QS
IV.25	211
VI.8	35
IX.16-23	185
XIII.7	35

CD

Rabbinic Literature

Mishnah, Sotah
1.1-2	184

Early Christian Literature

Augustine
Enarrationes in Psalmos
72.4	297

Didache
1:5	149

John Chrysostom
Homiliae in epistulam I ad Corinthios
15:1	3

Homiliae in epistulam II ad Corinthios
4:3	3

Lactantius
De ira Dei
17.33	53

Polycarp
Philippians
3:2	102

Tertullian
Apologeticus
15	144

De pudicitia
13-14	1, 3, 13, 43

Greco-Roman Sources

Aeschines
Against Ctesiphon
176   120
791-92   43

Aeschylus
Agamemnon
791   44

Alciphron
3.60   153

Alexis
121   145
183   143
215   143
233   143
263   143

Anaxilas
32   144

Andocides
2.8   44

Antiphanes
82   143
193   144, 146

Antiphon
107   44
262   120

Apollonius of Tyana
Epistles
35   58
44   285, 461
45   50, 58, 221, 285, 453, 464, 465, 466
46   55
58   53

Apollonius Rhodius
Argonautica
1.208   242

Appian
Bella civila
1.39   32
3.94   308
4.133   35
4.521   32
Punica
136   241, 290

Aristophanes
Pax
174   355
Plutus
563-64   51
Thesmophoriazusae
1026   42

Aristophon
5   146
10   146

Aristotle
Athenain politea
45.3   198

Ethica eudemia
7.1.2   430
7.1.2-3   438
7.1.3   381
7.2.19   382, 430
7.2.39   383, 443
7.2.40   202, 385
7.2.45-48   409
7.3-5   137
7.3.2   381, 390, 423
7.5.3   383, 443
7.5.3   383
7.6.8   382
7.8   153
7.9-10   137

Index of Ancient Sources

7.9.1	423
7.9.5	423
7.10.10	423
7.10.12	423
7.10.13	423
7.11.7	430

Ethica nichomachea
4.3.21	51
5.2	57, 171
5.8	53
6.12.9	169
7.6.4	51
8.3.8-9	202, 385
8.4.2	427
8.5-6	137
8.5.5	423
8.6.4	429
8.6.7	423
8.7-8	137
8.7	153
8.7.1	381, 390
8.7.2	137, 138, 166, 425, 428
8.7.4	381
8.8.5	384, 443
8.9.1-2	384
8.9.3	382, 430
8.10	137
8.11.2	139
8.12.1	384
8.12.5-6	139
8.13-14	427, 431
8.13	381, 427
8.13.2-4	427
8.13.7-8	431
8.13.8	200
8.14	137, 431
8.14.1	431, 432
8.14.2	138
8.14.2-4	139
8.14.3	428
8.14.3-4	138
9.1	427
9.1.3	381, 427
9.3.2	381, 429
9.11.4	383, 436
9.12.1	384

Politica
4.12, 1295b18-21	72, 73
5.10, 1312b24	120
5.11, 1315a18	51
7.7, 1327b40-1328a16	47
8.3, 1337b12-15	73

Rhetorica
1.9.24	200
1.10-14	57
1.10.3	10, 53
1.10.6	57
1.11.22	153
1.11.29-12.2	52
1.12.2	59, 204
1.13.5	53
1.13.10	59
2.2.3-4	51
2.2.5	50, 51, 59
2.2.6	51
2.2.7	116
2.2.8-9	47, 220, 382
2.2.15	220, 384
2.3	47, 220, 461
2.5	51
2.5.3-8	200
2.11.1-7	455
2.13	219
2.16.1-4	51
3.1	115
3.6.1-3	213
3.14.11	461, 488

Athenaeus
Deipnosophistae
4.164b-d	144
6.237b	145
6.238b-c	146
6.238d-e	146
15.698d-699a	117

Aulus Gellius
Noctes atticae
1.22.5	365
1.26	46

Caesar
Bellum civile
1.4   219
1.22.5   217

Chion
Epistles
16   221

Choricius of Gaza
Apol. Mim.
26   117
109   117

Cicero
De amicitia
6.20   390
8.26   391
9.31   390
15   443
17.62-21.81   390
18.65   202
19.69-20.73   390
46-48   383
59   219
61-81   443

Pro Archia
6   367, 407, 409

Epistulae ad Atticum
1.12.4   365, 402
1.13   217
4.13.2   283
13.52   360
17.5-6   390

Brutus
37   116

Pro Caelio
41   367, 407

Epistulae ad Familiares
1.9.4   286
1.9.10   215, 220
1.9.19   286
1.9.20   215, 226, 283, 450

3.7.2   286
3.8   221
3.8.2   286
3.8.7   286
3.10.1   286
3.10.5   286
3.10.9   286
3.12.2   286
3.12.4   286
3.13   390
4.13.2   226
5.1   286, 382
5.1.1   450
5.2   221, 286, 450
5.2.3   151
5.2.5   287
5.2.6   382
5.8   50, 221, 438, 450
5.8.2   450
5.8.3   226, 451, 452
5.8.5   220
5.9.2   365, 402
6.10.1   438
10.11.3   438

De finibus
1.13   367, 407
1.25   367
2.26.85   165, 428
2.44   367, 409
2.81   367
3.24   161

De inventione rhetorica
1.55.109   461

Pro Murena
70-72   366

De officiis
1.15.47   289
1.39   356
1.42.150-51   75
1.45-46   390, 443
1.109   226, 283
3.75   226, 283

De oratore
2.82.334　　109
3.133　　　366

Orator ad M. Brutum
17　　　　116

Epistulae ad Quintum fratrem
1.2.12-13　436
2.12.2-3　　286

Pro Rabirio Postumo
5.16　　　96, 417

Pro Sexto Roscio Amerino
93　　　　413
111　　　202

Tusculanae disputatione
2.7　　　　367, 407
3.13.27　　471, 474
3.31.74-75　474
3.32.77　　473, 474
3.50　　　367
3.76　　　475
3.79　　　475, 475
4.6　　　　367
4.6.12-14　472
4.6.14　　444, 471, 473
4.21　　　53
4.26-29　　171
5.28　　　367

Columella
De agricultura
1.*Praef.* 9　137
1.*Praef.* 12　137

Demetrius
De elocutione
4　　　　　120
57　　　　469
153　　　117
240-304　109, 204
240　　　116
245　　　109, 114
246　　　114
248　　　109, 114
250　　　114
253　　　109, 114
263　　　114
268-73　114
270　　　109
277-80　114
280　　　109
283　　　109

Demosthenes
Epistulae
2　　　　　221
2.1　　　451, 456
2.1.6　　55
2.1.18　　464
2.1.20　　464
2.2　　　222, 227. 441
2.8　　　227, 441
2.25　　456
2.26　　223, 225

Orationes
1.16　　43, 459
4.18　　120
18.178　77
21.129　53
23.122　219
41.25　　41, 171

Digesta
7.8.2-3　148
9.3.5　　148

Dio Cassius
36.43.1　32
37.39.3　220
39.10　　226, 283
43.50.3-5　241, 290
44.34.7　284
46.7　　　117
48.29.3　284
48.30.1　284
48.30.2　284
52.37　　41, 171
54.7.2　310
57.18　　173
59.9　　　311
67.2　　　355

Dio Chrysostom
Orationes
1.67	97
4.57	198
7.17	97
16.1	472, 473
16.4	472
17	171, 172
17.6	172
17.8	171, 172
30.19	97
42.3	130
43.7	223
45	216, 223, 224, 227, 229
45.2-3	216
45.3	44, 216, 227
45.5	216
45.7	216, 217
45.8	216
45.9	224, 227
45.9-10	216
4.10	224, 225, 227, 441
45.11	224, 441
45.11-13	225
45.12-13	216
45.14	224, 441
45.15	217
45.16	217, 227
46	215
46.6	215, 227
50	223
50.3	223, 441
50.6	223, 441
50.9	223, 441
50.10	223, 441
59.1	40
67.8	41
73.3	157
73.5	202
74.10-11	202
76.7	51

Diodorus
2.31	144
3.67.2	459
12.20.3	219

Diogenes Laertius
1.87	219
1.91	220
3.46	272
7.92	161
7.113	53
7.119	475

Dionysius of Halicarnassus
Antiquitates romanae
3.7.3	381
4.9	35
8.32.3	70
8.34.1-3	382
8.50.4	453
8.73	35
9.7	41

De compositione verborum
3	120
11	106, 204

De Demosthene
8	114
21	109, 204
22	109, 114, 204
34	106, 204

De Lysia
3	131

Epistula ad Pomeium Geminum
3	107, 204

De Thucydide
23	107
55	107

Diphilus
60	143
61	143

Ennius
14	147
14-19	147

Epicharmus
35.7   143
99   170

Epictetus
Diatribai
1.2.7   100
1.2.14   100
1.2.28   100
1.2.30   100
1.20.6   157
1.28.10   454
1.29.45   100
1.29.57   100
2.1.1-7   476
2.2.9   454
2.10.7-8   100
2.19.24   447
2.22   452
2.22.3-4   443
2.22.6-7   444
2.22.8   442
2.22.25   443
3.9.15   103
3.23.30   474
3.24.81   53
4.1.11   103
4.1.151   103
4.1.158   103
4.8.17   103
4.8.25   103

Enchiridion
24.2   103

Epicurus
Vatican Sayings
34   385
39   385

Epigenes
2   143, 144

Eupolis
162-69   143
166   143

Euripides
Andromache
164-65   68, 69, 72

Fragmenta
438   51
716   69

Orestes
396-98   44
1105   43

Phoenissae
1071   32

Troades
609   32

Fronto
Ad amicos
1.10   148

Ad M. Caesarem
5.59   436

Ad Verum
2.7   136

Galen
De placitis Hippocratis et Platonis
4.6.24   444
5.7.52   471

Hermogenes
Περὶ ἰδεῶν
2.8   112
2.9   110

Herodas
Mimiambi
2   117
5   44, 46

Herodotus
5.66   159
7.14   69
7.16   43

Hesiod
Opera et dies
707-708   431
707-14   449

Hippocrates
De arte
48   134

Homer
Ilias
15.532   242

Odyssea
8.543   242
9.406   170
12.494   170

Horace
Epistulae
1.3.30-36   411
1.7.22-24   390, 443
1.7.37-38   97
1.7.61-70   407
1.15.26-35 144
1.18.10-14 143
1.18.10-20 411
2.1.1-2-107 366
2.1.245-47 443
2.2.95-101 411

Satirae
1.1.23   439
1.3   411
1.5   411
1.6.47   409
1.6.52-64   390, 443
1.8.11   145
1.9   411
2.1.21-22   145
2.3.33-34   347, 407
2.3.296   367
2.5.33   292
2.6.41-45   411
2.7   143, 439, 440, 443
2.7.37-39   144
2.7.39-40   440
2.7.46-67   440

2.7.68-72   440
2.7.83-87   440
2.7.95-101 440
2.7.102-11 440
2.7.111-15 440
2.8.7   360

Hyperides
2.10   116

Iamblichus
De vita pythagorica
102   429

Isocrates
Orationes
6.108   120
10.12   77
16.48   461

Juvenal
Satirae
3.119-25   411
5   137, 360, 364, 401
5.1.1-11   143
5.14   97, 419
5.130   97, 419
5.137   97, 419
5.156-73   143
5.161   97, 419
6.219-23   417
7   137
7.45   97, 419
8.187-88   417
10.161   97, 419

Laus Pisonis
68   409
84-96   400
104-15   137
128-37   390, 443
133-37   148, 411
133-208   400
218   390, 443

Livy
5.13.6-7   401
29.37.10   286

Longinus
De sublimitate
3.1	120
12.4	114
14.1	114
14.2	114
31.1	131
31.2	131
34	109, 204
34.1-4	114
34.4	109, 111

Lucian
Juppiter tragoedus
14	117

De mercede conductis
1	136, 149
3	136, 146, 149, 369
4	149
8	97
10	135
13	149
17	411
19-20	149
20	407
20-21	136
26	135, 149, 411
26-27	411
27	135
30	135
39-40	411

Nigrinus
4	473
21-24	137

De parasito
5	142
21	145, 170
22	142

Somnium
13	73

Toxaris
6	383

Lysias
9.20	200
14.29	32
16.3	198

Macrobius
Saturnalia
2.7.2	439
2.7.6-7	439

Marcus Aurelius
10.37	198

Martial
Epigrammata
1.20	364
2.18	137
2.32	137
2.55	137
2.68	137
2.68	137
3.30	137, 360
3.36	137
3.37	137
3.46	137
3.50	365
3.60	364, 401
4.61	149
4.85	364
6.11	364
6.51	147
8.67.9-10	147
10.11.6	149
10.14	137
10.18	137
10.70	137
10.74	137
10.75	137
10.49	364
12.36	137
12.82	147

De Spectaculis
7	417

Maximus of Tyre
5	103
33.7	163

Menander
Misoumenos
A36   142
A37-40   142
A41-98   142

Monostichoi
259   41, 171

Samia
297   120

Sententia
456   383

Musonius
11   76

Naevius
27-29   144

Nepos
Atticus
14.1   365

Ovid
Fasti
1.135   401

Tristia
1.8.29   409
3.6.19   409

Pausanias
2.1.2   242, 290
2.4.6   306

Persius
Satirae
439

Petronius
Satyrica
26-74   360
30   292, 307, 359
50   292
53   417
53.12-13   365

62   292
74   292
77   329
90   368, 407
111-13   417

Philodemus
Volumina rhetorica
2.175   120
2.210   161

Philostratus
Vitae sophistarum
1.18   58, 285
1.361.25   53
2.1.550-61 57
2.1.559-63 53, 54, 55, 225, 285
2.1.562   225
2.1.562-63 50, 54, 221, 286, 436,
            441, 465, 466, 467
2.1.563   227, 453, 461
3.33   58, 285
8.2   58, 285

Phrynichus
198   374, 403

Plato
Alcibiades major
1.246C   198

Apologia
41E   473
23B   473

Charmides
158D   198

Epistulae
5.322D   272
6.323A   272

Leges
728E   68
759D   198

Menexenus
244A   453

Phaedo
85A   43
66E-67A   447

Phaedrus
257C   72
66E-67A   450

Philebus
31B-F   43, 44
36A   44

Respublica
331E   200
364A   115
371C   256
387D   32

Symposium
215E-216C 473

Plautus
Asinaria
273   401
650-54   143
670-702   143
Captivi
177   143
877   144

Curculio
280-90   146
309-25   143
358   144

Menaechmi
77-109   143
973-77   135

Miles gloriosus
9-78   143
667   143
948   143

Mostellaria
359-64   417

Persae
59-60   143

Stichus
155-56   143
159-60   144
233   144
286   144
395   144
575   143

Pliny the Elder
Naturalis historia
35.199   305

Pliny the Younger
Epistulae
2.6   364, 401
2.6.1-4   360
2.6.2   388
2.17   360
3.1   400
3.1.9   367
3.3   409
3.5.11   365, 402
3.21.6   409
5.6   360
5.19.3   365, 402
7.3.2   388
9.36.4   365, 402
10.96   277

Plutarch
De adulatore amico
55C   474
66B   474
69E-F   473
70D-E   474
73D-E   474

Quomodo adulator ab amico internoscatur
27   443

Alcibiades
4   473

Antonius
67	312, 313

Caesar
57.5	241, 290

Cato Minor
32	77

Cicero
49.5	374, 403

Comparatio Aemilii Pauli et Timoleontis
31.5	217

Caomparatio Demonthenis et Ciceronis
26.1	284

De laude ipsius
539D	439
540C	439
542E	439

Demosthenes
7.3	118
7.4	118
7.5	118
7.6	118

Marcellus
315	41

Moralia
26A	168
27A	168
28A	168
54B	144
67E	446
86C	201
86D-E	200
87C-D	201
89B	201
90F	200
91B	168
101B	163
135C	163
143C	166
207F	315
237E	168
457A-B	45
457B-C	45
457C	53
459B	45
460C	46
460D	47, 51, 220
460D-464C	382
461E	47, 220
462B	47, 220
463A	45
463A-B	45
463B	47, 220
463C	47, 220
464C-D	45
476E	457, 458
488	319
498D	457
526A	165
538E	200
554E-F	457
556A	457
672E	163
688D	163
734A	163
776B	136
777B-D	148
777D	148
777E-F	150, 151
777E-778A	148
778A	148
778A-B	136, 137
778D-F	148
778E	148
778D-E	148
779A-C	148
825E	459
1087B	163
1089E	163
1096C	163

Quaestionum convivialum
711A-F	365
711C	365, 402
712E	365

De recta ratione audiendi
47A	474

Regum et imperatorum apophthegmata
14   315

De tranquilitate animi
476F   474

De virtute morali
452C   474

Pollux
Onomasticon
7.189   355

Polyaenus
6.36   52
8.47   46

Polystratus
7.297   292

Pomponius
151-52   143

Poseidonius
Fr.
155   53

Pseudo-Andronicus
Περὶ Παθῶν
2.44   457

Pseudo-Aristotle
Epistulae
5   55, 221, 227

Pseudo-Callisthenes
72.19   120

Pseudo-Demetrius
Τύποι Επιστολικοί
2   253

Pseudo-Euripides
Epistulae
5   54, 55, 58, 221, 227

Pseudo-Hippocrates
Epistulae
17.45   474

Pseudo-Libanius
Ἐπιστολιμαῖοι χαρακτῆρες
19   49, 221, 464, 466
66   50, 56, 60 386, 464, 466
90   47
107   50, 467

Pseudo-Lucian
Amores
27   41

Pseudo-Plutarch
De Fluviis
12.1   120

Vitae decem oratorum
845B   116

Moralia
107F   163
308E   120
310E   120

Publilius Syrus
142   220
245   219

Quintilian
Institutio oratoria
8.3.3   109
8.6.59-61   213
9.1.35   213
9.3.91   213
9.4.124   213
11.3.2   116
11.3.5-6   116
11.3.7   116
11.3.12-13   116

Rhetorica ad Herennium
3.11.9   116

Sallust
Bellum catalinae
10.5   219

Seneca
De beneficiis
1.1.6	421
1.4.2	391
2.2.1	421
2.18.6-7	369
2.25.2	476
3.1.5	139
3.11.2	165
5.5.2	139
5.6.2-7	369
6.24.1-2	139
7.23.1	289
7.23.3	289

De clementia
2.7.1	477
2.7.2	478

De Constantia Sap.
2.1.3	473

Epistulae morales
9.6	136
9.10	166
41.4	447
88.18	75
88.21	75
88.23	75
90.3	171
90.8	171
90.36	171
90.38	171
90.39-40	171
94.14	388
95.63	220
108.22	173

Hercules furens
251-53	396

De ira
1.12.2-5	53

Quomodo amicitia continenda sit
Fr. 1	202, 220, 381, 430, 433, 437, 442, 461

Sextus Empiricus
Adversus mathematicos
11.90	161
11.207	161

Solon
Fr. 13.5	200

Sophilus
7-8	143, 144

Sophocles
Ajax
338	43
774	453

Antigone
300	169
301	170

Elektra
654	43

Oedipus coloneus
1217	44

Philoctetes
101	170
107	170
108	170

Stobaeus
Eclogae
2.7.105	162
2.58.5	161
2.59.4	161
2.67.20	162
2.91.10	53, 477
2.102.11	161
2.104.10	161

Florilegium
40.9	317

Strabo
Geographica
8.4.8	290
8.5.1	312

Index of Ancient Sources

8.5.3 315
8.5.5 315
8.6.23 241, 290
13.608 272

Suetonius
Gaius Caligula
57 417

Divus Claudius
16 311
25 71, 392

Tiberius
36 173

Tabula Cebes
10 455, 456
11 458

Tacitus
Annales
2.85 173
6.18 317

Dialogus de oratoribus
5.2 400, 409
6.2 148, 400, 414

Terence
Phormio
327-45 143
339-42 147
340 147

Theognis
74 202
87-92 443
93-94 443
119-28 429, 442
416 442
529-30 202
751 51
851-52 443
979 443
1080 442
1082

1097-1100 429
1219-20 429

Theophrastus
Characteres
142

Thucydides
4.28.1 43, 459
6.59 44

Timocles
13 143
31 143

Ulpian
9.3.5.1 407

Varro
De lingua latina
5.25 96, 417

Saturarum Menippearum
517B 368, 407

Valerius Maximus
2.9.6 286
7.3 219
8.14.6 75

Vita Aesopi
G80 p.60 120
W77b p.96.37 120
W77b p.97.2 120
W100, 6-7P 452

Vitruvius
De architectura
5.11.2 368, 407
6.5 356, 357

Xenophon
Anabasis
1.1.10-11 242
2.4.15 242
2.5.13 69

Cyropaedia
1.6.28 200
8.1.30 115

Hellenica
6.4 120

Hiero
5.4 69, 72

Memorabilia
1.6.12 76
2.6.35 200
2.9.1 52
3.5.2 41, 171
3.10.5 68, 70, 72, 73, 77

Inscriptions and Papyri

BGU
I.22 52
I.115 324
II.248 48, 58, 284, 285, 453
II.531 48, 58, 221, 227, 453, 465, 466
III.846 449
IV.1062 177
IV.1079 45, 46
IV.1117 120
IV.1147 85

CIG
269 272
1241 272
1249 272
2512 262
2717 262
2811 263, 279
3151 262, 279
3162 262, 279
3777 248, 263
3793 263
6378 272

CIJ
I.5 377

CIL
6.9148 363
10.3377 297

I.Ephesos
IV.1008 272
VI.2054 40

IG
2.1104 42
2.1368 460
2.1369 460
2-3.11492 263, 280
3.550 313
3.551 313
3.805 312
4.126 362
4.203 265
5.1.40 263, 279
5.1.80 291
5.1.141-42 313
5.1.7 263
5.1.117 291
5.1.153 263
5.1.206-12 313
5.1.212 291
5.1.463 313
5.1.970 313
5.1.1172 314
10.2.255 242

IGR
3.300 320
4.813 262, 265
4.1435 262, 265, 279
4.1630 265, 279

ILLRP
116 368, 407
680 368, 407

ILS
1503 320

1514	235	706	52
9502	320	743	52
9503	320	1481	44
9485	320		

I.Smyrna

		PPetr.	
761	262	2.13	44
771	262		
772	262	*PRyl.*	
		1.28.211	44
OGIS		2.113.13	52
90.3	198		
383.122	40	*PTebt.*	
595.15	83, 164	118.4	242
669.43	43	294.16	40

PAmh.

SEG

97.14	40	9.8	173
		9.50	265
PFay.		11.558	291
21.9	164	11.622	272
		11.994	272
PGiss.		24.194	272
17	449, 452	24.496	263
		25.194	273
PGrenf.		28.1010	272
2.36	44	28.1033	263, 279
2.82.17-18	32	28.1034	263
		28.1045	263
PHal.		38.710	264, 279
1.208	42	39.409	291
		39.1316	264

PLond.

SIG

46.73	169	344.55	43, 459
2710.13-17	459	368.25	40
		695.68-69	40
PMich.		786	314
V.243	460	790	312
V.244	460	807.16	35
V.245	460	985	363
VII.477	120	1170	362
VIII.502	449, 452		
		TAM	
POxy.		2.437	263
413	135, 143, 157, 417	4.276	263, 279
483	177	5.743	262

Index of Modern Authors

Abramenko, A.   307
Adams, J. N.   214
Aejmelaeus, L.   65, 199, 208
Agamben, G.   296, 297, 298
Agosto, E.   251, 253, 254, 256
Alexandre, M.   395
Alföldy, G.   275
Allo, E.-B.   10, 12, 13, 14, 22, 27, 28, 29, 30, 34, 35, 36, 40, 44, 51, 87, 99, 102, 155, 159, 176, 180, 181, 183, 186, 192, 193, 194, 197, 199, 210, 434
Alpern, K. D.   429
Amandry, M.   290, 301, 303, 304, 308
Anderson, J. K.   336, 337, 341
Anderson, R. D.   XXVII, 108, 110
Anderson, W. S.   143
Andrews, S. B.   63
Andringa, W. van   355
Arangio-Ruiz, V.   260
Arnaoutoglou, I. N.   460
Arnott, W. G.   142, 144, 145
Arzt-Grabner, P.   236
Ascough, R. S.   42
Atkinson, K.   91
Aune, D. C.   162, 472
Aune, D. E.   67
Azar, M.   XI

Babbitt, F. C.   120
Bachmann, P.   13, 14, 25, 29, 30, 33, 35, 36, 39, 40, 43, 61, 68, 80, 88, 99, 104, 131, 155, 159, 180, 182, 183, 184, 194, 197, 434, 459, 478, 479
Badiou, A.   397, 398
Bailey, D. R. S.   215, 226
Balch, D.   244, 246, 247, 248, 321, 322, 324, 325, 327, 328, 329, 330, 331, 332, 333, 334, 335, 357, 359, 381, 301
Balot, R. K.   51
Balsdom, J. P. V. D.   365
Banks, R.   213, 244, 521
Barclay, J. M. G.   X, 275
Barclay, W.   451
Barker, D.   XI, 324, 460
Barnett, P.   X, 74, 83, 84, 102, 127, 168, 181, 203, 208, 235, 434
Barré, M. L.   124
Barrett, A.   395, 396
Barrett, C. K.   1, 13, 14, 16, 17, 18, 19, 21, 24, 25, 27, 30, 32, 33, 34, 35, 36, 40, 43, 52, 63, 65, 66, 68, 69, 73, 76, 77, 78, 79, 81, 82, 84, 85, 86, 87, 88, 89, 99, 102, 103, 104, 110, 111, 114, 115, 122, 125, 126, 127, 128, 129, 131, 133, 140, 148, 154, 155, 159, 160, 163, 164, 166, 167, 168, 170, 171, 174, 176, 180, 181, 182, 183, 184, 185, 190, 193, 195, 196, 197, 198, 199, 203, 209, 210, 218, 230, 232, 233, 249, 296, 300, 362, 370, 375, 392, 393, 394, 404, 405, 406, 407, 426, 434, 444, 458, 459, 478, 479
Barrier, J.   X, 163
Barsky, B.   X
Bartin, S. C.   245, 363
Baslez, M.-F.   293
Bauckham, R.   294
Bauernfeind, O.   168, 169, 170
Baur, F. C.   5, 9, 25, 125, 126
Becker, J.   178
Behm, J.   40, 41
Bengel, J. A.   XXI, 34
Berger, K.   49
Bertram, G.   51, 156, 157, 160, 161
Best, E.   393

Betz, H. D.   IX, XIX, XX, XXII, XXV,
   9, 14, 18, 21, 23, 24, 43, 45, 47, 61,
   62, 63, 66, 67, 74, 75, 78, 80, 90,
   100, 104, 108, 113, 125, 129, 130,
   132, 139, 140, 153, 158, 163,
   164,165, 166, 167, 168, 169, 170,
   171, 174, 176, 177, 178, 179, 180,
   181, 190, 196, 198, 207, 218, 256,
   258, 368, 384, 398, 420, 421, 422,
   424, 425, 428, 429, 437, 438, 440,
   445, 462, 463, 479, 480
Beyschlag, W.   6, 26, 194
Bickel, E.   432
Bieringer, R.   XIX, 25, 114, 179
Billerbeck, P.   184
Birge, M. K.   90
Bitner, B.   XI
Bitzer, L. F.   62
Bjerkelund, C. J.   78
Black, M.   92
Blanton, W.   X
Blasi, A. J.   237
Blass, F.   112
Bleek, F.   4, 5, 8, 25, 179, 424, 469
Blue, B.   337, 338, 345, 349
Blundell, M. W.   200
Bodel, J.   307
Boismard, M.-E.   375
Boman, T.   297
Bonaria, M.   365
Bonhöffer, A.   100
Bookidis, N.   336, 337
Bornkamm, G.   XXIV, XXV, 1, 9, 23,
   31, 36, 207, 360, 362, 401, 437,
   445, 446, 462
Borse, U.   128
Bourguet, E.   320
Bousset, W.   7, 14, 159, 183, 434
Bove, L.   260
Bowditch, P. L.   137, 388, 390
Bowersock, G.   X, 75, 107, 261, 266,
   291, 292, 310, 312, 313, 314, 315,
   316, 317, 318, 397
Box, H.   315
Boyle, A. J.   396
Branham, R. B.   292
Braun, H.   35
Braund, D. C.   173

Braund, S.   470
Brendle, A.   462
Brennan, T.   470, 471, 472
Breytenbach, C.   448, 451, 475
Brink, L.   61, 442
Broneer, O.   265, 267, 269
Brown, A.   X, 98
Brothers, A. J.   325
Brown, P. G. McC   141, 144
Bruce, F. F.   13, 14, 25, 29, 30, 32, 42,
   61, 87, 128, 174, 176, 182, 299
Brugnoli, G.   367
Brunt, P. A.   100, 387, 388
Bultmann, R.   9, 14, 23, 25, 33, 34,
   35, 36, 37, 42, 44, 69, 79, 81, 84,
   86, 87, 88, 104, 120, 126, 128, 129,
   131, 134, 140, 152, 154, 155, 156,
   159, 163, 164, 165, 167, 168, 171,
   180, 183, 190, 196, 197, 198, 199,
   203, 210, 428, 438, 447, 448, 452,
   459, 462, 478
Bünker, M.   XXVI, 93
Burnett, A.   301, 303, 304, 308
Burton, E. D.   362

Cadbury, H. J.   248, 261, 263, 264,
   265, 267, 273, 274, 277, 276, 277,
   278, 295, 296
Cairns, D.   51
Cairns, F.   49
Calvin, J.   182
Cancik, H.   363
Caragounis, C.   152
Carr, A. W.   99
Carter, T. L.   77, 366
Cartledge, P.   310, 311, 312, 313,
   314, 315, 316, 318, 319
Caspari, W.   160
Castelli, E.   79, 420
Charlesworth, J. H.   92
Cheesman, G. L.   320
Chester, A.   91, 92
Chester, S. J.   247
Chow, J. K.   132, 149, 152, 220, 228,
   230, 235, 239, 243, 248, 250, 258,
   259, 288, 289, 317, 318, 366, 399,
   400, 406, 408, 411

Index of Modern Authors

Chrimes, K. M. T. 310, 311, 312, 313, 314, 315, 316, 318, 397
Christensen, D. L. 188
Christol, M. 320
Clarke, A. 241, 243, 248, 251, 259, 261, 264, 265, 266, 270, 272, 273, 275, 276, 277, 278, 279
Clarke, J. R. 335, 357, 358, 359, 360, 402
Classen, C. J. 113
Clemen, C. 8
Coenen, J. 117
Cohoon, J. W. 172
Collange, J.-F. 446
Collins, J. J. 92
Collins, R. F. 61, 83, 84, 91, 94, 96, 97, 98, 112, 232, 239, 244, 248, 251, 252, 253, 256, 257, 258, 259, 288, 289, 321, 323, 360, 361, 362, 373, 375, 394, 406, 411, 412, 416, 417, 418, 419, 420
Concannon, C. X
Conzelmann, H. 1, 83, 98, 230, 240, 251, 252, 256, 257, 361, 393, 420
Cooper, J. M. 471
Corbett, B. P. 142, 143, 145
Cotter, W. 42
Courtney, E. 147
Cranfield, C. E. B. 243, 273, 299
Crook, J. A. 180
Crosby, H. L. 215, 216, 223, 229
Crusius, O. 117
Cumont, F. 363
Cunningham, C. 441

D'Agostino, F. 67
Dahl, N. XXI, 234, 251, 257, 371, 406, 413
Daly, L. W. 120
Damon, C. 141, 142, 143, 144, 145, 146, 147
Danker, F. 355, 392
Dantes, S. P. 272
D'Arms, J. H. 360, 365
Daux, G. 266, 291
Davenport, G. L. 91
Deiss, J. J. 325

Deissmann, A. 152, 238, 294, 295, 296, 449
De Jonge, M. 91
Delcor, M. 186, 192, 194
Delling, G. 41, 99, 167, 171, 172, 177, 255, 256, 260
Demacopoulos, G. XI
Denney, J. 10, 34
Denniston, J. D. 105, 415, 469
Derrida, J. 409
Dessau, H. 294, 295, 296
De Vos, C. S. 230, 242, 243, 245, 246, 247, 248, 264, 266, 273, 275, 279, 289, 321, 322, 323, 324, 333, 376, 400
De Vos, M. 328
De Waele, F. J. 267, 268, 269, 270, 271, 276, 280, 349
Dewey, A. 69
DeWitt, N. J. 222, 223, 225
DeWitt, N. W. 222, 223, 225
Dibelius, M. 98
Dilley, M. E. 141
Dillon, J. 45
Dirlmeier, F. 202
Dobbins, R. F. 100
Dobschütz, E. von 231, 235, 259
Dodd, C. H. 446
Dover, K. J. 51, 200
Downs, D. J. 178, 424, 428
Drescher, R. 7, 19, 24, 25, 31, 38, 174, 175, 176, 421, 435
Drew-Bear, T. 320
Driver, S. R. 188
Dufallo, B. 394
Dunbabin, K. M. D. 329, 330, 338, 346, 360, 364, 365, 402
Duncan-Jones, R. 275
Dunn, J. D. G. 232, 236, 242, 250, 321
Dunning, B. XI
Düring, I. 321
Dutch, R. S. 205
Duthoy, R. 307

Eastman, S. X
Ebel, E. 244, 321
Eden, P. T. 440

Edwards, K. N.   303, 304, 308
Ehrenberg, V.   173
Elliot, N.   X
Ellis, E. E.   38, 184, 417
Emmerling, C.   XXII, 445
Engberg-Pedersen, T.   161, 470
Engels, D.   153, 242, 266, 267, 290, 291, 334
Entralgo, P. L.   470
Epstein, D.   IX, 214, 220, 226, 283, 284, 286, 480
Erskine, A.   471
Evans, C. A.   91, 92
Ewald, H.   5, 6, 7, 8, 13, 19, 25, 30, 39, 41, 43, 63, 153, 179, 424, 445

Fairweather, J.   108
Fallon, F. T.   128, 446
Fantham, E.   390
Fee, G.   76, 179, 230, 231, 235, 239, 241, 242, 245, 251, 257, 259, 288, 375, 394, 406, 412, 419, 420
Feldman, L. H.   377
Field, F.   149, 374, 403
Filson, F. V.
Finley, M.   298
Finn, T. M.   371
Fisher, N. R. E.   51
Fitch, J. G.   396, 397
Fitzgerald, J.   X, 67, 97, 108, 380, 383, 385, 386, 387, 388, 389, 391, 419, 448, 449, 450, 451, 453, 456, 470
Fitzmyer, J. A.   XXII, 240, 242, 251, 254, 255, 371, 412, 445
Fontaine, M.   141
Forbes, C.   X, 108, 112, 115, 218, 439, 440
Fortenbaugh, W. W.   470
Foss, P. W.   329
Fotopoulos, J.   278
Fowler, R. L.   435
Fränkel, H.   431
Fraschetti, A.   355
Fraser, P. M.   272
Fredrickson, D. E.   43, 424, 426, 434, 435, 436, 457, 474
Freudenberg, K.   439, 440

Frey, J.-B.   237, 238, 239
Friedländer, L.   137, 148, 149
Friedrich, G.   125, 126, 393
Friesen, S. J.   X, XIX, 153, 230, 237, 242, 243, 245, 247, 248, 251, 259, 261, 264, 265, 267, 268, 269, 270, 272, 274, 275, 278, 279, 281, 322, 357, 377, 98, 401
Furley, W. D.   470
Furnish, V. P   12, 13, 14, 16, 18, 24, 25, 26, 30, 31, 33, 34, 35, 36, 37, 39, 40, 41, 42, 52, 61, 62, 66, 68, 69, 70, 72, 74, 78, 79, 80, 81, 83, 84, 85, 86, 87, 88, 89, 96, 99, 102, 103, 105, 106, 110, 114, 122, 124, 125, 128, 129, 130, 131, 133, 140, 152, 153, 154, 155, 156, 160, 163, 164, 165, 166, 167, 168, 170, 171, 174, 176, 178, 180, 181, 183, 184, 185, 186, 190, 192, 193, 194, 196, 197, 198, 199, 200, 203, 208, 209, 210, 211, 220, 228, 273, 424, 425, 426, 434, 436, 438, 454, 455, 456, 458, 459, 478
Fürst, A.   219, 381, 427, 429, 430, 432, 442, 443

Gadbery, L. M.   326, 327
Gager, J.   371
Geagan, D. J.   265, 311
Gehring, R. W.   360, 452, 362, 365
George, M.   329, 357, 358, 359, 360, 401, 402
Georgi, D.   X, XXI, XXV, 9, 18, 21, 23, 25, 28, 81, 83, 86, 87, 88, 96, 125, 126, 127, 128, 129, 130, 139, 153, 163, 166, 178, 189, 195, 207, 211, 212, 233, 256, 258, 371, 394, 398, 422, 424, 437, 438, 445, 446, 462
Georgia, A.   XI
Gill, C.   470
Gill, D. W. J.   250, 259, 264, 265, 266, 270, 273, 279, 280, 281, 366, 376
Gillman, F.   230, 232, 264
Gillman, J.   232, 236, 290, 299, 300
Glad, C.   456, 459, 474

Glibert-Thirry, A.   457
Gnilka, J.   258
Godet, F.   243
Gold, B. K.   387, 390
Goldbeck, F.   359
Goldstein, J.   222, 223, 314, 461
Golla, E.   24
Goodrich, J. K.   278
Goodspeed, E. J.   233, 290, 293, 299, 300
Gordon, M.   298
Gösswein, H. U.   54
Grahame, M.   330, 358
Grässer, E.   14, 462
Graver, M. R.   470, 471, 472, 473, 474, 476
Griffin, M.   421
Grimaldi, W.   47, 50, 51, 53, 59
Grindheim, S.   99
Griswold, C.   477
Groag, E.   319
Grube, G. M. A.   109
Gruen, E. S.   314
Grundmann, W.   67, 68, 69, 77, 78, 83
Gulick, C. B.   145
Gunther, J. J.   125, 126

Haas, C.   404
Hadot, P.   161
Haenchen, E.   232, 233, 239, 249, 294, 295, 296, 300, 370, 392, 393, 403, 405
Hagedorn, D.   110
Hall, D. R.   11, 16, 25
Hall, J.   X, 136, 214, 226, 283, 284, 286, 382, 438, 450, 451, 480
Halmel, A.   XIX, XXV, 209, 385, 445, 469
Harding, M.   XI
Harnack, A. von   67
Harrer, G. A.   294, 296, 297
Harris, M. J.   18, 27, 29, 30, 32, 35, 36, 37, 39, 40, 42, 52, 80, 88, 89, 102, 133, 154, 182, 184, 185, 186, 425, 456, 459
Harris, W. V.   43, 44, 53, 162, 426, 470, 472

Harrison, J. R.   XI, 134, 139, 369, 422, 428
Hartman, L.   119
Hartwig, C.   231
Harvey, A. E.   434, 463
Hausrath, A.   XXII, XXIII, XXIV, 8, 60, 205, 207, 437, 444, 445, 446
Heath, M.   48, 108, 113
Heckel, T. K.   94, 119, 393, 417
Heidland, H. W.   83
Heinrici, C. F. G.   XXI, 3, 4, 8, 9, 10, 11, 14, 15, 25, 27, 28, 29, 34, 36, 37, 42, 68, 88, 98, 105, 106, 113, 133, 154, 157, 166, 185, 406, 412, 415, 416, 417, 419, 469
Helmbold, W. C.   205
Hemer, C. J.   267, 272, 275, 294, 297
Hengel, M.   294, 296, 417
Henry, D.   396
Henry, E.   396
Hercher, R.   54, 55, 58, 221
Héring, J.   9, 14, 84, 88, 155, 164, 235, 259
Herrington, C. J.   396
Herzog, R.   362
Highet, G.   137, 419
Hilgenfeld, A.   6, 7, 8, 19, 30, 126
Hinck, H.   464
Hinze, B.   XI
Hock, R. F.   61, 73, 74, 75, 76, 96, 114, 134, 135, 138, 139, 149, 151, 152, 165, 228, 368, 386, 390, 400
Hoffer, S. E.   450
Hoffmann, A.   328
Hofius, O.   361, 362
Hofmann, J. C. K. von   9, 34
Hogan, K.   XI
Holland, G. S.   440
Holloway, P.   X
Holmberg, B.   278
Holsten, C.   8, 10
Holtzmann, H. J.   5, 8, 10, 23, 25
Hooker, M. d.   372
Horn, F. W.   251, 255, 256, 412
Hornbeck, P.   XI
Horrell, D. G.   65, 71, 246, 289, 325, 326, 327, 333, 334, 335, 337, 338, 339, 348, 349, 357, 392

Horsfall, N.   389, 390, 407
Horsley, G. H. R.   55, 225, 235, 242, 261, 296, 363
Horsley, R. A.   374, 404, 405, 408, 410
Hughes, F. W.   434
Hughes, P. E.   3, 4, 8, 9, 10, 15, 25, 27, 31, 32, 33, 34, 36, 37, 39, 40, 41, 52, 61, 68, 69, 74, 81, 87, 88, 102, 111, 131, 151, 152, 160, 166, 168, 170, 171, 180, 186, 192, 193, 202, 203, 455
Hultgren, S. J.   XXII, 445
Humphries, R. A.   98
Hurd, J. C.   411
Hyldahl, N.   XXI, 11, 15, 194

Inwood, B.   471

Jaekel, S.   383
Jewett, R.   X, XXVI, 81, 231, 232, 233, 235, 236, 243, 245, 253, 256, 264, 273, 278, 280, 293, 297, 325
Johnson, E.   XI
Johnson, L. T.   423
Jones, A. H. M.   173, 313
Jones, C. P.   55, 205, 215, 223, 364, 365, 366, 402
Jones, R. E.   305
Jongkind, D.   325, 327, 334, 335, 337, 351
Joshel, S. R.   75
Joubert, S.   178
Judeich, W.   262
Judge, E. A.   IX, 74, 102, 119, 130, 132, 152, 213, 214, 230, 231, 232, 234, 235, 236, 237, 241, 243, 249, 250, 266, 288, 290, 293, 294, 295, 298, 299, 300, 323, 366, 368, 369, 371, 385, 391, 399, 403, 418, 430

Kajanto, I.   241, 291, 297
Kamudzandu, I.   X
Kant, L. H.   377
Käsemann, E.   18, 61, 89, 139, 243, 380
Kaser, M.   43, 180
Kasher, A.   374
Kassel, R.   145
Katzoff, R.   314
Kehnscherper, G.   295
Kendall, B.   XI
Kennedy, G. A.   463
Kennedy, J. H.   XXII, XXIII, XXIV, XXVI, 9, 36, 64, 80, 160, 207, 209, 437, 444, 445, 446, 458, 476
Kent, J. H.   264, 265, 266, 267, 268, 269, 270, 271, 273, 274, 278, 280, 281, 290, 301, 302, 303, 304, 305, 309, 311, 376
Ker, D. P.   82, 156, 372, 373, 374, 414
Kim, B.-M.   178
Kim, C.-H.   253
Kim, Y. S.   X
Kinney, D.   292
Kirner, G. O.   132, 152, 289, 318, 364, 366, 368, 375, 380, 399, 401, 406, 407, 408, 419
Klauck, H.-J.   XXVI, 54, 65, 199, 208, 244, 321, 361, 362
Klinghardt, M.   246
Klöpper, A.   5, 8, 9, 10, 25, 39, 88
Knibb, M. A.   92
Knox, J.   71
Koch, D. A.   112
Koch, L. J.   84
Koester, H.   X, 127, 462
König, K.   7, 8, 18, 19, 25, 31, 40, 44, 65, 104, 122, 445, 449
Konstan, D.   X, 43, 53, 136, 137, 142, 151, 202, 380, 381, 382, 385, 387, 388, 389, 390, 407, 410, 470, 477
Kornemann, E.   313
Koskenniemi, H.   225, 464
Kraabel, A. T.   371
Krenkel, M.   XIX, XXII, 6, 7, 11, 12, 13, 14, 20, 23, 24, 25, 26, 27, 29, 30, 34, 36, 37, 38, 52, 80, 174, 175, 176, 194, 421, 445, 458, 459, 476
Kretzer, A.   253
Kristeva, J.   426
Kritzer, R. E.   236
Kroll, W.   359
Kruse, C. G.   1, 3, 16, 25

Kubutschek, J. W. 275
Kuck, D. W. 91
Kuhn, H.-W. 94, 417
Kümmel, W. G. 11, 18, 36, 39, 40, 42, 59, 174
Kyrtatas, D. 276

Lagrange, M.-J. 243
Laird, M. L. 307
Lake, K. XXIII, XXIV, 2, 9, 36, 64, 80, 207, 446, 458, 476
Lamberton, R. 205, 319
Lambertz, M. 296, 297
Lambrecht, J. XIX, 63, 167, 182
Lamouille, A. 375
Lampe, G. W. H. 9
Lampe, P. 232, 322, 330, 359, 361, 362, 365, 369, 377, 380, 398, 401, 407
Landvogt, P. 248, 261, 262, 263, 265, 279
Lassen, E. M. 79
Laurence, R. 331, 332, 355, 356, 359, 401, 402
Leivestad, R. 67, 78
Leon, H. J. 295
Lepenioti, C. 291
Levick, B. 320, 374
Levinson, B. M. 188
Lichtenberger, H. 92
Lietzmann, H. XX, 13, 14, 25, 29, 30, 33, 34, 35, 36, 37, 42, 68, 84, 131, 134, 154, 157, 182, 184, 185, 196, 210, 243, 252, 459, 478
Lieu, J. M. 90, 233, 370, 371
Lifschitz, B. 238
Lim, T. 119, 404
Lincicum, D. 188
Lincoln, A. T. 163
Lindemann, A. 90, 96, 97, 99, 240, 246, 251, 252, 253, 254, 255, 256, 257, 259, 260, 289, 318, 324, 361, 370, 371, 406, 412, 414, 417
Lisco, H. 180
Litfin, A. D. 82, 96, 374, 404, 409
Littlewood, C. A. J. 396
Loisy, A. 23, 49, 462
Long, F. J. XX

Longenecker, R. N. 235
Lüdemann, G. X, 18, 71, 94, 126, 127, 139, 173, 174, 177, 178, 232, 233, 237, 239, 243, 249, 294, 295, 296, 300, 370, 374, 392, 393, 398, 403, 404, 405, 480
Lütgert, W. 81, 88, 126
Lutz, C. 76, 317
Luz, U. 186

MacDonald, M. Y. 250, 276, 363
McDonald, W. A. 267, 269, 273, 278
McDonough, S. M. 296
MacDowell, D. M. 51
McElduff, S. 396
McGowan, M. XI
Mackintosh, R. 27
McLean, B. H. 324
MacMullen, R. 75, 77, 153, 275, 318, 363
Maiuri, A. 325
Malherbe, A. 47, 49, 50, 56, 60, 61, 221, 230, 232, 237, 241, 242, 243, 244, 245, 250, 253, 259, 275, 280, 300, 321, 323, 357, 386, 390, 464
Manson, T. W. 2
Marek, C. 320
Marquardt, J. 365, 402
Marshall, B. A. 226, 283, 450
Marshall, P. IX, X, 28, 51, 75, 97, 102, 106, 107, 108, 109, 111, 122, 130, 132, 133, 134, 135, 136, 138, 139, 149, 151, 152, 165, 166, 200, 202, 211, 213, 214, 217, 218, 219, 220, 222, 228, 250, 258, 288, 289, 368, 369, 380, 386, 391, 398, 399, 406, 407, 411, 427, 428
Martin, D. X, 97, 187, 261, 262, 263, 264, 276, 279, 410, 419
Martin, J. 115
Martin, R. P. 13, 14, 35, 43, 61, 84, 88, 102, 103, 114, 125, 128, 129, 152, 155, 159, 168, 171, 178, 180, 181, 184, 196, 197, 198, 203, 425, 478, 479
Mason, H. J. 264, 265, 267, 279
Matera, F. J. 26
Matthews, E. 272

Matthews, S.   363
Mau, A.   359
Meeks, W. A.   38, 230, 231, 232, 233, 234, 235, 237, 239, 241, 242, 243, 244, 245, 247, 248, 249, 250, 259, 262, 264, 275, 278, 280, 288, 289, 290, 293, 300, 307, 308, 318, 321, 322, 323, 324, 357, 394, 398, 404, 420
Meggitt, J. J.   153, 237, 243, 248, 261, 264, 267, 269, 272, 274, 275, 277, 278, 279, 394, 417
Mell, U.   211
Menzies, A.   102, 111, 115, 122, 183, 186
Meritt, B. D.   290, 301, 302, 309
Merklein, H.   97, 99, 420
Merritt, H. W.   122
Metzger, B. M.   405
Meyboom, P. G. P.   350
Meyer, H. A. W.   28, 29, 33, 89, 183, 186, 415
Michaelis, W.   232
Michel, O.   235, 243
Millar, F.   270
Milleker, E. J.   305
Miller, P. A.   394
Miller, S. G.   246, 333, 318, 338, 339
Milligan, G.   449, 450
Mitchell, L. G.   202
Mitchell, M. M.   XIX, XXIII, XXV, XXVII, 9, 21, 24, 65, 87, 103, 108, 113, 127, 132, 175, 176, 199, 207, 208, 229, 375, 410, 413, 420, 421, 444, 462, 497
Mitchell, S.   320
Mitchell, T. N.   215, 283
Mitteis, L.   450
Modrzejewski, J.   374, 404
Moffatt, J.   9, 11, 30, 231, 235
Momigliano, A.   314
Mommsen, T.   277
Morgan, C.   339
Morris, L.   232
Moule, C. F. D.   104, 110, 154, 155, 166, 167, 362
Moulton, J. H.   166, 362
Mowery, R. L.   320

Moyer, H.   159
Mrozek, S.   298
Müller, F.   168
Mullins, T. Y.   343
Munck, J.   297
Murphy-O'Connor, J.   18, 127, 128, 156, 235, 237, 244, 245, 246, 259, 273, 279, 288, 289, 290, 294, 296, 297, 300, 321, 322, 323, 324, 326, 327, 330, 333, 334, 335, 336, 338, 342, 349, 357, 359, 374, 375, 393, 406, 424, 480

Neander, A.   5, 7
Nesselrath, H. G.   141, 142, 145, 170
Neusner, J.   184
Nicholson, J.   226
Nickle, K. F.   177, 178
Nicoll, A.   156
Nicols, J.   360
Nobbs, A.   XI
Nock, A. D.   459
Nongbri, B.   X
Norden, E.   113
North, J.   306
Noy, D.   238
Nussbaum, M.   470

Ogereau, J.   XI
Oliver, A.   351, 352
Oliver, J. H.   55, 57
Ollrog, W-H.   38, 231, 233, 255
Olsson, B. H.   48, 58, 284, 285, 453, 466
Oostendorp, D. W.   61, 89, 126, 139
Osiek, C.   246, 247, 322, 328, 330, 331, 332, 334, 335, 357, 359, 363, 401
Ostrow, S. E.   307
Overman, J. A.   371

Packer, J. E.   325
Pagano, M.   325
Pakaluk, M.   137, 138, 200
Pallas, D. I.   272
Palmer-Bonz, M.   394
Panayotakis, C.   365
Pangle, L. S.   137, 383, 427, 431

Pani, M.   314
Papathomas, A.   236
Patte, D.   X
Peachin, M.   365
Pearson, L.   200
Penella, R.   XI, 58, 285
Peppard, M.   XI
Perkins, J.   77
Pernot, L.   113
Pervo, R. I.   XXII
Peters, W. J. Th.   350
Peterson, B. K.   62, 65, 103, 104
Pfleiderer, O.   6, 26, 27, 194
Pickard-Cambridge, A. W.   170
Pickett, R.   98
Piper, L. J.   311, 312, 313, 314, 316, 317
Plank, K.   71, 97, 420
Pleket, H. W.   305
Plezia, M.   55
Plummer, A.   XXIII, XXIV, 4, 9, 11, 12, 13, 14, 25, 28, 29, 32, 33, 34, 35, 36, 37, 42, 43, 52, 61, 62, 63, 68, 69, 74, 79, 80, 84, 85, 87, 89, 102, 103, 105, 110, 115, 121, 124, 131, 133, 134, 135, 151, 154, 156, 159, 165, 166, 167, 168, 170, 171, 174, 179, 180, 181, 183, 186, 192, 193, 197, 199, 203, 210, 234, 375, 434, 446, 458, 459, 476, 478, 479
Pogoloff, S.   96, 119, 413
Preston, R.   319
Pritchett, W. K.   107, 109
Prümm K.   26, 41, 42
Puech, B.   265

Räbiger, J. F.   8
Rajak, T.   238, 239
Ramsay, W. R.   230, 234, 290, 292, 293, 294, 320
Ramsden S. E.   340
Rawson, B.   283, 286
Rawson, E.   283
Reich, H.   117
Relihan, J. C.   439
Rendall, G. H.   9, 435
Renehan, R.   162, 472
Ribbeck, O.   141, 142, 143, 144, 145

Richardson, P.   375, 393
Riesner, R.   174, 295, 296
Rigaux, B.   393
Ripolles, P.   301
Rist, J. M.   161
Rives, J. B.   277, 306, 307
Rix, H.   241
Rizakis, A. D.   266, 291, 293
Robert, L.   262, 265
Roberts, C.   459
Roberts, W. Rhys   109, 111, 114, 131
Robertson, A.   234, 375
Robertson, A. T.   166, 242
Robinson, H. S.   337, 338
Robinson, O. F.   42
Roetzel, C.   9, 14, 24, 65, 102, 104, 122, 153, 187, 191, 425, 446
Roller, M. B.   396
Roos, A. G.   267, 269, 276, 277, 278
Rosner, B.   188
Rossbach, O.   432
Rothwell, K. S.   422
Rudich, V.   396
Rüpke, J.   363
Russell, D. A.   110

Sabatier, A.   9
Salies, G. H.   339, 347
Saller, R.   80, 135, 136, 137, 148, 289, 323, 356, 359, 366, 369, 387, 388, 389
Salmeri, G.   215, 223
Salmon, E. T.   242
Salomies, O.   241, 290, 291
Sampaolo, V.   328
Sand, A.   81
Sargeaunt, J.   147
Schenk, W.   XXVI, 93
Schlier, H.   232, 243
Schmeller, T.   X, 246, 324, 361, 363, 400, 401
Schmid, W.   295
Schmiedel, P.   XXIII, XXIV, 6, 7, 8, 14, 25, 30, 34, 63, 444, 445, 446
Schmithals, W.   XXIV, XXV, 9, 81, 86, 87, 88, 126, 296, 462
Schnabel, E. J.   251, 290, 370, 371
Schneider, G.   239, 393

Schneider, J.   417
Schneider, K.   401
Schnelle, U.   90, 94, 95, 231
Schniewind, J.   98
Schoeps, H.-J.   154, 157
Schowalter, D. N.   XIX, 326
Schrage, W.   72, 94, 98, 99, 228, 237, 242, 257, 259, 412, 420
Schreiber, A.   245, 252, 322
Schrenk, G.   57
Schulze, W.   291
Schüpphaus, J.   92
Schürer, E.   173, 237
Schwartz, D. R.   395
Schwartz, E.   203
Schwegler, A.   126
Schweizer, E.   70, 81, 82, 163
Schwemer, A. M.   296
Seesemann, H.   83
Segal, E.   135, 143
Seitz, J.   XI
Sellin, G.   93, 99, 127
Semler, J. S.   XX, 174
Senft, C.   XXVI, 93
Shaw, G.   420
Shear, T. L.   267, 268, 276, 335, 341, 342, 343, 344, 345, 346, 347, 348, 349, 350, 352
Sherk, R. K.   235
Sherwin-White, A. N.   173, 296
Shiell, W.   366
Sickenberger, J.   24
Sihvola, J.   470
Skeat, T. C.   459
Smit, J. F. M.   82, 96, 156, 278, 372, 373, 374, 405, 414, 415, 416
Smith, D. E.   305, 306, 360, 364
Smith, J. T.   334
Smith, M. S.   292
Smith, W. D.   474
Smyth, H. W.   105, 236, 415, 469
Sokolowski, F.   363
Solin, H.   234, 235, 236, 241, 290, 291, 293, 297, 300, 305
Solmsen, F.   115
Sorabji, R.   470, 471
Spawforth, A.   263, 273, 290, 292, 298, 299, 301, 302, 303, 304, 306, 308, 309, 311, 312, 313, 314, 315, 316, 317, 318, 319
Spencer, A. B.   108
Spicq, C.   40, 258, 451
Stählin, G.   242, 245, 250, 321
Stansbury, H. A.   242, 243, 266, 309
Starr, R. J.   365
Stegemann, E.   X, 247, 275
Stegemann, W.   X, 247, 275
Steinhauer, G.   310
Stemmer, K.   328
Stepheson, A. M. G.   11, 15
Steveson, T. R.   139
Stone, M. E.   92
Stillwell, R.   269, 352
Stowers, S. K.   XX, 45, 49, 50, 162, 221, 368, 386, 392, 407, 444, 466, 472, 480
Strachan, R. H.   9, 14, 166, 183
Strack, H.   184
Strecker, G.   380, 437
Studemund, W.   432, 433
Stuhlmacher, P.   211, 243
Sumney, J. L.   87, 88, 95, 101, 102, 125, 127, 139
Sundermann, H.-G.   62, 66, 164
Swain, S.   107, 108, 113
Sykutris, J.   49, 54, 55, 225, 464
Syme, R.   317

Taillardat, J.   202
Tasker, R. V. G.   14, 80, 82, 187
Taslialan, M.   320
Taylor, C. C. W.   201
Taylor, H.   146
Taylor, J. J.   392
Taylor, L. R.   234, 309, 310, 311, 312, 316
Taylor, N. H.   XXIII, XXIV, 209, 445
Theissen, G.   76, 86, 88, 95, 96, 97, 98, 115, 148, 153, 159, 228, 230, 231, 232, 234, 235, 237, 238, 239, 241, 242, 243, 244, 245, 247, 248, 250, 255, 258, 259, 261, 262, 263, 264, 265, 271, 273, 275, 276, 278, 280, 281, 282, 288, 289, 290, 307, 309, 318, 321, 322, 324, 537, 359, 360, 361, 364, 365, 370, 376, 394,

398, 399, 400, 401, 403, 408, 412, 413
Thiselton, A. C. 82, 83, 90, 98, 235, 237, 241, 242, 251, 256, 288, 289, 297, 309, 335, 338, 361, 365
Thom, J. C. 423
Thomas, G. S. R. 295
Thrall, M. E. XIX, XXI, 1, 11, 13, 14, 16, 18, 19, 20, 21, 24, 25, 26, 27, 28, 29, 30, 32, 33, 34, 35, 36, 38, 39, 40, 41, 42, 52, 56, 57, 58, 59, 61, 63, 68, 69, 70, 75, 76, 78, 84, 85, 87, 88, 89, 100, 102, 103, 104, 114, 124, 125, 128, 129, 131, 133, 134, 135, 154, 155, 159, 164, 165, 166, 167, 168, 170, 171, 174, 176, 178, 180, 181, 182, 183, 184, 185, 186, 190, 192, 196, 197, 198, 199, 200, 202, 203, 209, 210, 211, 220, 228, 424, 425, 434, 435, 456, 458, 463, 464, 468, 477, 478, 479
Thurén, L. 113
Tieleman, T. 470, 471
Till, R. 439
Tilley, M. XI
Tilley, T. XI
Too, Y. L. 201
Treggiari, S. M. 367, 407
Trillitzsch, W. 432
Trümper, M. 329, 330
Tylawsky, E. I. 141, 142, 143, 145, 146

Van de Weerd, H. 269, 270, 271, 272, 273, 274, 279
Van Vliet, H. 183, 184, 185, 191
Vegge, I. XX, 37, 84, 103, 182
Venticinque, P. F. 460
Vermes, G. 186
Veyne, P. 323, 359, 360, 396
Vielhauer, P. XIX, XXI, XXII, XXVI, XXVII, 9, 114, 207, 462
Vogliano, A. 324, 363
Volf, J. M. G. 197
Volkmann, R. 115
Vos, J. S. 96, 372

Walbank, M. E. H. 290, 325, 334, 336
Walker, D. D. X, 63, 67, 78, 79, 89, 121, 193
Wallace-Hadrill, A. 77, 137, 247, 260, 289, 323, 324, 325, 327, 328, 329, 330, 331, 332, 333, 354, 355, 356, 357, 358, 359, 369, 401, 402
Walters, J. 278, 364
Wan, S.-K. 446
Watson, F. 9, 60, 61, 62, 63, 64, 65, 67, 103, 104, 122, 199, 208, 392, 437
Waywell, S. E. 347
Weaver, P. R. C. 323
Weber, M. 175
Webster, T. B. L. 141, 145
Weichert, V. 49, 50, 464
Weinberg, S. 337, 337, 338, 341
Weinreich, O. 440
Weiß, A. 320
Weiss, B. 34
Weiss, J. XIX, XXIII, XXV, XXVI, 6, 7, 8, 9, 19, 23, 25, 29, 38, 39, 49, 52, 63, 64, 65, 69, 70, 71, 72, 76, 79, 82, 83, 87, 89, 90, 91, 93, 94, 96, 97, 98, 99, 104, 112, 113, 153, 156, 157, 160, 174, 175, 176, 179, 181, 207, 209, 234, 236, 240, 242, 247, 249, 251, 252, 254, 255, 256, 257, 259, 260, 281, 288, 289, 290, 292, 293, 299, 318, 361, 370, 371, 372, 373, 374, 375, 400, 404, 405, 406, 408, 409, 410, 411, 412, 414, 415, 416, 417, 418, 419, 420, 421, 424, 425, 426, 428, 444, 445, 451, 462, 463
Weizsäcker, K. H. von 6, 7, 19
Welborn, L. L. XXI, 9, 23, 31, 60, 71, 82, 83, 84, 87, 94, 95, 96, 97, 98, 100, 113, 115, 122, 156, 158, 159, 221, 228, 235, 243, 275, 276, 298, 366, 367, 372, 373, 375, 376, 384, 385, 386, 392, 397, 406, 409, 413, 414, 415, 416, 417, 418, 419, 420, 434, 437, 438, 439, 440, 441, 455, 460, 462
Wendland, P. 14, 198, 199

West, A. B.   280, 290, 298, 302, 303, 304, 306, 307, 308, 309, 310, 311, 312, 315, 316, 317, 318, 319, 320
West, M. L.   431
Wettstein, J. J.   106
Wheeler, M.   325
White, J. L.   434, 449
White, L. M.   360, 380, 456
White, P.   75, 136, 137, 148, 149, 151, 290, 367, 386, 387, 388, 389, 390, 400, 407, 409, 411, 419
Wiefel, W.   392
Wiemken, H.   143, 157
Wilamowitz-Moellendorf, U. von   113, 431
Wilcken, U.   295, 450
Wilckens, U.   99, 157, 243, 258, 417
Wilcox, M.   371
Wiles, G. P.   199
Williams, C. K.   326, 327, 335, 336, 341, 342, 349, 350, 351, 352, 353, 354, 392
Wilson, A. J. N.   306
Windisch, H.   10, 11, 13, 14, 16, 20, 21, 24, 25, 26, 27, 28, 29, 30, 31, 32, 33, 34, 35, 36, 37, 39, 40, 41, 42, 49, 51, 52, 53, 56, 57, 58, 61, 62, 63, 67, 68, 69, 70, 72, 73, 74, 78, 80, 81, 82, 84, 85, 86, 87, 88, 89, 99, 100, 101, 102, 104, 105, 106, 110, 111, 113, 114, 115, 120, 121, 122, 124, 125, 128, 129, 131, 133, 134, 139, 140, 148, 151, 152, 154, 155, 156, 158, 159, 163, 164, 165, 166, 167, 168, 169, 170, 171, 174, 175, 176, 180, 182, 183, 185, 190, 194, 195, 196, 197, 198, 199, 203, 210, 211, 213, 218, 221, 258, 384, 386, 421, 424, 425, 426, 428, 429, 437, 438, 439, 440, 441, 444, 448, 454, 455, 457, 458, 459, 461, 463, 468, 469, 476, 477, 480.

Winter, B. W.   20, 42, 61, 76, 82, 83, 104, 105, 106, 107, 110, 115, 119, 122, 130, 131, 132, 218, 250, 257, 259, 264, 265, 266, 276, 278, 279, 280, 361, 362, 368, 374, 375, 404, 405, 409, 416
Winter, F.   236
Winter, J. G.   449
Winterling, A.   407
Wiseman, J.   266, 267, 271, 279, 291, 292, 311, 333, 334, 335, 336, 337, 349
Wiseman, T. P.   136, 331, 356, 365, 366, 367, 368, 401, 407
Witherington, B.   133, 246
Wolff, Ch.   14, 18, 30, 42, 74, 85, 87, 88, 99, 100, 154, 197, 208
Wolter, N.   99
Woodward, A. M.   268, 276
Wooten, C. W.   110
Wright, K. S.   305
Wright, R. B.   91, 92, 93
Wright, W. C.   286
Wulf-Rheidt, U.   329, 330
Wüst, E.   141

Yavetz, Z.   77
Young, F.   1
Young, N. H.   71
Youtie, H. C.   449
Yuen-Collingridge, R.   XI, XXI

Zahn, T.   9, 10, 11, 20, 25, 36, 52, 56, 59, 194, 243, 249
Zanker, P.   328, 330, 331, 332, 333, 335, 356, 357
Zeilinger, F.   462
Zervos, O. H.   328, 329, 344
Zerwick, M.   29
Zmijewski, J.   62, 75, 84, 129, 131, 133, 140, 154, 158, 163, 164, 438
Zoumbaki, S.   291